The History of Brenau University, 1878–2013

The History of Brenau University, 1878–2013

A Study of Student, Faculty, and Staff
Negotiation to Shape the Collegiate Experience

Charles H. "Trey" Wilson III

\<teneo\> //press
AMHERST, NEW YORK

Copyright 2014 Teneo Press

All rights reserved
Printed in the United States of America

No part of this publication may be reproduced, stored in or introduced into a retrieval system, or transmitted, in any form, or by any means (electronic, mechanical, photocopying, recording, or otherwise), without the prior permission of the publisher.

Requests for permission should be directed to:
permissions@teneopress.com, or mailed to:
Teneo Press
University Corporate Centre
100 Corporate Parkway
Suite 128
Amherst, NY 14226

Library of Congress Control Number: 2014960260

Wilson, Charles Hooper, III.
The History of Brenau University, 1878–2013: .
p. cm.
Includes bibliographical references and index.
ISBN 978-1-934844-66-3 (alk. paper).

Dedication

To Ana and Celia with all my love.

Table of Contents

List of Figures ix

List of Tables xiii

Preface xv

Acknowledgements xxvii

Introduction: Placing Brenau into Context 1

Chapter 1: Parties to the Parley 31

Chapter 2: The History of Academics at Brenau 115

Chapter 3: Institutional Policymaking as Staff & Faculty
    Forte 187

Chapter 4: Building Brenau 239

Chapter 5: Organizations and Traditions at Brenau 269

Chapter 6: Smoking, "Night Riding," & other Serious
    Offenses 311

Chapter 7: "No imitations of masculine sports" 373

Chapter 8: Bringing Home the Gold[en Tigers] 395

Chapter 9: Student Success at Shaping Space 439

Conclusion: Brenau University Today 489

Figures 503

Tables 537

Bibliography 543

Index 573

List of Figures

Figure 1: Students of the Georgia Baptist Female Seminary circa 1890 503

Figure 2: Brenau students circa 1920 504

Figure 3: Brenau students in 1938 in a photograph taken by Ramsey (Gainesville, Georgia) entitled, "Tri-Delta Chapter 1938." 505

Figure 4: Brenau students entertaining dates from nearby Riverside Military Academy circa 1955 506

Figure 5: Students participating in Brenau's annual spring Class Day event circa May, 1980 507

Figure 6: Brenau students circa 1992 508

Figure 7: Brenau students in 2013 509

Figure 8: Dr. H. J. Pearce and Prof. Azor Van Hoose 510

Figure 9: Dr. Josiah Crudup 511

Figure 10: Dr. James T. Rogers 512

Figure 11: Dr. John S. Burd 513

Figure 12: Dr. Edward L. Schrader 514

Figure 13: Image showing damage caused by the tornado of April 6, 1936 to Brenau's campus 515

Figure 14: Domestic science laboratory circa 1950 516

Figure 15: A sample of music performed at Brenau in the early 1900s 517

Figure 16: Brenau Choral circa 2007 518

Figure 17: Brenau students in a 2005 production by the Gainesville Theatre Alliance 519

Figure 18: The Tri-Kappa Society of Brenau College 520

Figure 19: The Georgia Baptist Female Seminary circa 1879 521

Figure 20: Wilkes Hall circa 1920 522

Figure 21: Photograph of the lobby of Yonah Hall circa 1900 522

Figure 22: From left to right, Yonah Hall, East Hall, Bailey Hall, and Pearce Auditorium circa 1940 523

Figure 23: Interior of Pearce Auditorium (circa 1920), featuring the ceiling painting entitled, "Aeneas at the Court of Dido." 524

Figure 24: Simmons Memorial Hall circa 1940 525

Figure 25: Brenau Trustee Library circa 2002 525

List of Figures   xi

Figure 26: The Crow's Nest circa 1925 showing elevated seniors and underclassmen 526

Figure 27: Elements of Brenau's Japanese gardens designed by Shogo Joseph Myaida 527

Figure 28: The Brenau campus in the early 1900s, depicting several halls connected to form a single, large edifice 527

Figure 29: The Alpha Delta Pi house circa 1920, which was typical of the several sorority cottages at Brenau during this era 528

Figure 30: May Day at Brenau circa 1925 529

Figure 31: R.A.T.T. week at Brenau circa 1995 529

Figure 32: One of Brenau's mysterious Dare Stones 530

Figure 33: Brenau's early aquatic facilities 531

Figure 34: A field day sports team (of sophomore baseball players) also showing appropriate costume for gym activities (circa 1920) 531

Figure 35: Brenau students playing volleyball circa 1950. (Note as well the presence of archery targets and bars for stretching in the upper left-hand corner of the frame.) 532

Figure 36: Brenau soccer circa 2011 533

Figure 37: The Stabs as depicted in the Bubbles circa 1920 534

Figure 38: Brenau's H.G.H. Society 535

Figure 39: One of Brenau's several stately sorority houses 536

List of Tables

Table 1: Number of Men and Women on the Brenau Faculty by Year 537

Table 2a: Undergraduate degrees offered by Brenau over time 538

Table 2b: Undergraduate degrees offered by Brenau over time (cont.) 539

Table 2c: Undergraduate degrees offered by Brenau over time (cont.) 540

Table 2d: Undergraduate degrees offered by Brenau over time (cont.) 541

Table 2e: Undergraduate degrees offered by Brenau over time (cont.) 542

Preface

This study examines the history of Brenau University, a private liberal arts institution located in Gainesville, Georgia, that was founded in 1878 as a college for the education of women. Set in the venerable and alluring Appalachian foothills, Brenau has in its many years enjoyed several successes, endured numerous struggles, and played host to some remarkable characters, each with many lessons to teach. As such, Brenau's history has all the elements of a good story, and so whereas it might appeal the most to people interested in the history of women's higher education or with some connection to Brenau (i.e., alumnae, faculty & staff members, students, and supporters), anyone could find it intriguing. Several questions concerning Brenau could be of interest to any constituency: How and why was a women's college founded in north Georgia? What is the history of academic life at Brenau? What was the history of such things as "physical culture" and athletics at the College? What is revealed by examining the history of traditions and organizations (such as secret societies) at Brenau? What challenges (such as integration) has Brenau faced in modern times and how did the institution cope? How has Brenau's physical environment altered over the years in response to changing societal attitudes about women and higher education? Answering these questions will both paint a more complete picture of Brenau and will contribute new knowledge to the historiography of women's higher education.

I propose to address these and other questions, framing my inquiries around the concept of college as being a "negotiated space." This idea suggests that the overall experience of any college or university is essentially constructed in a process of negotiation between two key groups, the institution's students and its official personnel, the faculty and staff. Of course, these negotiations might, at times, take the form of actual face-to-face meetings between these two parties. Far more often, the negotiating occurs over time and not at arm's length in something like an ongoing, give-and-take process spanning the life of the institution. Each side might take years to do something that impacts the college experience or take years to respond to something promulgated by the other party. The end result, though, is that both sides—institutional employees and students—play a role in refining their school.

The idea that a college is, in effect, a negotiated space is certainly not anything unique to Brenau, nor is it any novel concept that I advance. Yet, whereas it should be intuitive to think of any college experience as the product of bilateral negotiation between students and college officials, in fact, the idea of student agency is often lost in many institutional histories. Rather, these works depict the lives of colleges and universities from the top down, focusing a great deal upon the actions of administrators, trustees and benefactors, and faculty and staff members. Typically, their very organization reflects this bias. Many institutional biographies periodize the history of the college or university around the terms of its presidents, making readers trudge chronologically through "The Smith Years," then "The Jones Years," etc. These orthodox histories can forget to adequately acknowledge the fact that students were also historical actors who often pushed back against institutional designs or even initiated their own campus policies and that they actually did so with some success to create their idealized version of what college should be. To better keep

Preface　　　　　　　　　　　　　　　　　xvii

a focus on student agency, the chapters in this history are organized not around years but around themes significant in the life of any college.

Chapter 1 begins by orienting the reader to Brenau by describing some of the significant characteristics of the present-day institution (enrollment, programs of study, etc.) and the region. Borrowing from scholarship on higher education, it then provides a brief overview of how women's colleges originated and evolved in the United States to place Brenau into a larger historical context. This discussion traces the emergence of women's colleges from institutions known as girls' "academies" and "French schools" to more academically rigorous places that adopted curricula rooted in classical study and so situates Brenau in a larger academic world. I then describe my methodology, which will be to examine Brenan's history topically within a framework of college as a negotiated space.

The first topic introduces Brenau's students, faculty members, and staff members to acquaint readers with some of the key players that have shaped the Brenau college experience over time. Despite their differences (which will become apparent), common ground has long existed between those seeking education at Brenau and those providing it. Both sides sought to create an ideal college experience—they just differed at times on what that would be. Brenau students and the Brenau faculty and staff frequently sparred over contested space between extremes. For example, socially speaking, students sought freedom and treatment as adults. At the same time, Brenau personnel (typically administrators, but also some other faculty and staff members) strove to implement social controls *in loco parentis*. Academically, students sought vocationally relevant knowledge whereas faculty members were content at times to dispense learning for learning's sake. Contests such as these occurred throughout Brenau's history between these identifiable groups.

Though typifying any group of students over more than a century can be challenging, chapter 1 shows that some consistencies have historically stood out among Brenau attendees. Brenau has generally attracted young women from all over the country and the world, often from educated households. The College has long stressed its affordability and its desire to expand educational opportunities for women. Brenau went beyond merely advertising its low cost. The College took pains in some of its promotional materials to stress that it discouraged lavish spending by students and that it offered generous scholarships for some of those enrolled. Perhaps encouraged by this, students came to Brenau from many socioeconomic backgrounds. Though Brenau would enroll some students from working class families and some from very wealthy homes, most Brenau students tended to be from "middle-class" backgrounds. This was true even as student numbers tended to fluctuate with the economy and, occasionally, became so low as to jeopardize Brenau's continued existence. Until fairly recently, there was relatively little outwardly apparent religious or racial diversity at Brenau, rendering the institution largely white and Protestant for much of its existence. Additionally, it perhaps goes without saying that, by design, there has likewise been very little gender diversity over the years at the Brenau Women's College, either. Many young women have attended Brenau over the years, many of them would graduate, and a few of these alumnae would achieve some prominence in various fields.

Though they surely could not have agreed on everything every time, enough similar traits and backgrounds and/or affinity for their *alma mater* have apparently existed over time between Brenau students to incline them to hold similar views when it came to negotiating with Brenau officials. Though it would go too far to claim that the student body always spoke with one clarion voice in negotiations with Brenau personnel, little evidence suggests that the students ever Balkanized significantly over any major issues. Rather, throughout its history, most Brenau students or their agents (such as the members of the Student Government Association, perhaps the oldest such body at a southern women's college) seemed to have been on more or less the same page in dealings with the faculty and staff.

Preface

The discussion on Brenau personnel examines Brenau's founders, subsequent administrators, and profiles a few of the remarkable professors the College has employed over time, but particularly in its earlier years. Powerful presidents with long tenures (especially Dr. H.J. Pearce and Dr. Josiah Crudup) played large roles in governance and negotiations with students. Chapter 1 also examines the demographics of the faculty, focusing on their education and gender distribution, to better appreciate how they might have influenced and related to their Brenau students.

Chapter 2 addresses academics at Brenau. To offer context, the chapter begins with an overview of what students studied at early American women's institutions as compared to the classical program of studies offered to students at early men's colleges. The chapter then touches on the development of academic departments and the elective system in academia before exploring how Brenau's curriculum changed over time and how those changes were the product of negotiation between students and faculty members. Though not widely acknowledged for having done so, Brenau innovated quite a bit, especially in its youth. For example, it was apparently the first college anywhere to let students count courses in art and music as electives toward traditional baccalaureate degrees, a practice commonplace today. Among Georgia's private women's colleges, Brenau innovated by creating programs in teacher education, commercial studies, and domestic sciences alongside its classical offerings. The institution also maintained a remarkable independent conservatory, one of the largest and best-reputed in the state, until its merger with the College. Brenau meant to uplift women with these programs in its early years. No doubt many graduates found success for having received a Brenau education, but, in a sense, the opposite may have also occurred. Instead of empowering women, some of Brenau's programs reinforced ideas that women should only occupy traditional gender roles. For example, until modern times, Brenau educated women to be teachers, but never to be school principals. Brenau trained women in stenography and other secretarial skills, but never taught them how to found and run their own businesses. Brenau taught women to sing and play music, but not to conduct symphonies. This is unfortunate because evidence shows that Brenau's students were often well-prepared for college work and might have benefited from a more rigorous and scholarly curriculum.

Despite its academic innovations, Brenau experienced difficulties that forced it to adapt and change. For example, owing to several factors that will be examined, the College lost regional accreditation in the 1940s. This prompted a curriculum overhaul. Brenau went from offering several different types of undergraduate degrees to offering only the Bachelor of Arts in the 1950s. This remained the norm for several decades, even after Brenau regained accreditation. In the late 1960s and early 1970s when many women's colleges struggled to survive, Brenau expanded its mission (and its enrollment numbers) by beginning to offer evening courses outside of its Women's College that were open to nontraditional students—and even to men, a move which produced some controversy. In the 1980s, Brenau expanded further by opening several satellite campuses throughout Georgia, offering weekend courses and developing a weekend-only baccalaureate degree program, and offering several graduate degrees. In 1992, reflecting growth and these many changes, Brenau College became Brenau University. Over the next twenty years, the institution continued to grow, added more degree programs (including its first doctorate), and started offering online courses and degree programs.

Throughout this rich academic history, negotiation between Brenau students and Brenau faculty and staff took place and shaped the academic landscape of the institution, but only to a degree. At Brenau, it was, by and large, the faculty and administration that determined degree requirements and what would be taught and when and why. Even so, students were not entirely without agency. Upon occasion, they successfully negotiated with the faculty and administration for some academic-related changes and brought about the rise and demise of several academic programs by "voting with their feet."

Chapter 3 examines institutional policymaking at Brenau and reveals an arena at the College in which administrators exercised almost absolute control in determining the character of the institution. This is well-illustrated in the historical trace of admissions rules about race and gender. Though presently a very diverse and inclusive place in terms of race, religion, etc., Brenau officials powerfully resisted integration and espoused a culture of racial segregation up until as late as 1972, making Brenau one of the very last colleges anywhere in America to desegregate. The chapter places this resistance into context by briefly examining the history of higher education for African Americans and for women, especially in the South, up until the Civil Rights Era. During this period when other educational institutions began dismantling segregationist policies, Brenau's governors held out. Administrators used somewhat novel and very calculated strategies to dodge integration that generally centered on avoiding taking *any* government funding for anything. The belief was that if the College had no ties to the federal government, then the federal government could not compel integration. With the blessing of Brenau's trustees, Dr. Josiah Crudup, Brenau's fourth president, acted so as to perpetuate segregation at the College by placing Brenau at a financial distance from government reach. Nothing suggests Brenau's students at the time either generally supported or objected to the College's policies respecting race. Moreover, even if students had objected, it is not likely their views would have been given much consideration by the faculty and staff as they set policy. After all, Brenau officials did not consult at all with students before flirting with a controversial, though short-lived, policy shift to admit men to the all-women's college.

Chapter 4 is concerned with Brenau's physical environment. As was the case with academics and institutional policy setting, students seemed to exercise little agency in negotiating with College personnel over Brenau's built and landscaped spaces. Still, students have never been completely without influence. The chapter reveals that as Brenau's Gainesville campus has evolved over the years, its very architecture and design have changed in response to changing institutional and societal views about femininity and the role of higher education for women. Reflecting conservative, patriarchal views about women in the nineteenth-century South, the Georgia Baptist Female Seminary (as the College was named until 1900) operated in one large edifice to better monitor and supervise its students. Later, society came to expect graduates of women's colleges to be suited to step quickly into the roles of wife and mother. Brenau evolved a system of residential cottages that emulated a family environment and served as laboratories in which future matriarchs could hone domestic skills. Finally, by the mid-twentieth century, as wider society began to acknowledge the intellectual equality of women to men, Brenau's campus became homologous to typical men's colleges and to coeducational colleges located elsewhere. Brenau developed the structures and forms common to these institutions (such as residence halls, athletic facilities, etc.) because any college simply required such things to adequately address the wants and needs of modern college-goers, whatever their gender.

Chapter 5 is entitled, "Organizations and Traditions: Those that Govern Students and those that Students Govern." It explores the negotiation between students and the faculty & staff over the Brenau college experience by examining organizations and traditions in which students exercised a great deal of agency and those in which they lacked agency. This chapter explains how Brenau's popular and officially sanctioned Y.W.C.A.; its literary, fine arts, and media clubs; and its several time-honored traditions have encouraged student conformity or remained under student control. Likewise, evident in some of Brenau's traditions are aspects of the college experience that are aloof from negotiation and official control whereas others serve to keep Brenau students governed.

Students found some voice in setting rules and discipline at the College, which chapter 6 discusses. Following an overview of the history of rules at colleges generally, an examination of Brenau's rules over time reveals the institution's regulations to be detailed and often atypically liberal—at least by Georgia women's college standards of the day. Brenau women

Preface   xxiii

gradually negotiated for much autonomy under the College rules, which evolved over the decades as did entities like disciplinary boards and honor courts. The chapter traces this evolution and examines changes in rules about card playing, church and chapel attendance (requirements for which Brenau dropped fairly early by Georgia standards, a novel thing for a women's college to do), class attendance, housing (especially rules relating to visitation, quiet hours, and curfew), dress code, smoking, and interacting with men (i.e., conversing, receiving callers, dreaded "night riding," dating, and even marriage).

Chapters 7 and 8 deal with Brenau's more physical side. Chapter 7 examines "physical culture" at the College, which is different from athletics as the term is generally taken to mean. Physical culture amounted to little more than demure activities like light gymnastic exercise and calisthenics. Sports, athletics, and physical education developed at northern women's colleges before heading south. For many years, southern women's colleges like Brenau promoted physical culture and not athletics for students, thinking the latter unhealthy and masculinizing for women. Despite stressing student health, having seemingly opulent sports facilities, and having faculty members, courses, clubs, and field days all dedicated to physical activity, up until the 1920s, Brenau actually sheltered women athletically.

Chapter 8 describes a protracted shift at Brenau as students began to prevail in negotiations with the faculty and staff over introducing true athletics at the College. Beginning in the 1920s, competition (once thought to be un-womanly and so discouraged) increased as Brenau class and club teams played tennis, basketball, and other sports against each other. Students founded an athletic society and promulgated ways to "letter" in a sport. Though Brenau once avoided intercollegiate athletic competition (fearing it would promote un-feminine qualities), students eventually negotiated successfully for this. Brenau athletes broke new ground by playing the "co-eds" of the North Georgia Agricultural College (now the University of North Georgia) in basketball in 1927, becoming the first women's college in Georgia and one of the first in the South to participate in an intercollegiate sport.

History shows that the vigor for athletics alive at Brenau in the 1920s would wane for several decades before resurging. Brenau would not participate in another intercollegiate contest in any sport for many years. Instead, intra-school "play days" and competition between classes and clubs again became the norm and more demure sports (like dancing and rhythmic gymnastics) resurfaced prominently. Owing to lagging student interest perhaps brought on by changing societal attitudes about femininity, athletics and sports declined even more in the 1950s and early 1960s as demonstrated by Brenau's yearbooks, which depicted little or nothing about sports. On the heels of the modern women's movement in America, a sporting revival occurred at Brenau in the 1970s as students and officials both began supporting athletics. The College started offering more physical education courses and built new athletic facilities. Intercollegiate athletics resumed in the late 1970s and the 1980s with the establishment of swimming and tennis programs, which became quite strong in both regional and national competition. Starting in the 1990s, Brenau began competing against other schools in soccer, rowing, volleyball, cross country, and basketball. The University would later add programs in softball, track and field, and competitive cheerleading as well. Such robust athletic offerings would likely not have emerged at Brenau were it not for earlier negotiations by students wanting more than demure exercises at the institution.

Chapter 9 examines spaces sacred to students and student secret societies at the College. This was the realm in which Brenau students arguably enjoyed the most success in their negotiations with faculty members and administrators to create their version of an idealized undergraduate experience. The chapter begins by providing a brief overview of the origins of collegiate secret societies (including sororities) before exploring these bodies at Brenau. Brenau students began forming secret societies in the early twentieth century, with names like "The

Skulls" and "The Stabs." They operated mostly clandestinely, beyond the reach of the faculty and staff. Most were short-lived, except for the prestigious and mysterious H.G.H. Senior Honor Society, which has been around Brenau since the 1930s, making it one of the very few truly timeworn secret groups at any women's college. Sororities have also been at Brenau for many decades. Chapter 9 discusses the origins of sororities at the College specifically and what accounts for the success of national sororities at Brenau when they exist at only three other women's colleges—and maintain houses only at Brenau. History shows how sorority membership has changed over time at Brenau, how sororities once discriminated in membership selection on the basis of race and religion (and, apparently, even smoking preference), and the kinds of events and functions sororities sponsored over the past century. Brenau's sororities created detailed rules for "rushing" and "pledging" that evolved over time. Ultimately, Brenau's sororities simultaneously and paradoxically both encouraged and subverted femininity as Brenau women created their idealized version of the college experience in this realm largely apart from the influence of the faculty and staff.

I conclude Brenau's history by coming full-circle. The book began by pointing out several of Brenau's distinguishing characteristics and by arguing that college is a contested space in which the overall experience of any institution is refined over time in a process of negotiation between students and the faculty & staff. This study ends by saying that Brenau's history shows that the College is distinguished *precisely by* this negotiation—Brenau is Brenau thanks to this process more than anything else.

The results of this negotiation between students and the faculty and staff at Brenau appear along a continuum. Often, Brenau's faculty members and administration gained the upper hand in negotiations with students and these officials enacted their desires absent much student agency. This was particularly evident in fashioning the College curriculum, in setting institutional policies about such things as admissions, and in constituting the College's physical environment. In other instances, this was not the case. At times, Brenau's students seemed to win these negotiations and exhibited a remarkable degree of autonomy in conducting affairs in some arenas. Brenau women had a prominent voice in effecting College rules and discipline, in bringing athletics to campus, and in running student organizations. Perhaps more important than noting who wins at what is acknowledging that *both* sides have agency in refining the college experience. Other scholars might utilize a methodological framework for their work that also contemplates the college experience as a negotiated space to produce accounts that will add to what is known about other institutions of higher learning. Many colleges and universities, especially in the South, still need their histories written and student agency should matter as much as anything else in doing so.

Acknowledgements

This work owes its completion to many people who assisted me and who inspired me to strive for high standards of scholarship. I hope I reached that bar, but, in any case, the fault for any shortfalls or errors occurring herein is mine alone and should not reflect negatively upon any other person or upon Brenau University. Also, though this work is *about* Brenau it is not *of* Brenau. The views and opinions expressed herein are those of the author and are not necessarily shared by Brenau University.

I particularly want to acknowledge that everyone associated with the University that I consulted in writing this book—current and former faculty and staff members, and students—gave me the distinct sense that whereas they admired her immensely, like me, they wanted the historical account of Brenau to be, above all, *genuine*. There are times in the life of any institution that are unflattering. Some colleges and universities might try to keep such episodes hidden. They might be aided in doing so by a sympathetic biographer—perhaps a member of the faculty or a graduate of the institution itself. Writers with such personal connections would be more likely to produce a celebratory history that trumpets an institution's triumphs and glosses over its tragedies. Other than having taught two history courses there as an adjunct faculty member, attending an occasional music recital or theatrical performance, and making use of its library and Archives from time to time for research, I have no ties to Brenau. Yet, even as I am perhaps able to avoid writing a celebratory account of Brenau's history, I found that there are, in fact, things to celebrate about the institution. Regarding what should not be celebrated, just as a college can try to sweep unflattering chapters under the rug, it can acknowledge negative episodes and learn from past mistakes. To their great credit, I believe those with ties to Brenau are of a mind to learn to better serve future generations by thoughtfully considering what came before—warts and all.

I am grateful to several current and former students and personnel at Brenau University for their help and encouragement. Drs. John S. and Patricia A. Burd and Dr. James Southerland provided a great deal of information and support in personal interviews and conversations. John Burd went on to very generously provide absolutely invaluable feedback on this entire manuscript. His extensive knowledge about Brenau and his keen eye for detail simply made the work far better than it otherwise could have been and I am truly beholden to him for this. The Brenau Trustee Library staff was always very accommodating, as was Mr. Michael McPeek, Brenau's Director of Multimedia Publishing, who assisted me with retrieving some electronic sources. Mr. David Morrison, Brenau's Vice President for Communications and Publications, and his staff were extremely helpful to me at multiple turns. Finally, I am particularly indebted to Ms. Debbie Thompson, who holds many titles at the University, including that of Official Archivist. Debbie was unfailingly knowledgeable, helpful, and, with her wonderful sense of humor and enthusiasm, always a joy to speak with.

Outside of Brenau, I am grateful to many past and present colleagues and students at Gainesville State College and at the University of North Georgia for their support as I pursued this project. Dr. Bonnie "B.J." Robinson and Mr. James Hinds rendered invaluable assistance to me with preparing the several illustrations included in this book for publication. Dr.

Acknowledgements   xxix

Paul Richardson and Toni Tan of Teneo Press were always professional and patient, traits a new author could never esteem highly enough. The outside reviewers employed by Teneo made many excellent suggestions to improve the manuscript for which I am thankful. Additionally, I am grateful to Dr. Peter Charles Hoffer for all he taught me in my first years of graduate training to become an historian.

My doctoral dissertation committee members at the University of Georgia were simply outstanding and guided me to produce the forerunner of what would eventually become this manuscript. Two members were Dr. Derrick P. Alridge and Dr. Todd D. Dinkelman. I learned much from their tutelage and they always provided me with invaluable feedback and support on this project. To Dr. Ronald E. Butchart, my committee chairman and my advisor in the doctoral program who supervised my work on this study, I owe a very, very great deal indeed. I have been the beneficiary of his insight, his wisdom, his intellect, his humor, and his indefatigable support more times than I could count. No student anywhere ever had a better mentor and friend.

Finally, for all they have done to help me bring this book about, I owe the most of all to my friends and family who have been there for me over the years. Two are first in my heart: my daughter, Celia, who, with her boundless spirit, kind heart, and vast talents, constantly amazes and inspires me beyond all words, and my wife Ana, with whom I am honored and grateful to have shared so much of life's journey. *Os quiero mucho.*

The History of Brenau University, 1878–2013

Introduction

Placing Brenau into Context

The name "Brenau" is derived from German (*brennan*, which means "to burn") and Latin (*aurum*, which means "gold") and means "gold as refined by fire." This motto reflects Brenau's desire to forge its students into remarkable beings. The main campus of the University is located about fifty miles northeast of Atlanta, Georgia, in the city of Gainesville, near the foothills of the Appalachian Mountains. Sixty-three buildings, some of which are on the National Register of Historic Places, are grouped in what approximates two quadrangles and occupy this verdant fifty-six acre site. Brenau is accredited by the Southern Association of Colleges and Schools and is a self-described private, selective, non-denominational, comprehensive university. Brenau maintains three points of matriculation for students: the Women's College, the Undergraduate School (consisting of evening and weekend, as well as online, course offerings), and the Sidney O. Smith Jr. Graduate School. Students locate their academic home in one of four colleges: Business and Mass Communication, Education, Fine Arts and Humanities, and Health and Science. Brenau also maintains an "Early College" program, which provides select young women with the opportunity to complete their final two years of high school while simultaneously earning an Associate of Arts degree from the institution.

In 2012, Brenau had a combined enrollment in all divisions of around 2,800 students. Commuting students take classes in Gainesville or at one of Brenau's satellite campuses elsewhere in Georgia in north and south Atlanta, Augusta, or at the King's Bay Naval Base on the Georgia coast. Several hundred students reside on the main campus in several dormitories and sorority houses. Student diversity is noteworthy. In 2011–2012, Brenau enrolled students from at least twenty-three states and twelve countries. Around one-fourth of Brenau's students were members of minority groups and many were over twenty-five years of age.[1]

At the heart of Brenau University is its Women's College, which, as of 2012, had been educating young women for over 133 years. This small liberal arts college was founded in 1878 as the Georgia Baptist Female Seminary and became Brenau College in 1900. From very modest beginnings, Brenau has matured greatly. It redefined itself as a university in 1992 to reflect its expanded offerings of undergraduate degrees in over thirty majors and of graduate degrees in teacher education, business administration, accounting, nursing, psychology, public administration, and interior design. In 2012, Brenau claimed thousands of alumnae, an endowment of over twenty-five million dollars, an economic impact to its community of over $60 million, and an established presence in various regional and national college rankings.[2]

Nothing about Brenau happened overnight. Indeed, like other American institutions of higher learning, Brenau can actually trace its distant roots back to the Middle Ages when colleges first emerged (in a somewhat haphazard fashion) in western Europe.[3] Brenau's more immediate ancestors formed in Britain's North American colonies as outgrowths of primary and secondary schools. Experiences varied by place, but these schools generally provided at least a rudimentary education (which focused on the famous three "'Rs") and typically enrolled both boys and girls. From these schools would emerge a handful of colonial colleges, mostly the institutions that today comprise the "Ivy League."[4] Jurgen Herbst, a scholar of American higher education, asserted that these first colonial colleges "were created as unincorporated provincial Latin grammar boarding schools governed by trustees."[5] Like their counterparts in European universities, colonial college trustees saw to it that students at these Spartanly-equipped schools studied the "classical curriculum," which consisted of Greek, Latin, philosophy, and rhetoric, among other things. This happened generally in preparation for entering careers in the ministry or government. Migrating graduates of these institutions founded other colleges elsewhere across the country in the late eighteenth and early nineteenth century, importing the classical curriculum as they went.[6]

Most early colleges enrolled only men. Women's colleges would come into being to offer women higher education. Like their male-dominated counterparts, these typically evolved from lower schools, but historians offer slightly different traces of this process owing to regional differences. Christie Anne Farnham, the author of *The Education of the Southern Belle: Higher Education and Student Socialization in the Antebellum South*, noted that, "Beginning in the late eighteenth century, wealthy southern families sometimes sent their daughters to 'French schools.'"[7] Often, but not always, boarding schools, girls attending these institutions received instruction in French (hence the name), arithmetic, dancing, art, and embroidery—the so-called "ornamental" courses. Farnham indicated that these were not academically rigorous places designed to educate girls in the same curriculum that boys received at the time. Rather, French schools existed chiefly to facilitate social gain on the part of a girl's family and actually had the effect of marginalizing women by relegating them to particular social roles. Farnham wrote, "French schools, by refining the rough edges of behavior and language and by emphasizing taste and the arts, improved the position of students in the marriage market."[8] Graduates of French schools were cultured and refined and, as such, were sought after by southern men from good families for marriage. Unsurprisingly, at French schools, developing intellect took a back seat to developing the social graces. Farnham asserted that French schools prepared women to become ladies and little else. According to Farnham, young southern women who desired more serious schooling "had to await the spread of academies before secondary education became widely available."[9]

This spread really began around the 1820s when southern academies either sprang up or, occasionally, developed as some French schools morphed into more academically demanding institutions.[10] Farnham determined that the widespread growth of southern academies signaled a shift in educational focus for women as the curriculum of French schools became more obsolete. She wrote:

> Herein lies a major difference between the French schools and the academies. Although the new academies initially offered few courses above the level of history, geography, and English grammar —which were to be found in many of the larger boarding schools —there is a shift in emphasis from a core curriculum consisting of French and the arts to one composed of academic subjects.[11]

According to Farnham, academies were more academically and intellectually rigorous places than the more ornamental French schools they replaced.[12] Some of these academies would become still more academically rigorous and eventually become southern women's colleges.

In the North, it was not French schools but "venture schools" that would eventually beget academies and, later, women's colleges. In her book entitled *Women's Education in the United States 1780–1840*, historian Margaret A. Nash wrote that:

> From 1780 to 1840, women's opportunities for advanced education burgeoned. In the 1780s, women who sought education beyond the rudiments found it primarily in temporary, short-lived schools... that were open for only a few weeks or months at a time.[13]

These were called "adventure" or "venture" schools and proprietor-owners often ran them out of private homes.[14] Nash noted that though subject matter varied from school to school, most "taught the English branches, geography, and arithmetic" as well as "any other subject for which there might be a market," like music or art.[15]

Nash wrote that by the late eighteenth century, elite families moved away from the home tutoring of adventure schools and instead educated their children in more permanent "academies." Nash pointed out that these were actually "variously called academies, seminaries, or institutes" and that they provided access to full-time teachers, scientific apparatuses, and possibilities for socialization that were not available in private homes.[16] In addition, according to historian Kim Tolley, "a school bearing the name 'academy' or 'seminary' differed from a venture school in having some form of financial support other than tuition, articles of incorporation, and the oversight of a board of trustees."[17] Occasionally, venture schools evolved into academies or seminaries as they acquired these things.[18]

In his well-respected, if somewhat dated, work on the history of women's higher education in the United States, historian Thomas Woody examined the girls' academies that would eventually give birth to women's colleges. In some instances, academies had actually existed for many years in America. Woody wrote that as far back as 1727, the convent of the Ursuline Sisters in New Orleans began teaching young women rudimentary subjects. Later, Pennsylvania was home to the Bethlehem Female Academy and the Female Academy of Philadelphia, which came into being in 1742 and 1792, respectively.[19] Also, Moravians founded the Salem Female Academy in North Carolina in 1772.[20]

Besides having existed in America for some time, girls' academies and seminaries had become surprisingly numerous in early America given the nation's largely rural character. Historian Mary Kelly asserted that "Between 1790 and 1830, 182 academies and at least 14 seminaries were established exclusively for women in the North and South."[21] At least 158 more schools would open by 1860.[22] Henry Barnard, an eminent nineteenth-century historian of American education, posited the number of academies in America at "more than six thousand" that were "spread across the land, in every state and territory" by 1850.[23] Theodore Sizer, author of *The Age of the Academies*, would deem even that figure to be conservative.[24] Many of these academies, like the forerunner of Brenau, educated only girls.

Whether academies and seminaries evolved from venture schools in the North or from French schools in the South, they would be among the institutions that would eventually produce women's colleges like Brenau. Prior to 1830, Nash observed that "virtually no institution called a college admitted women."[25] Still, heads of girls' academies and seminaries "frequently asserted that, even though their institutions did not take on the name 'college,' they offered college-level curricula for women."[26] It was the adoption of this increased academic rigor on the part of some academies and seminaries that created women's colleges like Brenau.

There were multiple reasons why such a shift in educational focus to providing more and more rigorous schooling for girls occurred. Nash noted that after 1830, views about women and college changed in the United States as religious revival had swept through America in the Second Great Awakening. Where once colleges had existed to simply prepare men for the professions, colleges came to prepare young men *and* women "to participate in creating a Christian nation."[27] At the same time, Enlightenment and women's rights movement notions about how amenable women were to education argued powerfully that women were just as capable of being students as men were.[28]

Another reason for increasing the rigor of women's education lay in changing attitudes about women themselves. Colonial American women had little access to higher education within their eighteenth-century sphere. Historian Frederick Rudolph wrote that, "The colonial view of woman was simply that she was intellectually inferior—incapable, merely by reason of being a woman, of great thoughts. Her faculties were not worth training. Her place was in the home, where man had assigned her a number of useful functions."[29] This was perhaps even more the case in the South. Woody wrote that "the standard for a girl's education in the southern colonies to the end of the eighteenth century" was "generally with reference to men and their own future sphere as home-makers."[30] Regarding this standard, Woody observed that "Beyond the merest rudiments, the ornamental subjects were clearly emphasized, inasmuch as these made them agreeable embellishments of society and attractive ornaments of the home."[31]

After the American Revolution, educating women more wherever they lived seemed to make more sense to Americans. After all, the fledgling country burgeoned with opportunity. Indeed, so much opportunity existed that many Americans believed that men simply could not take advantage of all of it all by themselves. They needed "the assistance of wives who knew how to help their husbands to make their fortunes" by sharing in the managing of finances, of correspondence, and of the increasingly complex American home.[32] Also, just as men had the important job of running the new country, American women needed "to help prepare the manhood of tomorrow for responsible citizenship" so he might better serve the Republic.[33] To become modern homemakers, business assistants, and "republican mothers" required a more robust, more general education. Academies and their more thorough curricula emerged to meet this need. Whereas such a better education would surely have empowered women, more might have been done. By preparing women to fit only these certain roles in society, academies did not prepare women to aspire to greater things.

The only real exception to this was in the area of teaching. As one team of authors put it, with the societal perception of their nurturing, patient natures, "Women were increasingly regarded as better teachers than men."[34] They would also work for less than men would. These factors, coupled with a growth in the numbers of schools in the country beginning in the early nineteenth century, created opportunity for educated women, which made more women want to be highly educated. In *A Century of Higher Education for American Women*, author Mabel Newcomer also contended that the advent of technological innovations like electric and gas lighting and washing and sewing machines helped the cause of women's higher education. Women gained more leisure time thanks to these labor-saving devices and often spent that time doing more reading, which increased their desire for education.[35]

Among academies that catered to women in the nineteenth century, a hierarchy emerged as the expanded depth and breadth of the curricular offerings of some institutions came to set those schools apart from others. These relatively more academically rigorous places, in turn, adopted names to set themselves apart from the pack. Farnham wrote that, "To distinguish their level of coursework from that of ordinary academies, the term female seminary came into use."[36] Though all seminary curricula still included at least some "ornamental" courses like art and music, Farnham revealed that at all serious seminaries, as at contemporary men's colleges, "the study of the classics at some level was generally attempted."[37]

It was this attempt at classical study that truly set some seminaries apart from lesser academies and made them wholly different from earlier French and venture schools. Some of these advanced seminaries would eventually evolve into women's colleges beginning around the 1830s. This occurred as these institutions deemphasized ornamental and secondary or preparatory-level educational programs in favor of adopting more advanced classical curricula on a par with that of contemporary men's colleges.

John R. Thelin, an historian of American higher education, noted that the "typical curriculum" of a men's college around 1830 "emphasized the study of classical languages, science, and mathematics with the aim of building character and promoting distinctive habits of thought."[38] Regarding nineteenth century women's colleges that strove to emulate men's colleges, Thelin asserted that the "'female seminaries' were usually comparable in academic rigor to the colleges for men in the same area."[39] Comparable, that is, but not identical. Thelin noted further that "Some evidence suggests that the curriculum for women usually emphasized English and modern languages over classics—not unlike the parallel offerings at men's colleges in the 'bachelor of science' track."[40]

Placing Brenau into Context

According to Nash, many historians have generally acknowledged such different emphases or even believed that the early female academies and seminaries that replaced venture and French schools were, with few exceptions, inferior to contemporary male institutions. She challenged this notion, contending that "both the curricula and the pedagogy were similar for men and women in most academies of the period."[41] Nash's findings dispelled notions that girls' academies and seminaries taught only "ornamental" subjects whereas boys' academies taught "classics" like Greek and Latin. In fact, she found that academic curricula for both genders almost invariably consisted of "English, geography (broadly conceived), arithmetic and mathematics, and ancient and modern languages."[42] Academies and seminaries also offered some vocational subjects, "like navigation and surveying for men and needlework for women," as well.[43] Pedagogically, most academies and seminaries shunned the rote memorization learning style that once dominated education and instead encouraged more active learning and academic competition among students.[44]

Both Nash and Thelin would agree that some of the most advanced of the female seminaries and academies would eventually become early women's colleges, Brenau's immediate predecessors. Exactly which institution became the first women's college in America is difficult to discern. In writing a report on women's colleges for the United States Department of Education, Irene Harwarth, Mindi Maline, and Elizabeth DeBra acknowledged several contenders. They pointed out that Wesleyan College of Macon, Georgia, "was the first school chartered in the United States in 1836, to confer on girls 'all such honors, degrees and licenses as are usually conferred in colleges and universities.'"[45] At the same time, the authors also pointed out that Woody identified Mary Sharp College, which was founded in Winchester, Tennessee, in 1851 and closed in 1896, as "the first U.S. women's college to require both Latin and Greek in a four-year course, and give an A.B. degree comparable to those awarded by men's colleges."[46] Harwarth *et al.* also observed that Elmira College in Elmira, New York, which was founded in 1855, and Vassar College in

Poughkeepsie, New York (founded in 1865), are also claimants to the title of oldest true women's college because they first developed academic standards "in a fair degree comparable with men's colleges" and a healthy endowment, respectively.[47]

Over time, other women's colleges would be established after these pioneering institutions. All of the notable "Seven Sisters" institutions (which are Barnard and Vassar colleges in New York; Bryn Mawr College in Pennsylvania; and Mount Holyoke, Smith, Wellesley, and Radcliffe Colleges in Massachusetts) had been founded by 1875. Beginning around 1900, educators founded many Catholic women's colleges throughout the country as well.[48] Also around the turn of the century, a handful of public women's colleges opened. The founding of these and other women's colleges throughout the country would swell women's college numbers in America into the hundreds. Many of these institutions would thrive for several decades into the twentieth century but see enrollments contract beginning around mid-century. This would have been primarily due to the simple fact that, as time passed, most American colleges became coeducational. Women thereby gained many more options for higher education and enrollment at women's colleges dropped. Precipitous enrollment drops closed many women's colleges and caused many others to become coeducational. Overall, Harwarth noted that, "The actual number of women's colleges [had] dropped from approximately 300 in 1960 to about 80 in 1998."[49] Still more women's colleges would cease to be in subsequent years. Brenau is one of the survivors.

Brenau can make no claim to being the first women's college, yet its development mirrors that of the institutions that can. Brenau began life as an advanced seminary, named the Georgia Baptist Female Seminary, in 1878. Despite its being relatively old, the story of Brenau, with but one short exception, remains largely untold. Biographies of educational institutions exist for other colleges and universities, many much younger than Brenau. These institutional histories provide a wealth of information on the places they were written about. These works also help us learn about history in a much broader context as we see in the microcosm of a single college or university a rendering of part of the larger world. Given its fairly long life and its relatively rare character as a single-gender institution, at the very least, shedding light on the past of Brenau University's Women's College would, at the same time, illuminate more about the history of higher education and the history of women. For these reasons, at least, Brenau is worth writing about.

To date, only one attempt has been made to reveal the history of Brenau. The "short exception" mentioned earlier is a brief (i.e., 100 double-spaced typed pages) work by Eleanor Rigney entitled *Brenau 1878–1978: Enriched by the Past, Challenged by the Future*.[50] Rigney, who taught at Brenau for several years, wrote *Brenau 1878–1978* upon the occasion of then Brenau College's one-hundredth anniversary. Rigney included chapters on the development of Brenau's music conservatory, its student organizations, town and gown relations, and campus life and traditions. Published in 1978 by Brenau itself, Rigney's work was presumably held to somewhat less rigorous standards of scholarship than it would be today. Consequently, it is quite brief and, by today's standards, sparingly researched. Rigney used and analyzed relatively few primary sources and only one piece of secondary scholarship in her writing. Also, Rigney's work is rather celebratory. Her tone throughout the dissertation indicated that she thought a great deal of her employer. Even so, what Rigney produced is a clearly written and interesting overview of Brenau's first hundred years. In particular, *Brenau 1878–1978* included a well-done study of the socioeconomic status of several families who sent their daughters to Brenau in the early twentieth century. Still, this socioeconomic study notwithstanding, Rigney's work left out more than it included about Brenau's early history and could not speak to Brenau's dynamic last three-and-a-half decades of existence at all. Consequently, it seems fair to state that, as of 2012, Brenau remained largely unstudied.

Compared to other subfields within the larger discipline of history, "unstudied" could describe the state of much of the history of higher education generally just as it describes Brenau's condition in particular. Bookshelves full of works on topics like military history or slavery or political history usually contain few books about the history of higher education. Also, there are fewer college and university histories than there are colleges and universities. Additionally, relatively few scholars have engaged individual topics within the history of higher education such as institutional discrimination and integration, the community college movement, "boosterism," and others. Perhaps most tellingly, only two works in this field could even approach being dubbed "synthetic."

A classic in the field of the history of higher education is Rudolph's 1962 book entitled *The American College and University: A History*. Using a bevy of primary and secondary sources, Rudolph chronicled the development in America of classically-oriented, colonial colleges inspired by English models. His book examined these institutions as they evolved and were joined in the mid-nineteenth century by universities, inspired by German models, which began to develop and thrive into the mid-twentieth century. He considered many aspects of colleges and universities in his account. Among other things, his topics included the curriculum, the "extracurriculum" (i.e., what Rudolph refers to as the "collegiate way," which contemplates the residential nature of American colleges and college life and traditions more generally), the changing character of faculty, the development of land grant and state colleges, and the rise of football. Rudolph's account is often witty, generally quite well-written, and does a thorough, if not definitive, job of examining many aspects of a very difficult-to-examine field. [51]

Thelin's *A History of American Higher Education*, which was published in 2004 and revised in 2011, built upon Rudolph's work in many respects. Like Rudolph, Thelin used multiple primary and secondary sources to examine institutions of higher education in the United States from the colonial era to the modern day. In particular, he focused upon the impact of economic, cultural, political, and social factors on the development of colleges and universities. Thelin has drawn particular praise in this work for his overview of women's college experiences, his discussion of historically black colleges and universities, and for examining southern colleges and universities.[52] Most impressive, perhaps, is Thelin's willingness to grapple with long-accepted assumptions regarding higher education. He persuasively argued that some views once taken for granted should be reexamined.[53]

Like Rudolph, Thelin contended that colonial colleges emerged to "identify and ratify a colonial elite" that would assume the leadership of colonial society. Thelin went on to say that antebellum colleges in America differed by region. Colleges in the North trained sons excluded from land ownership as a result of primogenitor for careers at the same time southern colleges nurtured the development of southern gentlemen-landowners. According to Thelin, following the disruptive periods of the Civil War and Reconstruction, the Progressive Era saw the rise of universities, the expansion of coeducation, greater emphasis placed on science in the curriculum, an increased professionalization of college faculty members, and the emergence of vibrant campus life and intercollegiate athletics. During the interwar period of the twentieth century, colleges struggled financially during the Great Depression and reached out to ever more diverse student clienteles to make ends meet. During the Cold War years, vocationally oriented colleges and graduate education expanded rapidly.[54] Though Thelin might perhaps have written more about the impact of the Civil Rights, feminist, or counterculture movements on college campuses during the 1960s, his penultimate chapter is an especially interesting description of American higher education as a "troubled giant" with problems to solve and potential to reach.

Both Rudolph and Thelin might have penned more about the higher education of women.[55] Indeed, within the field of the history of higher education (particularly in America), more might be said on this subject because women have been regularly attending college for over 150 years. It is telling that the benchmark work in this field is often still considered to be Thomas Woody's two-volume *A History of Women's*

Education in the United States, despite the fact that it was first published in 1929.[56] Woody's history engaged such topics as the origins of the women's education movement, opposition to women's education, the rise of coeducation in colleges and universities, and, perhaps more sparingly, the development of women's colleges. Given when it was written, more than this it could not address.

Only a handful of more recent works on the higher education of women are well-known. Among these are John Mack Faragher and Florence Howe's *Women and Higher Education in American History* and Barbara Miller Solomon's *In the Company of Educated Women: A History of Women and Higher Education in America*. The essays in Faragher's collection examine a variety of topics such as single-sex colleges, pioneering women educators like Lucy Sprague Mitchell and Alice James, and the history of black women in higher education.[57] Solomon's book examines women's struggles for access to institutions of higher learning, the dimensions of the college experience for women, the connection between feminism and women's education, and the effects of higher education upon women's life choices. Her book also focused on the early history of women's higher education and on how differences in regional culture effected the development of women's education.[58]

In *Women's Education in the United States 1780–1840*, Margaret Nash argued that education prior to 1840 was not as gendered as many historians have claimed. Rather, "both the curricula and the pedagogy were similar for men and women in most academies of the period."[59] Nash determined that "Enlightenment beliefs and the ethos of civic republicanism" were behind the growth of women's education.[60] Women went to school for several reasons. Some sought learning to be better able to "Christianize the nation."[61] Others wanted "some degree of economic self-sufficiency" by obtaining jobs as teachers.[62] Still others studied for the "sheer longing for learning."[63] Ultimately, Nash found that "education was key to the project of class formation" and that "class and race were more salient than gender in the construction of educational institutions."[64]

Like Nash's work, Mary Kelley's *Learning to Stand and Speak: Women, Education, and Public Life in America's Republic* dealt with the history of early higher education for women. Kelley found that advanced women's academies and seminaries taught not just skills necessary for becoming republican mothers, but for entering public life. Educated women yearned for more than inhabiting domestic spheres. They became teachers, school founders, writers, lecturers, and community association leaders. Kelley's painstaking analysis of early women's academy and seminary catalogs showed that men and women studied many of the same subjects, attended class for similar lengths, and paid similar fees—all facts suggesting that Americans greatly valued education for daughters as well as sons. Still, all was not equal. Kelley illustrated that, besides teaching content, women's institutions took pains to inculcate modesty in students. This was done so young women would not "show off" their learning and reach beyond their feminine spheres—exactly what many women did.[65]

In *Gender and Higher Education in the Progressive Era*, Lynn D. Gordon described how the second generation of American women to attend college challenged prevailing female stereotypes to take part in the intellectual and political life of the time. These women sought educations on par with those received by men and, unlike earlier generations of educated women, sought careers in addition to marriage. Gordon deftly used writings of female students that were published in literary magazines to craft her narrative. She learned that female students at the University of California were often resented and snubbed by their male counterparts whereas women at the University of Chicago integrated well—at least until administrators feared the "effeminization" of the university and began to exclude women from college life. Students at Vassar, Sophie Newcomb, and Agnes Scott women's colleges enjoyed vibrant campus life, but owing to regional cultural differences negotiated pursuing marriage and career differently than northern women. Perhaps what Gordon did best in this book was to correct historical misconceptions about women students in this era as being frivolous and socially preoccupied. Their writings indicated that these students were often thoughtful and serious and focused on their educations.[66]

Amy Thompson McCandless picked up about where Gordon left off and studied an academically neglected region of the country in her book entitled *The Past in the Present: Women's Higher Education in the Twentieth-Century American South*. McCandless asserted that social, political, cultural, and economic forces operated in the South to create a distinctive educational climate for women. Around 1900, a poor economy and conservative attitudes about gender made for few educational opportunities for southern women compared to elsewhere. As southern states resisted coeducation, the opportunities that did emerge for women were often at private colleges, which were expensive and emphasized manners and deportment over scholarship. McCandless found that these adverse circumstances actually united the students who did manage to attend southern women's colleges. A heightened spirit of sisterhood developed, which prepared women well to participate in clubs and civic organizations later in life.[67]

Linda Eisenmann's book, *Higher Education for Women in Postwar America, 1945–1965*, also dealt with the twentieth century. Her research eroded a prevalent notion that the postwar years in America was a period of educational listlessness for women. Despite the facts that the numbers of women students and faculty members at American colleges declined during this period and that the number of women who left education to have families increased, the period between 1945 and 1965 was significant. These decades would see built a "generational bridge from the energetic women of World War II to the activists of the late 1960s."[68] Women during this era worked more quietly than their later feminist counterparts to effect change, but they still managed to draw attention to women's needs as evidenced by the expansion of things like continuing education programs for women in American colleges and universities.[69]

The titles in this handful of stand-out general histories of women's higher education in America do not concentrate on women's colleges particularly. Relatively few works do, actually, which is why studies like Louise Schutz Boas' *Woman's Education Begins: The Rise of the Women's Colleges* still receive attention today despite having been first published in 1935.[70] When historians do examine women's colleges, they tend to look at northern institutions. One scholar has noted that, "Studies of women educators and institutions outside New England have been relatively few, and on the college level, attention to the eastern women's colleges still prevails."[71] Each of the historic Seven Sisters colleges has its own institutional history (or two) and, generally speaking, books dealing with women's colleges almost invariably focus on these and other northern women's schools. A case in point is Helen Horowitz's *Alma Mater: Design and Experience in Women's Colleges from Their Nineteenth Century Beginnings to the 1930s.* This book discussed the history of women in American higher education by examining several selected colleges, specifically the Seven Sisters as well as Bennington College in Vermont and Sarah Lawrence College in New York—all northern schools.[72]

Horowitz asserted that concern over social control and discipline determined how many women's colleges initially developed. As evidence of this, she cited how several older institutions were contained entirely in one building to promote student supervision at all times. She also indicated that, early on, most women's colleges tried to cultivate a sense of family among students, which was actually an extension of popular notions of domesticity. Later colleges like Smith and Bryn Mawr had architecture more resembling that of men's colleges, which demonstrated that these institutions wanted to produce scholars and not merely well-acculturated women. The other Sisters eventually followed suit in changing their designs. Horowitz indicated that women faculty members at these colleges eschewed their roles as monitors of female students and preferred instead to become serious scholars. Horowitz also examined student culture at the colleges and determined, perhaps unsurprisingly, that some students just wanted to have fun at college whereas others more seriously pursued education. She related that concerns over college-educated women not marrying and female homosexuality prompted some women's colleges in the 1920s to try to steer women back to domesticity and to further ties with men's institutions.[73]

Horowitz's focus on northern schools is typical of much of the scholarship about women's colleges. *The Education of the Southern Belle: Higher Education and Student Socialization in the Antebellum South* is rare because it examined early southern women's colleges. Farnham asserted that, despite the South's backward reputation regarding education, many more institutions of higher learning were created for women there than in the North. Though some of these colleges were really little more than finishing schools, Farnham found others to be academic institutions on a par with many men's colleges. These women's colleges pioneered the study of modern foreign languages and the sciences in higher education whereas contemporary, predominantly men's colleges retained educational curricula focused on the classics—subjects thought to be too deep for women to grasp.[74]

Farnham determined that alumnae of southern women's colleges were often very well educated compared to their northern counterparts. Even so, few of these women's college graduates would utilize their educations in a practical sense. Rather, education for a southern woman occurred to make her more refined, to make her more of an object of desire for potential mates, and to reify upper-crust Southern society's social power and influence. It was the northern, not the southern, women's colleges that produced radicals and reformers.[75]

Besides the works of Farnham and McCandless, by 2012, only a pair of doctoral dissertations dealt with southern women's colleges as a whole. In 1985, Florence Fleming Corley published "Higher Education for Southern Women: Four Church-related Women's Colleges in Georgia, Agnes Scott, Shorter, Spelman, and Wesleyan, 1900–1920."[76] Prior to this, only Elizabeth Barber Young's 1932 dissertation entitled "A Study of the Curricula of Seven Selected Women's Colleges of the Southern States" dealt with southern women's colleges generally.[77]

To these works about southern women's colleges generally, only a relative few books about particular institutions can be added. Many are rather dated. For example, Lillian Adele Kibler wrote a history of South Carolina's Converse College in 1973 whereas Edward Alvey wrote a history of Mary Washington College in Virginia in 1974.[78] Two decades earlier, Roberta D. Cornelius wrote about Virginia's Randolph-Macon Woman's College in 1951 just as Mary Lynch Johnson wrote about Meredith College in North Carolina in 1956.[79] Frances J. Niederer wrote an illustrated history of Virginia's Hollins College in 1973 and Florence Read wrote *The Story of Spelman College* in Atlanta in 1961 a few years after Martha Lou Lemmon Stohlman wrote *The Story of Sweet Briar College* in Virginia in 1956.[80] Some works date from the 1980s and include Mildred Morse McEwen's history of Queens College in North Carolina (1980), Walter Edward McNair's history of Agnes Scott College in Georgia (1983), Frances Dew Hamilton and Elizabeth Crabtree Wells' history of Judson College (1989), and Bridget Smith Pieschel's 1984 book about the Mississippi University for Women.[81] Only Phinizy Spalding's 1994 history of the Lucy Cobb Institute in Athens, Georgia, Jeffrey R. Willis' 2001 brief history of Converse College, Judith T. Bainbridge's 2001 history of the Woman's College of Furman University in Greenville, South Carolina, Susan Tucker and Beth Willinger's 2006 history of Newcomb College, and Darin S. Harris' unpublished 2008 dissertation about Tift College could be considered recent.[82] As of 2012, many prominent southern women's colleges—some well over 100 years old—have never had their histories written thoroughly and/or recently. These include Wesleyan College in Georgia, Midway College in Kentucky, Salem College in North Carolina, Columbia College in South Carolina, and Brenau.[83]

This historiography should suggest that, compared to other historical themes, women's colleges both individually and collectively could bear more scholarly scrutiny. Developing a history of Brenau will add to what is known about what were really the only viable higher educational outlets for roughly half of the population of a large segment of the country for many years. Several questions deserve examination and serve as organizing topics for the chapters in this book: How and why was Brenau founded? What is the history of academic life at Brenau? What is the history of such things as physical culture and athletics at the College? What is revealed by examining the history of traditions and organizations (such as narratives and secret societies) at Brenau? What policy challenges (such as integration) has Brenau faced in modern times and how did the institution cope? How has Brenau's physical environment altered over the years in response to changing societal attitudes about women and higher education? I selected to address these topics in specific because they should be of interest to a wide audience and because they cut across the full spectrum of American college life. By design, the organization of this history is thematic as opposed to chronological, though, like a chronology, it will cover every major period in Brenau's long life. Though a few more traditional historians of higher education may find this thematic approach unorthodox, I believe it will actually produce a less staid, less pedestrian, and much more readable account of Brenau's past.

I explore these themes by utilizing secondary sources (such as those mentioned earlier) to offer historical context and, in the main, materials contained in the Archives of Brenau University, which are located in the Brenau Trustee Library in Gainesville, Georgia. The Archives contains a modest holding of primary source materials dating back to the earliest years of the institution. For example, included in its collections are many yearbooks, a few literary journals, some notes & minutes from several years of faculty meetings, and some editions of Brenau's student newspaper, the *Alchemist*, dating from various years. Also included in the Archives are many College bulletins and student handbooks, the papers of several University presidents, and a myriad of photographs. Yet, though the Brenau Archives has much, it likewise lacks much. The collection holds few student records or things like course materials, completed assignments, and syllabi and virtually no presidential papers and correspondence appear since the early 1970s. In addition, many primary sources that are conventionally consulted in writing college histories simply do not exist in the Archives for Brenau. For example, there are no personal letters or student diaries, nor do the Archives contain complete collections of Brenau literary journals and student newspapers. Also, there is very little material produced by or about Brenau alumnae in the Archives such as oral histories, correspondence, or first-person anecdotes. Materials such as these that would help to better capture the "voice" of the people closest to Brenau would have been informative. Hopefully, the Archives will acquire them with time. In their absence, one can only make do with the archival sources that *are* available, as I have tried to do.

Augmenting these sources are newspapers. The *Atlanta Constitution* and the *Gainesville Eagle*, which were both daily newspapers published in the late nineteenth century and early twentieth century, revealed much in—mainly—two types of formats: articles and narrative advertisements. Journalists have written many articles about Brenau over time that cover a range of topics, from sporting events to personnel changes to social happenings. In the first half of the twentieth century, these frequently appeared in the society pages of Atlanta's largest newspaper, the *Atlanta Constitution*, under the heading "Brenau Notes." Narrative advertisements typically resembled actual newspaper articles though they were written by people either with ties to Brenau or in Brenau's employ. These appeared periodically until the early 1900s. Given their obvious bias, they must be carefully used as historical sources, but it would be a mistake to discount them entirely. After all, the narrative advertisements contained a great deal of information and this had to stand up to both public scrutiny and the newspapers' due diligence. Hence, though Brenau might be expected to put its best foot forward in its ads, it would not have printed misinformation or false claims. Doing so would have been a quick route to losing popular respect and credibility and alienating one of the best advertising mediums of the day. So, though newsprint sources about Brenau may not be perfect, they are far from useless.

Using these sources, I frame the history of Brenau around a concept of college as essentially being a "negotiated space." This idea suggests that the overall experience of any college or university is constructed in a process of negotiation between two key groups, the college's students (both past, present, and future) and its personnel, its faculty and staff, which would include its administration. Of course, these negotiations might, at times, take the form of actual face-to-face meetings between representatives of these two parties. Far more often, the negotiating occurs over time and not at arm's length in something like an ongoing, give-and-take process spanning the life of an institution. Each side might take years to do something that impacts the college experience or take years to respond to something promulgated by the other party. The end result, though, is that both sides—institutional employees and students—play a role in refining their school.

The idea that the collegiate experience is a product of negotiation is certainly not anything unique to Brenau, nor is it any novel concept that I put forward. It should be intuitive to think of any college experience as the product of bilateral negotiation and place this theme squarely in an institution's history. Yet, in fact, the idea of student agency is often lost in many institutional histories. Rather, these works depict the lives of colleges largely from the top down, focusing upon the actions of administrators, faculty members, and staff members. These histories can forget to adequately acknowledge the fact that students often pushed back against institutional designs or even initiated their own campus policies and that they actually did so with some success to create their idealized version of what college should be.

The story of Brenau bears out that this process of negotiation took place from 1878 until the present day. Throughout the institution's history, Brenau's students and its faculty and staff have each jockeyed to create and refine what I call "their Brenau," their ideal version of what the Brenau University experience should be. Often, Brenau's faculty and staff won out in these negotiations with students. This was particularly evident in fashioning the College curriculum, creating Brenau's physical environment, and in setting institutional policies about such things as integration. In other instances, this was not the case. At times, the students essentially prevailed in negotiations over the collegiate experience at Brenau and exhibited a remarkable degree of initiative, solidarity, and autonomy in conducting affairs in some arenas. Brenau women had a prominent voice in effecting College rules and discipline, in influencing student organizations, and in bringing athletics to campus. Ultimately, both sides enjoyed success in this process because they seldom worked at truly cross purposes. Everyone, officials and students alike, wanted Brenau to enjoy a long and prosperous life.

Few institutional histories are likely to be exhaustive or definitive. Though I do believe this one covers much, even some deserving topics had to receive less attention than others. For example, so as to maintain a focus on the ongoing negotiation between Brenau's students and the faculty and staff, I did not examine in great detail Brenau's trustees. Though they appear in this book from time to time, a separate stand-alone history would really be required to adequately examine these important men and women and their contributions to the institution. Incidentally, such a history might validate a first for Brenau. The 1932 edition of the *Brenau Bulletin* catalog related, "It will be noted in the list of members of the board that several are women. Two of these were first elected in 1920 and it is believed that Brenau College is the first college in the South to have a woman on its Board of Trustees."[84] Historical research focused on the institution's trustees could speak to this assertion and many others. Indeed, it would take many histories to report on everything and everyone that Brenau has known in its long life. But, as one historian discerningly put it, when it comes to writing, "faced with the impossible vastness of the past, historians have no choice but to leave out most of it."[85] I focus here on what I deemed to be the most meaningful aspects of Brenau's past and hope that I made selections that are informative and representative of the whole.

Just as few college histories will be the last word on their subject, it is a rare institutional biography that will bring about any grand paradigm shifts in thinking about higher education. Hopefully, this study will at least enrich understanding of both a place (Brenau) and a process (negotiating between interested parties for an idealized collegiate experience). In addition, it will make new claims about several "firsts" in women's higher education in Georgia. Examining Brenau's experience will furthermore shed additional light on themes of persistent importance in the study of women's higher education, such as the advent of sport and the development of rules & discipline at women's colleges. All of this will contribute, even if only modestly, to what is known about women's history generally—which anyone with an affinity for women's colleges would consider to be a worthwhile endeavor.

Notes

1. Information informing this introduction about Brenau came primarily from Brenau's 2011 admissions *Viewbook*, its 2011–2012 *Catalog* (hereinafter abbreviated as "*Catalog* (2011)"), and the website of the Brenau University Office of Research and Planning. These are available online at Jensen Design Studio, "Brenau Undergraduate Viewbook," http://jensendesignstudio.com/wp-content/uploads/2011/11/brenau_viewbook_spreads.pdf (accessed 16 October 2012); *Brenau University Undergraduate and Graduate Catalog 2011 – 2012, vol. 127* (Gainesville, GA: Brenau University, 2011), http://catalog.brenau.edu/index.php (accessed 30 November 2012); and Robert Cuttino, "Research and Planning," Brenau University, http://intranet.brenau.edu/facts/Demographics/default.htm , respectively (accessed 16 October 2012).
2. Ibid. A comprehensive report about Brenau's economic impact upon its community prepared around 2005 is located at Atlanta Regional Council for Higher Education, "Economic Impact Report for Brenau University," Brenau University, http://intranet.brenau.edu/pr/update/ARCHE%20Brenau.pdf (accessed October 16, 2012).
3. A.B. Cobban related that before the fifteenth century, the term *universitas* referred "to [a] guild of masters or of students or of masters and students combined" (2). See Alan B. Cobban, *The Medieval English Universities: Oxford and Cambridge to c. 1500* (Berkeley, CA: University of California Press, 1988), for more about the origins of Universities.
4. See Frederick Rudolph, *The American College and University: A History* (New York, NY: Alfred A. Knopf. 1962; reprint, Athens, GA: University of Georgia Press, 1991) to learn more about early American colleges.
5. Jurgen Herbst, "The First Three American Colleges: Schools of the Reformation," *Perspectives in American History* 8 (1974): 7.
6. Ibid.
7. Christie Anne Farnham, *The Education of the Southern Belle: Higher Education and Student Socialization in the Antebellum South* (New York, NY: New York University Press, 1994), 43.
8. Ibid.
9. Ibid.
10. Ibid.
11. Ibid., 49.

12. Ibid.
13. Margaret A. Nash, *Women's Education in the United States 1780–1840* (New York, NY: Palgrave MacMillian, 2005), 5.
14. Ibid., 36.
15. Ibid., 5, 36.
16. Ibid., 5.
17. Kim Tolley, "The Rise of the Academies: Continuity or Change?" *History of Education Quarterly* 41 (summer, 2001): 233.
18. Ibid.
19. For more information about the development of academies, see Thomas Woody, *A History of Women's Education in the United States. 2 Vols.* (New York, NY: Science Press, 1929; Reprint, New York, NY: Octagon Books, 1966).
20. "About Salem: Our History," Salem College, http://www.salem.edu/about/our-history/ (accessed 26 January 2013).
21. Mary Kelley, *Learning to Stand and Speak: Women, Education, and Public Life in America's Republic* (Chapel Hill, NC: Published by the Omohundro Institute of Early American History and Culture, Williamsburg, Virginia, by the University of North Carolina Press, 2006), 67.
22. Ibid.
23. Henry Barnard as cited by Diane Ravitch, "American Traditions of Education" in Terry M. Moe, ed., *A Primer on America's Schools* (Stanford, CA: Hoover Institution Press, 2001), 6.
24. See Theodore R. Sizer, *The Age of the Academies* (New York, NY: Teachers College Press, 1964), 1–22.
25. Nash, *Women's Education*, 6.
26. Ibid., 83.
27. Ibid., 7.
28. Ibid.
29. Rudolph, *American College and University*, 307–8.
30. Woody, *A History of Women's Education in the United States*, vol. I, 273.
31. Ibid. Note that some scholars, most notably Margaret Nash, disagree with this assertion of Woody's.
32. Rudolph, *American College and University*, 309.
33. Ibid.
34. Irene Harwarth, Mindi Maline, and Elizabeth DeBra, "'Women's Colleges in the United States: History, Issues, and Challenges'; Report prepared for the National Institute on Postsecondary Education, Libraries, and Lifelong Learning of the Office of Educational Research and Improvement in the

Department of Education," U.S. Department of Education, http://www.ed.gov/offices/OERI/PLLI/webreprt.html (accessed 29 September 2012).

35. Mabel Newcomer, *A Century of Higher Education for American Women* (New York, NY: Harper and Brothers, 1959), 16. Not all historians would agree with this proposition. In her book *More Work For Mother: The Ironies of Household Technology From the Open Hearth to the Microwave*, Ruth Schwartz Cowan argued that the advent of "labor-saving devices" actually led to women taking on more work and enjoying less leisure time. Ruth Schwartz Cowan, *More Work for Mother: The Ironies of Household Technology from the Open Hearth to the Microwave* (New York, NY: Basic Books, 1983).
36. Farnham, *Education of the Southern Belle*, 65.
37. Ibid., 73.
38. John R. Thelin, *A History of American Higher Education* (Baltimore, MD: The Johns Hopkins University Press, 2004), 64.
39. Ibid., 56.
40. Ibid.
41. Nash, *Women's Education*, 12.
42. Ibid., 47.
43. Ibid., 49.
44. Ibid.
45. Harwarth et al., "Women's Colleges in the United States: History, Issues, and Challenges."
46. Woody, *A History of Women's Education in the United States, vol. I*, 184 as cited in Harwarth et al., "Women's Colleges in the United States: History, Issues, and Challenges."
47. Ibid. Incidentally, both Vassar and Elmira became coeducational in 1969.
48. See Mary J. Oates, ed., *Higher Education for Catholic Women: An Historical Anthology* (New York, NY: Garland Publishing, Inc., 1987) for more information about Catholic women's colleges.
49. Irene Harwarth, "A Closer Look At Women's Colleges," U. S. Department of Education, http://www.ed.gov/pubs/WomensColleges/index.html (accessed 17 October 2012).
50. Eleanor Rigney, *Brenau College 1878–1978: Enriched by the Past, Challenged by the Future* (Gainesville, GA: Brenau College, 1978).
51. See Rudolph, *American College and University*.
52. Michael W. Simpson, review of *A History of American Higher Education* by John R. Thelin, *Education Review*, 12 September 2004, http://www.edrev.info/reviews/rev303.htm (accessed 12 October 2012).

53. See Thelin, *History of American Higher Education.*
54. Ibid.
55. Thelin, in particular, is reproached a bit by historian Ronald Butchart for his omission of anything truly substantive about the educational experience of African American women. This is especially disappointing for Butchart since Thelin wrote his synthesis after quite a bit of fine scholarship on this subject had been published. Ron Butchart, conversation with author, 16 March 2008.
56. See Woody, *A History of Women's Education in the United States.*
57. John Mack Faragher and Florence Howe, *Women and Higher Education in American History* (New York, NY: W. W. Norton & Company, 1988).
58. See Barbara Miller Solomon, *In the Company of Educated Women: A History of Women and Higher Education in America* (New Haven, CT: Yale University Press, 1985).
59. Ibid.
60. Nash, *Women's Education*, 12.
61. Ibid., 13.
62. Ibid.
63. Ibid.
64. Ibid., back cover.
65. See Kelley, *Learning to Stand and Speak.*
66. See Lynn Gordon, *Gender and Higher Education in the Progressive Era* (New Haven, CT: Yale University Press, 1990).
67. See Amy Thompson McCandless, *The Past in the Present: Women's Higher Education in the Twentieth-Century American South* (Tuscaloosa, AL: The University of Alabama Press, 1999).
68. Linda Eisenmann, *Higher Education for Women in Postwar America, 1945–1965* (Baltimore, MD: Johns Hopkins University Press, 2006), 233.
69. See Eisenmann, *Higher Education for Women.*
70. See Louise Schutz Boas, *Woman's Education Begins; the Rise of the Women's Colleges* (Norton, MA: Wheaton College Press, 1935).
71. Sally Schwager, "Educating Women in America," *Signs*, vol. 12, no. 2 (winter, 1987), 336.
72. See Helen Lefkowitz Horowitz, *Alma Mater: Design and Experience in the Women's Colleges from Their Nineteenth-Century Beginnings to the 1930s* (New York, NY: Alfred A. Knopf, 1984).
73. Ibid.
74. See Farnham, *Education of the Southern Belle.*
75. Ibid.

76. See Florence Corley, "Higher Education for Southern Women: Four Church-Related Women's Colleges in Georgia, Agnes Scott, Shorter, Spelman, and Wesleyan, 1900-1920" (PhD diss., Georgia State University, 1985).
77. See Elizabeth Barber Young, *A Study of the Curricula of Seven Selected Women's Colleges of the Southern States* (New York, NY: Teachers Colleges, Columbia University, 1932).
78. See Lillian Adele Kibler, *The History of Converse College, 1889-1971* (Spartanburg, SC: Converse College, 1973) and Edward Alvey, *History of Mary Washington College, 1908-1972* (Charlottesville, VA: University Press of Virginia, 1974).
79. See Roberta D. Cornelius, *The History of Randolph-Macon Woman's College* (Chapel Hill, NC: The University of North Carolina Press, 1951) and Mary Lynch Johnson, *A History of Meredith College*: 2nd *Ed.* (Raleigh, NC: Meredith College, 1972).
80. See Frances J. Niederer, *Hollins College: An Illustrated History* (Charlottesville, VA: University of Virginia Press, 1973); Florence Read, *The Story of Spelman College* (Princeton, NJ: Princeton University Press, 1961); and Martha Lou Lemmon Stohlman, *The Story of Sweet Briar College* (Sweet Briar, VA: Alumnae Association of Sweet Briar College, 1956).
81. See Mildred Morse McEwen, *Queens College: Yesterday and Today* (Charlotte, NC: Heritage Printers, Inc. for Queens College Alumni Association, 1980) and Walter Edward McNair, *Lest We Forget: An Account of Agnes Scott College* (Atlanta, GA: Tucker-Castleberry Printing, Inc., 1983); Frances Dew Hamilton and Elizabeth Crabtree Wells, *Daughters of the Dream: Judson College 1838 – 1988* (Marion, AL: Judson College, 1989); Bridget Smith Pieschel, *Loyal daughters: One hundred years at Mississippi University for Women, 1884-1984* (Oxford, MS: University Press of Mississippi, 1984).
82. See Jeffrey R. Willis, *Converse College* (Charleston, SC: Arcadia Publishing, 2001); Phinizy Spalding, *Higher Education for Women in the South: A History of Lucy Cobb Institute, 1858-1994* (Athens, GA: University of Georgia Press, 1994); Judith T. Bainbridge, *Academy and College: the History of the Woman's College of Furman University* (Macon, GA: Mercer University Press, 2001); Susan Tucker and Beth Willinger (eds.), *Newcomb College, 1886-2006: Higher Education for Women in New Orleans* (Baton Rouge, LA: Louisiana State University Press, 2012); and Darin S.

Harris, "Polishing cornerstones: Tift College, Georgia Baptists' separate college for women," (PhD diss., Georgia State University, 2008).

83. Some brief works exist about a few of these colleges, but none attempt to relate the entire history of the institution examined and/or are quite old. For examples, see Samuel Luttrell Akers, *The First Hundred Years of Wesleyan College, 1836–1936* (Savannah, GA: Beehive Press, 1976); F. N. Boney, "'The Pioneer College for Women': Wesleyan over a Century and a Half," *Georgia Historical Quarterly* 72 (fall, 1988): 519-32; Richard W. Griffin, "Wesleyan College: Its Genesis, 1835–1840," *Georgia Historical Quarterly* 50 (March, 1966): 54–73; Caryl L. Martin, "The Evolution of Intercollegiate Athletics at Wesleyan College: A Historical Perspective," *Journal of the Georgia Association of Historians* 19 (1998): 54–106; Jerold J. Savory, *Columbia College: The Ariail Era* (Columbia, SC: R. L. Bryan, 1979); Evelyn Barksdale Winn, "A History of Columbia College" (master's thesis, University of South Carolina, 1928). Incidentally, for a listing of many books written about the history of many colleges, consult Linda Sparks, *Institutions of Higher Education: An International Bibliography* (Westport, CN: Greenwood Publishing Group, 1990).

84. The board was also described as non-sectarian. *Brenau Bulletin, 1932 – 1933, v. XXIII, n. 3* (Gainesville, GA: Brenau College, 1932), 16; Brenau University Archives, Gainesville, Georgia. Hereafter, references to this source are indicated as "*Catalog* (1932)."

85. Jared Farmer, review of *Massacre at Mountain Meadows: An American Tragedy* by Ronald W. Walker, Richard E. Turley Jr. and Glen M. Leonard, *BYU Studies*, 47, no. 3 (2008): 175 – 179, 175; http://sunysb.academia.edu/JFarmer/Papers/280382/Review_Massacre_at_Mountain_Meadows_by_Turley_et_al (accessed 12 October 2012).

CHAPTER 1

PARTIES TO THE PARLEY

MEETING THE STUDENTS AND OFFICIALS OF BRENAU, BOTH PAST & PRESENT

Like all colleges and universities, Brenau is fundamentally a product of human relations. Almost everything the institution was, is, or will become is the result of a remarkable and long-lived negotiation between two key groups: Brenau's students and Brenau officials, who are collectively the institution's faculty, administration, and other student services staff.[1] In the arenas of such contested spaces as college athletics, college rules and regulations, and academics, these negotiators sparred, more or less amicably, toward constructing what each side saw as "their Brenau," their ideal version of the College. Brenau, then, is also a product of compromise—oftentimes (but not always) of the willing variety between these contesting sides. This chapter offers a glimpse of Brenau's students and employees over time to inform an understanding of both who each side was and the roles each would play in negotiating for their Brenau.

From the outset, note that Brenau's students and Brenau's faculty and staff members have never worked entirely at cross purposes. Though they have had their differences, since the founding of the College, there has actually been much common ground between the two camps about what the character of the institution should be. In particular, both sides of negotiators would have worked to cultivate what historian Frederick Rudolph termed the "collegiate way." Rudolph wrote that:

> The collegiate way is the notion that a curriculum, a library, a faculty, and students are not enough to make a college. It is an adherence to the residential scheme of things. It is respectful of quiet rural settings, dependent on dormitories, committed to dining halls, permeated by paternalism. It is what every American college has had or consciously rejected or lost or sought to recapture.[2]

This was Brenau from inception, which both the faculty & staff and students (who came annually by the dozens and hundreds, respectively) embraced. What the two sides differed on were the details.

Two areas of friction really predominated. On the one hand, students and College officials contested the very vision of what it meant to be educated. Students tended to reject what they perceived as archaic subjects (such as a Latin-based curriculum) favoring instead more marketable, more practical learning. Conversely, College faculty and staff members tended to reject the vocationalized mentalities that many students possessed, believing instead that learning for learning's sake had value. The other great divide involved the amount and degree of paternalism that would exist at the College. Many in the administration and on the faculty would have viewed their role as being *in loco parentis* while simultaneously acknowledging that students needed at least some independence, some room to grow. Most students would have seen themselves largely as adults entitled to independence, but would likewise have acknowledged that at least some boundaries set by someone made sense. What the two sides jockeyed for was the middle ground between their opposing views.

Of course, no college could function without its students. As at any college, it would be the students at Brenau that would play a large role in determining the character of the institution. Among other factors, their backgrounds in terms of characteristics such as class and socioeconomic status, place of origin, religion, race, age, and, of course, gender, would contribute much toward the nature of the collegiate way that would emerge at Brenau. These student characteristics will be examined in turn in this chapter. (See Figures 1 through 7 for glimpses of various members of Brenau's student body over the years.)

Compared to other women's colleges, the student body at Brenau has generally been diverse in some respects and quite homogenous in others. Speaking of New England women's colleges, Helen Horowitz wrote that, "By the 1890s, the women's colleges attracted a new clientele—young, well-educated women of the wealthy strata who had no thought of a career after college."[3] These young women were different from the kind of students that most college founders had hoped to attract—namely, young women that were "serious, hardworking, daughter[s] of the middle class preparing to teach."[4] These New Englanders were in some ways similar to, and in some ways quite different from, their southern counterparts.

With few exceptions since its emergence in the region, higher education for women in the South had been restricted to the daughters of elite families for generations. As late as the mid-nineteenth century, a college education for a woman (where it occurred at all outside of New England and the Midwest) was largely a luxury item. Some affluent southern families sent their teen-aged daughters to what amounted to private, all-girls, southern "finishing schools" to learn social graces and to study "ornamental" material deemed suitable for young women, such as modern languages, botany, and arts and music. Young women in these institutions would likely have had much more in common with each other than just age and gender, including Protestant beliefs, wealthy upbringings, and white, Anglican roots.[5]

This archetype predominated in southern women's higher education until the late nineteenth century. It was then, in the decades leading up to the Progressive Era, that things changed. Some of the finishing schools that had sprouted throughout the region to teach wealthy girls the social graces gradually became more academically rigorous and eventually evolved into all-women's colleges. This shift likely occurred at this time in response to the financial distress brought about by the Civil War and Reconstruction. Their fortunes gone, many southern families became unable to support the leisurely lifestyles of ladies promoted by earlier women's schools. Instead, they demanded better education for daughters to improve their prospects of making a living. Over time, women from more diverse backgrounds began attending southern colleges in more significant numbers. The type of concerns for social justice that had often catalyzed the development of women's colleges in other regions eventually prompted some educators of women in the South to enroll non-elite students in their institutions. These women brought with them to college very different worldviews from those of earlier students and radically changed the face of higher education for southern women.[6]

Founders established the Georgia Baptist Female Seminary, the institution that would become Brenau College, in 1878 and embraced this desire to expand educational opportunities for women. The best evidence for this comes in the form of newspaper advertisements for the institution that appeared in the late nineteenth century and the early twentieth century. The *Atlanta Constitution* published a plethora of ads for the Seminary and, later, the College during this period. Economy was a prevalent theme in many of these as Brenau's founders clearly sought to make the institution inexpensive enough so that any young woman could afford to attend. The Seminary's catalog echoed this theme. In describing the aim of the institution, the catalog read, "The prime object is, by rigid economy, to bring the highest order of Collegiate instruction within the reach of the middle and poorer classes of society. This we can and will do by our Cottage System, by cheap board and low rates of tuition; and as soon as our collections shall reach $25,000, tuition in our Literary Department will be virtually free."[7]

Tuition never became free. In 1900, Brenau's catalog indicated that board for a single eighteen-week term ran from $65 to $80.[8] Tuition in 1900 was $22.50 per term for freshmen and sophomores and $30 per term for juniors and seniors.[9] The catalog listed separate tuition charges for conservatory (music) subjects. Students taking art, voice, and elocution paid $25 whereas students taking piano and organ paid up to $40 and $60, respectively. Roughly $7.00 in other fees covered usage of the library, the science laboratories, and medical facilities.[10] All told, the full annual cost of a Brenau education in 1900 might run around $275, or roughly one-third of the average family income at the time of $800.[11] By comparison, in 2008–2009, the average household income for the United States was $50,221 and the average total cost of a year of private, four-year college education was $31,233—more than one-half of what average families made in a year.[12]

In 1910, Brenau's catalog published a paragraph dealing with "Minimum, Average, and Maximum Expense" for "a girl taking an average course."[13] In this section, the College added together charges for the following expenses for a single term: board, room, literary tuition, music tuition, piano practice, books and music, and fees and incidentals. Brenau found the minimum expense to be $149, the average expense to be $201, and the maximum expense to be $259 per term.[14] According to census data, the average family income in 1910 was about $1200.[15] Brenau's costs had doubled during a decade when annual household income increased by half. By 1930, Brenau estimated that the minimum annual expense for attending the College during the Great Depression would be $547 and the maximum expense would be $647.[16] These estimates included $150 for tuition and $280 for board.[17]

Examining expenses at other collegiate institutions during these decades bears out that Brenau, though not a bargain, was competitively priced. This could well have served to attract a wider spectrum of young women to Gainesville. For example, Yale College charged $155 per year for tuition in 1900 and 1910 and estimated that an average student would spend around $545 for tuition, room, board, and other expenses during this period.[18] This was just a bit more than the "Maximum Expense" a Brenau student could anticipate paying. By 1930, tuition at Yale was $450 per year and room rent averaged around $250 per student per year

—numbers again on a par with costs at Brenau.[19] At the University of Georgia in 1899:

> Students paid no tuition, which had been eliminated by the Legislature in 1881. The average student fee total was about $200, which included a $10 matriculation fee, a $5 library fee, and a $2 fee for initiation into one of the literary societies. Fees for laundry, board, furnishings, books, stationery and utilities varied depending upon usage (the catalog offered a range from "low" to "very liberal"). Every student also paid $16 for his uniform for drill.[20]

The $200 in fees (plus board) for Georgia students in 1899 seems comparable to the $220 approximate total cost of Brenau in 1900. By the nineteen-thirties, tuition had made a comeback in Georgia's public colleges. For example, in 1938, tuition at Georgia Tech was $50 per semester.[21] Coupling fees to this would have brought the educational expenses (sans room and board) of a Tech student close to matching the $75 per term expenses paid by Brenau women in the same decade. Regarding expenses at Emory University in Atlanta, a former Emory professor wrote that:

> In 1919 tuition per quarter was $25. This was increased to $35 in 1920. Everyone paid a general fee of $5.00 per quarter and laboratory courses had variable fees. The lab fee for general chemistry was $2.00 in 1919 and $5.00 in 1920. A breakage deposit was required and was refundable if no apparatus was broken.
>
> Examples of living expenses were: Alabama Hall, $54.00 per year for a double room with three occupants. A double room with two occupants in Winship and Dobbs was $58.50 and a single room could be had for $81.00 per year. Meals were $25.00 per month in the Dining Hall.[22]

In all, at Emory in 1919, "total expenses for the year were estimated as $450 to $695, with $500 being the average."[23] The average cost of Emory was roughly double what a Brenau student would have paid only a few years before. At all-women's Vassar College in 1905, the annual fee for tuition and residence was increased from $400 to $500.[24] By 1920, the fee was $880.[25] By 1931, Vassar charged $1,200 for tuition and residence.[26] These figures prove that a Vassar education cost roughly twice that of a Brenau education during the early twentieth century.

By the late twentieth and early twenty-first centuries, the cost of a Brenau education remained modest compared to other schools. In 1965, Brenau charged $1,620 in annual tuition and residential fees.[27] By 1970, students paid $2,325.[28] For the same year, the U.S. Census Bureau declared that "the median money income for all families" was about $9,870.[29] A decade later, the annual comprehensive fee at Brenau totaled $4,650.00 per year.[30] By comparison, the average total annual cost of attendance at a 4-year institution in the U.S. in 1980 was $13,670.[31] By 2008, the "comprehensive fee" of the Women's College at Brenau totaled $26,450 per year and paid for tuition, room, board, and other services.[32] Though this cost was a far cry from the figures of the early 1900s, it was still quite inexpensive compared to other private institutions in the region and accounted for a relatively low percentage of an average family's income.[33] According to a Cornell University report, "in 1980 college tuition took an average bite of 26 percent of the median family income; in 2004, it more than doubled to 56 percent."[34] Even Brenau's entire annual comprehensive fees did not match these percentages in these years.

As at any college, administrators established fees at Brenau over the years and would have done so with little, if any, active student input. Yet, even in this seemingly one-sided process, a type of negotiation occurred between students (and potential students) and College officials because Brenau could charge no more than students and their families were willing to pay. In essence, students negotiated with the institution on financial matters through their very enrollment. If the College charged too much, students would enroll elsewhere, which would induce the administration to moderate costs. Consequently, by voting with their feet, students exhibited some agency.

Besides keeping tuition and fees low in an effort to make Brenau accessible even to young women of modest means, Brenau also discouraged spending lavishly on fashion extravagance and offered some scholarships for study at the College. Several early newspaper advertisements and catalogs iterated what Brenau's 1910 catalog stated, which was that "expensive dressing is discouraged" and that "décolleté and elaborate or very expensive toilets are prohibited."[35] The College banned extravagant clothing for several decades in the early 1900s—and made much of this ban—so that young women of modest means would not be discouraged from attending Brenau for fear of looking out of place. To further attract students from middling socioeconomic backgrounds, Brenau offered a handful of scholarships. These issued even from early on. The 1910 catalog indicated that, "Thirty scholarships of the value of $60 are awarded yearly to students who have been distinguished in their high schools, and to others who may be found worthy of same."[36] Additionally, for a number of years, several early editions of Brenau catalogs indicated that daughters of clergymen could attend Brenau at reduced rates. Merit aid appears to have become more modest in the ensuing decades. Though catalogs mentioned scholarships, none seemed numerous. Moreover, it is unlikely that Brenau's endowment, which remained relatively small until the 1980s, could have supplied any significant amount of financial aid to students. Still, each year, at least a handful of very capable students appear to have had their Brenau educations paid for in whole or in part throughout the history of the College.

Though students played no active role in determining the fees the College charged, they would have been in a position to resist Brenau's policies regarding extravagance. Young women in the early twentieth century might have pushed the limits of permissible fashion at Brenau by simply trying to out-do one another with what they wore until the administration saw fit to step in. Moreover, the students themselves might have set the bar of what constituted extravagance quite high had they all adopted rather elaborate dress. None of this apparently happened. Rather, as illustrated by many photographs in Brenau's college yearbooks (both old and recent), students tended to dress on a par with one another.

On the matter of extravagance, then, students and administrators seemed to be in accord that it had little place on campus.

Besides facilitating the enrollment of young women of various means, Brenau's affordability may have contributed to attracting a more geographically diverse student body to the College. Archival records show that students came from many states to attend the Baptist Female Seminary and Brenau College and from several states and countries all around the world to study at Brenau University. It seems unlikely this would have happened if Brenau was overpriced.

Eleanor Rigney, a member of Brenau's faculty during the 1970s, produced a socioeconomic study of the College in the 1930s that spoke to this geographic heterogeneity. In the first half of this decade, Rigney determined that roughly a quarter of Brenau's then 1,019 students that reported a place of origin to the College came from outside the Southeast. Twenty or more students came from each of four states: Ohio, Pennsylvania, Illinois, or West Virginia. Several Brenau women also called New York, Texas, and Kentucky home. Brenau students came from as far north as Vermont and Michigan and as far west as California, Oregon, and Washington. Perhaps more so than some other women's colleges operating during this period (particularly in the South), Brenau's student body was diverse in terms of place of origin.[37]

The institution celebrated this geographic diversity. Beginning in the early twentieth century and lasting until mid-century, Brenau held an event it called its "State's Day" pageant. An edition of the "Brenau Notes" society column in the *Atlanta Constitution* from 1908 indicated that the pageant showcased floats from over twenty-five states and from England and Cuba.[38] Various later editions of the "Notes" indicated that, to celebrate stately diversity, the event came to consist of several performances, recitals, and other festivities.

Over time, state clubs formed at Brenau and existed until around 1950. Yearbook photographs from the 1920s and 1930s indicated that some clubs, mainly those from the southeastern states, had several dozen members. Clubs representing more distant states were either smaller or joined together with other neighboring states to form a regional club. Still, the fact that these clubs existed at all and that they frequently had several members proves that Brenau had students from across the continent from early on, something not all southern colleges could boast of.

As Brenau matured, the College attracted students from not just faraway states but from American territories such as Hawai'i and from some foreign countries as well. Beginning in 1950 and lasting for several years, the Gainesville Rotary Club occasionally sponsored international students. Young women from at least three countries (Denmark, Finland, and Honduras) attended with this support.[39] Also around mid-century, Brenau created a "Special Department for Latin American Students," which operated for a handful of years and brought native Spanish-speaking women to Gainesville to study from various places. Brenau Spanish instructors oversaw the program, which required students to take "certain special courses" designed to acquaint them with "the language and customs of an American college."[40]

Even despite programs like these, international student numbers at Brenau were never large until fairly recently. Since becoming a university, Brenau typically enrolled a few dozen international students annually. By 2012, international students hailing from a dozen countries comprised around six percent of Brenau's student body in the Women's College.[41] Many of Brenau's finest athletes have been from outside the United States. Throughout the 1990s and 2000s, several members of Brenau's tennis team were from Europe or Asia and helped guide the University to many winning seasons and several conference championships.

Around the time that international students began attending Brenau in greater numbers, the percentage of out-of-state students enrolled at the University declined somewhat. In 2005, this figure was at twelve percent, lower than in years past.[42] Students represented at least twenty-three states in 2011–2012.[43] It is probable that the actual number of out-of-state students did not decrease markedly from recent years so much as the number of in-state students increased as Brenau's enrollment grew in the 1990s and 2000s. This growth would have been stimulated by the advent of Georgia's H.O.P.E. Scholarship in 1993. H.O.P.E. stands for "Helping Outstanding Pupils Educationally." Sales of state lottery tickets funded H.O.P.E. awards, which annually granted eligible Georgia students a few thousand dollars to apply toward in-state private college tuition and expenses. This induced many students to remain in Georgia for higher education.[44]

Because Brenau officials have always handled the institutional admissions process, students could have played no active part in geographically diversifying the student body other than by encouraging girlfriends they happened to know living in far-flung places to apply. Even so, students did play a role in sustaining Brenau's geographic diversity by creating a welcoming environment on campus for students everywhere. Student-driven state clubs, residence hall associations, sororities, organizations, and athletic teams thrived at Brenau and provided social outlets and stability for students far from home. Even though membership in any group would have been at least somewhat selective (and, in some cases, perhaps highly selective), overall, what students created to nurture each other at Brenau was inclusive enough to suffice to keep many students who were not from anywhere near Georgia enrolled.

Wherever they called home, Brenau women as often as not came from educated families. Rigney analyzed the level of educational achievement of the parents of Brenau students during the 1930s by dividing the decade in half. For the first half of the decade, Rigney gathered data from 1,031 fathers of Brenau students. This is not to say that in any given year there were 1,031 young women enrolled at Brenau. Rather, this many fathers completed surveys from 1930 to 1935. Rigney determined that just under half of these fathers of Brenau students who reported their educational achievement in the several years of the early 1930s had attended at least some college. The fathers of several Brenau students worked white-collar jobs and served as physicians, attorneys, college professors, or in other professions. About twice as many fathers were businessmen and another large contingent farmed. Rigney indicated that fathers who were businessmen reported a "great variety" of occupations and that there was "no obvious pattern to these occupations which would point to any particular degree of affluence."[45]

The story was essentially the same in the second half of the 1930s. Rigney reported that of the 668 fathers of Brenau students who reported on their education to the College during these five years, 318 (just under half) had attended at least some college. Rigney noted that among the fathers who reported having attended college, more obtained advanced degrees in the period of 1935–1939 than had obtained advanced degrees in the previous half-decade. Despite this, the types of occupations maintained by the fathers of Brenau students remained constant throughout the decade. Most fathers were businessmen, followed by professionals and farmers. The fathers in business worked at many different jobs though none appeared to be very high-level corporate executives. Additionally, no data indicated that any of the Brenau fathers were either skilled or unskilled laborers.

Throughout the 1930s, Rigney determined that fewer than one-half of the mothers of Brenau students had attended at least some college. Several mothers, in fact, had actually attended Brenau themselves.[46] Indeed, alumnae often thought enough of Brenau to encourage their daughters to attend as well. In 1906, the *Atlanta Constitution* reported on one set of these "legacy" students, noting that, "Miss Mary Callie Reynolds of Sylvania, Ga., and Miss Emma Welchel, of Gainesville, Ga." were "the first granddaughters of Brenau College. Miss Reynolds' mother was Miss Lucy Wallace, of the class of 1884" and "Miss Welchel's mother was Miss Emma J. Thompson, a member of the class of 1881."[47]

Rigney's study showed that, prior to mid-century and compared to the general population of the United States, Brenau women came from well-educated homes given that roughly half of the mothers and fathers of students were college educated. Beginning in 1940, the U.S. Census

Parties to the Parley   43

Bureau began tracking the "Percent[age] of People 25 Years and Over Who Have Completed High School or College." In 1940, the Bureau reported that fewer than six percent of the U.S. population (male or female) had completed four or more years of college.[48] The percentage of college graduates probably would have been even lower in the 1930s and, very likely, even smaller still in Georgia and other southern states as opposed to the country at large.

Read one way, Rigney's findings might argue against Brenau's having a diverse student body in the 1930s. After all, the data appear to show a number of young women from college educated households going to college themselves. Yet, the other half of Brenau's students were first-generation college attendees. And, though many young women attending Brenau had fathers with similar occupations (businessmen, professionals, etc.), many others did not. These considerations imply that Brenau students were not at all as homogenous as they might otherwise have been.

Several decades later, Brenau still attracts many young women who are the first in their immediate families to attend college. The results of a March 24, 2004, survey taken of 457 mostly undergraduate students found that 139 young women (or 31%) described themselves as "First generation students."[49] This was slightly fewer than the national average for the same year, which one researcher put at 40%.[50] As Americans generally pursue college degrees in greater numbers in the years to come, one would anticipate that even more Brenau students would hail from educated households.

Though Brenau has, over the years, succeeded in attracting a student body that cut across many socioeconomic lines, some of its students admittedly were still drawn from that "wealthy strata" of society that Horowitz described. Brenau's administrators acknowledged as much, just as they would contend that, to be truly diverse, rich and poor alike should be represented among the student body. A portion of the 1910 catalog mentioned that Brenau was "fortunate in having a large patronage among the wealthier classes of the South, who demand for their daughters the conveniences of life to which they have been accustomed at home."[51] The 1940 catalog stated, "While some of the critics of Brenau have characterized it as a 'society school,' which is not true in the sense implied, it is true that the students have come from the best homes in more than thirty-five states. Both financial and social references are required of all applicants for admission. Good character and reputation are required."[52] Brenau began discarding these requirements in the 1970s as admissions became largely need-blind and indifferent to social reputation.

Though indifference to students' social reputation would come with time, Brenau seemed to manifest a refreshing indifference to a student's religion since almost its inception. Brenau's stand on religion beginning in the early twentieth century is interesting. The institution was, after all, a women's college in the Deep South Bible Belt during a very pious age. By all accounts given this triumvirate, Brenau should have been a very religious place. Yet, in terms of religion, moderation and tolerance seem to have always been the rule at the institution.

Brenau was originally founded as the Georgia Baptist Female Seminary. Despite its early name, the College never received much more than the appellation from the Baptist denomination. No funding came to Brenau from any large Baptist organizations, though many individual Baptists and smaller congregations likely did donate. Additionally, no evidence suggests that the Baptist denomination (or any denomination, for that matter) ever held any influence over Brenau's curriculum or over the governance of the College. This was certainly not the case at other area women's colleges. Agnes Scott College in Atlanta was, from its inception, affiliated with the Presbyterian Church.[53] True to its name even if Brenau's forerunner was not, the Cherokee Baptist Female College (later Shorter University) in Rome, Georgia, has always held strong ties to Baptists.[54] Wesleyan College "was founded through the efforts of a group of Macon citizens and the Georgia Conference of the Methodist Episcopal Church."[55] Founded in 1881, Spelman College "was supported by the

Woman's American Baptist Home Mission Society and named the Atlanta Baptist Female Seminary."[56] Moravians, a Protestant sect, founded Salem College in Winston-Salem, North Carolina, in 1772.[57] In nearby Raleigh, Meredith College was the Baptist Female University from its inception in 1891 until 1909 when it adopted its present name.[58] On February 8, 1854, "representatives of the South Carolina Methodist Conference voted to establish Columbia Female College in Columbia, S.C.," whose mission would be, in part, "to educate young women for fruitful service to church."[59] Members of Siloam Baptist Church established the forerunner to Judson College in Marion, Alabama, in 1838 and the institution has since remained "church related, embracing Christian principles and values."[60] It appears that in the entire southeastern region of the country, the only other private women's college to end up with by-and-large secular origins besides Brenau was Converse College, which formed as a kind of stock company with shares held by some Spartanburg, South Carolina, citizens.[61]

Although the institution has never held official ties to any religious organization, most of the people who have been associated with Brenau over the years (including students) apparently were religious and the institution has long tried to maintain a virtuous—if not religious—environment on campus. Several photographs in every edition of the College annual yearbook dating back to Brenau's founding depict robust numbers of students in groups like the Young Women's Christian Association and various fellowship organizations. Also, early in its history, Brenau required church attendance of students. Even when officials later relaxed this mandate (which happened relatively early for a southern women's college, as discussed in the chapter on rules and regulations), Brenau continued to strongly encourage churchgoing. Brenau's early official literature, such as the 1900 catalog, said of the College, "It is a Christian institution, and young ladies entrusted to its care will receive instruction in all that pertains to the development of their spiritual nature."[62]

Despite these sanctimonious elements, Brenau has maintained an exceptional degree of religious toleration from its start and throughout its life. The College advertised itself as being "undenominational" in early promotional materials and attracted young women from many faiths. A 1911 article in the *Atlanta Constitution* reported of Brenau that "here nearly every denomination is represented during the scholastic year—Methodists, Baptists, Presbyterians, Roman Catholics, Jews, Episcopalians, daily mingle with each other, and daily, as they go to and from their classes, as they play, talk and work they are receiving from each other the tolerance which the interchange of varied opinions always brings out. Prejudices disappear, while each girl is strengthened in her own affiliations."[63]

Exactly what those affiliations have been over time is hard to say. Very early on, Brenau must have polled students for their denomination to facilitate enforcing the mandatory Sunday morning church attendance and to inform its advertising. None of those records or any others that might have inquired about student religion since then are in the Archives. Presumably, Brenau's student body at any given time would mirror that of wider American society. According to one pair of scholars writing in 2001 about religious diversity over time in the United States, "Protestants decreased from being almost 80 percent of the population 100 years ago to about 60 percent today."[64] This suggests that a significant majority of Brenau's students have always been Protestant. Still, they have definitely not all been Protestant.

Several sources indicate that many Roman Catholics and several Jewish students have attended Brenau over the years.[65] In the early twentieth century, about 18,000 Roman Catholics lived in Georgia, though few apparently lived in northeast Georgia.[66] The history of the Saint Michael's Catholic Church in Gainesville related that the Gainesville congregation numbered just five people in 1912 and held Communion service in private homes.[67] Gainesville would not get a Catholic Church until 1933. Yet, by 1945 "a growing number of Catholics at Riverside Military Academy and at Brenau College, both located in Gainesville, necessitated the provision of a resident pastor" in the parish.[68] This suggests that there were, indeed, a number of Catholic students in attendance at both institutions. Nothing short of many Catholic students would have been enough to drive parishioner numbers up sufficiently to merit stationing a priest in the city. This is because Gainesville's resident Roman Catholic population could not have been large. Even as late at 1957, the Archdiocese of Atlanta (which encompassed Gainesville and all of north Georgia) had only 23,659 members and fewer than 100 priests in its entire range.[69] By the late 1950s, fewer than 125 families called the entire seven-county parish in which Gainesville was a part home.[70] Whereas the Archdiocese probably could not justify posting a priest to Gainesville to service so few families, sending a priest to minister to those families *and* a number of college students would make much more sense.

Additional evidence suggests that a fair number of Brenau students have been Catholic over the years. According to an article published in the newspaper of the Catholic Archdiocese of Atlanta, "in 1951 the students attending Brenau College received their charter in the National Newman Federation."[71] Newman Clubs began appearing on American college and university campuses in the 1880s to "help Catholics live their faith" in non-Catholic environments.[72] The photographic spreads of the club in the *Bubbles* never depicted many members compared to other campus social organizations, but they would demonstrate the presence of at least several Catholics at the College in any given year for some years after mid-century.

The existence of other organizations on campus also offers proof of the presence of non-Protestant students at Brenau. From 1926–1930, Brenau sustained a chapter of the Delta Phi Epsilon social sorority. At the time, ΔΦE was largely Jewish. As with the Newman Club, yearbooks never revealed more than a handful of members in the group in any given year. Yet, despite this and ΔΦE's short lifespan, that enough young Jewish women attended a small, southern women's college in rural Georgia in the 1920s to even contemplate founding a chapter of a Jewish sorority is remarkable.[73] It is reasonable to assume that Jewish and Roman Catholic students would not have come to Brenau in numbers—or at least would not have stayed—if Brenau had not proven to be as accepting of multiple religious faiths as it claimed to be.

Though open-minded about its students' faith, Brenau has been closed-minded in other respects. Regarding admissions, there was a time when race mattered as much to the institution as religious denomination mattered little. Though the College would enroll a small handful of women from Asia and Latin America over time, for its first hundred years, Brenau severely lacked any racial diversity among its student body. The institution was homogenous and was overwhelmingly white. This would not change until the early 1970s when Brenau finally began enrolling African American students. Black student enrollment would gradually increase until, by the twenty-first century, Brenau claimed very respectable numbers of minority students. According to Brenau, in 2011, twenty-three percent of students are from minority groups (not including international students).[74] This compares quite favorably with other colleges in the region around this time. For example, only fourteen percent of the students at Piedmont College in Demorest, Georgia, were from racial minority groups in 2012–2013. The same year, such students comprised only 9.7% of the student body at the University of North Georgia in Dahlonega.[75]

Student organizations came into being at Brenau as the campus welcomed students of color. Two African American sororities established themselves at Brenau and an organization called the Brenau Silhouettes formed on campus. The Silhouettes were and are "devoted to the purpose of strengthening awareness of minority concerns and strengthening relationships among all students" and have sought "to provide occasions for social interaction related to all cultural experiences."[76] The growth of organizations such as these and Brenau's minority student population, as well as the enrollment of several international students each year since about the 1980s, have helped to transform Brenau's modern student body into one that is quite racially diverse.

Though various sources speak to student race at Brenau, sources about other student attributes are lacking—some severely so. For instance, demographic profiles of student populations at some institutions of higher education can speak (even if only in a limited sense) to the attribute of student sexual orientation. A profile of Brenau could not. Though in 2012 a growing number of U.S. colleges and universities had specific courses, majors and minors, graduate programs, campus organizations, and/or campus centers or offices dedicated to lesbian, gay, bisexual, and transgender themes, Brenau is one of the many that had yet to develop such things. Other than a 2011 catalog course description reference to "gay/lesbian history" as a possible emphasis for a gender studies special topics course (one of just three gender studies courses then offered by the University), nothing at all in any of Brenau's materials or in its Archives relates to sexual orientation.[77] It is only in a few instances in the online archives of Brenau's student newspaper, the *Alchemist*, that one can find any association between Brenau and homosexuality at all. From 2008 until 2010, one student, Rachel Thurman, wrote a dozen often quite engaging op-ed columns that addressed L.G.B.T. themes.[78] Herself a lesbian, she occasionally referenced personal experiences to inform her writing. Nothing suggests that anyone ever censored her work in the least, nor had her columns ever elicited any negative comments from readers in the *Alchemist*'s online comments section by July of 2012. Perhaps these things suggest that even if Brenau is not at the vanguard of promoting the inclusion of homosexuals on campus, neither is it at all engaged in excluding gays and lesbians from campus life either. The same could not be said for other institutions in the state, even in the twenty-first century.[79]

Whatever their backgrounds and characteristics, at times, many students came to Brenau. For a growing liberal arts college, Brenau generally enjoyed fairly large enrollments from the turn of the century to the 1920s. In 1900, Brenau's catalog indicated that the institution enrolled 213 students in all of its collegiate programs.[80] Brenau's 1910 catalog indicated that the College enrolled 370 students that year in all of its programs combined.[81] By 1920, enrollment had increased to 554 students.[82] Until the late twentieth and early twenty-first centuries, this would be near the peak enrollment of the institution.

A memorandum prepared in 1950 by Ella D. Winfield, a former registrar at Brenau, gave a concise picture of enrollment at the College over the years between 1930 and 1950. In 1930, enrollment was at 483.[83] With the onset of the Great Depression, enrollment fell sharply at Brenau, bottoming out during that decade at 320 students in 1934.[84] A report prepared by Brenau officials and ominously entitled "Freshman Mortality 1929 – 1939" indicated that freshman attrition, in part, explained the decline in enrollment. On average, Brenau lost fully 50% of every year's freshman class as half of the students did not return to Gainesville for their sophomore year.[85] Because of this factor and dynamism in recruiting, enrollment from 1935 to 1950 often fluctuated a great deal from year to year with the College literally gaining or losing over a hundred students from one year to the next.

This fluctuating enrollment at Brenau apparently hit bottom in 1949–1950. In that academic year, Winfield's memo indicated that only 228 students attended the College, fewer than half the number of young women that had studied at Brenau only three decades before. This was likely due to more young women dropping out of college or foregoing college altogether to get married earlier in post-World War II America. By 1950, "the age of marriage for American women had dropped below twenty" and "the percentage of divorces reached an all-time low."[86] Over the next half-century, enrollment would gradually, though steadily, increase. By 2000, Brenau's Women's College had tripled in size from its low in 1950 and by 2012 just over 800 students enrolled at the Gainesville campus, with many hundreds more enrolled in the University's evening, weekend, and online programs.[87] By 2012, students from twenty countries enrolled in the Women's College and, importantly, Brenau's retention rate had climbed to 69%, far above the 50% rate of the 1930s.[88]

In the face of fluctuating enrollment, selectivity in Brenau's admissions policies varied over time. To be admitted to the freshman class of the Collegiate Department in the Baptist Female Seminary, Brenau examined students to gauge their ability in mathematics (mostly arithmetic and fundamental algebra), English (grammar and composition), Latin (two books of Caesar), United States history, and physical geography. Students could apply for entrance into higher classes and would be given more difficult exams to judge their fitness for skipping grades. Conversely, if a student did poorly on the freshman examinations, but still seemed able to do the work, she might gain admission on a trial basis.[89]

The 1910 Brenau College catalog indicated that admissions requirements to Brenau had become more stringent since 1900. In 1910, the College offered a single entrance examination, which still covered English, Latin, math, and history, but also expected students to demonstrate some proficiency in either science, Greek, French, or German. Alternatively, Brenau admitted without examination students who could present certificates from "other schools of recognized standing" proving their mettle or who were "graduates of high schools which have been accredited by the University" of Georgia.[90] The College also advertised around this time that "The standard A. B. course is based upon a fourteen-unit entrance requirement."[91] By the 1960s, Brenau dispensed with its own examination and required the Scholastic Aptitude Test for freshman admission.[92] In 1970, Brenau recommended a student score a minimum of 400 in each area of the S.A.T. and also required applicants to take the English Composition Achievement Test and a Foreign Language Achievement Test.[93]

By 1980, Brenau required standardized test scores, high school transcripts, and a recommendation from a high school counselor for admission of U.S. students to the Women's College.[94] Though combined S.A.T. scores of 800+ guaranteed admission, the College declared that, "A significant number of students who submit S.A.T. scores below 800 or even below 600 are admitted to Brenau in recognition of the fallibility of standardized testing devices."[95] As a result, "of the 513 students who applied for admission for fall quarter, 1980, 496 were accepted."[96] By the twenty-first century, Brenau's average S.A.T. scores had risen to just over 1000.[97]

As at any institution, Brenau's admission requirements attempted to ensure that only students prepared and able to do its college-level work enrolled. Evidence exists for much of its history to suggest that capable students attended. Brenau began by seeking students from accredited high schools, even early on. The university Archives contain some materials dating from around 1930 from the Southern Association of Colleges and Schools that ask Brenau officials to provide first-semester grades for new freshmen. In essence, S.A.C.S. planned to use the data to validate that students who graduated from high schools it accredited were, in fact, being adequately taught what was needed to succeed in college. Regarding its freshmen, Brenau's registrar indicated "a very few will be seen to be from schools not on the full accredited list, but are admitted as graduates with the understanding that standing depends on quality of work."[98]

Any notion that Brenau's Women's College might have ever routinely enrolled very underprepared or young high-school-aged applicants lacks foundation for many reasons, but one stands out: Brenau already had an alternative for them. In 1928, the institution founded and thereafter maintained its own separate college-preparatory secondary school, Brenau Academy, which could serve these students without turning away business.[99] Though in the modern era some advanced Academy students would joint-enroll in college classes, earlier in its history, Brenau emphasized that the two schools were separate. In response to a question posed in an early S.A.C.S. report officials completed on October 11, 1930, Brenau stipulated that no college faculty members taught in the preparatory school and that no students of the preparatory school attended college classes.[100]

Beginning around the mid-twentieth century, Brenau made mention of merit scholarships in its catalogs to attract particularly good students. The 1940 *Brenau College Bulletin* spoke of twelve "College Scholarships," valued at $250 a year for four years, which were competitively awarded to applicants as well as a limited number of $150 scholarships set aside for "honor graduates of accredited high schools."[101] By 1950, Brenau awarded a limited number of $100 "Freshman Honor Scholarships" and also distributed a few "Senior College Honor Scholarships" that paid $200 a year for sophomores who continued on to the A.B. at Brenau.[102] These still existed in 1960 and 1970 and, as during the earlier decades, covered much of Brenau's cost.[103] Curiously, by 1971, the *Brenau Bulletin* made no mention of scholarships. A decade later, Brenau again discussed academic scholarships in its catalog, but more generally, saying only that funding would be awarded for "academic excellence."[104] By then, Brenau also awarded scholarships in fine arts and athletics.[105] According to the 1990 catalog, students with a 1200 S.A.T. score and a 3.5 grade point average in high school could vie to become "Brenau Scholars" and earn $10,000 of funding annually. "Brenau Trustee Scholarships" were awarded in lesser amounts to students scoring 1000 on the S.A.T. and graduating high school with a 3.0 G.P.A.[106] Brenau retained these awards into the twenty-first century to, as ever, attract academically bright young women to attend.[107]

Other evidence also suggests that many Brenau students were capable collegians. As a case in point, many national honor societies have established chapters at Brenau over the years. Rigney wrote that:

> In 1909, the honorary literary society, Phi Beta Sigma, was founded at Brenau to stimulate scholarship, foster the "love and truth and worth", [sic] and to promote the interest and ideals of Brenau. Zeta Phi Eta, the national professional speech arts fraternity was established October 10, 1893. Mu Phi Epsilon, organized in 1911,

is a national honorary music fraternity. Alpha Delta, an honorary journalistic fraternity; Tau Sigma, an honorary dancing fraternity; Tau Kappa Alpha, national honorary forensic fraternity; and Delta Psi Kappa, an honorary physical education fraternity were active in 1935.[108]

Rigney also indicated that Brenau would claim chapters of the following honoraries at one time or another:

Sigma Pi Alpha (an honorary society connected with foreign culture)

Gamma Sigma Epsilon (a chemistry honorary society)

Sigma Theta Tau (a nursing honor society)

Pi Theta Epsilon (the National Honor Society of Occupational Therapy)

Alpha Lambda Delta (a society honoring freshman scholarship)

Kappa Pi (an international honorary art fraternity)

Tau Sigma (an honor society for dance students)

Omicron Delta Kappa (a national leadership honor society)

Kappa Delta Pi (an honor society for education majors)

Lambda Iota Tau (a national honorary society for literature students)

Phi Alpha Theta (a history honor society)

Psi Chi (a psychology honor society)

Sigma Tau Delta (an English honor society)

Order of Omega (an honor society open only to sorority members)[109]

As well, the faculty pursued establishing a chapter of Pi Gamma Mu (a social sciences honor society) in April of 1928.[110] In the spring term of 2007, Brenau announced that it had been granted a charter of Phi Kappa Phi, the "oldest and largest national honor society" in America.[111] National honor societies such as these with reputations to uphold set nationally-normed requirements of eligibility for membership. It is unlikely any would have chartered at Brenau unless they perceived that the College offered a respectable education and enrolled students on a par with those attending other colleges.

Though data such as these suggest that Brenau has enrolled capable students during much of its institutional history, other materials occasionally suggested otherwise. For example, in a letter dated September 28, 1948, the executive secretary of the Southern Association of Colleges and Secondary Schools wrote Brenau's president to relate that Brenau students had done poorly in a recent administration of the Graduate Record Examination. He wrote:

> The showing at Brenau is rather disappointing, because it reveals weaknesses and does not reveal the outstanding strength one would expect. Few students reach the average of 500 points in any subject, and almost none goes above that figure. The showing on General Education raises the question as to whether the entrance program is strong enough to secure well prepared girls.[112]

Additionally, some years, college admissions seemed almost non-selective—even in relatively modern times. As a case in point, in 1980, Brenau's admissions committee reviewed 181 applications and denied admission to just 17 applicants.[113]

Finally, it is difficult to gauge overall student ability at Brenau over time because the Archives apparently do not contain any historical records of perhaps the most telling indicator of students' ability to do college-level work: student graduation rates. Multiple sources (catalogs, especially, which list alumnae by year) indicate that the College has long graduated at least a few dozen young women annually, but these do not indicate if students made regular annual progress in their academics or if they struggled en route to earning a degree. In modern times, roughly one-third of Brenau students reportedly graduate in four years, but no records for years prior to this period seem to have been archived.[114]

Among graduates, Brenau at times saw relatively few alumnae go on to graduate and professional school. Some materials completed in 1930 for S.A.C.S. accreditation purposes represented that only twelve percent of Brenau graduates had gone on for graduate study during the last ten years.[115] Though this percentage was not high, a memorandum elaborating upon this indicated that the handful of Brenau alumnae who did undertake graduate study went to some fine schools, such as the University of Georgia, Columbia University, Vanderbilt (Peabody), The University of Texas, and the University of California.[116] Also, this number has increased slowly over time. In Brenau's 1948–1949 S.A.C.S. "Report Form for Senior Colleges," a page lists by name and year of graduation students who enrolled in graduate or professional school. Between 1941 and 1948, an average of seven students each year from graduating classes that numbered around 45 to 55 continued their studies, most at nationally-known universities.[117] In more recent years, Brenau alumnae have gone on to a variety of graduate and professional schools. The Brenau University Office of Alumni Relations maintains an alumnae magazine entitled *Brenau Window*, which frequently publishes life updates from graduates. These updates show that Brenau graduates work or continue studying in many fields.[118]

While Brenau graduates have been finding personal and professional success for well-over a century, unlike some other women's colleges, Brenau cannot claim many famous alumnae. Still, a few women who studied at the College have gained notoriety. Helen Dortch became the second wife of the much older former Confederate General James

Longstreet on September 8, 1897, after her roommate at Brenau (who happened to be the general's daughter) introduced the pair. Mrs. Longstreet became the first woman to hold State office in Georgia when Governor W. Y. Atkinson appointed her assistant state librarian in 1894. She was also an avid environmental and historical preservationist who worked to preserve scenic Tallulah Gorge in north Georgia from development.[119] Another Brenau College graduate landed an even higher political appointment as described in a rather colorful 1929 *Time Magazine* article:

> A great advocate of The Home during the campaign, President Hoover has surprised nobody by the fewness of his appointments of women to public offices. But lately he put aside his feeling against women as officeholders long enough to listen to arguments by his Secretary of the Treasury Andrew William Mellon in behalf of Miss Annabel Matthews of Gainesville, Ga. The arguments seemed so irresistible that President Hoover last week appointed Miss Matthews to the U. S. Board of Tax Appeals ($10,000 per year), the first woman ever named to this potent buffer agency between the Treasury and the taxpayer.
>
> A graduate of Brenau College in her home town, Miss Matthews taught school for a dozen years in Georgia, went to Washington 15 years ago as a clerk in the Treasury's Bureau of Internal Revenue. Ambitious, she studied law, became a double taxation expert, and accompanied U. S. delegations abroad to international tax conferences.[120]

Ellnora Decker Krannert graduated from Brenau around 1912 with a degree in music. She later married Herman C. Krannert, a Midwestern industrialist, and the pair became very wealthy from founding and running a cardboard container company. Ellnora and her husband went on to make very generous contributions to education and the arts. In particular, the millions they donated created the Krannert School of Management at Purdue University, the Krannert Center for the Performing Arts at the University of Illinois, and the Krannert Memorial Library at the University of Indianapolis.[121] Another alumna, Dr. Elizabeth Parker, graduated from

Brenau in 1924 and by 1934 had earned a master's degree in zoology and a medical degree from George Washington University. She became "an authority on female endocrinology, a medical school teacher and administrator, a writer and a research scientist" who headed up G.W.U.'s female endocrinology research laboratory from 1932 to 1945.[122]

Someone else who pursued a career in academia was Katharine Du Pre Lumpkin. After graduating from Brenau in 1915 at the young age of 19, she studied sociology, earning a master's degree from Columbia University and later a Ph.D. from the University of Wisconsin in 1928. She went on to teach at several women's colleges and wrote several books. Lumpkin is perhaps most remembered for her work entitled *The Making of a Southerner*. Published in 1947, *The Making of a Southerner* has been described as "part family history, part autobiography, and part sociological study" that described Lumpkin's transition "from passive inheritance of white supremacy to conscious rejection of the racial values of a segregated South."[123] Lumpkin found at Brenau "a small group of students...who, like her, were open-minded and inquisitive and found a single (though curiously unnamed) faculty member who encouraged them all to 'use our minds, go to the sources, have no truck with undocumented hearsay, [and to] keep our eyes on the vast play of forces.'"[124]

Another prominent Brenau associate was actress Amanda Blake, who attended Brenau's girl's preparatory school for a time. Blake played "Miss Kitty Russell" for nineteen seasons on the very popular television series "Gunsmoke." Television aficionados will know that Kitty was "the proprietress of the Longbranch saloon in Dodge City" and "the girlfriend of the series' leading character, Sheriff Matt Dillon."[125] Blake visited Brenau frequently, went on to serve on the College's Board of Trustees, and made several public appearances throughout the country on behalf of Brenau.

Other Brenau alumnae include Florence Reville Gibbs, who graduated from Brenau around 1910 and went on to become the first woman from Georgia to be elected to the Federal House of Representatives.[126] Lera

Millard Thomas attended Brenau in the 1920s and would go on to become the first woman elected to the U.S. Congress from the state of Texas.[127] Terry Coleman, a graduate of the Evening and Weekend College, served as Speaker of the House in the Georgia State Assembly from 2003–2004.[128] Roslyn E. Wallace graduated from Brenau in 1944 and went on to earn both a doctorate in biology from Harvard University and a Fulbright award for cancer research at the Sorbonne in Paris. She became the first woman to receive the prestigious Cyanamid Scientific Achievement Award for chemotherapy research in 1979.[129] Del Ward, who graduated from Brenau in 1947, became a prominent broadcasting personality in the 1950s. Known as "Del from Dixie," she has been called the nation's first "gal disk jockey." Many thousands of listeners tuned into her popular music radio show that ran for several years on W.G.N. in Chicago and also heard her in the New York and St. Louis markets as well.[130]

Candice Dyer is a younger alumna of the Women's College who is making her mark in the twenty-first century as an up-and-coming writer. Dyer graduated from Brenau in 1992 where she majored in journalism and served as the editor for the student literary journal, the *Elixir*.[131] She has authored several articles on various topics for a number of publications that include *Men's Journal, Paste, Garden & Gun, Georgia Trend, Brightleaf: A Journal of Southern Writing*, the *Macon Telegraph*, and the *Atlanta Journal-Constitution*, among others.[132] In 2009, she won a coveted "Green Eyeshade" award for excellence in Southern journalism for a piece published in *Georgia Music Magazine*.[133] Dyer also wrote a well-received book about the Macon, Georgia, music scene in the twentieth century. Published in 2008, *Street Singers, Soul Shakers, Rebels with a Cause: Music from Macon* chronicles such rock legends as Little Richard, Otis Redding, James Brown, the Allman Brothers Band, and several other artists with ties to central Georgia.[134]

Regrettably, the Brenau Archives contain relatively little official documentation relating to alumnae more generally. Though catalogs at times mention associations of alumnae as far back as the early 1900s, a fully organized alumnae office that would keep thorough records—such as Brenau presently has—appears to have come relatively late to the College. Brenau apparently did not even employ a full-time Alumnae Director until February of 1971.[135] More alumnae-related sources could have better described the role played by Brenau graduates in creating the Brenau College experience. That they influenced in various ways and to varying degrees negotiations with the faculty and staff to shape the College must be a given. Alumnae have shaped Brenau as alumnae shape any institution by doing such things as helping recruit new students, assisting graduates in job placement, and, of course, donating money.

Alumni donations to a college or university can serve as an indicator of student satisfaction. A high alumni giving rate would suggest an institution's graduates were satisfied with their college experience. Though the Archives do not contain any materials showing past rates of alumni giving, several alumnae have gifted money to Brenau over the years.[136] In 2008, the average alumnae giving rate for Brenau was twelve percent—right at the national average.[137] Earlier, one alumna's gift was particularly noteworthy. In the late 1920s, Ada Little attended Brenau, where "she majored in education...served as treasurer for three student groups and was voted 'most cheerful' by her peers."[138] She "graduated in 1930, married, moved to Virginia, and began playing the stock market" with a small inheritance her mother left her. She played it pretty well.[139] Ada died in July of 2000 and, roughly a year later, her estate finalized a donation of $2.5 million to Brenau, the "largest gift in the university's history" to date.[140]

Though the University Archives contain relatively little material pertaining to alumnae, a few artifacts (such as personal correspondence or references in presidential papers or other documents) suggest that graduates had (or attempted to have) some influence at Brenau beyond that likely to be associated with donations. Indeed, every time an alumna wrote a check or wrote a letter to their alma mater, they were to some degree engaging themselves in the process of negotiation for the ideal

Brenau college experience. As the Archives come to contain more—and more detailed—matter on Brenau graduates, it should become possible to better discern exactly what they brought to the discussion.

Whenever they attended en route to graduating, students at Brenau's Women's College have historically hailed from a number of places and economic backgrounds and have also been mostly white, mostly Christian, and, according to conventional wisdom about undergraduate college attendees, mostly between the ages of 17 to 24. Of course, they have also been women. Once at Brenau, most of these students seemed to have largely come together. Though they surely could not have agreed on everything all the time, something (perhaps their similar traits and backgrounds, a sense of "sisterhood," etc.) apparently existed that inclined many Brenau students to hold concordant views about many things—at least when it came to important matters of negotiating with the Brenau faculty and staff. Though it would go too far to claim that the student body always spoke with one clarion voice in negotiations with Brenau personnel, history suggests that the students rarely Balkanized over any significant issues. If they had, one would expect to find evidence of such division, perhaps in the form of conflicting opinion pieces in the student newspaper or perhaps even administrative correspondence noting diverging student views. Some examples of these kinds of things exist in the Archives, but not many. Moreover, other evidence suggests that, over time, Brenau students have joined together, particularly in support of the voice of the student body, the Student Government Association.

Students founded Brenau's S.G.A. around the turn of the twentieth century, making it quite possibly the oldest such organization at a southern women's college.[141] Though its structure would change somewhat over time, it has always been, essentially, a representative body comprised of several Brenau students elected annually by the student body. In 1947, "A recent faculty investigation revealed that the Student Government at Brenau College was working efficiently and was more than satisfactory in every respect."[142] The investigation determined that,

"The chief contribution of the Student Government has been the creation of a high morale among the students and a maintenance of a fine quality of citizenship among the student body at large."[143] The 1971 *Institutional Self-Study* that Brenau prepared for review by the Southern Association of Colleges and Schools read, "The Student Government of Brenau is highly effective and commands the respect and support of the students as well as of the faculty and administration. A questionnaire sent to a random sample of students indicates that sixty-nine percent feel that they are represented by Student Government."[144] By a decade later, S.G.A.'s reputation had apparently diminished, but it still commanded no small amount of student support. Another survey prepared for S.A.C.S., this one of 40 residential upper-class students, found that 53% "disagreed that students supported S.G.A."[145] The opinion of S.G.A. was higher among the College's more active students: "Of twenty-two peer advisors polled, eighty-six percent agreed that students supported S.G.A."[146]

Members of the Student Government Association at any time in Brenau's history would have appreciated the support of the student body as they engaged in negotiations with Brenau's faculty and staff over an idealized Brenau College experience. There have been many men and women who, over time, served as faculty members, staff members, and administrators at the institution. Like the students, they sought to shape Brenau in very deliberate ways that reflected their beliefs and desires. Throughout the College's history, a handful of presidents in particular served long tenures and would have loomed large in negotiations with students. These administrators and other faculty and staff members —especially when Brenau was relatively young—were in positions to effectively shape much about the character of the College.

A few powerful presidents figure in Brenau's history. The first of these was the Reverend William Clay Wilkes. Wilkes is credited with founding the Georgia Baptist Female Seminary in Gainesville, Georgia, in 1878. Born in 1819 in South Carolina, Wilkes graduated from Mercer University, then a Baptist college in Penfield, Georgia, in 1843. Prior to this, it was said that Wilkes had "been a teacher of youth in Georgia for about thirty-five years" whose "record in Eatonton, Forsyth, Spalding, Dalton and Gainesville" was "part of the educational history" of Georgia.[147] This educational history included building two women's schools from the ground up. In 1850, the board of directors of the Forsyth Female Collegiate Institute in Forsyth, Georgia, hired Wilkes as the school's first president and his efforts promoted early growth at the Institute.[148] Around 1867, Wilkes founded the Spalding Seminary in the county of the same name. Wilkes eventually moved north to escape the "malarial" climate of central Georgia, became the pastor of the Baptist church in Gainesville, and led efforts to found a seminary there.[149]

At the fifty-fifth anniversary of the Baptist Convention held in Gainesville from April 19 to April 23, 1877, Wilkes and his supporters broached the idea of founding a seminary with the denomination. Their proposal read:

> Proposition from the City of Gainesville for the
> Establishment of a Female College
> State of Georgia - Hall County - City of Gainesville.
>
> The Mayor and Council of the City of Gainesville submit to the Baptist Convention of the State of Georgia the following proposition, to wit:
>
> If the Baptist denomination, under the management and control of the Convention of the State of Georgia, will establish, at Gainesville, a female seminary of high order, the city of Gainesville, by her regularly constituted authorities, binds herself to donate to said convention, for the use of said college six acres of land, wherever the said convention may select for a location for said college, in the corporate limits of said city, provided there shall be no valuable building on the land selected.
>
> The city of Gainesville further binds itself to donate to the said Baptist Convention, the sum of twenty-five thousand dollars,

> in the bond of the city of Gainesville, each bond to be of the denomination of one hundred dollars, for the use of said college; the bonds to be delivered, and the interest to commence at once, at eight per cent per annum, from the time that said college shall be located, and building commenced, said interest to be promptly paid annually.
>
> We further submit that we believe that twenty thousand dollars can be raised in the next twelve months, by voluntary contribution from the Baptist people, and other citizens of the surrounding counties, in aid of said enterprise.
>
> All of which we submit, and ask a favorable consideration.
>
> Done by the order of the Council. Witness our hands and the seal of the corporation this April 20, 1877: A.B.C. Dorsey, City Clerk, D.G. Candler, Mayor.[150]

The Convention responded:

> Resolved: That we take under our control the institution of learning for girls, which the city authorities of Gainesville, and the citizens thereof and vicinity propose to build, and which they have so generously tendered this body, through their Mayor, the Hon. D. G. Candler, and the pastor of the Baptist Church, Rev. W. C. Wilkes.
>
> Resolved: That in accepting this proposition from Gainesville, we do not disparage the claims of any similar institution which may now be in existence, or may hereafter be established.
>
> Resolved: That in accepting this proposition, we do not assume any financial liability whatsoever.[151]

In fact, the resolutions amounted to little more than a vote of confidence for Wilkes' project. The Baptist Convention would never attempt to control the institution in any way, nor would it contribute at all financially to the Seminary. It was Reverend Wilkes who took on these tasks until his death.

The Georgia Baptist Female Seminary came into being with much fanfare. The *Gainesville Eagle* proclaimed that, "On the 4th day of July [1878], the people of Gainesville—Ladies especially—and the citizens of Hall and adjacent counties" were invited to witness "the interesting ceremonies of laying the Corner Stone of the First Edifice of the Georgia Seminary, by the Odd-Fellows and the Masons; and to hear able speeches by Hon. W. P. Price of Dahlonega, and by our worthy representative, just from Congress; the Hon. Hiram P. Bell, in the interest of our great enterprise."[152] The *Eagle* reported that a procession consisting of a band; the student bodies, faculties, and trustees of other Gainesville-area schools; eminent speakers; and area pastors marched from the town square to the Seminary lot for the auspicious ceremony. The *Eagle* related that, in addition to taking in the spectacle, attendees would be permitted "to make a small, suitable deposit of papers, coin, grains of corn, wheat, oats, rye, &c., and especially a list of the names of contributors" to deliver to Wilkes' seminary on the occasion of its founding.[153]

Rev. Wilkes died in 1886. According to the February 23, 1968, edition of the *Alchemist*, Seminary governors "felt it was too great an expense to try to continue without Wilkes' leadership, and so they put the Seminary up for sale."[154] Leadership of the institution passed to Dr. Azor Van Hoose (see Figure 8) when he bought the school. Born in 1860, Van Hoose spent a lifetime working in the field of education. He earned his A.B. at The University of Georgia in 1882 and later received an advanced degree from Mercer University.[155] After earning his credentials, the *Atlanta Constitution* reported that:

> Professor Van Hoose ... taught in Howard College, Alabama, and his *alma mater* in Athens. Feeling that the life of a professor was too circumscribed for him he resigned his position in the university in 1885, came to work in Gainesville and entered upon his life work. His friends endeavored to persuade him not to leave the university and Major Lamar Cobb, then secretary of the board of trustees, wrote him a letter requesting him not to send his resignation to the board. All this advice was of no avail...for he

saw that Gainesville, of all southern cities, possessed superior advantages for a great female college.[156]

In fact, Van Hoose originally went to Gainesville to found a municipally-supported, coeducational institution with Wilkes that would come to be called Gainesville College.[157] This functioned for several years, but the idea of taking control of and growing the female seminary apparently appealed to the two men more than maintaining the municipal college.

The *Constitution* reported that when Reverend Wilkes died, "Professor Van Hoose bought the building of the Baptist seminary and combined the two schools, changing their names to the Georgia Female Seminary" and, apparently, sent the men packing.[158] Van Hoose personally purchased the Seminary and became its president in March, 1886, a position he would hold until 1910. The school retained an association with the Baptist denomination, but in name only. No financial support ever came to Brenau from large Baptist organizations. Perhaps as a result of this, the institution Van Hoose inherited from Wilkes struggled. An article in the July 8, 1897, edition of the *Atlanta Constitution* indicated that, "Professor Van Hoose secured the seminary property in 1886 after it had been closed for debt for eight months. At that time, a one-story brick house served the purpose of the institution, and without equipment of any kind Professor Van Hoose opened the school in September 1886 with twenty-five pupils and two boarders."[159]

In 1893, Dr. Haywood Jefferson Pearce (see Figure 8) purchased half-interest in the Seminary from Van Hoose and joined the faculty as a co-president of the institution. Dr. Pearce was born near Columbus, Georgia, in 1871. He went on to graduate from Emory College in 1891 and later took a master's degree from the University of Chicago.[160] He was well-educated and well-traveled for a man for his time.[161] He toured Europe and Japan, went on to earn a Ph.D. at the University of Würzburg in Germany, and, in 1917, published a book entitled, *Philosophical Meditations; Talks to College Girls.*[162] According to the *Atlanta Constitution,* Dr. Pearce "had just begun a female college [in Columbus, Georgia]" when "he and

Professor Van Hoose, becoming acquainted through an article in the *Constitution*, decided to unite their interests and combine or unite both institutions at Gainesville."[163] Dr. Pearce set aside plans to build a $25,000 college building in Columbus and joined Professor Van Hoose to create "the most thorough and best equipped school in the South."[164]

A remarkable school required a remarkable name. According to the University website, "In 1900 H. J. Pearce purchased the institution and renamed it Brenau, a linguistic blend formed from the German word *brennen*, 'to burn', and the Latin *aurum*, 'gold'."[165] Therefore, Brenau means burned or refined gold and this meaning is what underlies the institution's motto, "As gold refined by fire." For Dr. Pearce and Prof. Van Hoose, the new name and motto were precisely "indicative of the aims and object of the [new] institution" and were thoughtfully arrived at.[166] The *Brenau College Catalogue* of 1900–1901 indicated that:

> A new name was wanted and many lexicons, cyclopedias, etc., were consulted in the search. Finally some one [sic] recalled that beautiful passage in Isaiah which says: "and I will make me a man finer than gold, yea, finer than the golden wedge of Ophir," which expresses so fully the work of the true teacher, elevating the soul, refining the character, taking the young woman through the crucible of college life and turning her out "finer than the gold of Ophir."[167]

The *Catalogue* did not indicate why the name change was wanted. Because the terms were not synonymous, deliberately replacing "seminary" with "college" could only have served to signal a change in the institution's character. Contemporaries would have understood a college to offer a less-preparatory, more rigorous education than a seminary. Brenau officials apparently sought such a re-identification. Additionally, in light of their never having provided the hoped for financial support to the institution or having had any role in its operation, retaining any nominal reference to the Georgia Baptists simply made little sense.

Around 1900, Dr. Pearce and Prof. Van Hoose formed a corporation called the "Brenau Association" to administer the institution, apparently in anticipation of Dr. Pearce's impending absence. The small association (only two others ever joined Pearce and Van Hoose on its board) existed for only three years, during which time Dr. Pearce traveled to Chicago and Europe. Upon his return in 1903, Dr. Pearce and Prof. Van Hoose again assumed joint control of the Seminary by purchasing the interest of the Association.[168]

In 1909, Dr. Pearce purchased the interest in the College held by Prof. Van Hoose, who left Gainesville to become president of Shorter College in Rome, Georgia, a position he held until 1922.[169] By virtue of this purchase, Dr. Pearce became, in essence, the sole owner of a college—an unusual, though not unique, arrangement at the time for a women's college.[170] He retained sole ownership of Brenau until 1917, except for the brief period between 1910 and 1913 when he invited the former president of Shorter, Dr. Thomas J. Simmons, and Mrs. Simmons to join him in Gainesville.[171] Interestingly, for a time, running Brenau was a family affair. A reporter doing a story on the College noted, "The Pearce family runs Brenau. Pearce, Senior, is president; Pearce, Junior, vice president. Both, along with Mrs. Pearce, Senior, the professor's stepmother are trustees. Thomas J. Pearce, a son, is treasurer. Miss Eva Florence Pearce is dean and professor of English. A son-in-law of the president also holds an administrative position."[172] The fifty years that the patriarch of the Pearce family ultimately served as president of the College (from 1893 until 1943) might have earned him "the distinction of probably the longest continuous service of any college president in the United States."[173]

Although Dr. Pearce would remain Brenau's president until his death, in 1917 he made arrangements to cede control of the institution to a board of trustees. In *Brenau 1878–1978*, Eleanor Rigney wrote:

> Dr. Pearce proposed to donate the entire property to a Board of Trustees consisting of eighteen non-resident members, none of

whom were to be nominated by the national alumnae organization of the College.[174]

The only condition to this donation—and it was a big one—was the raising of an endowment fund of $200,000, which was subsequently increased by agreement to $500,000, something like $8 million today when adjusted for inflation.[175] In 1927, Mrs. Aurora Strong Hunt, a Baptist Female Seminary alumna of the class of 1882, donated the Dixie-Hunt Hotel in downtown Gainesville, valued at $250,000.00, to Brenau.[176] This very generous gift, coupled with other donations, brought the endowment to half-a-million dollars by 1928, and solidified the establishment of the Brenau Board of Trustees.

Despite the establishment of the Board and its adoption of a governing role at the College, Dr. Pearce remained a significant presence at Brenau. He would have thrown around much weight in any negotiation with anyone, be they students or employees. Perhaps the best evidence for this is how Dr. Pearce dealt weightily with his own faculty. The faculty meeting minutes book entry for October 6, 1931, indicated that the faculty received a communication from Dr. Pearce. In it, he addressed the difficult financial times that Brenau and, indeed, much of America had fallen upon in the era of the Great Depression. He wrote, "I have decided that it is to the mutual interest of the institution and its faculty to pay only 75% of the salaries due during the nine month school session."[177] With a stroke, and apparently without consulting the faculty at all, Dr. Pearce cut salaries. Though arguably not an unusual move to make during difficult economic times, its repercussions illustrate Dr. Pearce's authority. (What is not similarly well-depicted is whether or not Pearce cut his own salary...)

The move would last for years. The minutes book entry of October 4, 1932, indicated that the College was still in financial difficulty owing to the Depression. Dr. Pearce wrote, "we have accumulated a diamond ring, several municipal bonds, [and] a mortgage on a house and lot" in payment for tuition from several families.[178] Because cash was tight, Dr. Pearce reiterated that paying full salaries would not be possible, at least not in the near future. On February 7, 1933, Dr. Pearce submitted a letter to the faculty saying that, thanks to some business wrangling, refinancing, etc., he hoped that "The actual total cut in salaries will amount to only 20%" as opposed to 25%. Still, with this good news, Dr. Pearce intimated that though he would hate to do so, he reserved the right to recommend to the Brenau Board of Trustees a cut in personnel or salaries should the need arise.[179]

By 1936, faculty member sentiment over the move had apparently reached a boiling point. On January 28, 1936, Dr. Pearce wrote an extraordinary letter to the faculty. In this, he indicated that it had come to his attention that "there is some dissatisfaction on the part of some faculty members with the present salary scale…and possibly with other features of the College."[180] Dr. Pearce went on to say that, "it is highly important that the faculty shall be united, sympathetic each with the other, loyal to the institution, both in conduct and speech" and that "indiscriminate destructive criticism must inevitably result in harm to the institution and to all those whose interests are thereby affected."[181] He then called for all faculty members to formally request in writing to be re-nominated for appointment in the coming academic year. His message was clear: Dissenters should "not apply for re-nomination."[182]

In the letter, Dr. Pearce went on to advocate for increased fundraising through the establishment of an endowment that would raise $50,000. He also personally pledged $10,000 to the effort if other funds would be raised to match his gift. Possibly moved by this gesture, on March 3, 1936, most faculty members subscribed to the endowment and pledged to match Dr. Pearce's contribution and also beseeched the Brenau Board of Trustees to enthusiastically support the endowment drive as well. A component of this, the Brenau Three Thousand Club, would be created in December of 1936 that would solicit donations from Brenau alumnae and acknowledge their gifts publicly. About a month later, Brenau's employees again affirmed their support for Dr. Pearce. The faculty met on April 7, 1936, the day after a tornado struck Gainesville, leveling much of the town (though it spared much of the College) and killing dozens, and offered their support for President Pearce's leadership during the difficult time of recovery.[183]

Dr. Pearce's move to cut salaries may have helped Brenau weather the depression, but it came with costs. As is suggested by his letter calling for dissenters among the faculty to ultimately leave the College, the move hurt his reputation with some of the faculty. Whereas the logical result of a pay-cut might seem to be a disruption in employee morale, this was apparently not always the case. A former administrator and later president at Emory University in Atlanta, Goodrich C. White, recalled that, "The Great Depression hit the campus hard in other ways. To keep the University solvent, [former Emory President Harvey Warren] Cox was forced to cut expenditures by nearly 30 percent between 1931 and 1935."[184] White said that the Emory faculty greeted the move with understanding, not hostility, which touched Cox deeply. He indicated that:

> The only time I ever saw him [Cox] give way to feeling was when he had to announce the imminent necessity of a salary cut, and the faculty had responded with a spontaneous expression of loyalty and confidence. He broke down then; and for some minutes he could not speak. The faculty whose interests were so deeply his had shown that they believed in and trusted him. That broke him, where difficulties and problems never could. In every crisis, great or small, his poise [was] unshaken, his courage undaunted his decision unfailing.[185]

Dr. Pearce apparently did not enjoy a similar spontaneous outpouring of support when it came to salary cuts, which might suggest that the Brenau faculty was more tepid toward their president in such matters.[186]

Dr. Pearce retained the Brenau presidency until his death in 1943. His widow led a small "operating committee" that governed the College for just over a year. In a way, as a result of this service, Lucile Townsend Pearce (who typically went by Mrs. Haywood J. Pearce, Sr.) might arguably be seen as the first female chief executive of a predominantly white women's college in Georgia, though she never laid claim to the title of president nor was she ever formally inaugurated into the position.[187] Moreover, only a year later in 1945, the Brenau Board of Trustees hired Dr. Josiah Crudup as president of the College (see Figure 9). Still, it is perhaps worth noting that for one year (1945), women held all of the senior administrative offices at Brenau: Mrs. Pearce served as Chairman of the Operating Committee, Miss M. E. Bentley served as College Treasurer, Miss Eva F. Pearce served as the Dean of Women, and Miss Ella Winfield held the position of College Registrar.[188] If this was not unique among southern institutions at the time, it must at least have been rare. The following year saw a return to normalcy at the College as Brenau hired an associate dean and a business manager who were both men to assist its new president. Dr. Crudup would be the first of six professional administrator-educators that would lead the institution over the next six decades. Under their leadership, Brenau became a more selective, nationally-recognized university that grew its campus, enrollment, curricular offerings, and endowment.[189]

Josiah Crudup was born in Hot Springs, North Carolina, and graduated from Mercer College in 1923.[190] He went on to earn a Ph.D. in physics from the University of Chicago in 1939.[191] Dr. Crudup returned to teach at his alma mater for a time before becoming an administrator.[192] At Mercer, thirteen ministerial students charged Dr. Crudup and several other faculty members with heresy for teaching evolution in violation of Southern Baptist policies.[193] The outcome of the accusations was that the professors "were warned 'to stick with their disciplines, to maintain Baptist orthodoxy, and to be sure and articulate their positions in the classroom lucidly.'"[194] Dr. Crudup left Mercer to assume the presidency of Brenau in 1945, a position he would hold for two decades. In Gainesville, Dr. Crudup was very active in his church and community and once won the local Rotary Club's "Man of the Year" honor.[195] According to Brenau's catalog, Dr. Crudup "is remembered for his efforts to beautify and restore the campus property as well as to improve Brenau's financial status."[196] Importantly, Dr. Crudup also deftly guided Brenau through the difficult process of re-obtaining accreditation from the Southern Association of Colleges and Schools, which Brenau had earlier lost. Dr. Crudup also played a significant role in keeping Brenau racially segregated after most other colleges and universities in America had integrated.

Upon Dr. Crudup's retirement in 1968, Dr. William K. Clark assumed the presidency of the College. A native of Virginia, Dr. Clark graduated from Texas A & M before earning his M.A. and Ph.D. at the University of Texas in ecology and botany.[197] He taught at Sam Houston State College in Texas for fifteen years before joining the Brenau faculty as its vice-president.[198] Dr. Clark would become president the following year, but he would hold the post for a short time. In February, 1970, he resigned from Brenau.[199] Whether Dr. Clark resigned voluntarily or was asked to resign for some reason is not clear from anything in the Archives or from interviewing long-time personnel, though it is perhaps conspicuous that he left in the middle of the academic year. Dr. Crudup returned to serve as acting president of Brenau until Dr. Clark's successor could be hired.

On May 31, 1970, Dr. James T. Rogers became the sixth president of Brenau College (see Figure 10). A native of Cleveland, Mississippi, Dr. Rogers graduated from Delta State University with a degree in biology in 1955 before joining the U.S. Navy.[200] He served as a pilot from 1956 to 1960 and attained the rank of lieutenant commander. Following his naval career, Dr. Rogers attended graduate school at Florida State University and earned a doctorate in administration and higher education. He worked as Director of Student Personnel at Pensacola Junior College and was the Dean of Student Affairs at Armstrong Atlantic State University in Savannah, Georgia, before becoming president of Brenau on May 30, 1970. At Brenau, Dr. Rogers presided over the integration of the student body and the expansion of several academic offerings, as well as additions to campus that included the College natatorium. Dr. Rogers left Brenau after serving fifteen years as president to take a position as the Executive Director of the Commission on Colleges of the Southern Association of Colleges and Schools. Following his departure, Dr. Hugh M. Mills,

Jr., a prominent area educator who had served as the first president of Gainesville Junior College from 1965 to 1983, succeeded Dr. Rogers and served as Brenau's interim president for one year.[201]

In November of 1985, Brenau's trustees appointed Dr. John S. Burd as Brenau's seventh president (see Figure 11). Dr. Burd studied music at Greenville College and Butler University before earning his Ph.D. at Indiana State University.[202] Dr. Burd served as Vice President for Academic Affairs at Maryville University in St. Louis, Missouri, before coming to Brenau. He and his wife, Dr. Patricia Burd (who was also a professional educator), had been long-time believers in single-gender education and were pleased to see their two daughters attend women's colleges.[203] Highlights of Dr. Burd's tenure as president are several.[204] Perhaps the greatest include "acquiring university status; increasing the endowment from $2.5 million to $47.6 million; [and] constructing a new library and a new performing arts center," as well as acquiring the Jacobs Business and Communication Arts Building and building the Northeast Georgia History Center.[205] Dr. Burd was responsible for initiating several innovative Brenau programs, including an Online College, an Evening and Weekend College, and a Learning and Leisure Institute for adults. He also oversaw the addition of seven graduate-level degrees as well as the growing of Brenau's overall enrollment by 60%. In addition, Dr. Burd can take credit for catalyzing the renovation of numerous campus buildings, including the Simmons Visual Arts Center and the Wheeler Alumni House, and presiding over the construction of Brenau's tennis and fitness centers. Several of Brenau's campus buildings ended up being placed on the National Register for Historic Places during his tenure as president as well.[206] Dr. Burd was also a vigorous supporter of a rare collaboration in higher education between a private institution (Brenau) and a public one (Gainesville State College) to form the Gainesville Theater Alliance, which had come into being just the year before President Burd arrived at Brenau.

Ken Stanford was a journalist who followed Brenau's search for its eighth president after Dr. Burd announced his retirement. He reported in April of 2004 that "the seven trustee members of the search committee" thought that each of three finalists they had visited with "brought strong qualifications" to the presidential search.[207] The trustees' statement additionally declared, "We were also impressed that the three were women, as we realized that the time has come for Brenau to have a woman president."[208] Stanford's article mentioned two by name: Dr. Helen Ray, who was serving as Brenau's Vice President for Academic Affairs at the time, and a Dr. Cynthia Farris. Though both were impressive, a woman's time to head Brenau had apparently *not* yet come after all. Neither was chosen to lead the University and the search continued.

Dr. Edward L. Schrader eventually became Brenau's eighth president on January 1, 2005 (see Figure 12). A native of Vicksburg, Mississippi, Dr. Schrader graduated from Millsaps College and earned a Ph.D. in geology at Duke University. Before coming to Brenau, Dr. Schrader worked in private industry, taught at the University of Alabama, and served as president of Shorter College in Rome, Georgia, for four years. While at Shorter, Dr. Schrader "increased enrollment and developed a new scholarship program of more than $1 million from outside funding."[209] Also at Shorter, Dr. Schrader drew fire from the Georgia Baptist Convention for taking steps to reduce the Convention's control over university governance, efforts supporters of liberal arts education should deem as laudable.[210] Upon assuming the Brenau presidency, Dr. Schrader announced plans to develop a large capital campaign to improve campus infrastructure and to continue work on increasing enrollment, efforts which were well underway by 2012. He also affirmed his commitment to Brenau's mission as a women's college, noting "Every woman here is given the opportunity for leadership and to reach her full potential."[211]

Over time, top administrators have not been the only noteworthy personalities among Brenau's personnel. From time to time, but perhaps especially in its youth, the Baptist Female Seminary and Brenau College had several celebrated professors. Along with administrators and other staff, these educators would have been greatly involved in negotiations with students over the Brenau College experience. Many taught music. Particularly in the College's infancy, conservatory faculty members frequently gave public performances. Brenau's promotional materials sang their praises. Speaking of the Conservatory, one ad read, "It has a faculty of the highest standing."[212] Another advertisement bragged about an early professor. It read:

> Chevalier Ferrata is a native Italian. He studied for ten years at the Royal Academy of Rome and during his stay there won fifteen medals for excellence in composition and technique. He also won three gold medals awarded by the Italian government for the excellence of his musical composition, and in 1897 won the second prize at the competition of the Music Teachers' National Association held in New York. Last January the University of the State of New York honored him with the doctor's degree after a critical examination of an opera upon which he is now at work.[213]

Brenau's catalogs indicated that during the first few decades of the twentieth century, virtually all of the faculty members in the music and voice departments were trained in Europe. Besides Ferrata, who studied in Rome, several attended the Royal Conservatory in Leipzig and one attended the Royal Conservatory in Stuttgart.[214] Many of Brenau's music teachers held advanced degrees in music, such as Ferrata and August Geiger, who also received a doctorate in music from the University of New York.[215]

Even professors without such degrees were acclaimed. One article in the *Atlanta Constitution* bore this out by describing another professor of music. It read:

> For the past ten or fifteen years the very highest and best musical advantages have been given young ladies attending Brenau Conservatory at Gainesville, GA. Professors Van Hoose and Pearce have a high ideal as to what constitutes a really great school of music

and have never faltered in their determination to give to the girls of Georgia the highest musical advantages. They have secured for the next year the services of Mr. Otto Pfefferkorn as director of the Conservatory. Mr. Pfefferkorn is one of the great musicians of the day. He recently gave two recitals in the auditorium of Brenau, where some of the greatest artists of the day have been heard, and it was the unanimous opinion of all who heard him that his equal had never been heard in Gainesville. It was after hearing him play that the management of the college decided that he must be added to Brenau's faculty.[216]

Brenau's 1910 catalog devoted several pages to reprinting letters and articles from prominent people praising Otto Pfefferkorn's ability.[217] Among even the less-prominent members of the Conservatory were apparently musicians of good quality. For example, the *Alchemist* reported that in 1919, one "Miss Fritzlen," an assistant to music professor Otto Pfefferkorn and herself a graduate of Brenau's conservatory, played a delightful "Liszt Concerto."[218] The *Alchemist* of December 3, 1924, reported that two faculty members, professors McCormick and Turnipseed, played to a packed auditorium.[219] The October 23, 1945, edition of the *Alchemist* ran a story with the headline "Dr. Ben J. Potter Will Be Presented In Organ Recital."[220] Potter was a member of the Brenau music faculty and was also an associate in the prestigious Royal College of Organists, London.[221]

Early Brenau students frequently traveled to Atlanta to see their teachers perform in front of large audiences. On one occasion, several tickets went unsold for a musical performance in Atlanta at which Otto Pfefferkorn was performing. When the news reached the Brenau students, they held an "enthusiastic meeting" at which "100 of them signified their desire to attend the concert."[222] The "Brenau Notes" reported that the Southern Railroad, "always ready to assist Brenau in every way," sent up two coaches "decorated most beautifully with college colors, streamers and flags" to take the students to the concert.[223] The "Notes" declared that the cars carried to Atlanta, "one of the jolliest, happiest and most enthusiastic crowds of college girls that ever went upon such a trip."[224]

In the early twentieth century, Brenau music faculty members grew their popularity and prestige by occasionally performing at benefits. The "Brenau Notes" reported in 1907 that faculty member Florence M. Overton, the head of the School of Oratory, gave a performance "for the benefit of the confederate monument that is being erected by the Longstreet chapter, Daughters of the Confederacy."[225] Some faculty members teaching in the Conservatory became so widely-known that they even got endorsement deals.[226]

Despite the celebrity of some of these early music instructors, most of Brenau's faculty members over time apparently chose to concentrate on teaching instead of seeking the limelight. Whereas other larger colleges and universities may routinely have many famous professors on staff ranging from best-selling authors to noted scientists, Brenau luminaries have been, relatively speaking, fewer in number. Still, among Brenau's stand-outs are some remarkable individuals.

During the nineteen-teens, Samuel Gayle Riley taught history at Brenau. He has been described as having "belonged to a new generation of southern intellectuals, often educated in the North, who were bringing a critical cast of mind and a familiarity with modern intellectual trends to colleges and universities across the [southern] region."[227] Brenau students praised Riley "as the school's 'most profound' and 'most exacting' teacher" and noted how he challenged them intellectually in such courses as "Women in Modern Society" and with readings from legends such as John Dewey and Charles Beard.[228] Some years after Riley's service at the College, Benjamin Julian Kaston earned a Ph.D. in zoology from Yale University and taught biology at Brenau from 1938 to 1945. During his day, he was one of the nation's foremost experts on spiders and wrote two books and over 86 scientific articles on them.[229]

Another faculty member who lectured at Brenau during the 1930s was quite controversial. Jeannette Rankin was a women's rights advocate who became the first woman elected to the U.S. Congress in 1916 to represent her native state of Montana. A committed pacifist, Rankin garnered notoriety for being one of only fifty representatives to vote against America's entering World War I. This stance likely contributed to her losing a bid for a U.S. Senate seat in 1918. Following this, Rankin traveled for a time and then settled down outside of Athens, Georgia, where she lived a rather Spartan lifestyle and worked on various social causes. Around 1934, Rankin and Brenau entered into discussions to establish at the College a professorship exploring alternatives to war that would be called the "Chair of Peace," which she would hold. The move drew fire from groups such as the American Legion, who accused Rankin and the College of being "un-American," claims both vehemently and publically denied. Though the furor would ultimately subside and Rankin would give several lectures at Brenau, the chaired professorship never materialized. Rankin would eventually leave Georgia and return to the national spotlight, even being elected by Montanans to another single term in congress. Her political career effectively ended for good when Rankin, ever the dove, became the only member of the U.S. Congress to vote against America's entering World War II following the Japanese surprise attack on Pearl Harbor, Hawai'i, a hugely unpopular (if principled) move on her part. After leaving congress, Rankin continued advocating for peace and women's rights in various capacities until her death in 1973.[230] In her very long life, the ties Rankin made with Brenau were arguably some of the closest she would ever forge with any college or university.

In more recent decades, one of Brenau's most renowned faculty members did not make news as Rankin did but, rather, reported on it. Zeke Segal taught journalism at Brenau from 1991 until 1996. A 1938 graduate of Yale, Segal had worked for C.B.S. news since 1962 and had risen to become the Southeastern Bureau Chief by 1973, a prominent position he held for a decade.[231] Segal seemed to know everyone who was anyone in news circles during his time at C.B.S., including news legends like Mike Wallace, Dan Rather, and Walter Cronkite.[232] According to close family members, he also loved teaching at Brenau, which he did right up until his death.

At least two Brenau faculty members will be regarded as being remarkable as much for their longevity with the College as for their exceptional ability in the classroom. Beth Nott has taught French and advised several student organizations at Brenau since joining the faculty in 1971. A long-time colleague praised her as "one of the best-liked and most-respected members of the faculty" who was "a detail-oriented person with the highest academic standards."[233] By 2012, only James Southerland had worked at Brenau longer than Nott. He completed his bachelor's, master's, and doctoral degrees in history at the University of Georgia and joined the Brenau faculty in September of 1969. Southerland was an award-winning history teacher for decades before serving as Vice President of Academic Services and Dean of the Faculty.[234] He would finally retire at the end of the 2012–2013 academic year after serving Brenau for fully 44 years.[235]

Though Brenau personnel such as these selected future students through the college admissions process, nothing in the Archives suggests that Brenau students exercised much agency when it came to making decisions regarding the College's faculty, staff, and administration. Though some colleges today invite students to give input during personnel searches and perhaps even place students on search committees, Brenau seems to have not historically emphasized this. Alumnae, too, seem to have played small roles even in big hires as demonstrated by a lack of correspondence on such matters in the Archives' presidential correspondence. Still, students could have influenced personnel decisions in more discreet ways. Student evaluations of instructors "began to become popular during the 1960s and early 1970s as a common evaluation tool for faculty."[236] Brenau catalogs do not mention evaluations during these decades, which may suggest the College adopted them somewhat later. When they appeared, through these, comments in student publications (such as the *Alchemist*), or just word-of-mouth, students could have easily expressed views about College personnel. That those views somehow influenced personnel retention or brought about changes is not evident

Parties to the Parley 81

from any archival sources, but it seems reasonable to think that this could have occurred.[237]

Over the years, many Brenau personnel have had at least one significant quality in common with their Women's College students—they shared the same gender. Like other colleges, Brenau publishes a list of its faculty members in every edition of its catalogs. Table 1 indicates the number of male and female faculty members at Brenau for several sampled years over an eight-decade period as determined by examining these lists. The table reveals that, importantly for a women's college, Brenau has employed several women throughout its relatively long history. It should be acknowledged, though, that the number of women teaching subjects in Brenau's collegiate divisions was, until 1970 or so, relatively small. Examining catalogs reveals that Brenau's earlier female faculty members were generally not high-ranking professors, but, rather, were librarians, typewriting tutors, or instrument or vocal coaches in the conservatory division of the College. Still, from time to time, some women would stand out among the traditional collegiate faculty.

In 1900, 1910, and 1920, Brenau had one, two, and four female Ph.D. holders on its faculty, respectively. In 1930, three women had doctorates (all from Ivy League schools) and taught in biology, German, and math & physics. By 1940, Brenau had eleven faculty members with terminal degrees but only one woman (an English professor) with a terminal degree. By 1950, three women held doctorates at Brenau and taught chemistry, psychology and philosophy, and modern languages. Beginning in 1960 when women were becoming more widespread in the academic workforce, Brenau still employed few women with Ph.D.'s.[238] Up until 1980, women with Ph.D.'s never comprised more than 25% of the personnel holding doctorates that taught at the College. Thereafter, the percentage gradually increased. By 2012, 129 of the 181 faculty and staff members listed in the Brenau Catalog (i.e., 71%) were women around a time when women, on average, comprised just 41 percent of the faculty at most baccalaureate and master's degree colleges.[239] Fifty-four of these women faculty members at Brenau held doctorates and several others held what are recognized as terminal degrees in their fields, such as the M.F.A. for theater or design.

Faculty member characteristics such as reputation, education level, gender, etc., may provide insight into how the faculty participated in the process of negotiation with students and administrators to shape the Brenau college experience. Well-known, well-qualified professors—those secure in their jobs or with many professional prospects—should have been more candid participants in these negotiations. Other faculty members would have been more likely to simply "rubber stamp" whatever Brenau's powerful presidents wanted and less likely to side in any negotiation with students.

Prior to the death of President Pearce in 1943, it seems doubtful that many members of the faculty would have felt secure in challenging many administrative decisions on any College matter. Until he ceded control of the College to the Brenau Board of Trustees, Dr. Pearce, as sole owner of Brenau, had the final say in everything—and held the power to terminate employees at will. Even with the advent of the board of trustees, Dr. Pearce must have remained a formidable presence at Brenau —perhaps too much so.

This seems to have been the opinion of a group that has for decades claimed to represent the interests of America's academics, the American Association of University Professors. In a February, 1934, publication entitled, "Academic Freedom and Tenure: Report of Committee A," Brenau came under scrutiny. The report explained, "when tenure conditions are unsatisfactory at a college or university and a professor is threatened with dismissal without adequate notice and proper hearings, a complaint is lodged," which prompts an investigation by the A.A.U.P.[240] On rare occasions when matters could not be cleared up via correspondence brokered by the A.A.U.P. between administrators and an aggrieved faculty member, the report indicated that the A.A.U.P. would form a committee to "pay a visit to the college under investigation."[241] The function of the

A.A.U.P. investigating committee was "essentially that of a grand jury...to ascertain the conditions of tenure at the institution under investigation."[242] Typically, but not always, the committee would subsequently publish its findings, unless the administration of the institution under investigation undertook "to correct the unsatisfactory conditions of tenure found to exist by the investigating committee."[243] Failing this, the A.A.U.P. would resort to asking its membership to vote to remove an offending institution from "the list of colleges in which professors are eligible for membership in the Association."[244] The punishment was meant to apply not to an institution at large but "specifically upon its present administration" and would be levied "for the sole purpose of informing [A.A.U.P.] members, the profession at large, and the public that unsatisfactory conditions of academic freedom and tenure have been found to prevail at these institutions."[245] Theoretically, this would make it harder for an institution to attract high-caliber professors and so be something a college would want to avoid.

A rather colorful *Time* magazine article described the events of 1934 that related to Brenau and the A.A.U.P. It read:

> Last week the American Association of University Professors met in St. Louis for the purpose, among others, of revising its list of "ineligible" universities & colleges. The institutions which spot this list are the black sheep of U. S. education, and the A. A. U. P. will not accept new members from their faculties. The "ineligible" pen contained five such black sheep. DePauw (Greencastle, Ind.), Brenau (Gainesville, Ga.) and Harris Teachers' College of St. Louis were penned up because their respective presidents had arbitrarily dismissed professors—in most cases outspoken liberals. So was Rollins (Winter Park, Fla.) [and] the U. S. Naval Academy at Annapolis. ... Scrutinizing the five black sheep in the pen, the professors decided that the least consequential of them had washed itself white. Opening the gate a crack, they allowed Harris Teachers College to scoot gratefully out.[246]

Unfortunately for Brenau, there would be no scooting. It remained firmly pent-up.

According to an A.A.U.P. website entitled, "List of Censured Administrations, 1930–2002," the investigating committee never published a report of its findings about Brenau.[247] The College may, indeed, have been censored for what the A.A.U.P. deemed to be wrongful termination of an employee, as per the *Time Magazine* story. It also probably did not help Brenau's case that institutional retention policies of the era seemed somewhat vague. Brenau's 1947 "S.A.C.S. Report Form for Senior Colleges" reported that, "After invitation to return to faculty membership for three years, it is assumed that faculty membership is permanent tenure."[248] It is also interesting that, according to this A.A.U.P. website, the censure for Brenau had technically never been removed in the twentieth century. This seems to be an error, though. The Spring, 1957, A.A.U.P. *Bulletin* indicated that "Membership in the American Association of University Professors is open by nomination and election to teachers and research workers on the faculties of approved colleges and universities."[249] The same edition of the *Bulletin* indicated that Brenau had two active members in the Association, suggesting that the College's censure had, in fact, been dropped at some prior point.[250] Moreover, Brenau's name did not appear on the A.A.U.P.'s 2011 website listing of censured institutions.[251]

The implication of Brenau's experience with the A.A.U.P. is that academic freedom and feelings of job security on the part of the faculty suffered under the administration of Dr. Pearce, but improved thereafter—hence the lifting of the censure. While these factors suffered, one would not expect the faculty to be full participants in any negotiation over the character of the College. Rather, fearing for their livelihoods, one would anticipate that the faculty would negotiate in lockstep with powerful administrators such as Dr. Pearce. Exactly how much things would have changed in a post-Pearce era at Brenau is unclear. The fact is that Dr. Crudup, Dr. Pearce's successor, appears to have been a very powerful president himself. Though, unlike Dr. Pearce, Dr. Crudup answered to the Brenau Board of Trustees, the impression one gets from the materials in the Archives is that personnel decisions stopped with the president. It really would not have been until 1970 that faculty members should have felt more at ease to voice any dissent they may have harbored about the College.

The *Institutional Self Study for 1969–1971* indicated that, "The jurisdiction of the faculty has been broadened since March, 1970, when faculty members were placed on the Admissions Committee and on the newly established Executive Council," the "primary advisory body to the President."[252] Also around this time, the College formalized its policies on tenure and academic freedom. Prior to this occurring, "the statement regarding tenure was both brief and general, and there was no record of its adoption by the Board of Trustees."[253] The sense is that faculty member tenure—if it truly had existed—had been granted on a case-by-case basis at the discretion of the administration. The formalized rules afforded more job security as they specified that a tenured faculty member could only be terminated for "adequate cause" and with "academic due process."[254]

The formalized rules of 1970 also safeguarded academic freedom—at least to a greater extent than the College apparently had heretofore. Brenau assured each faculty member of their freedom to research & publish and the freedom "to express both his religious convictions and his views as a citizen."[255] (Presumably, *her* views would likewise have been safeguarded.) Academic freedom was not completely unfettered. The *Self-Study* noted that a faculty member was "entitled to freedom to discuss his subject in the classroom, though he is reminded that he has the responsibility of avoiding 'controversial and/or inflammatory matter' unrelated to his subject."[256] The rules furthermore explained what a faculty member needed to do to "correct any abridgement of his freedom," but also spelled out "the recourse that may be taken by administrative officials if a faculty member fails to assume those responsibilities which accompany the privilege of academic freedom."[257]

Faculty members pleased with the changes at the College starting around 1970 would likely have become displeased only a few years later. This is because "Brenau did away with its policy of tenure in 1976 in favor of the continuing contract policy for full-time faculty."[258] A 1997 study determined that only around 9% of private U.S. colleges and virtually no public colleges used such a contractual system.[259] According to the *Chronicle of Higher Education*:

> Advocates of tenure say it is the surest protection of academic freedom, creating a system of due process in which the burden of proof is upon administrators to demonstrate that a professor's dismissal is for cause, rather than a response to controversial scholarship. But critics say that tenure's protections make it difficult to get rid of incompetent faculty and can promote a culture of complacency among those who have attained the status.[260]

Brenau acknowledged that its contract system created "a degree of professional insecurity" at the College as several faculty members surveyed expressed concerns that the scheme did not ensure academic due process or adequately protect their rights.[261] Under this system, the most job-secure arrangement a faculty member could hope for would be a five-year "reappointment" to their position. This would be true "even for those with long years of service to the College."[262] More junior faculty members would receive shorter-duration reappointments amounting to probationary periods before they could attain a five-year appointment. All faculty members would be periodically evaluated by supervisors on a range of factors that would focus on assessing teaching competency and service to the institution. Though a faculty member terminated during a contracted period could theoretically appeal their firing, there was no appeal for non-renewal of contract. Brenau was not even obligated to provide a non-renewed faculty member with the reasons why he or she had been let go and, in fact, administrators were "advised…not to do so."[263]

Though faculty member job security had arguably decreased by the 1980s, Brenau's stance on academic freedom had apparently not changed much. The College still reminded its faculty that their academic freedoms carried with them "the responsibilities of performing all regularly assigned academic duties so that controversial matters bearing no relation to the subject are not introduced into the classroom."[264] Additionally, by 1984, Brenau expected faculty members to exercise "discretion so that an individual's private opinions may not be construed as an official institutional position."[265]

In light of Brenau's policies for retention and academic freedom, some faculty members over time may have felt much like the faculty members around 1980 who "expressed concern about their rights and opportunities to voice within the College community opinions contrary to those of the administration" for fear of "being labeled disloyal or malcontent."[266] Perhaps sensing that its policies were, from the standpoint of faculty members, somewhat lacking, the College acknowledged, "Professional security...is essential to high faculty moral and to the College's ability to retain an experienced, qualified faculty. It is, therefore, imperative that this issue receive the serious attention of the administration."[267] Serious attention consisted of revising "for greater clarity" the rules on reappointment and termination and restructuring the appeals process.[268] One thing it did not consist of was establishing a faculty senate. Though some faculty members expressed an interest in doing this around 1980, the administration had "reservations that such a forum might serve as a divisive force."[269] As of 2012, Brenau still lacked a faculty senate and tenure for faculty members.[270] Moreover, institutional policies apparently still gave administrators wide discretion in making employment decisions regarding members of the faculty. In 2000, a study on colleges without tenure noted that a faculty member at Brenau may be terminated not only for financial exigency (which is an accepted practice in higher education), but also for "reduction in academic program, or need to reorganize, as determined by the administration of the university."[271] Also, although some colleges without tenure followed A.A.U.P. procedures for faculty member dismissal for cause that included components such as timely official notification and hearings with witnesses for presentation of defense, Brenau was not one of them. The article noted that Brenau's policy stipulated that "the president...may, at any time, remove or suspend any faculty member or other employee for adequate cause by giving written notice."[272]

Given the history of academic freedom and retention policies at Brenau, one might expect to find there a faculty possessed of limited agency and little job security—certainly not a group inclined to negotiate far apart from its administration about anything. Though this may have been the case at one time or another in Brenau's history, it has certainly not always been the case. Several pieces of evidence suggest that the Brenau faculty in general has often been both content and capable of speaking its own mind.

The minutes books of the Brenau faculty meetings kept through the mid-1950s show that the faculty voted on many important measures pertaining to the institution. Members of the faculty cast votes to expel students, to modify the College disciplinary rules and curriculum, and to assent to bringing intercollegiate athletics to the campus, among other things. This suggests that the faculty did exercise at least some role in College governance. Also, Brenau's presidents generally attended, spoke at, and, when matters came up, apparently voted at these meetings. It is significant that not all votes were unanimous. Some faculty members felt comfortable voting against Brenau's presidents—even Dr. Pearce— on some matters. In addition, note that throughout its history, Brenau has employed several members of its faculty and staff for many years, if not literally decades. It seems unlikely so many people would have remained attached to the institution for so long if its leadership practiced intimidation. Also, whatever its policies on academic freedom may have been, it is worth acknowledging that there are no records in the University Archives that document either a faculty member's claim of a violation of his or her academic freedom or any records indicating that administrators ever disciplined a faculty member for irresponsible academic behavior. And, other than the instance in January of 1936 when Dr. Pearce noted "dissatisfaction" on the part of some of the faculty members with their pay, nothing in the Archives speaks to extensive conflict between the faculty at large and any of Brenau's administrations. Rather, members of the Brenau faculty and staff went from complaining about their workplace in the 1930s to lauding it around 2011. In that year, Brenau ranked among the top ten small universities nationwide in the areas of "collaborative governance; professional and career development programs; teaching environment; confidence in senior leadership; relationships with supervisors and faculty chairs; and respect and appreciation for employees" according to the "Great Colleges to Work For" rankings released by the *Chronicle of Higher Education*.[273] Taken together, this should suggest that, over the years, at least some faculty members at the institution have been comfortable being genuine participants in the negotiations for the Brenau college experience and not simply followers of the administration.

Of course, being able to take a different stance in a negotiation and actually doing so are two different things. The reality has been that when it comes to creating the Brenau college experience, the faculty and the administration would seldom need to work at cross-purposes. Rather, more often than not, most of the faculty and members of the College administration would likely have found themselves on the same side of an argument opposing the students. This was evident time and again from the entries in the Brenau faculty meeting minutes book.

Throughout its history, negotiations over what the Brenau experience would be between the faculty, the College staff (including its administrators), and Brenau's students would have occurred—to some extent, at least—whenever College personnel and students interacted, be it in the classroom, the College dining room, or in some other setting. Perhaps the most outright negotiations between these two camps occurred in Brenau's faculty meetings. For most of the life of the institution, the faculty generally held its meetings at least monthly during the school year and occasionally had "called" faculty meetings if something important came up that needed more immediate attention. Upon occasion, the faculty and staff at these meetings entertained, evaluated, and passed judgment on petitions submitted by Brenau students. These petitions dealt with multiple requests. Some examples include Brenau students requesting that certain campus regulations be modified or that dates of examinations be adjusted for one reason or another. Occasionally, the faculty permitted a few students to appear briefly at the faculty meetings to speak in support of their petitions. Most commonly, student petitions came to the faculty from the Executive Council of Brenau's Student Government Association. All Brenau students were members of the Association and the elected officers of the Association comprised the Executive Council. Additionally, each class elected officers who would occasionally present petitions to the faculty on behalf of their fellow classmen.

The fate of any given student petition varied depending upon a variety of factors. What is significant is that over time the faculty and administration did not decline *all* the student petitions; far from this, most were actually approved. This indicates that there was give-and-take in these negotiations, but this should not be overstated. The very fact that the students had to petition the faculty and staff (and not the other way around, for instance) and that those students did so in a venue completely controlled by the College personnel would obviously diminish student agency. Yet, the fact that this petitioning could occur at all suggests official receptivity to working things out with students. Through these official channels, the students negotiated and lobbied for what they wanted. Sometimes, given the influence of the faculty and the administration in so many areas, the students came away empty-handed or had to settle for what they could get. Yet, at other times, students drew closer to creating the college experience they desired through success in these processes. The following chapters discuss both outcomes.

Notes

1. For purposes of this study, I define the term "student" broadly, to include anyone having enrolled at Brenau, be it in a full-time or part-time capacity, as an undergraduate or as a graduate student, as a resident or as a commuter, as someone who graduated as well as non-graduates, etc. I utilize several terms to describe as a group the employees of Brenau that negotiated with students. Some include "faculty," "staff," "administration," "officials," "governors," "employees," and "personnel." Admittedly, many more people comprise the faculty and staff of a college or university than its teachers, administrators, and the other individuals who work in traditional student-services offices, such as student life, the Registrar's Office, etc. However, I confine my examination here to what might be termed Brenau's "white collar" employees. I do not mean at all to diminish the importance of other institutional personnel by not focusing on their interactions with students in this study. Indeed, students probably had frequent interactions with such Brenau employees as maintenance personnel, housekeeping staff, groundskeepers, cafeteria staff, etc. These interactions would surely, at times, have involved negotiation and could have shaped the college experience at Brenau every bit as much as interactions between students and Brenau's faculty and administration. These interactions are not dealt with here simply because sources speaking to what took place between students and these personnel are lacking. A subsequent project, perhaps using oral history interviews with former students and staff, might shed light on interchanges between Brenau's "blue collar" employees and its students that this study cannot.
2. Rudolph, *American College and University*, 87. Scarcities of money, potential students, and housing may have induced colleges to adopt residential characters. See Thelin, *History of American Higher Education*, 10.
3. Horowitz, *Alma Mater*, 147.
4. Ibid.
5. See Farnham, *Education of the Southern Belle*.
6. See McCandless, *Past in the Present*.
7. *Twenty-Second Annual Catalogue of Brenau College and Brenau Conservatory* (Atlanta, GA: The Foote & Davis Company, 1900), 14; Brenau

University Archives, Gainesville, Georgia. Hereafter, references to this source are indicated as "*Catalog* (1900)."
8. *Catalog* (1900), 76.
9. Ibid.
10. Ibid.
11. Camille DeBell, "Ninety Years in the World of Work in America," *Career Development Quarterly*, 50, no. 1 (Sept., 2001): 77–88.
12. "Small Area Income and Poverty Estimates (SAIPE): 2009 Highlights," U.S. Census Bureau, http://www.census.gov/did/www/saipe/data/highlights/files/saipe_highlights_2009.pdf (accessed 17 October 2012); "Fast Facts: Tuition Costs of Colleges and Universities (Chapter 3)," U.S. Department of Education National Center for Education Statistics (2009), http://nces.ed.gov/fastfacts/display.asp?id=76 (accessed 17 October 2012).
13. *Thirty-second Annual Catalogue of Brenau College-Conservatory, 1910, v. 1, n. 2* (Gainesville, GA: Brenau College, 1910), 76; Brenau University Archives, Gainesville, Georgia. Hereafter, references to this source are indicated as "*Catalog* (1910)."
14. Ibid.
15. Wesley Clair Mitchell (ed.), *Income in the United States, its Amount and Distribution, 1909–1919, Issue II* (New York, NY: National Bureau of Economic Research, 1922), 293; available from Google Books, http://books.google.com/books?id=L-JCAAAAIAAJ&printsec=frontcover#v=onepage&q=293&f=false (accessed 17 October 2012).
16. *Brenau College Catalogue, 1929–1930, v. XXII, n. 2* (Gainesville, GA: Brenau College, 1929), 25; Brenau University Archives, Gainesville, Georgia. Hereafter, references to this source are indicated as "*Catalog* (1929)."
17. Ibid.
18. George W. Pierson, *A Yale Book of Numbers: Historical Statistics of the College and University 1701–1976* (New Haven, CT: Yale University Press, 1983), 578; Yale University, http://oir.yale.edu/1701-1976-yale-book-numbers (accessed 17 October 2012).
19. Ibid., 590.
20. Michael F. Adams, "State of the University Address 2000," University of Georgia, 12 January 2000, http://president.uga.edu/index.php/speeches/sotu/state_of_the_university_2000/ (accessed 17 October 2012).
21. "Tech Timeline – 1885," Georgia Institute of Technology, http://livinghistory.gatech.edu/new/timeline/1880.html (accessed 17 October 2012).

22. R. A. Day quoting from Thomas H. English, *Emory University 1915–1965 - A Semicentennial History* (Atlanta, GA: Higgins-McArthur Co., 1966); Emory University, http://www.chemistry.emory.edu/department_info/history/chapter1.html (accessed 17 October 2012).
23. Ibid.
24. "1900–1909," Vassar College, http://chronology.vassar.edu/records/1900-1909/ (accessed 17 October 2012).
25. "1920–1929," Vassar College, http://chronology.vassar.edu/records/1920-1929/ (accessed 17 October 2012).
26. "1930–1939," Vassar College, http://chronology.vassar.edu/records/1930-1939/ (accessed 17 October 2012).
27. Brenau College, *An Institutional Self-Study, Under the Auspices of The Southern Association of Colleges and Schools, September 1969 – May 1971* (Gainesville, GA: Brenau College, 1971), 104. This and similar sources are more colloquially known as Brenau's SACS Self-Studies and are available in various boxes labeled "Self Study" in the Brenau University Archives, Gainesville, Georgia. Hereafter, references to this source are indicated as "*Institutional Self- Study, 1969 – 1971.*"
28. Ibid.
29. U.S. Bureau of the Census, Current Population Reports, Series P-60, No. 80, "Income in 1970 of Families and Persons in the United States," U.S. Government Printing Office, Washington, DC, 1971, http://www2.census.gov/prod2/popscan/p60-080.pdf (accessed 17 October 2012).
30. *Brenau College 1980-81 Undergraduate Bulletin* (Gainesville, GA: Brenau College, 1980), 35; Brenau University Archives, Gainesville, Georgia. Hereafter, references to this source are indicated as "*Catalog* (1980)."
31. "Fast Facts: Tuition Costs of Colleges and Universities (Chapter 3)," U.S. Department of Education National Center for Education Statistics (2009), http://nces.ed.gov/fastfacts/display.asp?id=76 (accessed 17 October 2012).
32. *Brenau University Catalog* (Gainesville, GA: Brenau University, 2007), 51. Hereafter, references to this source are indicated as "*Catalog* (2007)."
33. Emory University, Agnes Scott College, Covenant College, Berry College, Mercer University, and Oglethorpe University, for example, all charged students over $30,000 per year in 2008. See "Special Report: American's Best Colleges (2008)," *Forbes.com*, http://www.forbes.com/lists/2008/94/opinions_college08_Americas-Best-Colleges_State_5.html (accessed 17 October 2012).
34. Susan Lang, "How competition for the best students, faculty and facilities -- and rankings -- sends tuition soaring," *Cornell Chronicle*, 8 November

2006, http://www.news.cornell.edu/stories/Nov06/tuition.so.much.sl.html (accessed 17 October 2012).
35. *Catalog* (1910), 76.
36. Ibid.
37. See Rigney, *Brenau College 1878–1978.* Some other women's colleges of the period do not seem to have drawn students from so wide a range even though they were located in far less bucolic environs than Brenau. For example, around 1900, Goucher College—even though located in urban Baltimore fairly near the nation's capital—drew fully 40% of its students from Maryland and "the majority of the remaining sixty percent [came from] the Middle States; Pennsylvania, New York, New Jersey, and the District of Columbia." Anna Heubeck Knipp, *The History of Goucher College* (Baltimore, MD: Goucher College, 1938), 539; Internet Archive, http://archive.org/stream/historyofgoucher00knip/historyofgoucher00knip_djvu.txt (accessed 17 October 2012). The *Meredith College Quarterly Bulletin of 1909* contains thirteen pages of student names listed under the heading, "List of Matriculates by Counties." Only a single page is devoted to "Matriculates from Other States," which suggests that fewer than 10% of the young women at Meredith were from outside North Carolina. *Quarterly Bulletin 1909–1910* (Raleigh, NC: Meredith College, 1909), 20; Internet Archive, http://archive.org/stream/meredithcollegeq1909mere#page/n25/mode/2up (accessed 17 October 2012). At Agnes Scott College during the early twentieth century, it was said that "The great majority of the students are from the southeastern states, but they are well distributed among these." See James Ross McCain, *The Story of Agnes Scott College: 1889–1939* (Atlanta, GA: Agnes Scott College, 1939), 55. In 1906, the Pennsylvania College for Women (later Chatham University) *Catalogue* listed only 10 of 84 students as being from out-of-state. See *Thirty-Sixth Annual Catalogue* (Pittsburgh, PA: Pennsylvania College for Women, 1905), 59–62; Internet Archive, http://archive.org/stream/pennsylvaniaco190510penn#page/n161/mode/2up archive.org (accessed 18 October 2012). The Agnes Scott College *Bulletin: 1912 – 1913*'s "Register of Students" listed 208 students for that year. Fully 106 hailed from Georgia with another 38 coming from neighboring Alabama. Only nine other states and one foreign country (Mexico) were represented. See *Agnes Scott College (Decatur, Georgia) Bulletin: 1912 –1913* (Lynchburg, VA: J. P. Bell Co., Inc., 1912); Internet Archive, http://archive.org/stream/agnesscott19121913agne#page/122/mode/2up (accessed 18 October 2012). While Brenau students were geographically

diverse compared to these institutions, other women's colleges operating around the same time could also boast of having students from many states. Referring to the period of time around the turn of the last century, one historian wrote, "The safest general statement which can be made about Wellesley students of the first forty years of the college is that more than sixty per cent of them have come from outside New England." Florence Converse, *The Story of Wellesley* (Boston, MA: Little, Brown and Company, 1915), 168. Also, the 1911 catalog of Sweet Briar College Catalogue indicated that around 225 young women from thirty states attended the institution that year. *The Sixth Year Book of Sweet Briar College* (Sweet Briar, VA: Sweet Briar College, 1911), 84; Internet Archive, http://archive.org/stream/sweetbriarcolleg1911swee#page/n5/mode/2up (accessed 19 October 2012).
38. "'States Day' at Brenau Was Splendid Pageant," *Atlanta Constitution*, 30 April 1908, p. 7.
39. No author, "Birte and Paula Host Rotarians," *The Rotarian: An International Magazine*, May 1954, 42.
40. *Brenau Bulletin, 1949 – 1950 v. XXXXI n. 3* (Gainesville, GA: Brenau College, 1949), 94; Brenau University Archives, Gainesville, Georgia. Hereafter, references to this source are indicated as "*Catalog* (1949)."
41. CollegeData.com, "College Profile: Brenau University," http://www.collegedata.com/cs/data/college/college_pg06_tmpl.jhtml?schoolId=513 (accessed 28 May 2013).
42. Princeton Review, *Complete Book of Colleges, 2005* (New York, NY: Princeton Review Publishing, 2004), 118.
43. "Brenau Undergraduate Viewbook," Jensen Design Studio, http://jensendesignstudio.com/wp-content/uploads/2011/11/brenau_viewbook_spreads.pdf (accessed October 19, 2012).
44. For more information about Georgia's H.O.P.E. scholarship, see https://secure.gacollege411.org/Home/_default.aspx (accessed 19 October 2012).
45. Eleanor Rigney, *Brenau College 1878–1978*, 48.
46. Ibid., 50.
47. Photo Standalone -- No Title, *Atlanta Constitution*, 20 May 1906, sec. D, p. 5.
48. "CPS Historical Time Series Tables, Table A–2—Percent of People 25 Years and Over Who Have Completed High School or College, by Race, Hispanic Origin and Sex: Selected Years 1940 to 2009," U.C. Census Bureau, http://www.census.gov/hhes/socdemo/education/data/cps/historical/index.html (accessed 20 October 2012).

49. "asmtday2004surveyresults," Course Hero, http://www.coursehero.com/file/1685890/asmtday2004surveyresults/ (accessed 20 October 2012).
50. Watson S. Swail, "Legislation to Improve Graduation Rates Could Have the Opposite Effect," *The Chronicle of Higher Education*, vol. 50, no. 20 (23 January 2004): B16.
51. *Catalog* (1910), 76.
52. *Brenau College Catalogue, 1939–1940, v. XXXI, n. 3* (Gainesville, GA: Brenau College, 1939), 17; Brenau University Archives, Gainesville, Georgia. Hereafter, references to this source are indicated as "*Catalog* (1939)."
53. Office of Communications, "History & Traditions," Agnes Scott College, http://www.agnesscott.edu/about/history-traditions/ (accessed 27 October 2012).
54. Alice Taylor-Colbert, "Brief History and Traditions of Shorter University," Shorter University, http://www.shorter.edu/about/history.htm (accessed 27 October 2012).
55. "History of the College," Wesleyan College, http://www.wesleyancollege.edu/About/HistoryoftheCollege/tabid/134/Default.aspx (accessed 27 October 2012).
56. Taronda Spencer, "Spelman College," *New Georgia Encyclopedia* (6/6/2006), http://www.georgiaencyclopedia.org/nge/Article.jsp?id=h-1460 (accessed 27 October 2012).
57. "History," Salem College, http://www.salem.edu/about/our-history (accessed 27 October 2012).
58. See Mary Lynch Johnson, *A History of Meredith College*: 2nd Ed. (Raleigh, NC: Meredith College, 1972).
59. "History," Columbia College, http://www.columbiacollegesc.edu/about/history.asp (accessed 27 October 2012).
60. "A Brief History of Judson College," Judson College, http://www.judson.edu/content.asp?id=84415 (accessed 27 October 2012).
61. "Our Mission and History," Converse College, http://www.converse.edu/about/our-mission-history (accessed 27 October 2012).
62. *Catalog* (1900), 9.
63. "Religious Influences in College Education," *Atlanta Constitution*, 30 July 1911, sec. D, p. 8.
64. Michael Hout and Claude S. Fischer, "Religious Diversity in America, 1940 – 2000." Paper prepared for submission to the Sociology of Religion Session, Annual meeting of the ASA, Chicago, IL, August 2001. http://ucdata.berkeley.edu/rsfcensus/papers/Hout_FischerASA.pdf (accessed 27 October 2012).

65. Of course, students of other faiths have attended Brenau as well, but in much smaller numbers. For example, at least four Muslim women have graduated from Brenau: Khadija Safi and Shamim Siddiqi (WC '10), Maria Ebrahimji (WC '98), and Zakiyyah Hassan (EWC '95). See "Brenau Project Management Master's Program Wins Recognition by International Standards Organization," PR Web (21 September 2010), http://www.prweb.com/releases/project/management/prweb4547344.htm (accessed 27 October 2012); Candice Dyer, "She Speaks for Herself," *Brenau Window*, Summer, 2011, pp. 8–11, http://artsweb.brenau.edu/brenauwindow/summer2011/Summer2011.pdf (accessed 27 October 2012); and "Ummah Image Awards ," Gamma Gamma Chi, http://gammagammachi.org/2008_gammafest/awards_program/recipients.html (accessed 27 October 2012).
66. Brendan J. Buttimer, "Catholic Church," *New Georgia Encyclopedia* (12/10/2005), http://www.georgiaencyclopedia.org/nge/Article.jsp?id=h-2922 (accessed 27 October 2012).
67. "History of Saint Michael Catholic Church," Saint Michael Catholic Church (Gainesville, Georgia), http://saintmichael.cc/index.php?page=history (accessed 27 October 2012).
68. Ibid.
69. "Archdiocese of Atlanta – Statistics," Roman Catholic Archdiocese of Atlanta, http://www.archatl.com/about/stats.html (accessed 21 October 2012).
70. Rev. R. Donald Kiernan, "St. Michael's Gainesville Parish In Ga. Vacationland," *The Georgia Bulletin* (23 January 1964), http://www.georgiabulletin.org/local/1964/01/23/d/?s=brenau (accessed 27 October 2012).
71. Ibid.
72. J.D. Long-García, "Newman Centers: A brief history," *U.S. Catholic* (16 January 2012), http://www.uscatholic.org/life/2012/01/newman-centers-brief-history (accessed 27 October 2012).
73. See the chapter on sororities and secret societies for more information about Delta Phi Epsilon.
74. Brenau University, "'Extraordinary Lives' Admissions Viewbook," Jensen Design Studio (2011–2012), http://jensendesignstudio.com/our-work/brenau/ (accessed 27 October 2012), back cover.
75. See "College Profile: Piedmont College," CollegeData.com, http://www.collegedata.com/cs/data/college/college_pg06_tmpl.jhtml?schoolId=1621 (accessed 28 May 2013) and "College Profile: North Georgia College &

State University," CollegeData.com, http://www.collegedata.com/cs/data/college/college_pg06_tmpl.jhtml?schoolId=1606 (accessed 28 May 2013).
76. *Bubbles* (Gainesville, GA; Brenau College, 1992), 111. Hereafter, references to this source are indicated as "*Bubbles* (1992)."
77. Catalog (2011), "'GS – 390: Special Topics' course description," Brenau University, http://catalog.brenau.edu/content.php?catoid=4&navoid=205&cpage=6 (accessed 27 October 2013). Sadly, sexual orientation was not mentioned alongside race, color, religion, etc., in the statements of non-discrimination published in Brenau's modern catalogs, either. Other regional women's colleges, such as Agnes Scott and Converse College, specifically mention sexual orientation in their policies. See "Accreditation and Non-discrimination," Agnes Scott College, http://www.agnesscott.edu/accreditation-nondiscrimination.html (accessed 27 October 2012) and *Converse College Student Handbook, 2011–2012* (Converse, SC: Converse College, 2011): 1, http://www.converse.edu/sites/default/files/site-files/Student_Life/2011_2012%20Student%20Handbook_WEB.pdf (accessed 27 October 2012). However, it is worth mentioning that Brenau's human resources webpage (https://intranet.brenau.edu/dnn/Operations/HumanResources/Benefits/tabid/196/Default.aspx) expressly indicated in November of 2013 that "domestic partners" would be eligible for several employee benefits.
78. See Rachel Thurman, "[various columns]," Brenau University, http://intranet.brenau.edu/dnn/Home/SearchResults/tabid/109/Default.aspx?Search=lesbian (accessed 21 October 2012).
79. Around 2011, Shorter University in Rome, Georgia, required employees to sign a "Personal Lifestyle Pledge," to retain their jobs. Among the provisions of the pledge was a promise to reject homosexuality. Philip Caufield, "Shorter University in Ga. requires employees to sign pledge saying they are not gay," *New York Daily News*, 31 October 2011, http://www.nydailynews.com/news/national/shorter-university-ga-requires-employees-sign-pledge-gay-article-1.969789#ixzz21yOZnKry (accessed 29 November 2012).
80. *Catalog* (1900), 20.
81. *Catalog* (1910), 92.
82. *Brenau College Catalogue, 1920–1921, vol. XI, no. 2* (Gainesville, GA: Brenau College, 1920), 121; Brenau University Archives, Gainesville, Georgia. Hereafter, references to this source are indicated as "*Catalog* (1920)."
83. "Enrollment of Brenau College," memorandum prepared by Ella D. Winfield, undated, but likely prepared in 1950, the last year of data provided

in the memo; Registrar Files, Box 1 of 1, Folder 6, Brenau University Archives, Gainesville, Georgia.
84. Ibid.
85. "Freshman Mortality 1929 – 1939," Registrar Files, Box 1 of 1, Folder 8, Brenau University Archives, Gainesville, Georgia.
86. Edward L. Ayers et al., *American Passages: A History of the United States* (Boston, MA: Wadsworth Cengage Learning, 2009), 793.
87. Petersons.com, "Brenau University," http://www.petersons.com/college-search/brenau-university-000_10004140.aspx (accessed 29 November 2012).
88. College Data, "College Profile: Brenau University," http://www.collegedata.com/cs/data/college/college_pg06_tmpl.jhtml?schoolId=513 (accessed 29 November 2012).
89. *Catalog* (1900), 22.
90. *Catalog* (1910), 11.
91. Advertisement. *Atlanta Georgian and News*, 8 July 1911, p. 17 [insert C].
92. *Brenau College Bulletin 1960 – 1961, v. L, n. 1* (Gainesville, GA: Brenau College, 1960), 26; Brenau University Archives, Gainesville, Georgia. Hereafter, references to this source are indicated as "Catalog (1960)."
93. *Brenau College Bulletin 1970 – 1971, Annual Catalogue Edition, Vol. LX, No. 1* (Gainesville, GA: Brenau College, 1970), 27; Brenau University Archives, Gainesville, Georgia. Hereafter, references to this source are indicated as "Catalog (1970)."
94. Brenau College, *An Institutional Self-Study Under the Auspices of The Southern Association of Colleges and Schools, September, 1979 – May, 1981* (Gainesville, GA: Brenau College, 1981), 35; Brenau University Archives, Gainesville, Georgia. Hereafter, references to this source are indicated as "*Institutional Self-Study, 1979–1981.*"
95. Ibid.
96. Ibid., 38.
97. College Data, "College Profile: Brenau University," http://www.collegedata.com/cs/data/college/college_pg06_tmpl.jhtml?schoolId=513 (accessed 30 November 2012).
98. "Key for Report" in response to a letter dated 15 February 1930 from Joseph Roemer of the Commission on Secondary Schools to the Brenau College Registrar's Office; Folder 8 (labeled "SACS Miscellaneous (1928 – 31)" in Box 5 (labeled "SACS Self-reports"), Brenau University Archives, Gainesville, Georgia.

99. AccessNorthGA.com, "Brenau Academy shifts focus to 'early college' program," 5 January 2011, http://www.accessnorthga.com/detail.php?n= 235036 (accessed 30 November 2012). There were apparently two other attempts to found a girls' school in Gainesville prior to 1928. "Founding," Brenau University Archived Webpages (formerly online at http://artsweb. brenau.edu/historic/Founding/default.htm from around 2004 until 2011); hard-copy print-out located in Box 1 of 1 labeled "Archived Webpages," Brenau University Archives, Gainesville, Georgia.
100. "Complete Copy of Southern Association Report as Filled Out October 1930 – 1931 for all General Material"; Folder 6 (labeled "SACS Forms 1927-33") in Box 5 of 6 (labeled "SACS Self-reports"), Brenau University Archives, Gainesville, Georgia.
101. *Brenau College Catalogue, 1939–1940, v. XXXI, n. 3* (Gainesville, GA: Brenau College, 1939), 31; Brenau University Archives, Gainesville, Georgia. Hereafter, references to this source are indicated as "*Catalog* (1940)." Brenau also provided $150 scholarships to daughters of ministers, teachers, and active-duty Army officers in 1940. Ibid.
102. *Brenau Bulletin, 1949 – 1950 v. XXXXI n. 3* (Gainesville, GA: Brenau College, 1949), 36; Brenau University Archives, Gainesville, Georgia. Hereafter, references to this source are indicated as "*Catalog* (1950)."
103. *Catalog* (1960), 29–30; *Catalog* (1970), 33–34.
104. *Catalog* (1980), 40.
105. Ibid.
106. *Brenau University Undergraduate and Graduate Catalog, Vol. 107, No. 1* (Gainesville, GA: Brenau University, 1990), 44; Brenau University Archives, Gainesville, Georgia. Hereafter, references to this source are indicated as "*Catalog* (1990)."
107. *Brenau University Undergraduate and Graduate Catalog, Vol. 117, No. 1* (Gainesville, GA: Brenau University, 2000), 50–51; Brenau University Archives, Gainesville, Georgia. Hereafter, references to this source are indicated as "*Catalog* (2000)."
108. Rigney, *Brenau College 1878–1978*, 68–69.
109. Ibid.
110. "Faculty meeting minutes book entry of 03 April 1928," *Faculty Journal for Twenty-five Years (1922 – 1947)*, 60; Brenau University Archives, Gainesville, Georgia. Hereafter, references to this source are indicated as "*Faculty Journal* (25 years), [entry date]."
111. "Brenau Tapped to Host Prestigious Phi Kappa Phi Honor Society Chapter," *The Weekly: Your Neighborhood Newspaper*, 18 April 2007,

http://www.theweekly.com/news/2007/April/18/Brenau.html (accessed 30 November 2012).

112. "Letter from M. C. Huntley to President Josiah Crudup, 28 September 1948;" Folder 9 (labeled "SACS Reports 1940s") in Box 5 (labeled "SACS Self-reports") in the Brenau University Archives, Gainesville, Georgia.
113. Brenau College, *An Institutional Self-Study, 1979-81*, 35.
114. *U.S. News & World Report*, "Brenau University," usnews.com, http://colleges.usnews.rankingsandreviews.com/best-colleges/brenau-university-1556/academics (accessed 30 November 2012).
115. "Complete Copy of Southern Association Report As Filled Out October 1930 – 1931 for all General Material"; Folder 6 (labeled "SACS Forms 1927-33") in Box 5 of 6 (labeled "Self-Study") in the Brenau University Archives, Gainesville, Georgia.
116. Ibid.
117. "SACS Report Form for Senior Colleges (1948–49)"; Folder 9 (labeled "SACS Reports 1940s") in Box 5 of 6 (labeled "SACS Reports") in the Brenau University Archives, Gainesville, Georgia.
118. See http://www.brenau.edu/about-brenau-extraordinary/office-commpub/brenau-window/ to locate current and past editions of *Brenau Window* (accessed 30 November 2012).
119. See the following: John William Leonard, *Woman's Who's Who of America: A Biographical Dictionary of Contemporary Women of the United States and Canada* (New York, NY: The American Commonwealth Company, 1915), 499; Sarah E. Gardner, "Helen Dortch Longstreet (1863–1962)," *The New Georgia Encyclopedia*, 25 May 2007, http://www.georgiaencyclopedia.org/nge/Article.jsp?id=h-881 (accessed 30 November 2012); "Longstreet, Helen Dortch," Georgia Women of Achievement, http://www.georgiawomen.org/2010/10/longstreet-helen-dortsch/ (accessed 30 November 2012).
120. "The Presidency: Appointments," *Time Magazine*, 30 December 1929, http://www.time.com/time/magazine/article/0,9171,929134,00.html#ixzz1NNBgHWJN (accessed 30 November 2012).
121. "Mrs. Herman C. Krannert, Philanthropist, 84, is Dead," *New York Times*, 8 July 1974, http://select.nytimes.com/gst/abstract.html?res=F1061FFF3F5B1A7493CAA9178CD85F408785F9 (accessed 30 November 2012).
122. "Gynecologist, Endocrinologist Elizabeth Parker Dies at 93," *The Washington Post*, 03 Nov 1996.

123. Scott Romine, "Katharine Du Pre Lumpkin (1897–1988)," *The New Georgia Encyclopedia*, 15 April 2009, http://www.georgiaencyclopedia.org/nge/Article.jsp?id=h-491&sug=y (accessed 30 November 2012).
124. John C. Inscoe, *Writing the South Through the Self: Explorations in Southern Autobiography* (Athens, GA: University of Georgia Press, 2011), 135.
125. "Amanda Blake kissed boy; Brenau put her on probation," *Gainesville Times* (Gainesville, GA), 11 September 1977, Brenau College Centennial Commemorative Section, p. 8.
126. Office of the Clerk, U.S. House of Representatives, "Florence Reville Gibbs," Women in Congress, http://womenincongress.house.gov/member-profiles/profile.html?intID=85 (accessed 30 November 2012).
127. Office of the Clerk, U.S. House of Representatives, "Lera Millard Thomas," Women in Congress, http://womenincongress.house.gov/member-profiles/profile.html?intID=244 (accessed 30 November 2012).
128. "Focus on EWC Alums: Terry Coleman, Speaker of the House," *Brenau Magazine*, published by the Office of Public Relations, Brenau University, Spring 2004, p. 10.
129. Mary Welch, "Roslyn Wallace Was Here," *Brenau Window* (spring, 2010): 10 – 11, http://artsweb.brenau.edu/Brenauwindow/Spring2010/default.htm (accessed 1 December 2012).
130. Candice Dyer, "Miss Hacksaw: Trody Trow!" *Brenau Window* (spring, 2010): 6 – 9, 7, http://artsweb.brenau.edu/Brenauwindow/Spring2010/default.htm (accessed 1 December 2012).
131. *Bubbles* (1992), 106.
132. "About Candice Dyer," http://anticsincandyland.wordpress.com/about/ (accessed 1 December 2012).
133. Green Eyeshade, "2009 Winners," http://www.greeneyeshade.org/past-winners/2009-winners/ (accessed 1 December 2012).
134. David Kirby, "The Maconian Renaissance? Candice Dyer's Street Singers Plumbs the Mystery of Macon Music," *Georgia Music Magazine*, http://georgiamusicmag.com/the-maconian-renaissance/ (accessed 1 December 2012).
135. Brenau College, *An Institutional Self-Study, 1969 –1971.*
136. For a time, the Brenau Alumni Relations Office maintained a web page entitled "Alumnae Giving - Women's College," which listed alumnae benefactors by class. Several dozen women from various classes dating back to the "Class of 1940" have made contributions to the institution. See http://www2009.brenau.edu/index.cfm?objectid=BF19AA3B-65B3-FE26-0873B7A9CD140FCE (accessed 14 April 2012).

137. See "Brenau University Ranking," GRE Explorer, http://www.greexplorer.com/Top-Universities/Brenau-University.html (accessed 1 December 2012), reprinting the "Rankings, Scores, and Key Indicators" of the 2008 *U.S. News and World Report* annual "College Rankings" issue. Regarding the national average of alumni giving, see Scott Jaschik, "Donations Are Up, But Not From Alumni," *Inside Higher Ed*, 20 February 2008 http://www.insidehighered.com/news/2008/02/20/gifts (accessed 1 December 2012). At best, just slightly more than one-half of a college's graduates will contribute as alumni donors. See Katy Hopkins, "Top 10 Most Loved Schools," *U.S. News and World Report*, 20 January 2011, http://www.usnews.com/education/articles/2011/01/20/top-10-most-loved-schools (1 December 2012).
138. Larry Hartstein, "Bullish on Brenau: Long-lost alumna's stock picks aid college," *The Atlanta Constitution*, 28 September 2001, Section D, p. 1.
139. Ibid.
140. Ibid.
141. See the chapter on student organizations for more information about the formation of Brenau's Student Government Association.
142. "SACS Report Form for Senior Colleges (1947–48)," in Folder 9 (labeled "SACS Reports 1940s") in Box 5 of 6 (labeled "SACS Reports") in the Brenau University Archives, Gainesville, Georgia.
143. Ibid.
144. Brenau College, *An Institutional Self-Study, 1969–71*, 192.
145. Brenau College, *An Institutional Self-Study, 1979 –1981*, 198.
146. Ibid.
147. "State Baptist Female Seminary at Gainesville, Hall County, Ga.," *Atlanta Constitution*, 16 December 1877, p. 4.
148. "Part 1: How Tift College was conceived," *Monroe County Reporter*, 22 September 2010, http://www.dcor.state.ga.us/NewsRoom/Publications/Tift.html (accessed 2 December 2012).
149. Hubert Bruce Fuller, *History of the Baptist Denomination in Georgia*, (Atlanta, GA: Jas. P. Harrison & Co. Printers and Publishers, 1881), 582; available at http://www.ebooksread.com/authors-eng/hubert-bruce-fuller/history-of-the-baptist-denomination-in-georgia-alt/page-129-history-of-the-baptist-denomination-in-georgia-alt.shtml (accessed 2 December 2012).
150. "The Founding Years," Brenau University Archived Webpages (formerly online at http://artsweb.brenau.edu/historic/Founding/default.htm from around 2004 until 2011); hard-copy print-out located in Box 1 of 1

labeled "Archived Webpages," Brenau University Archives, Gainesville, Georgia.
151. Ibid.
152. "The Georgia Seminary: Interesting Ceremonies by the Odd-Fellows and Masons," *Gainesville Eagle*, 28 June 1878, p. 1.
153. Ibid.
154. Jo Hall, "Four Presidents Charter Progressive Course," *Alchemist*, 23 February 1968, p. 4.
155. Ibid.
156. "The Georgia Female Seminary and Conservatory of Music," *Atlanta Constitution*, 6 August 1893, p. 18.
157. Ibid.
158. Josiah Carter, "A Day at Brenau," *Atlanta Constitution*, 31 July 1904, sec. C p. 4.
159. "A Creditable Success," *Atlanta* Constitution, 8 July 1897, p. 4.
160. Jo Hall, "Four Presidents Charter Progressive Course," *Alchemist*, 23 February 1968, p. 4. In fact, this article says that Pearce graduated Phi Beta Kappa from Emory. However, Phi Beta Kappa would not come to Emory until 1929. See "Honor Societies," Emory University, http://college.emory.edu/home/life/societies.html (accessed 15 December 2012).
161. Pitts Theological Library Archives and Manuscripts Department, "Callahan, William Jackson. Papers 1890–1936," Manuscript no. 063, Emory University, http://www.pitts.emory.edu/Archives/text/mss063.html (accessed 15 December 2012).
162. Haywood J. Pearce, *Philosophical Meditations; Talks to College Girls* (Boston, MA: The Stratford Company, 1917); available from Hathi Trust Digital Library, http://babel.hathitrust.org/cgi/pt?id=uva.x004216859; seq=1;view=1up (accessed 15 December 2012).
163. "The Georgia Female Seminary and Conservatory of Music," *Atlanta Constitution*, 6 August 1893, p. 18.
164. Ibid.
165. Brenau University, "Brenau at a Glance," http://www.brenau.edu/about-brenau-extraordinary/brenau-at-a-glance/ (accessed 16 December 2012).
166. *Catalog* (1900), 8.
167. Ibid.
168. Rigney, *Brenau College 1878–1978*, 3.
169. Alice Taylor-Colbert, "Brief History and Traditions of Shorter College: The Shorter Heritage," http://www.shorter.edu/about/history.htm (accessed 16 December 2012).

170. Though college governance arrangements varied throughout the nation, few women's colleges—at least in Georgia—seem to have been singularly owned as Brenau was. A board of trustees affiliated with the Georgia Conference of the Methodist Church governed Wesleyan College in Macon from inception. Samuel Luttrell Akers, *The First Hundred Years of Wesleyan College, 1836–1936* (Macon, GA: Beehive Press, 1976), 11. Agnes Scott College "began its career in a rented building September, 1889, under the auspices of the Decatur Presbyterian church" and remained governed by a board of trustees thereafter. *Eleventh Annual Catalogue and Announcement of the Agnes Scott Institute (1900)* (Atlanta, GA: Agnes Scott Institute, 1899), http://www.archive.org/details/eleventhann189 91900agne (accessed 16 December 2012). "A board of trustees formed to run" the Forsyth Female Collegiate Institute (later Tift College) of Forsyth, Georgia, when it formed in December of 1849. The board "included three Baptists, three Methodists and one Presbyterian." "Part 1: How Tift College was conceived," *Monroe County Reporter*, 22 September 2010, http://www.dcor.state.ga.us/NewsRoom/Publications/pdf/Part_ 1_how_tift_college_was_conceived.pdf (accessed 16 December 2012). "Spelman College's history began on April 11, 1881," when "Sophia B. Packard and Harriet E. Giles, schoolteachers and Baptist missionaries from New England," founded the Atlanta Baptist Female Seminary in the basement of Atlanta's Friendship Baptist Church. "The school was legally organized with a charter and a board of trustees in 1888 under the presidency of Packard." Taronda Spencer , "Spelman College," *New Georgia Encyclopedia*, http://www.georgiaencyclopedia.org/nge/ Article.jsp?id=h-1460 (accessed 16 December 2012). The Cherokee Baptist Female College (present-day Shorter University) of Rome, Georgia, opened in 1873 and, sometime prior to 1910, developed a board of trustees for governance. Alice Taylor-Colbert, "Brief History and Traditions of Shorter University: The Shorter Heritage," http://www. shorter.edu/about/history.htm (accessed 17 December 2012). Outside of Georgia, the Union Female College in Eufaula, Alabama, which opened in 1854, operated with trustees until its purchase by Brenau and subsequent closure, as indicated by materials published in 1893. Mary Rosser, *President Thomas Jackson Simmons and Mrs. Simmons: An Appreciation* (Gainesville, GA: Brenau College and Conservatory, 1910), 13; available at http://catalog.hathitrust.org/Record/009587573 (accessed 17 December 2012). Peace College in Raleigh, North Carolina, "was founded in 1857 by Raleigh's First Presbyterian Church." Around

1872, the college "was leased to the Reverend Robert Burwell" and family, who operated Peace Institute until 1890. Technical ownership, however, remained with the church and "local Presbyterians composed the board of trustees of Peace in the early twentieth century." Jonathan Martin, "Peace College," North Carolina History Project, http://www.northcarolinahistory.org/encyclopedia/754/entry (accessed 18 June 2013). In 1889, Converse College in Spartanburg, South Carolina, was founded "as a stock company and Mr. Converse," a prominent local businessman, "headed the first board of directors, comprised entirely of Spartanburg citizens." Then, "In 1896, by the voluntary act of the stockholders, Converse College was incorporated under the laws of the state of South Carolina and a self-perpetuating board of trustees was established." "Converse College: Our Mission and History," http://www.converse.edu/about/our-mission-history (accessed 17 December 2012). Whitworth College in Brookhaven, Mississippi, operated briefly as a partnership and then as a sole-proprietorship in 1859, closed for the Civil War, and reopened in 1865 under the ownership of the Mississippi Methodist Conference. "Whitworth College Archive," http://www.llf.lib.ms.us/LLF/Archival%20Project%202002-2003/Whitworth/M1f.html (accessed 17 December 2012). See also Kathleen George Rice, "A History of Whitworth College for Women" (Ph.D. diss., University of Mississippi, 1985).

171. Rigney, *Brenau College 1878–1978*, 3. T.J. Simmons graduated with an A.M. from Wake Forest University in 1883. He went on to teach public school for about a decade in North Carolina and Georgia before becoming the president of the Union Female College at Eufaula, Alabama. He served in this capacity for five years before departing for Rome, Georgia, to assume the presidency of Shorter College. He held that post for twelve years before becoming co-president with Dr. Pearce at Brenau. When he moved to Brenau, a number of the faculty at Shorter apparently went with him, as did a large number of fine pianos, which Simmons personally owned. See Mary Rosser, *President Thomas Jackson Simmons and Mrs. Simmons: An Appreciation* (Gainesville, GA: Brenau College and Conservatory, 1910), 13; available at http://catalog.hathitrust.org/Record/009587573 (accessed 17 December 2012). When his wife, Lessie Muse Southgate Simmons died in 1913, Thomas Simmons sold his interest in Brenau to Dr. Pearce.

172. Boyden Sparkes, "Writ on Rocke," *Saturday Evening Post*, 26 April 1941.

173. Jo Hall, "Four Presidents Charter Progressive Course," *Alchemist*, 23 February 1968, p. 4.
174. Rigney, *Brenau College 1878–1978*, 41-42.
175. Ibid. I arrived at the figure adjusted for inflation by utilizing an "Inflation Calculator" maintained by S. Morgan Friedman at http://www.westegg.com/inflation/ (accessed 17 December 2012). The calculator "adjusts any given amount of money for inflation, according to the Consumer Price Index, from 1800 to 2007."
176. Ibid.
177. *Faculty Journal* (25 years), entry dated 6 October 1931.
178. Ibid., entry of 4 October 1932.
179. Ibid., entry of 7 February 1933.
180. Ibid., entry of 28 January 1936.
181. Ibid.
182. Ibid.
183. Ibid.
184. Emory University, "Stability and Growth: Harvey Warren Cox's Presidency," *Emory History*, http://emoryhistory.emory.edu/people/presidents/Cox.htm (accessed 17 December 2012).
185. Ibid.
186. Agnes Scott College also reduced faculty and staff salaries, apparently with no negative repercussions. Walter Edward McNair, quoting Agnes Scott's president in 1931, wrote that the faculty showed "the finest co-operation possible during this period of financial difficulty, voluntarily offering any reduction in salaries that may be necessary." Walter Edward McNair, *Lest We Forget: An Account of Agnes Scott College* (Atlanta, GA: Tucker-Castleberry Printing, Inc., 1983), 85.
187. Sophia Packard led Spelman College through its first decade until 1891, making her the first female chief administrator of a women's college in Georgia. Spelman College, "A Brief History of Spelman College," *Bulletin 2010–12*, http://www.spelman.edu/docs/default-document-library/bulletin_2009-2010_final.pdf?sfvrsn=10 (accessed 17 December 2012). Nora Kizer Bell was named the first woman president of Wesleyan College in 1997. Sen. Saxby Chambliss, "Honoring Dr. Nora Kizer Bell," *Congressional Record*, v. 144, n. 11 (12 February 1998): 173; available from Capitol Words, http://capitolwords.org/date/1998/02/12/E173-3_honoring-dr-nora-kizer-bell/ (accessed 17 December 2012). Ruth Schmidt became Agnes Scott's first woman president in 1982. Rick Badie, "Ruth A. Schmidt, 79: First female president at Agnes

Scott College," *Atlanta Journal-Constitution*, 26 May 2010, http://www.ajc.com/news/news/local/ruth-a-schmidt-79-first-female-president-at-agnes-/nQgMF/ (accessed 17 December 2012). Neither Shorter College, LaGrange College, Andrew College (formerly Andrew Female College), nor the Georgia Normal and Industrial College (later Georgia College and State University) have had women presidents as of 2012 and none remain single-sex.

188. Brenau College, *Bubbles* (Gainesville, GA; Brenau College, 1945), 11–12. Hereafter, references to this source are indicated as "*Bubbles* (1945)."

189. Under the watch of these presidents, Brenau increased overall enrollment to over two-thousand students; expanded curricular offerings to include many undergraduate majors and several graduate degrees; regained accreditation by the Southern Association of Colleges and Schools (which had been lost in the 1940s); and amassed an endowment that, at one time, amounted to over thirty million dollars. Brenau University, "Brenau At a Glance," http://www.brenau.edu/about-brenau-extraordinary/brenau-at-a-glance/ (accessed 17 December 2012).

190. "Notable Alumni," http://about.mercer.edu/notable-alumni/ (accessed 17 December 2012). While at Mercer, Crudup helped to build the college's original radio tower and establish WMAZ at Macon.

191. Dr. Crudup's 1938 dissertation was entitled, "*The absorption of the shower-producing component of cosmic radiation in iron and lead.*" See http://adsabs.harvard.edu/abs/1938PhRv...54..483C (accessed 17 December 2012).

192. "$20,000 Chimes to Memorialize Battle," *Atlanta Daily World* (4 Feb. 1940), 8.

193. J.C. Bryant, "Mercer University," *The New Georgia Encyclopedia*, 15 Sept. 2008, http://www.georgiaencyclopedia.org/nge/Article.jsp?id=h-1448 (accessed 17 December 2012).

194. Ibid.

195. Jo Hall, "Four Presidents Charter Progressive Course," *Alchemist*, 23 February 1968, p. 5.

196. Brenau University, "History of Brenau," *Brenau University Undergraduate and Graduate Catalog* (2010 – 2012), http://catalog.brenau.edu/content.php?catoid=3&navoid=140#History (accessed 17 December 2012).

197. Jo Hall, "Four Presidents Charter Progressive Course," *Alchemist*, 23 February 1968, p. 4.

198. Ibid.

199. *Catalog* (2001), 9.
200. Some of the biographical information about Dr. Rogers was drawn from a personal website he maintained up until around 2011, http://www.jamestrogers.com/about.asp. As of December, 2012, Dr. Rogers no longer maintained the website. For additional biographical information about Dr. Rogers, see Delta State University, "Delta State alums Rogers, Thrash to be awarded honorary degrees at University's May commencement," *DSU Headlines*, 12 May 2007, http://www.deltastate.edu/pages/1073.asp?item=2449 (accessed 17 December 2012).
201. James J. Lorence, "Gainesville State College," *New Georgia Encyclopedia*, 21 Oct. 2005, http://www.georgiaencyclopedia.org/nge/Article.jsp?id=h-1440 (accessed 17 December 2012).
202. Dr. John S. Burd, "Brenau College: Self-Study Report Georgia Department of Education," 15 December 1990, p. 15; Brenau University Archives, Gainesville, Georgia.
203. Dr. John S. Burd, interview by author, tape recording, Gainesville, Georgia, 23 September 2010. Dr. Patricia Burd actually wrote a dissertation that compared the role of women on the boards of trustees of coeducational colleges with the roles played by women on the boards of women's colleges.
204. The following account of Dr. Burd's accomplishments is distilled from Hon. Nathan Deal, "Tribute to Dr. John S. Burd, President, Brenau University," speech in the House of Representatives, 21 April 2004, http://votesmart.org/public-statement/40116/tribute-to-dr-john-s-burd-president-brenau-university#.UM_LxORX0kQ (accessed 17 December 2012).
205. "Dr. Burd Announces Retirement After 19 Years of Leadership," *The Link*, vol. 1, no. 1 (fall, 2003), Brenau University Office of Public Relations, p. 1.
206. Ibid.
207. Ken Stanford, "One candidate for Brenau president remains 'under serious consideration," AccessNorthGA.com, 3 April 2004, http://www.accessnorthga.com/detail.php?n=160946 (accessed 17 December 2012).
208. Ibid.
209. Jeff Gill, "Schrader has big plans for Gainesville university," *Gainesville Times*, 9 January 2005, http://archive.gainesvilletimes.com/news/stories/20050109/localnews/66156.shtml (accessed 17 December 2012).

210. J. Gerald Harris, "Shorter soars like a hawk with new president and accreditation affirmed," *The Christian Index*, 2 February 2006, http://www.christianindex.org/1942.article (accessed 17 December 2012).
211. Jeff Gill, "Schrader has big plans for Gainesville university," *Gainesville Times*, 9 January 2005, http://archive.gainesvilletimes.com/news/stories/20050109/localnews/66156.shtml (accessed 17 December 2012).
212. "Educate Your Daughter," *Atlanta Constitution*, 24 July 1900, p. 9.
213. "A Noted Musician Comes to Georgia and Will Locate at Gainesville," *Atlanta Constitution*, 29 July 1900, p. 18.
214. Josiah Carter, "A Day at Brenau," *Atlanta Constitution*, 31 July 1904, sec. C, p. 4.
215. "High Degree for Geiger," *Atlanta Constitution*, 30 August 1908, sec. A, p. 5.
216. "The New Director at Brenau," *Atlanta Constitution*, 19 July 1902, p. 8.
217. *Catalog* (1910), 100–102.
218. "Miss Fritzler [sic.] Plays in Chapel," *Alchemist* (Gainesville, GA: Brenau College), vol. 7, no. 3 (8 November 1919), p. 3.
219. "Mr. McCormick In Recital," *Alchemist* (Gainesville, GA: Brenau College), vol. XII, no. 6 (3 December 1924), p. 1.
220. "Dr. Ben J. Potter Will Be Presented In Organ Recital," *Alchemist* (Gainesville, GA: Brenau College) vol. XXXII, no. 3 (23 October 1945), p. 1.
221. Ibid.
222. "Brenau Notes," *Atlanta Constitution*, 17 January 1904, sec. B, p. 4.
223. Ibid.
224. Ibid.
225. "Society Notes," *Atlanta Constitution*, 14 April 1907, sec. A, p. 7.
226. Display Advertisement --No Title, *Atlanta Constitution*, 10 April 1904, sec. B, p. 5.
227. Jacquelyn Dowd Hall, "'To Widen the Reach of Our Love:' Autobiography, History, and Desire," *Feminist Studies*, Spring 2000, vol. 26, issue 1, p. 231–248, 239.
228. Ibid.
229. See Leonard S. Vincent, "B. J. Kaston, American Araneologist 1906–1985: A Biography and Bibliography," *Journal of Arachnology*, vol. 14 (1987): 283–291.
230. Johnny Vardeman, "Congresswoman who opposed wars brought big brouhaha to Brenau," *Gainesville Times*, 1 April 2007, http://

gainesvillelegals.com//news/stories/20070401/opinion/164960.shtml (accessed 22 May 2013).

231. "Zeke Segal, Journalist, 78," *The New York Times*, 1 September 1996, http://www.nytimes.com/1996/09/01/us/zeke-segal-journalist-78.html (accessed 22 May 2013).

232. Nick Taylor, "Hauling Ashes," *Brenau Window*, Summer 2008, 10–11, http://artsweb.brenau.edu/brenauwindow/Summer2008/HaulingAshes_sum08.pdf (accessed 22 May 2013).

233. Brenau University, "Brenau University celebrates professor's 40th year," *Brenau News*, 11 May 2011, http://www.brenau.edu/news/brenau-university-celebrates-professor%E2%80%99s-40th-year/ (accessed 18 December 2012).

234. Brenau University, "Brenau adds vice president and strengthens provost position," *Brenau News*, 06 July 2010, http://www.brenau.edu/news/brenau-adds-vice-president-and-strengthens-provost-position/ (accessed 18 December 2012).

235. Nick Dentamaro, "A Message from Jim Southerland," *Brenau University Update*, 08 May 2013, http://update.brenau.edu/2013/05/08/a-message-from-jim-southerland/ (accessed 22 May 2013).

236. Richard Vedder, "Student Evaluations, Grade Inflation, and Declining Student Effort," *Chronicle of Higher Education*, 19 June 2010, http://chronicle.com/blogs/innovations/student-evaluations-grade-inflationdeclining-student-effort/24926 (accessed 18 December 2012).

237. Nothing in Brenau's archived student newspapers or other publications, letters to administrators, alumnae materials, etc., indicated that students seemed to be especially satisfied—or especially dissatisfied—with any Brenau faculty member in particular.

238. Brenau's percentage of women faculty members about this time seems to have been on a par with at least one other southern women's college. A photograph of the faculty of Converse College taken in 1958 showed 31 men and 25 women, which meant that 45% of the Converse faculty were female as opposed to 49% at Brenau. Jeffrey R. Willis, *Converse College* (Charleston, SC: Arcadia Publishing, 2001), 78.

239. See Mary Ann Mason, "The Pyramid Problem," *The Chronicle of Higher Education*, 9 March 2011, http://chronicle.com/article/The-Pyramid-Problem/126614/ (accessed 29 May 2013).

240. S. A. Mitchell, "Academic Freedom and Tenure: Report of Committee A," *Bulletin of the American Association of University Professors*, vol. 20,

no. 2 (February 1934): 97 –104, 98; available from http://www.jstor.org/stable/40219014 (accessed 18 December 2012).
241. Ibid., 99.
242. Ibid., 100.
243. Ibid., 101.
244. Ibid., 102.
245. "Academic Freedom and Tenure," *Bulletin of the American Association of University Professors*, vol. 24, no. 1 (January, 1938): 5.
246. "Education: Blackest Sheep," *Time Magazine*, 13 January 1936, http://www.time.com/time/magazine/article/0,9171,755641,00.html#ixzz1NNDHS8l4 (accessed 24 December 2012).
247. "List of Censured Administrations, 1930-2002," American Association of University Professors, http://www.aaup.org/AAUP/pubsres/academe/2003/JF/FTR/cenlist.htm (24 December 2012).
248. "SACS Report Form for Senior Colleges (1947–48)," Folder #9 (labeled "SACS Reports 1940s") in Box 5 of 6 (labeled "Self Study"), Brenau University Archives, Gainesville, Georgia.
249. "Membership," *AAUP Bulletin*, vol. 43, no. 1 (spring, 1957): 122.
250. Ibid., 136.
251. See American Association of University Professors, "Censure List," Our Programs: Academic Freedom, http://www.aaup.org/AAUP/about/censuredadmins/ (accessed 28 December 2012).
252. Brenau College, *Institutional Self Study, 1969–1971*, 121.
253. Ibid., 127.
254. Ibid., 128.
255. Ibid.
256. Ibid.
257. Ibid., 128–129.
258. Brenau College, *Institutional Self-Study, 1984–1985* (Gainesville, GA: Brenau College), 174. Hereafter, references to this source are indicated as "*Institutional Self-Study, 1984–1985*."
259. Richard Chait and Cathy A. Trower, "Where Tenure Does Not Reign: Colleges with Contract Systems," *New Pathways: Faculty Career and Employment for the 21st Century Working Paper Series Inquiry #3*, American Association for Higher Education, Washington, DC, 1997, http://www.eric.ed.gov/ERICWebPortal/detail?accno=ED424814 (accessed 25 December 2012).
260. Jack Stripling, "Most Presidents Prefer No Tenure for Majority of Faculty," *The Chronicle of Higher Education*, 15 May 2011, http://

chronicle.com/article/Most-Presidents-Favor-No/127526/ (accessed 18 December 2012).
261. Brenau College, *Institutional Self-Study, 1979–1981*, 129–130.
262. Ibid., 130.
263. Ibid.
264. Brenau College, *Institutional Self-Study, 1984–1985*, 174.
265. Ibid.
266. Brenau College, *Institutional Self-Study, 1979–1981*, 129.
267. Ibid., 130–131.
268. Ibid., 131.
269. Ibid., 129.
270. In the University's defense, Brenau is not alone in its abandonment of tenure. In his 2002 book entitled *The Questions of Tenure*, Richard Chait identified 88 four-year colleges without tenure (71). None were among the most elite schools in the country. See Richard Chait, *The Questions of Tenure* (Boston, MA: Harvard University Press, 2005).
271. William T. Mallon, "Standard Deviations: Faculty Appointment Policies at Institutions Without Tenure" in Cathy A. Trower (ed.), *Policies on Faculty Appointment: Standard Practices and Unusual Arrangements* (Bolton, MA: Anker Publishing, Inc., 2000). Reprinted with permission from Anker Publishing, Inc., http://www2.acenet.edu/resources/chairs/docs/Mallon.pdf (accessed 20 December 2012).
272. Ibid.
273. "Brenau Gains Highest Status in National 'Great Colleges to Work For' Survey," Brenau News, http://www.brenau.edu/news/brenau-pianists-demonstrate-that-four-hands-are-better-than-two-at-sept-1-concer/ (accessed 25 December 2012). (Note that while this URL seems mislabeled, it does direct to the correct article.)

Chapter 2

The History of Academics at Brenau

Derived by the Faculty & Staff, Complied with by Students

Colleges and universities publish statements of mission to explain their *raison d'être*, statements that are revised periodically as times change. Brenau has explained its reason for being in different ways since its founding. In 1917, Brenau's president, Dr. H. J. Pearce, believed Brenau existed to produce a young woman able:

> To find satisfaction in being rather than seeming; to find joy in doing rather than dreaming; to be prepared for service thereby earning the right to be served; to be pure in heart; vigorous in mind, discreet in action; to love deeply, to fear nothing, hate never; to enjoy that freedom which comes from knowledge of the "Truth"; to be modestly conscious of the limitations of human knowledge and serenely confident of the limitless reaches of human endeavor –[1]

"This," wrote Dr. Pearce, "is the ideal of Brenau."[2] Though he no doubt meant well, aspects of his philosophy, rooted as it was in patriarchal notions about womanhood, could do little to uplift women. Though the advice to find satisfaction in being, not seeming, might have discouraged putting on airs, it also urged women to know their place. Encouraging a woman to "do" rather than "dream" implied that women were prone to flights of fancy and discouraged them from setting sights high. And urging discretion, modesty, and serenity meant women should be reserved, not assertive. Almost a century later, much had changed. Brenau University now challenged students to "live extraordinary lives of personal and professional fulfillment" in preparation for "a lifetime of intellectual accomplishment and appreciation of artistic expression."[3]

Since its founding, whether striving toward an ideal or accomplishing a mission, Brenau has relied upon physical culture or athletics to nourish student bodies, religion and campus life to attend to students' spirits, and academics for the mind. As at other colleges generally, Brenau at one time or another has offered various degrees, which students earned by taking a few years' worth of various combinations of prescribed and elective coursework. Within this otherwise routine scheme, two themes deserve particular attention: How Brenau's academic curriculum has changed over time and the degree to which the development of the academic curriculum has been a product of an ongoing negotiation between Brenau's students and Brenau's faculty and staff. This chapter will explore these themes and make two claims.

The first claim is that in its youth and compared to other southern women's colleges, Brenau was an academic innovator that adopted novel academic policies and that created several novel programs for young women in the belief that such programs would be popular and empowering. In particular, Brenau blazed trails among southern women's colleges by supporting early on a business division, a teacher education division, a domestic science program, and uncommonly robust conservatory offerings. Brenau was also apparently the first college anywhere to let students count courses in art and music as elective credits toward a regular baccalaureate degree. Over time, though, this innovative spirit waned. Beginning around the mid-twentieth century, Brenau ceased trying to adjust its curricular offerings according to its perception of the changing ideals and status of womanhood. The College did this because its novel programs never achieved their much hoped-for popularity with students and because of a need to restructure the curriculum to regain regional accreditation, which it had lost. Brenau's innovative spirit returned in the 1980s when it created Georgia's first weekend college program and the first evening degree program in the Atlanta area. In the 1990s, Brenau reinvented itself as a university, making many curricular changes and expansions attendant to this.

The second claim is that Brenau's academic curriculum has historically developed largely from the top-down. The faculty and staff (in particular, the institution's administration) have clearly dictated academic marching orders to students regarding their programs. This has occurred despite the fact that Brenau's students have been quite capable of contributing to a discussion about their own studies. The only real exception to this top-down style of development involved the termination of some of the College's programs. Over the years, Brenau has discontinued some programs in response to student disinterest. After a fashion, this actually does reflect some ability on the part of students to effect academic change —but not at all of the sort students would prefer to possess.

Prior to 1900, Brenau was, in most academic respects, what one might consider to be a typical southern women's college. Examining the core curriculum of studies in Brenau's early years bears this out. Brenau was founded as the Georgia Baptist Female Seminary in 1878. According to Eleanor Rigney, seminary students studied the following subjects by class up until about 1900:

> Freshman Class – Analytical Arithmetic; Caesar concluded (Caesar 1st book was begun the year previously in what was called Preparatory School); Algebra concluded (this was also begun the year previously); Analysis of English Grammar, Green; English Composition; Mythology and Roman History; Geometry commenced; French continued (like Caesar and Algebra, French was begun the

previous year); Virgil commenced; Plain Bookkeeping; Penmanship.

Sophomore Class – Virgil concluded; French continued; Geometry completed; Algebra completed; Trigonometry; Surveying, Latin Prosody; Navigation; Botany, Wood; Composition and Elocution, Green; Introductory [sic.]; Natural Philosophy commenced.

Junior Class – Cicero's Orations, Greek Testament; Rhetoric; Greek Anabasis; Conic Sections; Analytical Geometry; Natural Philosophy completed; Astronomy; Physiology; Cutter's Natural History; Homer's Iliad; Horace, Chase and Stuart; Composition and Elocution; Chemistry commenced.

Senior Class – Philosophy concluded and illustrated with apparatus; Logic; Intellectual Philosophy, Upham; Latin, Livy, Chase and Stuart; Graham's Synonyms; Moral Science; Paley's Theology; Geology; Greek: Memorabilia; Composition and Elocution; General review preparatory to graduation. [4]

By examining the curriculum of a few neighboring collegiate institutions, Rigney concluded that, academically, Brenau's forerunner compared favorably to other southern colleges of the day (both women's and men's) in depth and rigor.[5]

This was to be expected. Regarding nineteenth century women's colleges that strove to emulate men's colleges, historian John R. Thelin asserted that the "'female seminaries' were usually comparable in academic rigor to the colleges for men in the same area."[6] He noted that the "typical curriculum" of a men's college beginning around 1830 "emphasized the study of classical languages, science, and mathematics with the aim of building character and promoting distinctive habits of thought."[7] Though once, as historian Margaret A. Nash put it, "some people vociferously objected to the idea of Latin and Greek for girls," this would change—especially in the Deep South.[8]

In her book entitled *The Education of the Southern Belle*, Christie Anne Farnham noted that "Southern fathers were much more willing than their counterparts in the North to expose women to the classical curriculum."[9] The belief was that a classical education refined a young woman and made her a better marriage prospect. The practice of educating women in the classical tradition continued into the late nineteenth century. The Baptist Female Seminary embraced classical studies as indicated by the presence of Livy, Cicero, and others in its plan of study. Additionally, the core curriculum of the Seminary focused on English, music, mathematics, sciences, and modern languages. Farnham pointed out that many southern women's colleges had long taught these subjects, believing them particularly appropriate for women. Indeed, she found that women's colleges had been innovators in encouraging the collegiate study of the sciences and modern languages.[10]

The curriculum of the Baptist Female Seminary remained largely set until 1900. In that year, the Seminary changed its name to Brenau College and reorganized itself. According to an article published in a 1904 edition of the *Atlanta Constitution*, the charter of Brenau College provided for two distinct institutions. These were:

> a college of high order, open only to girls and young women, furnishing full courses in literary and scientific schools and having the right to grant diplomas and to confer degrees upon all who finish its prescribed courses; [and] also a conservatory of music, art, oratory and kindred subjects with full power to grant diplomas and confer degrees upon all who complete satisfactorily the courses prescribed in its curriculum.[11]

Whereas an institution's rechristening of itself might portend much curricular change, in fact, little immediately occurred at Brenau. This was because the reason for the change was apparently not to usher in new academic programs, but rather to acknowledge the strength of the programs that had already developed.

Though the subjects at the heart of Brenau's degree programs would remain constant, the organization of the institution did change with the adoption of collegiate status. The 1900 *Catalogue* indicated that the

College created four departments: a Conservatory, a Business Department, an "Intermediate or Subcollegiate Department, of two years," and a "Collegiate Department, of four years."[12] Brenau subdivided the Collegiate Department into several schools, such as English, Ancient Languages, etc.[13] Each school constituted "a complete course in the subject taught" and was "conducted by a Professor with such assistants as are necessary."[14] Early catalogs listed the several courses available in each school and even indicated the textbooks that would be used in each individual course. Each school typically offered one or more courses as a component of the universally required core curriculum. Though nomenclature would change over time, Brenau's basic scheme would not. "Schools" eventually became "departments" and "majors" replaced the notion of "a complete course." The presence of core courses remained constant from 1900 on.

Some professors and assistants teaching these core courses garnered praise in an article in the July 31, 1904, edition of the *Atlanta Constitution*. Their credentials suggested that they were qualified to teach college-level material. Speaking of the school of moral science and philosophy, the article related that it was "under Professor Pearce," Brenau's co-president, and embraced "four departments—logic, psychology, aesthetics and history of philosophy." [15] The article continued, saying:

> The various subjects are presented by means of lectures and the parallel use of a text-book. The aim of the department is not only to lead the pupil to a thorough knowledge of the fundamental principles, but to familiarize her with some of the best literature of the several subjects, thus preparing the way for subsequent original investigation.[16]

The article focused particular emphasis on the study of psychology at Brenau and asserted, "It is doubtful if any institution in the south has a more thorough course in psychology than Brenau."[17] In Dr. Pearce, Brenau had a department head that was "recognized as one of the leading psychologists of the day."[18] The article pointed out that Dr. Pearce had "studied at the University of Chicago for two years, then spent a year at Wurzberg [sic], Germany, where he received his doctor's degree, and has but lately returned from a six months' stay in Paris, where he was intimately associated with some of the leading men of Europe."[19]

Other professors and departments of the day also received praise. The *Constitution* reported:

> Every department of Brenau College is upon a very high plane and the school is especially proud of its high literary curriculum. If there is one department in which the education of a young lady should be more thorough than in any other, it is that of English, and in this the work of Brenau is unusually high. No college or university in the south does more or better work in this department than does this splendid institution, within our own border. At its head is Mrs. Irene Tisinger, who has enjoyed the finest advantages for study, having studied at Columbia, The University of Chicago and Chautauqua.[20]

Despite the College's emphasis on the study of English, Brenau did not neglect other subjects. Lydia B. Essex, "an honor graduate of Wellesley college [sic], who has had several years' successful experience in teaching," assisted Professor Van Hoose in the department of science. According to the *Atlanta Constitution*, "The scientific laboratories are well equipped. Young ladies do the same work in practical chemistry, botany, zoology [and] astronomy that young men do in our larger universities."[21] Brenau apparently tried to keep its labs current. By 1907, the *Constitution* related that, "The new scientific laboratory is another important improvement recently completed. Under the direction of E. H. Murfee most excellent work is being done in this department. Apparatus for the illustration of wireless telegraphy and the Roentgen rays has recently been installed."[22] Also in 1907, the *Constitution* reported that, "The new department of history under the direction of Miss Florence M. Rohr is also doing excellently. A course in current history is being followed with much interest by a large body of students."[23]

The article suggested that early Brenau's faculty members were generally well-credentialed with expertise that permitted them to offer college-level courses in more than merely the core curriculum. From very early on, Brenau students took courses outside of Brenau's core as they had the option of enrolling in electives. In the early 1900s, the concept of electives was still novel to many colleges. The idea had emerged in 1869 when, as historian Christopher J. Lucas put it, in his inaugural address as president of Harvard College, Charles W. Eliot "threw down a gauntlet before defenders of the old order."[24] Lucas asserted that, "Against traditionalists committed to the notion of a fixed, uniform course of studies required of everyone, Eliot announced that from now on under his regime, students would have more freedom to select from among different classes and course of study."[25] In this way the "elective system" came into being.

Lucas contended that the system caught on. He wrote:

> The first four decades of the 20th century witnessed a remarkable flurry of curricular reform and experimentation in American higher education. The supplanting of the more or less fixed, uniform classical curriculum of the mid-1800s with an elective system and the introduction of a vast array of utilitarian courses of study by century's end had marked an important shift in academic thought.[26]

Things would change. Lucas went on to say that more remarkable reforms occurred and observed that:

> There was irony possibly in the fact that some were inspired by dissatisfaction over the results of just those innovations enacted in the period immediately preceding. In a sense, with the pendulum of academic opinion having swung far in one direction, it now began describing an arc leading in precisely the opposite direction. Specifically, the target of much criticism was the elective principle or system pioneered at Harvard under President Eliot.[27]

According to Lucas, at many colleges and universities, "The original idea of allowing undergraduates to select their own patterns of study had been prompted by a desire to make academics more interesting and relevant. Instead of being compelled to submit to a single regimen of subjects selected for their supposed disciplinary value, students were allowed to pick and choose, based on their own individual interests, preferences, and career aspirations."[28] Yet, at many of these same institutions, officials came to believe that whatever gains had come from allowing students to take electives had been offset "by a concomitant loss of coherence and intellectual integration." [29] In short, Lucas concluded that, "The elective system, in a word, had borne bitter fruit." [30]

This was not the case at Brenau, which embraced electives warmly almost from the start. The July 2, 1905, edition of the *Atlanta Constitution* reported that, "It has recently been determined to make a still more radical innovation than any which has yet been adopted, viz.: the recognition of music as an elective study looking toward the A. B. degree," Brenau's Bachelor of Arts.[31] The *Constitution* indicated that, despite the fact that music had a long and storied place in human history, "in no college for women has definite provision been made for the study of music as a part of the regular college course."[32] Brenau would be the first to do so. The article related that, "The faculty of Brenau after extended discussion, pro and con, have decided that since an intelligently directed study of music has an intellectual value equal at least to the study of many of the 'ologies,' the former should be placed on a par with the latter and equal credit given—under conditions which cannot be outlined here."[33] Other colleges would follow suit. For example, Amy Thompson McCandless wrote that, "In 1908 Converse College in South Carolina became the first liberal arts college to allow courses in music and art to count toward an A.B. degree."[34] In fact, Brenau seems to have been technically the first to do so, having beaten Converse to the mark by three years.[35] A 1911 entry in the Trustees' minutes for Agnes Scott College indicated that "the Scientific and Literary part of Music" could be counted "'under conditions' for the B.A. degree."[36] Several decades later, virtually all colleges, male and female, would routinely permit students to take courses in the arts for elective credit in earning degrees. Brenau was on the cutting edge of this curricular revolution because of its strong arts programs. In a similar way, in 1941, Brenau began allowing "15 hours of credit" for "two years of successful work in [its] Commercial Dept."[37]

Of course, whenever they attended, Brenau undergraduates took electives, courses in the core curriculum, and courses in specific disciplines to ultimately earn a degree. Brenau has offered many different types of undergraduate degrees throughout its history. Some, like the A.B. (literally, the "*artium baccalaureus*"), have been common to many colleges and have been offered by Brenau since its inception. Others seem to be particular to Brenau and were relatively short-lived, such as the B.D., the Bachelor of Domesticity. Others came and went and, occasionally, came again as was the case of the Bachelor of Science in Education. (See Table 2 for a summary of Brenau's undergraduate degree offerings over time.)

Throughout its history, Brenau made changes to its academic offerings for many reasons identified by the faculty and administration to be important. Some of these demonstrated an early innovative spirit by southern women's college standards of the day, such as with the development of programs in domestic science, stenography, and teacher education, presently to be addressed. Brenau made other curricular changes over the years in deference to accreditation. The U.S. Department of Education has noted that college and university accreditation "arose in the United States as a means of conducting nongovernmental, peer evaluation of educational institutions and programs."[38] The practice of accrediting colleges began in the 1890s when "private educational associations of regional or national scope," such as the Southern Association of Colleges and Schools, "adopted criteria reflecting the qualities of a sound educational program and ... developed procedures for evaluating institutions or programs."[39] The criteria in question would alter a bit over time, but, among other things, earning or maintaining accreditation has always required that an institution have: qualified faculty members with terminal degrees (i.e., earned doctorates), adequate physical and capital resources (including such things as ample library materials and endowment funds), rigorous academic programs, and institutional policies in place to guarantee academic freedom, student rights, and honest, accurate recordkeeping.[40] Representatives from the regional accrediting bodies, themselves faculty members at accredited institutions, would evaluate written materials (called "self-studies") submitted by schools seeking accreditation or reaccreditation and also travel to inspect schools personally. The process was frequently long and arduous for institutional applicants, but it was worth the trouble. Becoming accredited by a regional accrediting body served as a means to publically validate the high quality of an institution's educational programs. A few women's colleges were actually at the forefront of the accreditation movement. Agnes Scott College became the first college in Georgia to earn accreditation when it did so in 1907.[41] By early 1912, "four southern women's colleges belonged to the Association of Colleges of the Southern States: Agnes Scott, Goucher, Randolph-Macon, and Sophie Newcomb."[42] Also in 1912, Converse College became the first college to be accredited in South Carolina.[43] Once gained, institutions had to maintain accreditation by keeping standards high and applying for periodic re-evaluation of their programs or risk losing their accredited status.

Becoming accredited by the Southern Association of Colleges and Schools turned out to be a challenging process for Brenau for a time. Things started off easily enough. Brenau initially earned accreditation from the Southern Association in December of 1929.[44] This was, incidentally, somewhat late compared to some other institutions in the region, but still quite a bit earlier than several others.[45] Yet, in 1936, S.A.C.S. withdrew its accreditation of the College. Brenau would become re-accredited a few years later, but what could have happened in less than a decade to warrant its initial removal?

Dr. Josiah Crudup addressed accreditation and what dissatisfied S.A.C.S. in a report to the Board of Trustees of Brenau College that he delivered on May 28, 1945. He remarked:

During the recent five day visit to Brenau College, I was immediately confronted with the disturbance and uncertainty of Brenau students and parents because of the fact that Brenau College is not on the approved list of the Southern Association of Schools and Colleges. Conference with some of these students and parents seemed to bring assurance to them of the quality of services and instruction at Brenau College. However, membership in the Southern Association is necessary to the future and progress of Brenau College and must be one of the purposes behind all programs and plans for the college in the future. It will not be wise to make application for membership in the Association until Brenau College has attained the standards and admission is assured.[46]

Dr. Crudup concluded, "I am sure that this day will draw nearer with the achievement of the following objectives" and proceeded to list what Brenau needed to work on.[47] To return to the good graces of the Southern Association, the College needed to focus on:

(1) Improvement of the Faculty and faculty salary schedule,

(2) Improvement of the Library and study facilities for the students,

(3) Erection of a Science Building and removal of the Chemistry Department from Van Hoose Hall [which was primarily a dormitory],

(4) The continued reduction of the debt and freeing of the Endowment to the support of the College,

(5) The Improvement of Buildings and grounds,

(6) The establishment of a sound business management and securing the services of a trained and competent business manager,

(7) The establishment of annual gifts to Brenau College from friends in the City of Gainesville, the Alumnae and friends of Brenau College throughout the Country.[48]

Dr. Crudup would tackle each of these items during his presidency, but three seemed to require more attention from him than others: the issues of finances, personnel, and library improvement. Dr. Crudup also streamlined the College's academic offerings in an effort to appease S.A.C.S.

Regarding finances, as strange as it sounds but in a very real sense, one of the factors that may have contributed to Brenau's losing its accreditation was the weather. Shortly before 9:00 a.m. on the morning of April 6, 1936, not one but *two* strong tornadoes tore through Gainesville doing terrible damage to the city's downtown, several residential districts, and part of the Brenau campus. (See Figure 13.) More than 200 people were killed in what remains the "fifth deadliest tornado episode in recorded United States history" as of 2012.[49] Rebuilding would have been costly for the College in good years; the Great Depression only magnified the hardship.

Brenau's financial problems were further exacerbated by the fact that the College apparently kept very little cash on hand. Brenau had established an endowment fund by 1928, which met the condition set by Dr. Pearce before he would turn over control of the College to a board of trustees. Yet, as late as 1950, Brenau's endowment remained relatively small at only $650,000.[50] Much of this amount was not held in cash but rather in real estate. In 1927, Mrs. Aurora Hunt, an 1882 alumna of the Baptist Female Seminary, "deeded $350,000 in property to Brenau," which included the Dixie-Hunt Hotel in Gainesville, as well as "some hotel stock and $100,000 cash."[51] For decades, Brenau relied heavily upon student tuition to cover most operating costs. As late as 1969–1970, "greater than ninety percent of all income was realized from student related fees."[52] Consequently, a significant dip in student enrollment would leave the

College financially strapped. Such dips were actually common at Brenau for many years. Ella D. Winfield's memo from the Registrar's Office indicated that Brenau's enrollment had fluctuated wildly during the 1940s. Enrollment went from 268 students in 1942 to 450 students in 1946 and back to 228 students in 1949.[53] This would have impeded Brenau's ability to budget and made for much financial instability—probably enough to alarm the Southern Association of Colleges and Schools.

If Dr. Crudup had an elaborate plan for improving Brenau's finances, it is not evident from any materials in the Archives. In large part, it seems he put the College on better economic footing by simply asking for—and getting—donations. Members of the community, alumnae, and trustees responded. The endowment grew, if not in great leaps, and this was apparently enough to placate the Southern Association at the time. Even so, several sources suggest that Brenau's finances were of frequent concern when the time came for re-accreditation. In his September 23, 1960, report to the Brenau Board of Trustees, Dr. Crudup wrote that since regaining accreditation in the late 1940s, Brenau "has been meeting satisfactorily the 21 standards of accreditation and has enjoyed an excellent standing among the colleges of America."[54] Ominously, though, he added, "It is with grave concern that I bring to your attention our problem in meeting 'Standard Seven' which deals with endowment and financial support."[55] Simply put, Brenau's endowment annual income was coming very close to falling below the S.A.C.S. required minimum. Dr. Crudup said, "May I urge every trustee to give his best thought and use every influence available in building up the Endowment of Brenau College."[56]

Financial difficulties still plagued the College decades later. In an interview, Dr. John Burd related that when he became Brenau's eighth president in 1985, he "came to a very, very troubled place financially."[57] In the late 1960s and the 1970s, Brenau had accumulated a substantial debt, mostly as a result of gradual operational overspending in some troubled economic times. Worse still, the institution still lacked a substantial endowment. Dr. Burd's first priority was to get Brenau operating in the black financially and to establish a robust endowment that would better enable the College to recruit talented staff by offering greater salaries. "Within two years," said Dr. Burd, "we had wiped out all outstanding debt."[58] The endowment grew spectacularly as well. "When I left [in 2005]," recalled Dr. Burd, "the endowment was around $50 million. We started with one million."[59] Dr. Burd credited the successful growth of the endowment largely to good economic times and to the talented development staff that worked for Brenau. Though the bad economic times of the 2000s would hammer college endowments everywhere, in 2008–2009, Brenau still had over $23 million on its books—more than enough to satisfy S.A.C.S. for the foreseeable future.[60]

Another hurdle Brenau had to clear to regain accreditation related to personnel. Dr. Crudup summed it up simply: "Brenau College faculty does not have enough professors holding the Ph.D. degree or equivalent."[61] Dr. Crudup indicated that this should change with future hires. For example, he noted in 1945 that Brenau needed to hire a Head of English and a Head of History. He declared, "It would be desirable if these two additions could be men holding the Ph.D. degree."[62] (One hopes that women with doctorates would have been desirable as well.) Adding terminal degree holders to the faculty took time. When Dr. Burd came to Brenau, he recalled that something like 40% of the faculty had terminal degrees. Through conscientious recruiting efforts, that figure more than doubled during the Burd administration. "It took a lot of money to do that," Burd recalled, "but it made S.A.C.S. happy."[63]

Besides addressing issues of finance and personnel, Dr. Crudup also streamlined the College's academic offerings for many years beginning in the 1940s, apparently in an effort to further appease S.A.C.S. Brenau focused on offering a single degree to increase its chances of re-accreditation. The sentiment among Dr. Crudup's administration, as is evident from several memoranda and pieces of correspondence in the Brenau Archives, was that Brenau should focus on doing one thing—and doing it very well—to impress S.A.C.S. President Crudup said as much in a speech to the College trustees. He indicated:

> About twelve years ago when we were trying to attain accredited membership in the Southern Association of Colleges for Brenau, the best strategy seemed to be that of developing a less expensive program with a high quality of work. This was necessary to meet Southern Association standards. At that time we limited the degree offering to the Bachelor of Arts degree and made no professional offerings. This strategy along with a successful financial campaign resulted in accredited membership for Brenau in 1947.[64]

In his May 27, 1949, report to the Brenau Board of Trustees, Dr. Crudup wrote:

> The attainment of membership and accreditation in the Southern Association of Colleges, American Council and New York Regents left Brenau College short of complete national accreditation only by recognition from the American Association of Universities. However, in December 1948, the American Association of Universities abandoned its thirty-five year old practice of accrediting colleges and universities. Thus, Brenau College has attained a position with no more fields to conquer in general academic accreditation.[65]

"Since that time," Dr. Crudup would later say, "Brenau College has enjoyed an excellent standing in the Southern Association of Colleges" and the other accrediting bodies.[66]

Brenau's academic bulletins reflected the results of the "less expensive program" strategy for many years. According to its bulletin for 1949–1950, Brenau entered the 1950s with a changed curriculum, which the catalog referred to as the "Brenau Plan." In regaining accreditation, Brenau had eliminated all of its degree programs except for the Bachelor of Arts degree. Students could essentially still major in everything that had been available to them before the overhaul, but could only earn the A.B. in doing so. Brenau offered majors in "English Language and

Literature, Speech Arts, Foreign Languages, Psychology, Mathematics and Physics, Sociology and Economics, History and Political Science, Biology, Chemistry, and Music."[67] By 1953, Brenau had added majors in home economics, physical education, and education.[68] All of these majors would essentially remain the same at the College until the mid-nineteen seventies. Multiple degrees would resurface at Brenau beginning in the 1960s, apparently after the institution had proven itself to S.A.C.S. over time. In 1965, Brenau began offering the Bachelor of Science degree alongside the Bachelor of Arts. According to the annual bulletin, "The Bachelor of Science degree is available only to those who are following the planned program for teachers approved by the State Department of Education, and those who complete the Nurses' Education program."[69] A decade later, Brenau had added programs of study in broadcasting, business administration, commercial arts, special education, general studies, interior design, journalism, pre-law, secretarial science, studio art, and theatre.[70] By the mid-1980s, several academic sub-fields such as accounting, computer science, special education, and church music became majors in the areas of art, music, business, and education.[71] The Women's College also supported majors in criminal justice and equestrian studies for a time.[72] With the development of a general/liberal studies major in the 1990s and the addition of a Bachelor's in Fine Arts degree, Brenau claimed roughly three-dozen major undergraduate programs of study heading into the twenty-first century.[73]

Throughout much of the twentieth century, roughly one-third of the bachelor's degrees at Brenau consisted of required "core curriculum" courses in English composition and literature, foreign language, social & behavioral sciences (including history), and a laboratory science sequence.[74] Brenau prescribed these "basic requirements" during a woman's freshman and sophomore year in the belief that they were "the broad and fundamental fields of human knowledge."[75] Brenau revised the core in the 1970s by dropping the foreign language requirement and including additional courses in mathematics and the fine arts.[76] The core curriculum underwent changes again in the 1980s as Brenau added some literature and philosophy courses to offer "exposure to both the Eastern and Western philosophical, historical, and literary traditions."[77] By 1995, the core curriculum had been replaced by "General Education Requirements" that were "designed to develop in all students a broad knowledge base in the liberal arts."[78] The subjects required of students in this new scheme actually resembled in many respects those of the pre-1970 core, right down to the re-introduction of a foreign language requirement for students in the Women's College.[79] By 2012, Brenau maintained "Liberal Education Requirements" for all students that it divided into four "learning portals." These were, "World Understanding, Scientific and Analytic Curiosity, Artistic and Creative Imagination," and "Communication and Language Fluency."[80] Each portal required three or four courses and students generally had many course options to choose from to apply toward any given portal. The remainder of the undergraduate degree requirements consisted of courses in the major area and elective course work.

Strictly speaking, during these many decades in which Brenau created and modified various aspects of its curriculum in deference to S.A.C.S., negotiation did not really occur between the College's students and its faculty and staff. Rather, the Brenau faculty and administration made unilateral decisions about what degrees would be offered at the College and what courses would be required to earn each degree. Brenau solicited little student input during this era simply because it would have been superfluous. Whether or not the students overtly liked or disliked any or all of the changes was incidental; Brenau simply had to implement modifications to gain and then preserve its good standing in the academic world. On this necessity, both the students and the faculty and staff would have been in agreement. Consequently, even though only the faculty and staff created the academic aspect of the Brenau College experience, both the Brenau faculty and staff and the Brenau students sought the same outcome.

Though Brenau personnel determined the vast majority of the character of the curricular life at the College, students were not completely without agency when it came to academics. Essentially, they had the ability to "negotiate with their feet" when Brenau implemented program changes. By simply enrolling in or not enrolling in some program in great numbers, students communicated their needs and desires to the faculty and staff, which would have to respond. The response could come in the form of changes to a program to make it more amenable to students. The response could also be the termination of a program if making it more attractive to students proved to be infeasible. In addition, Brenau would, at times, also try to anticipate student needs and desires and build academic programs accordingly. This chiefly occurred as Brenau established a few vocationally-oriented programs for students in fields like domestic science, music, business, and education. Its aim was to supplement a student's liberal studies with an education that would equip her to enter a profession, such as teaching, stenography, musical performance, or even homemaking. Though some of these vocational kinds of programs existed or would come to exist in a few state normal schools of the day, they were less common in a private white women's college like Brenau.

Such a trade-oriented aspect of higher education was frequently absent in American colleges in the nineteenth century, despite the fact that precedent for it dated far back to the Middle Ages. Historian Alan B. Cobban wrote that medieval society "expected its universities to be vocational institutions responding to vocational needs."[81] Course offerings reflected this. Medieval university students typically studied theology, law, rhetoric, and *dictamen* (essentially, letter writing) to prepare for careers in government (e.g., as administrators, counselors, diplomats, or notaries) or in the church (e.g., as administrators, notaries, or preachers). But universities supported "lesser" intellectual pursuits as well. For example, even at venerable Oxford University, there were "a number of teachers who specialized in the 'useful subjects' which had a direct application to the practical problems of business administration."[82]

Most all early American colleges had little use for the useful subjects. McCandless observed that, "White private and church-affiliated women's colleges seldom offered any professional or vocational courses at all, preferring to emphasize instead a general education that provided 'an enriching heritage for life.'"[83] Such institutions as these had long grounded curricula in classical studies believing that the study of the classics "itself forms the most effectual discipline of the mental faculties."[84] Brenau and the Baptist Female Seminary innovated by following both paths. The institution emphasized the classics in its core and simultaneously offered what amounted to professional coursework in several areas, which set it apart from many similar southern institutions of the time.

Many women studied to become teachers at the Seminary and, later, at Brenau College. In an 1893 interview in the *Atlanta Constitution*, Brenau's president, Professor Van Hoose, related that:

> We have connected with the school a regular Normal Department in which we give girls who wish to teach special advantages. This department is presided over by a graduate of the Peabody Normal, Nashville, and has been of incalculable benefit to young ladies in their efforts to become teachers. I believe that, for its age, the seminary has given to Georgia more enthusiastic teachers than any institution in the state. This fact is rapidly becoming known and we can scarcely supply the demand made upon us for good teachers.[85]

Dr. Van Hoose provided proof of the Seminary's good preparation of teachers by quoting a June 30, 1892, letter from a state education official. He indicated that G. L. Carsson of Carnesville, Georgia, wrote: "I write you this morning simply to tell you of the success of our, or rather your, girls in the pubic examination last Saturday. Eighty persons, many of whom were old teachers, stood the examination. Claudia led the whole number, making a 99 3-7 on her paper. Delia came next, scoring 98, and Cora next, with 97 2-7. Seven of your pupils stood the examination and all of them received first-grade" scores.[86] "The young ladies," the article indicated, "are pupils of the seminary."[87] Other officials were also pleased with the teachers produced by the Seminary. The *Constitution* reported:

> Mr. John T. Wilson, the efficient commissioner of Hall county [sic], says: "For the past five or six years I have examined a large number of girls trained at the seminary. In this number I believe that there are only two who have failed to receive the highest grade certificate. The penmanship, spelling and general manner of expression of these girls is excellent. I have never known one who did not make a successful teacher.[88]

Wilson concluded by saying, "The seminary does the most thorough work of any institution of my acquaintance" in preparing women to become teachers.[89]

Brenau would continue its tradition of teacher preparation in the twentieth century. Around 1910, the College began offering a two or three year "Licentiate of Instruction" (L.I.) degree. The College catalog of that year indicated, "The L.I. degree is a new course which has recently been arranged by the faculty of Brenau. It is intended to be something of a Normal Course, and is especially adapted to young ladies wishing to fit themselves to teach in the public schools of Georgia and other States."[90] The degree changed names to become the "Junior College Teachers Certificate" by 1930, but its requirements essentially remained the same.[91] Though a two-year teaching degree had disappeared by about 1940 as teacher preparation came to require four years of study, Brenau students could still study education. The catalog for that year indicated that students could earn an A.B. with a major in "Psychology and Education."[92] Also by 1940, Brenau had created a Bachelor of Science in Education degree program, wherein students could study "Physical Education or the Biological and Natural Sciences."[93] Examining many editions of Brenau's catalogs revealed that this degree would be discontinued in the late 1940s with the S.A.C.S. reforms, revived in the 1970s, and discontinued again before being revived yet again in the 1980s. Also in the 1980s, Brenau created graduate programs in education. Students would eventually be able to earn M.Ed. degrees, M.A.T. degrees, and Ed.S. degrees in elementary and middle grades education at Brenau or at one of its satellite campuses.

Brenau's early education offerings were innovative for a private women's college in Georgia and rare in the state generally. Only one state-supported school offered teacher training for women at the same time the Georgia Baptist Female Seminary began doing so in the early 1880s. The North Georgia Agricultural College in Dahlonega, Georgia, added a "Normal Department" in 1877. Graduates of the department "could teach in the primary common schools of the state without examination by or license from any board of education or county school commissioner."[94] Amy Thompson McCandless noted that, "In the state of Georgia a women's normal and industrial school had been established in Milledgeville in 1889 and a coeducational normal school in Athens the same year, but there were no public liberal arts institutions for women in the state before World War I."[95] The forerunner of Tift College in Forsyth, Georgia, offered teacher training in the 1890s.[96] Wesleyan College would not offer such training until later and Agnes Scott College had only just been founded in the early twentieth century. The Seminary was already training teachers years before any of these institutions would start doing so.

To some extent, supporting teacher education programs in the late nineteenth century and early twentieth century uplifted women. Historian J. L. Rury wrote that, "The fact that women were restricted to a narrow range of professional career options meant that teaching attracted a disproportionately large number of well-educated and talented women from relatively high-status backgrounds."[97] This lack of career options combined with a growth in teaching jobs led women to the profession. Scholars have observed that schools grew markedly in number beginning in the mid-1800s to accommodate increased immigration and increased urbanization brought on by the Industrial Revolution. This led to an increased demand for teachers.[98] Schools employed women as teachers chiefly because they would work for less than men. Rury wrote that "feminization occurred because school districts were unwilling or unable to pay the rising costs of retaining male teachers as school terms became longer and teaching became less attractive to men."[99] At the same time, educated men found other, more lucrative careers thanks to the changing economy. Male administrators also saw women as being more tractable than men, which may have led to their hiring in greater numbers. Finally, another "rationale for [women's] presence in the classroom replicated the sentimental rhetoric of child nurturance that was being heaped on motherhood."[100] In other words, because women were seen as nurturing, employers believed they would make good teachers of children.

Though doubtlessly appreciated by many, the uplift provided to women from teaching jobs in the late nineteenth century and early twentieth century was imperfect. Rury noted that just because more women came to teach did not translate into more than modestly improved opportunity for women generally. Rury indicated that, "Feminization in teaching did not mean more power or prestige for most women who became teachers."[101] Instead, it contributed to the development of what Rury called a "two-tiered system of employment in education, one in which women did the bulk of the teaching under the supervision of an increasingly authoritative cadre of male administrators."[102] This may have discouraged some women from joining the profession as time progressed. At the same time, as office jobs opened to women in the early 1900s, women moved into those professions, often viewing them as more attractive. Brenau continued to support its teaching programs even in the face of such factors. The College did so because Brenau was committed to educating educators. Brenau trained women teachers from an early date when relatively few other Georgia colleges did and helped women pursue better careers than they otherwise might have been able to pursue.

The fate of Brenau's teaching degrees over time should also not detract from viewing Brenau's early efforts as forward-thinking. To be sure, said degrees came and went at the College, but nothing in Brenau's

Archives suggests that the College ever stopped offering any teaching degree because it doubted the appropriateness of a program. When the institution cut back on its offerings, it apparently did so for other reasons, such as to appease S.A.C.S. This history suggests that Brenau has always believed in preparing women to be teachers even when it was forced to curb that preparation.

Besides leading the way in teacher preparation in Georgia, the Baptist Female Seminary and Brenau College also broke ground in the state around the turn of the century by preparing women to fill office jobs. Historian Jane Bernard Powers wrote that, "commercial education emerged as an important field of study during the latter years of the nineteenth century."[103] The emergence came as a result of America's vast economic growth. Powers noted that "the workplace required an army of clerical workers" and that women often filled these needs as employers deemed them "inexpensive" and "docile" compared to men.[104] By 1913, "offices were thoroughly redeemed as centers of female employment."[105] Some private colleges like Brenau "adapted their curriculum to meet workplace needs"; Brenau did so relatively early.[106]

An 1893 edition of the *Atlanta Constitution* related that, "The Commercial Department which Professors Van Hoose and Pearce propose to establish by the opening of the school year, is a new departure in female colleges."[107] The intention of the Seminary management, the article continued, was "to make the departments of the school so thorough and comprehensive that a young lady may fit herself for any work in life."[108] The reasons for doing this were obvious: "Every one [sic] knows that women are today filling hundreds of places whose duties have heretofore been performed by men. Lady bookkeepers, stenographers, typewriters, etc., are to be found everywhere."[109] Though such jobs were everywhere, training for them was scarce in women's colleges. The *Constitution* indicated that, "For want of a thoroughly equipped business department in our female colleges, ladies desiring to perfect themselves in these branches have been compelled to attend the business colleges of Atlanta and other cities."[110] The article asserted that:

> It is proposed to organize a commercial department at the seminary, equipped with every known faculty for teaching stenography, typewriting, bookkeeping, etc., practically and invite young ladies to come here, where they can have all the surroundings and influence of a pleasant home, and obtain the same advantages at about half the cost of a course at the average city business college. A large room is being furnished with all appliances and conveniences for such a course, and a gentleman, a graduate of one of the best commercial schools, will be in charge of the department.[111]

The article concluded that, "The cost of a business course will be much less than that usually paid, while the instruction will be of the highest character."[112]

Students could continue to study some aspects of business at Brenau at the turn of the twentieth century. The *Atlanta Constitution* reported in 1904 that:

> Brenau maintains a business department in which bookkeeping is thoroughly taught. The students become familiar with all the work of a bookkeeper in a business establishment, learning to handle properly all forms of business correspondence and the meaning of checks, drafts, bills of lading, invoices, receipts, notes, etc. Stenography and typewriting are also taught.[113]

The article indicated that, "Many young ladies who have mastered those useful branches of an education in business methods at Brenau have good positions."[114] In addition to bookkeeping, the College offered courses in shorthand, spelling, punctuation, reporting, typing, and stenography. Brenau continued to claim that stenographers, in particular, were in very high demand. To meet this demand, the catalog went so far as to indicate that, "Rooms will be opened in the city in addition to the department at the College and to accommodate a large and increasing demand for instruction in the commercial department, young men and young women will be admitted to these classes."[115] Long a women's college, Brenau seemed willing to get into the business of educating men in business.[116]

Examining contemporary advertisements in several newspapers placed by other educational institutions in the Deep South revealed that the Baptist Female Seminary and, later, Brenau College had few peers when it came to offering a business course around the turn of the twentieth century. The *Macon Telegraph* reported in 1887 that, "The addition of stenography, typewriting and telegraphy to the curriculum of Wesleyan Female College...has been made and the teachers in these departments secured." [117] And, over a decade later, a Montgomery advertisement for the Judson Institute for young ladies in Alabama indicated that school offered business courses.[118] Yet, no other women's college in Brenau's region (such as Agnes Scott or Shorter College) ever advertised bookkeeping, stenography, or similar programs around the turn of the century. Brenau filled an uncommon niche as it sought to enable women to obtain comfortable and fairly well-paying white-collar positions.

Although Brenau's early business offerings may have been uncommon, they were not long-lived. Brenau ceased to advertise these programs or mention them in its catalogs by about 1910. Brenau probably discontinued its early programs simply because of competition that eventually did emerge and not because of any erosion in the belief that the programs benefited women. Beginning in the twentieth century, secretarial trade schools grew in numbers and size throughout the country, including in Georgia.[119] These schools could offer women adequate (if not collegiate) training to enter office environments cheaper and closer to home than could Brenau. Brenau likely folded its programs as students chose to enroll in such trade schools in increasing numbers.

Business studies would eventually return to Brenau. In the 1940s, Brenau offered a two-year certificate in "Secretarial Studies." To earn the certificate, students took a year of courses in the College in such subjects as English, modern languages, and history and then took a year of courses

The History of Academics at Brenau 141

on typing, shorthand, stenography, office methods, dictation, and the like.[120] Beginning in 1950, Brenau taught these business-related courses through a department of "Commerce."[121] Brenau offered the certificate for some time, even during the restructuring period in which the College had eliminated all but its Bachelor of Arts degree. In the 1980s, Brenau began offering degrees dedicated to business. A Bachelor's degree in Business Administration came first and would eventually be followed by an M.B.A. degree beginning in the 1990s. In modern times, these ubiquitous degrees and the College's certificate could not be considered novel. Yet, although they are today fairly commonplace, Brenau's earliest efforts at business education were not.

Also uncommon around the turn of the last century in Georgia were Brenau's offerings in domestic science. Barbara Miller Solomon wrote that, "in the 1900s home economics gained a solid place as an academic offering" in colleges.[122] This gain "derived from the interest of students" as college officials responded to their desires to acquire practical skills.[123] The movement for home economics study was not without detractors. Feminist educators saw this as a setback as they believed women would gravitate to "Home Ec." departments and not study other disciplines, which did occur to some degree. Also, colleges with home economics departments often relegated female academics to those departments regardless of their credentials, as was the case of one woman historian Solomon described. Still, student demand (quite probably stoked by parental and social views) won out in places like Brenau.

By 1904, the *Atlanta Constitution* reported of Brenau that, "The college believes that its highest duty and privilege is to fit its girls to become homemakers; to know every duty pertaining to the care of a well ordered home, and to this end it has established its department of Domestic Science."[124] College officials believed that, "Brenau's ideal woman is one who is not only well educated from a literary or musical standpoint, but who can, when occasion demands, make a garment, cook a meal, or keep a home in beautiful order."[125] Consequently, the Department of Domestic Science taught Brenau women "to cook, sew, receive and dispense homelike hospitality."[126] Times demanded that a woman of good standing have such knowledge. Brenau contended that, "In this day of poor help such instruction is greatly needed and it is believed that the department will soon become one of the most popular and prominent in the college."[127]

Indeed, even prior to this prediction, the Domestic Science department had already garnered attention. The *Constitution* reported in 1903 that:

> The school of domestic science at Brenau College is growing rapidly in interest and is commanding attention under the able management of Miss Estelle Allen, of Atlanta, who is a graduate of the Oread Institute, Worcester, Mass. Special zeal is evidenced by the Brenau students of the cooking classes. They are taught first the chemistry of foods and the principles underlying the cookery.[128]

Brenau students applied what they learned in their "frequent and instructive lectures."[129] The *Constitution* indicated that, "After taking the course in cooking, both from a practical and theoretical standpoint, the girls frequently entertain their friends in the city at breakfast, lunch or dinner, some acting as hosts, while others prepare and serve the meal."[130] Brenau considered each of these occasions to be a "pleasant feature of the school" and "a social evening" when outside friends of the class were "invited to come in and test the good things to eat as prepared by the students."[131] Domestic science students entertained in the mornings as well. The *Constitution* reported that:

> It is a matter of college interest that the cooking class is soon to serve a breakfast to a limited number of friends. The breakfast is to be planned, prepared and served by the girls of the class. The delightful menu selected will be all the more appetizing when served by dainty misses in their white aprons, caps and cuffs.[132]

Classes in the Domestic Science department were "conducted in a cottage adjoining the college, which is furnished with every convenience that goes to make the study a delightful pursuit."[133] In other words, Brenau students had their own "model home" to work in. [134]

By 1910, Brenau offered a degree called a "B.D." (a "Bachelors of Domesticity") for that "large class of girls who desire to spend two or three years in college to fit themselves for the duties of society and the home."[135] Brenau envisioned that the course of study for this degree "will be planned with special reference to a preparation for the life which is distinctly womanly."[136] Consequently, "Household Economics" and "Child Study" were part of the B.D. curriculum. Officials acknowledged that the majority of Brenau graduates would work in the home and asserted that if "a college for women has any practical mission at all, that mission must be the preparation of its students for the kind of life which circumstances will necessarily determine for them."[137] Over time, Brenau upgraded its model home and its domestic science kitchen laboratory to prepare students for this life. (See Figure 14.) Students could continue to take a turn at doing such things as "planning menus and color schemes, inviting guests, marketing, keeping accounts, apportioning work, laying the table for formal and informal meals, and general entertaining."[138] Importantly, though, Brenau stressed that its aim was *not* "to train cooks, dressmakers, etc." but, rather, to train ladies who expected "to require the services of cooks and dressmakers."[139] Clearly, the College sought to prepare women for not just any home, but rather for upper-class homes —assuredly white—that could afford to hire "help."

Though home economics thrived early on at Brenau, the subject failed at other nearby women's liberal arts colleges around the same time. McCandless wrote that, "Converse College offered home economics as early as 1914," but that in 1927, "all home economics courses were discontinued."[140] She continued, writing that "Home economics suffered a similar fate at Agnes Scott in Georgia."[141] As early as 1921, the president of Agnes Scott had proposed to its board of trustees to establish "a

Department of the Home."[142] In 1934, J.R. McCain, the college's next president, supported the establishment of a department of the home where students could take courses in child psychology, nutrition, and household budgeting, among others. Neither the faculty nor students at Agnes Scott seemed overly enthusiastic about McCain's plans, so the school continued to offer only a traditional bachelor's degree. By contrast, by 1930, Brenau students who completed sixty-six hours of course work that included courses like "Cookery" and "Dietetics" and "Household Physics" and who satisfied all other requirements for the A.B. degree would be granted a "Home Economics Certificate" in addition to the baccalaureate.[143] By 1940, as one of its bona fide four-year degrees, Brenau offered a "course leading to the A.B. degree with [a] major in Home Economics."[144]

Curiously, by around 1950, Brenau students could no longer earn a Bachelors of Domesticity as the degree had been discontinued. They could still major in home economics and choose from among about a dozen courses to use as electives in their program.[145] At first blush, this discontinuation might seem somewhat odd given the widespread assumption that the popularity of domesticity actually increased in post-war America. In light of this, one would think that Brenau would not want to eliminate a rare degree that focused on the subject.[146] It is likely that Brenau eliminated this and some other degree programs so as to focus on its liberal arts subjects in an effort to appease S.A.C.S. Whatever the case, home economics remained a major option at the College even into the 1970s.[147] Indeed, judging by increases in course offerings relating to home ec., the major grew in popularity. Again, this timing was somewhat ironic as the increase in popularity coincided with the rise of the quite progressive modern women's rights movement, which generally sought to liberate women from the confines of the home. At any rate, home economics would remain a major at Brenau for some years before being dropped again by the twenty-first century. Although Brenau would ultimately discontinue its domestic science programs as times changed, the College's initial decision to offer such programs was, for the time and place, conspicuous for a Georgia women's college.

Among Georgia's several women's colleges, white and black, public and private, Brenau was among the first—if not the first—to offer degree programs for women in education, commercial studies, and/or domestic science. Thinking these fields appropriate areas of study for young women in the late nineteenth and early twentieth centuries, Brenau's faculty and administration sought to prepare women for work or homemaking. Though the longevity and success of each of these programs would vary, what seems constant over time is the College's interest in offering young women the option to pursue vocationally-oriented education alongside its more traditional liberal arts courses. From 1950 until 1965, Brenau catalogs described what the College referred to as "career courses." The description read:

> While Brenau continues to be a standard Liberal Arts college, with no lessened emphasis on the classical A.B. degree, career courses may be worked out in the following fields: art, physical education, speech (including dramatic arts and radio broadcasting), secretarial science, sociology and economics, journalism and advertising, music, home economics and nutrition and science preparatory to the field of laboratory technician.
>
> Accredited and recognized majors may now be taken in speech, music, home economics, physical education, and science. The other career courses may be pursued as electives, equivalent to a second major. In all of these fields, Brenau offers enough electives so that a student, while completing her major, may still take enough 'career work' to qualify her either for graduate work in that field or for some more immediate, practical use.[148]

The College noted that, "Out of the 120 hours needed for graduation, 72 must be taken in fulfillment of requirements for the A.B. degree, including a major in one of the approved fields" and that "the remaining 48 hours may be taken by the student as electives and concentrated in the student's desired career field, with a vocational emphasis."[149] Beginning in the 1958–1959 school year, Brenau added another vocationally-oriented program in the form of a degree in medical technology. Earning this degree required completing three years of course work and then spending a final year working as a trainee in the Hall County Memorial Hospital in Gainesville.[150] In 1960, Brenau created in cooperation with the hospital the Hall County School of Nursing.[151] Initially consisting of "36 consecutive months of intensive training," this program would eventually transition to a baccalaureate degree and, by 2012, graduate several dozen nurses a year.[152]

Though nothing in the Archives indicates Brenau officials consulted with students in developing these programs, students did get to participate in negotiations for the programs' futures—at least after a fashion. Because student enrollment over time largely determined a program's success or failure, students could, in a sense, negotiate with the faculty and staff over the academic character of Brenau by "voting with their feet." Generally speaking, the more receptive students were to a program, the more it became entrenched as a part of Brenau's academic life.

One firmly entrenched component of academic life at Brenau has always been the fine arts. Many women's colleges have historically showcased terrific fine arts programs; Brenau is no exception. The College's early offerings for students studying music, dance, the visual arts, and elocution (i.e., public speaking or theater), were quite good—perhaps among some of the strongest in the region as Brenau maintained a large and active conservatory in the late nineteenth century and early twentieth century. The *Atlanta Constitution* identified Brenau's conservatory with glowing terms. It reported that, "Another great feature of the seminary is the Conservatory of Music, which, under the direction of Professor C. J. Wallace, has become one of the best known and most popular music schools in the entire south. The course is regularly graded and is as high as that of the New England Conservatory and other northern institutions."[153] In an interview published in the *Constitution*, Professor Van Hoose described the Conservatory:

> We have a music department unsurpassed and hardly equaled in the southern states. To obtain a diploma from the conservatory, a pupil must study and thoroughly master all the principles of theory, harmony, thorough bass, etc., and be able to write a melody of two strains, or thirty-two measures, from a given theme of four measures. The pupil is also thoroughly grounded in all the principles of orchestration. She must be able to arrange a given theme for ten instruments; this is where the principles taught in theory, harmony, etc., are put into practice. The idea that anyone who can play well can [not] teach well is an exploded one, and those teachers who understand the science of music are rapidly taking precedence over those who know only how to execute. I simply state a fact when I say that the conservatory is unable to supply the demand made upon it for teachers. Our course is everywhere recognized as thorough and complete and people appreciate the good work we do.[154]

The *Constitution* went on to describe the "Full Orchestra" that worked in connection with the Conservatory. The orchestra was comprised of "some twenty-five or thirty pieces, consisting of cornets, clarinets, violins, piccolos, trombones, flues, drums, etc."[155] For a time, it was apparently unique: "As far as we have been able to discover," Van Hoose related, "this is the largest female orchestra in the United States."[156] In addition to its orchestra, the Seminary could boast of a reputable department of voice grounded in "the pure Italian school."

Some of Brenau's conservatory faculty members were quite accomplished, especially in music. The 1900 college catalog devoted several pages to reprinting short newspaper articles that lauded performances given by Brenau's voice and instrumental instructors.[157] Brenau also took pains to relate the credentials of several of those faculty members in advertisements and stressed that the College's principle teachers had been trained abroad. A 1904 article in the *Atlanta Constitution* trumpeted,

"Virtually all of the faculty members in Brenau's music and voice departments were trained in Europe. Several attended the Royal Conservatory in Leipsic [sic] and one attended the Royal Conservatory in Stuttgart."[158]

Like its music faculty, Brenau's early facilities for musical study seemed ample. The College had dozens of pianos in many practice rooms. Brenau also trumpeted that, "No other institution in the south, so far as we know, can boast of being the possessor of two pipe organs."[159] Brenau's primary stage for musical, dance, and dramatic performances during the twentieth century was its Pearce Auditorium. Brenau constructed this lavish venue in cooperation with the city of Gainesville, which provided the College with a $10,000 no-interest loan in the 1890s for construction. Builders completed the 720 seat Victorian opera house in 1896. The facility's acoustics have always been exceptional and the auditorium has played host to many prominent performers over the years.[160] Other area women's colleges would wait years to get facilities on a par with Pearce Auditorium.[161]

Many students availed themselves of Brenau's noted faculty and facilities in earning their music degrees at the Conservatory. Students studying music could focus on "Pianoforte, Violin, Organ, Voice, and Theory."[162] To obtain a Mus.B. (i.e., a Bachelor of Music) degree from the Conservatory, the 1900 catalog indicated that a pupil must have "completed a literary course equivalent to that required to obtain our B.L. degree [the "Bachelor of Letters," Brenau's literary degree] when the applicant may be eligible [for] the degree Associate in Music."[163] This would have been a very rigorous program. Brenau expected students to work in the collegiate courses for the B.L. (i.e., history, math, English, etc.) while simultaneously devoting many hours of study and practice to their conservatory courses. The catalog published the names and compositions of famous composers that Brenau expected students to master in each year of study. Many were quite challenging. A sample from an advertised performance in the *Atlanta Constitution* of December 20, 1903, shows how varied and advanced selections could be. (See Figure 15.)

Brenau's conservatory continued to garner praise in the nineteen-teens. An encyclopedia devoted to Georgia said of Brenau in 1917, "Its musical conservatory in particular, is said to be the largest conservatory in the South in the number of professors engaged, students in attendance, and extensiveness of equipment."[164]

Conservatory instruction remained focused on piano and certain orchestral instruments. By now, though, the Conservatory also offered a course "arranged for those intending to prepare themselves thoroughly for the profession of teaching music."[165] The Conservatory continued to offer the Mus.B. with performance emphases in piano, voice, violin, and organ. Also, the Conservatory required its music and voice students to gain stage experience by playing in periodic recitals. According to summaries published in the weekly "Brenau Notes" column of the *Atlanta Constitution*, which ran for many years in the early 1900s, these were numerous and generally very well-attended public performances in Pearce Auditorium.[166] One early group, the Euterpean Club, was "composed of a number of the music pupils" who supported fellow Conservatory students and, at some performances, arranged the musical "programme" themselves."[167] Brenau staged traveling performances of groups like this as well around this time. For example, in 1920, the student newspaper of the University of Georgia, *The Red and Black*, noted of a performance of Brenau's Glee Club in Athens that "The club was far above the standard glee clubs and the voices of the principals and cast were exceptionally fine."[168]

Conservatory students practiced long and hard to prepare for these recitals, efforts not lost on their schoolmates. One former professor at Brenau during the 1940s recalled a tradition that after a young woman gave her senior recital, she would enter the cafeteria for dinner that evening to a standing ovation given by all of the students.[169] Though this was a small gesture, it is telling. The applause signaled nothing less than how students sought to add their imprimatur on an aspect of Brenau academic life that was otherwise entirely the province of the faculty and staff. Students could not set academic requirements respecting performance, but they could support each other as such requirements were met.

Despite the rigors of the requirements to earn a degree in music at the Conservatory, over the years, Brenau graduated students who met them. Some students apparently did more than just meet minimum standards. In the early twentieth century, Brenau's catalog indicated that the institution offered a Bachelor of Music degree to students who met the requirements for the lower degree and completed additional work. Also, exceptional piano students could undertake what amounted to post-graduate study as Brenau offered a seventh-year "University Course" beyond the five or six year normal period of study for the "Collegiate Course."[170]

Brenau's music program would be revised heading into mid-century. The 1930 catalog spoke of the Brenau Conservatory as a separate entity from Brenau College proper, having a separate charter and a separate board of trustees. The catalog indicated, though, that Brenau College students pursuing the A.B. degree were still welcomed to take conservatory work to apply toward their degrees. In addition, the Conservatory continued to offer the Bachelor of Music and bachelor's degrees in other fine arts and continued to make use of courses in Brenau College. The catalog mentioned little more than this about the Conservatory. Where past catalogs had described conservatory course offerings and faculty member qualifications in detail, the 1930s catalog dispensed with this. By 1940, the Conservatory had changed status again. It went from separating from Brenau College to being completely absorbed by it. As the Conservatory had done, Brenau College still maintained robust offerings in the fine arts courses previously governed by the Conservatory. Brenau discontinued offering the Bachelors of Music degree, but many Brenau students still studied music as part of the B.A. curriculum.

After mid-century, articles in the *Alchemist*, the *Atlanta Constitution*, and in other newspapers indicated that Brenau still gave many musical performances and recitals annually as it always had. For example, in

1950 in Daytona Beach, Florida, "The Brenau College Concert Choir of 30 feminine voices opened Music Week at the Bandshell last night before nearly 1,800 persons."[171] In 1958, Barbara Owens "was presented in a voice and piano recital" that "included compositions of Clementi, Bach, Beethoven, Field and Palmgren."[172] In April, 1960, Thelma Clay gave a piano recital that included works by Beethoven, Chopin, and Mendelssohn.[173] Five years later, Carolyn Turpin performed a piano recital that included works by "Bach, Beethoven, Chopin, Fuleihan, Prokofieff, and Liszt," as well as by Mendelssohn.[174] In 1979, the *Alchemist* reported that forty women from Brenau's Choir spent Spring Break touring several European cities and giving recital-like performances.[175]

Complementing these announcements about Brenau's modern musical performances were no pieces reporting on the celebrity of Brenau's music faculty and facilities, articles that had once been commonly published. Still, even decades after the much-praised conservatory ceased to be, Brenau students, faculty and staff members, and the Gainesville community cooperated to promote impressive musical endeavors. In 1978, the Gainesville Symphony Orchestra formed and affiliated with Brenau. It would grow from 36 to 75 members and for years maintain an active performance schedule, typically in Brenau facilities.[176] According to Dr. Burd, the choir, which had long been present at Brenau, became a "phenomenal group" beginning around the late 1990s under the direction of Dr. Michelle Roueché.[177] Under her watch, Brenau choirs were invited performers at "numerous Georgia Music Educators conventions, for Spivey Hall's prestigious concert series in Atlanta, and for two Southern Division conventions of the American Choral Directors Association."[178] (See Figure 16.) Roueché left big shoes to fill at Brenau when she departed in 2011 to become the Director of Choral Studies and Professor of Music at the University of Mary Hardin-Baylor in Texas. In September 2005 Brenau created the Brenau International Opera Center to develop undergraduate and graduate degree programs "in a conservatory-type continuing education curriculum geared to the growth and nurturing of the young operatic singer/actor."[179]

Like music, visual arts have long thrived at Brenau. Early Conservatory visual art students focused on two-dimensional art and worked with charcoal, crayon, pen and ink, and watercolor, in addition to paint. Art students also studied both portraiture and landscape painting under the tutelage of personnel the College touted as being very talented.[180] In 1920, Brenau's art department continued to emphasize drawing and painting (though ceramic work was offered as well) and students now had to study four years to earn a diploma in art.[181] Three-dimensional art courses would eventually be added to the curriculum by mid-century, as later would courses in interior and fashion design. By the twenty-first century, Brenau had developed an extensive library of vintage clothing from the eighteenth, nineteenth, and twentieth centuries to support fashion students.[182] Two exceptional collections comprised the nucleus of this library. The Bete Todd Wages Vintage Clothing Collection, named in honor of its alumna benefactor, holds over five thousand pieces of many origins dating from 1780–1920. Contained in the Princess Lucie Shirazi Jadot-Rops Collection is "a treasure trove of dresses, sportswear, purses and accessories owned by the princess Lucie Jadot Shirazi," the very fashionable daughter of a wealthy Belgian viceroy/railroad magnate who lived through much of the twentieth century, married into royalty with a son of the Shaw of Iran, and co-founded the World Wildlife Fund.[183]

Other than Princess Shirazi's royal couture, what visual art students at Brenau lacked for many years was actual art to scrutinize and gallery space in which to see it displayed. Even though Brenau had offered visual art programs since its inception and by the mid-1990s had even contemplated creating a dedicated satellite campus devoted exclusively to arts programs in Savannah, the College owned little visual artwork of any renown until the late 1980s.[184] One of the most visible contributions President Burd made to Brenau was to expand the institution's permanent visual art collection. In a 2000 interview with *Georgia Trend* magazine, Dr. Burd noted, "When I arrived here, I was disappointed that an institution with so fine a reputation in the arts had so [little] art—even by students— hanging on the walls."[185] To change this, with the support of the Brenau

Board of Trustees, Dr. Burd placed advertisements in *The Wall Street Journal* and *The New York Times* asking for art donations. He also secured the help of Leo Castelli, a world-renowned art dealer, to grow the College art collection.[186] To reap tax breaks, wealthy art patrons responded.

The first significant piece of artwork Dr. Burd acquired was a still life by William Merritt Chase.[187] Other donations followed. Major works in the collection would eventually include "early oil paintings by Cézanne and Renoir, watercolors by Delacroix, pre-Columbian artifacts, a large oil painting by Anna Elizabeth Klumpke, sculptures by Jean Arp, Clyde Connell, William King and Maria Artemis, a gouache by Amelia Peláez and prints by Jasper Johns."[188] By 2012, Brenau had amassed a collection of over 6000 pieces that included works by Robert Rauschenberg, Roy Lichtenstein, James Rosenquist, Andy Warhol, and Darryl Pottorf with an estimated value of several million dollars.[189]

To display its world-class visual art, Brenau needed gallery space. Prior to 1985, student and faculty member work "was presented informally in various buildings on campus."[190] Dr. Burd established the Brenau University Galleries in 1986. By 2012, three separate exhibition spaces on the Gainesville campus comprised the Galleries: The President's Gallery located in the upstairs lobby of Pearce Auditorium; the Sellars Gallery located on the first floor of the Simmons Visual Arts Center; and The Leo Castelli Art Gallery, located on the first floor of the John S. Burd Center for the Performing Arts.[191] Once established, the Galleries began attracting prominent artists, scholars, and critics for exhibitions and events, as well as hundreds of schoolchildren each year as part of an award-winning museum education program.[192] The Galleries also served to greatly enrich the experience of Brenau's students studying art appreciation or studio arts.

As was the case with visual arts, Brenau has supported study in some of the more physical fine arts (such as drama and, later, dance) for many years. In the institution's earliest days, drama was known as "elocution" or "oratory." Elocution students at Brenau in 1900 studied such topics as gesturing, dramatic interpretation, Shakespeare, speech, and even anatomy to become better actresses. These students also took many courses in "physical culture" (roughly akin to modern physical education, albeit of a much more demure variety) to prepare themselves for the rigors of stage work. By 1910, oratory students at Brenau Conservatory could earn a Bachelor's of Oratory degree. One-fourth of the requirements for the degree were "Literary Interpretation and Expression" whereas another quarter were divided among English (mostly) and mathematics.[193] As in 1900, oratory students continued to take more physical education than other Brenau students. Beyond this, Brenau's general catalog of 1910 said little about the school of oratory. Instead, the College instructed interested parties to write for a publication focusing on Brenau's dramatics in particular. Brenau's conservatory continued to offer the four-year diploma in art and the B.O. degree in 1920.[194] That degree would be discontinued around 1940, about the time the College absorbed the Conservatory and the curriculum changed to focus on the A.B. degree.

As early as 1903, the school's Cushman Club, which was named for Charlotte Cushman, a famous actress of the nineteenth century, entertained the Gainesville area with organized productions and supported Brenau drama students.[195] The College began putting on plays in the early twentieth century, such as "As You Like It" in 1905 and "Twelfth Night" in 1907.[196] Drama student recitals were also common over the years.[197] A 1930 edition of the *Alchemist* lauded Nonie Clark's senior recital and said that she "very charmingly portrayed the characters of 'The Makropoulos [sic] Secret.'"[198] A 1935 edition of the *Alchemist* published write-ups congratulating three seniors on their recital performances and mentioned that each girl played all of the parts in the play she selected.[199] In 1943, "Miss Jean Drane...was presented in the first speech recital of the year last week at the college Theater Workshop."[200] Opulent performances would continue to be offered for decades.[201] In 1950, Brenau's speech department planned to present "Alice in Wonderland" and "Watch on the Rhine," as well as a Shakespearean play.[202] In 1960, the *Alchemist* reported that Brenau staged a production of "Sorry, Wrong Number," which required an unusually large number of light and sound effects.[203] In 1970, the *Alchemist* indicated that the College put on "My Fair Lady," which was a joint effort on the part of the music and drama departments.[204] Drama generally thrived at Brenau because of faculty member and, more importantly, student support. An early article in the *Alchemist* reflected this appreciation for dramatics at the College when a student declared, "We get entertainment fully as good as a lot of professional work seen on the state in Atlanta...and we get in cheap, girls!"[205]

Various editions of the student newspaper from the 1940s, 1950s, and 1960s suggest that drama at Brenau soldiered on through much of the mid-twentieth century as students and faculty members staged popular performances regularly. In 1979, drama at the College underwent a renaissance. That year, the administrations and faculties of Brenau and of Gainesville College (a two-year liberal arts college in Oakwood, Georgia, near the city of Gainesville) combined forces to create The Gainesville Theatre Alliance. The collaborative venture expanded and improved Brenau's already strong dramatics program. The G.T.A. was more than an academic theater program; it was a semi-professional performance company. Talented guest artists—some even with experience on Broadway—frequently performed with and provided valuable coaching to G.T.A. students in several performances each year. (See Figure 17.) By 2007, the Alliance had established an endowment of over $400,000 and a children's theater. Also by 2007, two of G.T.A.'s many performances ("The Heir Transparent" and "The Scarlet Pimpernel") had achieved national recognition. Both plays beat out over 600 other entries from colleges and universities around the country to place in the top ten of the American College Theater Festival in the years they were performed. The Alliance has enjoyed great personnel stability, having had only two directors in its 26 year history: Ed Cabell, who led the organization from 1979–1989, and Jim Hammond, who began directing GTA in 1990. By 2012, Hammond supervised over a dozen full-time staff and faculty members. Also by this year, G.T.A. had developed a full prop and costume shop and it performed many of its productions in Gainesville's Burd Center, an opulent and spacious arts facility built in 2002.[206]

Dance has been a prominent art form at Brenau for decades. The Conservatory and, later, the College have taught several dance styles over the years, including ballet, tap, jazz, and modern. Campus dance groups such as Tau Sigma, a national dance honor society, frequently held recitals. For example, in 1950, the group gave a performance of "New York City." For this recital, Brenau's dancers did numbers that corresponded to several of the Big Apple's colorful ethnic neighborhoods.[207] Even though the College has offered many dance courses, supported organizations devoted to dance, and held dance recitals for decades, Brenau women could not major in any type of dance until relatively recently. Prior to 1978, Brenau housed its dance courses and students in its physical education department. In that year, Brenau began offering bachelors of arts degrees in "Ballet Pedagogy" and "Ballet Performance." The College required students to take a minimum of forty-five hours in dance classes and also required participation in a professional dance company to earn a dance degree.[208]

Dance at Brenau and in the north Georgia area benefitted immensely from the coming of Diane Callahan to Gainesville in the late 1960s. Callahan was a very accomplished professional dancer who had studied under several imminent dance instructors and choreographers, including Russian-born prima ballerina Alexandra Danilova and George Balanchin, who co-founded the New York City Ballet.[209] As a young woman, Callahan toured Central America, Europe, and Asia with the well-respected Ballet Nacional de Cuba before joining the San Francisco Ballet as a soloist. She went on to serve as a principal dancer with the Atlanta Ballet before relocating to Gainesville where she founded the Gainesville School of Ballet in 1969. In 1974, Callahan founded the Gainesville Ballet Company. Brenau's most accomplished dance majors have been able to perform with the company or with the Brenau Dance Ensemble, which Callahan also helped to establish. Some of her former students and company members have gone on to perform on Broadway and with several prominent big-city ballet companies.

By 1988, Brenau had added a major in "Dance/Theater," which permitted dance students to study more than just ballet "to prepare the major for professional alternatives in dance."[210] By 1998, Brenau's dance offerings had become much more nuanced. The College offered a bachelor in fine arts degree with majors in dance education, dance pedagogy, and dance performance.[211] It required of all students "command of a broad range of movement idioms coupled with depth in at least two areas of technique," as well as coursework in choreography, production, and dance history.[212] Articles in the *Alchemist* and various photographs from the 1980s and 1990s housed in the Archives show that dance performances and recitals continued to occur regularly throughout these decades.

In 2005, Brenau's dance program became the first at a college or university in the state of Georgia to become accredited by the National Association of Schools of Dance. The Association is the only dance accreditation agency recognized by the U.S. Department of Education and its members have to meet very rigorous standards to earn accreditation. The N.A.S.D. noted in its acceptance letter that, "There are many excellent characteristics of the Brenau University Dance Program."[213] These included "Highly qualified, dynamic, caring, motivated and professional faculty members," "Serious and motivated students," and "supportive administration."[214] By 2012, only two other programs in the state had achieved accreditation: the Atlanta Ballet Centre for Dance Education and the University of Georgia.[215]

Although this chronology of Brenau's Conservatory and fine arts programs shows flashes of exceptional novelty, Brenau was not an unrivalled arts innovator among women's colleges. Many of these institutions have long been strong in the arts. For example, the School of Music of all-women's Converse College in Spartanburg, South Carolina, developed outstanding programs and "received a national rating as a professional school of music" in the early 1900s.[216] Still, though not peerless, the depth and breadth of Brenau's fine arts offerings set the institution apart from many others over the years. Brenau was one of the few private, southern institutions that could offer first-rate artistic training of the sort that could secure the best opportunities for young women.

Although "innovative" could mean many things, it fairly applies to Brenau in its early days. Until just before the mid-twentieth century, the Georgia Baptist Female Seminary and Brenau College offered programs in teacher education, business, home economics, and fine arts that were uncommon, especially for a southern women's college. Still, "uncommon" did not necessarily mean "successful." Student receptivity to these novel programs varied and was generally very modest, except in the case of Brenau's fine arts offerings. The 1930 edition of the *Brenau Bulletin* included a section entitled "Alumnae of the College" in which Brenau published information about each of its graduating classes to-date including what degree or certificate each graduate received. These data revealed the popularity of the College's various programs and may explain why Brenau's innovative non-conservatory programs were generally short-lived.

Enrollment in Brenau's conservatory and fine arts programs had always been quite robust. Several dozen (or more) young women routinely received degrees or certificates in music each year during the first few decades of the twentieth century, which suggests that Brenau's innovative artistic programs were quite popular. By contrast, it is not evident that Brenau's bookkeeping and stenography programs ever truly took off as no student is listed as having received a certificate from the program, though some students apparently did enroll. For example, Brenau's 1910 catalog listed eleven students as being in the "Bookkeeping and Stenography" program.[217] Still, it appears that the program's numbers must have remained small for its brief existence.

According to the 1930 *Brenau Bulletin*, the vast majority of Brenau's non-conservatory students in the first quarter of the twentieth century took A.B. or B.L. degrees rather than pursue one of Brenau's more unique

The History of Academics at Brenau

programs.[218] From 1900 until 1925, Brenau conferred 380 Bachelor of Arts degrees, making the A.B. the institution's most granted degree by far. Another 111 students received the B.L. during this period. None did so after 1914. The College's catalogs indicated that the degree was still offered at Brenau, but was apparently nowhere nearly as popular as the A.B. The same was true for the Bachelor of Science. Although the College offered the degree for many years, only eighteen students earned a B.S. prior to 1909 and none received the degree from 1909 until 1930. The A.B and B.L. degree programs overshadowed Brenau's programs in domestic science and teacher education, but some students still enrolled in these programs. Brenau offered its first teacher education degree, the L.I., from 1907 until 1913, though it had been training teachers since years before. Eighteen students earned the degree during this period. The Domestic Science Certificate was more popular, but still never enrolled many students. Brenau offered the certificate from 1908 until 1922, during which time only 41 students earned it.

Beginning in the late 1920s and into the 1930s, Brenau's more uncommon curricular offerings faded. This culminated in the 1940s when Brenau began offering only a single degree (the Bachelor of Arts) and would be more or less the norm until Brenau expanded its programs as it became a university. Brenau's promotional materials for its earlier programs suggest that the College innovated regionally in the belief that it was uplifting women. Recall that Brenau offered the L.I. and the B.D. degree to women to "fit themselves to teach in the public schools" or to "fit themselves for the duties of society and the home," respectively. Brenau wanted to give women opportunities they might otherwise not have had absent its uncommon programs. Were there other reasons for offering such programs? Perhaps. For example, could the Baptist Female Seminary and Brenau College have made the somewhat unusual moves into vocational training as a means to retain or attract students? Might the institution have created these programs in the belief that doing so would generate more tuition revenue? We can only speculate about the answers to questions like these because insufficient evidence exists to provide more exact claims.

Interestingly, the failure of many of Brenau's unusual programs might have left women better off than they would have been had the programs been widely successful. Despite its good intentions, by offering degrees in fields like teaching and domestic science, Brenau inadvertently reified a pre-war social status quo in America that relegated women to occupying only a few selected and accepted roles in society. McCandless wrote that southern women's colleges like Brenau that embraced the liberal arts "were careful to complement their 'masculine' liberal arts curriculum with a 'feminine' atmosphere conducive to ladylike deportment and cultured elegance." [219] In part, Brenau created this atmosphere through its regionally innovative academic offerings, which were geared toward preparing women students to occupy "suitable" roles in society.

As a case in point, although early on the Baptist Female Seminary and Brenau College prepared women for the suitably feminine role of office worker (to support businessmen with dictating and stenographic skills and the like), the institution offered no courses such as economics, finance, or business or personnel management. Brenau kept with the prevailing view in late nineteenth- and early twentieth-century American society that women should not or could not run businesses, but rather only serve as functionaries to the men who ran them. Consequently, Brenau's programs prepared women to assume only a support role in business. Similarly, Brenau prepared women to teach school, but did not prepare them to become administrators. Consequently, the College contributed, perhaps unwittingly, toward the continued marginalization of women in the field of education by producing no lady principals. Also, Brenau prepared women to perform or teach music, but, as demonstrated by its course offerings, it did not anticipate that they would become leaders of the band. And, finally, with its domestic science offerings, Brenau encouraged women to avoid working outside the house altogether and to embrace fully the traditional woman's spheres of hearth and home.

It would take roughly a hundred years, but Brenau would eventually empower women to lead more extraordinary lives. Starting in the 1970s, Brenau began offering a number of undergraduate and graduate academic programs that gave students access to many careers and not just the few that society had once deemed suitable for women. The College also began reaching out to male and nontraditional students at this time and extended its educational offerings well beyond Gainesville.

Changes began in earnest in 1971 when Brenau "chose to enlarge its constituency" by offering evening classes to nontraditional students—mainly working students and men, by Brenau's definition.[220] Brenau formed a "Community Services Division" to oversee this in "response to rapid growth of the nontraditional student population" in its service area.[221] Some restructuring and a few name changes later, this became the School of Professional Studies and eventually simply the Professional College in 1983. This component of the institution offered "bachelor's degree programs and master's degree programs to men and women who elect to study in the evening or at off-campus locations."[222]

During the 1970s and early 1980s, judging by the catalogs of the Professional College and the Women's College, things like institutional policies, admission standards, and degree requirements respecting undergraduate study were generally the same for the two divisions. The most notable difference between the two entities was that the Professional College supported few undergraduate and no graduate degree programs in the liberal arts. Early on, undergraduates in the Professional College could only major in career-oriented subjects such as education, business, performing arts, social work, and nursing.[223] Early graduate programs focused on master's-level studies in early childhood or elementary education.[224]

By 1986, the Professional College offered undergraduate and some graduate programs at a dozen sites all around Georgia, including Gainesville.[225] The aim was to make higher education accessible. Dr. Burd noted in an interview that, "[Brenau] had started an evening college to address that—there was no question in my mind. And it was a smart move, financially."[226] Dr. Burd also indicated that having "a part of the school in Atlanta" made good sense. "Atlanta," he noted, "was a prime area for doing this because many of the state schools at the time would not do it, they did not feel [establishing an evening and/or weekend college] was academically what they should do."[227] Having a part of the school in other places made sense, too. Brenau had actually operated a satellite campus before in its history. Around 1905, presidents Van Hoose and Pearce opened "Alabama Brenau" on the campus of a failed women's college (the Union Female College) in Eufaula, Alabama.[228] The location never thrived and ceased operations after a few years. Brenau's modern expansion efforts would be far more successful. Dr. Burd indicated that Brenau opened its King's Bay Naval Base campus at the request of the base's commanding officer, who even provided some exceptional facilities for the College to use. Brenau would eventually offer quite-full classes at one time or another in several locations throughout Georgia besides Atlanta and King's Bay, including in Augusta, Norcross, and Waleska.

Student demand had prompted the addition of several new academic programs as well as new academic centers. In addition to its vocationally-oriented degrees, the Professional College now awarded bachelor of science and bachelor of arts degrees to students majoring in general studies as well as in several humanities disciplines, including history, English, and political science.[229] The College also offered elective courses in eleven fields as well.[230] Also by this time, the Professional College permitted students to petition officials to apply up to a year's worth of credit for "experiential learning" toward a degree. Such credit could come from things like military service or from "employment or other life/learning experiences."[231] Graduate degree and course offerings remained occupationally oriented. Beginning in the early 1980s and continuing throughout the decade, the College offered master's degrees in education and business administration.[232]

Even as Brenau began planning for its statewide expansion, up until the 1980s, the College had enjoyed a higher education monopoly on four-year degrees in the Gainesville area. Around this time, rumblings of competition came. The March 11, 1984, edition of the *Atlanta Journal-Constitution* reported that, "Bad blood is boiling in North Georgia because of a proposal by state-run North Georgia College to offer third- and fourth-year business courses at Gainesville Junior College in direct competition with Gainesville's private Brenau College."[233] In a position paper Brenau prepared in 1984, the institution pointed out that the College had a beneficial "economic impact on the Hall County area of over $26 million each year" and that "duplicate course offerings" in its immediate service area would jeopardize the Professional College, which would in turn jeopardize "Brenau as a whole."[234] Brenau's logic may have impressed the powers-that-be. The *A.J.C.* later reported that, "After weeks of name-calling, North Georgia withdrew its request to the Board of Regents."[235] The article noted that, "the issue may re-emerge in the future." It eventually would, and, despite Brenau's reasoning, North Georgia would establish degree programs in business, education, and nursing at the Gainesville College campus by the twenty-first century.

The late 1980s saw continued academic program growth at Brenau. In 1987, Brenau created an Honors Program for its most gifted students.[236] The previous year, Brenau inaugurated the academic innovation that was its Weekend College program, which was a part of the Professional College at Brenau. This was billed as the first such program in the state of Georgia, if not the entire southeast. Though several colleges and universities offered weekend coursework to students, Brenau was the first Georgia institution to enable students to complete all work for a four-year degree—and some graduate degrees—solely via weekend courses. Students in the program could major in several subjects, including business administration and education, and took courses at either Brenau's Gainesville or Atlanta campuses on Friday evening, all day Saturday, and Sunday afternoon. Each course required attending "six four-hour class sessions stretched over a 10 week period," in addition to outside work.[237] The College even offered dormitory space for overnight students studying in Gainesville.

As was the case with the Professional College generally, Brenau created its weekend college program in part in response to its perception of potential student needs. A July 21, 1986, news release prepared by Judy Bolyard Purdy quoted Dr. Burd as saying, "Our purpose in creating the weekend college format is to carry out the objective of the Brenau Professional College, which is dedication to excellence in education with the most convenient and effective formats for the adult learner."[238] Dr. Burd had served as the Dean of the Evening and Weekend College at Lindenwood College in St. Louis, Missouri, and helped to establish the weekend college at that institution.[239] His experience overseeing a similar program in his previous position in St. Louis boded well for establishing an evening and weekend program at Brenau. In addition, Dr. Burd said that Brenau had been fortunate to have on staff Dr. Jack Sites, who he described as "about as creative as any academic I've ever known." Dr. Burd noted that Sites "really worked on the evening and weekend program and got the faculty behind it."[240]

Students who were willing to pay for weekend courses induced Lindenwood, Brenau, and other institutions with similar programs to add weekend college programs to their curricula. This was no mean feat. Purdy's news release indicated that, "Everyone from the librarian to the registrar has had to make changes in the way each performs his or her duties."[241] Student needs induced these often radical changes, which, in a way, suggests that College personnel shared at least some agency with students when it came to shaping academics.

Offerings for nontraditional undergraduate students and graduate students would change at Brenau in the 1990s. By 1993, Brenau had restructured its undergraduate organization. The Professional College had been replaced by the Evening and Weekend Programs division, which operated alongside the Weekend College. The *Brenau Undergraduate and Graduate Catalog* of that year indicated that the two programs "have evolved slightly different core curricular requirements" from those of the Women's College.[242] The difference essentially boiled down to requiring Women's College students to take an additional foreign language course and an additional physical education course.[243] The remaining degree requirements were similar. Depending on the remote site they attended (there were still several campus centers across the state), Evening and Weekend College students could major in education, business administration (including law enforcement), and nursing. By 1993, Brenau no longer sponsored undergraduate majors in the humanities outside of the Women's College, although by 1998 the University would let students take a bachelor's degree in either general studies or liberal studies.[244]

Brenau's graduate division also saw major changes beginning in the 1990s. These had been many years in the making. An "Institutional Self-Study" prepared for the Southern Association of Colleges and Schools in 1984 indicated that Brenau had implemented graduate programs for several reasons. Mainly, the College sought to provide continuing education for both teachers and private sector employees and to offer up-to-date training and programs for its service area.[245] Brenau had created a Graduate Division and offered its first graduate program, a master's degree in elementary education, in 1975. Master's degrees in business and public administration followed in 1977 and 1981.

Even as Brenau personnel crafted the College's graduate degrees, they did so mindful of student and prospective student needs. The development of what would become the Master of Public Administration degree particularly illustrated that Brenau could be responsive to student interests. The Self-Study indicated that the M.P.A. was "designed specifically for in-service students in the public sector who felt that the graduate business program did not meet their needs."[246] Many students switched to the public administration degree program upon its implementation, suggesting that Brenau made a good choice.[247] Both administrative programs catered to the "needs of the community." The 1984 Self-Study indicated that "96 percent of the current students occupy positions in local industry, government, and financial institutions."[248] A handful of other graduate students studied at satellite campuses in such cities as Athens, Augusta, and Rome.[249] By 1985, 447 students had earned graduate degrees from Brenau in programs that enjoyed regional accreditation and that employed several faculty members, many of whom had both terminal degrees and years of work experience.[250]

Increased enrollment is not the only evidence that students were receptive to the College's graduate offerings. Brenau administered a survey to its graduate division alumni and to current students in 1984. The vast majority of the 270 or so respondents praised the flexibility and quality of Brenau's graduate programs. Additionally, of the handful of students who had undertaken graduate study at other institutions, roughly 80% thought Brenau's programs were comparable or stronger to those elsewhere.[251] The College took all of this as evidence that it was, as it desired, meeting "the needs of the working professional."[252] It is likewise evidence that Brenau's students could subtly influence the development of academics in ways they could not have in times past when the faculty taught students what they felt was needed, irrespective of student wants.

In 1992, Brenau College became Brenau University. This occurred as the Brenau Board of Trustees voted to more accurately reflect in name what Brenau had become. According to the University, the name change "reflected the comprehensive programs of study, the diverse student body, new and stricter employment criteria for professors, and the scope of available graduate programs."[253] In the year Brenau acquired university status, its graduate school offered an M.B.A. and an M.Ed. with several areas of specialization.[254]

Another program that suggested that students could influence Brenau's academic offerings emerged a year after Brenau adopted university status. According to the Spring, 2004, edition of *Brenau Magazine*, the University created its Brenau University Learning and Leisure Institute (known as "B.U.L.L.I." or "BULLI") to give the many retirees who called north Georgia home "a place to continue their life-long learning, a place to meet, develop new friendships and expand their knowledge without the constraints and pressures of applications, homework, deadlines, and grades."[255] Initially subsidized by an anonymous donor, by 2004, BULLI would become self-sustaining and even awarded an annual scholarship to a deserving Brenau student.[256] Over the years, BULLI has offered short-term classes on a variety of subjects, including history, fitness, literature, and religion, to name but a few. Classes are taught by members of the Brenau faculty or by subject matter experts drawn from the community. BULLI even fostered several clubs as retirees met and formed interest groups to indulge in favorite pastimes like bridge or chess. The program also found a new cadre of supporters for the University as members volunteered to help out at functions like career day or to serve as research subjects for students in the occupational therapy department. Speaking of the program, one student, Margaret Ellett, said, "BULLI has kept me young."[257] BULLI periodically repeated trips and courses that garnered robust enrollments and eliminated those that did not. Consequently, perhaps more so than any of Brenau's other educational programs, student interests determined precisely what would be taught.

In keeping with the newly-acquired university label, Brenau's graduate offerings continued to grow and evolve after 1992, often in response to student desires. By 2001, to accommodate student demands for convenience, Brenau began offering "a 10-course, 36-semester-hour MBA that [could] be completed online in four semesters."[258] Other online programs would follow, notably in education. Brenau had been offering the education specialist degree for a number of years before it became offered online as well. Besides the staples of business administration and education, other Brenau master's programs that developed in the 1990s and 2000s emphasized the health sciences, such as nursing, occupational therapy, and counseling.

Brenau planners began work on the institution's first doctoral degree in 2008. Approval from the Southern Association of Colleges and Schools to officially become a doctoral degree-granting institution came in December of 2010.[259] This allowed Brenau to launch its Doctor of Nursing Practice program for licensed RNs holding master's degrees in August of 2011.[260] In its first year, thirteen students enrolled in the seven semester doctoral program, which was only the second one of its kind in Georgia.[261] On October 22, 2009, the Brenau University Board of Trustees voted unanimously to name its graduate school after a native of Gainesville whose ancestors had served as trustees for Brenau since the institution's founding. Sidney O. Smith, Jr., continued the family legacy after graduating from Harvard and the University of Georgia School of Law and serving as an attorney and U.S. District Judge. Smith played an important role in the establishment of Brenau's clinical doctorate in nursing.[262]

As of 2012, besides the Ph.D. in nursing, the University planned to offer two other doctoral degrees in adult education and occupational therapy.[263] The addition of these programs was a key component of an ambitious strategic vision adopted by Brenau in late 2011 called "Brenau: 2025." According to its strategic plan, by the year 2025, Brenau would become "an internationally recognized leader in innovative higher education with a unique blend of the liberal arts and professional preparation resulting in accelerated and advanced degrees in areas that meet the essential needs of the 21st century."[264] In response to "demands by students and prospective employers for people to complete better educations in less time than that required in older models," Brenau planned to adopt more accelerated degree programs and distance-learning modalities.[265] The central idea would be to yield undergraduate and graduate students whose education was "extraordinary" and "demonstrably life-changing."

To craft such an experience, Brenau took a multi-faceted approach. It first adopted what it called an "innovative 'Four Portals of Learning' curriculum" for undergraduate students. This would "mix the required content for [a] discipline" with between one and four "liberal arts ingredients" that are world understanding, scientific and analytic curiosity, artistic and creative imagination, and communication and language fluency. Brenau stated that this interdisciplinary curriculum would reduce most students' time-to-degree by "at least one year." Alongside these curricular changes, the University likewise began a "systematic upgrade" of virtually every corner of its Gainesville campus and encouraged more collaborative research between professors and students guided by expert faculty members in interdisciplinary scholarship. Finally, Brenau would greatly encourage study abroad experiences for undergraduates and require undergraduates to develop facility in a second language. At the graduate level, the University resolved to develop "market-driven" programs with "industry-leading potential" in areas such as health sciences and fine & performing arts. Largely thanks to aggressively marketing such programs, Brenau anticipated growing its enrollment "beyond 5,000 students by 2025." [266] At the same time, according to Dr. Southerland, Brenau planned "to limit enrollment in the Women's College to about 1,000 students" to preserve the institution's small-college feel.[267] For all of its programs, Brenau resolved to continue to "attract and support students from diverse social, economic and ethnic backgrounds," including older and working students, with funding where possible.[268]

Whatever their backgrounds and numbers, future students at Brenau will enjoy a wide array of academic offerings to choose from. Whether those students will have a hand in shaping the curriculum as opposed to simply receiving what University personnel disseminate remains to be seen. Modern research suggests that students can offer meaningful input into shaping what they study.[269] Brenau could very well recognize this and give students a seat at the table when it comes to negotiating over academic policies. The products from such interaction might even prove to be as innovative by today's standards as aspects of Brenau's curriculum were in days gone by.

Notes

1. H.J. Pearce, "The Brenau Ideal," http://www.brenau.edu/about-brenau-extraordinary/about-the-campus/ (accessed 27 December 2012).
2. Ibid.
3. "Brenau University Mission Statement," *Brenau University Athletic Department Student Handbook*, http://www.brenautigers.com/f/Student-Athlete_Handbook.php (accessed 25 December 2012).
4. Rigney, *Brenau College 1878–1978*, 24–25.
5. Ibid.
6. Thelin, *History of American Higher Education*, 56.
7. Ibid., 64.
8. Nash, *Women's Education*, 46.
9. Farnham, *Education of the Southern Belle*, 6.
10. Ibid., 25–26.
11. Josiah Carter, "A Day at Brenau," *Atlanta Constitution*, 31 July 1904, sec. C, p. 4.
12. *Catalog* (1900), 21.
13. Ibid., 23. These were stated at one point as being the schools of English, Ancient Languages, Modern Languages, History and Political Science, Mathematics, Physics, Chemistry, Astronomy and Geology, Moral Science, and the school of the Bible and Sacred Literature. The catalog went on to say that Brenau had organized the schools of chemistry, physics, geology, and astronomy into what could probably best be described as a sub-department (though the catalog confusingly referred to it as another "Department"), and added to this group the study of biology. Additionally, the catalog indicated that a school of pedagogy existed to prepare teachers.
14. Ibid.
15. Josiah Carter, "A Day at Brenau," *Atlanta Constitution*, 31 July 1904, sec. C, p. 4.
16. Ibid.
17. Ibid.
18. Ibid.
19. Ibid.
20. Ibid.
21. Ibid.

22. "Brenau College Completes New Buildings, Plans for the New Year," *Atlanta Constitution*, 8 December 1907, sec. A, p. 2.
23. Ibid.
24. Christopher J. Lucas, *American Higher Education: A History* (New York, NY: St. Martin's Press, 1994), 165.
25. Ibid.
26. Ibid., 210.
27. Ibid.
28. Ibid.
29. Ibid.
30. Ibid.
31. Display Advertisement—No Title, *Atlanta Constitution*, 2 July 1905, sec. D, p. 8.
32. Ibid.
33. Ibid.
34. McCandless, *Past in the Present*, 57.
35. Converse may lay claim to being the first *accredited* college to do so as it was "the first college in South Carolina to be admitted to membership in the Southern Association of Colleges and Secondary Schools" in 1912. Jeffrey R. Willis, *Converse College*, 33. Brenau would not achieve S.A.C.S. accreditation until several years later. There is also some evidence suggesting that Hollins College, a women's college in Virginia, may have employed a type of elective system as early as the nineteenth century. However, elective credit was apparently applied toward earning "certificates of graduation," not college degrees. See W. R. L. Smith, *Charles Lewis Cocke: Founder of Hollins College*, (Boston, MA: The Gorham Press, 1921), 107; available at http://www.ebooksread.com/authors-eng/william-robert-lee-smith/charles-lewis-cocke-founder-of-hollins-college-tim/page-6-charles-lewis-cocke-founder-of-hollins-college-tim.shtml (accessed 25 December 2012). Also, an historian of the history of Wesleyan College has noted that, "By 1888, although the elective system had not yet become established, the offerings under the heading 'optional studies' had increased to an even dozen" at the college. Samuel Luttrell Akers, *The First Hundred Years of Wesleyan College, 1836–1936* (Macon, GA: Beehive Press, 1976), 106. In 1897, Wesleyan "adopted the plan of elective courses of study." Ibid., 118. The college offered the BA, the B of Literature, and the B of Science, but it is not clear that courses in art and/or music could count as elective courses in a baccalaureate plan of study. Ibid.

36. Walter Edward McNair, *Lest We Forget: An Account of Agnes Scott College* (Atlanta, GA: Tucker-Castleberry Printing, Inc., 1983), 46.
37. *Faculty Journal* (25 years), 4 November 1941, 247.
38. U.S. Department of Education, "Accreditation in the United States," 30 November 2012, http://www2.ed.gov/admins/finaid/accred/accreditation_pg2.html, (accessed 27 December 2012).
39. Ibid.
40. For more detailed information on the standards for and process of accreditation, see Southern Association of Colleges and Schools Commission on Colleges, "The Principles of Accreditation: Foundations for Quality Enhancement," http://sacscoc.org/pdf/2010principlesofacreditation.pdf (accessed 27 December 2012).
41. Walter Edward McNair, *Lest We Forget: An Account of Agnes Scott College* (Atlanta, GA: Tucker-Castleberry Printing, Inc., 1983), 30.
42. Elizabeth Avery Colton, "Standards of Southern Colleges for Women" *The School Review*, vol. 20, no. 7 (September, 1912):458-475, 459.
43. Willis, *Converse College*, 33.
44. "Copy of new information sent to Southern Ass'n. Sept. 1, 1932," Folder 8 (labeled "SACS Miscellaneous Reports 1928-31 [sic]") in Box 5 of 6 (labeled "Self-Reports"), Brenau University Archives, Gainesville, Georgia.
45. The University of Georgia was accredited in 1909, as was Mercer in 1911 and Emory in 1917. Georgia College and State University was not accredited until 1925. North Georgia College & State University (which became the University of North Georgia in January, 2013) received accreditation in 1935. LaGrange College, Piedmont College, and Oglethorpe College (now Oglethorpe University) were all founded in the nineteenth century, but did not receive accreditation until 1946, 1965, and 1950, respectively. Southern Association of Colleges and Schools Commission on Colleges, "Membership Directory," http://sacscoc.org/search.asp (accessed 27 December 2012).
46. "A Report to the Board of Trustees of Brenau College (Monday, May 28, 1945)," Dr. Crudup Files, Box 34 of 40, Folder 10, p. 3, Brenau University Archives, Gainesville, Georgia. To try to placate students and parents, Brenau even produced a pamphlet in 1942 entitled "Accreditation of Colleges" that essentially said that the SACS accreditation process was deeply flawed and that state accreditation (which Brenau had) should be the true measure by which the quality of a college should be gauged. Bre-

nau College, "Accreditation of Colleges," *Brenau Bulletin* (insert), vol. 33, no. 5, 1 March 1942, Brenau University Archives, Gainesville, Georgia.
47. Josiah Crudup, "Report to the Board of Trustees of Brenau College (Monday, May 28, 1945)," p. 3.
48. Ibid., 3-4.
49. Leigh Ann Ripley, "Introduction to the Gainesville Tornado Disaster of 1936," Digital Library of Georgia, 30 June 2008, http://dlg.galileo.usg.edu/tornado/about/history.php (accessed 27 December 2012).
50. "Letter from Walter Yust, Editor, Encyclopedia Britannica, to Dr. Josiah Crudup inquiring about the vital statistics of the college for publication in the Encyclopedia's 1950 Britannica's Book of the Year, dated October 21, 1949." Available in Registrar Files, Box 1 of 1, Folder 6, Brenau University Archives, Gainesville, Georgia. By comparison, the endowment of Sweet Briar College, another southern women's college had a "book value of $995,827 in 1950–51." Sweet Briar College, *Bulletin of Sweet Briar College: State of the College* (Sweet Briar, VA: Sweet Briar College, 1960), 20; available at http://www.archive.org/stream/bulletinofsweetb434swee/bulletinofsweetb434swee_djvu.txt (accessed 27 December 2012). Also, Wesleyan College had maintained an endowment fund since the late 1800s. Samuel Luttrell Akers, *The First Hundred Years of Wesleyan College, 1836–1936* (Macon, GA: Beehive Press, 1976), 110.
51. Johnny Vardeman, "Hunts of Dixie-Hunt Hotel became wealthy, generous Hall Countians," *Gainesville Times*, 18 June 2006, http://archive.gainesvilletimes.com/news/stories/20060618/opinion/104196.shtml (accessed 27 December 2012).
52. Brenau College, *Institutional Self-Study, 1969–1971*,101.
53. "Enrollment of Brenau College." Memorandum prepared by Ella D. Winfield, undated, but likely prepared in 1950, the last year of data provided in the memo; Folder 6 in Box 1 of 1 (labeled "Registrar Files"), Brenau University Archives, Gainesville, Georgia.
54. Josiah Crudup, "A Report to the Board of Trustees of Brenau College (Friday, September 23, 1960)," Dr. Crudup Files, Box 29 of 40, Folder 5, Brenau University Archives, Gainesville, Georgia, p. 9.
55. Ibid.
56. Ibid.
57. Dr. John S. Burd, interview by author, tape recording, Gainesville, Georgia, 23 September 2010.
58. Ibid.
59. Ibid.

60. "U.S. and Canadian Institutions Listed by Fiscal Year 2009 Endowment Market Value and Percentage Change* in Endowment Market Value from FY 2008 to FY 2009," National Association of College and University Business Officers and Commonfund Institute, 2010, http://www.nacubo.org/Documents/research/2009_NCSE_Public_Tables_Endowment_Market_Values.pdf (accessed 28 December 2012).
61. Crudup, "A report to the Board of Trustees (May 28, 1945)," p. 4.
62. Ibid.
63. Dr. John S. Burd, interview by author, tape recording, Gainesville, Georgia, 23 September 2010. Speaking of faculty members he hired, besides being good educators, Dr. Burd recalled in particular that, "The faculty was also very good with dealing at the undergraduate level with the parents."
64. Josiah Crudup, "A Report to the Board of Trustees of Brenau College (May 31, 1957)," Dr. Crudup Files, Box 35 of 40, Folder 5, p. 4, Brenau University Archives, Gainesville, Georgia.
65. Josiah Crudup, "A Report to the Board of Trustees of Brenau College (May 27, 1949)," Dr. Crudup Files, Box 34 of 40, Folder 10, p. 10, Brenau University Archives, Gainesville, Georgia.
66. Crudup, "Report to the Board of Trustees (May 31, 1957)," p. 4.
67. *Catalog* (1949), 43.
68. *Catalog* (1953), 43.
69. *Catalog* (1965), 39.
70. *Brenau College Bulletin 1973–1975, Annual Catalogue*, vol. 85, no. 2 (June 1973): 44–45.
71. *Catalog* (1984–1986), 74.
72. Ibid.
73. *Brenau University 2001–2002 Undergraduate and Graduate Catalog* (Gainesville, GA: Brenau College, 2001): 68–69. Hereafter, references to this source are indicated as "*Catalog* (2001)."
74. Brenau College, *Institutional Self-Study, 1979 – 1981*, 42.
75. *Catalog* (1950), 42.
76. Ibid., 42-43.
77. Ibid., 41.
78. *Brenau College Catalog* (Gainesville, GA: Brenau College, 1995), 66; Brenau University Archives, Gainesville, Georgia. Hereafter, references to this source are indicated as "*Catalog* (1995)."
79. Ibid., 68.

80. *Brenau University Undergraduate and Graduate Catalog 2008–2009*, v. 124 (Gainesville, GA: Brenau University, 2007), 70; Brenau University Archives, Gainesville, Georgia. Hereafter, references to this source are indicated as "*Catalog* (2008)."
81. Cobban, *The Medieval English Universities*, 15.
82. Ibid., 224.
83. McCandless, *Past in the Present*, 55.
84. *Reports on the Course of Instruction in Yale College: By a Committee of the Corporation and the Academical Faculty* (New Haven, CT: H. Howe, 1828): 6-7.
85. "The Georgia Female Seminary and Conservatory of Music," *Atlanta Constitution*, 6 August 1893, p. 18.
86. Ibid.
87. Ibid.
88. Ibid.
89. Ibid.
90. *Catalog* (1910), 15. According to historian Ronald Butchart, most contemporary normal schools that trained teachers required three years of study. Ronald Butchart, email message to author, 12 November 2007.
91. *Catalog* (1929), 48.
92. *Catalog* (1939), 56.
93. Ibid., 52.
94. Camillus J. Dismukes, "North Georgia College Under the Trustees," *The Georgia Historical Quarterly*, vol. 56, no. 1 (spring, 1972): 94. In 1883, the N.G.C. trustees claimed that the college sent "more teaching force into the schools of the State than all the [other] colleges of the State combined."
95. Amy Thompson McCandless, "Maintaining the Spirit and Tone of Robust Manliness: The Battle against Coeducation at Southern Colleges and Universities, 1890–1940," *NWSA Journal*, vol. 2, no. 2 (spring, 1990): 199–216, 207.
96. Starr Miller, "Was This Voice First to Question the Value of Homework?" *The Clearing House*, vol. 29, no. 6 (February, 1955): 359.
97. J. L. Rury, "Who became teachers? The social characteristics of teachers in American history," in D. Warren, ed., *American Teachers: Histories of a Profession at Work* (New York, NY: Macmillan, 1989), 41.
98. See Carl F. Kaestle, *Pillars of the Republic: Common Schools and American Society, 1780–1860* (New York, NY: Hill and Wang, 1983) for an overview

of the emergence of public schooling and the profession of teaching in the nineteenth century.
99. Ibid., 27.
100. Madeleine R. Grumet, *Bitter Milk: Women and Teaching* (Amherst, MA: University of Massachusetts Press, 1988), 84.
101. Rury, "Who became teachers?", 29.
102. Ibid.
103. Jane Bernard Powers, *The "Girl Question" in Education: Vocational Education for Young Women in the Progressive Era* (Washington, DC: Falmer Press, 1992), 39.
104. Ibid., 40.
105. Ibid.
106. Ibid., 39.
107. "The Georgia Female Seminary and Conservatory of Music," *Atlanta Constitution*, 6 August 1893, p. 18.
108. Ibid.
109. Ibid.
110. Ibid.
111. Ibid.
112. Ibid.
113. Josiah Carter, "A Day at Brenau," *Atlanta Constitution*, 31 July 1904, sec. C, p. 4.
114. Ibid.
115. *Catalog* (1900), 34.
116. Brenau's advertised foray into coeducation was apparently brief and unremarkable as nothing in the archives or in newspaper advertisements of the day makes more mention of the experiment. It is not even officially clear that any men even ultimately enrolled.
117. Display Advertisement—No Title, *Macon Telegraph*, 10 September 1887, p. 5.
118. Display Advertisement—No Title, *Montgomery Advertiser*, 1 August 1901, v. LXXII, n. 171, p. 4.
119. See Amy Eagle, "A Job Once Filled by Men Became a Pink Profession," *Chicago Tribune*, 26 April 2006, http://www.goucher.edu/documents/MediaHits/Chicago%20Tribune%20news_%20A%20job%20once%20filled%20by%20men%20became%20a%20pink%20profession.pdf (accessed 28 December 2012).
120. *Catalog* (1939), 117.
121. *Catalog* (1949), 55.

122. Solomon, *In the Company of Educated Women*, 85.
123. Ibid., 86.
124. "Domestic Science," *Atlanta Constitution*, 29 July 1904, p. 7.
125. "Girls are Trained as 'Home Makers'," *Atlanta Constitution*, 31 July 1904, sec. C, p. 5.
126. "Brenau Notes," *Atlanta Constitution*, 24 January 1904, sec. B, p. 6. It is interesting to note the effort to elevate the course work to the status of a "science." This would have been done in an effort to legitimize it in the college curriculum. Other institutions similarly called course work of this nature "home economics" to imply an association with another legitimate academic subject, economics.
127. "Girls are Trained as 'Home Makers'," *Atlanta Constitution*, 31 July 1904, sec. C, p. 5. Note the class consciousness on the part of the administration in this quote.
128. "Brenau College Notes," *Atlanta Constitution*, 15 November 1903, sec. C, p. 5.
129. Ibid.
130. "Girls are Trained as 'Home Makers'," *Atlanta Constitution*, 31 July 1904, sec. C, p. 5.
131. "Brenau College Notes," *Atlanta Constitution*, 15 November 1903, sec. C, p. 5.
132. Ibid.
133. Ibid.
134. "Brenau Notes," *Atlanta Constitution*, 24 January 1904, sec. B, p. 6.
135. *Catalog* (1910), 16.
136. Ibid.
137. Ibid, 32.
138. Ibid.
139. Ibid.
140. McCandless, *Past in the Present*, 58.
141. Ibid.
142. James Ross McCain, *The Story of Agnes Scott College*, 67.
143. *Catalog* (1929), 79.
144. *Catalog* (1939), 95.
145. *Catalog* (1949), 66-67.
146. But see Susan Lynn's essay entitled, "Gender and Progressive Politics: A Bridge to Social Activism of the 1960s" in Joanne Meyerowitz, ed., *Not June Cleaver: Women and Gender in Postwar America, 1945–1960* (Philadelphia, PA: Temple University Press, 1994). Lynn takes on

the popular view of post-war domesticity, claiming it to be largely unsubstantiated. She claimed that "scholars...often assumed, rather than demonstrated, the all-pervasiveness of that ideal. The notion that domestic ideology suffused American society, popularized by Betty Friedan's *The Feminine Mystique*, gradually made its way into standard accounts of the period" (104).

147. *Brenau College Bulletin 1970 – 1971/Annual Catalogue Edition/Vol. LX No. 1* (Gainesville, GA: Brenau College, 1970), 81; available in the Brenau University Archives, Gainesville, Georgia. Hereafter, references to this source are indicated as *"Catalog* (1970)."
148. *Brenau College Bulletin 1950–1951*, vol. XXXXII (Gainesville, GA: Brenau College, 1950), 41.
149. Ibid.
150. *Brenau College Bulletin 1958–1959*, vol. L (Gainesville, GA: Brenau College, 1958), 43.
151. William L. Norton, Jr., *Historic Gainesville & Hall County: An Illustrated History* (San Antonio, TX: HPN Books, 2001), 122.
152. Savannah King, "First class of Hall nurses honored," *Gainesville Times*, 26 September 2013, http://www.gainesvilletimes.com/archives/89242/preview/ (accessed 27 March 2014).
153. "The Georgia Female Seminary and Conservatory of Music," *Atlanta Constitution*, 6 August 1893, p. 18.
154. Ibid.
155. Ibid.
156. Ibid.
157. *Catalog* (1900), 46-48.
158. Josiah Carter, "A Day at Brenau," *Atlanta Constitution*, 31 July 1904, sec. C, p. 4.
159. Display Advertisement—No Title, *Atlanta Constitution*, 12 July 1905, p. 8.
160. Council of Independent Colleges, "Pearce Auditorium," Historic Campus Architecture Project, November 2006, http://hcap.artstor.org/cgi-bin/library?a=d&d=p271 (accessed 28 December 2012).
161. Agnes Scott College's spacious Gaines Chapel opened in 1941. Walter Edward McNair, *Lest We Forget: An Account of Agnes Scott College* (Atlanta, GA: Tucker-Castleberry Printing, Inc., 1983), 106. At Meredith College in 1925, one of "three temporary frame buildings east of the quadrangle...was to serve as an auditorium." It was not until 1949 that "a new auditorium replaced the temporary wooden one, which had

been in use for twenty-three years." Mary Lynch Johnson, *A History of Meredith College*: 2*ⁿᵈ Ed.* (Raleigh, NC: Meredith College, 1972), 177, 219.

162. *Catalog* (1900), 63.
163. Ibid.
164. Lucian Lamar Knight, *A Standard History of Georgia and Georgians: Volume Five* (Chicago, IL: The Lewis Publishing Company, 1917), p. 2424; Internet Archive, http://archive.org/details/astandardhistor03 kniggoog (accessed 28 December 2012).
165. *Catalog* (1900), 42.
166. See also *Catalog* (1900), 69–70.
167. "Brenau College Notes," *Atlanta Constitution*, 15 November 1903, sec. C, p. 5. The club often garnered much praise, such as when it did "honors in a most finished manner at the social entertainment following the programme" of one Conservatory performance.
168. "Brenau Glee Club Presents Good Act," *Red and Black*, 22 April 1920, p. 1, http://redandblack.libs.uga.edu/xtf/view?docId=news/1920/rab1920-00 65.xml&query=brenau&brand=rab-brand (accessed 28 December 2012).
169. "Interview with Dr. Barbara Webster, faculty member at Brenau for 13 years beginning in 1943," transcribed interview, p. 3; Box 1 of 1 (labeled "Dean of Women Files"), Brenau University Archives, Gainesville, Georgia.
170. *Catalog* (1900), 51–52.
171. "College Singers Draw Audience of 1,800," *Daytona Beach Morning Journal*, vol. XXV, no. 124, 8 May 1950, p. 1.
172. "Miss Barbara Owen Presents Senior Recital At Brenau," *Gadsden Times*, vol. 91, no. 23, 1 May 1958, p. 7.
173. "Clay Gives Piano Recital," *Alchemist* (Gainesville, GA: Brenau College), vol. XLVI, no. 7, 12 April 1960, p. 6.
174. "Carolyn Turpin Gives Recital," *Alchemist* (Gainesville, GA: Brenau College), 29 April 1965, p. 6.
175. "Brenau Choir Goes European," *Alchemist* (Gainesville, GA: Brenau College), March 1979, p. 3.
176. Gainesville Symphony Orchestra, "About Us," http://www.gainesvillesymphony.com/aboutus.html (accessed 5 February 2011).
177. Dr. John S. Burd, interview by author, tape recording, Gainesville, Georgia, 23 September 2010.
178. "Dr. Michelle Roueché Bio," University of Mary Hardin-Baylor, http://hr.umhb.edu/profile/Rouech%C3%A9/Michelle (accessed 28 December 2012).

179. "Introduction," Brenau University, http://catalog.brenau.edu/content.php?catoid=3&navoid=140 (accessed 28 December 2012).
180. *Catalog* (1900), 62.
181. *Catalog* (1910), 16.
182. Tasha Biggers, "Brenau exhibit puts a spotlight on the fashion of the 1950s," *Gainesville Times*, 12 November 2008, http://www.gainesvilletimes.com/archives/11116/ (accessed 29 December 2012).
183. Kristen Morales, "A good fit: Two Brenau University students take their fashion skills to China for a new exchange program," *Gainesville Times*, 13 June 2008, http://www.gainesvilletimes.com/archives/6041/ (accessed 29 December 2012).
184. Robert J. Vickers, "Brenau Mulls Opening Art School in Savannah," *The Atlanta Constitution* [Atlanta, GA] 11 Aug 1992, p. C2.
185. Jerry Grillo, "A Work in Progress," *Georgia Trend*, vol. 16, no. 2 (October 01, 2000): 88.
186. Catherine Fox, "Leo Castelli's Famous 'Circle' Included Brenau University," 3 October 2010, http://www.brenau.edu/news/leo-castellis-famous-circle-included-brenau-university/ (29 December 2012). Castelli was actually the agent for acclaimed American contemporary artist Jasper Johns, who had family members who had attended Brenau.
187. Ken Stanford, "Brenau University Galleries marks 20th year," *AccessNorthGA.com*, 19 December 2005, http://www.accessnorthga.com/detail.php?n=119828 (accessed 29 December 2012).
188. Ibid.
189. Ibid.; Sarah Ruth Long, "History of the Brenau Art Gallery and Permanent Collection." Unpublished essay, 15 April 1998; Box labeled Essays, Brenau University Archive, Gainesville, Georgia; Dr. John S. Burd, email message to author, 1 November 2013.
190. Ken Stanford, "Brenau University Galleries marks 20th year," *AccessNorthGA.com*, 19 December 2005, http://www.accessnorthga.com/detail.php?n=119828 (accessed 29 December 2012).
191. "Brenau University Galleries," Brenau University, http://www.brenau.edu/about/brenau-university-galleries/ (29 May 2013).
192. Ken Stanford, "Brenau University Galleries marks 20th year," *AccessNorthGA.com*, 19 December 2005, http://www.accessnorthga.com/detail.php?n=119828 (accessed 29 December 2012).
193. *Catalog* (1910), 16.
194. Ibid.

The History of Academics at Brenau 181

195. "Notes from Brenau," *Atlanta Constitution*, 13 December 1903, sec. C, p. 7.
196. "State Society," *Atlanta Constitution*, 30 April 1905, sec. A, p. 8; "Brenau Notes," *Atlanta Constitution*, 10 March 1907, p. 5.
197. "Nonie Clark Gives Senior Recital," *Alchemist* (Gainesville, GA: Brenau College), v. XVI, n. 26, 16 April 1930, p. 1; Frances Nunn, "Senior Dramatic Recitals," *Alchemist* (Gainesville, GA: Brenau College), v. XXI, n. 9, 14 May 1935, p. 2.
198. "Nonie Clark Gives Senior Recital," *Alchemist* (Gainesville, GA: Brenau College), v. XVI, n. 26, 16 April 1930, p. 1.
199. Frances Nunn, "Senior Dramatic Recitals," *Alchemist* (Gainesville, GA: Brenau College), v. XXI, n. 9, 14 May 1935, p. 2.
200. "Personals," *The Miami Daily News*, vol. XLVIII, no. 322, 1 November 1943, p. 7.
201. "Brenau Notes," *Atlanta Constitution*, 4 March 1906, p. 5.
202. "Grandma Would be Shocked: Drama Brings Men to Brenau?" *Alchemist* (Gainesville, GA: Brenau College), v. XXXVII, n. 2, 27 September 1950, p. 1.
203. "Gail Chitwood Casts Play Production Students in 'Sorry, Wrong Number,'" *Alchemist* (Gainesville, GA: Brenau College), v. XLVI, n. 7, 12 April 1960, p. 3.
204. "'My Fair Lady' Opens Wednesday," *Alchemist* (Gainesville, GA: Brenau College), v. LXI, n. 7, 23 February 1970, p. 1.
205. "Twelfth Night," *Alchemist* (Gainesville, GA: Brenau College), v. XII, n. 6, 3December 1924, p. 1.
206. "Gainesville Theater Alliance," http://gta.gsc.edu/Pages/default.aspx (accessed 30 December 2012).
207. "'New York City' Theme of Tau Sigma Recital," *Alchemist* (Gainesville, GA: Brenau College) v. XXXVIII, n. 9, 11 March 1952, p. 3.
208. *Brenau College Catalog, 1978–79* (Gainesville, GA: Brenau College, 1978), 98–99; Brenau University Archives, Gainesville, Georgia. Hereafter, references to this source are indicated as "*Catalog* (1978)."
209. "Diane Callahan, Founding Artistic Director," Gainesville Ballet, http://www.gainesvilleballet.org/comp_artisticdir.htm (accessed 30 December 2012).
210. *Brenau College Catalog, 1988–90* (Gainesville, GA: Brenau College, 1988), 112–113; Brenau University Archives, Gainesville, Georgia. Hereafter, references to this source are indicated as "*Catalog* (1988)."

211. *Brenau University Undergraduate and Graduate Catalog 1998–1999, vol. 115, no. 1* (Gainesville, GA: Brenau College, 1998), 77; Brenau University Archives, Gainesville, Georgia. Hereafter, references to this source are indicated as "*Catalog* (1998)."
212. Ibid.
213. Ken Stanford, "Brenau Dance Program receives accreditation," *AccessNorthGA.com*, 21 February 2005, http://new.accessnorthga.com/detail.php?n=140629 (accessed 30 December 2012).
214. Ibid.
215. "Accredited Institutional Members," National Association of Schools of Dance, http://nasd.arts-accredit.org/index.jsp?page=List_Accredited_Members (accessed 30 December 2012).
216. Converse College, "Our Mission and History," http://www.converse.edu/about/our-mission-history (accessed 30 December 2012).
217. *Catalog* (1910), 20.
218. See the section on "Alumnae" in *Catalog* (1929), 10.
219. McCandless, *Past in the Present*, 55.
220. Brenau: The Professional College, *An Institutional Self-Study Under the Auspices of The Southern Association of Colleges and Schools, 1984–1986* (Gainesville, GA: Brenau College), 343–344; Box labeled "Self Study, 79–81, 84–85, 93," Brenau University Archives, Gainesville, Georgia. Hereafter, references to this source are indicated as "*Institutional Self-Study, 1984–1986.*"
221. Ibid.
222. *Brenau College Annual Catalog: School of Professional Studies Edition, January, 1981, vol. 103, no. 2* (Gainesville, GA: Brenau College, 1981), 11: Brenau University Archives, Gainesville, Georgia. Hereafter, references to this source are cited as "*The Professional College Bulletin* (1981)."
223. Ibid., 59.
224. Graduate Study Program: Brenau College, 1975–1976 (Gainesville, GA: Brenau College, 1975), 25: Brenau University Archives, Gainesville, Georgia.
225. *Brenau College Annual Catalog: School of Professional Studies Edition, 1983–1986* (Gainesville, GA: Brenau College, 1981), 18–19: Brenau University Archives, Gainesville, Georgia. Hereafter, references to this source are cited as "*The Professional College Bulletin* (1983–1986)."
226. Dr. John S. Burd, interview by author, tape recording, Gainesville, Georgia, 23 September 2010.

227. Ibid.
228. Isabella Margaret Elizabeth Blandin, *History of higher education of women in the South prior to 1860* (Washington, DC: The Neale Pub. Co., 1909), 78; Internet Archive, http://archive.org/details/historyofhighere00blanrich (accessed 31 December 2012).
229. *The Professional College Bulletin* (1983–1986), 76.
230. Ibid.
231. Ibid., 82.
232. *The Professional College Bulletin* (1981), 19–20.
233. Kevin Sack, "Off-campus centers vie for students," *Atlanta Journal-Constitution*, 11 March 1984, pg. 1-d.
234. Brenau College, "Position Paper on Duplicative Higher Education Offerings: The Impact on the Gainesville-Hall County Area," 3, 2: Box labeled "Miscellaneous," Brenau University Archives, Gainesville, Georgia.
235. Kevin Sack, "Off-campus centers view for students," *Atlanta Journal-Constitution*, 11 March 1984, pg. 1-d.
236. Rudi Kiefer, "Brenau's Best and Brightest," *Brenau Window*, Fall 2012, http://window.brenau.edu/featured/honorable-mention/ (accessed 31 December 2012).
237. Hank Ezell, "Brenau to open the state's first weekend college," *The Atlanta Constitution*, 23 July 1986, np.
238. Judy Bolyard Purdy, "Brenau's Weekend College Makes Learning More Convenient," Brenau News Release, 21 July 1986, p. 2; Box labeled "Weekend College Materials," Brenau University Archives, Gainesville, Georgia.
239. Dr. John S. Burd, interview by author, tape recording, Gainesville, Georgia, 23 September 2010.
240. Ibid.
241. Judy Bolyard Purdy, "Brenau's Weekend College Makes Learning More Convenient," Brenau News Release, 21 July 1986, p. 2; Box labeled "Weekend College Materials," Brenau University Archives, Gainesville, Georgia. Apparently, not everyone at Brenau was eager to make changes. Dr. Burd related that, "As much as I love them—I even was one—faculty have a strong tendency to not be experimental in education." However, Dr. Burd indicated that Brenau's faculty would eventually see the necessity of making changes. "They were fairly convinced of the potential benefits of evening programs, but they had had a very negative experience with a government program" to offer limited evening

classes that Brenau had piloted a few years before. That program in which state employees took classes from Brenau faculty members had not measured up to expectations for a number of reasons. The newer incarnation of evening courses would be a much better experience. Dr. John S. Burd, interview by author, tape recording, Gainesville, Georgia, 23 September 2010.

242. Brenau University, *Undergraduate and Graduate Catalog, 1992–1993, vol. 110, no. 1* (Gainesville, GA: Brenau University), 66. Hereafter, this source will be cited as "*Catalog* (1992)."
243. Ibid., 68.
244. Ibid., 66.
245. Brenau: The Professional College, *Institutional Self-Study, 1984–1986*, 343-344.
246. Ibid., 346.
247. Ibid., 347.
248. Ibid., 368.
249. Ibid., 374.
250. Ibid., 349.
251. Ibid., 393.
252. Ibid., 380.
253. "Brenau at a Glance: History," Brenau University, http://www.brenau.edu/about-brenau-extraordinary/brenau-at-a-glance/ (accessed 17 January 2013).
254. *Catalog* (1992), 233.
255. "BULLI for Brenau: Going Strong 10 Years On," *Brenau Magazine*, Office of Public Relations, Brenau University (spring 2004): 11.
256. Ibid.
257. Ibid.
258. Robert Haddocks, "Earn MBA Online," *The Atlanta Journal/Atlanta Constitution* [Atlanta, Ga] 31 May 2001: p. JJ.2.
259. Elizabeth Burlingame, "Brenau to offer doctoral degrees," *Gainesville Times*, 16 December 2010, http://www.gainesvilletimes.com/archives/42893/ (accessed 17 January 2013).
260. Ibid.
261. Dallas Duncan, "Brenau students start class today," *Gainesville Times*, 29 August 2011, http://www.gainesvilletimes.com/archives/55143/ (accessed 3 January 2013).
262. "Trustees Name Graduate School for Judge Smith, Approve Nursing Doctorate Program for 2011," Brenau University, 27 October 2010,

The History of Academics at Brenau 185

http://www.brenau.edu/news/trustees-name-graduate-school-for-judge-smith-approve-nursing-doctorate-program-for-2011/ (accessed 3 January 2013).
263. Elizabeth Burlingame, "Brenau to offer doctoral degrees," *Gainesville Times*, 16 December 2010, http://www.gainesvilletimes.com/archives/42893/ (accessed 3 January 2013).
264. "Extraordinary Lives: Brenau 2025," Brenau University, 1 October 2011, http://artsweb.brenau.edu/brenauwindow/strategicplan.pdf (accessed 3 January 2013).
265. Ibid.
266. Ibid.
267. "New Undergraduate and Graduate Schools Enhance Brenau's 2025 Vision," 12 August 2010, http://www.brenau.edu/publications/news/new-undergraduate-and-graduate-schools-enhance-brenau%E2%80%99s-2025-vision/ (accessed 3 January 2013).
268. "Extraordinary Lives: Brenau 2025," Brenau University, 1 October 2011, http://artsweb.brenau.edu/brenauwindow/strategicplan.pdf (accessed 3 January 2013).
269. See Adam Fletcher, *Meaningful Student Involvement: Guide to Students as Partners in School Change 2nd edition* (Olympia, WA: SoundOut.org, 2005); available at http://www.soundout.org/MSIGuide.pdf (accessed 3 January 2013).

CHAPTER 3

INSTITUTIONAL POLICYMAKING AS STAFF & FACULTY FORTE

THE CASE OF SEGREGATION STRATEGY AT BRENAU COLLEGE

I first taught at the Women's College of Brenau University in the fall semester of 2006. Among the 35 remarkable young women in my "Survey of World Civilizations I" course were eleven African American students, two Hispanic students, one international student (from Zimbabwe), and two students in wheelchairs. This was an invigorating change for someone who routinely taught classes at another nearby college in which the vast majority of the students were white, male, and from the United States. In fact, leaving out gender, I had never had such a diverse class as the one I taught at Brenau in a decade of involvement in college teaching at five institutions.

Such diversity, it turns out, is fairly typical of Brenau in the twenty-first century. For instance, in 2009–2010, the Women's College enrolled 930 students from 23 states and 12 countries. Twenty-three percent of these students were from minority groups (not including international students) and several were older than 25.[1] Besides the historic Women's College,

Brenau also maintains The Undergraduate School and The Sydney O. Smith Jr. Graduate School that offer undergraduate and graduate degrees to women and men in online programs and in evening programs held on multiple campuses throughout Georgia. According to Brenau's Office of Research and Planning, in 2011, 1925 undergraduates enrolled in these programs along with 993 graduate students.[2] Roughly a quarter of the students in each of these two divisions were from racial minorities and the vast majority of students were women.[3]

Much about the student diversity that was typical of Brenau around 2011 would have been unfathomable some two centuries earlier when minority students (particularly African Americans) were generally barred from attending college with white students—or barred from attending college at all. Setting aside race, historically speaking, there was a time in North America when *none* of the students currently in Brenau's Women's College division could have obtained a college education simply because of their sex. The story of African American women overcoming the dual strikes of race and gender to obtain higher education—both in the United States generally and at Brenau College in particular—is a fascinating tale of overcoming obstacles.

This chapter describes how Brenau's governors went to great lengths to retain segregation at the College when other similarly situated institutions integrated, assenting as they did (if, at times, reluctantly) to both the spirit and the letter of the Civil Rights legislation and judicial holdings of the 1950s and 1960s. Thanks to very careful planning on the part of one of its powerful presidential administrations in particular and the implementation (sometimes at some cost) of unique and, at times, arguably crafty institutional policies, Brenau successfully resisted integration for much longer than other colleges. Despite this past, Brenau would go on to become a diverse institution committed to non-discrimination. Throughout this entire saga, relatively little negotiation between Brenau students and the Brenau faculty and staff actually occurred. The story about segregation at Brenau illustrates that in the realm of institutional

Institutional Policymaking as Staff & Faculty Forte   189

policy making, Brenau employees enjoyed virtual *carte blanche* to shape the College as they saw fit.

Understanding Brenau's experience requires some background information. Although black women have been an integral part of the American experience since the early 1600s, racism and sexism kept them from higher education in any great numbers until the nineteenth century. Historian Linda M. Perkins determined that a handful of northern female "seminaries" emerged in the 1820s and 1830s to educate white women in curricula that resembled those of modern secondary schools. Although a very few of these forerunners of women's colleges opened their doors to black women, none did so "on a continuous basis."[4]

The continuous enrollment of African American women in an institution of higher education would not commence until 1842. In that year, Oberlin College in Oberlin, Ohio (a pioneer in black men's and in white women's education), admitted its first black female student, Sarah J. Watson Barnett. Others would follow. In 1850, Lucy Stanton became the first black woman to earn a four-year degree from an institution of higher education in America.[5] Mary Jane Patterson became the first black woman in the United States to receive the Bachelor of Arts degree, doing so at Oberlin in 1862. Oberlin would go on to graduate 128 black students by 1900, many of them women.[6]

Oberlin College blazed a trail educating black women in the nineteenth century that some other colleges would follow. The eminent African American historian and scholar W.E.B. DuBois documented this in a landmark work entitled, *The College-Bred Negro: Report of a Social Study Made Under the Direction of Atlanta University*, which he published in 1900. The report explained that, "Before the [civil] war ten [black] women graduated [from college], as far as we have been able to ascertain; from 1861 to 18[79, forty-four]; from 1880 to 1889, seventy-six; 1890 to 1898, one hundred and nineteen." In addition, three women graduated "Class Unk'n," making a total of 252 African American women who "finished a college course" prior to 1899, according to DuBois.[7]

The first half of the twentieth century saw expanded educational opportunities for black women and men alike. Historian Jeanne Noble wrote that, "For the first fifty years of the century, the vast majority of these students were enrolled in black colleges," which would have accounted for thousands of graduates by mid-century.[8] Strong enrollment in black colleges continued past 1950. According to the United States Department of Education, "By 1953, more than 32,000 students were enrolled in such well known private black institutions as Fisk University, Hampton Institute, Howard University, Meharry Medical College, Morehouse College, Spelman College, and Tuskegee Institute, as well as a host of smaller black colleges located in southern and border states."[9] At the same time, "over 43,000 students were enrolled in public black colleges."[10] These were institutions established by states under the "separate but equal" doctrine created in the 1896 United States Supreme Court case of *Plessy v. Ferguson*.[11] Though they were separate, racially segregated higher educational facilities were seldom equal. Still, in an era largely lacking any policing of racial inequality, these separate institutions sufficed legally to forestall the enrollment of black men and women into predominately white state colleges and universities.

Whatever college they attended, most African American students in the twentieth century would have been women because black women have historically attended college in far greater numbers than black men. Noble observed, "A pattern of black women's superiority over black men in degree attainment begins in high school, continues in college, and includes one or two years of graduate work."[12] This pattern began in 1910 and, with the exception of the decade of the 1920s, has continued until the present day.

The landmark Supreme Court case of *Brown v. Board of Education of Topeka, Kansas* (1954), overturned the decision in *Plessy* and, coupled with Title VI of the Civil Rights Act of 1964, set in motion events that would expand the enrollment of African Americans (both men and women) in colleges and universities.[13] Title VI stated that, "No person in the

United States shall, on the ground of race, color, or national origin, be excluded from participation in, be denied the benefits of, or be subjected to discrimination under any program or activity receiving Federal financial assistance."[14] Within what was then called the Department of Health, Education, and Welfare, the federal government established the Office for Civil Rights (O.C.R.) to police the provisions of Title VI. Many states and many private entities both received federal financial assistance for higher education and operated racially segregated colleges and universities, which could not stand. Though told to desegregate by the O.C.R., very few did so speedily. It would be years before all major state systems and virtually all private colleges receiving public funds integrated. The last institutions of higher education to integrate were in the Deep South where, driven by prejudiced (if not racist) mindsets, segregation remained official policy at a handful of schools as late as the 1970s. A study of United States Census Bureau data by the National Center for Education Statistics revealed that the number of African Americans under the age of 35 enrolled in institutions of higher learning "rose to a high in 1977 of 1.103 million students, or 10.8 percent of the nation's college population, from 234,000, or 5 percent, in 1965, the first year such comparisons were made."[15] Again, most of these students would have been young African American women owing to historical trends.

Just as Title VI guards against racial discrimination in higher education, Title IX of the Education Amendments of 1972 to the Civil Rights Act of 1964 guards against gender discrimination in colleges and universities and facilitates the enrollment of black women in programs of higher education. The act indicated that, "No person in the United States shall, on the basis of sex, be excluded from participation in, be denied the benefits of, or be subjected to discrimination under any education program or activity receiving Federal financial assistance."[16] Prior to the passage of this statute, little more than good common sense induced many colleges to become coeducational—but this good sense often sufficed for much. Historian Rosalind Rosenberg wrote that women's access to higher education "owed much to the efforts of the early women's rights movement, whose leaders declared that coeducation was an essential precondition of woman's emancipation from her 'separate sphere.'"[17] These efforts had paid off somewhat handsomely as, "by the end of the nineteenth century coeducation had become the predominant form of higher education in this country."[18] Still, whereas many colleges and universities did admit women by this time, relatively few did so in great numbers.

Although coeducation predominated in the United States at large prior to 1900, only a few southern institutions contributed to this. Rosenberg wrote:

> As a consequence of the Civil War and the conservative social tradition that lingered in the South, collegiate education developed more slowly than in the rest of the country, and sexual segregation persisted longer in both public and private institutions. Where traditions were weaker and economic constraints pronounced, however, coeducation was adopted. Thus, coeducation in the South came first to the state universities of Texas, Arkansas, and Mississippi and to the black colleges. Only slowly did it spread eastward to the old South.[19]

Until well into the twentieth century, Guilford College in North Carolina (founded in 1837) and Texas Christian and Rice universities in Texas (founded in 1873 and 1912, respectively) were the only southern colleges to be coeducational from establishment. Among public colleges and universities in the South, only the University of Mississippi and the University of Kentucky admitted women prior to 1890 in 1885 and 1888, respectively. The University of South Carolina, Auburn University, the University of Tennessee, and the University of Alabama all began admitting women in the 1890s. The slow spread of coeducation in the Old South continued into the twentieth century as the Universities of Georgia, North Carolina, Florida, and Virginia eventually accepted female students.[20]

Although coeducation was lacking in parts of the South, women who could not study alongside men in many state systems or in all-male private colleges could attend a women's college. This was especially true in Georgia. In 1878, William C. Wilkes founded the forerunner of Brenau University, the Georgia Baptist Female Seminary in Gainesville, Georgia. Prior to this year, perhaps three dozen other women's colleges had been established throughout the region, all catering to white students.[21] Three were neighbors to Brenau: LaGrange College in LaGrange, Georgia, was founded in 1831 as a female academy and became a college in 1851; Wesleyan College in Macon, Georgia, was originally named the Georgia Female College and was first chartered in 1836; and Tift College near Macon was founded in 1849 as the Forsyth Female Collegiate Institute. Agnes Scott College in Decatur, Georgia, would be founded as a female seminary in 1889. Several other women's colleges existed in Georgia at one time or another, though few survived into the twentieth century. Americus Female College in Americus closed in 1879. Bethel Female College in Cuthbert closed in 1875. The Madison Collegiate Institute and Methodist Female College in Madison and the Houston Female College in Perry closed in 1880 and 1896, respectively. While they functioned, the presence of these and the several other institutions mentioned earlier actually made Georgia a center for women's private collegiate education in the nineteenth century.[22]

Unfortunately for black women in Georgia, thanks to prevailing prejudicial attitudes, the presence of many women's colleges in the state did not provide them with much educational opportunity. Of these institutions, only Spelman College, which was founded in 1881 to educate black women, admitted African Americans prior to the 1950s.[23] Although African Americans and women generally shared the common problem of discrimination, this shared experience never fostered integration into higher education in the state during the first half of the twentieth century. Women's colleges discriminated against African Americans in the same manner in which women were discriminated against by men in other colleges.

In *The College-Bred Negro*, DuBois observed, "Among the women's colleges the color prejudice is much stronger and more unyielding."[24] He cited several examples of this prejudice against admitting black students in women's colleges prior to 1900. DuBois indicated that, in response to a letter he penned, the secretary of Vassar College wrote:

> We have never had but one colored girl among our students, and as no one knew during her course that she was a Negro there was never any discussion of the matter. This young woman graduated from the college, and although it is now well known that she is a Negro, the feeling of respect and affection that she won during her college course has not been changed on the part of those who knew her here. There is no rule of the college that would forbid our admitting a colored girl, but the conditions of life here are such that we should hesitate for the sake of the candidate to admit her and in fact should strongly advise her for her own sake not to come.[25]

The administration at Barnard College in New York indicated to DuBois that:

> No one of Negro descent has ever received our degree, and I cannot say whether such a person would be admitted to Barnard as the question has never been raised, but there is nothing in our regulations that excludes anyone of any nationality or race.[26]

Regarding black applicants, the trustees of Mills College for women in Alameda, California, "decided some years ago that it was not best for us to receive such students."[27] The Randolph-Macon Woman's College of Lynchburg, Virginia (a "prominent Southern Institution"), related to DuBois that, "We entirely favor the education of Negroes to any degree they may wish but are not prepared to enter upon that work ourselves. We believe that in all boarding schools and colleges the races must, for the good of both, be educated separately."[28]

In the nineteenth century, only in Massachusetts, DuBois wrote, was there "usually no barrier" to the entry of African Americans to women's colleges. He cited Smith College, Wellesley College, and Radcliffe College as all having Negro students. Yet, even in Massachusetts, not all institutions favored integration. DuBois indicated that Mount Holyoke College "puts the statement negatively" when it responded to an inquiry about their willingness to admit black students: "We do not refuse admission to colored persons, but we seldom have application for this class of candidates."[29]

Whether at a coeducational institution or an all-women's college, the implication of this data is that even if gender might not have barred a black woman from attending college prior to the mid-twentieth century, with only a few exceptions, race would have. If the integration of African American women into institutions of higher education came slowly to the United States and even slower to the South, it came even slower still to private colleges and universities in the Deep South. Far below the Mason-Dixon Line, an entrenched segregationist mentality prevailed well into the twentieth century in the minds of many whites. This simply would have prevented the consideration of—let alone the occurrence of—racial integration at almost all southern institutions of higher education until after the *Brown* decision. This was decidedly the case at Brenau College. Much historical evidence suggests that, led by powerful administrators who were likely segregationists themselves, and apparently without ever consulting then-current students on the matter, Brenau defiantly resisted integration until very late in its history, often going to great lengths to do so.

This historical evidence takes many forms. Over the years, Brenau University has conscientiously maintained a thorough history of itself in pictures. Brenau's University Archives contain a plethora of vintage and modern photographs of students dating back years to its days as a female seminary. In addition, the College began producing a robust yearbook (called the "*Bubbles*") as early as 1900. It was not until 1973 that any African American students appeared in any College photographs.[30] This photographic record suggests that Brenau did not receive African

Americans as students until after the 1960s. Other evidence also supports the view that Brenau was not interested in admitting black students during much of its history.

Some of this evidence speaks to student attitudes toward race. In a memorandum written on November 27, 1973, Brenau Dean John E. Sites addressed the establishment of secret societies at Brenau. Part of his memorandum references a photograph of a club that appeared in the 1912 edition of *Bubbles*. Sites wrote:

> The clubs that were developed during this time [at the college in the early 20th century] seem to have secret ideals that were not like the sororities of today, even though many local sororities did begin to spring up. It is suggested that these organizations at that particular time had a lighter touch, stressing fun and fellowship rather than scholastic goals.
>
> In 1912, history indicates that the first of these organizations developed. It was called Tri-Kappa and had no affiliation with any other chapter. It appears to have been planned and originated at Brenau College.[31]

Dean Sites continued, describing the Tri-Kappas:

> One wonders whether KKK was borrowed from the infamous racist organization of the South, the Klu Klux Klan [sic]. A number of features seem to be similar, but no official record or mention is made of the other organization. The dress of each member was a white robe, covering most of the body except their heads. As a symbol, the members displayed three K's and two pictures of the palm of the hand. As was usually the case, the group adopted a password which we're unable to determine today. However, it is indicated that it had no origin but probably had some symbolic meaning to the girls that made it up. Their flower was the Bleeding Heart.[32]

Although Sites is very likely correct in saying that no direct linkage with the Klan could be made, in the group's yearbook photograph, the dress of members does perhaps bear a resemblance to that of hooded Klansmen. (See Figure 18.) An Internet search conducted in 2012 returned no information at all about the meaning of the group's motto, "Devilamenger." Several websites associated the Tri-Kappas' password (which, contrary to what Dean Sites says, is easily determined because it was printed in the annual) "didiki" as meaning "gypsy" or "traveler." No association of either word with the Ku Klux Klan appeared. Likewise, neither the Black Hand nor the Bleeding Heart seem to be Klan-related.

Although much of this evidence suggests that there was no linkage between the Tri-Kappas and the Ku Klux Klan, some aspects of the club's founding might be conspicuous. Originally founded in the 1860s in the aftermath of the Civil War, the Ku Klux Klan suffered a decline in the late nineteenth century as federal and state authorities cracked-down on violent Klan activities against blacks. Largely in response to white dissatisfaction with urbanization and massive immigration from eastern and southern Europe, the Klan would rise again. The organization was re-formed around 1915 in Atlanta and went on to garner millions of members throughout the country by the 1920s. Brenau women founded the Tri-Kappas by the nineteen-teens in close proximity to Atlanta. Though it seems rather far-fetched, one might wonder whether more than coincidence accounted for the close birth dates and places of the two organizations.[33]

The existence at Brenau of student groups that may have supported segregation and the absence of African American students in photographs for much of the College's history are not the only evidence that suggests Brenau may have harbored an institutional culture of prejudice for a number of years. A 1924 edition of the *Alchemist*, Brenau's student newspaper, included a description of the College's traditional freshmen initiation week (called "Rat Week") that spoke to Brenau's views on race. The paper read:

> Friday night...all 'rats' were initiated into the holy order of Brenau. This ceremony was very beautiful and impressive. The "rats" were

dressed in black bathing suits and blacked to represent slaves. The name of every Freshman was read out and on the reading of her name she came forward to give her sacrifice of fruit and one dime to the Holy Cat of the Sophomore class. Along with her other offering each one offered to the fire some undesirable trait.[34]

Nothing suggests that the depiction of freshmen as lowly slaves fazed any of Brenau's students or faculty members. A later edition of the *Alchemist* (this one from 1935) also spoke to Brenau's views on race. This edition described the College's annual May Day Fete of that year. It read:

The title of the program was May Fete At The Old Plantation. The manor was covered with Dorothy Perkins roses, and in the midst of this southern atmosphere the arrival of the queen was awaited on the eleventh day of May, 1850, to accept the crown to be presented by the Colonel. All the slaves and their children were allowed to come out and have a part in the festival by singing, dancing, or saying a word of greeting, for that was the day the Queen met her Prince Charming, the Beau of the Fifties, and received her crown.[35]

Brenau underclassmen would have played the roles of the singing and dancing slaves and their children in this spectacle. Despite knowing of the evils of the "peculiar institution," the College chose to gloss over history and instead presented a sanitized version of slavery in a pageant that celebrated and sanctified the Old South.

Brenau's views on race were evident from more than such ceremonies; official documents occasionally addressed the issue. Applications to the College have at times inquired about an applicant's racial background. This apparently began at Brenau as it did at many places in the nineteen-seventies for purposes of tracking institutional compliance with federal regulations. Judging by actual archived copies of Brenau admission applications from the mid-twentieth century, inquiring about race on applications did not occur prior to this time. One reason for this is that it probably would have been a foregone conclusion to everyone with their eye on the College that all applicants to Brenau would be

Institutional Policymaking as Staff & Faculty Forte 199

(and should be) white.[36] Another reason Brenau applications need not have inquired about race was because, from at least the 1950s and until the 1970s, Brenau required applicants to attach a passport-style photograph with their application. Indeed, regarding this, the application itself read in capital letters, "This is VERY IMPORTANT." Clearly, admissions personnel at Brenau could have used these photographs to exclude any applicants on the basis of race.

These sources suggest that Brenau possessed a segregationist mentality through much of the twentieth century. Some other schools were different. Because they wanted to or because they wished to continue receiving federal funding, many southern state colleges and universities and many private colleges in the South on the public dole integrated (speedily or otherwise) in the 1950s and 1960s. Yet, at this time when other colleges and universities throughout the United States were breaking down color barriers, some private institutions in the South held out. Brenau was one such school. The College's institutional leadership went to great pains to try to ensure that Brenau would remain all white. This backward mindset contrasts sharply with both Brenau's twenty-first century diversity and the forward-thinking in the nineteenth century that called for the creation and sustenance of an institution of higher learning in north Georgia dedicated exclusively to educating young women.

Dr. Josiah Crudup was arguably a guiding force behind Brenau's resistance to integration. He became the fourth president of the College in 1945 and served until 1968. Prior to joining Brenau, Crudup was a graduate of Mercer University, where he was a member of the Kappa Alpha Order men's fraternity, and the University of Chicago. When the new president came to Brenau, the College's student newspaper, the *Alchemist*, published an article written by a friend of Crudup's, Elliot Dunwody, describing him. Dunwody wrote glowing praise for Crudup. He lauded Crudup for having "a fresh and original way of saying everything;" for being "a great teacher, a great leader, [and] a great speaker;" for being a nationally famous Kiwanian; for having "a fine

Christian character;" and for being a person who "stimulates and inspires you."[37] According to Dunwody, Crudup would "teach you to admire without envy, to disagree without bitterness, to fight injustice without hatred, and to cultivate humility without surrender of conviction."[38] A fellow employee at Brenau remembered Dr. Crudup "for his efforts to beautify and restore the campus property as well as to improve Brenau's financial status."[39] In the first two years of his administration, Dr. Crudup eliminated half-a-million dollars' worth of debt incurred by the College over the years. He also guided the College in its difficult process of re-securing national accreditation from the Southern Association of Colleges and Schools, which Brenau had earlier lost. In addition, archived correspondence indicates that Dr. Crudup oversaw the construction and renovation of several buildings on campus.

These significant contributions earned Dr. Crudup the esteem of many people associated with Brenau. His popularity did not stop there. The following article with the headline, "Last Four-Year Class Graduates; Dr. Josiah Crudup Gives Address" appeared in the *Chatsworth Times* on May 17, 1951:

> Fifty-six Murray County High School graduates donned caps and gowns to receive their diplomas Sunday and had the distinction of being the last class to graduate under the old four-year high school program. There will be no graduating class next year since the first five-year class will still have another years [sic] work to complete.
>
> Dr. Josiah Crudup, president of Brenau College at Gainesville, gave the commencement address.
>
> Introduced by Elswick Keith, school principal, as the "most popular speaker in the state," Dr. Crudup held his audience's attention by relating a series of humorous anecdotes, by congratulating everyone connected with the class, including the Dads [sic] "who had to pay the bills" and by giving the graduates some sound advice about the problems confronting them in the world today.

> The speaker urged the class not to stop in the pursuit of education with a high school diploma. With thousands of war veterans taking advantage of government-paid college training, the present high school graduate has no particular advantage unless he goes on with his education, Dr. Crudup said.
>
> In the face of such questions as whether or not we will have atomic warfare and how strong Communism will become, the graduate will do well to "Be faithful to your training, to the things that endure," Dr. Crudup said.[40]

This and other sources suggest that Dr. Crudup was a personable individual and a dedicated educator. He was, at the same time and like many of his contemporaries, most likely a dedicated believer in the idea that members of different races should be educated separately.

Desegregation was a concern for Dr. Crudup for at least two decades before Brenau would integrate. This is revealed by several addresses to the Brenau College Board of Trustees that Dr. Crudup delivered in annual meetings as Brenau's president beginning in 1953. In the annual meeting of the College Board of Trustees for that year, Dr. Crudup said:

> [A] problem confronting many colleges in the future is a matter of racial segregation. With continued rulings from the United States Supreme Court to the effect that Negroes have the right of enrollment at colleges supported by public taxation, the problem of segregation becomes more acute. While a mild interest has been aroused recently on our campus by the attendance of a few Negroes at recitals in Brenau Auditorium, yet [sic] segregation will never be an acute problem at the independent colleges such as Brenau.[41]

Dr. Crudup brought up the topic of segregation again in 1957 and 1958 in regard to Brenau Academy, the College's secondary school for girls, which had been established in 1928. In 1957, he indicated that, "Recent national developments have brought about increasing popularity in private boarding schools for high school girls. Last summer 125 applications for enrollment were received and we could admit only 80 girls. If this condition continues, we should be making plans to expand the facilities of the Academy."[42] He reiterated this point in 1958:

> Because of the problems of segregation, more people are thinking of private schools. Several years ago, the Westminster schools in Atlanta were founded. The success has been spectacular. Last week, the papers gave an account of another private school development on the north side of Atlanta. Except for being coeducational, the schools are very much in design like Brenau Academy, which has had more than 30 years of very successful operation.[43]

These early addresses indicated that Dr. Crudup, though cognizant of desegregation, was not truly concerned about it. The integration of Brenau's concert performances was only mildly interesting to Dr. Crudup and he saw the integration of public schools as presenting not threats but business opportunities for the College. In this regard, Dr. Crudup was being savvy.

In the 1950s, many southern states adopted a policy of "massive resistance" toward school integration. U.S. Senator Harry F. Byrd, Sr., of Virginia originated this policy, which had as its linchpin "a law that cut off state funds and closed any public school that agreed to integrate."[44] Private schools offered alternatives for whites to public schools that either closed or integrated. Correctly or not, the term "segregation academies" came to be applied to many of these private institutions (like the Westminster schools Dr. Crudup spoke of) that came into being during the Civil Rights era and that ended up accommodating white flight from public schools. Though Brenau Academy had existed for decades prior to the formation of these segregation academies, Dr. Crudup saw the Academy as an alternative to integrated public education. He viewed school integration not as something for Brenau to fear but rather for Brenau to capitalize on. This tone would change.

Institutional Policymaking as Staff & Faculty Forte   203

Dr. Crudup raised the red flag regarding segregation in his 1961 address to the Trustees. Indeed, much of his speech related to the topic. He began by referring to several "new trends in American education." He said:

> The newspapers and magazines this week of May, 1961, tell the story of new trends in American education. *U.S. News* this week tells a story of serious objections in the Congress to the Kennedy plan for federal aid to education. There has been an increase in the number of educational leaders who have raised serious questions concerning the federal government's student loan plan and loans of federal funds for school buildings. There is the unanswered question concerning the extent of government control which will follow the use of federal funds.[45]

Dr. Crudup went on to relate how fearsome government control could be. He indicated:

> In the *Atlanta Journal* of May 7 appears a story telling that the federal government has gone to court to force Prince Edward County in Virginia to reopen its schools and on a desegregated basis. According to the story, Attorney General Robert Kennedy has asked the court to enjoin Virginia from operating any public schools until they force Prince Edward to reopen on a desegregated basis. There is a suggestion that financial support be withdrawn until there is compliance with federal demands.[46]

Dr. Crudup predicted that this phenomenon would not be confined to Virginia and drove home the point that integration enjoyed governmental support at the highest levels. He said:

> Last Saturday, May 6, Attorney General Robert Kennedy made an address at the law day exercises at the University of Georgia. In this speech Mr. Kennedy reaffirmed the present federal government administration's determination to use all means within its power to bring about desegregation in our schools and colleges. Also on the radio last week was the account [that] over 250 colored

students in the 11th and 12th grades in Atlanta had applied for admission to white high schools next September.[47]

Dr. Crudup likewise contended that integration efforts would not be confined to primary and secondary schools. He told the trustees, "All of this action brings before us again the possibility of complications in a college administration when federal funds are used in the promotion of the institution."[48]

Dr. Crudup went on to intimate to the Brenau Board of Trustees that these "complications" would soon become very problematic for most other nearby independent colleges. Dr. Crudup revealed that these schools had made the mistake of accepting government funding for various purposes. He told the College trustees that, "seven out of the 10 members of our Georgia Foundation for Independent Colleges have applied [for] and are receiving federal government loans for new buildings."[49] Dr. Crudup implied that, for having done so, these unfortunate institutions would now be subject to some federal governmental control, which would ultimately mean that they would be subject to forced integration.

But this fate would not befall Brenau. Dr. Crudup proudly stated that, "Brenau College continues to make progress without federal aid."[50] Though other institutions could be forced to integrate, the government simply had no leverage on Brenau. Dr. Crudup concluded this section of his 1961 address to the Brenau Board of Trustees by declaring that, "All of the above accounts confirm our convictions in the wisdom of our policy to remain free of debt preserved by independence, and continue the promotion of Brenau College according to its traditional plans."[51] Of course, a very large part of Brenau's "traditional plans" embraced segregation. Dr. Crudup reminded the trustees of this, pointing out that "nationality, race and personal background are acceptable considerations in our plan of student selection at Brenau College."[52]

This, then, was Dr. Crudup's strategy: keep Brenau white by keeping away from government money. It was a point he would try to drive

Institutional Policymaking as Staff & Faculty Forte   205

home repeatedly over the years. In 1962, Dr. Crudup again addressed the Brenau Board of Trustees and again spoke on desegregation. He said:

> During the past year there has arisen much evidence that this rapid evolutionary change in our country is including some of our independent colleges, both from the standpoint of independence and racial segregation. This spring news reports revealed the intention of Agnes Scott College to consider the applications of Negro girls next year. A recent lawsuit in Atlanta permitted Emory University to admit a Negro boy to enrollment. Last week a news item told of the admission of Negro boy to a fraternity at the University of North Carolina and another report revealed that Tulane is soon-to-be desegregated.
>
> There are also indications that the completely independent colleges will become modified in future years as more of these colleges will receive federal government financial aid. Among the ten colleges in the Georgia Foundation for Independent Colleges, there remain only two or three of these institutions who had not sought and been granted financial aid from the federal government. I am pleased to report to you again that Brenau College remains free of debt and has not sought any financial aid from the federal government.
>
> As we survey our Brenau College heritage we are proud of the record. Through the past years Brenau College has been selective and granted the right to enrollment only to those who seem to be qualified to benefit from the atmosphere of this campus and the training offered by this faculty. Without financial obligation to the federal government and without coercion from any controlling church organization, it seems to be reasonable that this policy can be continued here at Brenau College.[53]

Needless to say, the only students qualified to benefit from the atmosphere of Brenau during that time were white.

Dr. Crudup used a huge portion of his 1965 report to the trustees to reiterate and clarify Brenau's strategy of maintaining whiteness by abstaining from partaking of government funding. He entitled this section of his speech, "The Civil Rights Act effect on higher education." Dr. Crudup told the board of trustees:

> Probably no single event in the history of American higher education has effected [sic] more colleges with the kinds of problems than the Civil Rights Act of 1964 passed by the Congress of the United States. In an effort to eliminate discretion and bring the full rights of citizenship to all people in this country, our government has posed more problems for its colleges. Along with the introduction of these many complicated problems, our federal and state governments have also instituted many ways in which these colleges can obtain financial assistance and guidance in meeting these critical situations. Many of our church-related and private colleges, along with all of our state-owned tax supported colleges, have been taking full advantage of this financial assistance with government money. Only very few of our private colleges have not made federal government loans or participated in financial benefits of government-sponsored projects.[54]

"Brenau College," Dr. Crudup declared, "is one of these independent colleges not yet receiving any governmental financial support whatsoever."[55]

Other institutions were not so lucky—or as foresightful in their financial planning—as Brenau. Dr. Crudup described the plight of one such school that happened to be much like Brenau:

> Recently, the president of Converse College, which seems to be under pressure because of the Civil Rights Act, sent me a letter asking our position in this matter. More recently, the Chairman of the Converse Board of Trustees sent to Mr. Thurmond [a Brenau Trustee] a letter revealing the same concern for Converse in the matter of dormitory housing and discipline. The use of borrowed federal government funds to build new buildings has some advantages and can easily implement big developments, but it also has its complications.[56]

Institutional Policymaking as Staff & Faculty Forte 207

In describing the "complications" of Converse College, Dr. Crudup told Brenau's trustees about the horror that might have been. The two institutions were, after all, very similar, both being small, private, southern liberal arts colleges for women with no church affiliation. Yet, because Converse College had made a deal to get funding with the devil that was the federal government, it would have to integrate—which it did in September of 1968, at least four full years earlier than Brenau.[57] But integration at Converse would not just mean that white students would have to attend classes with black students. Dr. Crudup intimated that white students would have to live alongside black students in the college dormitories as well. Brenau students would not have to suffer this indignity thanks to the foresight of Brenau's leadership in not taking money from the government. Dr. Crudup declared, "Mr. Thurmond and I agree that we feel quite happy that Brenau College has been making its progress on a cash basis without borrowing any funds whatsoever."[58]

Elsewhere in his 1965 report to the Brenau Board of Trustees, Dr. Crudup took pains to validate his strategy with the mantle of legal expertise. He told the trustees:

> Last December, the Southern Association of Colleges invited Dr. Jerry Williams, Rex Baker Professor of Law, University of Texas Law School to address the Association on the implications of the Civil Rights Act of 1964. Copies of this address were delivered to the college presidents following the meeting. I carefully studied Dr. William's analysis of the Civil Rights Act and its effect on our colleges. As Dr. Williams analyzes the act from Title I to Title VIII, it becomes evident that this law requires all college recipients of federal financial support from tax moneys to desegregate. However, Dr. Williams concludes the analysis with this statement, "This law has nothing to do with the segregation or integrating of students or faculty of a purely private school. If there is no question of public accommodations, nor employment question, and if it has not had federal programs, state aid of one kind or another, then this law simply does not apply to it."[59]

Dr. Crudup concluded, "It is my opinion that Brenau College falls in the category of a purely private College and the mandates of the Civil Rights Act do not apply to this college."[60]

Although Dr. Crudup believed that not complying with the mandates of the Civil Rights Act left Brenau free to remain segregated, noncompliance came at some cost. Dr. Crudup told the trustees that:

> Recently, Brenau College received a form from the US Department of Health, Welfare, and Education asking this college to sign the Assurance of Compliance with the Civil Rights Act and return it to Washington. This has not been done. Later, we received a notice from the Georgia State Government Surplus Agency in Atlanta informing Brenau that we can no longer take advantage of their bargain purchases without signing the assurance of compliance. This has not been done and we have not attempted to make any purchases from this agency since that time.[61]

Records do not indicate how much Brenau might have benefited from this program. It was apparently worth something to many other institutions. Minutes from the trustee's meeting reveal that, "[Dr. Crudup] reported that according to information received, all colleges in Georgia had signed certificates of compliance as to non-segregation except Mercer, LaGrange, Shorter, and Brenau, and that Brenau cannot receive any surplus United States property" for having not signed.[62] Among other reasons, it is possible that most schools had signed on to keep availing themselves of this or other government programs.

Another cost of non-compliance was minor, but real. The minutes of some of the trustees' meetings indicated that because Brenau chose to remain segregated, the institution could not "continue with students under Vocational Rehabilitation programs."[63] This had little immediate impact on the College because, according to the minutes, Dr. Crudup determined that "only two students were at Brenau under that program when he recently checked the situation."[64] Of course, how much Brenau might have been able to take advantage of these programs had it not remained

Institutional Policymaking as Staff & Faculty Forte 209

segregated cannot be determined. It seems reasonable to assume that some benefits would accrue to institutions that chose to avail themselves of such programs supported by the vast federal largess.

Other programs might have helped Brenau as well, chief among them being programs that provided federal government financial aid to students. Brenau's Archives include several pieces of correspondence from Dr. Crudup that indicated Brenau wanted no part of this. In a September 1, 1964, letter, Dr. Crudup wrote, "Our philosophy of education here at Brenau College and Academy does not involve acceptance of any responsibility in helping parents pay tuition fees."[65] In a letter to Congressman Carl Elliot dated April 6, 1964, Dr. Crudup expressed that, "Brenau College has not participated in any federal grant programs nor any state-financed educational projects."[66] Another letter to the congressman written on May 28, 1964, drove the point home further as Dr. Crudup indicated, "Brenau College does not participate in any Federal Government program of student assistance."[67] Had Brenau assisted students in obtaining federal financial aid, tuition money to the College might have been more forthcoming. Contained in the archived correspondence of Dr. Crudup are copies of literally dozens of very polite letters written to parents to inform them of a balance due on their daughter's account and to point out to parents that because Brenau obtained no government money, it relied heavily on prompt and full payment of tuition to cover operating costs. Some of the outstanding bills were for several months' worth of education-related expenses and amounted to several hundred dollars. Had parents enjoyed the assistance of Brenau in obtaining federal aid for their students, it stands to reason that more tuition might have been paid more promptly, which would have empowered Brenau financially.

Another great cost of resisting integration related to donorship. Large corporate and philanthropic foundations had been financial benefactors of private colleges like Brenau for decades, often donating several thousand dollars or more to these schools. Such gifts were godsends for institutions with modest financial resources. Brenau itself received large donations from the Ford Foundation in the 1950s.[68] At a segregated Brenau, this well might run dry. Dr. Crudup told the trustees that, "many of the larger Foundations seem to be inclined to continue their support only to those independent colleges which have completely desegregated in harmony with the purpose of the Civil Rights Act of 1964."[69] Colleges like Brenau that refused to integrate did so at the risk of losing this significant financial support. This was a high price to pay for adherence to segregationist principles, but it was apparently one Brenau was willing to stomach. Even after hearing this information, the Brenau trustees supported their president's strategy for remaining an all-white institution: "Upon motion of Trustee Carter Estes, Brenau's policy of student selection in keeping with Brenau's traditions was approved."[70] Of course, keeping with tradition at Brenau meant barring African American women from attendance.

Despite these several and sometimes significant costs, Brenau College resisted integration primary by relying on the notion that it could not be forced to integrate because of its policy against accepting government money of any kind. One record indicated that so great was the desire on the part of College officials to remain segregated that they contemplated other means to resist integration as well. Dr. Crudup revealed this information in a portion of his 1965 report to the Brenau College Board of Trustees dealing with the Hall County School of Nursing. This was a joint venture between Brenau and local government, which opened its doors to its first students, a class of ten women from local communities, on September 11, 1960.[71] Dr. Crudup related:

> Hall School of Nursing will complete its fourth year and present its third class of registered nurses for graduation this summer. The enrollment of the school has now reached its full enrollment and will be graduating approximately 20 registered nurses each year from this time forth. It requires no imagination to clearly see the tremendous service to society being rendered by Hall School of Nursing and Brenau College in this splendid joint enterprise. But,

we are now confronted with some very serious problems brought about by the Civil Rights Act.[72]

In keeping with his view that any educational institutions that received government funding would be subject to integration, Dr. Crudup acknowledged that the joint educational enterprise that was the Hall County School of Nursing would be affected by the Civil Rights Act of 1964. Nevertheless, Dr. Crudup stated that other measures would suffice to forestall desegregation of the school for some time. He indicated:

> The pressure to desegregate Hall School of Nursing because of its federal government financial support has already made itself known in applications for enrollment. Because the school is small and applications for enrollment far exceeding the capacity of the school have come in early, we have temporarily solved the problem of integration. However, this procedure will not be satisfactory as a regular practice in the years ahead. Ultimately, all tax supported educational institutions must desegregate.[73]

This passage specifies that Brenau would also rely on simple white applicant volume to keep blacks out of school. By implication, Brenau could have passed over a very qualified black applicant in favor of admitting one of the many more average white applicants in its large applicant pool. But even if this measure failed, Dr. Crudup indicated that other measures might be taken. He warned the trustees that, "When the problem of integration at Hall School of Nursing becomes acute, the Trustees of Brenau College will be faced with a major decision concerning integration."[74] He went on to say that, "While this is not an acute problem at the present time and there are several possible solutions to this matter, yet [sic] I call this to the attention of the Trustees so that their thinking can prepare us for careful consideration when this time comes."[75] Dr. Crudup did not indicate what the several other possible solutions to the problem of integration might be, but, based upon his statements, he presumably had some backup plans in mind. Exactly what lengths Dr. Crudup would have gone to in keeping Brenau's doors closed to blacks is uncertain. What is certain is that Brenau remained firmly segregated during Dr. Crudup's nearly twenty-five year tenure as the College president.

Though Dr. Crudup arguably played a key role in keeping Brenau segregated, it would be unfair to blame him alone for perpetuating the College's resistance to integration. For segregation to have succeeded at Brenau as well as it did for as long as it did would have required more of an institutional culture of indifference to racial equality or even prejudice. It is probable that this existed and was maintained by Brenau's faculty and, perhaps, its students as well as its administration prior to the 1970s. Dr. James Southerland, a long-time employee of the College who taught history at Brenau from 1969 until 2013 and who would go on to serve as Brenau's Provost and Vice President for Academics, spoke about this culture in correspondence. Regarding integration, he indicated:

> I came in with about 20 new faculty in 1969 in anticipation of a [Southern Association of Colleges and Schools] self-study. We were brought in to change the complexion of the campus to secure reaccreditation. Dr. Crudup had recruited folks who were retired from high school teaching. He paid them very little but gave them housing. Most of them were in their sixties. By the time African American students came to Brenau, they had retired. They might have objected, I suppose, had they still been there.[76]

The faculty members photographed in the *Bubbles* annuals of the 1950s and 1960s were all white and mostly male; indeed, the only photographs of black people included in these or any other yearbooks at all for many years were of the dormitory and sorority house maids and custodians.[77] Dr. Southerland's estimation that these members of the old guard might have been likely to join Dr. Crudup in resisting integration is perhaps given more credence by this observation.[78] Regarding the new faculty members and the students, Dr. Southerland also said that, "I don't recall any controversy on campus, at least not with the new faculty. There may have been some among the students, but it wasn't apparent. The average faculty member had no problem with integration; in fact, most of the faculty were pretty liberal and wanted that to happen."[79]

The faculty members who joined Brenau in the late 1960s were not the only new personnel who seemed amenable to integration. With the retirement of Dr. Crudup in 1965, Dr. William K. Clark became Brenau's fifth president. He would serve until 1970. The Archives contain relatively few papers from the Clark administration, but one bit of correspondence offers some telling insight into Dr. Clark's attitude regarding race. In a letter dated October 6, 1969, Ms. Marion Vickers, a Brenau alumnae and teacher in Cherokee County, Georgia, inquired with Dr. Clark about the possibility of some of her students attending a concert series at Brenau. She wrote:

> There is one question I have that may present problems. There are three black students in our companion group from Cherokee County. Being a Brenau graduate, I do not wish to cause any discomfort; therefore, please advise me as to whether it would be permissible for them to attend these events.[80]

Dr. Clark responded, saying:

> I am sure no one in North Georgia can tell when the presence of some black people in an audience will cause discomfort to some other party in that audience. Certainly I can assure you that your three black students would cause me no discomfort and I am sure that in your company they would bring only credit to the program in which you include them.[81]

If this letter is any indication, Dr. Clark was no segregationist.

Whether or not, like Dr. Clark, the white students at Brenau during the decades of the fifties, sixties, and seventies wanted integration to happen or whether they wanted Brenau to remain segregated is difficult to discern. No archived student correspondence or articles in student publications ever spoke about integration, pro or con. Even so, it might be telling that despite the fact that African American students began enrolling in Brenau in 1972, the photographs in the *Bubbles* of some student organizations generally depict no black women members until the mid to late 1980s and then often depict only one or two. This may suggest that these organizations did not recruit blacks—though, in fairness to these groups, they may not have discouraged African American young women from joining either.

Brenau's sororities were even slower to integrate than most campus organizations. They would remain all-white until as late as 1994. In that year, photographs in the *Bubbles* indicated that a single African American woman had joined Alpha Gamma Delta, likely making this the first sorority at Brenau to admit a black member. Even a decade later, only one or two African American women are listed as being members of any of Brenau's predominately white sororities, despite the fact that Brenau had increased its enrollment of black women significantly. Granted, it may be that black students at Brenau around this time preferred to join one of the two or three African American sororities that came to exist alongside Brenau's other Greek groups. Still, the fact remains that the University's Panhellenic sororities could scarcely be described as diverse. This might suggest that, historically, some students in some of Brenau's Greek organizations may have been indifferent toward integration.[82]

At least some Brenau students apparently knew about and actually appreciated Brenau's policies of fostering institutional independence from government interference. In an April 1965 edition of Brenau's student newspaper, the *Alchemist*, editor Zella Octavia Buttram demonstrated this. She wrote an editorial that dealt with Brenau's image and essentially responded to an unfavorable article about Brenau published in the *Red and Black*, the student newspaper of the University of Georgia. Buttram wrote of Brenau that "we are one of two absolutely free and independent institutions left in Georgia" and that "As yet, we are not coerced by having accepted state, federal, or church funds, and so our opinions like our campus are still our own."[83] Though she never engaged the subject of segregation, Buttram's sentiments about Brenau's independence echoed those of Josiah Crudup. Such sentiments could have led either to conclude that Brenau had the ability to exclude from attendance whomever it saw fit.

Whether students agreed or disagreed with Dr. Crudup's stance regarding the admittance of African Americans to the College is unclear. It is probable that opinions about this varied among students over time. In the final analysis, though, student opinion on the matter apparently would have counted for very little. Nowhere in any of his speeches or correspondence regarding desegregation did Dr. Crudup mention what Brenau students might have thought or wanted. The implication of this is that Brenau's governors assumed they knew best and simply never took student views on the matter into account. Any ongoing negotiation regarding race on campus was, therefore, decidedly one-sided. Yet, this may have been an instance where no negotiation was needed. During the Crudup administration, many members of the student body and of the faculty and staff may have all been on more or less the same page. Students may not have pressed the administration for a voice in any negotiation over admitting blacks simply because they were silently assenting and agreeing to the College's practices and policies. On some other college campuses during the Civil Rights era, students rallied and protested racially restrictive admissions policies and perhaps contributed to the rescission of such policies at some institutions. Nothing in the Archives suggests that Brenau students ever raised their voices on the subject either way—or that they were given ample opportunity to do so by College officials.

But what if some Brenau students *had* protested the College's stance on segregation? Would this have induced Brenau's faculty and staff to enter into a dialog with students to shape the Brenau college experience? Or was making policy decisions simply the non-negotiable province of Brenau personnel? Examining the development of another of Brenau's institutional policies—this one permitting the enrollment of men—may suggest answers to these questions.

Since its founding as a women's college and for decades thereafter, Brenau had remained a completely single-gender institution. However, in 1969, though it maintained its focus on educating women, Brenau "began offering evening classes to male students at the junior and senior levels."[84] Two years later, officials amended the Brenau charter to include mention of male students. Despite appearances, according to administrators, these policy moves were "not to coeducation."[85] They were also apparently not moves that Brenau officials made in consultation with students or that students endured without comment

Dr. Southerland was involved in the changes that facilitated the enrollment of men. He related:

> We began an evening program and felt that it would be more successful if men were admitted. I think there was a feeling of serving the community behind the move as well as financial considerations. We did admit some men to day classes if they were experiencing a financial hardship and could not go to a coed school in another city. We did this for a few years in the 80's. I was a division chair and had a little to do with the decision.[86]

Dr. Southerland added, "If we had not added an evening program here and in several distant locations along with a later weekend program including graduate programs, I am sure the school would not have survived. We had to move with the times."[87]

Brenau did survive and, in the process, ultimately remained faithful to its mission to educate women. The fate of other American women's colleges was different. Many closed or became entirely coeducational. In 1960, almost 300 women's colleges existed nationwide. By 2001, only 74 remained.[88] Scarcely a decade later, that number had dropped to just 46.[89] In a rather tragic irony, women's colleges fell victim to their own success. For generations, graduates of these institutions had proven that women could thrive in college—which, in turn, induced most colleges and universities (state and private alike) that had not done so before to begin admitting women. As more educational opportunities opened for women, fewer women enrolled in women's colleges. It was the resulting loss of tuition revenue from this decreased enrollment that forced most women's colleges to either close or become coeducational.

Often, the decision to admit men was a difficult one for a women's college to make. Scott Jaschik, a writer for *Inside Higher Ed*, noted, "Many colleges that have gone coed have done so over the objections of students enrolled at the time the decision was made."[90] For example, at Wells College, the decision to become coeducational "was met with protests and legal threats by some students who wanted the institution to remain all-female."[91] At Randolph College (formerly Randolph-Macon Woman's College), women students who felt they had been promised a single-gendered education upon enrollment filed suit for breach of contract when the institution began admitting men in 2006.[92] At Mills College, "the board voted in 1990 to admit men, but the board reversed itself following student protests."[93]

As had been the case with Brenau's racial admissions policies, officials seem to have made institutional policies regarding gender absent student input. The issue of coeducation garnered attention from students that the issue of race never seemed to. The November 4, 1970, edition of the *Alchemist* reported, "The 93-year-old liberal arts college for women in Gainesville has now adopted a policy for admitting non-resident male students."[94] Dr. James Rogers, Brenau's president at the time, made the announcement at a weekly College convocation attended by both Brenau faculty members and students. The *Alchemist* article indicated that the move was necessary for Brenau to continue its relationship with the Hall County School of Nursing, which had begun admitting males. Additionally, Dr. Rogers pointed out that men who had earned two-year degrees at junior colleges would be able to complete their bachelor degrees at Brenau. The *Alchemist* related:

> The opinion of the students presently enrolled at Brenau was mixed. Some voiced the opinion that they wanted Brenau to be

free from male students. Others were delighted that men would now be able to take courses at the college.[95]

One student interviewed noted, "that when men start attending classes, the girls might 'dress up a little more.'"[96]

The November 17, 1970, edition of the *Alchemist* ran a feature entitled, "Co-Education—Pro and Con" in which two student writers addressed the merits and the demerits of the decision. Sally Collins explained that, "By admitting male students, Brenau is filling extra spaces and doing a service to the community," particularly by giving male teachers living in Gainesville a convenient place to take continuing education courses.[97] The College seconded these reasons in its 1979 *Institutional Self-Study*, as officials stated:

> [I]t is important to question why a college such as Brenau decided to implement such new programs. The answer to this question is found by looking at several factors. First, the State Board of Education discontinued the issuance of "life certificates" for teachers in 1975; all persons receiving teaching certificates thereafter have been required to earn staff development units or college credit in order to renew their certificates. Secondly, each year more elementary and secondary schools are applying for S.A.C.S. accreditation, and teachers in these schools are required to earn ten hours of staff development or college credit every five years to meet accreditation requirements. Thirdly, Gainesville is the popular and industrial center of Northeast Georgia, and many businesses encourage their employees to obtain additional educational training in administration. Finally, Brenau College continually tries to identify areas of growth and development for the purpose of broadening its resource base, servicing the North Georgia area, and offering the alternative of graduate study at a private college.[98]

Prior to Brenau's move, opportunities for higher education were limited for men living in or near Gainesville. Gainesville Junior College, which was a state school actually situated in Oakwood, Georgia, just south of the city of Gainesville, opened in 1966 and offered associate's degrees.[99]

State-run North Georgia College in Dahlonega, Georgia, and private Piedmont College in Demorest, Georgia, were the closest four-year-degree granting institutions to Gainesville. Although both had enrolled men for decades, each was about twenty-five miles from Gainesville.

Some students were unmoved by these considerations. Cindy Francis wrote in the November 17 edition of the *Alchemist*, "Two weeks ago, a tradition held supreme by most girls on this campus was broken. BOYS WERE ADMITTED. ... With boys on campus, Brenau will lose its uniqueness as being a small liberal arts college for women."[100] Francis related an anecdote about how Limestone College in South Carolina became coeducational "to illustrate the downfall Brenau could encounter with this new co-ed policy."[101] Limestone's decision of a few years ago had led to "12 boarding males who live in an old faculty building located ON CAMPUS."[102] Moreover, "While talking to people within the Limestone community, they said that the standards of the girls have decreased rapidly."[103] Francis intimated that the same could happen at Brenau.

Evidence suggests that many people in the Brenau community about this time shared Francis' views. In 1971, Brenau commissioned a third-party study of "attitudes toward the College."[104] In response to the question, "Should Brenau Be Coeducational?" the report indicated:

> One issue which was repeatedly brought to the attention of the Study Director was the decision of the Board to admit male students to Brenau College. As this matter emerged early as a predominant factor, your director made every effort to explore the feelings of all persons interviewed concerning this move. Of the 103 interviewed, 34 were adamant in expressing their dislike of young men on campus, 4 felt they should have been more selective, and 2 were in favor of admitting young men; 63 persons offered "no comment" on this issue. Of the 18 Board Members interviewed, 6 (30%) were opposed to admitting young men, 2 were dubious and expressed a "wait and see" attitude, and 10 were agreeable if it would be of benefit to Brenau.[105]

"In addition to those listed," the study continued, "a group interview was held with 15 students."[106] The young women interviewed, "were 100% opposed to having males admitted to the College."[107] Some faculty and staff members may also have had reservations about enrolling men. Speaking of the Brenau personnel, President Burd noted, "A lot of the people who were there came there because it was a women's college."[108] It is quite conceivable that some might have preferred that the College remain exclusively so.

Francis closed her critical piece in the *Alchemist* with an interesting commentary. She wrote:

> One advantage to this small college system is that the student is allowed to voice opinions representing the entire study body in such groups as the self-study committee and faculty-trustee relationship programs. If we are asked to participate in these such groups—WHY WERE WE NOT QUESTIONED ABOUT THE CO-ED POLICY???????????[109]

The October 21, 1970, edition of the *Alchemist* reported on some of these groups. For example, it described "a meeting of the college's board of trustees, a part of which was taken up with a student-trustee dialog program."[110] The article read:

> At Brenau, the college administrators have in the past years placed students on key committees within the organizational set-up of the college. Students sit on numerous college committees, including the admissions committee, the concert committee, the library committee, the student affairs committee, the student conduct committee, the student faculty current events committee and the teacher education committee.[111]

This article suggests that by 1970, Brenau's faculty and staff were setting up ways for students to become more involved with some of the bodies that determined institutional policy matters. There was actually some precedent for this at the College.

Institutional Policymaking as Staff & Faculty Forte 221

In his May 30, 1952, report to the Brenau Board of Trustees, President Josiah Crudup told the Trustees:

> The morale of the student body at the close of this year has been excellent, though it was most unsatisfactory last October as manifested by a one meal strike at supper on October 10. There was justification for complaint on the part of the students and we took immediate steps to correct this matter. We are continuing to study our dining hall problems and feel that more improvements can be made, though no student dissatisfaction was made known this spring.[112]

From this collective action on the part of students, Dr. Crudup sought to open lines of communication. He informed the trustees that, "A student-faculty committee was organized and meets just before regular faculty meetings to review the needs of the students and recommend improvements. This committee has worked well."[113]

Exactly how the committee worked well or for how long it did so is unclear. Nothing mentioned in any of the materials in the Brenau Archives qualifies its contribution to policy making at the institution. Presumably, it would have wanted to give input on a matter as important as coeducation. Yet, taken at face-value, Francis' article suggests that, committee or not, Brenau women were not consulted in making what might arguably be the biggest policy decision a women's college could make. This would seem to beg the question of whether or not student views were really being given serious attention by the faculty and staff around the 1970s.

Some evidence may suggest not. The Institutional Self-Study prepared by Brenau in 1979 indicated that "the controls exercised by the faculty over various groups and activities are varied."[114] In some instances, the faculty maintained a great deal of control; in others, faculty members served as little more than informal advisors. Moreover, though, the study stated that, "One strong control exercised by the administration is financial support. Presently, the student activities budget is allocated by the administration."[115] Though student organizations could make recommendations about "the division of the budgetary figure," students had no control over purse strings.[116] It seems doubtful that students could have exercised much influence in negotiations over institutional policies like coeducation (or much else, for that matter) without a significant voice in how funds would be spent.

The Self-Study also addressed "Student Participation in Institutional Government." It read:

> Inherent in the philosophy of Brenau is the creation of a small-college, interpersonal atmosphere, which, in turn, encourages a community, a College family. It is, therefore, necessary to open lines of communication and encourage participation at all levels, from students to faculty to administrative staff. In light of this goal, student participation in the governing of the College becomes desirable, if not imperative.[117]

To facilitate this "imperative" participation, Brenau students were represented on several standing committees. No appointment procedure existed; rather, the Dean of Student Development made committee assignments "with suggestions from the Faculty/Student Affairs Committee."[118] The arrangement apparently did not impress many students. The results of a 1980 survey taken by the College indicated "that many students think they do not have a role in decision-making processes at Brenau."[119] Indeed, of six faculty committees on which students served, the Self-Report indicated that students had voting rights only in the Faculty/Student Affairs Committee.[120] The ensuing years seemed to bring few changes. Both the 1995 and the 2007 undergraduate and graduate catalogs mentioned various committees at several places, but never indicated specifically that students served on any committees or suggested that students played significant roles in setting institutional policy.[121]

If Brenau seemed to do little to involve students in negotiations over institutional policies like admitting men or African Americans, it was not alone. In *Should Students Share the Power?: A study of their role in college and university governance,* Earl James McGrath noted that in 1970, "No comprehensive body of fact showing the extent of student involvement in academic government has existed before...; accordingly, the American Academy of Arts and Sciences in late 1969 instituted [a] survey to determine how far the developments of student participation had proceeded."[122] Speaking of the survey results, McGrath concluded:

> The main generalization which these facts permit is that although until three or four years ago American colleges and universities severely limited the involvement of students in academic government, now membership in one or another "faculty" committee is becoming the rule rather than the exception. The findings reveal that in the fall of 1969, 88.3 per cent of the 875 institutions that supplied usable information had admitted some students to membership in at least one policy-making body. It is, therefore, the atypical institution which has not moved in this direction, and such institutions are now for the most part actively considering doing so.[123]

Despite appearances, this was actually no cause for celebration. McGrath concluded:

> Those who believe that students have a right to a role in shaping educational policies will doubtless be reassured by the fact that almost nine out of ten institutions have already adopted such a policy. It would be a mistake, however, to jump from the foregoing figures to the satisfying conclusion that students are now in a position to exert strong influence on basic educational policy. Such an inference must be qualified by ... the kinds of committees on which students serve and their status in those bodies. No exhaustive documentation is required to demonstrate that, in terms of influence, membership in committees on social activities and entertainment, traffic and parking, homecoming, a spring festival, or a parents' day is not equivalent to voting status in the executive committee, the committee on the curriculum, on faculty selection and tenure, on admissions, or on degree requirements.[124]

Research suggests that, at most institutions of higher learning, little has changed in almost three decades. College and university students everywhere—including at Brenau—still enjoy relatively little actual policymaking influence on campuses compared to the faculty and staff.[125]

Another constituency that would have been concerned about Brenau's policy changes to admit men and African Americans was the alumnae. Alumni, one expert observed, "do take a very strong interest in their alma maters and do feel, legally or otherwise, that they have a stake in the future of the institution."[126] The Brenau Archives contain relatively few materials related to alumnae, and so little documentation exists to qualify alumnae views on these matters. Yet, according to other sources, some Brenau alumnae did not embrace the changes at the College easily. For example, regarding the establishment of the evening and weekend program that would admit men, Dr. Burd noted, "There were a lot of men who wanted to be in those programs," but some alumnae resisted their creation.[127] "It took some convincing," Dr. Burd recalled, "but when they saw how it helped the school financially, they were not going to argue with that."[128] He added, "And as long as we kept only women living on campus, that showed that we really did want to educate only women at the undergraduate level in the Women's College."[129]

What also helped assuage both women students and alumnae regarding the admission of men to Brenau was the fact that the policy change simply did not open the floodgates for male enrollment in the Women's College. Few men have apparently ever attended the women's division at Brenau under any circumstances. No official count exists, but other evidence bears this out.

For a handful of years after 1971, each edition of the *Bubbles* yearbook published one or two photographs of male students—just that and no more. After this time, there are no male student photographs. Had many men ever enrolled in the Women's College, one would expect to find more photographic evidence of this in yearbooks. Additionally, the window in which men might have enrolled in the Women's College proper absent extenuating circumstances was apparently quite narrow. Brenau's 1984–1985 *Institutional Self-Study for the Professional College* noted that, "After a one-year trial in which male students were admitted into classes in The Women's College, the Board [of Trustees] decided to restrict enrollment by male students to The Professional College."[130] Thereafter, only very few men would attend day classes.

By 2000, officials estimated that males made up "about 20 percent of the students at Brenau University" (including those in the evening and weekend programs) and that "between five and 15 of the Women's College's 658 students" were males who were allowed into the University's nursing, theater and dance programs.[131] Dr. Burd noted that some of these programs actually needed at least some men to truly function (such as dance and theater, which required male leads for some performances) and so permitted a handful of males to take particular classes through the Women's College.[132] Still, even this was rare and required special administrative permission. Males could only enroll in the Women's College "as irregular students for special course work or to meet specific schedule or program requirements on a permission basis only" provided by the Dean of the College.[133]

In addition, taking an occasional class at the Women's College was one thing; taking a degree from the Women's College was entirely another. By President John Burd's recollection of what he had heard over the years at Brenau, only four men reputedly ever actually graduated from the Women's College in the early 1970s before the evening and weekend programs launched and absorbed almost all male enrollment.[134] Other accounts bespoke even less. A newspaper article published in the year 2000 reported that "a college trustee thinks a male may have taken part in a graduation ceremony for the Women's College many years ago, but school officials aren't sure."[135] Even men studying dance, drama, or nursing who would take an occasional class in the Women's College were expected to graduate from the evening and weekend/professional division. An isolated exception that occurred to this practice actually led Brenau to firmly re-embrace this policy.

Brenau's catalogs have long let males know before they enrolled in the nursing program that they could not be part of the Women's College graduation ceremony because they were to be admitted as part of the separate Evening and Weekend College division.[136] In May of 2000, after a bit of wrangling that, at one point, even involved an "anti-discrimination lawyer," administrators permitted three male nursing students to take part in the graduation ceremony at the Women's College—the first and last time such a thing happened.[137] Thereafter, Brenau has taken pains to apprise all male students that future Women's College graduations would be all-women's affairs.

The histories of bringing African Americans and men to Brenau suggest that the process of policy making at the institution has been largely monopolized by the faculty and staff, even in the face of student concern. Throughout much of Brenau's history, little, if any, negotiation seems to have taken place with students over truly significant policy matters. Though the process may have been one-sided, some of the results—at least in recent history—seem to have benefitted everyone.

Given its history, it is striking how far Brenau has come with respect to race. The College was once truly remarkable for the lengths to which it went to remain racially segregated. Few—if any—other colleges anywhere in the country employed so successfully for so long such a calculated strategic policy to avoid integration as did Brenau. Indeed, Brenau may very well have been the last college of its kind to integrate in America. Prior to 1970, predominately white northern and western women's colleges had admitted African American women for some years. With the exception of Salem College in North Carolina, southern women's colleges as a whole were typically the last to integrate.[138] Among them, as mentioned earlier, Agnes Scott and Converse colleges desegregated before 1970. Columbia College in South Carolina "integrated without incident" in 1966.[139] In the fall semester of 1963, Sophie Newcomb College in New Orleans admitted its first black student.[140] "The first black student to graduate from Tift College in Macon "received her diploma in 1970," as did the first African-American woman to attend Hollins University in Virginia, meaning these women would have first enrolled in the late 1960s.[141] In 1968, Alabama's Judson College "accepted six African American women as students" and the first African American students enrolled at Meredith College in North Carolina and Wesleyan College in Georgia.[142] Marshalyn Yeargin became the first black student at Virginia's Sweet Briar College in 1968 as well.[143] Juanita Symmonds and Lelia Anne Lytle became the first African American graduates from Mary Baldwin College in Virginia in 1972, after having first enrolled in the late 1960s.[144] In that year, Ms. Belinda Harrison, the daughter of a school principal in Gainesville, became the first African American to enroll at Brenau College.[145] Three other African American young women (Michelle Gray, Lois Green, and Natalee Roberts) would join her in attending Brenau as freshmen in 1972.[146] These students intrepidly blazed a trail that many others would follow.

By 2012, it almost seemed as if Brenau was trying to make up for lost time, trying to make amends for its segregated history. The University aggressively recruits both students from racial minority groups and international students, which accounts for its current diversity. Where they were once excluded from campus, today African American students thrive at Brenau. Recent yearbooks repeatedly depict these young women as being integral members of the University community. Many hold important leadership positions. A number of resident assistants in campus dormitories are African American. Since the year 2000, some of the officers in Brenau's Student Government Association have been African American, including the president. Several African American young women have won the coveted "Miss Brenau" contest, which showcases scholarly activity and artistic expression. Some of Brenau's star athletes are black as are many of the College's brightest students. Put simply, Brenau in the twenty-first century fully embraces an ethos of racial inclusion and is doing as much to encourage integration today as it did to discourage integration only a few decades ago. At the same time, Brenau remains—for all intents and purposes—a women's college, one of only a handful still in existence. When other women's colleges closed or became entirely coeducational, Brenau stayed its course. True, Brenau did adopt policies that ultimately permitted a very small number of men to enroll at the College even before it created a separate unit (the Evening and Weekend College) open to men. Yet, the mission and focus of the Women's College has never wavered from serving the educational needs of young women as it has for well over a century. Like the policy decisions that created this diverse women's college—whether made for philosophical reasons, pragmatic reasons, or, as is likely, out of concern for both—many future questions about institutional policies will surely be of keen interest to Brenau students as well as University personnel. Whether or not faculty members and staff members will continue to command negotiations over such policy questions as they have in the past or will collaborate more with students to set institutional policy remains to be seen. What is certain is that both Brenau's faculty & staff and its students will hope for answers to such questions that will benefit the institution in which both share a common interest.

NOTES

1. Jensen Design Studio, "Brenau Undergraduate Viewbook," http://jensendesignstudio.com/wp-content/uploads/2011/11/brenau_viewbook_spreads.pdf (accessed 17 January 2013).
2. Office of Research and Planning, "Fast Facts - Fall 2012," Brenau University, http://intranet.brenau.edu/facts/ (accessed 17 January 2013).
3. Ibid.
4. Linda M. Perkins, "The Education of Black Women in the Nineteenth Century," in John Mack Faragher and Florence Howe, eds., *Women and Higher Education in American History* (New York, NY: W.W. Norton & Co., 1988), 70.
5. According to Ronald Butchart, Stanton received the "Lit.B" degree, which "was a college degree, intended for women, as a somewhat 'softer' course than the one open to men; it was Oberlin's way of handling coeducation, and gave women a less rigorous education than they would have received at a women's college." Ronald Butchart, e-mail message to author, 27 June 2008.
6. Roland M. Baumann, "A History of Recording Black Students at Oberlin College and the Story of the Missing Record," Oberlin College, 2002, http://www.oberlin.edu/archive/holdings/finding/RG5/SG4/S3/2002intro.html (accessed 17 January 2013).
7. W.E. Burghardt DuBois, *The College-bred Negro: Report of a Social Study Made Under the Direction of Atlanta University, Together with the Proceedings of the Fifth Conference for the Study of the Negro Problems, held at Atlanta University, May 29–30, 1900* (Atlanta, GA: Atlanta University Press, 1900), 54–55; available from The Digital Library of Georgia, http://fax.libs.uga.edu/E185x5xA881p/aup05/ (accessed 17 January 2013).
8. Jeanne Noble, "The Higher Education of Black Women in the Twentieth Century," in John Mack Faragher and Florence Howe, eds., *Women and Higher Education in American History*, (New York, NY: W.W. Norton & Co., 1988), 98.
9. U.S. Department of Education Office for Civil Rights, "Historically Black Colleges and Universities and Higher Education Desegregation," http://www2.ed.gov/about/offices/list/ocr/docs/hq9511.html (accessed 17 January 2013).
10. Ibid.

11. See *Plessy v. Ferguson*, 163 U.S. 537 (1896).
12. Noble, "The Higher Education of Black Women," 99.
13. See *Brown v. Board of Education of Topeka, Kansas*, 98 F. Supp. 797 (1951), 347 U.S. 483 (1954), 349 U.S. 294 (1955). As pertains to higher education, the 1955 court case of *Frasier v. Board of Trustees of the University of North Carolina* (134 F. Supp. 589, 592–93 (M.D.N.C. 1955)) may be as relevant as *Brown*. In *Frasier*, the Supreme Court upheld a lower court ruling that required a state to adopt racially nondiscriminatory undergraduate admissions policies at its public colleges and universities. Seeing the writing on the wall, those private colleges that had not by now desegregated began falling into line—some sooner than others.
14. "Civil Rights Act of 1964." (Pub.L. 88–352), *United States Statutes at Large*, 78 Stat. 241 (2 July 1964).
15. Reginald Stuart, "New Trend in College Desegregation Emerges"; *The New York Times on the Web*; 3 September 3 1981, http://partners.nytimes.com/library/national/race/090381race-ra.html (accessed 17 January 2013).
16. "Title IX of the Education Amendments of 1972 to the Civil Rights Act of 1964." (Pub. L. 92–318), *United States Statutes at Large*, 86 Stat. 235 (23 June 1972).
17. Rosalind Rosenberg, "The Limits of Access: The History of Coeducation in America" in John Mack Faragher and Florence Howe, eds., *Women and Higher Education in American History* (New York, NY: W.W. Norton & Co., 1988), 107.
18. Ibid., 109. Rosenberg indicated that, "Today more than 95 percent of all college women are enrolled in coeducational institutions" (109).
19. Ibid., 111.
20. "List of mixed-sex colleges and universities in the United States," *Wikipedia*, http://en.wikipedia.org/wiki/List_of_mixed-sex_colleges_and_universities_in_the_United_States (accessed 17 January 2013).
21. Count generated from "Timeline of women's colleges in America," *Wikipedia*, http://en.wikipedia.org/wiki/Timeline_of_women%27s_colleges_in_America (accessed 13 February 2014).
22. Several other women's colleges existed in Georgia at one time or another. Among them were Andrew College (co-ed since 1956), Cox College (closed in 1934), Georgia College & State University (co-ed since 1967), Shorter College (co-ed since the 1950s), and Valdosta State University (co-ed since 1950). Ray C. Brown, "List of Colleges and Universities that have Closed, Merged, or Changed their Names: Georgia," 9 July 2012, http://www2.westminster-mo.edu/wc_users/homepages/staff/brownr/

GeorgiaCC.htm (accessed 17 January 2013). Dr. Brown is the Director of Institutional Research at Westminster College in Missouri and he maintains a superbly detailed website that describes transformations of higher education institutions throughout the nation.
23. Though not a woman's college, Atlanta University also admitted black women before the 1950s. Ron Butchart, email message to author, 28 June 2008. Additionally, though not in Georgia, Salem College in Winston-Salem, North Carolina, apparently "educated girls of African-American heritage as early as 1785." "History," Salem College, http://www.salem.edu/about/our-history (accessed 17 January 2013). Salem began conferring college degrees in the 1890s.
24. DuBois, *College-Bred Negro*, 34.
25. Ibid.
26. Ibid.
27. Ibid., 35.
28. Ibid.
29. Ibid.
30. Brenau College, *Bubbles* (Gainesville, GA; Brenau College, 1973), 111. Hereafter, references to this source are indicated as "*Bubbles* (1973)."
31. Memorandum written on November 27, 1973, by Dean John E. Sites as quoted in Rigney, *Brenau College 1878–1978*, 66. In fact, at least one other secret society apparently preceded the Tri-Kappas on campus. See the chapter on secret societies *supra.*
32. Ibid.
33. For more on the history of the second Ku Klux Klan, see Nancy MacLean, *Behind the Mask of Chivalry: The Making of the Second Ku Klux Klan* (New York, NY: Oxford University Press, 1994).
34. "Freshman—Sophomore Week," *Alchemist* (Gainesville, GA: Brenau College), vol. XII, no. 6 (3 December 1924), p. 1.
35. "Vernice Hurst is Queen of May Day Fete," *Alchemist* (Gainesville, GA: Brenau College), vol. XXI, no. 9 (14 May 1935), p. 1.
36. Staff member of the Brenau University Office of Admissions. Interview by author, 31 October 2006, Gainesville, Georgia. Written notes. The interviewee requested that her name be withheld from publication.
37. Elliot Dunwody, "Dunwody Writes His Impression of Dr. Joe Crudup," *Alchemist* (Gainesville, GA: Brenau College) vol. XXXII, no. 3 (23 October 1945), p. 1.
38. Ibid.

39. Brenau University, *Annual Catalog, Vol. 122* (Gainesville, GA: Brenau University, 2006), 12; available in the Brenau University Archives, Gainesville, Georgia. Hereafter, references to this source are indicated as "Catalog (2006)."
40. "Last Four-Year Class Graduates; Dr. Josiah Crudup Gives Address," *Chatsworth Times*, 17 May 1951; available from http://murraycountymuseum.com/mchs_5p_rev.html (accessed 17 January 2013).
41. Crudup, "Report to the Board (May 29, 1953)," p. 4.
42. Crudup, "Report to the Board (May 31, 1957)," p. 8.
43. Crudup, "Report to the Board (May 30, 1958)," p. 8.
44. Virginia Historical Society, "The Civil Rights Movement in Virginia," http://www.vahistorical.org/civilrights/massiveresistance.htm (accessed 17 January 2013).
45. Crudup, "Report to the Board (June 2, 1961)," p. 2.
46. Ibid., 2-3.
47. Ibid., 3.
48. Ibid.
49. Ibid.
50. Ibid.
51. Ibid.
52. Ibid.
53. Crudup, "Report to the Board (June 1, 1962)," p. 2.
54. Crudup, "Report to the Board (June 4, 1965)," p. 4.
55. Ibid.
56. Ibid.
57. Jeffrey R. Willis, *Converse College*, p. 117.
58. Crudup, "Report to the Board (June 4, 1965)," p. 4.
59. Ibid., 4-5.
60. Ibid., 5.
61. Ibid., 4.
62. Brenau Trustees, "Minutes of Meeting of Trustees of Brenau College (Friday, June 4, 1965)," William Clark Files, Box 7 of 7, Folder 3, p. 1, Brenau University Archives, Gainesville, Georgia. While what exactly constitutes "surplus United States property" is never qualified in the minutes, the term presumably relates to the Surplus Property Act of 1944 (49 U.S.C. 47151). Property is defined broadly in the Act to permit the government to sell anything from desks and chairs to boats, aircraft, and

even real estate. Congress apparently intended that the Act primarily facilitate the disposition of surplus military equipment.
63. Ibid.
64. Ibid.
65. Josiah Crudup, "Sept 1, 1964, letter to Mr. Malcolm Reese, Chairman of School Committee, Committee of 1000, Perry, Georgia," Dr. Crudup Files, Box 34 of 40, Folder 9, Brenau University Archives, Gainesville, Georgia.
66. Josiah Crudup, "April 6, 1964, letter to the Honorable Carl Elliot, Congressman, United States House of Representatives, Washington, D.C.," Dr. Crudup Files, Box 34 of 40, Folder 9, Brenau University Archives, Gainesville, Georgia.
67. Josiah Crudup, "May 28, 1964, letter to the Honorable Carl Elliot, Congressman, United States House of Representatives, Washington, D.C.," Dr. Crudup Files, Box 34 of 40, Folder 9, Brenau University Archives, Gainesville, Georgia.
68. See "Ford Foundation Annual Report 1957."
69. Crudup, "Report to the Board (June 4, 1965)," p. 5.
70. Brenau Trustees, "Minutes of Meeting of Trustees of Brenau College (Friday, June 4, 1965)," p. 2.
71. Brandee A. Thomas, "Women remember early years of nursing at 50-year reunion," *Gainesville Times*, 24 September 2010, http://www.gainesvilletimes.com/archives/38367/ (accessed 18 January 2012).
72. Crudup, "Report to the Board (June 4, 1965)," p. 13.
73. Ibid.
74. Ibid, 14.
75. Ibid.
76. James E. Southerland, Ph.D., former history professor, Provost, and Vice President for Academic Affairs, telephone interview by author, written notes, 03 November 2006, Gainesville, Georgia.
77. In an impressive gesture, even though they could not have attended Brenau themselves at the time, African American employees of the College occasionally supported the College with donations. "Negroes Aid Brenau Col." *Atlanta Daily World*, 31 July 1936, p. 1.
78. Another possibility is that Dr. Crudup kept a very heavy hand on Brenau's tiller and that faculty opinion regarding integration (or anything else) would not have mattered one way or the other to an administration that ran the entire show, so to speak. However, minutes of several faculty meetings at Brenau do document that faculty members were vot-

ing on matters pertaining to the College's curriculum, discipline, degree conferment, and student admissions, among other things. This suggests that the faculty was at least in the habit of giving input to the administration on matters of importance to the College. Of course, how much credence Dr. Crudup gave such input is the greater question for which an answer is difficult to discern.

79. Ibid.
80. "Letter from Ms. Marion Vickers to Dr. William K. Clark," 6 October 1969, from Box 3 (labeled "Correspondence June 1969 to May 1970"), Folder 3, Brenau University Archives, Gainesville, Georgia.
81. Ibid.
82. Parents, too, may not have all supported integration when it came to Greek life. Dr. Burd related one anecdote in which a parent met with him to express displeasure that their daughter would be rooming with a newly-admitted African American member in a sorority house, an arrangement which apparently suited the daughter just fine. Dr. Burd gave the parent a very cool reception. He went on to say that he later learned that the two sorority sisters remained roommates in subsequent years and became close friends. Dr. John S. Burd, interview by author, tape recording, Gainesville, Georgia, 23 September 2010.
83. Zella Octavia Buttram, "Image Controversy Continues," *Alchemist* (Gainesville, GA: Brenau College), 29 April 1965, p. 2.
84. Ann Mahefkey, "Brenau University," *New Georgia Encyclopedia*, 6 June 2006, http://www.georgiaencyclopedia.org/nge/Article.jsp?id=h-1449 (accessed 18 January 2013).
85. James E. Southerland, Ph.D., former history professor, Provost, and Vice President for Academic Affairs, email message to author, 7 September 2010.
86. Ibid.
87. Ibid.
88. Jingle Davis, "3 women's colleges in state beat odds Nationally, many are closing or allowing men," *Atlanta Journal Constitution*, 17 June 2001, sec. A, p. 1.
89. "Colleges & Universities by Name," The Women's College Coalition, http://www.womenscolleges.org/colleges/byname (accessed 13 February 2014).
90. Scott Jaschik, "Male Impact," *Inside Higher Ed*, 19 July 2005, http://www.insidehighered.com/news/2005/07/19/men (accessed 19 January 2013).
91. Ibid.

92. "Virginia Supreme Court Rules for Randolph College Over Its Move to Coeducation," *Chronicle of Higher Education*, 6 June 2008, http://chronicle.com/article/Virginia-Supreme-Court-Rules/41106 (accessed 19 January 2013).
93. Scott Jaschik, "Male Impact," *Inside Higher Ed*, 19 July 2005, http://www.insidehighered.com/news/2005/07/19/men (accessed 19 January 2013).
94. Letter to the Editor, *Alchemist* (Gainesville, GA: Brenau College), vol. LXI, no. 4 (4 November 1970), p. 2.
95. Ibid.
96. Ibid.
97. Sally Collins and Cindy Francis, "Co-Education – Pro and Con," *Alchemist* (Gainesville, GA: Brenau College), vol. LXI, no. 5, 17 November 1970, p. 2.
98. Brenau College, *Institutional Self-Study, 1979 – 1981*, 294–295.
99. James J. Lorence, "Gainesville State College," *New Georgia Encyclopedia*, 12 October 2005, http://www.georgiaencyclopedia.org/nge/Article.jsp?id=h-1440 (accessed 19 January 2013).
100. Sally Collins and Cindy Francis, "Co-Education – Pro and Con," *Alchemist* (Gainesville, GA: Brenau College), vol. LXI, no. 5, 17 November 1970, p. 2.
101. Ibid.
102. Ibid.
103. Ibid.
104. The Cumberland Corporation, "Survey-Study Report: Brenau College," 1 September 1971, p. 1, box labeled "Survey-Study Report," Brenau University Archives, Gainesville, Georgia.
105. Ibid., 7.
106. Ibid., 8.
107. Ibid.
108. Dr. John S. Burd, interview by author, tape recording, Gainesville, Georgia, 23 September 2010.
109. Sally Collins and Cindy Francis, "Co-Education – Pro and Con," *Alchemist* (Gainesville, GA: Brenau College), vol. LXI, no. 5, 17 November 1970, p. 2.
110. "Students, Trustees Voice Opinions," *Alchemist* (Gainesville, GA: Brenau College), 21 October 1970, p. 6.
111. Ibid.

112. Josiah Crudup, "A Report to the Board of Trustees of Brenau College (Friday, May 30, 1952)," Dr. Crudup Files, Box 29 of 40, Folder 5, p. 9, Brenau University Archives, Gainesville, Georgia.
113. Ibid.
114. Brenau College, *Institutional Self-Study, 1979 –1981*, 193.
115. Ibid., 194.
116. Ibid.
117. Ibid., 197.
118. Ibid.
119. Ibid.
120. Ibid., 198.
121. See *Catalog* (1995) and *Catalog* (2007).
122. Earl James McGrath, *Should Students Share the Power? A Study of Their Role in College and University Governance* (Philadelphia, PA: Temple University Press, 1970), 38.
123. Ibid.
124. Ibid.
125. See Michael Lenard Sanseviro, "Student Government Presidents' Perceptions of their Role in Institutional Decision-Making at a Two-year Public College" (2007). Educational Policy Studies Dissertations. Paper 7. http://digitalarchive.gsu.edu/eps_diss/7 (accessed 20 January 2013); Alf Lizzio and Keithia Wilson, "Student Participation in University Governance: The Role Conceptions and Sense of Efficacy of Student Representatives on Departmental Committees," *Studies in Higher Education*, vol. 34, no. 1 (February 2009): 69–84.
126. Andy Guess, "Board Rights vs. Alumni Rights," *Inside Higher Ed.*, http://www.insidehighered.com/news/2007/10/05/trustees (accessed 20 January 2013).
127. Dr. John S. Burd, interview by author, tape recording, Gainesville, Georgia, 23 September 2010.
128. Ibid.
129. Ibid.
130. Brenau College, *Institutional Self-Study, 1984–1985*, 1.
131. James Salzer, "Pomp and circumvent: Men break rules," *The Atlanta Constitution*, 05 May 2000, sec. D, p. 1.
132. Dr. John S. Burd, interview by author, tape recording, Gainesville, Georgia, 23 September 2010. Indeed, the college began the practice of permitting men to perform with Brenau students in some artistic productions in the 1950s. See "Grandma Would be Shocked: Drama

Brings Men to Brenau?" *Alchemist* (Gainesville, GA: Brenau College), v. XXXVII, n. 2, 27 September 1950, p. 1.

133. Brenau College, *School of Professional Studies Undergraduate Bulletin, 1982–83* (Gainesville, GA: Brenau College, 1982), 22.

134. Dr. John S. Burd, interview by author, tape recording, Gainesville, Georgia, 23 September 2010.

135. James Salzer, "Pomp and circumvent: Men break rules," *The Atlanta Constitution*, 05 May 2000, sec. D, p. 1.

136. Ibid.

137. Ibid.

138. Moravian missionaries founded Salem in 1772 and "educated girls of African-American heritage as early as 1785." See "About Salem: Our History," Salem College, http://www.salem.edu/about/our-history/ (accessed 26 January 2013).

139. "About Columbia College: History," Columbia College, http://www.columbiacollegesc.edu/about/history.asp (accessed 12 February 2013).

140. Georgen Coyle and Susan Tucker, "Newcomb: A Brief History of the College," Tulane University, http://www.tulane.edu/~wc/collections/newcombhistory/newcomb.html (accessed 12 February 2013).

141. "Sylvia Williams First Black Tift College Student" *Atlanta Daily World* (1932–2003), 05 October 1973, http://search.proquest.com/docview/491404572?accountid=12774 (accessed 13 February 2013); "First African-American Graduate is Commencement Speaker," *Newswise.com*, 12 April 2002, http://www.newswise.com/articles/first-african-american-graduate-is-commencement-speaker (accessed 13 February 2013).

142. Elizabeth Crabtree Wells, "Judson College," *Encyclopedia of Alabama*, http://www.encyclopediaofalabama.org/face/Article.jsp?id=h-2492 (accessed 13 February 2013); "Meredith Timeline," http://www.meredith.edu/library/archives/meredith_timeline.html, Meredith College (accessed 13 February 2013); No author, "In Memoriam: Dr. Earl Strickland, 19th President of Wesleyan College," *Wesleyan Magazine* (winter, 2011), p. 46, http://issuu.com/wesleyancollege/docs/wesmagfall11 (accessed 13 February 2013).

143. Mary Molyneux Abrams, "The First: Marshalyn Yeargin '68, Sweet Briar's First African-American Student, Arrives on Campus," 5 February 2007, http://oldnews.sbc.edu/news/items/6997 (accessed 13 February 2013).

144. "Mary Baldwin College Bluestocking 2005," http://archive.org/details/marybaldwincolle2005mary (accessed 14 February 2013).

145. Barbara D. Wilson, Brenau University Registrar and Director of Student Records, email message to author, 3 August 2011.
146. Deb Prince Kroll, Brenau Women's College Alumna (1973) and Adjunct Professor of History, email to Mr. David Morrison, Vice President of Communications and Publications for Brenau University, 25 September 2013. Peace College in Raleigh, North Carolina, also integrated in 1972. In that year, for the first time in the history of the college, the student yearbook entitled *The Lotus* depicted a photograph of a young woman named Ms. Pat McCullers. *Lotus 1973*, http://library.digitalnc.org/cdm/singleitem/collection/yearbooks/id/1950/rec/72 (accessed 16 January 2014). McCullers also described herself "As the first African American to be accepted and graduate from Peace College more than thirty-five years ago" when she made a post in the "Comments" section of an online obituary dedicated to a former pastor of the First Presbyterian Church in Raleigh, Mr. Albert George Edwards, on August 10, 2011. "Comments," http://www.bryan-leefuneralhome.com/recentobituaries/preview.php?id=196&p=1&search= (accessed 16 January 2014). However, unlike Brenau, Peace College was a two-year college at this time. This is also true for Midway College, the only other southern women's college in operation around the time Brenau desegregated. No readily available source indicates when Midway integrated, but is unlikely to have been after 1972.

CHAPTER 4

BUILDING BRENAU

HOW PERCEPTIONS OF WOMEN AND FEMININITY DICTATED THE EVOLUTION OF PHYSICAL SPACE ON CAMPUS

In her well-respected book entitled *Alma Mater: Design and Experience in the Women's Colleges from Their Nineteenth-Century Beginnings to the 1930s*, Helen Horowitz suggested that people may "think about buildings and landscapes as historical texts."[1] The buildings and landscapes of American college campuses are particularly revealing texts. Since the founding of Harvard College in 1636, literally thousands of college and university campuses have been established in the United States. Many differ from institutions of higher learning found elsewhere. For example, though European colleges and universities often occupied cities, in America, colleges "were frequently located in rural landscapes with views to natural surroundings that were thought to have a favorable impact on students' mental and physical health."[2] Also, whereas European colleges like Oxford "tended to be inward-looking with buildings based around a courtyard," American colleges "were extroverted with separate buildings set in open landscapes" surrounded by green spaces.[3]

Architectural historian Paul Venable Turner noted that the college campus is "a uniquely American place" that is both a "city in microcosm" and "a vehicle for expressing the utopian social visions of the American imagination."[4] Above all, Turner claimed that "the campus reveals the power that a physical environment can possess as the embodiment of an institution's character."[5] The campuses of women's colleges may reflect this notion of physical environment embodying institutional character even more plainly than at other institutions.

Helen Horowitz determined that the physical spaces of many of American women's colleges evolved and changed over time in response to changing institutional and societal views about femininity and the role of higher education for women. Horowitz wrote that "the large seminary structure" that characterized several early women's colleges "kept its inmates physically in place and thus secure in a limited sense, but proved to have unintended consequences [as] students began to develop the autonomous culture—characterized by independence and intense friendships—that they called college life."[6] Though intriguing to young women in college, the culture of college life that developed distracted women from what many at the time thought they should be learning in college.

Horowitz noted that, "while the seminary protected women from men, it did not protect them from other women or from their own imaginations. The close supervision of women in a single building clearly guarded the virtue of young women; but what did this all-female world do to female character?"[7] Certainly, it could do little to make women better wives and mothers, roles even college-educated women were expected to play in the late nineteenth century and early twentieth century. To recreate a family environment that might nurture those who were expected to one day become nurturing homemakers themselves, some women's colleges created a system of "cottages" to complement academic buildings. Because these modest-sized houses and their occupants emulated a family environment where older family members supervised younger members with chores and other duties, they served as laboratories for future matriarchs to hone skills important to guiding a family.

The twentieth-century saw attitudes about higher education for women shift even more as society gradually acknowledged the intellectual equality of women to men and abandoned patriarchal attitudes and practices. Horowitz found that many women's colleges adopted structures and architecture "that boldly proclaimed descent from the male collegiate tradition."[8] The structures and forms of women's colleges (such as residence halls, academic buildings, quadrangles, clock towers, libraries, gymnasia, student unions, etc.) became not unlike those at American colleges everywhere—in some cases, right down to the collegiate classical or Gothic architecture.

Of course, throughout this progression, college officials have always been the driving force behind physical changes to campuses simply because erecting buildings and altering landscape generally requires a great deal of time and money, commodities students are usually short on. Still, students have not been completely without agency on the matter of campus design. Whether a college constructs a new residence hall in response to increased student enrollment or fixes an uneven walkway in response to student complaints, students are behind some physical alterations. Indeed, modern research has shown that college students were "able to clearly identify classroom attributes that enhanced their learning as well as those aspects of the built environment that inhibited their learning," suggesting that actively consulting students about some campus design elements might reap benefits.[9] Ultimately, what is clear is that though largely governed by college personnel, the evolution of a college's campus can, at some levels, be a product of negotiation between officials and students.

The development of Brenau's campus offers glimpses of this process of negotiation at work and also closely follows the historical trace of women's college physical development identified by Horowitz. From the outset, it bears mentioning that Brenau has apparently operated for much of its history without any kind of overarching campus master plan.[10] Though the College had such a plan in place by the 1990s, prior to relatively recent years, Brenau seemingly grew in a manner similar to that of Mills College in California, which reputedly "grew rather unheeded in its early years, with no apparent plan or guidelines."[11] In architectural terms, institutions such as Mills and Brenau "grew organically" over time according to need, as opposed to being constructed in a deliberate fashion. This is not at all an indictment; it simply reflects one process as opposed to another. The end result of either organic growth or fully-planned growth could potentially be both a functional and aesthetically pleasing campus environment—such as Brenau presently maintains. Several of the more prominent structures that have been on campus as components of this environment bear description.

The history of Brenau's campus begins in the late nineteenth century.[12] The earliest image in the Brenau Archives of the Georgia Baptist Female Seminary is from an April 10, 1879, newspaper advertisement. A drawing, it depicts a simple, two-story structure with several windows and chimneys. (See Figure 19.) The Seminary outgrew this edifice quickly. In 1887, the first permanent structure on campus, Wilkes Hall, was built. According to the University, "The original two-story Queen Anne structure featured a semi-circular porch with balustrades and Victorian bracketing, but it was destroyed by a storm in 1947. It was replaced by a two-story portico supported by four square columns."[13] (See Figure 20.) Wilkes has served as a dormitory/classroom building at Brenau and, more recently, as a dining facility.

The Baptist Female Seminary added Bailey Hall to campus in 1888. It was named in honor of Dr. J.W. Bailey, "a physician of great prominence in Southern medicine," who lived in Gainesville and supported the Seminary.[14] Bailey Hall has served as a dormitory for the College since it opened and has also housed faculty and administrative offices. In 1890, the Seminary added East Hall adjacent to Bailey Hall. The first floor of East Hall "originally functioned as a classroom building and library," though the College converted this space to dining rooms several decades ago.[15] The second floor of East Hall is a small dormitory capable of housing around a dozen women.

The Seminary completed Yonah Hall in 1893. It has three stories and abuts the southern wall of Wilkes Hall. Yonah Hall was built in the Georgian Revival style and features an arched entranceway and Corinthian pilasters. Yonah has served as a residence hall for most of its life. For many years in the early twentieth century, Yonah Hall contained a reception room on its first floor that Brenau women would use when receiving male guests. (See Figure 21.) College staff members always chaperoned such "dates."

Together with Bailey Hall, the 720-seat Pearce Auditorium forms the most prominent structure on campus. (See Figure 22.) Pearce was built in 1896 in the French Second Empire style. Characteristic of this, the auditorium has a large rectangular tower and several dormers that jut out from a mansard roof line. Four gracefully arched doorways facilitate access to the building. Gainesville architect M. Garland Reynolds, Jr., said of Pearce Auditorium that "The design for this building is taken from the Louvre Museum in Paris" and that "the placement and composition of the center portion's arched-over windows is very fine."[16] Pearce Auditorium served as a recreation hall in Brenau's early years and the remains of a heated swimming pool are still evident in its basement. In 1897, Brenau installed a pipe organ and added a large ceiling mural entitled, "Aeneas at the Court of Dido." (See Figure 23.) Some of Brenau's promotional material quotes a passage from the 1887 minutes of the Chattahoochee Baptist Association regarding the painting. The minutes read:

> Aeneas at the Court of Dido is the subject of the beautiful allegorical picture in the dome of the Auditorium. It is about 30 feet long by 15 feet wide and was enlarged from a 3 inch picture printed in a book. We don't know who Aeneas was, nor Dido either, but suppose they were people who lived way back in some of them old ancient

times when people didn't go much on dry goods. Be that as it may, the picture is as pretty as you will see in a week's journey.[17]

In fact, the painting is based on an opera entitled "Dido and Aeneas," composed by Englishman Henry Purcell around 1685. It recounts the tragic story of Dido, Queen of Carthage, who takes her own life in despair upon learning that her lover, the Trojan hero Aeneas, has abandoned her. The work has been hailed as "the greatest operatic achievement of the English seventeenth century."[18] In 1963, Brenau added a raised porch and white columns to the building and named it in honor of Dr. Pearce. Two decades later, the College closed Pearce Auditorium for extensive renovations. Though workers painted the nineteenth century brick white in the 1960s, many of the building's other architectural features (including a large stained glass window) were preserved in the renovation. At one time or another, several administrative offices and Brenau's President's Art Gallery have called Pearce Auditorium home.

Though design choices about any building are seldom (if ever) accidental, it is particularly worth noting that nothing about the architecture of Brenau's earliest permanent structures (such as Pearce and Yonah halls) was inadvertent. The College's leadership deliberately set out to communicate specific messages to the general public through their choices of interior and exterior style. For centuries in America, many college buildings have been built in the Greek Revival architectural style so as to evoke the intellectual spirit of the Classical Age. This explains the presence of Greek design motifs (such as columns and temple facades) in several Brenau campus buildings. Later period styles had significance at Brenau, too. According to one architectural historian, the Second Empire style which graces Pearce Auditorium "stood prominently at the center of an urbane and sophisticated Paris that had become the cultural and artistic center of Europe" during the nineteenth century.[19] This architectural style also facilitated a "fusion of rich ornamentation and rational planning" and so found use in many prominent U.S. government buildings during the age.[20] In Pearce Auditorium, Brenau sought to proclaim itself as an important center of culture and sophistication in the region through its use of the French Second Empire style without and a grand fresco within.

In the early 1900s, Brenau built several more structures on campus. The College erected Butler Hall in 1905. The building was named for the Honorable E.W. Butler from Madison, Georgia, who served as the first chairman of Brenau's Board of Trustees.[21] It has served mostly as classroom and office space since its creation. Brenau extensively renovated Butler Hall in the early 1980s and again in the late 1990s, this last time converting the building into a student center. Brenau renamed the building the Louise Hancock Owens Student Center in 1997 in honor of Mrs. Owens, who attended Brenau briefly in the 1930s and went on to serve as a Brenau trustee, as chairman of the building and grounds committee, and as the president of the Alpha Delta Pi alumnae association.[22] Overton Hall lies contiguous to Bailey Hall and was built in 1909 as the home of the Brenau School of Oratory. It was named in honor of Miss Florence M. Overton, who was the principal in the school for several years. Over the years, it housed the theatre faculty as well as a classroom and accesses to Pearce Auditorium. By 2012, Overton Hall served as the location of the Brenau University Security Office. Centennial Hall and Simmons Hall (not to be confused with Lessie Southgate Simmons Memorial Hall) "were built in the early 1900s and were substantially remodeled and veneered in brick in 1950 and 1964, respectively."[23] Both were built as and have remained small residence halls.

Though not built by the University, Brenau acquired another building that dated from the earliest years of the twentieth century. Maude Hunter Martin, a 1931 alumna of the College, gifted what would become the Jim Walters House to Brenau in 2001. According to journalist Ken Stanford, the house "was built around 1903 by Dr. E.E. Dixon and his wife Annie Perry Dixon," who were prominent Gainesvillians.[24] Many of their descendants (including two daughters) attended Brenau. The Dixons built the house "in the Georgian Revival style with neo-classical detailing," including a large veranda.[25] From 1910–1915, "the house was home to the Alpha Delta Pi sorority."[26] In 2005, Brenau named the house in honor of Jim Walters, a Brenau trustee and benefactor. As of 2012, the Jim Walters House was home to the Department of Institutional Advancement.

Brenau continued construction into the nineteen-teens and the Roaring Twenties. Originally built as a chapel in 1914, President Simmons oversaw the construction of the two-story Lessie Southgate Simmons Memorial Hall, so-called in memory of his late wife. The façade is in the Beaux-Arts Classical style with large fluted Ionic columns in front. Many features original to the building remain, including several stained glass windows, an Italianate tile floor in the entryway, and fireplaces and mantels in several rooms. Simmons Memorial Hall has served many purposes at Brenau. It was home to the College's Y.W.C.A. chapter for some years, the president's office, and also housed the College's library until 1988. By 2008, it contained the Office of the President, the Art Department, and the Sellars Art Gallery and had become known as the Simmons Visual Arts Building. (See Figure 24.)

The Geiger Memorial Hall Music Building is located adjacent to the stage area of Pearce Auditorium and houses the offices, studios, and classrooms of the music faculty. Workers completed Geiger Memorial in 1915 and remodeled the building twice, in 1931 and 1965. Brenau named the building for Dr. August Geiger, who for many years was the "head of the department of theoretical music" at the College.[27] Brenau built two dormitories, Sidney Lanier Hall (named for the poet) and Oglesby Hall (named "in honor of Lieutenant Wilbur Oglesby, who died in France while serving with the American Expeditionary Forces") in 1916 and 1919, respectively, though these were later demolished in the 1980s as upgrading became too impractical.[28] It was also around the nineteen-teens that Brenau began acquiring a few homes adjacent to campus to convert into club and sorority cottages. These would be renovated occasionally over the years or replaced with larger dwellings as groups outgrew their houses. Alonzo C. Wheeler, for many years a prominent Gainesville attorney and judge, built what would later become the Wheeler Alumni House in 1920. It remained in his family for many years until Brenau acquired the residence. The College utilized the classic Greek Revival structure as its president's house for several decades before locating the offices of Public Relations, Admissions, and Alumni Affairs there around 2004.

An era of modern construction began at Brenau with the completion of the Jewel Building in 1955. The building was named in honor of Mary Tallulah Jewell, mother of J. D. Jewell, who, with contributions from the Brenau Board of Trustees, provided funds for its construction. It housed the home economics department and laboratories in addition to faculty member offices and classrooms. In 2012, it was the main home of the School of Education. In the early 1960s, Brenau built the Crudup Hall dormitory, a science building, and a physical education building, which also contained dance studios and offices for the dance faculty. The College completed Virginia Hall, which has served as part dormitory, part faculty office location, in 1954. The building fell into disuse for around fifteen years in the 1990s, but reopened in 2006 with 32 new housing units after a $400,000 renovation.[29] Brenau completed its natatorium in 1974. The structure houses a six-lane, 25-yard, heated swimming pool approved by the Amateur Athletic Union of the United States for Olympic-caliber competition in addition to a spectator area, weight room, and sauna.

The major campus building project of the 1980s was without a doubt the Brenau University Trustee Library. The Trustee Library serves as the intellectual heart of the campus. It contains more than 100,000 volumes in addition to several hundred periodicals and tens of thousands of microfilm and audiovisual resources. (See Figure 25.) The library also houses computer and language laboratories, the College Archives and rare book room, and several conference and group study rooms. The Trustee Library had a quick birth—barely three years passed from its conception to its completion. Shortly after he assumed the Brenau presidency, Dr. Burd received the news from S.A.C.S. that the College would be expected to build a new library or risk shortly losing accreditation. Dr. Burd described the ultimatum as "rather myopic" because it seemed to offer little window for compliance. Nevertheless, though "slightly irritated," Dr. Burd planned to comply. Having just gotten the College out of financial difficulties, Dr. Burd was unwilling to assume any debt for the institution to finance the library construction. Instead, he approached the Brenau Trustees to raise funds. They responded admirably. Construction began on the Brenau Trustee Library in 1987. The Architectural firm of Bailey & Associates designed the library, which was built by the Tipton Construction Company.[30] The Brenau Trustee Library "was paid for when it opened" in the fall of 1988, which "made for an excellent start to future building projects."[31]

Among the Trustee Library collection's highlights include the personal library of one of Georgia's best known—if controversial—politicians. Thomas E. "Tom" Watson was a populist firebrand who served in the Georgia Assembly, the U.S. House of Representatives, and the U.S. Senate around the turn of the twentieth century. He was also a populist candidate for both the presidency and vice-presidency. Watson was a good writer and orator who both championed agrarian interests and attacked blacks and religious minorities with his rhetoric. He died in 1922. Two decades later, a Florida judge who had acquired Watson's several thousand volume collection donated it to the Brenau library in memory of a Brenau trustee.[32] It resides today in the rare book room.[33]

Also housed in the rare book room are several limited edition works of naturalist John James Audubon. Dr. J. Delano and Caroline Mixon donated these works to the Trustee Library between 1993 and 2008. Their donations included copies of the nineteenth-century naturalist's 435 "Birds of America" prints, produced in very elaborate, oversized commemorative editions. Brenau is one of only thirteen libraries in the United States to own this four-volume, leather-bound, double elephant folio.[34]

In 1982, Brenau constructed its Tennis Center adjacent to the Wallis Field athletic practice fields. The College noted that the facility cost "almost a half a million dollars" and provided Brenau "with one of the finest collegiate tennis complexes in the country."[35] In 2006, Brenau added a 14,000-square-foot indoor tennis facility and created the Smithgall Tennis Center. Funding for the center came from a donation made by Lessie Smithgall, the wife of local media mogul and philanthropist Charles Smithgall, who was herself a former Brenau Trustee and an avid tennis player for over 70 years.[36] Another 1990s-era building was largely devoted to mass communications. Built in 1994 on Gainesville's grand Green Street, the John W. Jacobs, Jr., Business and Communication Arts Building houses classrooms, studios, faculty & administrative offices, the Brenau University Learning and Leisure Institute (B.U.L.L.I.), and Brenau's radio and television broadcasting stations. John W. Jacobs, Jr., has been described as a man who "turned a small radio station in Gainesville into a broadcasting and Internet conglomerate now operated by his children."[37] Jacobs is also a noted philanthropist who served on the Brenau Board of Trustees for an impressive 48 years.[38]

By the twenty-first century, Pearce Auditorium, though still a respectable venue thanks to periodic renovations, was being stretched thin by the annual demands of multiple dance, music, and theater performances. To better serve the University and the surrounding community, Brenau opened the John S. Burd Center for Performing Arts on April 19, 2002. Designed by the architectural firm of Lord, Aeck & Sargent, the $11.5 million, 51,000-square-foot, state-of-the-art facility houses a 350-seat theatre, a recital hall, a lecture hall, a rehearsal theatre, and an art gallery. In the Center's opening ceremony, then trustee John Jacobs, Jr., dedicated the building to Brenau's eighth president, praising Dr. Burd's vision to improve the University.[39]

In addition to showcasing Brenau's performance arts, Dr. Burd also sought to put items of material culture on display for students and the community by building a first-rate regional history museum on campus.

The Northeast Georgia History Center at Brenau University replaced the Georgia Mountains History Museum, which had operated in a converted firehouse for twenty years in downtown Gainesville prior to 2004.[40] Five years of planning and fundraising preceded construction of the Center.[41] Officials broke ground on the $4 million, 25,000-square-foot facility designed in the late 1800s Empire Period style on August 16, 2002.[42] Dr. Burd hailed the Center as "a major addition to the cultural base and the quality of life in Northeast Georgia."[43]

The History Center envisioned itself as "the leading resource for promoting a greater understanding of the cultural, social, economic and political history" of the area with a companion mission of "preserving and sharing the history" of the region.[44] To fulfill its vision, the History Center has showcased many events and exhibitions since it opened. Among the Center's permanent exhibits include a hall devoted to the multi-million dollar poultry industry in the region.[45] Also on site is a reconstructed nineteenth century cabin belonging to a Cherokee Indian leader named Chief White Path.[46] Other exhibits showcase the work of "Mark Trail" cartoonist and long-time Gainesville resident Ed Dodd, depict Cherokee Indian lifeways, and chronicle the founding and early years of the city of Gainesville, with emphasis on revealing the aftermath of a large tornado that struck the city in 1936, killing hundreds.[47] The History Center also has a Freedom Garden to honor military veterans from north Georgia and a Sports Hall of Fame to pay tribute to area athletes who have achieved regional or national recognition.[48] In addition to such permanent exhibits, the History Center has hosted numerous community events for families and several traveling exhibits.

Besides exhibiting material and serving as an educational center for students, in keeping with its mission of preservation, the Northeast Georgia History Center also serves as a repository for historical memorabilia collected from area residents.[49] A menagerie of items (including clothing, furniture, farm equipment, toys, and collections of personal correspondence, to name but a few) fills the Center's basement.[50] Such a vast collection of material culture equips the Center to become, as Dr. Burd anticipated, an "interpretive teaching museum to encompass all of Northeast Georgia."[51]

Throughout its history, most of Brenau's main campus buildings have been situated on park-like grounds. Beginning with the earliest photographs contained in the Archives and continuing until the present day, pictures of several parts of campus show many mature trees growing amongst manicured lawns and flower beds, bisected here-and-there by walkways. There are several sizable green spaces on campus. Some are decorative, such as a smaller quadrangle and island lawn adjacent to the campus' Sorority Circle drive. Others are functional, such as the outdoor amphitheater near the Wallis Field athletic training area. The main quadrangle, which is near the heart of campus and fronts both Yonah Hall and Pearce Auditorium, is Brenau's verdant, very well-maintained centerpiece.

For over a century, the most prominent landmark on the main quad was Brenau's Crow's Nest. Essentially an elevated wooden deck reached by a set of stairs, this structure was originally built by the class of 1905 around the base of a large oak tree as a gift to the College. (See Figure 26.) Thereafter, the Crow's Nest had, as one newspaper article put it, "something of a nomadic existence."[52] Various factors (including a lightning strike that killed one anchor tree and wood deterioration) necessitated its relocation roughly every two decades. In 2008, Brenau made plans to construct a free-standing, steel-reinforced Crow's Nest on the lawn that would endure for generations. Admittedly, the new structure lacked some of the tree house charm evoked by previous Crow's Nests, but what the University built is accessible and sturdy in ways its predecessors never could have been.

According to campus tradition, only Brenau seniors are allowed to ascend the Crow's Nest completely. The only exception to this is during one weekend late each spring when graduating students assemble to escort members of the junior class to stand on the top as rising seniors.

Underclassmen otherwise scale the Crow's Nest at their peril. Tradition holds that any student who climbs higher on the Crow's Nest than is permitted could be brought to trial before the student Honor Court.

Besides the Crow's Nest, two other structures stand out on the main lawn. A circular, white-brick fountain with a three-tiered cascading statue at its center has adorned the quadrangle for decades. By tradition, Brenau women who become engaged as students get tossed into the fountain by friends and sorority sisters. (It is said that good friends and sisters will bring a towel and a change of clothes for the bride-to-be.) The newest edition to the lawn is the Daniel Pavilion, which the University installed in 2008–2009. The classical marble structure replaced an older arched entryway to the campus. The pavilion was named in honor of Carole Ann Carter Daniel, a Brenau alumna and a member of the University's Board of Trustees. The Brenau Master Facilities Plan noted that the pavilion identifies the "four portals of the University's strategic plan and mission," which encourage students to expand their worldview, discover the beauty of science and math, develop creativity and imagination, and refine language skills.[53]

Other than the main quadrangle, perhaps the most remarkable landscape feature in Brenau's history was its Japanese garden. (See Figure 27.) Johnny Vardeman, a former editor of the *Gainesville Times*, wrote a feature on the gardens for the newspaper in 2008.[54] His research revealed that in 1922, Brenau hired a landscape architect named Shogo Joseph Myaida to design and build several Japanese features on the campus. Myaida was a native of Japan who immigrated to America. He studied landscape architecture and "went on to become a nationally known landscape architect and designed Japanese gardens for several prominent people."[55] Myaida's strength was that he "readily adopted...American culture and developed a style of garden construction that blended the traditions of Japanese architecture and garden design with the practicality of American tastes."[56] His most famous work is the Japanese-style Garden at Hillwood Estates in Washington, D.C.[57]

Building Brenau 253

At Brenau, Myaida built a terraced garden, planted bamboo and other plants, installed a small lake, and "such additions as a pagoda, bridge, lanterns and arch" near where the University tennis courts presently sit.[58] The lake was called Lake Takeda in honor of two Japanese students who attended Brenau, "Kazuko Uyehara Vance (class of 1953) and her mother, Aya Takeda Uyehara," who was at Brenau from 1911–1914.[59] These young women from a prominent Japanese family made quite an impression on the College.

In 1910, the *Atlanta Constitution* reported, "The old world will be represented in a few weeks in the person of Miss Aya Tokada [sic], who sails from Japan during the present month. She will be educated for three years at Brenau under the auspices and at the expense of the Brenau Young Women's Christian Association."[60] Aya attracted much attention at Brenau. One edition of the "Brenau Notes" reported that, "little Aya Tokada, aged 12, a winsome Japanese student at Brenau" failed to show up at roll call one day, which threw the institution into a tizzy.[61] She was found, "seated in the middle of her room half covered in scores of Japanese flags, made by herself, with the walls adorned by the same national emblem" in celebration of the birthday of the Japanese emperor.[62] Touched by her patriotism, "Brenau pupils at once set about arranging a celebration in honor of the emperor's birthday."[63] At the celebration, the girls sang the Japanese national anthem, which brought tears to Aya's eyes.

Brenau must have impressed Aya as much as Aya impressed Brenau. Years after she studied in Gainesville, Aya arranged for her daughter to attend Brenau as well. President Josiah Crudup wrote the Brenau trustees on the matter. He indicated that:

> In 1910 Miss Aya Takeda came to Brenau College from Tokyo, Japan, and established herself with affection and high esteem by all who knew her while she was a student here in America. She was graduated from Brenau in 1914 and returned to Japan. She married Mr. G[eorge] Etsujiro Uyehara…who became one of the leading

> political figures of his country during the decades preceding World War II. Mr. Uyehara was a liberal democrat, a strong advocate of friendship with America, and opposed to the militarists of his country who were driving Japan to war with the United States. ...
>
> Since World War II, Mr. Uyehara has returned to public life in Japan and is now a member of the Japanese Diet and holds the high esteem of American representatives there."[64]

Dr. Crudup indicated that, "The above account explains the desire of Brenau College to do something for Miss Kazuko Uyehara," who was the daughter of Aya and George Uyehara and was in her second year attending Brenau.[65] Dr. Crudup went on to relate that, "Since [Kazuko] has been at Brenau College, I have received several letters from leaders of the Japanese people expressing appreciation. One of these letters came from Shigeru Yoshida, Prime Minister of Japan."[66] All the correspondence expressed gratitude to Brenau for facilitating the enrollment of Kazuko in the States.

The lake that bore Aya's name would become the centerpiece of a fairly long-lived enterprise sponsored by Brenau called "Camp Takeda." According to Johnny Vardeman, it was "a popular summer camp for girls operated right in the middle of Gainesville in the 1930s and '40s."[67] Located adjacent to Brenau's campus, the camp consisted of "cabins, infirmary, recreation hall, dining hall, theater, two lakes and stables" and campers indulged in "horseback riding, hiking, tennis, swimming, canoeing, dance and arts and crafts."[68] A former director noted that as many as 300 girls would come from all over the South and from right in Gainesville for one- or two-month terms. Vardeman noted that the camp "followed a Japanese theme" as cabins had names like "Maieda, Honzon and Shinshoku" and "pagoda-like structures stood in the lakes."[69]

Today, the only vestige of Brenau's Japanese garden that remains on campus is a thick stand of bamboo that grows near the northeast edge of campus. Long ago the garden yielded to Brenau's needs for a tennis complex and an athletic practice field. Nothing at all remains of the camp or of Lake Takeda today—except some photographs in Brenau's Archives and perhaps some memories of several women who attended the camp as girls.

Since its inception over 125 years ago, Brenau's campus—its grounds and buildings—has grown and changed markedly. During this evolution, the College added, removed, and altered its built environments in response to changing attitudes about women. Its general trajectory has been along the historical trace common to many women's colleges that Helen Horowitz identified: first came a single, large seminary building with which to better monitor and safeguard students; then came cottages to promote a familial atmosphere among residents; then came the typical trappings of men's colleges (with dormitories, a student union, etc.). Because it was younger and in the socially more conservative South, Brenau progressed through these stages in later decades than did northern women's colleges—but progress through them it would. Importantly, though it was College officials who did the building, students were not entirely without agency in bringing about physical changes to campus.

Very early on, in an age that sheltered young women (especially in the South), the Baptist Female Seminary and Brenau College essentially consisted of one grand, insulating edifice. (See Figure 28.) A 1910 Brenau advertisement read, "The magnificent new dormitory which is now being erected has been named North Hall. This building has every modern convenience and is connected by a covered passageway with Wilkes and Yonah Halls, which in turn connect with the Academic and Conservatory buildings."[70] Connections to everywhere on campus eventually became fusions. Brenau's 1979 S.A.C.S. Self-Study noted "as a result of renovations and structural alterations, these buildings have been connected to form a continuous architectural structure."[71] As Horowitz put it, such a single structure "contained all components for learning, working, and living."[72] It likewise restricted access to students as comings and goings could be easily monitored through a handful of entrances and exits. This, in turn, safeguarded feminine virtue.

Even as Brenau safeguarded womanly virtue, women's historian Catherine Lavender wrote that, "women's lives at the end of the nineteenth century were changing dramatically on various fronts," particularly as women became more educated and more employed.[73] Such women, Lavender claimed, were "determined to extend boundaries" and demanded greater societal recognition of their freedom and autonomy.[74] Some of this same spirit that would go on to produce suffragettes and flappers would eventually make its way to Brenau. There, it induced officials to relax some control over some students when it came to housing. Beginning around 1910 to 1915, cottages appeared on the Brenau campus as they had on the campuses of the northern women's colleges Horowitz studied. (See Figure 29.) Horowitz noted that at the northern schools, cottages were "structures designed inside and out to look like family dwellings" as they "broke up the all-female community of the seminary and dispersed students among situations of home."[75] The cottages at institutions like Smith and Vassar "fit perfectly the new collegiate order" as "living in smaller units fostered comradeship among students, the development of house loyalty, and a large number of house traditions" and generally "allowed a more informal life without regulations."[76]

Although at Brenau, unlike at northern schools, sororities occupied the cottages (or "clubhouses," as they were sometimes called), these houses were in other respects analogous to the cottages at northern women's colleges. Brenau cottages fostered the same "situation of home" as an article that appeared in the *Atlanta Constitution* demonstrated. It read:

> Of the students in the completion of their sorority houses, the story is told that last year a member of the faculty noticed a young woman washing windows in the little club house and doing other work not generally pursued by a girl of college age. "Why, my dear," she was asked, "why are you doing that?"
>
> "Because we must save every cent to fix up our little home, and we have each of us resolved to do our part of the housework."[77]

Another newspaper article suggested that living in the cottages taught students much more than merely how to keep house. An edition of the "Brenau Notes" related:

> The members of the Beta Sigma Omicron Society of Brenau have just completed what is probably the first clubhouse to be built by the students of any southern college for girls. The pretty little cottage has just been completed and when the grounds around it have been beautified, it will be one of the most attractive spots connected with Brenau Conservatory. The girls raised the money themselves for this building and have superintended its construction. It is beautifully furnished, and the members of the society are exceedingly proud of their new home.[78]

The sisters of BΣO had their cottage-living experience to thank for learning lessons in nothing less than finance and building construction, which would make them very knowledgeable family matriarchs indeed.

Just as living in cottages recreated the "refined home" and "secured '... desirable moral and social influences'" for young women, cottage living taught Brenau students the lessons of "comradeship" that Horowitz described.[79] The *Atlanta Constitution* related:

> These sorority club houses stand as an expression of cooperation. The student members of the chapter reside in them, and each house is presided over by a member of the faculty. Through these sororities, a social system along the most approved plan is established and the spirit of it lives with the students after they leave school. At present there are chapter houses representing the Phi Mu Gamma, the Sigma Phi Epsilon [sic], the Alpha Beta Tau, the Beta Sigma Omicron, added to the beauty of Brenau College, Gainesville.[80]

Brenau garnered laurels for the environment the cottages fostered. The January-February 1913 edition of the *Brenau Journal*, the College literary magazine, related that, "In the National Pan-Hellenic Council of Women's' Fraternities and Sororities held in 1912, Brenau was cited as a college where ideal chapter house life exists."[81] The *Journal* article concluded saying, "We are glad and proud that at Brenau the spirit of the sororities is one of democracy and good fellowship and not of selfishness and exclusion" as existed at other institutions.[82]

In the College's several chapter houses, Brenau women came together. Though all Brenau students shared common ties, the ties fostered among cottagemates produced a great degree of solidarity. It is likely owing to this that, of everything on campus, the faculty and staff exercised the least degree of control over sororities. In a sense, living in the cottages may have actually empowered the Brenau women to a degree and improved their odds at negotiating effectively with College personnel.

Like the northern women's colleges that Helen Horowitz studied, Brenau would eventually adopt on its campus the structures and architecture typical of men's colleges. This happened because views about college women changed. By the mid-twentieth century, society no longer believed college women needed fortresses to safeguard their virtue or cottages to teach home management skills. Rather, they needed the same facilities any male college student needed. At Brenau as elsewhere, residence halls and sorority houses replaced cottages, dedicated gymnasia emerged, and student unions were built alongside libraries and classroom buildings. Of course, this happened in part for practical reasons. For example, as health and safety regulations toughened across the nation over time, colleges everywhere moved to house students in fewer, larger residence halls with centralized cooking facilities as opposed to multiple small cottages, each with its own kitchen. Consolidating in this way both decreased the hazard of fire on campus and made for fewer spaces requiring cleaning and sanitation. Also, accrediting bodies such as the Southern Association of Colleges and Schools occasionally catalyzed campus construction as colleges built or modified facilities to meet accreditation standards. But whereas practical reasons mattered in campus design, so, too, did student interests. In part, colleges simply would not have built any living, recreational, and educational facilities unless students sought to use them. The negotiations over campus space, therefore, have been and will continue to be two-sided from this standpoint.

Students have also exerted some influence in the ongoing negotiations over Brenau's physical environment in the *way* they make use of structures and landmarks on campuses. Consider Brenau's Crow's Nest as an example of this dynamic. Brenau officials built, tore down, and rebuilt this iconic structure several times not because doing so was cost-effective or efficient. Rather, officials rightly sensed that they were simply not at liberty to deprive the students of a campus landmark they treasured and used frequently. The same should be the case for Brenau's dunking fountain and for several other smaller statutes and decorations around campus that have significance to various student organizations. As Brenau students co-opted these campus landmarks for their own purposes over time, they acquired something a bit akin to an ownership interest—albeit not in fee simple. It may not give them much else, but possessing this interest does mean that students should at least expect to be consulted on matters involving particular components of physical space on campus. Actual negotiation with campus officials over matters concerning idealizing Brenau's built environment might then begin there.

By 2008, Brenau had in place a master facilities plan for the University. All told, in that year, Brenau's main campus encompassed 76 buildings situated across 46 acres near downtown Gainesville.[83] Big changes were in the works. Brenau planned to build a $6 million Academic Complex and a $3.5 million University Student Center. Brenau's biggest project would be building three 17,000-square-foot duplexes at a cost of $2.5 million each. These would be located along Sorority Circle and would become new homes for Brenau's sororities. This planned change apparently riled some alumnae. One alumna, Anna-Elizabeth McCloud, felt strongly enough about this and other changes at Brenau that she corresponded with President Schrader and posted the letters they exchanged as part of a website she developed, "brenauthewayitshouldbe.com." In response to her concern about the proposed changes in Greek housing, Dr. Schrader wrote:

> [F]our of the six sorority houses are becoming structurally unsound and, hence, will become unsafe. Engineering firms have informed us that to preserve them would be substantially more costly than to replace them. We have to make some long term plans to attractively and safely house the sororities. The example you give of the ADP house being originally an old barn is exactly its problem. It has the deteriorating structure of an old barn and will be soon beyond our ability to add extra support to a deteriorating substructure. The current plan was reviewed with the sororities and their national house foundations two years ago and they very largely accepted it. The plan is to build a complex around sorority circle restoring that area to a central prominence in campus life. Each sorority would design the interior and exterior of its own house within the constraints of similar costs and safety codes. The houses would be a "Brown Stone" design with each having its own distinct exterior and interior but covered by one main utilities supply plan and roofed as if they were adjacent brownstone buildings in Savannah, or the like, sharing structural support and one roofing system. The sororities have generally liked the idea but it is not in concrete![84]

Besides delivering a cogent response to Ms. McCloud's concerns, Dr. Schrader's reply revealed something else of importance: the institution now actively sought student input on campus modifications. Nothing in the Archives suggests that this had ever been done in building the rest of campus. By involving students in negotiations over the physical character of the University, officials stand to both build trust with students and to benefit from their suggestions while creating a college environment that will be pleasing and functional for all Brenau constituents.

Notes

1. Helen Lefkowitz Horowitz, *Alma Mater: Design and Experience in the Women's Colleges from Their Nineteenth-Century Beginnings to the 1930s* (New York, NY: Alfred A. Knopf, 1984), xvi.
2. "Chapter 3: Historic Contexts of Campus Planning," *The University of Cincinnati Campus Heritage Plan*, p. 3–1, http://www.uc.edu/content/dam/uc/af/pdc/campus_heritage_plan/Chapter_3.pdf (accessed 14 February 2013).
3. Ibid.
4. Paul Venable Turner, *Campus: An American Planning Tradition* (Cambridge, MA: M.I.T. Press, 1984), 305.
5. Ibid.
6. Horowitz, *Alma Mater*, 5.
7. Ibid.
8. Ibid., 6.
9. S. Veltri, J.H. Banning, and T.G. Davis, "The community college classroom environment: Student perceptions," *College Student Journal*, vol. 40, no. 3 (2006): 517–527, 517.
10. The Brenau Archives contain a "Master Site Plan" that dates from the late 1930s to the early 1940s. However, although this indicated which buildings, roads, and landmarks were where on campus, it did not speak to planned future expansion.
11. Karen Fiene, "A Tale of Three Campuses: Planning and Design in Response to Cultural Heritage at Mills College, the University of California, Berkeley, and Stanford University," *Planning for Higher Education*, 1 April 2011, http://www.readperiodicals.com//201104/2325179311.html#ixzz1SkmwngW7 (accessed 14 February 2013).
12. The physical history of the campus—its many buildings, grounds, etc.—that follows is distilled from several sources. Brenau catalogs from various years and several of the "Institutional Self-Studies" prepared by the College for S.A.C.S. (materials which are all housed in the University Archives) contain descriptions of the institution's physical resources that I borrowed from. Also, several newspaper articles from the *Gainesville Times* and *Access North Georgia* provided various tidbits that informed the campus history. The Council of Independent Colleges' Historic Campus Architecture Project maintains "the first national architecture

and landscape database of independent college and university campuses" at http://hcap.artstor.org/cgi-bin/library?a=p&p=home, which yielded information about some structures as well. This site frequently cited another source ("Waskiewicz, Lyn. *Brenau College District. National Register of Historic Places designation report.* Washington, DC: U.S. Department of the Interior/National Park Service, 1978") that related material about campus architecture. Brenau maintained an information-packed webpage related to the campus physical environment, traditions, legends, etc., from at least 2004 through 2011. This webpage was located at http://artsweb.brenau.edu/historic/Uniquely/default.htm. The University's Office of Communications and Publications worked with Drs. Jim Southerland and Catherine Lewis to develop the content for this webpage, which consisted of much useful information and several web-quality images. Brenau retired this and several other webpages in early 2012 when it redesigned its entire website. In October of 2012, Mr. Michael McPeek, Brenau's Director of Multimedia Publishing in the Office of Communications, very kindly provided me with electronic copies of the retired webpages, which I printed out and placed as hard-copies in the Archives in the Brenau Trustee Library. A printed copy of what the pages related is contained in the Brenau University Archives in Gainesville, Georgia, in a box labeled "Archived Webpages." Hereafter, references to this source are cited as "Brenau University Archived Webpages." Finally, various photographs and documents in the Brenau Archives contributed bits and pieces of information toward forming an overall picture of the history of Brenau as a place.

13. "Architecture," Brenau University Archived Webpages (formerly online at http://artsweb.brenau.edu/historic/Uniquely/default.htm from around 2004 until 2011); hard-copy print-out located in Box 1 of 1 labeled "Archived Webpages," Brenau University Archives, Gainesville, Georgia.
14. "Deaths: Dr. J. W. Bailey," *Charlotte Medical Journal*, vol. 61 (January – June, 1910), 261, http://archive.org/stream/charlottemedical611910char #page/260/mode/2up (accessed 14 February 2013).
15. "Architecture," Brenau University Archived Webpages (formerly online at http://artsweb.brenau.edu/historic/Uniquely/default.htm from around 2004 until 2011); hard-copy print-out located in Box 1 of 1 labeled "Archived Webpages," Brenau University Archives, Gainesville, Georgia.
16. "The Hall of History Tour," http://archive.gainesvilletimes.com/communities/history/premier_buildings2.htm (accessed 14 February 2013).

17. "Architecture," Brenau University Archived Webpages (formerly online at http://artsweb.brenau.edu/historic/Uniquely/default.htm from around 2004 until 2011); hard-copy print-out located in Box 1 of 1 labeled "Archived Webpages," Brenau University Archives, Gainesville, Georgia.
18. Ellen T. Harris, *Henry Purcell's Dido and Aeneas* (New York, NY: Oxford University Press, 1990), 3.
19. Mark Gelernter, *A History of American Architecture* (Manchester, UK: Manchester University Press, 1999), 169.
20. Ibid.
21. From the field notes describing a photograph of the "Hon. E.W. Butler and Mrs. E.B. Thompson, Brenau College, Gainesville, Georgia, 1920-," Digital Library of Georgia, Georgia Archives, http://dlg.galileo.usg.edu/cgi/meta.cgi?query=id%3Adlg_vang_hal136&_cc=1&Welcome (accessed 14 February 2013).
22. Erin Behan, "Obituary of Louise Owens, 88, longtime Brenau supporter," *The Atlanta Constitution*, 3 April 2001, p. B-4, http://archiver.rootsweb.ancestry.com/th/read/OWENS/2011-09/1316475224 (accessed 14 February 2013).
23. Brenau College, *Institutional Self-Study, 1979 – 1981*, 234.
24. Ken Stanford, "Brenau honors Walters," *AccessNorthGA.com*, 15 October 2005, http://www.accessnorthga.com/detail.php?n=124009 (accessed 13 March 2013).
25. Ibid.
26. Ibid.
27. Lucian Lamar Knight, *A Standard History of Georgia and Georgians: Volume Five* (Chicago, IL: The Lewis Publishing Company, 1917), p. 2425, Internet Archives, http://www.archive.org/stream/astandardhistor03kniggoog#page/n6/mode/2up (accessed 13 March 2013).
28. Brenau College, *Institutional Self-Study, 1979 – 1981*, 226.
29. "Brenau to reopen former residential hall," *AccessNorthGa.com*, 25 July 2005, http://www.accessnorthga.com/detail.php?n=129589 (accessed 30 May 2013).
30. From the caption of "BW Photo – Scene at Brenau on day contract for Trustee Library Building was signed on August 18, 1987," Box 36, Folder 2, Academic Libraries, Georgia Library Association Collection at the Valdosta State University Archives, available at http://www.valdosta.edu/library/find/arch/archon/index.php?p=collections/findingaid&id=536&q=&rootcontentid=21157 (accessed 13 March 2013).

31. Dr. John S. Burd, interview by author, tape recording, Gainesville, Georgia, 23 September 2010.
32. Johnny Vardeman, "Brenau library houses books from Watson," *Gainesville Times*, 9 January 2011, http://www.gainesvilletimes.com/archives/43975/ (accessed 15 February 2014).
33. For more about Watson, see C. Vann Woodward, *Tom Watson: Agrarian Rebel* (New York: Macmillan, 1938; reprint, New York, NY: Oxford University Press, 1963).
34. Staff, "Brenau Trustee Library gift enhances Audubon book collection," *AccessNorthGA.com*, 8 October 2008, http://new.accessnorthga.com/detail.php?n=214044 (accessed 13 March 2013).
35. Brenau College, *School of Professional Studies Undergraduate Bulletin, 1982-83* (Gainesville, GA: Brenau College, 1982), 19.
36. Ken Stanford, "Brenau plans indoor tennis facility for students, community," *AccessNorthGA.com*, 10 March 2005, http://www.accessnorthga.com/detail.php?n=139428 (accessed 13 March 2013).
37. Dick Yarbrough, "Paying homage to 3 wise men," *CovNews.com*, 2 December 2009, http://www.covnews.com/archives/10055/ (accessed 13 March 2013).
38. Jeff Gill, "Chairman of Brenau trustees steps down," *Gainesville Times*, 8 October 2005, http://archive.gainesvilletimes.com/news/stories/20051008/localnews/24510.shtml (accessed 13 March 2013).
39. Jerry Gunn, "Brenau dedicates performing arts center," *AccessNorthGA.com*, 19 April 2002, https://www.accessnorthga.com/detail.php?n=195767 (accessed 13 March 2013). For more about the Burd Center and Lord, Aeck & Sargent, see http://www.lasarchitect.com/profile/project_list/arts_and_culture/brenau_university.
40. Ken Stanford, "New history center getting ready for grand opening," *AccessNorthGA.com*, 23 February 2004, http://www.accessnorthga.com/detail.php?n=163314 (accessed 13 March 2013).
41. Ibid.
42. Jerry Gunn, "A new name, a new museum in Gainesville," *AccessNorthGA.com*, 15 July 2002, http://www.accessnorthga.com/detail.php?n=192480 (accessed 13 March 2013).
43. Ibid.
44. "About Us," Northeast Georgia History Center, http://www.negahc.org/about/ (accessed 10 May 2013).

45. "It's all about chickens at the NE Georgia History Center," *AccessNorthGA.com*, 13 September 2008, http://www.accessnorthga.com/detail.php?n=213257 (accessed 10 May 2013).
46. "Museum Info.: Northeast Georgia History Center, Gainesville, Georgia," Museums U.S.A., 21 August 2009, http://www.museumsusa.org/museums/info/2502565 (accessed 10 May 2013).
47. "History Center ready to open in Gainesville," *AccessNorthGA.com*, 7 May 2004, http://www.accessnorthga.com/detail.php?n=159253 (accessed 10 May 2013).
48. "History Center celebrates first anniversary of Freedom Garden," *AccessNorthGA.com*, 3 May 2008, http://www.accessnorthga.com/detail.php?n=209616 (accessed 10 May 2013); Jerry Gunn, "NE Ga. History Center Sports Hall of Fame inductions," *AccessNorthGA.com*, 29 August 2009, http://www.accessnorthga.com/detail.php?n=222811 (accessed 10 May 2013).
49. Jeff Gill, "Northeast Georgia History Center serves as area's basement," *Gainesville Times*, 27 January 2009, http://www.gainesvilletimes.com/archives/14046/ (accessed 10 May 2013).
50. Ibid.
51. Jerry Gunn, "A new name, a new museum in Gainesville," *AccessNorthGA.com*, 15 July 2002, http://www.accessnorthga.com/detail.php?n=192480 (accessed 10 May 2013).
52. "Century of Brenau tradition continues," *AccessNorthGA.com*, 7 April 2009, http://new.accessnorthga.com/detail.php?n=219361&c=10 (accessed 10 May 2013).
53. "Brenau University's Master Facilities Plan," Brenau University, http://artsweb.brenau.edu/campus/6%20Master%20Facilities%20Plan.pdf (accessed 3 January 2013); Jensen Design Studio, "Brenau Undergraduate Viewbook," http://jensendesignstudio.com/wp-content/uploads/2011/11/brenau_viewbook_spreads.pdf (accessed 10 May 2013).
54. Johnny Vardeman, "Thick bamboo part of former Brenau garden," *Gainesville Times*, 2 November 2008, http://www.gainesvilletimes.com/archives/8515/ (accessed 10 May 2013).
55. Ibid.
56. "Japanese-Style Garden," Hillwood Estate, Museum, and Gardens (Washington, DC), http://www.hillwoodmuseum.org/about-hillwood/gardens/japanese-style-garden (accessed 10 May 2013).
57. Ibid.

58. Johnny Vardeman, "Thick bamboo part of former Brenau garden," *Gainesville Times*, 2 November 2008, http://www.gainesvilletimes.com/archives/8515/ (accessed 10 May 2013).
59. "Architecture," Brenau University Archived Webpages (formerly online at http://artsweb.brenau.edu/historic/Uniquely/default.htm from around 2004 until 2011); hard-copy print-out located in Box 1 of 1 labeled "Archived Webpages," Brenau University Archives, Gainesville, Georgia.
60. "Brenau Has Opened," *Atlanta Constitution*, 8 January 1910, p. 8.
61. "Miss Aya Tokada At Brenau Loyal to Flag of Japan," *Atlanta Constitution*, 4 November 1910, p. 10.
62. Ibid.
63. Ibid.
64. Letter of January 16, 1951, from Dr. Crudup to Mr. Thomas C. Law. Dr. Crudup files, Box 35 of 40, Folder 7, Brenau University Archives, Gainesville, Georgia.
65. Ibid.
66. Ibid.
67. Johnny Vardeman, "Girls camp in middle of Gainesville was antidote for summer doldrums," *Gainesville Times*, 5 February 2006, http://archive.gainesvilletimes.com/news/stories/20060205/opinion/64212.shtml (accessed 10 May 2013).
68. Ibid.
69. Ibid.
70. Advertisement. *Atlanta Georgian and News*, 9 July 1910 -- page 21 [insert]
71. Brenau College, *Institutional Self-Study*, 1979 – 1981, 225.
72. Horowitz, *Alma Mater*, 24.
73. Catherine Lavender, "The New Woman," http://www.library.csi.cuny.edu/dept/history/lavender/386/newwoman.html (accessed 10 May 2013).
74. Ibid.
75. Horowitz, *Alma Mater*, 5, 90.
76. Ibid., 232.
77. "A Word About the Social Organization," *Atlanta Constitution*, 2 August 1908, sec. A, p. 5.
78. "Pretty Club House Built by Brenau College Girls," *Atlanta Constitution*, 19 April 1908, sec. A, p. 7.
79. Horowitz, quoting a former president of Smith College. Horowitz, *Alma Mater*, 110.
80. "A Word About the Social Organization," *Atlanta Constitution*, 2 August 1908, sec. A, p. 5.

81. *Brenau Journal, January-February, 1912*, p. 168, Box 1 Labeled Literary Journals, folder 2, Brenau Archives, Gainesville, Georgia.
82. Ibid.
83. "Brenau University's Master Facilities Plan," Brenau University, http://artsweb.brenau.edu/campus/6%20Master%20Facilities%20Plan.pdf (accessed 3 January 2013).
84. Letter from Dr. Ed Schrader, President, Brenau University, to Ms. Anna-Elizabeth McCloud (Nix), February 22, 2008, http://brenauthewayitshouldbe.com/ [LINK: "What Started it All"] (accessed 10 May 2013).

CHAPTER 5

ORGANIZATIONS AND TRADITIONS AT BRENAU

THOSE THAT GOVERN STUDENTS AND THOSE THAT STUDENTS GOVERN

Historian John R. Thelin observed that as American colleges developed, "undergraduates...created an elaborate world of their own within and alongside the official world of the college."[1] In this world, student clubs, secret societies, athletic teams, campus traditions and the like emerged and became key components of the college experience. Indeed, some students were more interested in this "extracurricular" aspect of college than in their schooling. Thelin wrote that, "For many undergraduates, compliance with the formal curriculum was merely the price of admission into 'college life.'"[2] Paraphrasing Frederick Rudolph, a pioneering scholar of American higher education, Thelin contended that:

> student initiated activities had a discernible life cycle. In the initial stage, an activity would surface informally and even spontaneously among undergraduates. If a particular activity enjoyed sustained popularity, it attracted scrutiny from the administration and then attempts at either official abolition or control. Such administrative efforts usually failed and the activity would resurface in the form

of a renegade organization. Ultimately the administration would try to control or co-opt the activity by assimilating it into the formal structure (and covenants) of the college.[3]

Sometimes the administration succeeded and established governance over the activity. Other times, students succeeded in keeping the activity as their own.

Negotiation pervades every aspect of this extracurricular activity life cycle as college students and college faculty & staff members jockey to create the college experience they find most desirable. Among other things, the organizations, traditions, practices, etc., that are formed and shaped thanks to this process of negotiation are tools wielded by students and officials. College faculty and staff members can often use some of the extracurricular activities they control in ways to govern student behavior. This is quite overtly what happens in the case of athletics and honor societies, for example, as students conform to the expectations of the faculty and staff to earn a place on a team or academic laurels. Yet, even organizations that lack a strong faculty member presence can still serve official ends. Colleges and universities are frequently thankful for entities like civic or religious clubs and student government associations because these organizations actually relieve officials of some of the burdens of policing undergraduates. These groups can often promote both conformity and good behavior on the part of even heterogeneous members of the student body and so earn institutional sanction, if not outright support.

Just as there are things beyond the curriculum that college officials can use to govern student behavior, there are those that lie beyond the reach of the faculty and staff. Such organizations, traditions, practices, etc., are the ones that, for various reasons, college governors failed to co-opt. Although aspects of these things do still govern students by inducing conformity among members of the campus community, they are likewise governed *by* students, not college officials. Greek organizations and secret societies are good examples of such largely autonomous entities

Organizations and Traditions at Brenau 271

in which little negotiation occurs between college students and college faculty & staff members over goings-on. Students form the organizations, populate them, elect officers, hold events and functions, and set policies and standards that bring about desired behaviors among members—all with relatively little (if any) tangible interference or involvement on the part of the faculty and staff. Although some of these organizations and some of the practices and traditions they foster may actually promote some kinds of behaviors that college officials would prize, faculty and staff members have little agency in obtaining such outcomes. They simply occur because, often, students and college personnel do not work at cross-purposes; both want many of the same good things for their institution.

Since the founding of Brenau College and its predecessor, the Georgia Baptist Female Seminary, institutional personnel and students have created a vibrant extracurricular collegiate life. This extracurricular life is chiefly apparent in print in the surviving editions of the *Alchemist*, Brenau's student newspaper, in columns referred to as "Brenau College Notes" or "Brenau Notes" in the *Atlanta Constitution* daily newspaper, and in a hundred years' worth of Brenau's annually-published student yearbook, the *Bubbles*. All of these sources began publication around the turn of the twentieth century and, for decades, would provide an exceptional insight into the organizations, traditions, and practices prevalent at the College.

This chapter looks at these and examines both some extracurricular organizations and some practices at Brenau that have tended to govern students and some that have tended to be established and regulated by students. Because Brenau's athletics, honor societies, sororities & secret societies, and student government association are addressed elsewhere in this book, these are not dealt with here. Rather, this chapter explains how Brenau's popular and officially sanctioned Y.W.C.A.; its literary, fine arts, and media clubs; and its several time-honored traditions have encouraged student conformity or remained under student control. Likewise, evident in some of Brenau's traditions are aspects of the college experience that are aloof from negotiation and control by the faculty or the administration.

Regarding student organizations, many more have existed at Brenau over the years than just the "Y" and the literary societies. Quite a few of these have related to academic pursuits. For example, the *Bubbles* and other sources bear out that, at one time or another, Brenau has supported organizations such as a science club or a debate team. Other organizations have championed civic causes, such as Brenau's League of Women Voters.[4] This group was particularly popular at Brenau in the first half of the twentieth century. A 1930s yearbook photograph showed around fifty students as League members.[5] Still other Brenau student organizations have been social interest groups, such as S.A.D.D. (Students Against Driving Drunk).[6] Other Brenau organizations existed to support student groups elsewhere. For example, the 1911 *Bubbles* had a section devoted to "Fraternity Clubs" and included groups such as the "Phi Delta Theta Girls" and the "Kappa Alpha Girls."[7] More recently, several Brenau student organizations have had a vocational emphasis, such as Students in Free Enterprise (S.I.F.E.) and the Brenau Association of Nursing Students.[8] Other Brenau student groups have been decidedly less serious, especially far in the institution's past. In 1901, for example, a group called the "Bo-Ketchers" existed. Lest there be any doubt about the club's purpose, members represented their goal in verse: "Let us all be up & doing, Hunting 'round in every place, With one common aim pursuing —Get a man or break a trace."[9] Club officers held such titles as "Chief Bo-Ketcher," "Biggest Ketcher of All," and "A Jewel Ketcher."[10] These Ketchers may have had some competition in their hedonistic pursuits. Also at Brenau that year was a club called the "Love Sick League," as well as a "Lotus Club."[11]

Whether they operated for business or pleasure, all of the student organizations like these that have existed at Brenau over the years did so because both students and faculty & staff members wanted them there. As the name suggests, students would play important roles in student organizations, but so, too, could some College personnel who served as club sponsors or advisors. Students and officials might conceivably have dickered over anything, be it as mundane as setting a time and place for a single officer's meeting or something as weighty as creating a club's constitution. Most likely, the faculty and staff (who already had plenty to do) interceded relatively little. This certainly seems to have been the case with some of Brenau's more prominent student organizations.

Virtually since its inception and for many decades in the twentieth century, Brenau supported a chapter of the Young Women's Christian Association that was quite active. The *Atlanta Constitution* first mentioned the group in November of 1903 when it related that, "The Halloween entertainment given by the Young Women's Christian Association on Saturday evening proved to be very interesting and enjoyable to those taking part, besides netting a neat sum for the association."[12] According to the "Brenau Notes," by just a year later, the Young Woman's Christian Association had "become one of the strong organizations of the college and its members are doing...work that will bear blessed fruit in coming years."[13] The Y.W.C.A. would continue to play a prominent role in campus life throughout much of the century. Over the next several decades, multiple editions of the "Brenau Notes" and the *Alchemist* would mention various events sponsored by the club, such as vesper services, parties, sing-a-longs, and scripture study. Vesper services, in particular, were large affairs at which guest speakers and musical performances occurred, some even by large groups, as in the case of the Riverside Band and Orchestra, which played at Brenau in 1935.[14] Members of Brenau's Y.W.C.A. even occasionally traveled to other colleges to give musical or dramatic performances.[15] For several decades, Brenau's student handbooks published a great deal of information about the Y.W.C.A. Among campus organizations, only the College's student government and Panhellenic association received more attention in the handbooks. The organization grew to be so large on campus that, for a time, Brenau became something of a regional Y.W.C.A. powerhouse that sent representatives to area conventions and supported its own opulent club house.[16] Eleanor Rigney noted that:

> A permanent home was built for the Y.W.C.A. in 1918 in memory of Lessie Southgate Simmons. It included a chapel for worship, rooms for the cabinet, the Y.W.C.A. secretary, and the college library. The fund for the erection of this building began with a donation for five thousand dollars by Dr. T. J. Simmons, her widower and Co-President [of Brenau] from 1910 to 1913.[17]

Rigney concluded that, "About twenty-five thousand dollars additional was subscribed by members of the faculty" and other admirers of Mrs. Simmons, a large sum that speaks to the prominence of the club on campus.[18]

The popularity of Y.W.C.A. organizations on most college campuses, including Brenau, began to wane beginning in the late 1960s.[19] At Brenau, other more faith-specific student fellowship organizations (such as a Baptist Student Association, a Cardinal Newman Society for Roman Catholics, and a club that was actually called the Brenau Fellowship Association) emerged at one time or another that apparently drew students away from the "Y." Examining the *Bubbles* yearbooks of the 1960s, 1970s, and 1980s reveals that membership fluctuated in these fellowship organizations over time and that some (such as the Newmans) actually ceased operations. Yet, in any given year, it was common to note at least a dozen women (often more) as being members of these religious student organizations.

Brenau's students would have joined these groups for fellowship, for a chance to build ties of friendship in a pious atmosphere. Brenau faculty members and Brenau's administration would have been grateful for the existence of such groups. Religious organizations were, in essence, groups of students encouraging other students to maintain good behavior. In so doing, such religious organizations generally saved the faculty and staff some trouble in enforcing discipline on campus. Students in the Y.W.C.A. and other such groups would, generally speaking, not break the rules because doing so would have been un-Christian and would have earned the disapproval of fellow students. Especially in the early twentieth century, these groups were so large and influential on campus that they could have thrown their moral weight around to induce even nonmembers to behave a certain way. From the perspective of the faculty and staff, the end result would have been a better-disciplined student body acquired by expending less effort themselves. Absent these fellowship organizations, something (presumably the faculty and staff) would have had to take up the task of enforcing discipline. This would have been a taxing chore the faculty and staff would have been happy to avoid. Ultimately, each side (students and the faculty & staff) got something of what they wanted out of the negotiation over the existence of fellowship clubs. The students got to have fun in their organizations as they followed their faith and membership promoted solidarity within the student body. At the same time, the Brenau personnel farmed out some of their responsibilities for keeping order on campus to these student organizations.

Like the Y.W.C.A., student-driven literary and debating societies and various student publications have long existed at Brenau. As far back as 1880, the catalog of the Georgia Baptist Female Seminary read:

> There are two Literary Societies in the Seminary, composed of the larger [sic.] young ladies who are sufficiently advanced to understand and appreciate the advantages afforded. Each Society meets weekly, has a President, Secretary, Treasurer, and Librarian, and is gathering a nice library.[20]

The catalog indicated that the societies were called the "Butler Society" and the "Wilkesonian Society" and were named after two of the Seminary's early leaders. Presumably, as was typically the case at other colleges in the nineteenth century, the two societies would have competed for members and would have engaged each other in spirited discussions about arts and letters. Although the two societies would fold by the time Brenau College came into being, debating and literary study would continue off-and-on at the College throughout the century. For example, a 1917 edition of the *Montgomery Advertiser* noted that an organization called the "Philomathesian Literary Society" was active at the College.[21] In 1938, a group of Brenau students traveled to Athens to debate women students at the University of Georgia.[22] The March 19, 1940, edition of the *Alchemist* reported that a pair of Brenau students would meet students from Auburn University in a debate. The paper related that, "The Brenau colleagues will uphold the affirmative side of the subject, 'The United States should follow a policy of strict economic and military isolation toward all nations outside the Western hemisphere engaged in armed international or civil conflict.'"[23] On the eve of World War II, this was certainly a timely topic.

In addition to debating, Brenau students have engaged in the publication of a literary journal. In one of the earliest editions published by Brenau, the April 1905 edition of the *Brenau Journal* featured "a clever little poem entitled 'I know; He's Played With Me,' a well told little romance by Miss Bessie Ledbeter, of Atlanta, which she calls 'True Worth Will Find its Own,' and a little bit of verse by 'M.E.P.,' dedicated to some one [sic] who yet remains undiscovered."[24] The January-February, 1913, edition of the *Brenau Journal* contained two romantic short stories, a poem entitled, "To Our Friends, The Boys," and several pages of writing on current events, particularly involving the Panama Canal.[25] This edition of the *Journal* also reprinted some very glowing comments about written selections in past editions of the *Journal* that appeared in the literary magazines of Georgia Tech and Wofford College.[26]

The *Brenau Journal* ceased publication sometime before 1940. In December of that year, the College began publishing another literary magazine entitled *The Flame*. Several of the poems and short stories in the first edition were about Christmas whereas others were about boys or dating. Two more serious selections dealt with the war in Europe and the role the United States would play in the conflict. Though uncertainty permeated those pieces, so did confidence. Perhaps the most remarkable line in the entire magazine appeared in the short play entitled, "With This

Sunlight on Your Shoulders." Speaking of a Brenau woman waiting to see her beau for the last time before he traveled under military orders, Carolyn Cobourn wrote, "She has the kind of glamor which only the American college girl of today possesses. It is the glamor of health, with shining hair, shining face, and glowing red mouth. Her long length is restless and as she taps her foot, she gives the effect of a powerful personality in one so young."[27] The spring, 1946, edition of *The Flame* rewarded this kind of woman for years of wartime waiting and suffering. Several of the short stories described lovers reunited as servicemen returned home. By 1947, the home front had apparently returned to normal. *The Flame*'s commencement issue of that year published selections on exams, dieting, and sunburns, as well as poems, jokes, and book reviews.

The Brenau Archives contain no post-1940s editions of *The Flame*, which suggests that the literary journal ceased publication around 1950. In 1975, Brenau began publishing another incarnation of a literary magazine, this time entitled *The Elixir*, a title "borrowed...from a source of symbolic names upon which Brenau has drawn," that being "the ancient tradition of alchemy."[28] Nearly four decades later, *The Elixir* continues to publish original student writing, artwork, and photography on a plethora of topics. Themes seemed to vary from edition to edition, as did the appearance of the magazine. The simply-bound 1978 edition mostly contained poems that dealt with mythology and nature as well as nine haiku verses.[29] Roughly a decade later, *The Elixir* consisted mostly of short stories that generally dealt with the dark themes of homicide, domestic violence, and loveless marriages.[30] In 1998, *The Elixir* consisted mostly of poetry whose themes touched on everything from tomatoes, sweat tea, and the six o'clock news to lost love and death.[31] Also in 1998, Brenau began publishing a literary magazine showcasing the writing of the University's Evening and Weekend College students. *The Syllabus*, as it was known, was apparently a short-lived venture as no copies exist in the Archives from after 2001. By 2012, *The Elixir* still thrived and had a glossy, magazine-like appearance. Its three-dozen poems, short stories, and images dealt with every topic under the sun and showcased quite a bit of young talent.

In *Gender and Higher Education in the Progressive Era*, historian Lynn D. Gordon mined the writings of female students published in literary magazines of the age at several institutions to say a great deal about their experiences at college from the 1890s to the 1920s. The writings of these students indicated that they were often much more serious and focused on their educations than was previously believed.[32] The few editions of *The Flame* that survive in the Brenau Archives and the several archived editions of *The Elixir* are similarly telling. Sometimes, they reveal Brenau women to be eager to engage even the most somber of subjects; at other times, they show a much lighter side of students. Dominant themes changed over time. The writings of the students in the 1940s were preoccupied largely with notions of love and marriage and reflected society's views that women should become homemakers. These themes were conspicuously absent in much of the material written by Brenau students in the near aftermath of the women's movement of the late 1960s and early 1970s.

In the creation of the Brenau college experience, students and faculty members alike appear to have supported Brenau's debating societies and literary journals. Although the College largely underwrote the cost of these extracurricular activities, it was students and not faculty members that were the driving force behind both. The members of the debating society or the literary magazines' editorial board made content decisions. It is conceivable that faculty advisors could have weighed-in on debating topics and literary submissions. Yet, at least respecting the literary magazines, if censorship occurred, it is not readily evident. Several issues of *The Elixir* included writing that either contained profanity or that was quite sexually suggestive. If the Brenau faculty was ever of a mind to restrict student expression, it seems doubtful such provocative pieces would have been published as they were. Rather, the fact that the journals printed edgy pieces suggests that the faculty, staff, and students agreed that there was value in nurturing such outlets of expression on a liberal arts campus.

Besides publishing literary journals, Brenau has a long tradition of publishing a student newspaper that dates back to the days of the Georgia Baptist Female Seminary. In its earliest incarnation, the newspaper was called the *Seminary Signal*. In the twentieth century, the paper came to be called the *Alchemist*. Like *The Elixir*, the name was associated with the mythical pursuit of turning base metals like lead into gold and was meant to complement the name of the College, which means "gold refined by fire." Throughout the newspaper's history, students wrote the articles and editorials and were generally the driving force behind the periodical's publication. Very early on, Brenau boasted in several newspaper advertisements of being the only college in the southeast to own its own newspaper printing press upon which the Seminary printed the *Signal*. By the twentieth century, local community newspapers in Hall and neighboring counties printed the *Alchemist*.

Although relatively few editions of the *Alchemist* survive given how long the newspaper has circulated, enough exist to determine that Brenau students published their paper more or less continuously for over a century. As one would expect from a college newspaper, the vast majority of the content in the *Alchemist* over the years related to campus events and personalities. Still, the newspaper at times published other types of material, including world events, a minister's column, book and movie reviews, and creative writing selections. In mid-century, the paper devoted quite a bit of space to something like a society page, which identified some students by name and wittily detailed how they had spent their recent free time.[33] These columns indicated that many young women traveled to spend time with boyfriends or had their beaus come up to Gainesville for visits. By the nineteen-sixties and early 1970s, the paper had assumed its most professional appearance and earned high ratings in many respects by the Associated Collegiate Press.[34] Despite such laurels, the *Alchemist* was not without its detractors. A

1965 editorial in the University of Georgia's college newspaper criticized Brenau journalists for their concern about Brenau's image. The editorial hinted that the *Alchemist* would censor stories that would tarnish the College's reputation and likewise intimated that the Athens paper would never compromise its First Amendment rights.[35]

Also in the 1970s, Brenau supplemented its print media with broadcast media by establishing a radio station.[36] W.B.C.X. came on-line in the fall of 1977 at 89.1 on the F.M. dial. Though the College has a small television presence (a campus-bound cable channel that broadcasts some original programming and announcements), its main media outlet is the radio station. The call sign for the station stands for "Brenau College Experiment." Randy Mullinax, a Gainesville resident who worked at a commercial radio station near Brenau, assisted with the technical arrangements of getting the radio station up and running.[37] Dr. Jim Bridwell, a member of Brenau's faculty, served as the station's first director. Originally, the station broadcast from 10:30 a.m. to 9:00 p.m. with only a 10-watt transmitter, which covered an area "roughly the size of the Gainesville city limits."[38] Programming for the station in those early days was student operated. Bridwell described material broadcast on the commercial-free, "wall-to-wall music" station by saying, "Our music will reach from classical programs to popular disco music."[39] The station trained students and volunteers from the community to work as disc jockeys, playing music, taking requests, and broadcasting some news and educational programming.

Enthusiasm for the station seemed to dip somewhat in the 1980s and 1990s if station programming is any indication. Programming became largely automated and focused on a jazz/classical "easy listening" format. The station also broadcast few hours of original local programming at all. Despite this, some Brenau students still maintained a role at the station. The 1985 *Bubbles* indicated that thirteen young women volunteered their time as staff members at W.B.C.X.[40]

The station experienced a revival in the twenty-first century. Its broadcasting power would grow to be 875 watts, giving the station a reach to about a million potential listeners throughout northeast Georgia and into the lower Carolinas. In 2004, the station changed its name to "Eclectic 89.1." The change reflected a move to a very diverse programming schedule. The station continued to play jazz and classical selections, but also began playing music from around the world in addition to playing gospel music, rhythm and blues, rock, and other styles as well. In 2007, the station acquired a "digital Studio to Transmitter Link," which replaced W.B.C.X.'s outmoded line-of-sight transmitter.[41] Disc jockeys were largely still students or community volunteers. Under the guidance of program manager J. Scott Fugate, the station adopted a new mission statement: "serving the educational needs of Brenau University, the cultural needs of Gainesville and the greater NE Georgia area, the artistic needs of the community, the business needs of our own organization, as well as the needs & goals of our dedicated community of volunteers who help in the professional operation and maintenance of this radio station."[42] Local programming and listenership increased and the station even won a "Gabby Award" from the Georgia Association of Broadcasting for its improvements.[43] By 2012, W.B.C.X. branded itself simply as "The Voice of Brenau" and delivered several hours of original programming each week via the airwaves and online streaming.[44] By this time, the station was also a member of the Corporation for Public Broadcasting. Though Brenau students and community volunteers still did most of the disc-jockeying, by now W.B.C.X. had on staff as well Jay Andrews, who was a veteran professional broadcaster with many years of experience in the greater Atlanta market.[45]

Although Brenau's radio station entered the twenty-first century on new legs, the modern *Alchemist* seemed somewhat less vibrant compared to its former self. For a brief time in the late 1980s, the newspaper's name changed to the *Aurum*, which is the Latin word for gold.[46] The name would revert back to being the *Alchemist* after only a few years. In the interval, judging by existing copies in the Archives, the general appearance of the newspaper seemed less professional than it had been. Also, the newspaper's production seems to have become less regular—in some instances, perhaps down to one or two issues a term. Beginning in 2005–2006, the newspaper went to an online format, which was accessible from the Brenau University website.[47] Unlimited online access may be translating into wider readership. By 2012, online counters associated with both current and archived online articles could indicate how many times a piece had been viewed and some articles and opinion pieces had been accessed several hundred times.

Regarding the press, Vladimir Lenin once said that the fourth estate could be "a collective organizer of the masses." Though he probably envisioned a more sinister use of mainstream media, Lenin's suggestion that things like newspapers or radio could be used to shape public opinion would not have been lost on Brenau students and College officials. Each group would have wanted its own voice doing the talking via Brenau media to project its priorities and concerns in a favorable light.

Over time, Brenau faculty and staff members have generally exercised a good deal of control over Brenau's electronic media. This is governed not by students but by faculty and staff station managers and, in the case of online matter such as Facebook pages or Internet sites, by Brenau webmasters. True, students have some creative license when hosting their own radio shows and television productions or making posts in online forums on Brenau's websites and social media sites. Yet, ultimately, the faculty and staff have the final say in what makes the air or is retained on the Internet. Given this, college officials have historically had a great deal of discretion about what material is electronically transmitted and, consequently, what information students will have access to.

The same was not necessarily true for print media. Students have historically seemed to exercise a great deal of autonomy in publishing Brenau's newspapers, at least up until recent decades. The surviving copies of the *Alchemist* from various years might acknowledge the editorial staff of the paper, but most do not mention faculty member

Organizations and Traditions at Brenau 283

sponsors. Moreover, for much of the twentieth century, the paper seems to have been financially supported by its advertisements and not from college funds. Finally, the tone of the paper, especially during the mid-twentieth century, suggests an absence of great faculty control. At times, it seemed to approach risqué. For example, in a column called "Murmurings" in the *Alchemist* edition of Tuesday, May 14, 1935, an unnamed authoress wrote, "Our bouquet of flowers goes to the Mae West of the Alpha Chi house this week. She sold every automobile firm in Gainesville an ad for the *Alchemist* right after the advisory committee again refused to allow girls to borrow, or use their own, cars here. You have what it takes, dearie."[48] The same edition also carried an article entitled "Faculty Foibles" written by "The Goone," which spoofed one or two absent-minded professors on campus.[49] In addition, this edition of the newspaper facetiously admonished Brenau women for taking their dates from the nearby Riverside Military Academy to the movies to "carry on behind that projection," saying that "You know they're just babies yet."[50] Although none of the material printed was scandalous, one might imagine an administrator or two wishing that the occasional story could be toned-down to safeguard Brenau's public image. That such stories ran in the first place suggests that the newspaper operated with some autonomy. This would have worked in the students' favor during their ongoing negotiation with Brenau officials over the character their institution would assume just as faculty and staff member control of W.B.C.X. might have worked in the favor of College officials. Yet, at the same time, even controlled as it was by students, the newspaper could benefit Brenau's faculty and administration because no student or organization would ever want to see their name in print for a negative reason. The fear of bad press in the *Alchemist* would have inclined students toward acceptable behavior. Moreover, the desire for good press coverage no doubt encouraged good behavior on the part of some students and student organizations. This, the Brenau faculty and staff would have appreciated.

Although campus organizations like the Y.W.C.A. and publications like the *Alchemist* were student-driven, College officials still appreciated them as potential instruments of governing student behavior. The same thing can be said for many of the College traditions that have long existed at Brenau. A "tradition" is properly defined as "an inherited, established, or customary pattern of thought, action, or behavior."[51] Social psychologists believe that these patterns serve "to maintain a synthesis and conformity in the behavior of individual members of [a] society," which may explain their ubiquity on college campuses.[52] To an extent, colleges, like any societal institution, require conformity to function. Placing hundreds or thousands of young adults on a campus and permitting each do entirely his or her own thing would not reap much education. Hence, colleges created various means—both formal and informal—to help acclimate each year's crop of new, uninitiated freshmen to the routine and protocol of college life. Traditions are one such informal means.

Both Brenau students and the Brenau faculty and staff have played important roles in establishing and maintaining College traditions. Depending on the tradition, one group or the other may have governed more, but neither group could truly sustain a tradition absent at least tacit support from the other. Many traditions were decidedly student-driven at the same time others entailed significant involvement by College personnel. Yet, even student-driven traditions tended to require at least some faculty sponsorship just as no tradition could really have thrived without student support no matter how much the faculty might have supported it.[53] Sustaining practically all of Brenau's traditions would have required cooperation—and negotiation—between all members of the Brenau community.

Perhaps the most significant and time-honored tradition at Brenau is "May Day," which has existed since the College's founding. (See Figure 30.) In fact, the celebration that historically began in Northern European cultures to commemorate the end of winter has been observed by many American women's colleges over the years. At Brenau, the event was always a lavish spring festival.[54] A 1935 edition of the *Alchemist* described the May Day fete of that year and gives a sense of its grandeur:

> The title of the program was May Fete At The Old Plantation. The manor was covered with Dorothy Perkins roses, and in the midst of this southern atmosphere the arrival of the queen was awaited on the eleventh day of May, 1850, to accept the crown to be presented by the Colonel. All the slaves and their children were allowed to come out and have a part in the festival by singing, dancing, or saying a word of greeting, for that was the day the Queen met her Prince Charming, the Beau of the Fifties, and received her crown.[55]

"Colonel" H. J. Pearce, the president of the College, crowned Vernice Hurst May Queen. Every edition of the *Bubbles* throughout the twentieth century published several photographs of similarly lavish May Day events. Besides crowning the May Queen, highlights of the event include the presentation of the May Court and a May Pole Dance. May Day also coincided with Brenau's annual alumnae weekend, which brought many graduates back to campus.

Over the years, May Day has doubtlessly been a fun time for many Brenau women. Yet, there is another side to such celebrations. In her book entitled *The Education of the Southern Belle*, Christie Anne Farnham explained the fascination of May Day at women's colleges. Farnham wrote that:

> The crowning of the May queen was a Durkheimian collective enactment of society's definition of femininity, whereby men offered women protection in return for deference. By placing them on a pedestal and paying homage to their beauty, purity, and virtue, men infused the realities of a patriarchal society with a romantic patina that made young women's position more palatable to them.[56]

Although outwardly appearing to be a celebration of women, in a very real sense, May Day actually subverted womanhood. Farnham is saying that men gave college women May Day and other similar celebrations, in essence, to placate them, to make women less likely to perceive and complain about a generally subservient social status when they thought they were being treated like royalty. Whether they themselves realized it or not, Brenau's faculty and administration—which were, over time, often men—would have been complicit in encouraging conformity to this notion by sanctioning May Day performances.

May Day has historically exemplified a Brenau tradition that required a great deal of cooperation between students and the faculty & staff. Each group would have borne substantial responsibilities for the official campus function. Working together would have necessitated negotiation over even small details. Such shared governance would be exhibited to varying degrees in association with other traditions at Brenau.

May Day has not occasioned the only beauty pageant hosted by the College over the years. Beginning in 1942, the Brenau Recreation Association (which has also been known as the Recreation Board) organized the "Miss Brenau Pageant" to annually find the Brenau student who, in the opinion of the pageant judges, best exemplified the ideals of the institution. Brenau yearbooks show that, over the years, anywhere between one and two dozen freshmen selected by Brenau's sororities and independent student organizations have participated in the pageant, which includes an essay contest, a talent demonstration, and an interview. For several months prior to the contest, contestants rehearse song and/or dance numbers for the production. The winner of the pageant would receive a scholarship. Over time, articles in the *Alchemist* and photographic spreads in the *Bubbles* revealed that the event was, frequently, quite lavish and a significant part of campus life.

Traditional feminist critiques of spectacles like May Day or beauty pageants would argue that these events objectify women or have the effect of "marginalizing the types of bodies that are not displayed."[57] To such critiques, Sarah Banet-Weiser (the author of *The Most Beautiful Girl in the World: Beauty Pageants and National Identity*) responded that, "The production of femininity is one characterized by pleasure, among other things, and the contestants' own accounts of their pleasure and desire when producing themselves as beauty queens should not be written off as mere acquiescence."[58] "Feminists," Banet-Weiser declared, "who oppose beauty on the ground that it is oppressive are not more authentic than beauty queens."[59] In other words, there exist good arguments both for and against the propriety of pageants like May Day and Miss Brenau. Whether such events serve or disserve women's interests, they are established traditions at Brenau that have encouraged student conformity as participants and observers alike both found roles to play in their production.

Besides these pageants, other student-driven College traditions have also encouraged conformity on the part of Brenau women throughout the years. Like several women's colleges, Brenau has claimed a "Rat Week" (spelled "R.A.T.T.", "R.A.T.", or simply "Rat" at Brenau) as a tradition for many decades.[60] At Brenau, the acronym version stands for "Remember All the Traditions." The week serves to acquaint two rival classes at the College with each other as sophomores oversee a period of freshman initiation into College traditions.[61] During R.A.T.T. Week, the sophomores demand that the freshmen dress in some conspicuous manner (e.g., as indicated by several archived photographs, wearing mouse ears or black robes) and grill freshmen on their knowledge of campus rules and traditions. (See Figure 31.) Freshmen whose answers were unsatisfactory could be made to perform some task, like reciting a particular funny rhyme or falling on the ground to simulate an air raid drill. Various editions of the *Alchemist* over the years indicated that, for some time, R.A.T.T. Week culminated with "Rat Court," a final dosing of humiliation for freshmen before they would be considered properly initiated members of the College community.

The *Alchemist* described the events of a typical early Rat Week (this one in 1924) in robust detail. The paper read:

> Friday night...all 'rats' were initiated into the holy order of Brenau. This ceremony was very beautiful and impressive. The "rats" were

dressed in black bathing suits and blacked to represent slaves. The name of every Freshman was read out and on the reading of her name she came forward to give her sacrifice of fruit and one dime to the Holy Cat of the Sophomore class. Along with her other offering each one offered to the fire some undesirable trait.[62]

Freshman-Sophomore week marked the final formal rite of passage for the freshmen. The College, convened in assembly, saw the juniors and seniors exit whereas the freshman and sophomores remained. As sophomores read College rules, freshmen "victims were led up [to] the paint pot and received applications of blue and yellow, the good old colors that all good sophs swear by."[63] The freshmen were then made to sing "Glory, Glory to the Sophomores," with those vocalists who substituted the word "freshman" for sophomore being corrected "by more or less gentle taps on the legs that it was Sophomores, not Freshmen, they were singing their praises to."[64] The singing continued at lunch where "the poor starved Freshies" were graciously permitted by the sophomores to "eat as much as they could grab between rendering various" tunes.[65] After lunch, a "shoe scramble" was held in the gymnasium and the last two freshmen to find their shoes were put down for a "Kangaroo Court."[66] Finally, at Friday night dinner, the freshmen "were made to wear green hose, one high heel shoe and one tennis shoe, evening dresses with middies...and tooth brushes in place of beads."[67] The freshmen then had a beauty contest that members of the faculty judged and the winner received a baby bottle of milk as her prize. The *Alchemist* did not report what happened at the Kangaroo Court, but mentioned only that "it was worth shivering at" and that this "brought to an end the dreadful ordeal of the Freshmen."[68] "No longer," chimed the *Alchemist*, were the freshmen "considered new girls but were true Brenau Girls."[69]

Rat Week was still quite the spectacle in 1945. The *Alchemist* ran a story with the headline, "Sophomores Exterminate Rats and Restore Peace." The article proclaimed, "Everywhere the Freshmen were seen in their green and white, bowing and scraping to the ever mighty sophomores; Rat Cap numbers backward, foreword, inside-out, squanch-wise, and every which way."[70] The article indicated that all Rats wore green beanies and, as in prior years, curiously sported toothbrushes all around campus—perhaps to be used for cleaning something like steps or a monument. The article implied that the sophomores had their fun at freshman expense until week's end, when there was a picnic by the lake and "Then the Freshmen had their fun!"[71] Presumably, sophomore dunking was in order.

A 1980 edition of the *Alchemist* reported that, "Rat Week started out with a Rat Scare Sunday night. The following morning at 1:00 a.m. the freshmen were pulled out of their beds by the sophomores with their black robes and shining paddles."[72] Additionally, the freshman and sophomore classes gave out awards. Deserving sophomores received such laurels as "Most Obnoxious," "Most Hateful," and "Worst All Around," whereas the freshmen class counted among their number "Nicest Rat" and "Best Rat."[73] A photograph in the newspaper suggested other components of Rat Week. Apparently, Rats could be made to "hit the deck" when a passing sophomore called for an "air raid." The photograph depicted a smiling young woman, wearing a beanie with mouse ears, diving to the sidewalk as other students, also smiling, look on in amusement.[74]

R.A.T.T. Week was still going strong in 2008 as indicated by a story in the *Alchemist* of that year. The article indicated that in its modern incarnation, seniors assisted sophomores in performing their R.A.T.T. Week duties by standing next to them and urging them to "keep their faces solemn" even as freshmen tried to make them laugh as they were pelted with questions.[75] Also, the awards had changed. Freshmen could vie for "Most Dedicated Ratt," whereas sophomores no doubt sought to earn the "Scariest Sophomore Award."[76]

Brenau's R.A.T.T. Week clearly involved polite (and, perhaps, sometimes less than polite...) hazing, which was the means to an end. Whereas Brenau officials would have interceded if any sophomore ever took things too far, the tradition was otherwise self-governed by students. Excesses, if any, would have been few because students understood that the desired end result was promoting conformity and college cohesion, not inflicting harm. The events of the week built class spirit for both freshmen and sophomores. The tradition cemented relationships between the students in these classes as they either received or dispensed friendly abuse. R.A.T.T. Week also reaffirmed that all Brenau students were part of something much larger than themselves: their alma mater. The camaraderie students constructed in playing their roles brought the student body together. This bit of cohesion, coupled with other unifying factors, would have helped students maintain a unified front in their negotiations with Brenau officials over how their college would be.

Other student-governed campus traditions would promote cohesion between students in the junior and senior classes. The tradition of the spring "Spade Hunt" did for these classes what R.A.T.T. Week did for freshmen and sophomores. The hunt spans three days. On day one, the juniors receive from the seniors a few clues that should lead them to a hidden bag of candy. Assuming the juniors can locate the candy, they will receive on day two clues that should lead them to a hidden "baby spade," which is apparently more of a handheld garden trowel than a shovel.[77] Finally, if the juniors could find the baby spade, they would receive from the seniors on day three the clues that should lead them to the campus hiding place of the actual spade. According to tradition, "If the spade is found, the juniors get to smear shaving cream on the seniors, and vice versa if the juniors fail to find it."[78] Also, very few clues are given, but ribbons are tied on the spade and are supposed to be left showing.[79] Incidentally, it is not precisely clear from any archival material why it is a spade (as opposed to some other implement) that is hidden. At any rate, the act of collectively hiding the spade on the part of the senior class and the act of collectively searching for the spade on the part of the juniors have reinforced bonds between classmates at the College for years.[80]

Other traditions have been likewise geared toward upperclassmen. One involves a prominent structure on campus called the "Crow's Nest." The Class of 1905 commissioned the construction of the original Crow's Nest on the spacious lawn in front of Pearce Auditorium. Workers built

Organizations and Traditions at Brenau 291

a large, wooden platform about one story high and accessible by a set of stairs around a large oak tree on the lawn. Though the Crow's Nest has relocated several times for various reasons, the traditions surrounding it have always remained intact. The seniors in 1905 dedicated the Crow's Nest "to subsequent senior classes and declared no underclassmen could ascend the steps."[81] According to Brenau's Public Relations Office, this tradition morphed somewhat over time. By the twenty-first century:

> a tradition developed that only seniors were allowed up in the hallowed and lofty heights of its balustraded balcony - while juniors can only go so far as to stand on the first step; sophomores may venture to stand on the steps around the large platform at the base and the freshmen - well, the freshmen just get to stand on the concrete base that surrounds it all.[82]

"This hierarchy," Brenau contended, "encourages an understanding and appreciation in each student of the importance of history, tradition and the time-honored progression of rising through the ranks from class to class."[83] Over the years, Brenau's student handbooks indicated that any underclassman that dared ascend all the way to the top of the Crow's Nest and was caught in the act could be subject to a very hefty fine. Despite the warning, no doubt countless Brenau freshmen, sophomores, and juniors have snuck onto the platform over the years to acquire bragging rights for having done so. Photographs in the *Bubbles* yearbooks over the last several decades occasionally depicted a very solemn event akin to a changing of the guard when Brenau's seniors, very near their graduation, officially turn over possession of the Crow's Nest to the rising senior class.

This tradition is known as "Class Day" and it honors Brenau's seniors. Like May Day and more so than some other campus traditions, governance of Class Day involves faculty members as well as students. The two groups would coordinate for the event because Brenau celebrated Class Day as an official College function. At the event, which attracts parents and alumnae as well as Brenau students and personnel, class songs are sung and "a reading of the prophecy and last will and testament" of departing seniors is held.[84] Then, the seniors, clad in black robes, and the rest of the student body, who are dressed in white, form a procession to the front campus for the ceremony that will celebrate the promotion of each class. In the procession, freshmen carry a chain made out of ivy just as sophomores bear a chain made out of daisies. At the ceremony, the seniors pass down their robes to the juniors who are permitted to ascend to the top of the Crow's Nest. The entire student body then sings a tune called "Seniors, We Honor Thee" to the rising senior class.[85]

Though much about traditions like Class Days and May Days were the product of actual face-to-face meetings and negotiations between both Brenau students and the faculty and staff, other campus traditions seemed to have developed a life of their own over the years. Among these, perhaps the most unusual ungoverned tradition at Brenau is the legend that the campus is haunted by a ghost named Agnes. Candice Dyer, a freelance writer and herself a Brenau alumna, once quipped in the *Gainesville Times* that Agnes is "More Casper than Amityville" and has "morphed from an occult figure into a cult figure" at the College.[86] Theories abound about how Agnes came to haunt Brenau's Pearce Auditorium, her spectral home. Earlier in the twentieth century, Pearce once housed a swimming pool in its basement. Campus lore says that "a student hanged herself from a beam or diving board during the 1920s" and that her ghost "still piddles around the older halls and dormitories, where she twists doorknobs, turns on study lamps, bangs loudly on piano keys...and generally goes bump in the night."[87]

Debbie Thompson, Brenau's archivist, indicated to Dyer in an interview that, "We've never found an obituary or article in old newspapers to explain any of this."[88] Thompson related that Agnes aficionados had "narrowed her identity down, possibly, to Agnes Galloway," a student from North Carolina who "appears in the *Bubbles*, Brenau's yearbook, as a freshman in 1926."[89] No other pictures of Agnes Galloway have been discovered anywhere else in the University Archives. Dyer indicated that this lone photograph:

reveals Agnes Galloway to be a pretty young woman from the Jazz Age, with the kind of plump face that could appear on a cameo brooch. Her hair is fashionably bobbed, and she has lively eyes and an open, mischievous smile.[90]

Dyer joked, "Actually, she looks ready to drink some bathtub gin and dance the Charleston at a 'Great Gatsby'-style party."[91]

Several legends purport to account for Agnes' suicide. In one, she is a talented, but shy, pianist who is seduced, impregnated, and then jilted by a music professor who leaves her for a flapper. Despondent, she took her life. In another version, Agnes was devastated at not receiving a bid from her sorority of choice, or, alternatively, was denied her perfect role in a play or dance recital, and so killed herself. In yet another variation, Agnes was part of a secret society at Brenau. The story goes that she either died accidentally in a hazing incident as the society inducted her or that she was killed by a rival society who arranged her murder to appear to be a suicide. In any version, Agnes' forlorn spirit ends up haunting the Gainesville campus.[92]

In a 2005 article in the *Atlanta Journal-Constitution*, reporter Mark Davis tried to shed more light on Agnes' story. He interviewed Tammy Pell, a librarian from Agnes' home town of Mount Airy, North Carolina, who researched Agnes Galloway's past. Pell learned from the records of a local funeral home that the Galloway family buried daughter Agnes "after she died of tuberculosis on April 28, 1929."[93] Shortly afterwards, the family moved away. Although this seems to belie the story of Agnes' suicide, Davis' article points out that the Galloway family was wealthy and speculated that they could have covered up a suicide if they had wanted to do so. Tuberculosis, a relatively common and frequently fatal ailment of the time, would have been the likely disease to resort to using in crafting a cover story. Still, the ghost of Agnes may not even be a product of the 1920s. In an interview, Debbie Thompson pointed out that "Alums from the '40s and '50s don't tell Agnes stories…Agnes stories don't show up until the '60s."[94] This may suggest that Agnes either died later than the 1920s or, for whatever reason, put off her haunting for some time.

Among the many questions the story of Agnes might beg, some are particularly noteworthy: Why was this ghost story ever created? Why has it thrived as it has? Also, what can the story of Agnes tell us about the interaction between students and College personnel over the form of the Brenau college experience? Of course, ghost stories themselves are common and timeless, dating back to at least the age of ancient Greece (if not before).[95] Writer Virginia Woolf once wondered why such stories have thrived for millennia: "How are we to account for the strange human craving for the pleasure of feeling afraid which is so much involved in our love of ghost stories?"[96] She determined that people simply find being frightened entertaining—at least so long as it is under circumstances that they can control.[97] Agnes certainly does entertain. According to Candice Dyer, many students have held midnight séances (complete with Ouija boards) in attempts to contact her. Also, students have held campus events celebrating her, most notably "'Agnespallooza' with a 'You go, ghoul!' theme and souvenir T-shirts that say 'Agnes is my homegirl.'"[98] Professional ghost hunters have ventured to campus seeking Agnes for television programs, but none has left with any conclusive proof of her existence. And, of course, Agnes has been the star attraction of many a Halloween ghost walk in Gainesville.

Although its potential to entertain may account for why students created and nurtured the Agnes ghost story for years, other explanations for it may also exist. This is because ghost stories like that of Agnes can do more than entertain. According to one scholar, "Ghost stories commonly provide an alternative structure of cause and effect, in which the supernatural…offers its own pseudo-explanation" for events that occur.[99] Moreover, a ghost story can create "a world that is potentially within our power to change by the energy of our thoughts."[100] People, then, tell ghost stories to recast reality, to offer explanations for things when conventional explanations seem not to suffice. Brenau women have done this with Agnes for years. Dyer noted that College personnel and students alike attribute odd happenings during rehearsals and performances in Pearce Auditorium to her spirit. Agnes has become a convenient and plausible explanation for everything from strange noises to misplaced items in and around the Brenau buildings.

Besides serving as a scapegoat for the difficult-to-explain, Agnes also edifies. Simon J. Bronner noted, "often the telling of ghost legends serves to provide transcendent moral lessons."[101] Bronner pointed out that, like Agnes, many spiritual "ladies in white" the world over "walk the earth in story to remind others of...the anguish of love forsaken."[102] One version of the story of Agnes seems like a cautionary tale Brenau women would relate to remind one-another that forbidden liaisons can end badly. The story would likewise have the effect of putting male faculty members on notice that their misconduct with the young women in their charge could lead to tragic results. Read this way, Agnes' story could be seen as a device for guiding the behavior of members of the Brenau community. Other evidence for this exists. Candice Dyer learned that Sandy Blankenship, a stage and theater manager of Pearce Auditorium, had employed Agnes "as an enforcer of good manners." Blankenship related to her performance students that, "Agnes cannot stand a prima donna...Anyone who tried to throw his or her weight around or behaved in a generally cranky, difficult manner would get an extraordinary reaction."[103] According to Dyer, Blankenship warned that, "If you behaved obnoxiously...a tree branch might fall on your car during a storm; theater lights might flicker or go black during your solo; or the sound system could make 'honking' noises during your pirouette or monologue."[104] Conversely, students who behaved themselves would avoid incurring Agnes' wrath.

Besides being interesting for its own sake, the story of Agnes is fascinating because of what it says about the process of negotiating to create the ideal Brenau college experience. Both Brenau students and the Brenau faculty and staff employ the story in defining aspects of the institution. Students wield Agnes stories to anonymously editorialize about life at Brenau. Though it might be difficult for a student to openly declare that male professors can abuse their positions or that sorority elitism can lead to despair, Agnes could communicate such themes with impunity every time her story was told. Perpetuating the Agnes legend might suit some Brenau personnel because, for superstitious students, anyway, it might encourage good behavior. For both groups, the tradition of Agnes haunting the Gainesville campus was self-sustaining. Neither side necessarily required the other to keep the tradition alive any more than either side could really govern how the Agnes legend morphed and spread.

The presence of another legend connected to campus also illustrates how stories serve to construct the college experience. In 1937, a tourist hiking near Edenton, North Carolina, came across a stone about twice as big as a shoebox with a bit of very old-looking English writing on it. He took the stone to the history department at Emory University for analysis. At Emory was Dr. H. J. Pearce, Jr., the son of Brenau's president and a future vice president at the College. Pearce, Jr., and his colleagues determined that the stone bore writing (seemingly in Elizabethan English) that was apparently carved by none other than Virginia Dare, the first child born in North America to English parents. The 130 or so words on the stone detailed the destruction by disease and warring Indians of the Lost Colony of Roanoke Island in North Carolina and the burial of the dead by the few survivors, including Dare. The colony had been founded by the English in 1587 and discovered mysteriously abandoned in 1590. The historians dubbed the rock the "Dare Stone" and Pearce, Jr., convinced his father to purchase the stone from the finder. Once in Brenau's possession, the stone brought the College some media attention—and quite a bit of controversy.[105] (See Figure 32.)

Pearce, Jr., published an article about the stone in the well-respected *Journal of Southern History* and obtained an opinion from members of the American Antiquarian Society that the stone was genuine. Hence, many historians came to believe that the stones put an end to the centuries-long debate over the fate of the Lost Colony of Roanoke and America's first colonial celebrity, Virginia Dare. Even so, the Pearces sought to further verify the stone's authenticity and went so far as to offer a bounty for anyone bringing in the headstone mentioned in the carved writing as marking the gravesite of the dead.

Brenau soon became chockablock with blocks, each one assuredly a genuine Dare stone—at least according to its purveyor.

In 1941, journalist Boyden Sparkes published an article in the *Saturday Evening Post* that supposedly proved the Dare Stones—the original one and the ones that arrived later—were hoaxes. Sparkes let it be known that Brenau purchased many of the stones in its collection from finders with questionable reputations. Moreover, according to Sparkes, forensic analysis of the actual writing on the stones, as well as linguistic analysis of the diction and syntax of the carved stories, suggested to experts that everything about the stones was modern, not Elizabethan. Though Brenau never officially took a position on the authenticity of the stones beyond asserting that the first one seemed quite genuine, after the *Post* article, people dismissed all as fakes. The College ultimately removed the Dare Stones from public display to archival storage where they remain to this day. Yet, despite Sparkes' article and subsequent research into the stones, debate persists over whether or not at least the first of the stones could, in fact, be genuine.

Establishing the authenticity of the Dare Stones will likely prove to be as difficult as substantiating the existence of Agnes the ghost. Yet, the presence of both legends at Brenau demonstrates the importance of lore to constituting the collegiate experience. Both Brenau students and Brenau faculty and staff members would have sought to use these and other curiosities to create a campus mythology that served particular ends. Faculty members and administrators hoped to style the institution as a home for novel and serious scholarship. Students found an indefatigable spokeswoman in Agnes who could give voice to concerns they could not. What both Brenau students and the College faculty & staff seem to agree on is that legends of Agnes and of the Dare Stones each have a unique place at Brenau.

Several other traditions at Brenau, though important, are not unique to the University; many schools have field days, homecoming, class retreats, Greek Week, and, of course, graduation. In addition, some other women's colleges have been known to pair up freshmen with juniors and sophomores with seniors in a "sister class system" as does Brenau. Also, social dances have long been popular traditions at Brenau as they have at many other colleges. Originally, as at many women's colleges, dances at Brenau were all-women's affairs, being open only to Brenau students. In time, beginning in the 1930s, Brenau invited men to attend. Brenau would eventually develop the tradition of a spring Cotillion Dance, which was put on by the Cotillion Club, a large organization at the College for many years. By the 1950s, articles in the *Alchemist* suggested the event was grand and important. A 1952 edition of the newspaper included a long article that described the parties and events that each sorority put on during the weekend of the dance to complement the Cotillion.[106] The popularity of campus-wide dances appears to have diminished somewhat in the last quarter of the twentieth century if photographic spreads in the *Bubbles* are any indication. Still, Brenau continues to holds its Cotillion annually. Also, individual organizations (particularly Brenau's sororities), hold smaller formal dances as well throughout the year.

Besides its extant traditions, Brenau has known some traditions to fade over time. The College once had a totem pole that stood in a grassy triangle in front of the old gymnasium. Through its carvings, it was to have represented the "progress of civilization."[107] Various dances and ceremonies took place in front of it until it rotted away, apparently by mid-century.[108] Also, Brenau used to have a lavish "State's Day" event in the early part of the twentieth century. Students who all hailed from the same state would form "states clubs" and would prepare songs and skits to celebrate their state in a series of performances given by the several states clubs. The event served to build bonds of attachment between students who had common points of origin and to showcase that Brenau attracted students from many states and not just Georgia or the South. Indeed, according to tradition, "A weather vane atop Butler Hall symbolizes that Brenau students come from all directions."[109] Interestingly, Brenau apparently has its own Blarney Stone. An edition of the *Gainesville Times* published in 1978 to commemorate the centennial of Brenau reported that, "The magic wishing stone lies in front of East Bailey Hall, engraved with 'The Class of 1907.' Tradition is for a Brenau student to touch it and make a wish."[110] For whatever reason, the tradition appears to be little celebrated in modern times.

Another traditional event at Brenau for many years that died out was the annual Gainesville "chautauqua." Chautauqua (pronounced "she-tah-qwah") were:

> any of various traveling shows and local assemblies that flourished in the United States in the late 19th and early 20th centuries, that provided popular education combined with entertainment in the form of lectures, concerts, and plays, and that were modeled after activities at the Chautauqua Institution of western New York.[111]

These were especially popular events in rural areas like the South because they brought entertainment and culture to otherwise remote communities. Chautauqua could last anywhere from a few days to a month and became the temporary focal point of life when their tents went up near town.

Brenau sponsored a chautauqua meeting annually for many years in the early twentieth century. The first such meeting was in 1907 in Gainesville. The *Atlanta Constitution* reported that:

> This Chautauqua is to be of the nature of a camp meeting and tenting accommodations are to be provided for all who desire them. It is intended by the promoters of the enterprise to conduct

it on the lines identical with those established by the original chautauqua in New York.[112]

The event was scheduled for two weeks and was quite the affair. People came to stay from all around. The *Constitution* reported that, "Tents are arriving for those who will camp for the fortnight on the hillsides in Chattahoochee overlooking the beautiful Lake Warner, and the quiet-flowing river" and that "The boarding houses and hotels will amply accommodate in town the many who do not care to camp at the park."[113]

At the chautauqua, there were events a-plenty. The *Constitution* indicated:

> Boating parties, races, fish fries, launch trips, barbecues, tennis, and ball games on the athletic field are some of the attractions planned for the entertainment of the physical, while the intellectual, spiritual, education, and musical will be abundantly appealed to.[114]

The program appealing to the non-physical included speeches by a United States senator, lectures by several university professors and respected preachers, musical performances and voice recitals, oratory contests, and plays, to name but a few diversions.[115] Brenau students and some members of the faculty figured prominently in many of these events.

Brenau hosted similarly lavish chautauquas for several years. Some of these, such as the 1908 event in Gainesville, lasted up to a month. Though grand for a time, the chautauqua movement declined as radio, television, and automobiles became more widespread in America. These technologies provided easy access to entertainment for rural dwellers, who began attending the chautauquas less and less. The tradition had apparently died out at Brenau by the 1920s as no mention of a chautauqua being held by Brenau occurs after the nineteen-teens.[116]

For many years around the time of the chautauquas, Brenau also held large outings where the classes or, in some cases, even the entire school would embark upon a day trip to a nearby destination. Traditionally, the student body and their chaperones went to Tallulah Falls, Georgia, in the spring (the site of a very high and picturesque waterfall) and to Dahlonega, Georgia, in the fall (the site of the first gold rush in the United States, which offered tours of gold mines).[117] A 1919 edition of the *Alchemist* described the trip to Dahlonega in glowing detail. The trip began as the Brenau geology class piled into five cars and drove three hours to reach Dahlonega, which is about 22 miles northwest of Gainesville on what where then very primitive roads. The class picnicked on fried chicken at the base of a lovely waterfall before touring a gold mine and later returning in the evening to Gainesville for ice cream at a favorite shop downtown.[118] Outings to these destinations ceased to be traditions at Brenau as Georgia modernized because this made Dahlonega and Tallulah Falls conveniently accessible by car. The notoriety of the trips simply faded. This would be the same fate of smaller junkets to Atlanta as well. Once, large groups of Brenau women took trains into the city to see concerts and plays. After mid-century, automobiles transported students to their entertainment and large outings to Atlanta became passé.

Another trip tradition that died out was an annual freshmen outing to nearby Riverside Military Academy in Gainesville for a chance to socialize with boys.[119] For several years around mid-century, cadets in white jackets met the freshman women, paired off with them, and then received clues to track down ice cream hidden on campus. It is not evident how long this tradition lasted. Beginning in about the 1960s, Riverside began moving away from being what could probably best be described as a junior college to being a residential high school. This move would have eventually made the students from the two institutions too different in ages to really socialize.

Another tradition at Brenau that was somewhat unusual and quite short-lived was the "onion party." Sources indicate that such parties existed at Brenau for a time in the mid-twentieth century. A 1945 edition of the *Alchemist* described the event, which attracted members of the faculty & staff and the Brenau College Board of Trustees, as well as the students. The article read that, "Between bites from an onion sandwich each sorority sang one of their songs, everyone danced, gave spontaneous entertainment and just generally made as much noise as possible."[120] Despite their gaiety, onion parties would eventually lose their appeal.

Brenau's defunct traditions met their demise because some significant constituency (either Brenau students, the College's faculty and staff, or both) ceased to support them. Likewise, any tradition that thrives at Brenau—and many do—does so because of its importance to some group or groups. The same can be said of campus organizations. During its history, Brenau has seen several traditions and organizations that were largely student-governed just as several traditions and organizations have existed at the institution that tended to help the Brenau faculty and staff govern student behavior. Student involvement is actually the common denominator for both. Even where traditions and organizations existed to govern students, such things could simply not exist apart from students. Consequently, the necessity of student presence translates into some agency. Because of student centrality respecting both governed and governing organizations and traditions, students should continue to play a role in the ongoing negotiation with College personnel to create the Brenau experience.

Notes

1. John R. Thelin, *A History of American Higher Education* (Baltimore, MD: The Johns Hopkins University Press, 2004), 64.
2. Ibid.
3. Ibid., 65.
4. "College 'Convention' Names Smith," *New York Times*, 14 May 1928, http://select.nytimes.com/gst/abstract.html?res=F40E1EFA3A58167A93C6A8178ED85F4C8285F9 (accessed 10 May 2013). The article relates that "At the conclusion of a mock Democratic National Convention staged by the International Relations Club and the League of Women Voters of Brenau College," the students chose Roman Catholic, anti-Prohibitionist candidate Gov. Al Smith of New York over contenders from Tennessee, Missouri, and Ohio.
5. Brenau College, *Bubbles* (Gainesville, GA; Brenau College, 1930), no page number. Hereafter, references to this source are indicated as *"Bubbles* (1930)."
6. *Bubbles* (1992), 64.
7. Brenau College, *Bubbles* (Gainesville, GA; Brenau College, 1911), no page number. Hereafter, references to this source are indicated as *"Bubbles* (1911)."
8. "Student Organizations," Brenau University, http://intranet.brenau.edu/dnn/StudentServices/StudentOrganizations/tabid/64/Default.aspx (accessed 10 May 2013).
9. Brenau College, *Bubbles* (Gainesville, GA; Brenau College, 1901), 100–101. Hereafter, references to this source are indicated as *"Bubbles* (1901)."
10. Ibid.
11. Ibid., 103, 106.
12. "Brenau College Notes," *Atlanta Constitution*, 8 November 1903, sec. C, p. 6.
13. "Brenau Notes," *Atlanta Constitution*, 28 February 1904, sec. B, p. 6.
14. May Pate, "Y.W.C.A.," *Alchemist* (Gainesville, GA: Brenau College), 14 May 1935, v. XXI, n. 9, p. 3.
15. "Brenau Deputation Team to Give Program Tuesday," *Red and Black*, 19 February 1937, p. 5, http://redandblack.libs.uga.edu/xtf/view?docId=news/1937/rab1937-0045.xml&query=brenau&brand=rab-brand (accessed 10 May 2013).

16. Advertisement, *Atlanta Constitution*, 13 November 1904, sec. E, p. 6.
17. Eleanor Rigney, *Brenau College 1878 – 1978: Enriched by the Past, Challenged by the Future* (Gainesville, GA: Brenau College, 1978), 70.
18. Ibid.
19. For more about the decline of the Y.W.C.A. see Nina Mjagkij and Margaret Spratt, eds. *Men and Women Adrift: The YMCA and the YWCA in the City* (New York, NY: New York University Press, 1997).
20. *Third Annual Catalogue* (Gainesville, GA: Georgia Baptist Female Seminary, 1880), 16.
21. "Brenau College News Notes," *The Montgomery Advertiser*, vol. LXXXVIII, 25 November 1917, p. 20,
22. "Women Meet Brenau Team In Debate on Labor Query," *The Red and Black*, 25 February 1938, p. 8, http://redandblack.libs.uga.edu/xtf/view?docId=news/1938/rab1938-0105.xml&query=brenau&brand=rab-brand (accessed 10 May 2013).
23. "To Meet Auburn In Debate Here," *Alchemist* (Gainesville, GA: Brenau College), v. XXVI, n. 12, 19 March 1940, p. 1.
24. "Brenau Girls Issue Journal," *Atlanta Constitution*, 23 April 1905, sec. B, p. 5.
25. *Brenau Journal, January-February, 1912*, p. 168, Box 1 Labeled Literary Journals, folder 2, Brenau Archives, Gainesville, Georgia.
26. Ibid., 212–213.
27. *The Flame*, Brenau College, December 1940, p. 16.
28. *The Elixir*, vol. 1, no. 2, Spring 1978, p. 1, Box labeled Literary Magazines, 1 of 1, kept loose not in folder, Brenau University Archives, Gainesville, Georgia.
29. Ibid.
30. *The Elixir: Literary Magazine*, Brenau College, Gainesville, Georgia, 1989, Box labeled Literary Magazines, 1 of 1, kept loose not in folder, Brenau University Archives, Gainesville, Georgia.
31. *The Elixir (1998)*, Brenau University, Gainesville, Georgia, 1998, Box labeled Literary Magazines, 1 of 1, kept loose not in folder, Brenau University Archives, Gainesville, Georgia.
32. Lynn Gordon, *Gender and Higher Education in the Progressive Era* (New Haven, CT: Yale University Press, 1990).
33. See, for example, Doris Smith and Lois Sadler's "Sorority Scribblings," in *Alchemist* (Gainesville, GA: Brenau College) v. XXXII, n. 3, 23 October 1945, p. 4.

34. "'The *Alchemist*' Receives Rating, Critique by ACP," *Alchemist* (Gainesville, GA: Brenau College), 29 April 1965, p. 7.
35. Ron Musselwhite, "College Press—Image Maker?" *The Red and Black*, 30 March 1965, p. 4, http://redandblack.libs.uga.edu/xtf/view?docId=news/1965/rab1965-0154.xml&query=the%20alchemist%20brenau&brand=rab-brand (accessed 10 May 2013). Curiously, though, on the same editorial page and despite what the First Amendment says about freedom of assembly, *The Red and Black* declared, "we don't recognize mass demonstrations...as legitimate or effective methods for ensuring or obtaining" civil rights.
36. Brenau had actually operated a radio station (WKAY) for two years in the 1920s, but permitted its broadcasting license to expire, likely for financial reasons. S. E. Frost, *Education's Own Stations: The History of Broadcast Licenses Issued to Educational Institutions* (New York, NY: Arno Press and The New York Times, 1971), 42.
37. "Brenau's new FM station to go on the air this fall," *Gainesville Times* (Gainesville, GA), 11 September 1977, Brenau College Centennial Commemorative Section, p. 16.
38. Ibid.
39. Ibid.
40. Brenau College, *Bubbles* (Gainesville, GA; Brenau College, 1985), 60. Hereafter, references to this source are indicated as "*Bubbles* (1985)."
41. "Brenau's Eclectic 89.1 Radio Stations Strengthens Signal With Digital Technology," Hometownhall.com, 13 August 2007, http://www.hometownhall.com/news2006/brenaus-eclectic-891-radio-stations-strengthens-si.shtml (accessed 22 August 2007).
42. "WBCX," *Wikipedia*, http://en.wikipedia.org/wiki/WBCX (accessed 10 May 2013).
43. "Brenau's Eclectic 89.1 Radio Stations Strengthens Signal With Digital Technology," Hometownhall.com, 13 August 2007, http://www.hometownhall.com/news2006/brenaus-eclectic-891-radio-stations-strengthens-si.shtml (accessed 22 August 2007).
44. "89.1 WBCX Gainesville – The Voice of Brenau!" Brenau University, http://www.brenau.edu/wbcx/ (accessed 10 May 2013).
45. "Brenau University's WBCX-FM 89.1 Returns Radio Personality Jay Andrews to North Georgia Airwaves," Brenau News, 6 September 2012, http://www.brenau.edu/publications/news/jay-andrews-returns-to-air-wbcx/ (accessed 10 May 2013).

46. Jody Duncan and Lynn Smith, eds., *Brenau Women's College Student Handbook, 1984–1985* (Gainesville, GA: Brenau College, 1984), p. 81.
47. See http://alchemist.brenau.edu/ (accessed 10 May 2013).
48. "Murmurings," *Alchemist* (Gainesville, GA) v. XXI, n. 9, 14 May 1935, p. 3.
49. Ibid.
50. Ibid.
51. Merriam-Webster.com, s.v. "tradition," http://www.merriam-webster.com/dictionary/tradition (accessed 10 May 2013).
52. Rajendra Kumar Sharma and Rachana Sharma, *Social Psychology* (New Delhi: Atlantic Publishers and Distributors, 1997), 247.
53. The degree of faculty involvement with campus traditions has actually changed over time. As evidence of this, by 2008, Brenau employed in its Student Services Division a Director of the Center for Greek Life and Campus Traditions. See http://intranet.brenau.edu/dnn/StudentServices/MeettheStaff/tabid/98/Default.aspx (accessed 10 May 2013). Prior to formalizing a position involving campus traditions, faculty members would have likely contributed to upholding traditions at Brenau in a more *ad hoc* manner.
54. Note, however, that despite the name, the event has often been held in April so as not to interfere with May graduation. See "Architecture," Brenau University Archived Webpages (formerly online at http://artsweb.brenau.edu/historic/Uniquely/default.htm from around 2004 until 2011); hard-copy print-out located in Box 1 of 1 labeled "Archived Webpages," Brenau University Archives, Gainesville, Georgia.
55. "Vernice Hurst is Queen of May Day Fete," *Alchemist* (Gainesville, GA: Brenau College), v. XXI, n. 9, 14 May 1935, p. 1.
56. Christie Anne Farnham, *The Education of the Southern Belle: Higher Education and Student Socialization in the Antebellum South* (New York, NY: New York University Press, 1994), 168.
57. Sarah Banet-Weiser and Laura Portwood-Stacer, "'I just want to be me again!': Beauty pageants, reality television and post-feminism," *Feminist Theory*, vol. 7 (2006): 255–272, 263.
58. Sarah Banet-Weiser, *The Most Beautiful Girl in the World: Beauty Pageants and National Identity* (Berkeley, CA: University of California Press, 1999), 12.
59. Ibid.
60. See Meredith Minter, "Traditions at Randolph-Macon Woman's College: Rat Court," *The Sundial*, vol. 66, no. 4 (2 October 1981), http://faculty.randolphcollege.edu/fwebb/traditions/ratcourt.html (accessed 10 May

2013); Jeffrey R. Willis, *Converse College* (Charleston, SC: Arcadia Publishing, 2001), 105, which described Rat Week as "an old tradition at Converse"; "Heart & Soul of a Small Town: A Visit with Alumnae in Summerville," *Columns* (Spring 2010), http://www.columbiasc.edu/about/news-info/columns-magazine (accessed 10 May 2013), in which a Columbia College alumna described rat week as "the key to getting over homesickness" (9).
61. "Traditions," Brenau University Archived Webpages (formerly online at http://artsweb.brenau.edu/historic/Uniquely/default.htm from around 2004 until 2011); hard-copy print-out located in Box 1 of 1 labeled "Archived Webpages," Brenau University Archives, Gainesville, Georgia.
62. "Freshman—Sophomore Week," *Alchemist* (Gainesville, GA: Brenau College), v. XII, n. 6, 3 December 1924, p. 1.
63. Ibid.
64. Ibid.
65. Ibid.
66. Ibid.
67. Ibid.
68. Ibid.
69. Ibid.
70. "Sophomores Exterminate Rats and Restore Peace," *Alchemist* (Gainesville, GA: Brenau College) v. XXXII, n. 3, 23 October 1945, p. 1.
71. Ibid.
72. "News Briefs," *Alchemist* (Gainesville, GA: Brenau College), Fall Quarter 1980, p. 6.
73. Ibid.
74. Ibid., 4.
75. Sarah Fell, "RATT, RATT, RATT: How Much Do You Know?" *Alchemist*, 8 October 2008, http://intranet.brenau.edu/dnn/StudentServices/CareerServices/JobBoard/tabid/92/mid/505/newsid505/1672/Default.aspx (accessed 10 May 2013).
76. Ibid.
77. "Traditions," Brenau University Archived Webpages (formerly online at http://artsweb.brenau.edu/historic/Uniquely/default.htm from around 2004 until 2011); hard-copy print-out located in Box 1 of 1 labeled "Archived Webpages," Brenau University Archives, Gainesville, Georgia.
78. "Spade Hunt to May Day, Brenau traditions continue," *Gainesville Times* (Gainesville, GA), 11 September 1977, Brenau College Centennial Commemorative Section, p. 6.

79. Ibid.
80. The Spade Hunt tradition may be expanding to other classes. An *Alchemist* article read, "Although junior and seniors are involved mostly in this tradition, all Brenau Women's College students are encouraged to participate in the Spade Hunt." Sable C. Bing, "And the Search for the Spade Begins..." *Alchemist*, 4 April 2008, available at http://intranet.brenau.edu/dnn/StudentServices/CareerServices/JobBoard/tabid/92/mid/505/newsid505/1366/Default.aspx (accessed 10 May 2013).
81. Ibid.
82. Ibid.
83. Ibid.
84. "Spade Hunt to May Day, Brenau traditions continue," *Gainesville Times* (Gainesville, GA), 11 September 1977, Brenau College Centennial Commemorative Section, p. 6.
85. "Traditions," Brenau University Archived Webpages (formerly online at http://artsweb.brenau.edu/historic/Uniquely/default.htm from around 2004 until 2011); hard-copy print-out located in Box 1 of 1 labeled "Archived Webpages," Brenau University Archives, Gainesville, Georgia.
86. Candice Dyer, "Calling Agnes: Brenau University's resident ghost fuels emotions and stories," *Gainesville Times* (Gainesville, GA), 31 October 2004.
87. Ibid.
88. Ibid.
89. Ibid.
90. Ibid.
91. Ibid.
92. In 2008, Brenau staff member Kathy Amos suggested that Agnes was actually not alone in haunting Pearce Auditorium and that she may have come to the campus much later than her many origin stories suggest. See Melissa Weinman, "Bigfoot not the first strange tale out of North Georgia's hills," *Gainesville Times* (Gainesville, GA), 4 September 2008, http://www.gainesvilletimes.com/archives/8349/ (accessed 10 May 2013).
93. Mark Davis, "His Mission: To Chat with a School Spirit," *Atlanta Journal-Constitution*, 31 October 2005, sec. A, p. 1.
94. Candice Dyer, "Calling Agnes: Brenau University's resident ghost fuels emotions and stories," *Gainesville Times* (Gainesville, GA), 31 October 2004.

95. Rose McIlveen, "Greeks and Romans knew how to spin a ghostly tale," *IU Home Pages*, 26 October 2001, http://www.homepages.indiana.edu/1 02601/text/ghost.html (accessed 10 May 2013).
96. David Punter, *A Companion to the Gothic* (Malden, MA: Blackwell Publishing, Ltd., 2001), 123.
97. Ibid.
98. Candice Dyer, "Calling Agnes: Brenau University's resident ghost fuels emotions and stories," *Gainesville Times* (Gainesville, GA), 31 October 2004.
99. David Punter, *A Companion to the Gothic* (Malden, MA: Blackwell Publishing, Ltd., 2001), 123.
100. Ibid., 124.
101. Simon J. Bronner, *American Children's Folklore* (Atlanta, GA: August House Publishers, Inc., 2006), 144.
102. Ibid.
103. Candice Dyer, "Calling Agnes: Brenau University's resident ghost fuels emotions and stories," *Gainesville Times* (Gainesville, GA), 31 October 2004.
104. Ibid.
105. This account of the Dare Stones is drawn from a few sources. The first is T. Mike Childs, "The Dare Stones," *Ncpedia*, 2013, http://ncpedia.org/dare-stones (accessed 4 January 2014). The second is Boyden Sparkes, "Writ on Rocke," *Saturday Evening Post*, 26 April 1941, and the third is Robert White, *A Witness for Eleanor Dare: The Final Chapter in a 400 Year Old Mystery* (San Francisco, CA: Lexikos, 1992).
106. Honey Lou Price, "Socially Speaking," *Alchemist* (Gainesville, GA: Brenau College) v. XXXVIII, n. 9, 11 March 1952, p. 2.
107. "Spade Hunt to May Day, Brenau traditions continue," *Gainesville Times* (Gainesville, GA), 11 September 1977, Brenau College Centennial Commemorative Section, p. 6.
108. Ibid.
109. Ibid.
110. Ibid.
111. Merriam-Webster.com, s.v. "Chautauqua," http://www.merriam-webster.com/dictionary/chautauqua (accessed 10 May 2013).
112. "Chautauqua at Brenau," *Atlanta Constitution*, 17 April 1907, p. 3.
113. "Big Chautauqua Opens on 18th," *Atlanta Constitution*, 14 July 1907, p. 5.
114. Ibid.
115. Ibid.

116. For more information about the chautauqua movement, see Andrew Rieser's, *The Chautauqua Moment: Protestants, Progressives, and the Culture of Modern Liberalism* (New York, NY: Columbia University Press, 2003).
117. "Campus Rings With Shout and Laughter," *Atlanta Constitution*, 31 July 1904, sec. C, p. 5.
118. "Dahlonega Trip," *Alchemist* (Gainesville, GA: Brenau College), v. 7, n. 3, 8 November 1919, p. 1.
119. Dolly O'Berry, "Freshmen Take Their Annual Trip to Riverside," *Alchemist* (Gainesville, GA: Brenau College), v. XXXII, n. 3, 23 October 1945, p. 3.
120. Jeane Morris, "The Onion Party," *Alchemist* (Gainesville, GA: Brenau College), v. XXXII, n. 3, 23 October 1945, p. 1.

Chapter 6

Smoking, "Night Riding," & other Serious Offenses

Negotiating the Evolution of Rules and Discipline at Brenau

Rules and discipline have long been a part of college life in the United States. As far back as 1790, Samuel Hall published *The Laws of Harvard College* to advise students of proper conduct. Some laws dealt with religion as Harvard decreed:

> Whoever shall profane the [Sabbath] day by unnecessary business, or visiting, or walking on the Common or in the streets or fields of the town of Cambridge, or shall use any diversions, or otherwise behave himself disorderly or unbecoming the season, shall be fined not exceeding three shillings, or be admonished, degraded, suspended, or rusticated, according to the aggravation of the offence.[1]

Other rules forbade association with "any person of dissolute morals."[2] Harvard even had a dress code. A rule stated that, "All the Undergraduates shall be clothed in coats of blue gray, and with waistcoats and breeches of the same colour, or of a black, a nankeen, or an olive colour."[3]

Decades later, rules still bound Harvard College students and students at America's other colleges and, indeed, had become more complicated. Laurence R. Veysey, an historian of American higher education, observed that:

> The hallmark of the college disciplinarian was an elaborate codification of rules and regulations. A glance at college rules during the decade after 1865 reveals the extreme particularity with which the conduct of students was prescribed. At Harvard the listing of such regulations required eight pages of fine print. Students there were prohibited from leaving the college on Sundays without special permission, and they were forbidden to loiter in groups anywhere on college property.[4]

But not all colleges were like-minded. The disciplinarian's strict code would begin to disappear at some forward-thinking institutions in the mid-1800s. Frederick Rudolph noted that, "before the nineteenth century was half over, many of the leading institutions had abandoned the strict discipline and the extended code of laws which had characterized so many of the colleges."[5] Still, some colleges persisted with old ways. These institutions maintained fairly strict rules and regulations well into even the twentieth century. This was true of virtually all of the women's colleges in America, especially those in the South.

Regarding rules at southern women's colleges, Amy Thompson McCandless observed that, "Southern women were expected to behave as 'ladies' on and off the campus."[6] Hence, "Regulations against smoking, drinking, cardplaying, and dancing with men remained in force longer at southern colleges" than at northern schools.[7] Brenau College was a typically southern institution in this respect, but it was far less typical than other southern women's colleges in other respects regarding rules, regulations, and discipline.

The history of rules and discipline at Brenau reveals much about the ongoing negotiation between Brenau students and Brenau's faculty and staff to refine the Brenau College experience. Throughout much of

Brenau's history, the College's faculty and presidential administrations promulgated regulations regarding a plethora of topics, including such themes as chapel attendance, dating, smoking, cheating, and student dress. In doing so, College officials sought to maintain student discipline. In response, students pushed back against these efforts—often through rule breaking—as they sought their independence. An unspoken negotiation ensued between the two parties. At some times in the institution's history, Brenau's faculty and staff won out in disciplinary matters. Students were made to abide by rules and suffered often stiff penalties for not doing so. Yet, the faculty and staff were actually not completely free to mold the College as they and they alone wished. Students had some agency and, upon occasion, successfully negotiated with College officials over disciplinary matters. In response to student pressure, many rules softened over time or, in some cases, disappeared altogether. Also, Brenau officials frequently left the job of policing student conduct to students themselves. Examining this evolution of rules and regulations at Brenau shows both the process and the product of the contest for space between Brenau's students and the College's faculty and administration.

According to a description by Professor A. W. Van Hoose, an early president of Brenau College, the system of student discipline developed at the College was atypical virtually from the institution's founding. A reporter interviewed Van Hoose for an article published in 1903 in the *Atlanta Constitution* that described in robust detail how this system originated. The article read:

> One day several years ago Professor Van Hoose was sitting in the "home building" looking out across, the cool, well-shaded campus, when he saw fifty of the college girls walking down the street, two abreast, under the supervision of four teachers who looked like so many overseers. This thought came to Professor Van Hoose: Now, is that the way to treat young ladies of from sixteen to twenty-five years, who have been reared in good families, and who are supposed to have had good home influences? They are not treated that way at home. A girl living with her parents who goes out for

> a short walk and seeing an acquaintance does not ignore him and stare straight before her. She recognizes him with at least a slight inclination of the head, and meets the obligations of courtesy. It would be rudeness to do less, and how can practicing rudeness develop politeness, or accustom any one to those easy and graceful manners which seem to sit so naturally upon those who are well-bred. And why should a young lady when she comes to college be always under surveillance—watched by half a dozen guards as if she were not to be trusted?[8]

The article related that, "From the incident described sprang what is known as the self-government system of Brenau College."[9] This system supposedly arose because Brenau's "great purpose" was "the development of good women, well-rounded, perfectly developed [in] character."[10] Brenau officials saw their system of self-government as an exceptional way to cultivate a woman's good character and so facilitated its adoption. Brenau students took to the system quickly, no doubt pleased at the degree of self-determination it afforded them.

The 1903 article continued, describing how the self-government system operated. It indicated that, "In Brenau there are three classes of students, an 'honor roll,' a 'self-governed list' and a 'privileged list'" and proceeded to explain the system "in a nutshell."[11] The article stated:

> When the term opens all the new girls are on the same footing, so far as the rules governing their conduct are concerned. The student body elects what is known as a board of honor, consisting of twelve of the older girls. The ballots are cast in a regular election by the students and the faculty. The tenure of office is for six weeks, and the board of honor constitutes the real governing power of the college. They take a general oversight of the conduct of the girls, and at the end of their term of office they recommend to the faculty such girls as they deem worthy of a place on the "honor roll," which is the first step toward being a "self-governed" or "privileged" student. If their recommendations meet with the approval of the faculty, these girls are placed on the honor rolls and certain of the usual school-girl restrictions are removed. Thus

> they may go to walk in groups of four without a teacher; they may attend church on the Sabbath without a teacher; they are not required to sit in the study hall, but may study in their rooms or in such places as may be most pleasant or convenient for them. At the end of another six weeks they are eligible to the self-governed list, and their privileges and responsibilities are correspondingly broadened. At the expiration of the third six weeks they are eligible to the privileged list when practically all restraint is removed from them and they become in the full sense of the word self-governed girls.[12]

Brenau put this system into operation in 1898. When the *Constitution* reporter asked Professor Van Hoose if the system was a success, he replied, "Why, we have not had a case of discipline in so long that I can hardly remember when we did have one."[13]

Van Hoose continued, describing how the system actually encouraged the Brenau students to abide by the rules. He said:

> Self-governing girls who do not govern themselves as they should are reduced in ranks and then they feel the full force of the rules and regulations. ... The Brenau college girl is relieved of many arbitrary restrictions which in the old times interfered with the liberty of the student, but she forfeits these privileges if she fails to appreciate them. The system rewards faithfulness of the careful, conscientious student and develops her capacity for independent action, while a powerful and usually effective stimulus is given the careless, negligent girl, impelling her to use every effort to prove herself worthy of receiving the same position and privileges attained by her classmates and companions.[14]

Van Hoose concluded, "If a girl is wasteful of her time and indifferent to her opportunities, or will not obey the rules of the college, her parents are notified and she is quietly sent home."[15]

A later article in the *Atlanta Constitution* indicated that the system of discipline worked well. It read, "Six years of actual trial have demonstrated the success of the system, and the management point with pride to the fact that many other colleges for girls have followed the example of Brenau and, abandoning the old system, have adopted, in whole or in part, [t]he system inaugurated here in 1898." [16] Since its inception, Professor Van Hoose observed that, "It has been a very long time since we have had a case of discipline."[17]

Though it seems to have garnered no notoriety for doing so, it appears that Brenau may actually have been the first Southern women's college to create any kind of a system of student self-government and discipline. In his short history of Converse College, historian Jeffrey R. Willis wrote, "A Student Government Association (S.G.A.) was established at Converse in 1905. It was the second such system at a Southern college, with Randolph-Macon Woman's College being the first."[18] According to a 1982 article published in the Randolph-Macon Woman's College student newspaper, *The Sundial*, R-M created its system of student government in 1900.[19] Brenau students had already been electing representatives to positions of authority and creating some campus policies for two years prior to this and several years prior to 1905.[20]

While Brenau's system of student government and discipline may have been remarkable among southern women's colleges in the early 1900s, it was not entirely novel. In *Alma Mater: Design and Experience in the Women's Colleges from their Nineteenth-Century Beginnings to the 1930s*, historian Helen Horowitz examined several women's colleges in New England in the nineteenth century and the twentieth century. Among other things, she commented on their systems of enforcing good behavior. Horowitz wrote that, "While college authorities kept one essential weapon, the right to expel students for academic failure or a serious breach of the rules, they lacked the ability to shape behavior within this broad limit. Thus…several of the colleges turned to student self-government, enlisting certain students to monitor the behavior of others."[21] This begs the question of how much Brenau might have emulated these northern women's colleges in developing its system of discipline. No source speaks to this, but President Van Hoose, the architect of Brenau's disciplinary system, could have known of the policies at northern schools. He was a graduate of the University of Georgia and had been working in higher education for almost a decade before associating with Brenau. Traveling in these circles could have placed him in a position to learn of and adopt "cutting edge" developments. Even so, it would have taken some temerity on the part of Van Hoose to pioneer implementing such a system in the more conservative South.

As was the case in the northern schools, students at Brenau, with occasional faculty and/or staff member input, monitored the behavior of their peers. Brenau expected all students to know its rules. Incoming students received a student handbook (called *The Brenau Girl* for a time) that spelled out the College's rules and regulations in great detail. By 1937, the College had additionally established an honor code. It read, "Honorable conduct in academic work and student activities is the spirit of conduct at Brenau College. Such is the command and decree of the Student Government Association; upon it rests the traditions of honor and machinery by which offenders of the tradition are brought to an accounting."[22] The student handbook of 1945 indicated that, "Every fall each new Brenau girl is asked to sign the Honor Code whereby she pledges her responsibility for her own actions."[23] The handbook continued, saying "When she signs the code, she legally acknowledges a thorough understanding of the system and agrees to abide by the rules and regulations."[24]

The essence of the code would remain the same for years, though it would evolve. By 1955, the College's student handbook indicated that the honor pledge had become more robust. It read:

> We, the undersigned, as students of Brenau College, do hereby pledge ourselves to uphold the honor of the College by refraining from every form of dishonesty in our college life, and to do all that is in our power to create a spirit of honesty and honor on the campus.

> We acknowledge that this Honor Pledge also applies to any infringement of the Student Government Regulations as set forth in the Student Handbook, and that failure on our part to treat these matters with due regard is considered a breach of the trust placed in us by the faculty and our fellow students, and thus, a violation of this Honor Pledge.[25]

The pledge would remain essentially the same for the next several decades and, as in 1955, occupy a prominent position near the front of the student handbooks during this time. By 1974, the formality of signing the pledge was, strictly speaking, optional; a student demonstrated their intent to abide by the honor system merely by enrolling at Brenau.[26] Though this may seem like a major shift, it likely occurred simply due to logistics. As Brenau began growing its evening and weekend courses for non-traditional students in the 1970s, holding multiple ceremonies for multiple honor code signings would have become unwieldy. Yet, because all students were expected to adhere to the honor code, it would have communicated the wrong message to only require that some students (i.e., those in the Women's College) sign but not others. Therefore, the institution attached acceptance to the honor pledge to enrollment. Note that an absence of ceremony should not signal any diminished importance of academic integrity at Brenau. As evidence of this, it was also in 1974 that the student handbook began to carefully define plagiarism, something it had not done before.[27] By the twenty-first century, the spirit of the honor pledge remained much as it had half a century before. It read:

> I promise to uphold the Brenau University honor code by refraining from every form of dishonesty and cheating in university life, and will strive to create a spirit of honesty and honor. Failure to do so is considered a breach of trust toward the faculty and student body. I accept this commitment as a personal responsibility to refrain from and to report all forms of dishonesty and cheating.[28]

Even if they did not sign the pledge, students routinely recited the honor code for many years at the beginning of all formal convocations from the 1980s onward.[29]

Despite Brenau's best efforts to encourage honesty and good behavior, disciplinary infractions did occur. This happened as students, in their negotiation with College faculty members and administrators to refine their college experience to their liking, pushed boundaries. The 1900 catalog indicated that, "the girls themselves become largely the governing power" in policing violations.[30] This they did in groups that evolved with the College. The 1900 catalog related that, "Should any one of our girls abuse any privilege granted her, she is at once reported by the Board of Honor (all of whose members are students) and her name is taken from the list to whom privileges are extended, until by six weeks of blameless conduct she shows that she regrets her misconduct and really wants the confidence of the faculty and students."[31] For several years in Brenau's early history, students elected other students to comprise the Board of Honor. By the nineteen-teens, Brenau's student handbooks revealed that students elected in campus-wide elections comprised the College's Executive Council. The council assumed the job of appointing students to Brenau's Honor Board or, later as it would come to be called, the Honor Court. Originally, students could be appointed from the general student body. By the mid-1920s, Honor Court appointments made by the Executive Council consisted of members drawn from the ranks of the Executive Council itself.[32]

The Executive Council acted on minor cases of discipline (generally violations that could not, by themselves, lead to expulsion) and passed on student petitions for changes in the rules to the faculty and staff for consideration. The Honor Court met as needed to consider more serious infractions of the rules or violations of the honor code. By the mid-1930s, the Honor Court was "composed of five Senior Executive Council members, including the President of the Y.W.C.A. as an honorary member."[33] By the mid-1940s and up until the 1970s, the president of

Brenau's Student Government Association served as the chairman of the Honor Court. She appointed four other young women (typically from the senior class) to serve on the court for the academic year. By the mid-1970s, the chairman of the Honor Board was elected by the student body and she, in turn, appointed the other members of the board to their positions.[34] By 1984, the Honor Court had morphed to become a Judicial Board and an Appellate Board comprised of student justices. Also by this year, Brenau's student handbook published eleven pages of impressively sophisticated and intricate text called the "Judicial Constitution and Procedures," which covered topics ranging from the rights of a respondent brought up on disciplinary charges to investigative procedures in discipline cases to trial and appellate procedures and sanctions in discipline hearings.[35]

What is interesting to note in this historical development is the consistent centrality of student agency in maintaining discipline at Brenau. Dating back to nearly the institution's inception, students, either directly or indirectly, selected several of their peers to serve on Brenau's honor boards or courts. Virtually any student was eligible for selection in this democratic process.[36] These selected students passed on disciplinary recommendations to the faculty and staff. Entries in the minutes books of the Brenau faculty meetings kept by officials throughout much of the twentieth century consistently indicated that the faculty and staff often went along with the student recommendations.

The operation of the disciplinary system at the College is an excellent example of the ongoing negotiation between students and the faculty & staff for each body to create "their Brenau." Students, through their generally good conduct, negotiated for self-discipline and proved to College personnel that they could successfully police their own behavior. The faculty and staff, in turn, were content to leave many aspects of creating rules and enforcing discipline to the students because the students demonstrated by their conduct that they were enthusiastic about the system.

Smoking, "Night Riding," & other Serious Offenses

Over the years, Brenau subjected students who violated the rules to a range of punishments commensurate with the infraction committed. A simple loss of privileges attended minor infractions of the rules. More serious wrong-doers might be "campused," which meant losing many privileges and being restricted to campus. Young women found guilty of very serious disobedience could be suspended from school, asked to withdraw themselves from the College, or, in the most severe cases, expelled from Brenau entirely. It is interesting to note that in instances requiring punishment, the student honor board representatives passed along a recommended punishment to the faculty and staff, which virtually always adopted the student recommendation. The practical effect of this was that students could essentially get other students expelled if their disciplinary breech was severe enough. Also, as early as the 1920s, serious honor violations led to a loss of status on campus. The faculty meeting minutes book entry for April 1, 1924, indicated that the faculty approved a motion that would bar from holding "important office" in any club any student guilty of "a serious breach of discipline."[37]

The Brenau University Archives contain, in various forms, copies of College rules and regulations dating back to the turn of the twentieth century. These show that Brenau's rules developed rather organically over the years in response to changing times. The rules also reflect that student discipline at Brenau touched on a wide variety of subjects. Importantly, Brenau women did not merely enforce rules handed down to them by the faculty and administration. Brenau's students had the ability to actually promulgate some new rules, to change existing rules, or to have obsolete rules revoked. This chiefly occurred as students submitted petitions to the faculty for consideration.

A 1951 edition of the *Alchemist* student newspaper described the collaborative rule making process. The article read:

> The order in which this was brought about was as follows. Jean Ann Bradley, then President of the Student Body, asked the girls to put their suggestions on rules for the coming year into the

suggestion box outside of the auditorium. She and the officers of Student Government met and decided just which rules sounded logical and which did not. Then at a student-faculty relations board meeting, the rules were presented to the faculty. Each rule was discussed and voted upon.[38]

Although the faculty & staff did not pass all petitions, they gave student petitions serious consideration and, often, approved them. For example, at one time, simply playing cards was forbidden at Brenau. The faculty meeting minutes book entry for April 1, 1924, indicated that the faculty approved a petition from the student union "to substitute the word 'gambling' for the word 'card-playing' in the College handbook."[39] Students were willing to accept that gambling was wrong just as the faculty and administration were willing to accept that simple cardplaying was harmless. This is typical of how many student requests fared. Sources intimate that there seemed to be relatively little friction between the rule making power and the rule enforcing power of students and personnel at Brenau because the students had this ability to petition for changes to rules.

One subject engaged by the rules for many years was attendance at religious services by students. In the early twentieth century, the College regulations stated that, "Pupils are required to attend church of their choice on each Sabbath."[40] Students missing church around the turn of the century would have been frowned upon by any Southern women's college. Yet, even this early on, Brenau demonstrated some flexibility on the matter. According to Brenau's 1900 catalog, a student could miss church on account of two factors. One, unsurprisingly, was illness. Brenau also let students forego services if her parents gave her permission "to remain away from church."[41] Nothing in the Archives indicates how often families invoked this rule. Yet, that the provision existed at all— especially in the early 1900s—is worth noting. Not all Southern women's colleges were as forward-thinking when it came to church. For example, regarding "Religious Exercises" in 1900, the Baptist Female University in Raleigh, North Carolina (which would eventually become Meredith

College), decreed that "the work of each day begins with religious services, which the students are required to attend."[42] (Indeed, they had better be punctual. The institution's 1899–1900 *Catalogue* noted that, "at the roll call, those who are not in their assigned seats three minutes after the bell ceases ringing for morning prayers are marked absent."[43]) In addition to requiring attendance at daily religious services, the Baptist university's policy was that "All boarding students are required to attend Sunday-School and church on Sunday morning."[44] The *Catalogue* mentioned no exceptions. The implication is that, with respect to religion, Brenau long ago created an environment that would have been more welcoming than other places to students who were either more agnostic in their beliefs or who embraced faiths that worshipped on other days of the week.

Beginning in the 1920s, required church attendance ceased to be the rule at the College. The student handbook for 1925–1926 stated, "Church attendance is not compulsory, but is encouraged."[45] Just how many students acted on Brenau's encouragement and went to church is a matter for speculation; in fact, it may have been very few. In a called faculty meeting of February 20, 1924, the faculty considered "a communication from the pastors of the city churches, calling attention to the fact that a goodly number of the Faculty and the great majority of the students do not attend the services of church or Sunday School, and asking for a larger cooperation on the part of the academic colony of the community."[46] The faculty and staff resolved to encourage greater church attendance on the part of the students (and, presumably, among themselves as well...), but stopped far short of any attempt to mandate this.

Taken together, the Brenau community's purportedly feeble church going and the College's progressive policy on church attendance might suggest the institution to be an irreligious place. This was not really so. Occasionally, Brenau's student government administration acted to try to strengthen the religious affiliations of students, whatever they may have been. For example, in 1938, the faculty approved a student petition that requested to "have a blessing asked regularly at the College tables" in the dining hall at meal times.[47] Albeit in a small way, this would seem to show that even as late as the 1930s, some members of the Brenau community maintained a view that piety, perhaps the most historically cherished of all feminine virtues, should still be cultivated at a women's college.

Views such as this explain Brenau's attitude about chapel. Although church attendance was optional for Brenau students in the early twentieth century, attendance at daily chapel service was mandatory. The College held services both mornings and evenings. By the 1920s, Brenau had established the position of "Chapel Monitor" and entrusted this student with the responsibility to police chapel attendance and the authority to keep order among students in chapel. Little short of illness excused one from chapel. Indeed, the rules required that, "Notice of illness must be filed with the Chaperon on the day of illness in order to obtain class and chapel excuses."[48] Late or retroactive filing was not acceptable. Whereas some students probably enjoyed attending chapel, others apparently did not. Some, it seems, even resorted to positively un-Christian means to get out of chapel. An entry in the faculty meeting minutes book for 1926 indicated that the faculty had to deal with "a number of young ladies who are guilty—according to their own confession—of having forged excuses for absences from classes and chapel."[49]

Rules regarding chapel attendance would soften over time. As late as 1946, Brenau's student handbook indicated that "Chapel and Vesper attendance is compulsory" and that "chapel monitors will be held personally responsible for order there."[50] But by the mid-1950s, chapel services had been reduced in number. The student handbook of 1955 indicated that:

> A regular chapel program is prepared Tuesday through Thursday from 12:00 – 12:30. On Tuesday and Thursday the administration presents the program. The Wednesday program is under the auspices of the Fine Arts Department and the Student Body.[51]

Ninety minutes of chapel per week was a much lighter commitment than Brenau had required of students in the past.

In addition to reducing the amount of chapel Brenau students had to attend, the character of the chapel services changed as well. At the beginning of the century, chapel services dealt with religious themes. By mid-century, articles in various editions of the *Alchemist* indicated that official business and entertainment were more the order of the day as evidenced by the involvement of the administration and the fine arts department. According to Brenau's student handbook, the College still required chapel attendance as late as at least 1966, but for just two times a week. By 1970, the weekly chapel attendance requirement no longer existed, though Brenau's catalog indicated that "Each Thursday, students are offered the opportunity to participate in a college chapel program."[52] Even then, the catalog indicated that these chapel sessions were "not always religious in nature."[53] Faculty members or guests of the College might speak during chapel or students might have enjoyed performances by musical or dramatic groups.

What is not evident from sources is how much of the reduction in chapel attendance was the result of student agency. Evidence does show that students at times altered or attempted to alter the character of existing chapel services. The minutes of the Brenau faculty meeting of December 6, 1932, noted that the student Executive Council submitted a petition that recommended "certain changes in the form of the noon chapel service, and setting forth their own ideas as to what the daily program ought to be."[54] The faculty received the communication then "as information." Yet, in February, 1937, the minutes related that the faculty granted a student request that "one day of the four chapel days...be turned over to the students for varied programs to be arranged under the general direction of the Vice President of the Student Government Association."[55] Given this success, it is conceivable that students might have negotiated for less chapel over time. Compulsory chapel attendance had once been the norm at virtually all American colleges and universities. Yet, over the course of the twentieth century, such requirements vanished. Historian George M. Marsden noted, "In the 1890s...almost all state universities still held compulsory chapel services and some required Sunday church attendance as well."⁵⁶ These services had become rare by World War II. The same was true for many private institutions. Marsden attributed the waning of religious influences at institutions of higher education to several possible factors, occasionally including student influences. Whether students were or were not behind the changes of Brenau's rules relating to compulsory chapel attendance, nothing suggests that students minded the reduction.

This is not to say that Brenau students were necessarily losing interest in religion. Rather, students often pursued religious interests. For example, the December 3, 1940, faculty meeting minutes noted that Brenau "granted to the Hebrew students official permission to effect an organization of their own."⁵⁷ A decade before, a Jewish sorority had existed on campus.⁵⁸ One of the largest and most active groups on campus since Brenau's founding had been the Young Women's Christian Association. Whereas the Y.W.C.A. at Brenau frequently engaged in secular activities (e.g., sponsoring musical performances or bringing guest speakers to campus), the group was, fundamentally, a religious organization. It was still going strong in the era when Brenau dispensed with mandatory chapel attendance. Also, even as late as 1984, Brenau still required students to attend any chapels and convocations occurring during the term that the College declared to be compulsory.⁵⁹ Some of these assemblies would have had religious elements.

Of course, Brenau rules dealt with more than religious services. Over time, the College published many rules that involved class attendance. The general thrust of these rules was that students should attend class and official College events unless they had some compelling reason (such as illness or a family obligation) that prevented them from doing so. Students on the honor roll or who were performing very well academically were able to "cut" more than other students. Surviving Baptist Female Seminary materials indicate that the institution greatly valued attendance—at least on paper. In the late nineteenth century, the society section of the *Atlanta Constitution* often published announcements indicating that seminary students made frequent and, at times, lengthy visits to home during the academic year. One might wonder if such visits were excused family obligations. Brenau College's 1904 policy regarding attendance stated that, "Absences from school duties for any other than strictly providential causes are not excused. Five unexcused absences during any one term are sufficient cause for the removal of a student from any position of honor or privilege which she may have attained under the self-governed system. Exceptions can be made to this rule only by unanimous vote of the faculty and the honor board."[60]

The 1925 student handbook published what seemed to be a stricter rule governing attendance. It indicated that, "Each student is allowed two unexcused absences from each class for each semester. If any student exceeds this number of unexcused absences, she forfeits her credit in that subject or subjects."[61] The 1937 handbook reiterated this rule, modifying it only to indicate that the College permitted but a single absence for a one-hour class and that "no student is allowed to cut a class before or after a holiday."[62] Presumably, some "excused" absences would have been tolerated in addition to the two "unexcused" absences (the "cuts") allowed to each young woman per class per term.

The "cut" policy at Brenau had become somewhat more complicated by the nineteen-forties. The *Faculty Minutes Book for Twenty-Five Years*, which recorded what transpired at Brenau faculty meetings for decades, indicated that in the early 1940s, the College began focusing much attention on student attendance. By 1945, Brenau's attendance policy had become more detailed. The College published in the student handbook of that year and in handbooks for the next decade a table which indicated how many classes students could miss based upon such factors as their class standing, academic standing, and the number of days per week a course met.[63] In essence, juniors and seniors doing "A" or "B" quality work could miss five or six days of a typical class, whereas students struggling in any class were not allowed any unexcused absences.

By 1965, Brenau had abandoned its college-wide attendance policy in favor of giving individual instructors discretion over attendance. The College retained some universality by indicating that more than twelve absences (excused or unexcused) from any three or four hour class would result in failure.[64] Likewise, in 1974, the student handbook indicated that any student on academic probation (i.e., those with below a 2.0 grade point average) could not miss more than one day per term per credit hour of class due to an unexcused absence and still receive academic credit for the course.[65]

Brenau's attendance policies clearly looked threatening on paper. In reality, they may have been only modestly enforced. The minute books of the Brenau faculty meetings kept up until the 1940s do not indicate that the College expelled any student for poor class attendance, though Brenau did expel several students on other grounds. This suggests that either Brenau students seldom cut class or that the spirit of the law was observed more than the letter of the law. If the former was the case, this would be made all the more remarkable by the fact that, around mid-century, Brenau actually held classes six days a week. Brenau's catalogs indicated that Saturday morning classes were common until at least the 1960s, which would have made each student responsible for attending one more day of school per week.[66]

What is more likely is that Brenau students did cut class and other official functions but received relatively mild punishments. The faculty meeting minutes entry for March 2, 1926, indicated that the faculty "put under restriction those students who confessed to having forged excuses for absences."[67] Several years later, in 1933, several young women were again found guilty of forging excuses for absences.[68] In neither instance did cutting class or even forging excuses for their absences lead to suspension, expulsion, or other severe punishment for those students.

Other College rules related to campus housing. Since its founding, Brenau students have lived on-campus in dormitory residence halls and, beginning in about the nineteen-teens, in sorority houses or "cottages" as they were sometimes referred to. Living on campus was not mandatory, though, and many "town girls" (as they were called) attended Brenau while living with their families in Gainesville. Brenau's modern sorority houses have apparently always been owned by the College since their establishment. Brenau has given each sorority the right to occupy its house and the right to restrict occupancy to members of the sorority, though, occasionally, non-sorority women lived in sorority houses as well. The faculty meeting minutes book entry for February 3, 1925, indicated that enough non-sorority students lived in some sorority chapter houses at times to prompt the faculty to pass a motion that would hold those young women to the same standards of scholarship sorority members were held to. Consequently, any student making an academic average below 80% could be ejected from the house and moved into a dormitory where life was more regulated.[69]

The College expected residents in each sorority house—and in each dormitory—to abide by housing rules. Throughout Brenau's history, these housing rules have typically dealt with such things as quiet hours, visitation, and "lights out" time. In 1904, the College promulgated three simple rules on these subjects. They were:

> [Rule] 4. At 9:45 o'clock in the evening all pupils are required to retire to their rooms, and at 10:45 all lights must be out and absolute quiet observed.
>
> [Rule] 12. Sunday afternoons, from 3 to 5 o'clock, shall be observed as quiet hour, during which time pupils are required to remain in their rooms and to preserve absolute quiet.
>
> [Rule] 13. During school hours and study hours in the evening, pupils are required to remain in their own rooms or in the school rooms or library. Visiting either in bed rooms or practice rooms or loitering in the halls during such hours is absolutely forbidden.[70]

Twenty years later, the rules on these subjects had become more complicated. The 1925 *Official Hand-Book of Information* for the College published expanded quiet hours. The handbook decreed:

> (a) Quiet shall be observed during the following hours:
> (1) 9 A.M. to 1:20 P.M., 2:30 to 3:30 P.M., 7:30 to 9:30 P.M.
>
> (2) On Mondays from 7:30 to 9:30 P.M.
>
> (3) On Sundays from 11:30 A.M. to 1 P.M., 3:00 P.M. to 5 P.M. and 6:30 to 7:30 P.M.
>
> (4) Quiet hour does not have to be observed on Saturday night
>
> (5) All members shall maintain quiet in the library.[71]

To further qualify what could be done during "quiet hours," the *Hand-Book* indicated: "Stringed instruments may be played in rooms on Sundays, except from 11:30 A.M. to 1:00 P.M., 3:00 to 5:00 P.M., 6:30 to 7:30 P.M. They may *not* be played during quiet hours on any other days. Pianos and Victrolas may be used for appropriate music between 7:30 and 10:00 P.M."[72] This rule, like several others, came into being thanks to a student initiative. The faculty meeting minutes book entry for October 7, 1924, indicated that, "A petition from the Executive Council [asking] that students be allowed to have appropriate music in their rooms" was considered.[73] The faculty granted the petition and, importantly, placed the onus not upon themselves but upon the Executive Council to police the "appropriateness" of the music the students played. Consequently, the council, so entrusted, had to "assume responsibility for seeing to it that there shall be no jazz and no dancing."[74]

The 1925 handbook also dealt with "lights out" time. It indicated that, "All students must extinguish their lights at 10:30, when the light bell is sounded."[75] If any campus performance ran past 10:30 p.m., students had a half-hour after dismissal to prepare for bed. Deserving students could obtain something called "light extension" through special permission, which would allow for lights out at midnight.[76]

The 1904 rules said little else that related to College housing. By contrast, in 1925, Brenau's student handbook required that, "All rooms shall be orderly in appearance by 9:00 A.M. each morning except Sunday, when the time [is] extended to 11:30 A.M."[77] Also, whereas students could spend the night in other dormitories or in sorority houses on weekends simply by informing their house chaperone that they intended to do so, sleeping "outside of one's own room on any night except Saturday and Sunday" required official permission.[78] Furthermore, day pupils were not permitted to spend the night with friends on campus.

Scarcely over a decade later, little had changed regarding housing-related rules and regulations. According to the 1937 *Brenau Girl* student handbook, quiet hours were essentially the same as they had been in the nineteen-twenties, though students no longer had to observe quiet hours on Sunday afternoons or on Saturday afternoons after 1:00 p.m.[79] Interestingly, the College now went to the trouble to spell out what had probably been assumed in early publications of the regulations—the 1937 handbook indicated that 11:00 p.m. to 7:00 a.m. were quiet hours. Rules regarding "lights out" were also pretty much as they had been, though students in the 1930s had until 11 p.m. to turn off their lamps and could not ask for "light extension" more than twice per month.[80] Also, by the mid-1930s, students were exempt from tidying up their rooms on Sunday, prohibited from bringing day pupils to meals in the dining hall at any time, and were forbidden from sleeping with friends in other dormitories during weekdays.[81]

By 1945, Brenau had eliminated quiet hours on Saturday entirely, but otherwise basically retained the schedule of quiet hours from previous decades. Also, regulations in the nineteen-forties now specified that neither musical instruments nor typewriters could be used before 7 a.m. Lights out on Saturdays extended to midnight, though students were required to be in their rooms by 11 p.m. In addition to speaking to the "lights out" time, the 1945 student handbook also included a housing rule that read, "Each student is responsible for the care of her room and any student may be campused for defacing the walls of her room."[82]

By 1955, students living on-campus had no quiet hours on weekends, save at night. The handbook for this year did require students to be quiet around the auditorium during performances or services. In addition, the lights out rule that had applied only to Saturdays in 1945 was now the rule throughout the week. In deference to studiousness, the 1955 handbook also indicated that, "During mid-semester exams and semester exams lights do not have to be extinguished by 12:00 midnight."[83]

Several room regulations in the 1950s had changed substantially from earlier times. The College now permitted day students to spend Saturday nights on campus with their friends in the dormitories. It was also easier for a dormitory resident to spend the night with another dormitory resident. In addition, students were cautioned that, "All rooms shall be in orderly appearance by 11:00 A.M. If the student's room is not orderly before the maid leaves then it is the student's responsibility to put the room in order."[84]

The 1965–1966 student handbook published the same scheduled quiet hours of the previous decade. This edition of the handbook also made a distinction between "complete quiet" and "quiet," with the former applied only to traditional sleeping hours. Presumably, then, "quiet hours" did not require absolute silence. The 1965 edition of the student handbook also set different standards for sorority houses and dormitories. Residents in sorority houses were permitted to "watch television from 7:30 P.M. – 11:00 P.M. any night if they maintained a C average and if the television is turned low."[85] No mention is made of dormitory residents being permitted to watch T.V. at all. Also, another rule stated "Students living in sorority houses and upperclassmen in dorms may leave their lights on indefinitely any night, but quiet must be maintained after 11:00 P.M."[86] Freshmen and sophomores living in sorority houses, then, had it better than their counterparts living in Brenau's residence halls. Regarding cleanliness,

Smoking, "Night Riding," & other Serious Offenses 333

the 1965 handbook stated: "Rooms are checked every morning, except Sunday, for neatness. The maid will clean the floor, sweep, and check the bathroom each day. The responsibility for the rest is yours."[87]

Housing rules and regulations changed substantially from the mid-nineteen-sixties to the mid-nineteen-seventies. Regarding quiet hours, the 1974–1975 edition of the student handbook published no schedule of hours and said only that "Reasonable quiet shall be maintained at all times in the residence halls and houses."[88] Campus officials now permitted overnight guests (apparently, females only) at any time in the dorms and houses and permitted guests to stay up to three days. Regarding tidiness, the regulations said only that "Students are expected to keep their rooms neat and orderly."[89] There was no longer any mention of a maid. By 1974, Brenau had also implemented a key policy. Under the policy, seniors received keys for their residences and enjoyed an unlimited curfew on Friday and Saturday nights. Duplicating or loaning a key to someone else was prohibited. Losing a key was a serious matter which resulted in a student having to pay for several new keys and for the installation of new locks in their residence hall or sorority house. The student handbook stressed that the key policy was "experimental" and that "the abuse of the key privilege by any student will mean the forfeiture of this privilege for all students."[90]

The unlimited curfew for seniors on weekends by the 1970s was a vast departure from earlier times. Up until about 1945, Brenau student handbooks indicated that curfew was at 10 p.m. on the days when Brenau women could go out. A decade later, students could stay out until 10:55 p.m.[91] By 1984, non-seniors in good academic standing could remain out until 2 a.m.[92] No curfew was mentioned at all in the housing regulations of a decade later and beyond.

By 1984, each dorm or house determined its own "Study Hours," which was an interesting example of Brenau's willingness to give the students a good deal of control over their own affairs. Quiet hours were a thing of the past, though students were "required to refrain from excessive noise."[93] The "key policy" experiment of the 1970s was apparently a success as Brenau retained it. Brenau still expected students to keep their rooms neat and now, to categorically promote this in case there had been any doubt about the matter, the rules specifically forbade pets in College housing. The 1984 handbook indicated that dorms would be open to all visitors from noon until 9:00 p.m. on weekends—including male visitors, something earlier handbooks did not speak to. Brenau even permitted men in student rooms, though doors were required to be left open.[94]

The evolution of rules and regulations regarding student housing at Brenau actually reflects much more than simply a college's concern with quiet and discipline in its houses and dormitories. This evolution mirrors the changing status of women in American society and the success of Brenau students in negotiating with the faculty and staff for some autonomy. Brenau's early housing rules had the effect of practically cloistering students. This reflected the staunchly conservative mindset in the Deep South regarding women during this time. Women were objects to be protected, their virtue something to be safeguarded. This attitude changed hesitantly over time as women's liberation ran a slow course through Dixie, but change it would. Officials of the Georgia Baptist Female Seminary would have been mortified at finding a man in a student's residence hall room, whether the door was open or not. Yet less than a century later, men could visit student rooms—albeit not behind closed doors—which reflected substantial changes in attitude that were responses to changed times and student agency.

Like its housing rules, Brenau's dress code also changed with the times. The 1904 rules said nothing about student dress, other than pointing out to students that, "No loose wrappers are allowed in the halls."[95] The 1925–1926 student handbook made no mention of dress at all. Other than an extensive description of "Sports Costumes" (which is dealt with elsewhere in this book), the 1937–1938 handbook said only that "Students must be properly dressed when crossing campus or going to the tea room [a small café on campus]."[96] In an interview much later in her life, a student at

Smoking, "Night Riding," & other Serious Offenses 335

Brenau in the 1930s qualified this by saying, "Oh—we really had to dress up. If you went to town, you [won't] believe this, but we wore hats and gloves, heels and always had on hose, and dresses, if we just walked up to the drug store. We couldn't even go to the tea room with a gym suit on—you'd have to put a raincoat over it, to go to the tea room."[97]

The reason that Brenau's early materials said little about dress was that little needed saying. Like this alumna, young women from polite society such as those that attended Brenau then simply would have known what to wear and when to wear it. They would have relied upon a lifetime of training in the social graces by their families for this knowledge. And when in doubt, Brenau women would have erred on the side of caution and elected to dress up rather than down.

It was the rapidly changing perception of what, exactly, womanhood meant in American society that eventually led to Brenau's adoption of a dress code. Rather than leave open to question whether or not wearing this or that item would render a young woman "properly dressed," Brenau students eventually began setting standards for themselves. By 1945, Brenau had fully developed its dress code, which the student handbook of that year spelled out. Regarding "Manner of Dress," it read:

1. By formal dress is meant evening dress, hose, and evening shoes.
2. By informal dress or semiformal dress is meant a formal street dress, hose, no oxfords.
3. No student is allowed to cross the campus or go to the Tea Room in irregular dress, such as pajamas, etc. A formal house-coat is acceptable at night.
4. Slacks may not be worn on campus except going from the houses to the woods and to play practice.
5. Only playsuits or tennis dresses may be worn on the tennis courts.[98]

Formal dress would have been required at campus performances, recitals, sorority open houses, and other similar functions. Informal dress would have been acceptable for attending class. As had previous handbooks, the 1945 student handbook also continued the tradition of spelling out what constituted a proper "Sports Costume" on campus.[99] This would be a fixture in student handbooks for the next several decades.

Brenau's dress code of the 1940s sought to ensure that Brenau women dressed femininely. Helen Horowitz indicated that northern women's colleges were generally ahead of southern institutions like Brenau in permitting students to wear saddle shoes, slacks, and pants. These changes would come to Brenau in the mid-1950s. The 1955 student handbook indicated that students could wear jeans, slacks, pedal pushers, and shorts—new, "hip" fashions for the day. Even so, Brenau went on to say that "semi-formal" dress (what had been "informal" dress in the 1945 handbook) was required at lyceum numbers, concerts, church, and Sunday dinner and asked students to wear a coat over sleeping-wear when traveling to the infirmary.[100] To the dress regulations in force in the 1940s was added the following:

1. Students may wear blue jeans, pedal pushers, and slacks
   a. On campus except to class
   b. To the library after 5:00 P.M.
   c. While riding if remaining in the car
   d. Picnics
2. Students may wear shorts on back campus after class hours without raincoats going to and from the tennis courts and physical education classes and during the months of April, May, and June.
3. Shorts may be worn while riding with Brenau girls if remaining in the car.[101]

Clearly, a decade had made quite a bit of difference. Brenau students went from not being able to wear pants at all—except for on very specific occasions—to being permitted to wear much less than pants—shorts, albeit again on very specific occasions.

Smoking, "Night Riding," & other Serious Offenses 337

The 1965–1966 student handbook opened its section entitled "Helpful Hints" by expounding, "The good old typical American college dress and a smiling 'hi' as you pass each student are your first introductions to the Brenau way."[102] The handbook went on to qualify what "college dress" was. One new regulation that students no doubt greatly appreciated in light of the oftentimes hot Georgia climate was a rule that said, "Students are not required to wear hose in hot weather as announced by Executive Council."[103] The College added Bermuda shorts to the permitted clothing rule concerning blue jeans, pedal pushers, and slacks. Brenau now permitted students to wear these articles while bowling or golfing (though a raincoat was required to be worn to and from the sporting venue) or while participating in sports off-campus. Also, Brenau women wearing shorts could egress cars by 1965 without fear of reprisal. The 1965 handbook permitted students to wear "sports clothes excluding short shorts any time in the sorority houses except on Sundays in the rooms where guests are entertained."[104] At the same time, the handbook cautioned that "Students may not leave the campus with their hair rolled-up."[105] Finally, the handbook emphasized that *Brenau girls are expected to be well-groomed and neatly dressed at all times.*"[106] The implication of this was, again, that students should dress up rather than down for any given occasion and err on the side of caution. Making the mistake of not dressing properly came with consequences. The handbook indicated that improper dress earned a student a "warning" and that three warnings would place a student on campus restriction for one week.[107]

Brenau had overhauled the section on dress by the publication of the 1974–1975 student handbook. The section read:

> Brenau students have traditionally been noted for their well-groomed appearance and taste in choice of clothing. As in other areas of campus life, individuality is encouraged. However, Brenau students are expected to dress neatly at all times.

A. Curlers may be worn only on back campus, and they must be covered.

B. Shoes must be worn to all meals, classes, administrative offices, and off-campus.

C. At Sunday lunch dresses or nice pantsuits should be worn.

D. In classrooms and at other meals, clean jeans and jerseys, and shorts in summer school are acceptable.

E. Students are expected to wear at least a swim suit when sun bathing.

Designated areas are:

1. Bailey Hall.

2. Crudup Sundeck.

3. Sorority property—not in general public view.

4. Natatorium sundeck.[108]

Elsewhere, the 1974 student handbook indicated that casual dress was acceptable any time in the dining hall (except for Sundays) and, regarding "Sports Costume," said only that gym uniforms would be sold during the fall for students. The 1984–1985 student handbook altered little the dress code published in the handbook of 1974, saying only that a t-shirt and shorts should be worn over a swimsuit when traveling to or from the pool and that nursing students were expected to wear uniforms to their clinical labs.[109]

As was the case with housing regulations, Brenau's dress code changed with the times. Throughout its history, the code was meant to ensure that Brenau students represented their alma mater well by maintaining a pretty and proper, lady-like appearance. As the institution matured,

Brenau became more about turning out talented young scholars than refined Southern ladies. As this happened, official concern over appearance diminished just as students exercised more control in establishing standards of dress. In essence, Brenau women had, over the course of years, successfully negotiated for the right to police the dress code themselves by simply dressing well. They proved that they needed no fashion oversight but their own. By the twenty-first century, dress at Brenau was essentially self-regulated. That said, a visit to campus in 2012 would have borne out that Brenau students continued to hold themselves to high standards regarding personal appearance.

Although Brenau's good fashion sense has remained consistent over time, the same cannot be said for attitudes about smoking at the College. In writing about the early twentieth century, Helen Horowitz wrote that smoking among young women at college was "the outward sign of acknowledged female sensuality," and, as such, became "the most highly charged issue" on women's college campuses in the North. [110] Horowitz explained that, "Its lure for the female collegian was that it announced her sexual maturity and her interest in men even when she remained in the weekday company of women."[111]

Interestingly, early students at Brenau apparently thought little of the habit. An April 1895 edition of the *Seminary Signal*, the student newspaper of the Georgia Baptist Female Seminary, decried it. In a column entitled simply "Advice to Boys," the author wrote, "Never smoke cigarettes; it is a habit that will undermine your health and character and render you despicable in the eyes of intelligent people."[112]

Times would certainly change. By the twentieth century, Brenau students wanted to smoke. Yet, well into the 1930s, College regulations expressly forbade smoking and, worse for would-be smokers, lumped the practice in with such mortal sins as drinking and gambling.[113] The 1925–1926 *Official Hand-Book of Information* declared simply that, "Drinking, smoking and gambling are not tolerated by the college."[114] A young woman could have been expelled for engaging in any of those three activities. Things would not change at Brenau until 1932. An entry in the minutes book of the Brenau faculty meetings for that year related to smoking and illustrated that students could prevail in negotiations with the College faculty and administration over disciplinary matters. The entry read:

> A petition is read from the Executive Council, approved by the Student Government Association, asking that smoking be hereafter allowed in the sorority houses and the dormitories—with the understanding that it is to be explicitly forbidden (and a 'probation offense') to smoke on the campus, in public places, or in cars.
>
> Certain young ladies, representing the Council and the students at large, appear before the Body and support the petition with oral statements.
>
> Dr. Haywood Pearce, Jr., offers the following as an answer to the petitioners: "Resolved that smoking at public functions, or in public places—whether on or off the campus—is expressly prohibited." After some discussion, the motion is passed. The Dean is directed to report and interpret this action to the students.[115]

Elizabeth "Lib" Wheeler Thurmond attended Brenau from 1929 until 1933 and recalled when the College lifted the moratorium on smoking. Speaking of her sorority sisters and their conduct in the sorority house, she said:

> I was over there when smoking was first allowed. Why we didn't burn that house up, I don't know. We used to climb up in the attic. That was back in the days when it was real classy to smoke, devilish, and we'd crawl up in that attic. Mrs. Cunningham was our housemother and she was gone most of the day. I remember when they found out that we had been allowed to have smoking. She came back in and there we all sat with cigarettes in our hand. She nearly fainted; she didn't know it had been passed. She didn't know what in the world to do. She was just horrified. And we

Smoking, "Night Riding," & other Serious Offenses   341

said, "Ah, we can do it now, we can do it." Why we didn't burn that house down, I do not know.[116]

Lib concluded by recalling, "It was that way all over the campus."[117]

The 1937–1938 *Brenau Girl* student handbook said nothing of the by-then-permitted practice other than, "Students are not to smoke while entertaining gentlemen friends."[118] The 1945–1946 student handbook had more to say on the subject. A section was devoted exclusively to smoking, which read:

1. Students may smoke only in rooms or sorority houses.
2. Students must not smoke in Atlanta when they are there for Concerts.
3. Students must not smoke when entertaining gentlmen [sic] friends at any time.[119]

By a decade later, the 1955 student handbook indicated that the smoking privilege had expanded from rooms and sorority houses to include permission to smoke "while riding in private cars with dates, close friends, relatives, families, or other students."[120] Additionally, Brenau permitted students to smoke "in eating establishments" but not in "drugstores, other public places, or taxis."[121]

Brenau had expanded smoking regulations still further by the mid-1960s. The student handbook of 1965 indicated that "Students may smoke in the following places:"

1. On property of sorority houses.
2. While riding in private cars.
3. During Open House in a specific room where there is no dancing and on porches of sorority houses.
4. On terraces of freshman dormitories.
5. In restaurants and beauty parlors; this does not include stores (drug stores), taxis, and other public places.
6. In the Y.W.C.A. recreation room.

7. In the Tea Room.

8. Lobby of Crudup Hall.[122]

The College prohibited smoking only in the halls of its dorms, in the library, and, curiously, in its English classrooms.

Smoking as a pastime arguably reached its zenith at Brenau in the 1960s if one alumna's account can be believed. This anonymous student wrote a letter to Brenau's president, Dr. Josiah Crudup, in 1964, which read:

> Knowing how interested you are in the health of the Brenau girls, I would like to call your attention to the serious problem of the smoking of cigarettes at the college. ...
>
> At present, for a Brenau girl to be considered at all by any of the sororities for membership she must smoke, or be willing to start smoking in order to be "one of the girls."
>
> Your consideration of the problem of smoking at Brenau will be greatly appreciated by all concerned.[123]

Nothing suggests that Dr. Crudup pursued the matter, but it is perhaps conspicuous that a young woman went to the trouble to raise the issue at all. Her letter suggested that smoking at Brenau went from being viewed as a bad habit at the turn of the century to being a requirement for social acceptance after mid-century.

Time would see the toleration of smoking come full circle at the College. Smoking was not mentioned at all in the student handbooks published in either 1974 or 1984. By the twenty-first century, Brenau had adopted a very restrictive smoking policy. Students could only smoke outside in certain designated areas. The College stated that, "No smoking or tobacco use is allowed in any buildings, entrance or exit doorways, or anywhere on the front campus. The designated outside smoking areas are limited and marked."[124] The move to create what Brenau called a "modified smoke-free environment" apparently enjoyed student support as no correspondence to College officials, letters to the *Alchemist* editor,

Smoking, "Night Riding," & other Serious Offenses 343

etc., exist to indicate any objection to the change. Given this, it is likely that the young women who advocated this policy at the turn of the twenty-first century were thinking very much like the students at the Baptist Female Seminary at the turn of the twentieth century who advised boys to steer clear of tobacco.

Although smoking came full circle at Brenau, it was decried for different reasons in this and the previous century. In the modern era, people vilify smoking largely because the practice is known to harm health. One hundred years ago, people saw smoking as harming not health but a woman's "pure" image, something that could not be countenanced at a southern women's college like Brenau during the time. The College's policies on smoking relaxed over time thanks to student negotiation with College officials. Other southern women's colleges and some women's divisions at coeducational colleges in the South would be much slower to lift smoking bans; Brenau was progressive in this regard.[125] For example, Agnes Scott College did not lift its ban on smoking until 1950 and even then only permitted smoking in one place on campus for many years.[126] At Meredith College, "the rule against smoking had been relaxed" only by 1965.[127] The 1968 Anderson College Student Handbook for Women declared, "Women known to be smoking will be warned on first offense and parents will be notified. On second offense women will be suspended from college."[128] Brenau students largely had themselves to thank for the liberalization in College policy. And, as they did with smoking, Brenau students would do their best to bring about changes in another aspect of college life: interactions with the opposite sex.

In her book *The Past in the Present*, Amy Thompson McCandless observed, "Purity was one of the most cherished qualities of the Southern woman."[129] McCandless asserted that in the first half of the twentieth century, southern women's colleges were largely homogenous places and decidedly more conservative than their northern counterparts. Rules at southern women's colleges reflected this, especially in regard to the perception of womanly virtue. Most notably, rules in southern women's colleges in the first few decades of the 1900s "provided little opportunity for unsupervised contact with the opposite sex."[130] The strict regulation of heterosexual contacts by institutions of higher education most definitely reflected this concern for virtuous behavior. Rules relating to virtually all social interactions—but especially interactions with men—were common to all the early women's colleges. Brenau was no exception.

Brenau's 1904 regulations actually said little about student interaction with men. One rule sought to ensure that any interaction with men that happened to occur in town would be supervised. The rule declared that, "Pupils are not allowed to leave the grounds without express permission, not to appear on the streets unchaperoned."[131] Another rule required that, "Young ladies who desire to correspond with gentlemen other than the immediate members of their respective families, must deposit in the office a written permission to this effect containing the names and addresses of those with whom correspondence is permitted."[132] Nothing beyond these two rules really touched on interaction between men and women. In fact, nothing else needed to be said. Given the time and place, it would simply have been a foregone conclusion in the South that Brenau students would have had no contact with men other than their professors and male relatives. Indeed, the fact that Brenau required parental permission for students to merely *correspond* with men in the very early twentieth is telling of its staunchly conservative ethos. In her book, McCandless listed several schools that required written permission from parents for students to date. Brenau required this for simply writing a letter to a man.

In fact, until the early 1920s, Brenau apparently had rules that forbade girls from even speaking to boys under some circumstances. An entry in the faculty meeting minutes book for February 6, 1912, read, "The Student Council petitions that the prohibition against conversing with young men in the ice cream parlors be rescinded. The petition is denied."[133] In 1914, Brenau suspended two young women for allowing young men to come to their dormitory window to engage in conversation.[134] It was not until 1922 when Brenau's students were able to negotiate for permission to engage in casual conversation with young men. The entry for December 12, 1922, in the minutes book for faculty meetings read:

> The Discipline Committee recommends that, with the beginning of the new year, the students be allowed the privilege of conversing with young gentlemen when they meet them in suitable places, and that the rule forbidding such conversations be repealed.[135]

The Brenau faculty members voted to adopt the recommendation—but only after adding "instructions to throw around such conversations all proper safeguards."[136] Precisely what those proper safeguards were or would have been was not indicated, but it says something that officials were content to entrust students with implementing them.

As the nineteen-twenties roared by, Brenau expanded its policies on associating with the opposite sex. By mid-decade, the College permitted its young ladies to receive male guests, albeit under very specific and very scrutinized circumstances. The 1925–1926 student handbook included a section of rules on "Callers." The handbook read:

> 1. All callers received in the Yonah Hall Parlors *only.*
>
> 2. All arrangements for callers to be made with the Counselor.
>
> 3. General calling hours, 8 to 10 Saturday evening, 3:30 to 5 Sunday afternoon.[137]

Built in 1893, Yonah Hall was Brenau's main dormitory for many decades in the early twentieth century.[138] A Brenau student in the early 1930s recalled the Yonah Hall Parlor by saying, "You had to sit in the Chinese Parlor on that uncomfortable furniture for a date ... every piece was heavily carved Chinese furniture."[139] Clearly, the setting was not meant to be inviting, which might have discouraged lingering on the part of men.

The 1925 handbook went on to say that, "Certain privileges are granted students in regard to their association with their men friends in the city and on the streets; details concerning which are outlined by the

Counselor and Dean."[140] Seniors held some of these privileges and they were quite telling. The handbook indicated:

> 4. Seniors may have callers at any time without chaperonage by filing at the office of the Counselor.
>
> 5. Seniors may accompany their men friends to entertainments in the auditorium.
>
> 6. Seniors may lunch down town with their men friends on any day, including Sunday. It is understood that this privilege is not to be used after 6:00 P.M.
>
> 7. Seniors may have the privilege of walking on campus with their men friends.[141]

These rules are so telling because they imply that other students could *not* walk, lunch, or see shows with "men friends," let alone receive callers outside of weekends. Indeed, other regulations essentially eliminated these and other social possibilities. One rule stated that, "Students are not allowed to leave the campus before 3:30 P.M. without permission."[142] Students who received permission to go off-campus had to return to campus by 6 p.m. Also, the College did not allow students "to attend the moving picture theatre in town at *any time*."[143] Brenau additionally required written permission and College chaperones for students to leave town for dances at other college towns or to shop in Atlanta.[144] Brenau students who broke the rules to be with men did so at their peril. The handbook indicated that "offenses for which students have, in the past, been expelled" included "clandestine meetings with men" and "attendance at public dances in Gainesville."[145]

Little changed regarding the rules for gentlemen callers from 1926 until 1937. The handbook of that year published essentially the same limited hours for calling (8 p.m. to 10 p.m. on Saturdays, and, now, 2:30 p.m. to 5:30 p.m. on Sundays), but added that male guests could, by now, also be received in sorority houses on Sundays. By the mid-1930s,

Smoking, "Night Riding," & other Serious Offenses 347

association with men at some other times would also be tolerated, but under very particular circumstances. For example, students could attend church with gentlemen friends, providing they apprised officials of their intention to do so. Also, officials added another rule that said, "Guests from distant places may be allowed to visit in fraternity [sic] houses when passing through Gainesville for a short period of time, providing the house chaperone is present." [146] The handbook noted that "This does not include guests from nearby towns, colleges and universities, such as Clemson, Atlanta, and Athens."[147] Additionally, the 1937 handbook forbade students to receive callers at the homes of friends in Gainesville or to smoke while entertaining gentlemen friends. Also, once per month on a Saturday evening, officials permitted Brenau's sororities to have an "Open House," to which gentlemen could be invited.[148]

Rules regarding off-campus activity remained quite strict in the nineteen-thirties as they had been in the nineteen-twenties. Still, some leniency had developed as the result of successful student negotiations with the faculty and staff. The minutes for the faculty meeting of March 2, 1926, indicated that, "The petition from the Junior Class has been granted as to going to town and visiting picture-shows," which put juniors on near equal footing with seniors in terms of movie-going privileges.[149] The senior class had less luck with a petition it submitted roughly a year later. On February 1, 1927, the faculty ruled that "A petition by the senior class to add to their privileges the ability to go down town at night in the company of a chaperone is denied."[150] Still, it is worth noting that the petition was not denied on the basis of principle but "on the basis of being inexpedient."[151] This is perhaps an indicator that the faculty and staff were not distrustful of the seniors, but rather appreciative of the fact that finding chaperones for outings would have simply been too challenging at late hours. The College did require chaperones for other occasions or, more rarely, let students go to select events unchaperoned altogether. For example, Brenau required students attending the Sunday afternoon parade at the Riverside Military Academy to be chaperoned. At the same time, no chaperone was needed for walking with boys, providing the walkers stayed on a few specific streets near the downtown Gainesville square.

Chaperones notwithstanding, there were some off-campus places even within the downtown area that Brenau students absolutely could not go. The Discipline Committee forbade "students to make use of a certain beauty parlor in the City" in a meeting of October 6, 1931.[152] It may have been the "beauty-parlor of the Newman Drygoods Co.," which was identified in the November 1, 1932, entry of the Brenau faculty meeting minutes book.[153] Why students could not use the salon is not indicated. Presumably, though, it attracted a questionable clientele that the College expected Brenau women to avoid in the interest of preserving their ladylike reputations. Finally, regarding off-campus activity, the handbook decreed that "Students are not permitted to use the cars of young men."[154]

Breaking the rule about using the cars of gentlemen incurred particularly serious consequences. Brenau personnel referred to this as "night riding," given that students typically committed the infraction in the evening. Almost nothing could get a young woman thrown out of the College faster. The minutes books of the Brenau faculty meetings report violations of this offense more than any other and the consequences to offenders were invariably severe. The first recorded expulsion of a student for night riding occurred on May 23, 1916. Brenau expelled two more students on April 20, 1917, and another two on January 16, 1919. In a meeting on November 4, 1919, the faculty voted that students living off campus were to be held to the same standards regarding automobile riding as students living on campus. This may have opened the door for increased prosecutions of the offense.[155]

The secretary for the Brenau College faculty meetings described these and other night riding prosecutions quite robustly in the minutes of the 1920s. The November 5, 1922, entry in the minutes reported that, "The Discipline Committee reports that misses Alice Cox and Dorothy Stauffer have been guilty of automobile riding, at night, with men, that the two students have made a full confession, and that the committee recommends

Smoking, "Night Riding," & other Serious Offenses

immediate expulsion."[156] The recommendation passed unanimously. The March 15, 1923, entry in the minutes reported that Louise McLeod was "expelled from the Institution, because of automobile riding with a young man after dinner in the evening."[157] November 4, 1924, saw two more young women in trouble again for "riding clandestinely with men." The faculty expelled one woman and permitted the other, for reasons unknown, to save some face and withdraw herself from school rather than be expelled.[158] Finally, on April 6, 1926, the minutes book of the faculty meetings reported that, "Eight young ladies have automatically expelled themselves, through violation of our regulation touching clandestine night-riding."[159] This mass expulsion may have sent a clear and lingering message to Brenau's other students. Outside of expelling four young women on January 3, 1928, and three young women on January 14, 1930, for night riding, no other violations of the night riding rule appear for about a decade. [160]

The 1937 *Brenau Girl* student handbook continued to assert that, "Students are not permitted to use the cars of young men."[161] Yet, by this decade, breaking the rule no longer appeared to incur automatic expulsion as had been the case in the not-so-distant past. The entry for the faculty meeting of May 27, 1935, as recorded in the faculty meeting minutes book, indicated that Brenau disciplined six young ladies for "night-riding." The students received very strict punishments, but were not expelled.[162] Likewise, in February, 1937, the faculty asked another student to withdraw for night riding (in fact, her second offense), but did not expel her.[163]

Again in 1945, Brenau's student handbook expressed that night riding was an offense that might make a student "liable to expulsion."[164] Night riding was now actually defined in such a way that would be less vexing for students. The handbook indicated that "Night riding is considered any riding which is not directly to and from a destination."[165] In other words, young ladies could now use the cars of young men to get from place to place, such as from campus to a restaurant or to the cinema; they simply could not *linger* in the cars of young men or cruise around. This simple distinction vastly altered the character of the offense. By 1955, Brenau's student handbook indicated that this rule had been softened even further. There was a section dedicated to riding, which essentially permitted students to ride around town (and not just directly to and from destinations) during daylight hours, providing parental permission was on file. Additionally, the College permitted students who obtained "standing permission" from home to ride with boys in the evening, but another regulation declared, "Parking while exercising night privileges is absolutely prohibited except in [the] driveway on front campus."[166] Said driveway would have been well-illuminated and quite visible from campus to discourage indiscreet behavior.

Just as students enjoyed the gradual relaxation of rules concerning "night riding" over the years, they also enjoyed the relaxation of rules regarding gentleman callers. By 1945, Brenau permitted student dating. The handbook for that year published the following "dating hours" and locations:

> Friday—7:00 P.M.—10:00 P.M. (moving dates, not Yonah)
>
> Saturday—2:30 P.M.—5:30 P.M. Yonah; Houses the afternoon of Open House and Cotillion.
>
> 7:00 P.M. — 10:00 P.M., Movies.
>
> 8:00 P.M. — 10:00 P.M., Yonah.
>
> Sunday—2:00 P.M.—6:00 P.M. Houses or Yonah.
>
> 8:00 P.M. —10:00 P.M. Yonah only.[167]

The hours were strictly enforced. A faculty member at Brenau from 1943 to 1946 recalled, "On Sundays, you couldn't meet your date until 1:30 or 2 o'clock. They weren't allowed on campus or at least not in Yonah Hall. Miss Winfield [Brenau's Dean of Women or Lady Principal] would stand out front and wave the boys away if they showed up too early."[168]

Smoking, "Night Riding," & other Serious Offenses

In addition to publishing hours permitted for dating, the 1945 student handbook published several dating rules. They were:

> 1. All date slips for dates in Yonah are received from the Counselor's office before the date arrives on Saturday and Sunday evenings.
>
> 2. Students may have dates in town during the day, but must be on campus by 6:30 P.M.
>
> 3. Students must remain on campus after 6:30 P.M. on evenings of Open House.
>
> 4. Guests from distant places may be allowed to visit in sorority houses when passing through Gainesville for a short time, providing the house chaperon is present. If they remain for more than thirty minutes the visit continues in Yonah Lounge.
>
> 5. Students are not to receive callers at the homes of friends in town.
>
> 6. Students are not to smoke when entertaining gentlemen friends. Gentlemen may smoke, except at Open House or other social functions.
>
> 7. On Sunday afternoons dates may walk on campus to and from sorority houses and Yonah until 6:00 P.M. No walking with dates in the Park or at the Lakes.
>
> 8. Dates may call for girls living in the Sorority houses after 6:30 P.M. for movie dates, but they must not linger.
>
> 9. Dates may call for girls at Yonah during recreation hours (3:30 to 6:30 P.M.) and at night for movie dates, during the weekend on Sunday mornings for Church.
>
> 10. Seniors, Juniors, and Sophomores may walk to the drugstore on Sunday afternoons with dates for one hour.[169]

Specific rules also existed regarding dining out, which Brenau permitted students to do on Sundays, providing they signed in and out.

Conditions for dating had improved immensely for students at the College by 1945. The October 23, 1945, edition of the *Alchemist* for that year published an article that described the new "Rec room" where students entertained dates. The article declared, "It's a perfect place to entertain and very soon [will be] fully equipped with card tables, ping pong tables, a shuffleboard, and many other games. And if you can furnish the ingredients, there is a place to make fudge for that special date sometime."[170] Additionally, the article read that "One of the most wonderful assets is the radio Victrola [sic] which made its appearance—so bring your records and come over!"[171]

The 1955 student handbook rules regarding dating reflected changing times. Brenau permitted seniors to go out with dates "on any night but not every night" during the week.[172] Juniors could date on weekends and two other nights a week whereas sophomores and freshman could date on weekends and one other night per week. Students could have dates in town during the day, but had to be back on campus by 7 p.m. On Saturdays and Sundays, young women could stay out until 10:55 p.m., providing they signed in and out properly with their dorm or house director. As in previous years, Brenau only permitted students to linger with their dates in cars parked on the front driveway, which was still the most visible spot on the campus.[173]

According to the 1965 student handbook, Brenau students were staying out later on dates and going out more often. Curfew had been moved to 11:30 p.m. Also, something called "Late Permissions" had been created. Providing she indicated so on her dating sign-out card, a student could have an additional thirty minutes of time for her date any day but Sunday. Seniors could exercise this privilege six times per year, juniors five times, sophomores four times, and freshman, after their first six weeks at Brenau, three times. Juniors and sophomores could also date one other night per week than their 1950s counterparts. Additionally, students who obtained parental permission to do so could visit Atlanta or Athens with dates during the day, providing they returned to campus by curfew.[174]

Smoking, "Night Riding," & other Serious Offenses   353

By 1974, the student handbook indicated that dormitory and sorority house residents who signed in and out properly could stay out until midnight during the week and until 2 a.m. on weekends for dating or for any other reason. These were the hours at which Brenau locked its campus residences. All students, irrespective of class, could request to stay out until 1 a.m. seven times per quarter. Seniors could stay out all hours on Friday and Saturday nights. The 1974 handbook mentioned no other regulations touching on dating.[175] The student handbook of 1984 said even less on the subject. "Permission Status" had replaced curfews, though students still had to return to campus by a certain hour. With parental permission, "C" or better students living on-campus could stay out until 1 a.m. during the week or 2 a.m. on weekends. Struggling students were to be in by midnight during the week. Other than freshmen, Brenau permitted students "unlimited off-campus overnights, unless prohibited by parental permission."[176] By 1984, the College no longer even required that students sign in and out, though students were asked to leave information about their whereabouts for emergency needs.

This was a very far cry from how Brenau had once been. One of the College's rules in 1904 stated that, "Pupils are not allowed to leave the grounds without express permission, nor to appear on the streets unchaperoned."[177] In the 1920s, Brenau reserved the right to expel students for "leaving the College without the knowledge of the Authorities" and for attending "an out-of-town dance and ball-game without being chaperoned."[178] This practice continued into the 1930s and 1940s. On December 6, 1932, the faculty asked three students to withdraw from Brenau for leaving campus without permission. The faculty pressured three more young women to depart Brenau on February 1, 1944, "because of their leaving the College without permission, and because of other conduct which, in the judgment of the Committee, makes them too great a liability for the College to carry."[179]

By 1974, leaving the College and dating were no longer "liabilities" to Brenau. Indeed, by this year, no section on "dating" in specific even existed in the student handbook. The student handbooks of the 1980s, the 1990s, and later did not speak to dating at all, either. Finally, roughly 100 years after the institution's founding, Brenau students had negotiated for the ability to fully manage their own relationship affairs. Precisely what won the faculty and staff over is not clear. They might have assented in part for recruiting reasons. By the 1970s, Brenau competed with many private and state-owned coeducational colleges for students. Most of these institutions would not have been strict about student dating. Brenau may have had to relax its posture simply so students would consider enrolling. Alternatively, the dating rules may have changed over time simply because Brenau personnel (like their students) also changed with the times over the years.

At times throughout its history, Brenau even frowned upon the most societally sanctioned of affairs between the sexes: marriage—or, more precisely, marriage of enrolled students. Like other Southern women's colleges during the early part of the twentieth century, Brenau was at least as conscientious about turning out refined homemakers for affluent homes as it was concerned with educating young women. Consequently, the institution wholeheartedly supported the marriage of its graduates. The same was not true for marriage of its current students. The 1965 student handbook indicated that "secret" marriages would not be tolerated at the College.[180] Four decades earlier, marriage of any variety led to expulsion. The faculty meeting minutes book entry for December 7, 1926, read, "That, in the case of Miss Hattie Picher, a motion be made to the effect that she is now married, and that her name is dropped from the list of students."[181] The minutes book indicated that the faculty expelled another young woman in 1932 when she left the College without permission and "arrived at home with a husband."[182] Indeed, on at least one occasion, a Brenau official went to great lengths to thwart a marriage from occurring. In 1913, the *Atlanta Constitution* told the story in its society pages about a Brenau student who had recently fled the College to get married. The newspaper reported that as soon as Brenau president

Dr. H. J. Pearce heard about the speedy departure of the girl, he acted. The paper reported that Pearce:

> caught the next train and hurried to this city. For hours he searched for the runaway student. He finally found her and her fiancé in the Terminal station. Taking charge of Miss Ramsey, he notified her parents and ordered West [Ramsey's fiancé] to wait until their arrival from their home in Washington, Ga.[183]

The paper did not report whether or not the couple lived happily ever after. It is likely that the article went a very long way to reassuring parents that their daughters' honor would be well-safeguarded by Brenau officials.

Of course, Brenau opposed marriage when it did out of a belief that a woman could not be fully attached to both a husband and her alma mater simultaneously. Over time, Brenau would eventually view the institution of marriage and women's roles differently and come to allow marriage of even enrolled students. By 1974, married women did more than merely attend the College; they sought to form their own sorority on campus. The student handbook for that year related that, "Mu Rho Sigma [note the initials: M.R.S.], a sorority for women who are married or have been married, was founded at Brenau in May of 1974. Its members attempt to establish a common bond through which they can share mutual experiences and provide special services to the college."[184] By now, Brenau not only tolerated marriage, it encouraged the development of institutions and organizations on campus to support women in such relationships.

Also in regard to relationships, Brenau rules had, at times, dealt specifically with that mainstay of American dating, going to the movies. The entry for February 1, 1916, in the Brenau faculty meeting minutes book indicated that the "seniors again request permission to see picture shows."[185] The faculty granted their request, but only for shows on Fridays and "with the understanding that the teachers will ascertain in advance the character of the picture to be shown, and will cancel the permission whenever they deem it expedient to do so."[186] The same year, Brenau showed the "photo-play" entitled "The Birth of a Nation" at its commencement. The 1926 handbook decreed that, other than seniors, "Students are not allowed to attend the moving picture theatre in town at *any time*," let alone with a date.[187] The minutes book of the Brenau College faculty meetings indicated that this privilege would be extended to the junior class in 1926, but still eluded freshmen and sophomores.[188] By 1937, Brenau permitted seniors "to go to the show any afternoon with gentlemen friends without filing," to see evening shows "in groups of two unchaperoned and be back on the campus by 10:30," and to "attend the show in the evening with gentlemen friends, three times a week" by filing with the house chaperone.[189] Juniors and sophomores could see matinee shows by themselves during the week. Also, juniors could attend the picture show with gentlemen friends on Friday and Saturday nights or on other evenings providing they went in groups of at least two. Sophomores could attend the show with a male friend on Saturdays evenings or on other evenings providing they went in the company of seniors or members of Brenau's Executive Council. Brenau permitted freshmen to see a show one night a week in the company of a junior or senior member of the Executive Council and to see a show on Saturday afternoon (but not Saturday evening) with a gentleman friend, providing the student double-dated with another couple.[190]

Rules such as these operated into the mid-nineteen forties, as upperclassmen enjoyed more lenient movie-going privileges than did lower classmen. The 1945 handbook also indicated that, "Students may not attend the State Theater on Friday and Saturday nights," possibly because this theater served alcohol and created an environment unsuitable for young ladies.[191] By 1955, after what must have been years of student urging, Brenau women had negotiated for the elimination of such class distinctions regarding the movies. The only regulation that dealt with the movies published in that year's edition of the student handbook was a hold-over from the 1940s that stated, "No Brenau student may sit in the balconies of Gainesville theaters."[192] Presumably, this rule existed

Smoking, "Night Riding," & other Serious Offenses 357

to prevent Brenau students from sitting in a section of a theater with the notorious reputation of being a good place to "make out" with dates. Also, the balconies of small-town theaters were generally the only parts of theaters in the Jim Crow South where African Americans could sit. Barring Brenau students from balconies therefore worked to minimize contact with other races as well.

By 1965, the only regulation regarding movies published in the student handbook was one that permitted students to stay and see the ending of a movie even if it ran a "little over" the regulation dating hours.[193] Over these decades, movies evolved from being new-fangled and suspect forms of entertainment to become thoroughly commonplace—so much so that they no longer merited regulatory mention by the College. By 1974, the College's student handbook was silent on the subject of movies, let alone students' conduct at the movies.

What did merit comment by 1974 was the use of mind-altering substances. No doubt as a result of the public fall out over the "Psychedelic '60s," the College had a drug policy in place by this year. The policy essentially condemned the abuse of prescription drugs and reminded students of the illegality of such drugs as marijuana and hallucinogens.[194] A 1970 edition of the *Alchemist* indicated that Brenau brought speakers to campus to discuss drug abuse with students.[195] Brenau also published policies regarding alcoholic beverages by 1974. In essence, the College permitted responsible drinking by those of legal age on-campus at special functions and at special places. Historically speaking, this was quite a departure for Brenau. Drinking had simply not been tolerated by the College since its inception. Even as late as 1966, various Brenau materials indicated that drinking could lead to summary expulsion.

Interestingly, the minutes books for the Brenau faculty meetings for the first half of the twentieth century mention only a single incident of rule breaking involving alcohol—and, curiously, this incident also involved a member of the Brenau faculty. The entry of March 21, 1927, indicated that several students "while visiting Lake Burton, on March

20th, were guilty—according to their own confession—of handling recklessly (though not maliciously) another person's automobile, of smoking cigarettes, and of partaking, to some extent, at least, of whiskey that happened to have been left by unknown persons near the place where the students were camped."[196] Moreover, "a member of the Faculty—viz., Miss Louise Howarth—was with this party of young ladies, in the capacity of chaperone, and that her conduct on the occasion was...indiscreet and unprofessional."[197] The faculty (in a "spirit of tolerance and Christian forbearance") voted to leave disciplining Ms. Howarth up to Brenau's president, Dr. Pearce.[198] The minutes do not indicate what discipline Dr. Pearce meted out, but he may have been less spirited than his faculty; Ms. Howarth was not listed as a member of the faculty by the time the College published its 1930 catalog.

Brenau's rules and regulations and its honor code also dealt with academic conduct as well as student conduct generally. As early as 1925, Brenau's student handbooks indicated that cheating could lead to expulsion, no doubt solemnizing what had been the unwritten practice of prior years.[199] Brenau students seem to have abided by the tenets of the code closely for much of the institution's history. The minutes of the faculty meetings for the first half of the twentieth century revealed that only two grave violations occurred. In 1935, the College suspended a young woman for cheating on a French examination.[200] Brenau asked another student to withdraw for cheating in 1942.[201] Nothing really exists in the Archives addressing academic honesty in the last several decades. Brenau's recent catalogs do indicate that the University reserves the right to employ plagiarism detection services to verify the originality of submitted student work.

Over time, most rules and regulations at Brenau have dealt with specific themes like night riding, cutting class, and cheating, but not all rules have done so. Indeed, what might be considered a "golden rule" was unwritten —yet vigorously and harshly enforced. The gist of this rule superseded the black-and-white regulations that Brenau women were expected to abide by. Brenau expected its students, in thought and deed, to live up to the high ideals and standards of the College. Expulsion or forced withdrawal was the consequence of not doing so. The minutes book of the faculty meetings for the first half of the twentieth century contain several entries that attest to the seriousness of this rule at Brenau and the tough consequences for violators. On March 1, 1927, Brenau placed two students under restrictions for "unbecoming conduct and violation of college regulations."[202] Brenau expelled three young women on May 6, 1930, "on the ground that the attitude and conduct of these students showed them to be wholly out of place" at the College.[203] Three other ladies "for the same general reasons" were asked to withdraw, which they did.[204] The College asked another young woman to withdraw on April 5, 1932, "for conduct out of harmony with the ideals and regulations of the College."[205] Two more students were asked to withdraw on April 3, 1934, as "the attitude and conduct of the two students…have not been such as to render them desirable campus citizens."[206] Roughly three years later, Brenau sternly disciplined two students and forced another to withdraw from the College for being "guilty of certain irregular and objectionable conduct during a visit to Atlanta."[207] Finally, Brenau requested that two women leave the College on November 7, 1939, and disciplined five students on May 5, 1942, for each having committed a "serious breach of…discipline."[208] None of these cases mentioned a specific violation of any particular regulation. Rather, the College seems to have disciplined these students for violating the spirit, if not the letter, of the law.

As important as the golden rule was, like virtually all of the rules and regulations at Brenau, it would eventually disappear. Student agency hastened the demise of these rules as student representatives successfully petitioned the faculty in meetings over the years for changes. Brenau's student handbooks indicate that by the mid-1960s, the College still retained rules about such non-academic things as dress, chapel attendance, smoking, dating, and night riding. Even so, these rules were, as a whole, much less strict and particular than Brenau's rules had been in decades past. This is a testament to the success of the students in negotiating for their desired college experience. Despite their successes, student victory was not yet complete because even modest rules still existed in the late 1960s and early 1970s. Smack in the middle of perhaps the most libertine decade of the twentieth century, with its counterculture movements and social revolutions, Brenau still maintained some rules that sought to prescribe aspects of proper student behavior. Yet, only a decade later, as evidenced by the student handbook of 1974–1975, virtually all such rules were gone. Other than a few lines regarding a dress code, the only rules reprinted in the 1974 handbook dealt with academics. To paraphrase McCandless, Brenau was no longer making rules for the purpose of making "ladies."

Throughout much of its history, Brenau may have made rules to make ladies, but some Brenau students clearly believed that Brenau made rules for breaking. In an advice column published in a 1935 edition of the *Alchemist*, an anonymous author named "Freshman" lamented:

> I have been here for nearly nine months, and I am still wondering. I have had the rules thoroughly drilled into me, and I try to obey them, but I do not see why I should deny myself the pleasure of night riding, clandestine meetings with men, smoking in town, and staying off the campus until ten-forty-five. Others do these thngs [sic], for I've a friend in town who's not a member of the student body, who is well acquainted with its members, and she tells me she often sees girls breaking these rules, and apparently nothing ever happens to them. I hadn't heard of special privileges on the campus, but evidently some persons do have them.[209]

The advice columnist, Doris Dean, replied:

> The reasons that these students are not reported, is because if any one sees them, she, too, is probably breaking the same rule, or because they are "friends!" It would be just a case of the "pot calling the kettle black." Therefore, what happens? Nothing.[210]

Indeed, rule breaking was apparently nearly as old as rule making. The 1901 edition of the *Bubbles*, in fact only the second edition of the

College yearbook, published the following playful exchange between two students:

> Miss New Girl: Pray tell me what's the good of being on the self-governed list?
>
> Miss Old Girl: Why, you see, it gives the Faculty the satisfaction of thinking that you won't break the rules. Do you catch?[211]

What is most interesting about these sources is that they prove that Brenau students, since very early on, were willing to push back against institutional constraints. This would have been the very first step in negotiating for changes to the rules that would have helped make Brenau the kind of negotiated space the students sought. The young women who took this first step did more than merely break rules. They pushed social boundaries and explored their independence. Their behavior could be seen to be as much pioneering as it was naughty. The first Brenau woman who smoked, or wore shorts, or rode clandestinely at night, whether she knew it or not, was taking an important first step in a process that would culminate with the eventual emancipation of her sisters from rules barring such conduct. To paraphrase Professor Van Hoose when he spoke over a hundred years ago, through the efforts of these pioneering young ladies, Brenau College women were eventually relieved of the many arbitrary restrictions which in the old times interfered with the liberty of the student.

Oddly, the fact that rule breaking occurred may even be a testament to the success of Brenau's efforts to educate young women. After all, as a liberal arts college, Brenau has always aimed to develop the intellectual capacities of its students and to broaden their minds. Perhaps Brenau opened the minds of its students to such an extent that they sought to subvert and, in some cases, redefine the regulations of the very institution that empowered them.

Notes

1. Samuel Hall, "The Laws of Harvard College (1790): Chap. II. -- On Devotional Exercises, and the Observation of the Lord's-Day, Rule III," 18th-Century Reading Room.com, http://18thcenturyreadingroom.wordpress.com/2006/02/23/item-of-the-day-the-laws-of-harvard-college-1790/ (accessed 10 May 2013).
2. Samuel Hall, "The Laws of Harvard College (1790): Chap. IV. Of Misdemeanors and Criminal Offences., Rule I," 18th-Century Reading Room.com, http://18thcenturyreadingroom.wordpress.com/2006/02/23/item-of-the-day-the-laws-of-harvard-college-1790/ (accessed 10 May 2013).
3. Samuel Hall, "The Laws of Harvard College (1790): Chap. V. Miscellaneous Laws., Rule IX," 18th-Century Reading Room.com, http://18thcenturyreadingroom.wordpress.com/2006/02/23/item-of-the-day-the-laws-of-harvard-college-1790/ (accessed 10 May 2013).
4. Laurence R. Veysey, *The Emergence of the American University* (Chicago, IL: University of Chicago Press, 1965), 33.
5. Rudolph, *American College and University*, 106–107.
6. McCandless, *Past in the Present*, 127.
7. Ibid., 128.
8. "'Self-Governed Girls' is the Plan at Brenau," *Atlanta Constitution*, 5 July 1903, sec. A, p. 4.
9. Ibid.
10. Ibid.
11. Ibid.
12. Ibid. It is particularly intriguing that teachers voted as well as the students.
13. Ibid.
14. Ibid.
15. Ibid.
16. "'Self-Governed Girls' is the Plan at Brenau," *Atlanta Constitution*, 31 July 1904, sec. C, p. 4.
17. Ibid.
18. Jeffrey R. Willis, *Converse College* (Charleston, SC: Arcadia Publishing, 2001), 78.

Smoking, "Night Riding," & other Serious Offenses   363

19. Meredith Minter, "Our Student Government System," *The Sundial*, vol. 66, no. 18, February 26, 1982.
20. Brenau's Student Government Association lists its founding year as 1902, the year when the lineal descendant of the present organization formed. See "About S.G.A.," Brenau University Student Organizations, http://intranet.brenau.edu/dnn/StudentDevelopment/StudentOrganizations/tabid/64/Default.aspx (accessed 10 May 2013). However, student-elected representatives had been governing on campus on the Honor Board prior to that year.
21. Horowitz, *Alma Mater*, 149. In fact, the first student government association ever established at an American college or university originated at a women's college in Pennsylvania, not New England. According to its website, "When students united to form the Bryn Mawr College Self-Government Association in 1892, the College became the first institution of higher education in the United States to give students responsibility not only for enforcing rules of behavior upon themselves, but also for deciding what those rules should be. It was considered a radical experiment at the time, and is still unusual." See "About," Bryn Mawr Self Government Association, http://sga.blogs.brynmawr.edu/about/ (accessed 10 May 2013). Other schools in the middle states also adopted systems of self-government around the turn of the twentieth century. Historians writing about Goucher College in Baltimore, Maryland, noted that, "In the spring of 1901 the movement toward self-government in the Woman's College took definite form." Anna Heubeck Knipp and Thaddeus P. Thomas, *The History of Goucher College* (Baltimore, MD: Goucher College, 1938), 501; available at Internet Archive, http://archive.org/stream/historyofgoucher00knip#page/n5/mode/2up (accessed 10 May 2013).
22. Louise Culler, ed., *The Brenau Girl: Official Handbook of Information, 1937–1938* (Gainesville, GA: Brenau College, 1937), 9; available in the Brenau University Archives, Gainesville, Georgia. Hereafter, references to this source are indicated as "*Handbook* (1937)."
23. Marguerite Duncan, ed., *Official Handbook of Information* (Gainesville, GA: Brenau College, 1945), 11; available in the Brenau University Archives, Gainesville, Georgia. Hereafter, references to this source are indicated as "*Handbook* (1945)."
24. Ibid.
25. Sarah Allen, ed., *Students' Handbook, Brenau College, 1955 –1956* (Gainesville, GA: Brenau College, 1955), 7; available in the Brenau

University Archives, Gainesville, Georgia. Hereafter, references to this source are indicated as *"Handbook* (1955)."
26. Margie Thrasher, ed., *Student Handbook, Brenau College, 1974–1975* (Gainesville, GA: Brenau College, 1974), 32; available in the Brenau University Archives, Gainesville, Georgia. Hereafter, references to this source are indicated as *"Handbook* (1974)."
27. Ibid., 32-33.
28. *Brenau University Undergraduate and Graduate Catalog 2007–2008, v. 123* (Gainesville, GA: Brenau University, 2007), 34; available in the Brenau University Archives, Gainesville, Georgia. Hereafter, references to this source are indicated as *"Catalog* (2007)."
29. Sharon A. Swanson, "Brenau Welcomes Senator Steen Miles," Brenau University, 13 February 2007, http://intranet.brenau.edu/dnn/StudentServices/CareerServices/JobBoard/tabid/92/mid/505/newsid505/765/Default.aspx (accessed 10 May 2013).
30. *Catalog* (1900), 64; see also, "Notes from Judicial," *Aurum: Weekly Newsletter of Brenau College*, October 21–27, 1985, p. 1.
31. Ibid., 65. Only much later did some colleges vest their students with the disciplinary authority that Brenau women began exercising early in the twentieth century. For example, the Student Government Association at Agnes Scott College apparently acquired this power in 1929. Walter Edward McNair, *Lest We Forget: An Account of Agnes Scott College* (Atlanta, GA: Tucker-Castleberry Printing, Inc., 1983), 85.
32. See the *Official Hand-Book of Information, 1925–1926* (Gainesville, GA: Brenau College, 1925); available in the Brenau University Archives, Gainesville, Georgia. Hereafter, references to this source are indicated as *"Handbook* (1925)."
33. *Handbook* (1937), 15.
34. *Handbook* (1974), 33.
35. Jody Duncan and Lynn Smith, eds., *Brenau Women's College Student Handbook, 1984–1985* (Gainesville, GA: Brenau College, 1984), 25–36; available in the Brenau University Archives, Gainesville, Georgia. Hereafter, references to this source are indicated as *"Handbook* (1984)."
36. While one might argue that the move toward appointing (as opposed to electing) honor board members shows an elitist shift, this was probably not the case. The appointments were, after all, made by students who had themselves been voted into office in campus-wide elections. Still, even if one could criticize the process as becoming more exclusive, this may have had good results. As an example, consider the United States judicial

system. Presidents appoint members of the federal judiciary to the bench precisely to establish an independent judiciary and to avoid the vagaries of participatory democracy. See Maeva Marcus, ed., *The Documentary History of the Supreme Court of the United States, 1789–1800: Volume 8* (New York, NY: Columbia University Press, 2007), 5.

37. *Faculty Journal (25 years)*, entry dated 1 April 1924.
38. "New Rules for 1951–52," *Alchemist*, 5 May 1951, p. 3.
39. Ibid.
40. "'Self-Governed Girls' is the Plan at Brenau," *Atlanta Constitution*, 31 July 1904, sec. C, p. 4.
41. *Catalog* (1900), 71.
42. *Catalogue of the Baptist Female University, Raleigh, North Carolina, 1899–1900* (Raleigh, NC: Edwards & Broughton, Printers and Binders, 1900), 50; available from Internet Archive, http://archive.org/details/catalogueofbapti1900mere (accessed 2 June 2013).
43. Ibid.
44. Ibid.
45. *Handbook* (1925), 34. Brenau dropped its church attendance requirements substantially before other southern women's colleges, perhaps suggesting the institution held an uncommonly progressive attitude regarding the subject in the region. For example, at Meredith College, church attendance only became voluntary in 1963. See Mary Lynch Johnson, *A History of Meredith College, 2nd Ed.* (Raleigh, NC: Meredith College, 1972), 280; available at Internet Archive, http://archive.org/stream/historyofmeredit00john#page/n7/mode/2up (accessed 10 May 2012).
46. *Brenau College Faculty Journal for Twelve Years (1910 – 1922)*, entry dated 12 December 1922; available in the Brenau University Archives, Gainesville, Georgia. Hereafter, references to this source are indicated as "*Faculty Journal (12 years)*."
47. *Faculty Journal (25 years)*, entry dated 3 May 1938.
48. *Handbook* (1925), 13.
49. *Faculty Journal (25 years)*, entry dated 19 February 1926.
50. *Handbook* (1945), 27.
51. *Handbook* (1955), 80.
52. *Catalog* (1970), 17.
53. Ibid.
54. *Faculty Journal (25 years)*, entry dated 6 December 1932.
55. *Faculty Journal (25 years)*, entry dated 2 February 1937.

56. George M. Marsden, *The Soul of the American University: From Protestant Establishment to Established Nonbelief* (New York, NY: Oxford University Press, 1996), 3.
57. *Faculty Journal (25 years)*, entry dated 3 December 1940.
58. See material about Delta Phi Epsilon in the chapter on students and secret societies.
59. *Handbook* (1984), 22.
60. "'Self-Governed Girls' is the Plan at Brenau," *Atlanta Constitution*, 31 July 1904, sec. C, p. 4.
61. *Handbook* (1925), 14.
62. *Handbook* (1937), 25.
63. *Handbook* (1945), 60.
64. Patsy Fargason and Cheryl Gibbons, eds., *Students' Handbook, Brenau College 1965–1966* (Gainesville, GA: Brenau College, 1965), 60; available in the Brenau University Archives, Gainesville, Georgia. Hereafter, references to this source are indicated as "*Handbook* (1965)."
65. *Handbook* (1974), 30.
66. The outbreak of World War II actually induced many American colleges and universities to take steps to accelerate their degree programs to produce more educated servicemen for the war effort. Institutions did this by increasing the length of academic terms and by lengthening the school week. The result was that, "Most institutions were conducting classes 48 weeks a year, six days a week." This was even true for colleges with no military students (such as schools maintained by pacifist religious groups like the Quakers) and for women's colleges. V.R. Cardozier, *Colleges and Universities in World War II* (Westport, CT: Greenwood Publishing Group, Inc., 1993), 110.
67. *Faculty Journal (25 years)*, entry dated 2 March 1926.
68. *Faculty Journal (25 years)*, entry dated 7 February 1933.
69. *Faculty Journal (25 years)*, entry dated 3 February 1925.
70. "'Self-Governed Girls' is the Plan at Brenau," *Atlanta Constitution*, 31 July 1904, sec. C, p. 4.
71. *Handbook* (1925), 12.
72. Ibid., 14.
73. *Faculty Journal (25 years)*, entry dated 7 October 1924.
74. Ibid.
75. *Handbook* (1925), 12.
76. Ibid.
77. Ibid.

78. Ibid.
79. *Handbook* (1937), 20–21.
80. Ibid., 21.
81. Ibid.
82. *Handbook* (1945), 24.
83. *Handbook* (1955), 24.
84. Ibid., 25. Responsibility for tidying up has always apparently rested with Brenau's students, despite the presence of maids. According to photographs in the *Bubbles*, the college employed maids since about the 1930s to clean housing bathrooms, floors, and common areas. Students were responsible for cleaning everything else.
85. *Handbook* (1965), 42.
86. Ibid.
87. Ibid., 14.
88. *Handbook* (1974), 24.
89. Ibid.
90. Ibid., 23.
91. *Handbook* (1955), 27.
92. *Handbook* (1984), 15.
93. Ibid., 17.
94. Ibid., 16.
95. "'Self-Governed Girls' is the Plan at Brenau," *Atlanta Constitution*, 31 July 1904, sec. C, p. 4.
96. *Handbook* (1937), 26.
97. Mary Helen Hosch, Brenau student (1931–1935), interview by Andrea Davis, typed transcript, 27 February 1995, p. 3; Box 1 of 1 (labeled "Dean of Women Files"), Brenau University Archives, Gainesville, Georgia.
98. *Handbook* (1945), 35.
99. Ibid., 42.
100. *Handbook* (1955), 29.
101. Ibid., 30.
102. *Handbook* (1965), 14.
103. Ibid., 50.
104. Ibid., 51.
105. Ibid.
106. Ibid.
107. Ibid., 53.

108. *Handbook* (1974), 25. One wonders what incident(s) prompted the handbook's language that women must wear "at least" a swim suit when sun bathing.
109. *Handbook* (1984), 17–18.
110. Horowitz, *Alma Mater*, 289.
111. Ibid.
112. "Advice to Boys," *Seminary Signal* (Gainesville, GA: Georgia Baptist Female Seminary), vol. 1, no. 6 (April, 1895), p. 13; Early Publications, Box 1 of 1, Brenau University Archives, Gainesville, Georgia.
113. *Handbook* (1925), 14.
114. Ibid.
115. *Faculty Journal (25 years)*, entry dated 14 March 1932. Converse College began permitting smoking a year after Brenau and other southern women's colleges likely followed suit. Jeffrey R. Willis, *Converse College* (Charleston, SC: Arcadia Publishing, 2001), 49
116. Elizabeth Wheeler (Lib) Thurmond, Brenau student (1929–1933), interviewer unknown, typed transcript, date unknown, p. 4; Box 1 of 1 (labeled "Dean of Women Files"), Brenau University Archives, Gainesville, Georgia
117. Ibid.
118. *Handbook* (1937), 24.
119. *Handbook* (1945), 29.
120. *Handbook* (1955), 23–24.
121. Ibid.
122. *Handbook* (1965), 44.
123. Letter written anonymously by a "Brenau Alumna" on 18 June 1964 to Dr. Josiah Crudup, President. Dr. Crudup Files, Box 29 of 40, Folder 4, Brenau University Archives, Gainesville, Georgia.
124. Brenau University, "Annual Security Report & Annual Fire Safety Report 2010," p. 50, http://intranet.brenau.edu/dnn/LinkClick.aspx?fileticket=B5x0QwmcaoE%3D&tabid=91 (accessed 10 May 2013).
125. Several northern women's colleges had apparently permitted smoking as early as the 1920s. Regarding Smith College, see Allison Lockwood, "Making of a president: Smith College's William Allan Neilson," *Daily Hampshire Gazette*, 8 May 2010. Medical historian Allan M. Brandt wrote that, "By the mid-1920s the faculty at Wellesley had reconsidered their opposition to smoking and opened Alumnae Hall for students' use. In 1925, Bryn Mawr College also opened smoking rooms to its students…Vassar and other women's colleges soon followed suit." Brandt

noted that, "By the late 1930s, most surveys at women's colleges confirmed that a majority of students were smokers." Allan M. Brandt, *The Cigarette Century The Rise, Fall, and Deadly Persistence of the Product That Defined America* (New York, NY: Basic Books, 2009), 65.
126. Walter Edward McNair, *Lest We Forget: An Account of Agnes Scott College* (Atlanta, GA: Tucker-Castleberry Printing, Inc., 1983), 125.
127. Mary Lynch Johnson, *A History of Meredith College: 2nd Ed.*(Raleigh, NC: Meredith College, 1972), 276.
128. *Anderson College Student Handbook for Women* (Anderson, SC: Anderson College, 1968), 53; available at Internet Archive, http://www.archive.org/stream/andersonhandbook1968#page/52/mode/2up/search/smoking (accessed 10 May 2013).
129. McCandless, *Past in the Present,* 123.
130. Ibid., 125.
131. "'Self-Governed Girls' is the Plan at Brenau," *Atlanta Constitution,* 31 July 1904, sec. C, p. 4. Also, Brenau only permitted students to enter town at certain times. Another 1904 rule read, "Pupils are allowed to visit the stores in the city for shopping purposes only on Thursdays and Fridays of each week."
132. Ibid.
133. *Faculty Journal (12 years),* entry dated 6 February 1912.
134. Ibid., entry dated 11 December 1914.
135. Ibid., entry dated 12 December 1922.
136. Ibid.
137. *Handbook* (1925), 13.
138. *Catalog* (1929), 13.
139. Mary Helen Hosch, Brenau student (1931–1935), interview by Andrea Davis, typed transcript, 27 February 1995, p. 3. Available in Box 1 of 1 (labeled "Dean of Women Files"), Brenau University Archives, Gainesville, Georgia.
140. *Handbook* (1925), 15.
141. Ibid., 17.
142. Ibid., 15.
143. Ibid.
144. Ibid., 16.
145. Ibid., 17.
146. *Handbook* (1937), 24.
147. Ibid.
148. Ibid.

149. *Faculty Journal (25 years)*, entry dated 2 March 1926.
150. Ibid., entry dated 1 February 1927.
151. Ibid.
152. Ibid., entry dated 6 October 1931.
153. Ibid., entry dated 1 November 1932.
154. *Handbook* (1937), 27.
155. *Faculty Journal (12 years)*, entries dated 23 May 1916, 20 April 1917, 16 January 1919, and 4 November 1919.
156. Ibid., entry dated 5 November 1922.
157. *Faculty Journal (25 years)*, entry dated 15 March 1923.
158. Ibid., entry dated 4 November 1924.
159. Ibid., entry dated 6 April 1926.
160. Ibid., entry dated 03 January 1928 and entry dated 14 January 1930.
161. *Handbook* (1937), 27.
162. *Faculty Journal (25 years)*, entry dated 27 May 1935.
163. Ibid., entry dated 2 February 1937.
164. *Handbook* (1945), 22.
165. Ibid.
166. *Handbook* (1955), 23.
167. *Handbook* (1945), 27. "Moving dates" apparently referred to outings to dinner, the cinema, etc., as opposed to dates held in Yonah Hall, which were confined to the parlor.
168. Mrs. J. Allen Webster, Brenau professor (1943–1946), interviewer unknown, typed transcript, date unknown, p. 2. Available in Box 1 of 1 (labeled "Dean of Women Files"), Brenau University Archives, Gainesville, Georgia.
169. *Handbook* (1945), 28.
170. Barbara Stockton, "'Y' Lights," *Alchemist* (Gainesville, GA: Brenau College), vol. XXXII, no. 3 (23 October 1945), p. 3.
171. Ibid.
172. *Handbook* (1955), 31.
173. Ibid.
174. *Handbook* (1965), 44–48.
175. *Handbook* (1974), 21–22.
176. *Handbook* (1984), 15.
177. "'Self-Governed Girls' is the Plan at Brenau," *Atlanta Constitution*, 31 July 1904, sec. C, p. 4.
178. *Faculty Journal (25 years)*, entries dated 4 December 1923 and 15 December 1923

Smoking, "Night Riding," & other Serious Offenses 371

179. Ibid., entry dated 1 February 1944.
180. *Handbook* (1965), 59.
181. *Faculty Journal (25 years)*, entry dated 7 December 1926.
182. *Faculty Journal (25 years)*, entry dated 4 October 1932.
183. "Pretty Brenau College Girl Accepts Telephone Proposal And Marries Football Star," *Atlanta Constitution*, 25 February 1913, p. 1.
184. *Handbook* (1974), 70.
185. *Faculty Journal (25 years)*, entry dated 1 February 1916.
186. Ibid.
187. *Handbook* (1925), 15.
188. *Faculty Journal (25 years)*, entry dated 2 March 1926.
189. *Handbook* (1937), 30.
190. Ibid., 30–34.
191. *Handbook* (1945), 28.
192. *Handbook* (1955), 23.
193. *Handbook* (1965), 37.
194. *Handbook* (1974), 26.
195. "Drug Committee to Lecture," *Alchemist* (Gainesville, GA: Brenau College), vol. LCI, no. 7 (23 February 1970), p. 8.
196. *Faculty Journal (25 years)*, entry dated 21 March 1927.
197. Ibid.
198. Ibid.
199. *Handbook* (1925), 17.
200. *Faculty Journal (25 years)*, entry dated 27 May 1935.
201. Ibid., entry dated 3 March 1942.
202. Ibid., entry dated 1 March 1927.
203. Ibid., entry dated 6 May 1930.
204. Ibid.
205. Ibid., entry dated 5 April 1932.
206. Ibid., entry dated 3 April 1934
207. Ibid., entry dated 2 February 1937.
208. Ibid., entries dated 7 November 1939 and 5 May 1942.
209. "Doris Dean," *Alchemist* (Gainesville, GA: Brenau College), vol. XXI, no. 9 (14 May 1935), p. 3.
210. Ibid.
211. *Bubbles* (1901), 57.

Chapter 7

"No Imitations of Masculine Sports"

'Physical Culture' at Brenau College

In speaking of the historical development of sports at college, historian John R. Thelin asserted that, "Although historians of higher education have often overlooked the fact, athletics were central to the campus culture."[1] Although doubtlessly true for most men's colleges as far back as the mid-nineteenth century, Thelin's generalization would often fail with early women's colleges, especially in the South. At these institutions, "athletics" in the conventional sense (i.e., competitive activities and sporting contests "that require physical skill and stamina") typically developed slowly.[2] This was especially true at southern women's colleges like Brenau. At such institutions, until well into the twentieth century, students generally came up short in negotiations with faculty members for athletics at their colleges. Conservative and paternalistic mindsets maintained by many southern educators denied women athletics and instead promoted something often called "physical culture." This generally amounted to little more than demure activities like rhythmic gymnastics exercises and calisthenics. Brenau embraced this, in essence thinking that young women needed coddling and protection from over exertion. This mindset would not change until at least the 1920s when students began negotiating successfully for sporting contests and intercollegiate athletics at their College. Yet, even well after the 1920s, vestiges of Brenau's anti-athletic mindset existed for decades—a testament, perhaps, to sheltering and paternalistic views left over from an earlier age.[3]

To place things into context at Brenau requires some background knowledge about the history of college athletics generally. Athletics and physical education occupy such a prominent position in the modern college experience that it is perhaps difficult to fully envision college without them. Despite this centrality, academic historians have generally overlooked college sport. There are relatively few scholarly studies of the development of sports and athletics in higher education. Instead, the field of sport history is mainly dominated by popular studies and trade books. Still, these works can provide some needed insight about the development of athletics in higher education.

Prior to about 1850, most colleges enrolled only men and simply did not emphasize athletics of any variety because they saw themselves as places for mental, not physical, exercise. Beginning around the second half of the nineteenth century, this began to change, albeit slowly. Inter-class contests that were often quite violent games of something resembling modern American football appeared at colleges throughout the country. Almost invariably in these contests, freshmen battled sophomores as juniors played seniors. Male college students also took up baseball and, later, basketball in the mid- to late-1800s. Other activities like track, tennis, and, in cooler climes, ice hockey came along later. Rules for all of these sports would be revised and refined over time. Games also evolved from being competitions between classes at a single college to become competitions between colleges. Harvard and Yale held the first intercollegiate contest (a regatta) in 1852 whereas Williams and Amherst played the first intercollegiate baseball game in 1859. As more colleges adopted more and different sports, competition increased and eventually became an accepted—even expected—part of the collegiate way of life.[4]

But it was largely a man's way of life for many years. Athletics (even of the "demure activities" variety) were initially slow in coming to college women. As late as the nineteenth century, many members of society—including many physicians—voiced objections against physical exertion for young women. In their book entitled *The Physician and Sexuality in Victorian America*, John and Robin Haller documented how the nineteenth-century scientific community depicted women as being physically inferior to men and afflicted with nervous disorders and conditions like "neurasthenia."[5] Frances B. Cogan echoed this finding. In *All-American Girl: The Ideal of Real Womanhood in Mid-Nineteenth-Century America*, she wrote that:

> According to popular tradition from earlier decades and from abroad, as well as "professional" medical opinion, women had a much more delicate nervous system than did men because of the peculiar function of their reproductive organs. Because of this, and a greater "natural" sensitivity, their fragile nervous systems were likely to be overstimulated or irritated, with disastrous results.[6]

Of course, this female condition precluded much physical exertion. Because many physicians deemed exercise unsuitable for women, competitive sports were out of the question. "Experts" voiced two primary concerns: "(1) competitive sport would damage the childbearing function, and (2) competitive sport would masculinize girls and women."[7] These mindsets retarded the development of women's college athletics for many years.

Like the development of competitive athletics, physical education for women college students evolved slowly. June A. Kennard, an historian of women in sport, observed that, "In the early and middle nineteenth century, Catharine Beecher had argued for the inclusion of physical training at all levels of education, but it was not until the 1870s and 1880s that this became a partial reality."[8] When exercise finally caught on for college women, Kennard indicated that it was "the expensive, private women's colleges" in the North that were "leaders in incorporating physical education into the curriculum."⁹ Nancy Theriot, a scholar of women's studies, observed that, "The first physical education for women involved gymnastics and calisthenics" because "it was easy to argue that these were within the limits of properly womanly activity."¹⁰ Not so much physical fitness but rather "gracefulness and ease of carriage, as well as better health, were the promised rewards of physical education for women before 1900."¹¹

In *Able-Bodied Womanhood: Personal Health and Social Change in Nineteenth-Century Boston*, Martha H. Verbrugge documented the development of physical education at one private women's college (Wellesley College just outside Boston) from 1875 to 1900. Concerned for student health, Verbrugge wrote that Wellesley outfitted a small gymnasium and required students to exercise daily. Early on, Wellesley prescribed "light calisthenics" for students, which consisted of "free movements and exercises performed by individuals or pairs, with simple apparatus, such as wands, dumbbells, and rings."¹² Over time, Wellesley adopted a somewhat more rigorous system of something called "Swedish gymnastics," which "involved both free movements and work on ropes, ladders, and portable floor apparatus."¹³ Eventually, outdoor exercise "became a part of physical education at the college, and soon prospered in the form of organized athletics."¹⁴ Beginning in the 1880s, Wellesley students played tennis, baseball, basketball, and engaged in rowing, among other sports, and actively sought to make themselves "able-bodied."¹⁵

Barbara Miller Solomon asserted that "several factors explain the surge in popularity of sports among students" at northern women's colleges like Wellesley.¹⁶ Images in popular magazines depicted more athletic women favorably, which impressed college women. Also, Solomon contended that, "for female collegians, physical exercise became a symbol of 'emancipated womanhood.'"¹⁷ Watching and playing sports, therefore, became liberating activities for students at some northern women's colleges in the late nineteenth century and the early twentieth century.

But this was typically less the case at women's colleges in the South. There, different mindsets (often more conservative and paternalistic) generally prevailed. Southern educators restricted women to only certain forms of "appropriate" physical activity for years after northern college women were already playing full-fledged sports. In place of a culture of athleticism, colleges like Brenau promoted "physical culture" along multiple dimensions.

One such dimension involved promoting general health, if not physicality. This seems to have been done mainly with an eye to reassuring parents that their daughters would remain well at Brenau. Early newspaper advertisements for Brenau and its predecessor the Georgia Baptist Female Seminary spoke to this. One advertisement reported of the College that, "Its location is practically perfect, being situated in a beautiful grove with ample grounds for out-door recreation."[18] Another indicated, "Gainesville, Ga., has been a noted health resort for years. Its water is as pure and clear as crystal; there is absolutely no malaria in its atmosphere; it has a splendid system of electric street cars; it has just put in a complete system of sewerage; it has an altitude of nearly 1,500 feet."[19] The advertisement trumpeted that, "Brenau College is located in this beautiful and healthful city; it has steam heat, electric lights, [and] an abundance of hot and cold water baths on every floor...".[20]

Early newspaper advertisements for Brenau indicated that even if—somehow—this perfect environment could not stave off illness, Brenau was prepared to treat any ailments that might manifest. Brenau published promotional materials in the *Atlanta Constitution* that indicated, "Dr. James W. Bailey, of Gainesville, who is one of the most distinguished physicians in the United States, is president of the board of advisers and one of the best friends of Brenau college."[21] Brenau asserted that:

> Dr. Bailey is the great specialist in the treatment of diseases of children and thousands of little sufferers from all over the south have made pilgrimages to Gainesville to receive the benefit of his skill. He is the physician to Brenau and it is a rare privilege for

the students of a school to be in the care of one so able in his profession and so eminent and so universally beloved. Dr. Bailey has made many large gifts to Brenau and he is warmly devoted to the institution.[22]

Such assertions would have gone a long way to convincing parents that Brenau was a healthy place to which they could entrust their daughters.

Indeed, parents would have been right to have been concerned. The late 1800s and early 1900s saw recurring epidemics of typhus, typhoid, scarlet fever, influenza, and yellow fever sicken thousands of people—children especially—throughout the country.[23] Georgia and her colleges were not exempt from outbreaks and so health was of interest. A turn of the century advertisement in the *Atlanta Constitution* for Wesleyan College in Macon, Georgia, acknowledged that disease impacted education in the region. The advertisement read, "Students detained by quarantine will be specially tutored as far as necessary" and claimed that "Present health conditions at Macon and Wesleyan are better than ever," which intimated that conditions had once suffered.[24] In 1909, Agnes Scott College suffered a "devastating typhoid epidemic" that left 30 students ill.[25] Brenau, too, had to deal with illness. For its 1905 opening, the College indicated that "A few places are being held for students who are detained by quarantine restrictions. Two young ladies from Mississippi were not allowed to leave the train at Gainesville by the state quarantine officials, but were carried to Seneca, S.C. and are compelled to remain there for ten days before being allowed to reenter Georgia."[26]

These sources indicate how Brenau's physical culture manifested itself even before students did anything physical. Yet, Brenau did not simply rely upon quarantine policy, a pleasant climate, and its top-notch physician to keep its students healthy. Christie Anne Farnham observed that very early concerns for health induced many southern women's colleges to require some form of light physical activity for students, most commonly walking. Brenau embraced this thinking, which had persisted into the late 1800s. Many early Brenau catalogs and informational materials described students walking around campus in pairs of two, at least, if not in lines by class, or taking in the invigorating air of the Appalachian Mountain foothills near Gainesville, Georgia, on excursions from campus, making this pastime an important part of the institution's physical culture.

Whereas walking did entail doing something physical, it was not, of course, true "physical education" simply because students required no instruction in walking. Neither was walking a thoroughly "athletic" activity inasmuch as Brenau did not expect students to truly exert themselves. Rather, young women at Brenau took a daily constitutional because the faculty and administration believed walking promoted health while not overtaxing students.

Brenau eventually supplemented mere walking with actual exercise—albeit of a very demure variety. The Baptist Female Seminary and, later, the College instituted a program specifically called "Physical Culture" for its students. The College bulletin of 1900 described the earliest components of this as being:

> Physical Training; Its Relation to Health and Expression. Development of Nervous Force. Exercises in Relation to the Nervous System. Poise, Personality, Psycho-Physical Culture. Development of Sympathy and Unity. Endurance. Refinement of the Entire Physical Person. Exercises to Overcome Defects. Marching. Repose, Strength, Dignity, Grace of Motion and Bearing in the Parlor, on the Street, or Platform.[27]

Brenau asserted that, "The education of the physical being has become a necessity. Every pupil in the school is required to participate in the Physical Culture Exercises, that by this training the body may become the true outward expression of the soul within."[28]

Although such a statement of philosophy might seem to be somewhat forward-thinking, the reality was different. In promoting physical culture, Brenau promoted light exercise, not "athletics" as the term is generally taken to mean. Around 1900, Brenau's faculty clearly preferred that students engage in such safe activities as "marching" and developing "grace of motion" over such more physical pastimes as running and ball-playing. Moreover, exercises were not to be undertaken at Brenau for the purpose of developing better, stronger, more physically-able bodies. Rather, up until at least the 1920s, Brenau's faculty and administration believed that light exercise was simply a proper way to tap into a woman's "soul within."

Other evidence supports the notion that Brenau's view of physical culture around the turn of the last century did not embrace much athleticism. This can be seen, for example, in Brenau's athletic facilities. At first blush, these seemed opulent. An article in the June 25, 1896, edition of the *Atlanta Constitution* focused on the growth and prosperity of the Georgia Baptist Female Seminary. In particular, much of the article described "the magnificent new building" of the Seminary that was partly funded by a $10,000 gift from the people of Gainesville. This new building housed a large auditorium and expanded music instruction facilities. The new building also contained Brenau's facilities for physical instruction. The article indicated, "Over the stage we find the gymnasium, a large room, fitted with modern appliances, and to be presided over by a teacher competent to instruct in their uses. Passing down a flight of stairs from the gymnasium we find ourselves in the large natatorium," which the article described as "a pool about four feet deep and 40 x 25 in size." [29] The pool was "surrounded by convenient dressing rooms and shower baths" and the pool water, as well as the room, was to be "heated in winter by means of steam pipes." [30] The article reported that, "This room will also be in charge of a teacher, who will see that no excess or imprudence will be indulged in."[31] Besides the pool, the gymnasium even had "a splendid bowling alley" adjoining the natatorium.[32]

Taken at face value, this article seems to describe facilities that might have rivaled the gymnasia of some much larger, male-dominated institutions of the day. Yet, a closer read of the article belies this. Despite impressions to the contrary, the Baptist Female Seminary's facilities were not designed to empower women athletically. Rather, the facilities only reinforced the institution's rather limited view about the scope of women's fitness. Contemporary descriptions of athletic facilities at major male institutions would have emphasized more strenuous exercise and a good deal of space for competitive athletics.[33] Brenau's gymnasium with its "modern appliances" referred to a place with dumbbells, hoops, wands, and other paraphernalia that constituted the standard fare of exercise in women's institutions in the South. Also, the natatorium was not built for strenuous swimming. At only four feet deep, it had to have been designed for standing rather than swimming, for engaging in something more akin to modern "water aerobics" than diving or logging laps. (See Figure 33.) Similarly, women using the bowling alley would have been unlikely to strain themselves in that activity. Finally, note that all student activity was overseen by an instructor whose job it was to ensure that "no excess or imprudence" would be indulged in. This was not a personal trainer encouraging the Brenau women to fitness by working them harder, longer; rather, this was a matron to ensure that the students did not work too hard.

Sources suggest that Brenau promoted the same stripe of physical culture in the early twentieth century that it had in the nineteenth. An advertisement in 1904 in the *Atlanta Constitution* read:

> So, on the tennis court or on the grounds for basket ball or in the classic shades of the campus, if a Brenau girl wishes to make the welkin ring [i.e., a very loud noise] with her happy voice or merry peals of laughter there is no solemn personage to look shocked, for the management knows that the girl's lungs are being expanded with every shout; that she is drinking in great draughts of the pure health-giving atmosphere; that the warm blood is pulsing to her finger tips and building her into a woman to whom existence will not be a burden. Under the same idea, Recreation Hall is all that its name implies. This hall is in the home building or dormitory. It is really a 'rotunda' . . . and is fully as large. It is the heart and

center of the dormitory and adjoins the large parlor, the dining room, the president's office, reception room, etc.[34]

As with advertisements about athletic facilities, at first glance, this ad might make Brenau appear to be physically progressive. This was not necessarily the case. Granted, the College now touted programs in tennis and basketball, bona fide sports which it lacked only years before. Yet, the College supported these activities because they were deemed acceptable and appropriate forms of activity for women that would not be overtaxing. Brenau officials went on to carefully assert that, "There is an athletic association at Brenau, but no feminine imitations of masculine sports are allowed. The girls play tennis and basket ball and never overstep the bounds of propriety in their games."[35] This reassurance would have doubtlessly been welcomed by many parents who would not have wanted their daughters' behavior to deviate wildly from how southern society expected young women to behave in 1904. Also, note that Brenau supported exercise only to ease a woman's existence. A somewhat more progressive view might have entailed making students able-bodied enough to live robust, active lives and not merely unburdened lives. Finally, note that the advertisement lauds "Recreation Hall" and not Brenau's gymnasium. The effect is to de-emphasize the availability of access to what athletic equipment Brenau did possess.

The job of limiting the activity of Brenau students fell to Brenau faculty members. As early as 1904, Florence M. Overton of the Emerson School, Boston, came to Brenau and served as both "Assistant in the School of Oratory" and "Director of Athletics," a title somewhat out-of-step with reality given what the College offered in the way of sport.[36] Rose Allen of the Brenau School of Oratory assisted Overton and oversaw physical activities at the College's "Chautauqua Gymnasium" (an outdoor tent gymnasium erected at summer camps held at Brenau).[37] The director's job was to "see that students of Brenau have an abundance of out-of-door exercise" because "Tennis, Basket Ball, Gymnastic Exercises, Boating and other games tend to develop the girl into a perfect physical woman."[38]

By 1906, Brenau boasted that it was, "one of the few institutions of the south that...employs a trained physical director, whose sole duty it is to see that its student do not overtax themselves in any way, taking care at the same time to see that all have enough work of the right kind to keep busy."[39] The College also assured parents that, "Every student is carefully examined at the opening of the school term and if she has any physical defect it is carefully noted, and her work is governed accordingly."[40]

These quotations from 1904 and 1906 talked about developing "the girl into a perfect physical woman" and of ensuring that students "do not overtax themselves in any way." Additionally, the faculty permitted Brenau students to only engage in certain prescribed activities, all of which were demure. This language indicated Brenau's continued concern at the time about young women overexerting themselves and shows the persistence of the institution's notions about physical culture.

Even as the College expanded its athletic offerings over the next few years, Brenau continued to focus on demure activities—when it focused on sports at all. The "Brenau Notes" revealed that, "The students in the fencing class are enthusiastic over their work, under the direction of Miss Jane Mitchell, who was teacher of Fencing at Emerson College last year."[41] The announcement described the activity as one might an academic subject, which seems to diminish its sporting character. By 1908, a "riding club" had been "formed by a number of the students, with Miss Brown and Miss Rohr as chaperones, and two afternoons in each week are spent in delightful and health-giving exercise."[42] The 1909 edition of the *Bubbles* elaborated on this club by relating in tongue-in-cheek fashion that its colors were "black and blue" and that its motto was "Hol' on! Don' go so fast," clear indicators that only modestly physical riding went on.[43] This same edition of the yearbook included photographs of the athletic club with around three dozen members and the tennis club with fourteen photographed members wearing long-sleeved, ankle-length, white dresses and hats. There were also two club basketball teams at Brenau that year, the "Tigers" and the "Trojans."[44] Each boasted only five members. That relatively few young women joined any of these sporting clubs around a time when Brenau enrolled over 300 students speaks to the general lack of emphasis placed on athletics at the College.[45] Still, at the same time, it is significant that any students joined at all and that the newspaper article related that students (not faculty or staff members) founded athletic clubs. This proves that some students sought athletic outlets and were willing to negotiate for these with College officials. This nascent student agency would later drive much athletic expansion at Brenau.

In 1910, the *Thirty-second Annual Catalogue of Brenau College-Conservatory* made no mention of formal course work in physical education. Instead, the catalog continued to emphasize physical culture over athleticism and mentioned a wooded park and a lake near the campus, surely excellent venues for hiking and rowing.[46] Additionally, the catalog mentioned the athletic club that all students were encouraged (though not required) to join and had this to say about physical culture specifically:

> Nothing is more important in the education of a young girl than her *physical* development. Brenau has always stressed this feature of its work, but during the coming year it proposes to lay greater emphasis than ever upon it.
>
> Each student is given a thorough physical examination by the director of the gymnasium, and she prescribes for her the kind of exercise which her physical condition indicates that she needs.[47]

No mention was made of what "greater emphasis" might entail or of when or how often the faculty and staff expected students to exercise. The catalog did indicate that, "No one is excused from these exercises except upon the advice of a physician or the director of the gymnasium."[48] Still, it is worth noting that in the kind of physical culture promoted at Brenau, only relatively low-impact forms of exercise like walking and rowing ever received anything approaching sanction—and this was true for a student only after she had undergone a thorough physical. The College clearly continued to give women little credit for having sturdy constitutions.

Curricular changes would come after 1910 that would illustrate that Brenau made more effort to include physical education in the curriculum. And, clearly, this came with the blessing of the College itself because Brenau hired personnel devoted to physical education. Still, this did not signal a grand change in mindset for the College. Much institutional concern still lingered on things like graceful carriage, refined movement, and good posture—markers of genteel social class. Brenau, in early post-Victorian southern fashion, still yearned to produce graceful young women.

Examining the College catalogs reveals that demure activities like walking and rowing remained largely the standards in Brenau's physical culture right on through the nineteen-teens and into the 1920s. From the institution's inception, regular outings in North Georgia had occurred every year as many of the student body went to places like Tallulah Falls in the spring and to the town of Dahlonega in the fall.[49] A 1924 edition of the *Alchemist* reported that, "A very happy party of students and several members of the faculty spent the week-end at Lake Burton. Fishing, possum-hunting and hiking whiled away the hours."[50] Another lake nearby Brenau also afforded chances for recreation. An article in the *Atlanta Constitution* reported that, "It is the intention of Brenau to have its own boats for its students on this beautiful sheet of water and to give its girls the benefit of the healthful and delightful exercise of rowing. A regatta is already planned for next spring."[51] Demure on-campus opportunities for recreation also abounded at Brenau by the nineteen-twenties. The December 3, 1924, edition of the *Alchemist* reported that Brenau's Physical Education Club presented a "Gymnastic Exhibition." The older club members planned and made costumes for each segment of the event and taught younger students their movements. The presentation consisted of an "Indian Club drill," "German Gymnasium tactics," an "English Folk dance," a "Swedish gymnastic lesson," and an "apparatus number."[52] The emphasis of such outdoor activities as hiking and rowing and the events of the gymnastics exhibition attest to a rather limited, almost turn-of-the-century view of women's athletics on the part of Brenau that was several years behind the times compared to some northern women's colleges.

A continued emphasis in Brenau's physical culture on "Play Days" or "Field Days" well into the twentieth century also attests to this view. Editions of the *Alchemist* indicated that these took place at the College long after many northern institutions had largely begun to diminish such traditions in favor of intercollegiate athletics. In these events, College officials expected students to engage in friendly, low-key competition with one another in various activities and games. (See Figure 34.) The aim of these field days was not to make women physically stronger or to prepare them for the competitive work-a-day world. Rather, women's colleges like Brenau merely expected their students to get some light exercise and to further bond with classmates while honing feminine virtues like supporting others and cooperating. In speaking of the end result of practices like field days at southern women's colleges, historian Amy Thompson McCandless concluded that, "In sports as in other social activities, women were to be ladies."[53]

Perhaps some of the best evidence for Brenau's preference for producing graceful ladies as opposed to athletes comes from a relatively innocuous source: the College's dress code, which had been an integral part of the physical culture of the institution from the start. Since the College's inception, there was always a "required costume" for gym class. Conservative dress that was not particularly conducive to vigorous athletic activities had ever been the order of the day and would remain so—remarkably—even into the College's fourth decade. Brenau's official catalog of 1930 described the gym uniform simply as a "white middy, black bloomers, black tie, black hose, white or black rubber soled shoes."[54] The 1937-1938 edition of the *Brenau Girl* student handbook elaborated a great deal more on the proper dress for the College's young women. The handbook read:

The proper costume for the various activities in which the Brenau students engage is as follows:

> Gymnasium costume for fall and winter is white middy, blue bloomers, blue socks and rubber soled shoes. For going to and from the gym in gym or swimming costume, a long coat or slicker (but not a transparent slicker), must be worn. Shoes and hose must be worn to and from gym when going swimming. Girls from Lanier, Van Hoose, Oglesby and the Phi Mu and Delta Zeta House need not wear coats providing they go the back way and not along the street. No girl should appear on the street with gym suits or bathing suits unless a long coat is worn. This is a campus offense. Every girl entering the pool must take a shower and wear a cap.
>
> Tennis may be played in sport dresses with full skirts. Track pants are not to be worn on tennis courts or anywhere, except on athletic fields or in gym, only as specified by a Physical Education teacher or team captain.
>
> Horseback riders should dress in habits, and hat and boots, or in low heeled shoes, wool hose, not silk, knickers, shirts, coats, or coat-sweaters, not slip-on sweaters, and hats. Every rider must have a ticket for each ride. These are purchased from the bursar and presented to the superintendent before the ride.
>
> Hikers to New Holland or anywhere on the streets must wear skirts. Hikers in the woods may wear knickers, but not track pants. Playground and Public School teachers of Physical Education may wear knickers and a long coat, or sport dress, with full skirt. Low heels must be worn during playground and public school teaching.[55]

Even as late as the 1930s, official College publications continued to stress demure activities like swimming, tennis, horseback riding, and hiking. And, for these activities, fitness clearly took a back seat to fashion. Brenau expected its students to dress conservatively, like proper ladies, no matter what the circumstances, even if doing so might do something like inhibit one's range of motion or physicality.

Although sources like the College dress code suggest that the notion of physical culture prevailed at Brenau for many years, things would change. Beginning in the 1920s, student handbooks indicated that athletics in the conventional sense were emerging at the College even as Brenau maintained its greater emphasis on physical culture. "Play days" would continue for years at the College just as they would at northern schools, but additional sporting outlets emerged. During this decade, Brenau women could earn varsity letters for participating on winning inter-class competition teams in such sports as basketball, volleyball, and baseball or for passing a rigorous swimming test.[56] In 1927, Brenau participated in the "first intercollegiate game that a girls' college in Georgia has ever played" when the institution's basketball team beat the women's team of the North Georgia Agricultural College by a score of 14 to 9.[57] By 1930, Brenau had five physical education instructors on its faculty. The department required all students to take four years of P.E., which consisted of two hours of instruction and two hours of outdoor activity each week. The catalog indicated, though, that "this work is not counted for college credit."[58] This would change as, by 1940, students could actually major in P.E. and earn a Bachelor of Science in Physical Education degree at Brenau.[59] Also, during both the 1930s and 1940s, a plethora of images in the student yearbooks attested to the fact that Brenau women were participating in many sports, some still rather demure, but others less so. The *Bubbles* showed women riding horses; canoeing; playing soccer, baseball, and basketball; attending badminton class; dueling in fencing; practicing archery; and playing Ping-Pong. The yearbooks also depicted young women brandishing field hockey sticks and golf clubs as well.[60]

Whereas primary sources suggest that actual student participation in sports at Brenau could wax or wane somewhat in any given year (as occurred particularly around the war years), the general trajectory of the institution heading into mid-century and beyond was away from notions of physical culture and toward the inclusion of more athletics at Brenau. As is described in the next chapter, by the twenty-first century, students had negotiated successfully with College personnel for sport and athletics had assumed a prominent place at the University. A number of competitive—or, in many cases, even nationally-ranked—intercollegiate sport teams, a vigorous intramural program, and a curriculum that emphasized physical fitness complemented the institution's academic programs. This would be a far cry from the Brenau of over a century ago that avoided athletics to promote instead a view of physical culture for its students.

Notes

1. Thelin, *History of American Higher Education*, 181.
2. Dictionary.com, s.v. "athletics," http://dictionary.reference.com/browse/athletics (accessed 27 March 2013).
3. Or, as suggested by Brenau's former President, Dr. John Burd, the College's stance may have just as arguably represented, "the idea of college being [in the main] academic in orientation." Comments to author, n.d., but communicated in edits to manuscript draft in 2013.
4. For an overview of scholarly materials pertaining to athletics, see Steven A. Riess, "The Historiography of American Sport," *OAH Magazine of History*, vol. 7 (summer, 1992), http://maghis.oxfordjournals.org/content/7/1/10.extract (accessed 27 March 2013). For more about the history of athletics in college, see James Michener, *Sports in America* (New York, NY: Random House, 1976); Wells Twombly, *200 Years of Sports in America: A Pageant of a Nation at Play* (New York, NY: McGraw Hill, 1976); Douglas A. Noverr and Lawrence Ziewacz, *The Games They Played: Sports in American History, 1865–1980* (Chicago, IL: Nelson-Hall, 1983); and Betty Spears and Richard A. Swanson, *History of Sport and Physical Education in the United States. 3rd ed.* (Dubuque, IA: Wm. C. Brown, 1988).
5. See "Chapter One: The Nervous Century" in John S. Haller and Robin M. Haller, *The Physician and Sexuality in Victorian America* (Urbana, IL: University of Illinois Press, 1974).
6. Frances B. Cogan, *All-American Girl: The Ideal of Real Womanhood in Mid-Nineteenth-Century America* (Athens, GA: University of Georgia Press, 1989), 29.
7. June A. Kennard, "Review Essay: The History of Physical Education," *Signs: Journal of Women*, vol. 2, no. 4 (summer, 1977): 841.
8. Ibid.
9. Ibid.
10. Nancy Theriot, "Towards a New Sporting Ideal: The Women's Division of the National Amateur Athletic Federation," *Frontiers: A Journal of Women Studies*, vol. 3, no. 1 (spring, 1978): 1.
11. Ibid.
12. Martha H. Verbrugge, *Able-Bodied Womanhood: Personal Health and Social Change in Nineteenth-Century Boston* (New York, NY: Oxford University Press, 1988), 149.

13. Ibid., 151.
14. Ibid., 155.
15. Ibid.
16. Solomon, *In the Company of Educated Women*, 103.
17. Ibid., 104.
18. Display Advertisement—No Title, *Atlanta Constitution*, 24 July 1904, p. 12.
19. "The Location of a School," *Atlanta Constitution*, 26 July 1904, p. 2.
20. Ibid.
21. "Health is Well Cared For," *Atlanta Constitution*, 31 July 1904, sec. C, p. 5.
22. Ibid.
23. For more about diseases in the United States in the late nineteenth and early twentieth centuries, see Gerald N. Grob, *The Deadly Truth: A History of Disease in America* (Boston, MA: Harvard University Press, 2002).
24. Display Advertisement—No Title, *Atlanta Constitution*, 12 September 1905, p. 5.
25. Walter Edward McNair, *Lest We Forget: An Account of Agnes Scott College* (Atlanta, GA: Tucker-Castleberry Printing, Inc., 1983), 47-48.
26. "Brenau Enrolls Many Students," *Atlanta Constitution*, 24 September 1905, p. 2.
27. *Catalog* (1900), 60 – 61.
28. Ibid., 61.
29. "Georgia Female Seminary," *Atlanta Constitution*, 25 June 1896, p. 9
30. Ibid.
31. Ibid.
32. Ibid.
33. For example, Stanford University began construction of its gymnasium shortly after 1900. A description of the facility read, "The gymnasium on the second floor has 10,000 square feet of space for a complete equipment of apparatus...At the rear are special rooms for boxing, fencing and wrestling. On the same floor is a laboratory for special investigation work with the gymnasts and athletes...In the annex to the main building will be a ten-lap running track, space for practice of athletics, baseball and football. In the rear of the building will be located the tennis courts, a football gridiron, oval for field sports and a baseball diamond. The completed building will cost over $1,000,000." "News Items in General: Stanford's New Gymnasium," *American Gymnasia and Athletic Record, Volumes 1–2* (Boston, MA: American Gymnasia Company, 1904), 22. Sadly, a subsequent edition of this publication indicated that

the near-finished facility was destroyed by the Great California Earthquake of April 18, 1906, and the subsequent fires that raged around San Francisco. Ibid., 194.
34. "Campus Rings with Shout and Laughter," *Atlanta Constitution*, 31 July 1904, sec. C, p. 5.
35. Ibid.
36. "A Day at Brenau," *Atlanta Constitution*, 31 July 1904, sec. C, p. 4.
37. Ibid.
38. Display Advertisement—No Title, *Atlanta Constitution*, 21 August 1904, p. 7.
39. Display Advertisement—No Title, *Atlanta Constitution*, 12 July 1906, p. 8.
40. Ibid.
41. "Brenau Notes," *Atlanta Constitution*, 9 December 1906, sec. G, p. 5.
42. "Brenau Notes," *Atlanta Constitution*, 1 November 1908, sec. A, p. 3.
43. Brenau College, *Bubbles* (Gainesville, GA; Brenau College, 1909), no page number. Hereafter, references to this source are indicated as "*Bubbles* (1909)."
44. Ibid.
45. *Thirty-second Annual Catalogue of Brenau College-Conservatory*, 1910, vol. 1, no. 2 (Gainesville, GA: Brenau College, 1910), 59–60; available in the Brenau University Archives, Gainesville, Georgia.
46. *Catalog* (1910), 59 – 60.
47. Ibid., 63.
48. Ibid.
49. "Campus Rings with Shout and Laughter," *Atlanta Constitution*, 31 July 1904, sec. C, p. 5.
50. "Athletics," *Alchemist* (Gainesville, GA: Brenau College), vol. 12, no. 6 (3 December 1924), p. 3.
51. "A Day at Brenau," *Atlanta Constitution*, 31 July 1904, sec. C, p. 4.
52. "Athletics," *Alchemist* (Gainesville, GA: Brenau College), vol. 12, no. 6 (3 December 1924), p. 3.
53. McCandless, *Past in the Present*, 148.
54. *Catalog* (1929), 81.
55. *Handbook* (1937), 45–46.
56. *Official Hand-Book of Information, 1925 – 1926* (Gainesville, GA: Brenau College, 1925), 23; available in the Brenau University Archives, Gainesville, Georgia.
57. "Brenau College To Meet N.G.A.C. Basketball Team," *Atlanta Constitution*, 11 February 1927, p. 11.

"No imitations of masculine sports"

58. *Brenau College Catalogue, 1929–1930*, 30.
59. *Brenau College Catalogue, 1939–1940, v. XXXI, n.3* (Gainesville, GA: Brenau College, 1939), 108; available in the Brenau University Archives, Gainesville, Georgia.
60. Brenau College, *Bubbles* (Gainesville, GA; Brenau College, 1943), 107. Hereafter, references to this source are indicated as "*Bubbles* (1943)."

Chapter 8

Bringing Home the Gold[en Tigers]

Establishing and Advancing Athletics at Brenau

During the first decades of the twentieth century, nothing approaching "athletics" (as the term is conventionally given to mean) really existed at Brenau College. Rather, the institution only supported "physical culture" for its students. This consisted strictly of demure exercises, like gymnastics, walking, or rowing—activities that Brenau's faculty and administration deemed "suitable" for women. But beginning in the 1920s, Brenau students began to prevail in their negotiations with the faculty over things physical. Students gained the ability to participate in bona fide on-campus and intercollegiate sporting events and enjoyed more physical education in the College curriculum. Still, despite student efforts in negotiating for activities, it would be many decades before Brenau supported athletics to a robust degree.

Since the College's founding, many Brenau students and some faculty members were apparently enthusiastic for athletics. Brenau women frequently cheered on local men's sports teams. An early edition of the *Atlanta Constitution* reported that on one November day in 1904, "Over 1,500 people witnessed the game of football this afternoon at Chattahoochee park between the North Georgia Agricultural college team from Dahlonega and the Stone Mountain team. Brenau college [sic] witnessed the game in force and added great beauty to the assemblage."[1] Dr. Pearce also offered the use of Brenau's grounds to a Gainesville amateur baseball team.[2] Brenau students frequently cheered on athletes at Gainesville's Riverside Military Academy as well. In one case, "Brenau was represented by quite a number of the fair sex" at a football game one rainy September afternoon in 1912 when Riverside defeated Boys' High School.[3] Also in 1912, several Brenau students took a train ride to Athens, Georgia, to watch sporting events at the University of Georgia.[4]

But some Brenau women did more than merely watch and cheer. In November of 1903, the *Atlanta Constitution* reported that "Every afternoon the grounds surrounding the college present a lively scene when the basket ball teams are playing in one place, the baseball game going on in another and the tennis court is alive with enthusiastic players."[5] One student author at Brenau described the College's early athletic facilities in positively reverent tones in a passage published in the 1908 edition of the *Bubbles*, Brenau's student yearbook. The passage read:

> Our gymnasium is located at the topmost part of Brenau. We're the highest birds on the whole roost. We're first in everything. When the sun appears over the hills of Habersham the tennis courts are dotted with rosy girls carrying rackets ready for the fight. Over the athletic field fence a basketball comes flying bringing a message of industry from the other side. The gymnasium room is the seat of all good times, of feasts and dances, after the teachers are safely in their rooms. What stories could the old room tell if words were possible. Apparatus lines its walls. Rings knock your head invitingly as you march beneath them. Our horse is a rival to the Kentucky thoroughbreds. It can beat any horse—standing still. We grow tall by work on ladders. Some girl is continually

hanging and praying to grow tall. If you are too large Gym will make you small.[6]

The glowing passage concluded, "A remedy for all evils is here. Here, too, is found the fountain of eternal youth with Miss Lansing as the goddess who guards the sacred 'spring.'"[7]

This passage bespoke both student enthusiasm for athletics and the continuing preoccupation on the part of Brenau officials with exercise in moderation—as opposed to athletics—for students. In the passage, students march and use rings, ladders, and a tumbling horse—in other words, they satisfy the faculty and staff preference and engage in moderate calisthenics as opposed to vigorous exercise. Yet, at the same time, the passage indicated that the students were negotiating their own version of athletic space. Young women enthusiastically played tennis and basketball instead of just performing calisthenics. Moreover, Brenau students even made use of the gymnasium when the teachers were out of sight, no doubt so that they could engage in precisely the "excess or imprudence" College personnel decried.

Of course, playing tennis and basketball entailed competition. Although this was once frowned upon by women's colleges, attitudes would change. Nancy Theriot noted that:

> While the idea of women's athletics began to spread to most women's colleges and to co-educational institutions, the program itself was changing. Before World War I, games had replaced gym exercise as the focus of physical education for women. The instructors justified the switch by pointing out all the virtues women would learn through games—sportsmanship, courage, team spirit—which were seen as being previously inaccessible to them. The gym teachers argued that these were human, not male, characteristics and that women should be trained in them.[8]

Helen Horowitz noted that a few games, particularly basketball, captivated students at the New England women's colleges in the early twentieth century. Then, women's intercollegiate athletics were uncommon, but intra-school competition emerged at most women's colleges. This was true at Brenau. A 1906 edition of the "Brenau Notes" column in the *Atlanta Constitution* reported that, "A match game of basket ball was played Monday afternoon between the Brenau School of Oratory team and the Brenau Athletic Club team. The score was 15 to 13, in favor of the Oratory team."[9] The winning team "was tendered an oyster supper by the Brenau School of Oratory" and later in the week both teams were "entertained by Miss Nellie White, the instructor in gymnastics."[10] Though it was hardly "March Madness," humble games like this still signaled the emergence of competitive athletics at Brenau in the conventional sense.

By the next decade, various photographs in the student yearbooks indicated that Brenau sported volleyball teams and "Base-ball" teams for the several classes, which competed with each other on campus.[11] There was also an annual "Track and Field Day" held at the College. A 1908 edition of the "Brenau Notes" indicated that, "Two basketball teams have been organized by the Athletic Club and on last Monday afternoon a match game was played between the 'Tigers' and the 'Trojans,' the 'Tigers' gaining the victory."[12] Other later basketball players were, apparently, somewhat less enthusiastic about the game. Brenau's student newspaper, the *Alchemist*, reported in 1919 that "Some complaints have been made by the authorities in charge of the Senior Basketball [team] to the effect that the Senior's time for practice rolls around every week...but no actors or only a few ever turn up."[13] Apparently, this problem was not unique to the senior class. In an effort to increase participation, the *Alchemist* staff wrote, "This failure to report for practice applies also to other classes. Everybody fall in and show us what you can do."[14]

By 1920, Brenau supplemented these extracurricular athletic activities with more formalized instruction in physical education. The College had two professors of "Physical Training" who were both graduates of the New Haven Normal School of Gymnastics.[15] There was also an "Elementary Course" and an "Advanced Course" in Physical Training for students to enroll in. The former focused on outdoor games like basketball, baseball, and volleyball, as well as hikes and indoor games like gymnastics. The latter included what the elementary course did as well as track and field activities like running, the shot put, and pole vaulting and the use of "apparatus work" in gymnastics. Horseback riding as well as private work in tennis and swimming were available for a fee.[16] Students in Brenau's School of Oratory had more physical training options than students in the literary department. This was because being part of dramatic productions, which is what oratory students studied to do, could be a very physical task and so required physical preparation. In addition to the material in the elementary and advanced courses, oratory students played at field hockey, fencing, and heavy apparatus work in gymnastics. Oratory students also underwent "Expressive Physical Training," which included work on posture and gesturing, and studied pantomime.[17]

Although mere movement as a means to improve health still existed at the College in the formal curriculum in the 1920s, more athletic activities surfaced outside of the formal curriculum. For example, a faculty minutes book entry from the year 1923 mentioned that Brenau held an "Annual Track Meet" on campus.[18] This increased number of athletic activities was further demonstrated by an expanded role for Brenau's Athletic Association. The 1925 student handbook indicated, "Any student is a member of the Athletic Association upon payment of $1.00 which must be paid at the regular pay day. This entitles her to the use of the tennis courts, basket ball field, all A. A. property (balls, etc.) and to the right to receive honors and emblems awarded by A. A."[19] The association's governing body largely had students as governors. The Athletic Council consisted of "the Director of Physical Education, the officers of the Association, and four other students to be chosen by the Association."[20]

By 1925–1926, Brenau's student handbook indicated that the association encouraged outright competition among students. The handbook listed the following athletic contests at Brenau:

Basket Ball—For class championship.

> Tennis—Doubles and singles for class championship.
>
> Swimming Meet—Interclass meet in fall and spring.
>
> Volley Ball—Interclass tournament in the fail.
>
> Base-ball—For class championship.[21]

Photographs in the 1925 edition of the *Bubbles* also bore out that Brenau women occasionally played the less commonplace sports of field hockey and soccer on class teams. Top athletes could earn the coveted varsity letter. At men's colleges, this was typically done by playing on an intercollegiate team sport. Lacking as they largely did intercollegiate athletics, women's colleges like Brenau devised different schemes to reward their best athletes. The handbook indicated that:

> The members of the championship basket ball team and such members of the scrub [i.e., non-champions] as have played in four halves of a victorious interclass game receive their B's.
>
> The tennis champions in singles and doubles receive the B. Also the winners of the standard track events receive a B. To each member of the winning team in the volley ball a B is awarded.
>
> In swimming the B shall be awarded for the highest number of credits, based on a chart including dives, strokes for form, and speed.[22]

The handbook also cautioned students that, "The wearing of all insignia and letters are strictly limited to those earned in athletics."[23] Accompanying individual honors were class honors. The handbook read that, "To the class winning the greatest number of points during the year a loving cup is presented."[24]

Tangible evidence of Brenau's growing openness to women's athletics is also revealed by changes to the College swimming pool. Brenau was now letting women get in over their heads. The once shallow pool had been replaced by one deep enough to dive in and long enough to swim laps in. The 1925 student handbook indicated that Brenau's Athletic Association recognized three grades of swimmers. "Elementary" swimmers received an "An orange felt shield" providing they could:

> Swim forty yards, or once up and down the pool, any stroke. Do one front dive in good form—standing, running or shallow dive. Do the life-saving kick on the back with arms folded.[25]

"Proficient" swimmers received a bar decoration for their shield and were those who could:

> Swim twice up and down the pool, or forty yard any two strokes. Do three dives as follows: Two front dives, and a choice of any dive, not of the above. Stay up in the water five minutes, without touching the sides or bottom of the pool. Dive from the surface of water and touch bottom of pool.[26]

"Expert" swimmers could:

> Swim one hundred and sixty yards, or eight times the length of the pool, any four strokes. Do ten to fifteen plain and fancy dives to show ability. Stand up in water ten minutes without touching sides or bottom of pool. Dive from surface of water and bring up an object weighing at least eight pounds. Knowledge of all breaks and carries in life-saving. Plunging, at least a knowledge of "how to plunge." Undress in seven feet of water and swim ashore. Swim length of pool under water.[27]

Expert swimmers received a varsity letter "B" in recognition of their accomplishments. Like other women's colleges, Brenau stressed swimming as much as it did because society saw the sport as being both suitably feminine and, at the same time, practical. Importantly, Brenau's rigorous expert swimmer requirements prove that the College acknowledged that at least some women could perform exceptional athletic feats.

By the nineteen-twenties, Brenau's most capable athletes desired to perform their feats against rival colleges. This decade saw the first mention of intercollegiate athletics at Brenau. The College had adopted the trappings of an intercollegiate competitor many years earlier as it acquired various fight songs, school colors (black and gold), and a school mascot (the "Golden Tiger"). Yet, Brenau had never competed in an intercollegiate contest, something it would first contemplate doing during this decade.

In this respect, Brenau did not really stand out from other southern women's colleges of its day. Theriot wrote that:

> With the introduction of games into physical education departments, women began to compete against each other in basketball, tennis, field hockey, and rowing. Intercollegiate competition was not well organized, however, and usually existed only between traditional rivals or schools of close proximity. Even in colleges where such competition took place, however, intramural games were always the dominant activity in women's physical education programs.[28]

Other historians have gone so far as to say that intercollegiate competition between women was actually discouraged outright. Historian Amy Thompson McCandless observed that, "by the twenties, physicians began to worry that the aggressive nature of athletic events might pose a threat to the feminine physique and psyche" just as others "noted that competitive sports created belligerent behaviors."[29] Many women's college officials, therefore, generally shunned the aggression, commercialism, and exclusivity that characterized men's college sports. Instead of encouraging the development of women's intercollegiate athletics, McCandless wrote that women's colleges "were discouraged from seeking publicity, going on road trips, and rewarding talented individuals at the expense of less athletic participants."[30]

Brenau certainly created its share of on-campus athletic activities in lieu of intercollegiate matchups. By the 1920s, students had convinced the faculty and the administration to accommodate intercollegiate competition where many contemporary "experts" elsewhere would not. To some degree, this bucked a national trend and made Brenau a trailblazing institution, at least by southern standards. The *Faculty Journal for Twenty-five Years*, which was the minute book of the Brenau faculty meetings from about 1920 to 1945, contains this entry from February 5, 1924:

> The Student Union submits a paper informing the faculty of its unanimous approval of intercollegiate athletics, and implying that the Student Body would be glad to have the faculty commit itself, in principle, to the athletic program which the students have in mind. A motion to this effect is carried (by a vote of 15 to 9), but with the distinct understanding that this action on the part of the Faculty does not carry with it permission for Brenau students to accept any specific challenge until the matter has been passed upon by the Executive Dept. or by a Faculty committee.[31]

About a month later, Brenau had booked its first game. The *Faculty Journal* reported:

> March 3, 1925: On motion, specific consent is given for Howard College basket ball team to come to our home grounds and play an intercollegiate game—the date to be determined later and the details to be subject to the approval of our Discipline Committee.[32]

For reasons unknown, the game apparently never took place. It would be another two years before Brenau scheduled another intercollegiate sporting event.

The February 11, 1927, edition of the *Atlanta Constitution* covered Brenau's first actual intercollegiate game. The article read:

> Brenau college [sic] will enter a new era in her athletic career with the basket ball game against the co-eds of of [sic] N.G.A.C. [North Georgia Agricultural College] at Dahlonega, Ga. This will mark the first intercollegiate game that a girls' college in Georgia has ever played. The two teams will meet Saturday afternoon,

February 12, at 2:30 o'clock at Dahlonega. A return game will be played at Gainesville February 26.[33]

The article continued, addressing the propriety of the game. It stated, "The question of intercollegiate athletics has been before the administrators of the colleges for women for many years, but before this time it was dismissed as inadvisable."[34] To this, Brenau's President Pearce responded:

> It is a moot question whether there should be intercollegiate athletics for women. By allowing Brenau to meet N.G.A.C. in a basketball contest, I am not presuming to settle the question. It is an experiment, the outcome of which will be of interest to all southerners engaged in education for women.[35]

The experiment would be witnessed by "The Physical Education club, members of the athletic association, representatives from the faculty and a group of interested Gainesville people," who would accompany the Brenau team to Dahlonega.[36] The article indicated that Brenau took the contest very seriously as "with the able direction of Miss Louise Howarth, director in physical education, and the coaching of Rhett Turnipseed, athletic director for the Pacolet mill at New Holland, first and second string squads have been selected and carefully drilled."[37]

The preparation paid off. The *Constitution* reported that Brenau's varsity basketball team "defeated the Co-Eds of N.G.A.C. by a score of 14 to 9" in the first game.[38] The margin of victory in the return game played at Gainesville was even larger. The *Constitution* reported that, "the Brenau varsity had the lead through the game, and soon ran up a large score which at the end of the game stood 56 to 7."[39] Brenau was gracious in victory and a good host. The *Constitution* reported that, "Following the game, a reception was given for the visitors in the Physical Education club room, where sandwiches sand [sic] punch were served. Prior to the game they were guests of the college at a luncheon."[40]

Whether Brenau considered the experiment a success is unclear. What is clear is that in the late nineteen-twenties, Brenau's faculty and staff members were not all behind intercollegiate competition in the first place. The vote to permit such competition was hardly unanimous. Also, Dr. Pearce's "experimental" words were anything but a solid endorsement of intercollegiate competition. Still, several editions of the *Bubbles* indicated that the College had a varsity basketball team through the early 1930s, which would seem to indicate the Brenau administration's willingness to continue intercollegiate play at student urging.[41] Also, photographs in various editions of the *Bubbles* yearbook indicated that the College also had a pair of cheerleaders in the early 1930s as well. While not ironclad evidence that Brenau supported the idea of intercollegiate competition, cheerleaders were something a college would probably not need unless it competed against other schools. Even so, nothing else about intercollegiate sports—including information like schedules or win/loss records—appears in either the College yearbooks, the faculty minutes, college correspondence, or in the few existing editions of the *Alchemist* that remain from this decade. In other words, there is no evidence that Brenau's varsity basketball team actually *played* anybody after their games against North Georgia. Moreover, by 1937, the *Bubbles* no longer featured the varsity basketball squad in pictures. Instead, when it came to athletics, photographic spreads describing inter-class competition predominated. Each class in 1937 had a volleyball team and a basketball team. Also, several students played tennis and there was even a six woman swimming club—but no more varsity basketball team.[42] Several decades would pass before Brenau's materials again mentioned intercollegiate athletics.

Exactly why intercollegiate athletics died out at Brenau during the 1930s is something of a mystery. The reason may have simply been that Brenau students found inter-class "play" or "field days" to be more fun. Alternatively, it is conceivable that, given their hesitancy, Brenau officials might have caved in to some negative sentiment regarding women's athletics and scrapped the program. Intercollegiate athletics might also have failed because there was a dearth of female opponents for Brenau athletes to play. Outside of the North Georgia Agricultural College in

Dahlonega, no other coeducational colleges of any size were really close enough to Gainesville to be easily traveled to. A logical opponent for Brenau might have been all-women's Agnes Scott College in Decatur, Georgia, which was only about fifty miles away from Gainesville, but Agnes Scott was not as experimental with athletics as Brenau in the early part of the century. A December 17, 1922, article in the *Atlanta Constitution* indicated that "Agnes Scott...in basketball, as in hockey, has class teams only."[43] Perhaps an even more plausible explanation for the elimination of intercollegiate sports at Brenau early in the century was a monetary one. Like colleges everywhere, Brenau was hit hard by the Great Depression. It is conceivable that Brenau simply could not afford to expend time, money, and energy on intercollegiate athletics during a difficult economy. Finally, the cessation of intercollegiate athletics at Brenau around 1930 may have been part of a larger national trend. According to one pair of scholars, it was none other than women physical educators themselves that "successfully eliminated women's intercollegiate sport in all but 12 percent of colleges" around this time.[44] These educators "preferred some competition for all rather than intensive competition for a few" and advocated "Play Days, Sports Days, telegraphic meets, and intramural sports" as the "correct outlets for the athletic girl to display her skills."[45]

The 1928 *Bubbles* indicated that although intercollegiate competition may have been starting to falter, competition between Brenau students was as alive as ever. By the late 1920s, athletic competition went on between some of the state clubs at Brenau and saw young women from Georgia playing various games against students from Virginia, the Carolinas, the Northeast, and elsewhere. Also, photographs in the *Bubbles* yearbooks indicated that Brenau students were playing newer sports in greater numbers. Soccer had arrived to campus by now in earnest as the juniors were champions in that sport. Field hockey, too, was being played more regularly. There was also a chapter of Delta Psi Kappa, the "National Honorary and Professional Physical Education" society, which had organized at the College. The establishment of such an honorary society further indicated Brenau's deepening commitment to athletics.

Finally, faculty members, too, were joining in athletic fun. A section in the 1928 *Bubbles* called "Some Famous Dates at Brenau 1927–1928" related that a faculty member basketball team had played against some of Brenau's club and class teams on a few occasions.[46]

By 1930, health-conscious Brenau officials required students to present upon entry "a physician's certificate showing that the applicant is not afflicted with any communicable disease and that she is physically able to undertake the duties of a college course."[47] Also by 1930, Brenau had five physical education instructors on its faculty. The department required all students to take four years of P.E., which consisted of two hours of instruction and two hours of outdoor activity each week. The catalog indicated, though, that "this work is not counted for college credit."[48] Students could earn a certificate in physical education along with their A.B. degree by spending many hours beyond the minimum P.E. requirements engaged in physical activity.[49] Juniors and seniors could have somewhat reduced P.E. requirements than underclassmen, providing they kept their studies up. There were also several non-activity P.E. courses (like kinesiology and anatomy) as well as several activity courses on offer, including dancing, canoeing, and even camping at Camp Takeda in Gainesville, a large campground in Gainesville which the College owned.

By the 1930s, Brenau required membership in its Athletic Association for all students.[50] Also, a point system had been devised for the purposes of earning athletic honors and prizes. For example, a student could earn 50 points for making a class baseball team, 50 points for being a part of a class canoe crew (a sport which had also made its appearance at Brenau by now), and 100 points for being a captain of a class team in any sport. Students could also earn 25 points for simply trying out for a sport, which encouraged even modestly athletic young women to give sport a chance.[51] Two-thousand points earned a "large Brenau 'B'."[52] Opportunities to earn athletic points abounded throughout the decade. Class competitions in many sports occurred annually. Also, the April 16, 1930, edition of the *Alchemist* reported on a very spirited annual individual tennis tournament that the College held.⁵³ Other individual competitions would eventually develop in badminton and archery, but such competitions seemed relatively rare. The aim of athletics at the College during this era was clearly not to give students the chance to garner individual glory, but rather to learn how to be part of a winning team.

By 1940, physical education at Brenau could be seen to have advanced in some ways as it had retreated in others. Brenau required juniors and seniors to take only a single hour of P.E. per week, which was a marked reduction from the requirements of the previous decade.⁵⁴ Yet, by 1940, students could actually major in P.E. and earn a Bachelor of Science in Physical Education degree at Brenau.⁵⁵ Also, at the February 4, 1941, faculty meeting, Brenau's dean announced that "college credit will be given for approved work in Physical Education," which meant that P.E. courses could now count as electives in the regular curriculum.⁵⁶ This was something not all colleges were doing at the time.

Various photographs in the 1940 *Bubbles* indicated that Brenau women were remaining active in time-honored sports at the College while, at the same time, several new sports had made an appearance at Brenau as well. The *Bubbles* showed women riding horses, playing soccer, playing baseball, attending badminton class, dueling in fencing, practicing archery, and playing Ping-Pong. The yearbook also depicted young women canoeing and brandishing field hockey sticks in 1940 and the 1943 edition of the *Bubbles* proved through photographs that golf had made it to campus.⁵⁷ In addition, by 1940, Brenau had a synchronized swimming team called the "Aquacade." The 1940 *Bubbles* also indicated how a young woman would "letter" at Brenau. To get her "B", a student would have to accumulate 1000 points, which were earned on the basis of participation in various athletic events.

Brenau admissions officials continued to require a physical for attending students in the nineteen-forties.⁵⁸ In addition, the College also had an infirmary in the charge of two registered nurses by 1940.⁵⁹ By 1945, athletic dress requirements had relaxed somewhat. Brenau required gym shoes and tennis shoes for activities and prohibited backless tennis outfits. Of course, long coats were still the order of the day when going to and from the pool, but other than these rules, strictures were relatively non-specific.[60]

Intra-campus sports were still the norm at Brenau by 1940. An edition of the *Alchemist* for that year reported on a spirited basketball game between the juniors and freshmen. The juniors won the game for the third year in a row, thanks to "hard work, constant operation, experience, and a spirit equaled by none."[61] It also helped that the juniors "exhibited the 'three-man' defense at its best" and had superstar Kit Wharton on their team, who scored twenty-two points in the game.[62]

Despite the increasing competition on campus in events like the basketball tournament, Brenau still clung to demure sports at late as the 1940s. The same edition of the student newspaper that described the spirited basketball game also described a "P.E. Exhibition" at the College. For this, P.E. majors and faculty members joined with students from the folk dancing and fencing classes. Students put on demonstrations of several kinds of dances, fencing and tennis displays, and maneuvers on several types of gymnastics apparatuses.[63]

The 1940s witnessed something of a turnaround for sports at Brenau. Although up until now the students had made modest progress in increasing the rigor of athletics at the College, progress seemed to slow in this decade. Besides endorsing the demure sports of the P.E. exhibition, the 1945 student handbook seemed to indicate that the College was deemphasizing athletics to a degree. For example, the handbook made no mention of how a student could earn a varsity letter. It said only that, "We also try to arouse interest in sports by having class competition in soccer, volley ball, basketball, and softball."[64] Also, by this year, the Athletic Association was in the business of sponsoring non-athletic events. The handbook reported that the association sponsored an annual "Miss Brenau" beauty contest, an annual scavenger hunt, and a "Miss

Posture" contest using a "Silhouette-O-Graph," which could be "used to aid correction of posture."[65]

The 1944 edition of the *Bubbles* also did little to emphasize athletics. With its star-studded, olive-drab cover and a handful of drawings of soldiers, canons, and fighter planes, the yearbook had a military theme in homage to the war that raged across the globe. While the '44 *Bubbles* related that the College had formed a "Defense Council" to sell war bonds and that the cotillion club cancelled its annual dance to purchase one, depiction of sport at the College approached being 4-F. Only six photographs in the entire yearbook showed women engaging in such athletic pursuits as golf, archery, basketball, soccer, and swimming.

A further erosion of female athleticism at Brenau would seem to be apparent in the decade of the 1950s. In the 1951 edition of the *Bubbles*, although shuffleboard appeared as a new activity, there were only two pages devoted to photographs of athletes engaged in sport. By 1955, the *Bubbles* contained not a single photograph devoted to physical education or sports at all. The 1955–1956 student handbook also indicated that the term "Athletic" had been dropped from the name of the College's sport controlling body. The "Brenau Recreation Association" stood in its place. Its purpose was:

> To endeavor to promote good sportsmanship and team cooperation.
>
> To keep in good condition the equipment of the association and to purchase new equipment when needed.
>
> To award all cups and letters won by students in direct keeping with the point system.[66]

No part of the association's purpose seemed overly "physical." The B.R.A. board grew its membership in a remarkable fashion. The handbook indicated that:

> The Recreation Board will choose at various times during the year girls from the student body whose interest and participation in the activities of the Association merits recognition of a lesser degree than permanent membership in the Board.
>
> These girls will be called "Termites" and will work in cooperation with the Board in all its activities with permanent election as their ultimate goal. To be eligible for membership in the Board a "Termite" must have earned a minimum of 25 points in the Recreational Point System from September to March of that year. In March of each year the Recreation Board will tap several from this club for permanent membership in the Board.[67]

Sadly, no indication is given as to why the name "Termite" was selected for sub-board members.[68]

Despite the de-emphasis of athletics in the 1950s, Brenau students did not completely abandon sports. According to the student handbooks, the recreational point system of the 1950s typically gave Termites points for coming in first or second place in college-wide contests in a good number of sports, which proved that physical activates were actually still taking place at the College. These included archery, badminton, basketball, hockey, tumbling, soccer, softball, swimming, tennis, and volleyball—more sports that had ever been offered at the College before. (See Figure 35.) In addition, points could be earned for assisting with association events (like the Miss Brenau contest) and for dancing. A young woman would earn a letter by earning 100 points. Classes still competed in team sports and were awarded trophies for excellence, but no individual awards existed except in archery, badminton, tennis, and swimming.[69] For the 1950s, the "sports costumes" regulations were unchanged since the 1940s.

By 1961, Brenau had diminished athletic offerings even a bit further. The College required only freshmen and sophomores to take P.E. and to earn four credit hours of activity work. For this, students had to earn one credit in swimming, at least one credit in an individual sport (such as tennis, golf, or archery) or recreational sports, and at least one credit in a team sport or in dance (including tap, folk, ballet, etc.). Physical education majors took substantially more sporting coursework than non-majors and Brenau required all students to buy a P.E. uniform.[70] The 1965–1966 student handbook devoted several pages to reprinting the recreation association's constitution. Despite this, little had evidently improved regarding College athletics in a decade. Recreation Association Board membership was now tied to brains as well as brawn as women had to maintain a "C" average to stay on the board or to become a termite.[71] Also, by 1965, Brenau had revived the dormant practice of holding a College "Field Day" in which sororities, residence halls, and honorary societies competed against each other in a variety of games and contests.[72] In addition, hockey, tumbling, and soccer were apparently no longer being played at the College although bowling had been taken up again for the first time in decades. An April 1965 edition of the *Alchemist* indicated that Brenau exposed students to esoteric as well as mainstream sports. The paper reported that a "karate expert" gave a demonstration at the College, which was both interesting and well-attended.[73] A 1960 edition of the *Alchemist* bespoke the continued popularity of on-campus, intra-collegiate athletic contests in the sixties and described in great detail the College's softball tournament for that year.[74]

It is not entirely clear why athletics at Brenau seemed to have experienced a general decline in the 1950s and early 1960s. After all, the trajectory of sport at the College heading into these decades seemed positive. In actuality, the de-emphasis of athletics at Brenau was likely part of a national trend. According to sport historians Jean O'Reilly and Susan K. Cahn:

> In a conservative post-World War II climate that emphasized family, marriage, and conventional femininity, the popularity of women's sports suffered further decline. Little League programs restricted to boys sprouted everywhere, crowding out informal sandlot and playground teams that had once opened doors to the determined tomboy who excelled at the sport. In high schools

and colleges, women's intramural activities vastly outnumbered more competitive interscholastic and intercollegiate events, while in municipal settings women's recreation programs emphasized activities like 'beauty culture' and crafts instead of athletic contests. As the number of playing opportunities declined, girls and women who continued to seek high-level competition faced stereotypes of female athletes as ugly, unnatural, and masculine. Even more damaging were insinuations linking women's sports with lesbianism, also stigmatized as masculine.[75]

"Such condemnation," O'Reilly and Cahn determined, "created powerful disincentives for female athletic involvement" during this age.[76]

Brenau revived its commitment to athletics in its 1970 catalog, no doubt buoyed by the women's rights movement of the late 1960s that expanded opportunities for women generally. At the same time, it acknowledged a gendered difference in college sports. The College's position was that, "Although women's colleges emphasize Physical Education less than the men's colleges, the modern women's college is eager to help every student gain health and the recreation, team spirit, and love of sports that can be so happily acquired in the games and contests of the campus."[77] To facilitate this, the 1970–1971 Brenau catalog essentially reiterated the physical education requirements laid out in the catalog of a decade earlier. The only significant change was that the College added credit hours in "Body Mechanics" and in "Stunts and Tumbling" to the physical education activity requirements.[78] Brenau required each student to take two hours of physical education per week during her freshman and sophomore years to accrue four credits of activity courses. The College still required a physician to complete a health certificate for enrolled students and still required all entering students to take a swim test to determine an appropriate level of instruction.[79]

In 1970, inter-class sport competitions were still very popular at the College. The *Alchemist* reported that the Alpha Delta Pi team beat the Alpha Gamma Delta team to win the College basketball tournament. A mixed-gender team of members of the faculty challenged the winners to a game and went on to win the close match by 15 to 13.[80] The same edition of the paper published an article that described how four students received specialized instruction in golf.[81] In addition, this edition of the *Alchemist* published an article lauding jogging as "an excellent exercise to take up."[82]

By the 1970s, a student could rest assured that the physical education she received at Brenau would be of good quality, personalized for her needs—and hard to avoid. The College bulletin asserted that:

> This work is done under the direction of thoroughly trained physical educators in a modernly equipped gymnasium, swimming pool, health and exercise room, and recently enlarged athletic fields. Each girl is advised on her selection of activity courses so that she may have an opportunity to participate in a balanced variety of skill classes and team and individual sports. Remedial training is given when needed. Excuses from work in the gymnasium may be given only by the college physician or the Physical Education instructor.[83]

The catalog of this year also offered a rationale explaining the physical education requirement. It read:

> The intent of the requirement…is to help each student develop proficiency in a variety of recreation pursuits of physical orientation. Students, therefore, are required to have skill, knowledge, and understanding in dance, swimming and sports.[84]

To facilitate this development, Brenau offered a plethora of physical education activity courses ranging from archery to fencing to square dancing to synchronized swimming.[85]

While activity course offerings rebounded in numbers from earlier years, by 1975, Brenau had actually dropped more sports from its recreational program. The Brenau College student handbook of that year indicated that students could earn points toward board membership only for playing volleyball, basketball, softball, and for bowling.[86] Otherwise,

Bringing Home the Gold[en Tigers] 415

termites could earn points by dancing, serving as scorekeepers and timekeepers at sporting events, and by working to organize tournaments and events like the Miss Brenau pageant. Also, by the mid-1970s, the student handbook no longer reprinted rules for proper gym attire, but instead said only that gym uniforms would be sold in the fall.[87]

The nineteen-eighties saw big changes in athletics at Brenau. Brenau had built a large physical education building and upgraded to a new natatorium that workers completed in 1974, which contained a large pool and other exercise and steam rooms. In speaking of this facility, the 1980 undergraduate bulletin declared, "When coupled with the other physical education and recreation resources, the combined physical plant provides Brenau College with one of the finest small college educational facilities found in the nation."[88] Brenau often shared these facilities with the community. Beginning in the 1980s and continuing over the next several decades, the *Gainesville Times* and the *Atlanta Journal-Constitution* ran occasional announcements for high school athletic camps being offered at Brenau. The College hosted several such camps, including softball for girls and wrestling for boys, and held several swim meets in its Olympic-caliber pool.

Brenau had also revised its physical education requirements by 1980. The College required students to take two or three "classroom offerings" of physical education courses and three or four hours of activity courses for a total of six hours.[89] Students could choose from six classroom courses that dealt with such themes as nutrition, first aid, drug abuse, and sex education. Activity course offerings remained as robust as ever and even included courses that accommodated students with physical disabilities.[90]

As in previous decades, in the 1980s, intra-collegiate athletic competitions still remained important. The fall quarter, 1980, edition of the *Alchemist* devoted a section of the paper to "Sports." It indicated that field day, with its several races and games, was still a festive event at the College. Also, this edition of the student newspaper reported the results of a "Kick-Ball Tourney" held on campus, which the Tri-Delta sorority won.[91]

As it entered the late 1970s and the 1980s, Brenau finally added bona fide intercollegiate athletics. Mind you, the College had engaged in "extramural activities" (as they were called) in the fall of 1969 when its "field hockey club...participated against other college clubs" and "attended the Deep South Hockey Tournament," but this was not termed a varsity sport.[92] The 1980 undergraduate bulletin indicated, "Brenau College has two teams that participate in intercollegiate athletics in the areas of swimming and tennis. Both teams play regular schedules with intrastate and southeastern colleges and universities."[93] Brenau had also dabbled with forming a basketball program in 1979. The March edition of the *Alchemist* for that year reported:

> Mr. Alex Taylor of the Brenau College Criminal Justice Department is coaching a women's basketball team at Brenau. The team had its first game...against Gainesville Junior College. Unfortunately, the first game was not a win, but there are high expectations for the second game. It is scheduled...against Agnes Scott College.[94]

Despite the optimism, the basketball team folded and would not be revived until 2006.

The size of the intercollegiate athletic teams that did exist at the College at first were modest. The 1975 edition of the *Bubbles* displayed photographic spreads of the swimming and tennis teams. Four students played on Brenau's tennis team in 1975 and five students swam for the College.[95] Half a decade later, the tennis team still remained small but Brenau's swim team had doubled in size. The 1980 *Bubbles* also related that Brenau's swim team often competed against several much larger National Collegiate Athletic Association (N.C.A.A.) Division I universities, including Clemson University, the University of Georgia, and Florida State University.[96] Brenau took the sports very seriously as evidenced by the fact that it offered both athletic scholarships to prospective athletes and had a Director of Intercollegiate Athletics on staff.[97] Besides tennis and swimming, the 1980 *Bubbles* revealed that fencing had made a comeback at Brenau.[98] Four young women participated in what would be a short-lived club sport that had not been mentioned in relation to the College since the early 1900s. Also, Dr. Burd indicated that competitive women's golf actually existed for a short time at the College in the mid-1980s before folding owing to the departure of its coach to work with the Ladies Professional Golf Association.[99]

Despite the fact that Brenau's intercollegiate athletic teams were among the newest and the smallest in the country in the 1970s, 1980s, and 1990s, they were also among some of the best. In 1977, on the occasion of losing a swim meet with Brenau, the women's swim team coach of the University of Georgia said that Brenau's team "was third in the nation last year in the women's small college championships" and conceded that tiny Brenau was "just a stronger team than we are."[100] Brenau became a member of the National Association of Intercollegiate Athletics (N.A.I.A.) and the Southern States Athletic Conference. Under the leadership of coach Bill Rogers, the 1998 and 1999 N.A.I.A. coach of the year, the Golden Tigers tennis squad generally dominated its competition during the 1990s. Rogers came to Brenau in 1992. He inherited a solid program, which had been ranked in the top 25 of the N.A.I.A. in 1988.[101] By 1993, the once-small tennis team had grown to ten members and continued to garner laurels.[102] The 1994 edition of the *Bubbles* indicated that, "At the end of the 1992–1993 season, Brenau was ranked tenth in the nation and won the N.A.I.A. District 25 Championship."[103] From 1995 until 1999, Brenau finished its seasons ranked in the top five teams in the country in the N.A.I.A. About 150 colleges and universities competed in N.A.I.A. women's tennis then. It was a very competitive division, especially in Georgia, where Brenau played other nationally-ranked teams like Shorter College and Berry College.

Articles in the *Atlanta Journal-Constitution* in the late 1990s routinely reported that Brenau's tennis players routed players from other, much larger schools like the University of Georgia or Georgia State University.

In 1998, Brenau finished third in the N.A.I.A. tournament. In 1999, Brenau held the number one ranking in the country for much of its season and had a roster that included "six singles players ranked in the top 36 in the country, and three doubles teams among the top 15."[104] That same year, Brenau's tennis team won the school's first national championship title in any sport.

The *Gainesville Times* reported that, "The Golden Tigers shared the National Association of Intercollegiate Athletics (NAIA) title with Auburn-Montgomery Sunday in Boca Raton, Fla. Each team finished [the N.A.I.A. tournament] with 37 points."[105] Also in 1999, "the NAIA selected six Golden Tigers as first-team All-Americans."[106] Brenau's best player, sophomore Leyla Ogan, was the runner-up for the 1999 individual title after losing in straight sets to a member of the 1996 Chinese Olympic tennis team who was playing at an American college. Ogan managed this feat despite having a cancerous growth removed from her knee the previous summer and undergoing months of rehabilitation.[107] Several other Brenau players also finished the year with high rankings.

The secret to Brenau's success in tennis was international recruiting. Besides Ogan, who was from England, Brenau fielded young players from France, Brazil, Japan, and Malaysia.[108] International players actually kept Brenau on top of tennis rankings for several years. Brenau went to the N.A.I.A. finals in 2000 and again in 2001, but came up short both times. In 2001, the Golden Tigers appeared again in the N.A.I.A. finals against Auburn-Montgomery, but lost 5 to 2.[109]

Then, in 2002, Brenau again won the national championship. A writer for the *Atlanta Journal-Constitution* quipped that, "If Brenau University women's tennis coach Bill Rogers had to summon the players who recently won the NAIA championship, he'd have to initiate a global search."[110] The articled continued, saying that:

> Shortly after the Tigers from Gainesville, Ga., won the national title at the Peachtree City [Georgia] Tennis Center, they headed home. Junior Antonina Grib, the No. 1 singles player on a team

that finished 25–0, flew to Belarus. Sophomore Katrina Mihaere is from New Zealand, freshman Vilijana Dimouska from Australia, junior Irina Yarikova from Russia and seniors Katrina Franjic and Shan Liew from Germany and Malaysia, respectively.[111]

In another article, the *AJC* indicated that, "Because most top American players choose NCAA Division I schools," smaller colleges like Brenau had to recruit internationally.[112] Coach Rogers put it more colorfully. Speaking of coaches at smaller colleges, he said, "the rest of us scurry around trying to get players from wherever in the world we can."[113]

Brenau's tennis players continued to perform well into the early twenty-first century. The team finished ninth in the N.A.I.A. in 2003 and 2004 and was ranked as high as number three in 2005.[114] Around this time, the Golden Tigers routinely had individual players and doubles teams ranked among the top twenty-five in the nation and many Brenau players became All-Americans. The tennis team continued to retain its international flavor with many players and a new coach, Gordon Leslie, coming from abroad. The year 2009 was a noteworthy one for Brenau tennis. Bookended by two pair of lackluster seasons (Brenau went 13–10 and 11–11 in 2007 and 2008, respectively, and 12–10 and 11–8 in 2010 and 2011), the tennis program found its serve and cracked the N.A.I.A. top 10 rankings in April of that year.[115] The team also gained an exceptional new home facility, the $300,000 Lessie Smithgall Indoor Tennis Center.[116] Brenau planned to return many veteran singles and doubles players to the courts in 2012, which boded well for a strong season. Indeed, the Golden Tigers tennis team finished the year "ranked No. 6 in the NAIA and reached the quarterfinal of the NAIA National Championship."[117]

In addition to tennis, a swimming and diving team represented Brenau in intercollegiate competition beginning in the 1970s. In 1978, a special section in the *Gainesville Times* written to commemorate Brenau's one-hundredth anniversary indicated that the team excelled. The *Times* reported that, "In 1977, Brenau's swimmers were ranked third in the nation after the national finals in Pennsylvania, and had nine swimmers named to U.S. All-American ranks."[118] In 1985, Brenau's swimmers competed against such very large schools as Auburn University, Florida State University, and the University of Georgia in the Southern Intercollegiate Championships and swam their home matches in a very nice aquatics center on campus.[119] Despite the early accolades garnered by Brenau swimmers and the apparent strength of the team, Brenau's swimming program went under in 1986. According to Dr. Burd, this occurred as a result of the mid-year departure of its coach, which left Brenau with no one to recruit new athletes.[120] Although it had no team, several articles in the *Gainesville Times* and the *Atlanta Constitution* indicated that Brenau continued to host swim meets on campus for youth teams well into the twenty-first century. Then, in 2006, Brenau revived its swimming program. To do so, the University hired James D. ("Jim") Young, who had over 40 years of experience coaching swimmers.[121] He recruited several talented freshman athletes and the young program showed great promise as it began to mature. Building upon the foundation set by Young, Gabby Matthews took the helm as Brenau's swimming coach in 2008. Matthews was the daughter of a one-time coach of the Brazilian national team and became the first Brazilian woman to ever serve as the head coach of a collegiate swimming program.[122] Under Matthews' coaching, the team finished 19th in the National Association of Intercollegiate Athletics Swimming and Diving Championship in 2009 and would improve to 13th place a year later.[123] Matthews left Brenau in 2010 and Blaire Bachman thereafter assumed the swim coach's role.[124] When she took the job at age 24, Bachman, who actually grew up in Gainesville, was the youngest college swimming coach in the nation.[125] Under her guidance, Brenau's swimmers set several personal bests at the 2011 N.A.I.A. championships and entered the 2013 season "having recorded top places at the Appalachian Swimming Championships (6th) and NAIA National Championships (8th)" in 2012.[126]

For a time, Brenau supported another water sport—fishing. The 1984–1985 edition of the student handbook described the "Brenau College Fishing Team" in colorful detail. The handbook related that, "As a true innovation in women's intercollegiate sports, the Brenau College Fishing Team was formed during Spring of 1981."[127] Brenau's close proximity to Georgia's Lake Sidney Lanier, a 38,000-acre, fresh-water reservoir with over 692 miles of shoreline, provided a perfect location for the team to fish. The handbook boasted that in the same year of its founding the team "won its first intercollegiate meet...against men's teams!"[128] Team membership was open to all female students who successfully tried out. Apparently, fishing foundered fast; no more mention of it was made in Brenau's publications after only a couple of years.

Intercollegiate soccer began at Brenau in 1988, which, according to the American Soccer History Archives, was only six years after the N.C.A.A. officially recognized women's soccer.[129] Perhaps more than most women's collegiate sports, soccer experienced terrific growth in the 1980s and 1990s thanks to the effects of Title IX of the Educational Amendments of 1972 to the Education Act of 1965. This legislation essentially required schools and colleges to support men's and women's athletic programs equally. Many N.C.A.A. Division – I institutions with large programs in men's sports like football created women's soccer programs in an effort to balance things out in compliance with the requirements of Title IX. By the late 1990s, there were actually more collegiate soccer programs for women in the United States than for men.[130] Brenau's program grew in the midst of this nationwide expansion. (See Figure 36.)

The 1988 edition of the *Bubbles* indicated that:

> The Brenau soccer team kicked off their first season last fall. The team, coached by Dr. Calvin Hanrahan, played a four game season against [all-women's] Agnes Scott and Wesleyan Colleges. The soccer team was formed through the Organization of Club Sports by the Athletic Department.[131]

The program matured slowly, enduring some hard seasons for a handful of years. The September 14, 1996, edition of the *Atlanta Journal* reported that soccer powerhouse Oglethorpe University in Atlanta blanked the Golden Tigers 9 – 0 in their opening match in 1996.[132] By 1997, photographs in the *Bubbles* revealed that soccer remained small as a program, apparently with just enough women to field a team.[133] The 1998 yearbook indicated, "Soccer...which started out at the club level began competing intercollegiately in the fall. They play their home games at nearby Lakeview Academy," a private, college-preparatory day school also located in Gainesville.[134] During its first real intercollegiate soccer season, Brenau's team racked up two wins and eleven losses.[135] The 1998 photographic spread for the soccer team showed thirteen players and two coaches, which was still not much depth for a college program. By 2000, Brenau's young program showed some improvement by winning four regular season games.[136] Brenau continued to play their home games at Lakeview until 2001 when the city of Gainesville opened the Allen Creek Soccer Complex.[137] Brenau moved its soccer program to the new facility.

Along with getting a new home field, Brenau's soccer program got a new coach. In 2002, Mike Lochstampfor came to Brenau. Lochstampfor had played soccer himself both as an undergraduate and at the semi-professional level for many years before beginning a career as a college coach.[138] He oversaw several winning teams in Texas and in Georgia, most recently at Oglethorpe University, before moving to Brenau. In just two short years, Lochstampfor coached the Brenau team to the Southern States Athletic Conference tournament for the first time in many years. In 2005–2006, Brenau had one all-region, three all-conference, and seven academic all-conference players on the soccer team.[139] A year later, the team still improved on the pitch. The Golden Tigers closed out their 2006 soccer season with a 10–7–1 record, the most successful year in the young program's history. Also in 2006, two Brenau soccer players were named to all-conference teams.[140] In 2007, Brenau's schedule included matches against several nationally-ranked N.A.I.A. soccer teams, including those of Oglethorpe University and Berry College.[141] The competition took its toll as Brenau recorded a losing season. Only 2010 proved to be a greater disappointment as Brenau went 4–11–1.[142] Later seasons saw the Golden Tigers soccer players chalk up winning records against challenging opponents while simultaneously earning academic honors off the field.

In 2012, the team finished with its best record ever (13–5–0) and three players earned "All-Academic Honors" from the Southern States Athletic Conference.[143] Esther Anyanwu of Nigeria received both the S.S.A.C.'s "Newcomer of the Year" and the "Player of the Year-Offense" for leading the conference with 27 goals and eight assists for the season.[144]

Students founded a crew program at Brenau in the mid-1990s. According to coach Bill Rogers, the coming 1996 Summer Olympic Games in Atlanta "combined with Title IX" catalyzed interest in doing so.[145] Indeed, the program developed as something of an offshoot of the Lake Lanier Rowing Club, which rowing enthusiasts formed in 1993 to make use of an excellent rowing venue created in Gainesville for the Games.[146] Personnel from the L.L.R.C. helped several colleges in northeast Georgia, including Brenau, establish rowing programs.[147] Brenau's program was the only one to thrive. The 1995 edition of the *Bubbles* depicted the rowers as very dedicated by saying that the eight-woman team "has practice every day, except Wednesday and Sunday, at the crack of dawn."[148]

In 2000, the Brenau yearbook reported that the crew team welcomed M. J. McNamara as a new head coach and participated in seven regattas.[149] In 2004, Brenau rowers participated in the prestigious "Head of the Hooch" regatta on November 6 and 7 of that year. Brenau fielded a single novice boat that rowed respectably against over two-dozen clubs from much larger colleges and universities, such as Georgia Tech, Emory University, the University of Texas, Duke University, the University of Florida, and North Carolina State University.[150] By 2006, crew was still a serious sport at Brenau engaged in by over a half-dozen young women.[151] In 2009, the Brenau University crew team finished sixth out of 18 teams and earned a bronze medal in the women's varsity four in the Clemson Sprints Regatta in South Carolina. As in the past, the competition included much larger schools such as Georgia Tech, Georgia, Clemson, Auburn, North Carolina, Florida State, Wake Forest, and Northwestern.[152] Around 2010, Kim Butler, who was a 2008 graduate of Berry College where she rowed varsity crew, assumed coaching duties of Brenau's program.[153] When she departed in 2012, she left behind a well-organized and tightly-knit competitive team that still routinely rowed against much larger colleges and universities.

In 1995, the same year the College founded its rowing program, Brenau began a volleyball program as well. The team would struggle for several years. By 1997, the team consisted of nine players, which provided only a modest reserve to support six first-string players.[154] The yearbook indicated that, in 2000, the "volleyball team had their best season yet with a 14 – 12 finish" when Scott Hanley joined the program as a new coach.[155] The volleyball team's next best season came in 2002 when the team went 14–17.[156] The somewhat lackluster results for multiple seasons did not diminish support for the team. In a 2001 interview published in the *Gainesville Times*, one player praised the Brenau community by saying, "The students are really supportive, and the professors are supportive."[157] Still, many lean years followed. From 2003 to 2011, Brenau had only one winning volleyball season, which came in 2009 when the team went 24–11 overall and 5–8 in conference competition.[158] Some years, Brenau won no conference games at all. In 2011, tennis coach Andre Ferreira stepped in as interim volleyball coach after Meredith Franklin (who had coached the team for four years) became the University's sports information director for all Brenau athletics programs.[159] Jeff White came to Brenau and coached the team to a 20–11 season in 2012, which boded well for subsequent seasons.[160]

In 1997, Brenau's cross country team made its debut. Nine women ran for the College team, which Glenn Bryant coached.[161] Team wins were few, but Brenau's runners remained competitive for the next decade. Lila Harste, a veteran runner of the Atlanta Track Club, coached the team from 2002 until 2006 when Susan McIntyre took over. McIntyre was also an experienced runner and bicyclist with an impressive record of coaching at the high school level.[162] Though championships would prove to be elusive, so, too, would poor finishes. The official University

Athletics website bears out that both women coached Brenau's runners to many years' worth of solid, if never stellar, finishes through 2012.

With the addition of so many sports teams, it was perhaps only natural that Brenau would need a cheerleading squad to animate fans. The 1999 yearbook published several photographs of a "Pep Rally" held at the College. Featured at the rally was "the newly formed team of Brenau Cheerleaders, accompanied by one very energetic mascot."[163] While the Golden Tiger wore her stripes, Brenau's dozen-or-so cheerleaders wore a simple uniform that consisted of a t-shirt and gym shorts. What began as a spirit squad would evolve into a true collegiate sport. In 2011, just a year after the N.A.I.A. officially sanctioned competitive cheerleading, Brenau inaugurated its program. The University hired Krista Britt, a 15-year veteran cheerleading coach with a strong background in choreography, as head coach of 19 mostly freshman cheerleaders.[164] Routines would combine dance moves with tumbling and stunts requiring an exceptional degree of athleticism—as well as a lot of school spirit. In 2012 in its very first season of competition, Brenau's cheerleading team finished second in its classification group out of several teams at the National Cheerleading Association Collegiate Cheer and Dance Championships.[165] The same year, thirteen new freshmen joined the squad, adding a wealth of talent to an already accomplished group.[166]

Since 2004, Brenau's cheerleaders could add softball to the list of sports they supported. After a disappointing 1–19 inaugural season, Devon Thomas, an award-winning member of the Georgia Athletics Coaches Association for multiple years, coached the team to several solid finishes. Within only four years of founding the program, Thomas' teams "achieved national rankings in 2006 and 2007" and "produced 13 All Conference players and 8 All Conference freshman players."[167] In 2010, the team achieved an impressive 41–9 overall record, including a 15–1 home record.[168] In 2011 and 2012, many juniors and seniors filled the softball ranks and the experience showed. In May of 2012, the Golden Tigers went to the N.A.I.A. Softball National Championship in Gulf

Shores, Alabama. Despite a strong start in which Brenau defeated two top-twenty tournament opponents, the team was eliminated by the two tournament finalists and finished the year 44–16.[169]

In 2006, the University's varsity basketball program took to the court amid much fanfare. For the occasion, Brenau refurbished its gymnasium and maintained a "countdown" clock on the University website for months in advance. Gary Bays, a former women's basketball coach for Warner Southern College in central Florida who was selected as an N.A.I.A. Regional Athletic Director of the Year in 2005, was Brenau's first coach.[170] The Golden Tigers won their inaugural first game against Tennessee Wesleyan University before proceeding to have a rocky first season.[171] The team finished the year with ten wins and twenty losses and a conference record of 3–18.[172] Though three modest overall winning seasons followed, conference successes were few. Bays resigned in 2011 and Brenau turned head coaching duties over to Mr. Kris Stewart, who had served as a former assistant collegiate head coach at liberal arts colleges in Texas and North Carolina.[173] Though the team again finished below .500 in 2011–2012, the anticipated return of many sophomores and juniors in the coming seasons was cause for optimism.

The creation of the basketball program at the University in 2006 was part of a "sports program expansion plan" undertaken by Brenau around that time. This plan was designed to ultimately leave the University with intercollegiate varsity programs in "basketball, crew, cross country, golf, soccer, softball, swimming, tennis and volleyball."[174] By 2012, Brenau had largely realized its goals. In November of 2011, Brenau announced the addition of women's outdoor track and field to its varsity sports lineup, which was slated to begin competition in the spring of 2013.[175] With an ultimate goal of recruiting between 20 and 30 athletes, the team would become one of Brenau's largest programs and would bring to nine the total number of varsity sports supported by the University.[176] About a year later, Brenau made good on its promise to revive golf as an intercollegiate sport. An article published in the *Gainesville Times* around mid-December of 2012 reported that women's golf would start in the fall of 2013 and that the program would bring six to eight players and a new head coach to campus its first year.[177]

Just as Brenau was engaged in building new athletic programs in 2012, the University also sought to build new athletic arenas. Toward the end of that year, Brenau began exploring the possibility of erecting its own softball and soccer facilities at a complex near campus. In another December *Gainesville Times* article, President Schrader revealed that the University had been in preliminary communication with Pacolet Milliken Enterprises about developing several fields adjacent to the company's "New Holland" plant on Jesse Jewell Parkway in the city of Gainesville.[178] If everything worked out as planned, Brenau would be able to cease using various community athletic facilities owned by Hall County, Georgia, which it had been doing for years, and bring its home sporting venues significantly closer to home.

Athletics enjoy a prominent place at Brenau in the twenty-first century. A plethora of competitive—or, in many cases, even nationally-ranked—intercollegiate sport teams, a vigorous intramural program, and a curriculum that offers emphasis in physical fitness complements the institution's academic programs. This result was not accidental. Rather, it was the product of a gradual and generally informal process of negotiation that occurred between Brenau's students and its faculty and staff for over a century. In the face of conservative views about the limited physical ability of women long-held by society (including members of the faculty and administration at Brenau), students clamored for actual sports instead of mere demure exercises. At first covertly (as they snuck into the campus gym after hours behind the backs of College personnel) and, later, overtly, often with the support of faculty and staff members whose views had changed over time, Brenau's young women pursued physical activity. They proved themselves capable of athleticism and brought about the expansion of physical activities at Brenau. Whereas students of different generations pursued negotiations for athletics with the faculty and staff to differing degrees, in differing ways, and with differing degrees of success, the general trajectory of athletic development at Brenau was positive. That development eventually culminated in recent years with the refinement of an institutional culture that prizes athletics today as much as it avoided athletics a century ago. Though Brenau's journey may not have been unique (especially among southern women's colleges, which might be expected to have undergone similar athletic development), it was, for the institution, certainly profound.

It is ironic that although Brenau's institutional culture has changed radically over time, the institution's policy on athletics could arguably be said to have come full circle. At one time, Brenau permitted no imitations of masculine sports for fear of de-feminizing students. By 2012, the Brenau community still conveyed the impression that the University invites no such mimicry—but now for different reasons. Brenau would doubtlessly prefer that its students not imitate men in the twenty-first century, not for fear of yielding anything unfeminine, but, rather, because doing so would diminish women's agency. After all, given past successes, the athletic culture that Brenau women might create on their own could surpass whatever they might copy. Brenau women, therefore, have proven that they would be better off not imitating anything—masculine or otherwise—but blazing their own trails.

Notes

1. "Game was Tied at Gainesville," *Atlanta Constitution*, 25 November 1904, p. 9.
2. "Gainesville Nine Should Be Good," *Atlanta Constitution*, 12 February 1911, sec. A, p. 2.
3. "Riverside Beats Boys High School," *Atlanta Constitution*, 29 September 1912, sec. A, p. 15.
4. "Brenau Notes," *Atlanta Constitution*, 31 March 1912, sec. D, p. 15.
5. "Brenau College Notes," *Atlanta Constitution*, 15 November 1903, sec. C, p. 5. Note that in the early days of the game, "basket ball" was spelled as two separate words.
6. Brenau College, *Bubbles* (Gainesville, GA; Brenau College, 1908), no page number. Hereafter, references to this source are indicated as "*Bubbles* (1908)."
7. Ibid.
8. Theriot, "Towards a New Sporting Ideal," 2.
9. "Brenau Notes," *Atlanta Constitution*, 2 December 1906, sec. E, p. 8.
10. Ibid.
11. Brenau College, *Bubbles* (Gainesville, GA; Brenau College, 1918). Hereafter, references to this source are indicated as "*Bubbles* (1918)."
12. "Brenau Notes," *Atlanta Constitution*, 15 November 1908, sec. D, p. 7.
13. "Athletic—Seniors," *Alchemist* (Gainesville, GA: Brenau College), vol. 7, no. 3 (8 November 1919), p. 1.
14. Ibid.
15. *Catalog* (1920), 67.
16. Ibid.
17. Ibid., 99–100.
18. *Faculty Journal (25 years)*, entry dated 3 April 1923.
19. *Handbook* (1925), 23.
20. Ibid.
21. Ibid.
22. Ibid.
23. Ibid., 24.
24. Ibid.
25. Ibid., 23.
26. Ibid., 24.

27. Ibid.
28. Theriot, "Towards a New Sporting Ideal," 2.
29. McCandless, *Past in the Present*, 146–147.
30. Ibid., 147.
31. *Faculty Journal (25 years)*, entry dated 5 February 1924.
32. Ibid., entry dated 3 March 1925. Howard College was founded in Marion, Alabama in 1842. It moved to Birmingham in 1887 and later become Samford University. Samford University, "History of Samford University," http://www.samford.edu/universityhistory/ (accessed 27 March 2013). According to an article on page four of the March 26, 1872, edition of the *Atlanta Constitution*, there were 130 pupils at Howard in 1872. More recent enrollment figures were not evident. Subsequent articles in the *Constitution* indicated that Howard became both coeducational and, for a time, a big enough school to play the likes of Auburn and Georgia Tech in football.
33. "Brenau College To Meet N.G.A.C. Basketball Team," *Atlanta Constitution*, 11 February 1927, p. 11.
34. Ibid.
35. Ibid.
36. Ibid.
37. Ibid.
38. "Brenau Notes," *Atlanta Constitution*, 20 February 1927, sec. D, p. 2.
39. "Brenau Notes," *Atlanta Constitution*, 6 March 1927, sec. D, p. 7.
40. Ibid.
41. Brenau College, *Bubbles* (Gainesville, GA; Brenau College, 1932), 123. Hereafter, references to this source are indicated as "*Bubbles* (1932)."
42. Brenau College, *Bubbles* (Gainesville, GA; Brenau College, 1937). Hereafter, references to this source are indicated as "*Bubbles* (1937)."
43. Olive Hall, "Agnes Scott Has Brilliant Basketball Season in View," *Atlanta Constitution*, 17 December 1922, sec. A, p. 4.
44. Jana Nidiffer and Carolyn Terry Bashaw, *Women Administrators in Higher Education: Historical and Contemporary Perspectives* (Albany, NY: State University of New York Press, Albany, 2001), 197.
45. Ibid.
46. Brenau College, *Bubbles* (Gainesville, GA; Brenau College, 1928). Hereafter, references to this source are indicated as "*Bubbles* (1928)."
47. *Catalog* (1929), 30.
48. Ibid., 46.
49. Ibid., 47.

50. *Handbook* (1937), 43.
51. Ibid.
52. Ibid., 44.
53. "Sport-O-Graphs," *Alchemist* (Gainesville, GA: Brenau College), vol. XVI, no. 26 (16 April 1930), p. 4.
54. *Catalog* (1939), 108.
55. Ibid.
56. *Faculty Journal (25 years)*, entry dated 4 February 1941.
57. *Bubbles* (1943), 107.
58. *Catalog* (1939), 27.
59. Ibid.
60. *Handbook* (1945), 42.
61. Mary Gresham, "Through the Sporthole," *Alchemist* (Gainesville, GA: Brenau College), vol. XXVI, no. 12 (19 March 1940), p. 3.
62. Ibid.
63. "P.E. Exhibition Presented Friday," *Alchemist* (Gainesville, GA: Brenau College), vol. XXVI, no. 12 (19 March 1940), p. 4.
64. *Handbook* (1945), 43.
65. Ibid.
66. *Handbook* (1955), 45.
67. Ibid.
68. An Internet search for the term "Termite" in the context of athletics in September, 2012, revealed that the word was in use by several schools and recreational associations across the U.S. Most commonly, these users employed "termite" to designate the very youngest group of players in an activity, even younger than children playing in a "pee wee" league.
69. Ibid., 47.
70. *Brenau College Annual Catalogue, 1961–1962, v. LIII, n.1* (Gainesville, GA: Brenau College, 1961), 64; available in the Brenau University Archives, Gainesville, Georgia. Hereafter, references to this source are indicated as "*Catalog* (1961)."
71. *Handbook* (1965), 74.
72. Brenau College, *Bubbles* (Gainesville, GA; Brenau College, 1965), 19. Hereafter, references to this source are indicated as "*Bubbles* (1965)."
73. Robbie Warner and Nevin Lenhardt, "Karate Expert Gives Demonstration," *Alchemist* (Gainesville, GA: Brenau College), 29 April 1965, p. 7.
74. "Seniors Down Freshmen to Walk Off With Softball Champion [sic]," *Alchemist* (Gainesville, GA: Brenau College), vol. XLVI, no. 7 (12 April 1960), p. 5.

75. Jean O'Reilly and Susan K. Cahn (eds.), *Women and Sports in the United States: A Documentary Reader* (Boston, MA: Northeastern University Press, 2007), xvi.
76. Ibid.
77. *Catalog* (1970), 13.
78. Ibid., 102.
79. Ibid., 30, 38.
80. "ADPI's Win Tourney," *Alchemist* (Gainesville, GA: Brenau College), vol. LCI, no. 7 (23 February 1970), p. 7.
81. "FORE!!," *Alchemist* (Gainesville, GA: Brenau College), vol. LCI, no. 7 (23 February 1970), p. 1.
82. "Accessories," *Alchemist* (Gainesville, GA: Brenau College), vol. LCI, no. 7 (23 February 1970), p. 3.
83. *Catalog* (1970), 13.
84. Ibid., 100.
85. Ibid., 104–105.
86. *Handbook* (1974), 51.
87. Ibid., 47.
88. *Brenau College 1980–81 Undergraduate Bulletin* (Gainesville, GA: Brenau College, 1980), 19; available in the Brenau University Archives, Gainesville, Georgia. Hereafter, references to this source are indicated as "*Catalog* (1980)."
89. Ibid., 134.
90. Ibid., 135.
91. "Tri-Delta Tops Zetas In Kick-Ball Tourney," *Alchemist* (Gainesville, GA: Brenau College), Fall Quarter 1980, p. 5.
92. Brenau College, *Institutional Self-Study, 1969 – 1971*, 199.
93. *Catalog* (1980), 26.
94. "A New Team on Campus," *Alchemist* (Gainesville, GA: Brenau College), March, 1979, p. 7.
95. Brenau College, *Bubbles* (Gainesville, GA; Brenau College, 1975), 135, 139. Hereafter, references to this source are indicated as "*Bubbles* (1975)."
96. Brenau College, *Bubbles* (Gainesville, GA; Brenau College, 1980), 76–77. Hereafter, references to this source are indicated as "*Bubbles* (1992)."
97. *Catalog* (1980), 26.
98. *Bubbles* (1980), 75.
99. Dr. John S. Burd, interview by author, tape recording, Gainesville, Georgia, 23 September 2010.

Bringing Home the Gold[en Tigers] 433

100. David Westin, "Swim team falls," *Red and Black*, Nov. 21, 1977 -- page 7, http://redandblack.libs.uga.edu/xtf/view?docId=news/1977/rab1977-0907.xml&query=brenau&brand=rab-brand (accessed 10 May 2013).
101. Brenau College, *Bubbles* (Gainesville, GA; Brenau College, 1988), 156. Hereafter, references to this source are indicated as "*Bubbles* (1988)."
102. Brenau College, *Bubbles* (Gainesville, GA; Brenau College, 1993), 57. Hereafter, references to this source are indicated as "*Bubbles* (1993)."
103. Brenau College, *Bubbles* (Gainesville, GA; Brenau College, 1994), no page number. Hereafter, references to this source are indicated as "*Bubbles* (1994)."
104. Bud Ellis, "Brenau Swinging for Title," *Gainesville Times* (Gainesville, GA), 20 May 1999, sec. B, p. 1.
105. Ryan Smith, "Brenau Basks in Glow of NAIA Tennis Title," *Gainesville Times* (Gainesville, GA), 3 June 1999, sec. B, p. 1.
106. Ibid.
107. Bud Ellis, "Brenau Swinging for Title," *Gainesville Times* (Gainesville, GA), 20 May 1999, sec. B, p. 1.
108. Earnest Reese, "Recruiting abroad helps small schools compete," *Atlanta Journal/Atlanta Constitution*, 22 May 1999, sec. D, p. 8.
109. Todd Holcomb, "Women's Tennis," *Atlanta Journal-Constitution*, 26 May 2001, sec. H, p. 10.
110. Earnest Reese, "Brenau Goes Global for Win," *Atlanta Journal-Constitution*, 1 June 2002, sec. C, p. 7.
111. Ibid.
112. Larry Hartstein, "International Pipeline Key to Brenau's Title Run," *Atlanta Journal-Constitution*, 23 May 2002, sec. JJ, p. 4.
113. Ibid.
114. College Tennis Online, "Rankings," http://www.collegetennisonline.com/Tennis/Ranking.aspx?pType=T (accessed 10 May 2013).
115. Staff reports, "College tennis: Brenau cracks top 10 in polls," *Gainesville Times*, 21 April 2008, http://www.gainesvilletimes.com/archives/4828/ (accessed 10 May 2013).
116. Ashley Fielding, "New indoor tennis court will help Brenau's sport," *Gainesville Times*, 7 September 2008, http://www.gainesvilletimes.com/archives/8413/ (accessed 10 May 2013).
117. "Tennis Season Outlook," http://www.brenautigers.com/outlook/10/5.php (accessed 17 March 2014).
118. "The first 100 years," *Gainesville Times* (Gainesville, GA), 11 September 1977, Brenau College Centennial Commemorative Section, p. 4.

119. Darrell Simmons, "Sportsbeat," *Atlanta Journal-Constitution*, 7 February 1985, sec. D, p. 2.
120. Dr. John S. Burd, interview by author, tape recording, Gainesville, Georgia, 23 September 2010.
121. "Young named first Brenau swim coach," AccessNorthGA.com, 2006, http://www.accessnorthga.com/detail-pf.php?n=124956 (accessed 10 May 2013).
122. "On the upstroke: young swim team wins with passion," *Brenau Window*, spring 2008, p. 10, http://artsweb.brenau.edu/Brenauwindow/Spring2008/sp08sports.pdf (accessed 1 June 2013).
123. Staff reports, "Golden Tigers take 13th in NAIA swimming meet," *Gainesville Times*, 8 March 2010, http://www.gainesvilletimes.com/archives/30441/ (accessed 15 May 2013).
124. Staff reports, "Brenau names new swimming coach," *Gainesville Times*, 1 June 2010, http://www.gainesvilletimes.com/archives/33811/ (accessed 15 May 2013).
125. Bill Murphy, "Brenau turns to homegrown coaches," *Gainesville Times*, 8 July 2010, http://www.gainesvilletimes.com/archives/35158/ (accessed 15 May 2013).
126. Staff reports, "Local college scoreboard: March 11," *Gainesville Times*, 11 March 2011, http://www.gainesvilletimes.com/archives/47361/ (accessed 15 May 2013); "Swimming Season Outlook," http://www.brenautigers.com/outlook/10/7.php (accessed 17 March 2014).
127. *Handbook* (1984), 81.
128. Ibid.
129. Dave Litterer, "Women's Soccer History in the USA: An Overview," American Soccer History Archives, http://homepages.sover.net/~spectrum/womensoverview.html (accessed 17 May 2013).
130. Ibid.
131. *Bubbles* (1988), 143.
132. "College Soccer," *Atlanta Journal/Atlanta Constitution*, 14 September 1996, sec. J, p. 9.
133. Brenau College, *Bubbles* (Gainesville, GA; Brenau College, 1997), 88. Hereafter, references to this source are indicated as "*Bubbles* (1997)."
134. *Aurum* (formerly *Bubbles*) (Gainesville, GA: Brenau College, 1998), 60.
135. *Aurum* (formerly *Bubbles*) (Gainesville, GA: Brenau College, 2000), 92.
136. Ibid.

137. Gainesville Parks and Recreation Division, "Allen Creek Soccer Complex," http://www.gainesville.org/allen-creek-soccer-complex (accessed 17 May 2013).
138. Brenau University, "2010 Soccer Coaches," http://www.brenautigers.com/coach/8/4.php (accessed 17 May 2013).
139. Brenau University, "Adding Value to Our Community," http://alum.brenau.edu/development/value.cfm (accessed 22 August 2007).
140. Coach Mike Lochstampfor for Hometownhall.com, "Brenau Tigers Soccer season wrap up...," 23 December 2006, http://www.hometownhall.com/sports/college/brenau-tigers-soccer-seas.shtml (accessed 30 August 2007).
141. Brenau University, "2007 Soccer Schedule," http://www.brenautigers.com/schedule/5/4.php (accessed 18 May 2013).
142. Brenau University, "2010 Soccer," http://www.brenautigers.com/schedule/8/4.php (accessed 18 May 2013).
143. "Soccer Team Garners SSAC Honors," Brenau Soccer News, 11 November 2012, http://www.brenautigers.com/article/961.php (accessed 17 March 2014).
144. Ibid.
145. Glenn Hibdon, "Brenau Adds Sports But Tennis Still King," *Tulsa World*, 23 May 1996, sec. B, p. 5.
146. During Dr. Burd's presidential administration, Brenau actually played a role in the 1996 Summer Olympic Games held in Atlanta. The University housed 130 rowers from many foreign countries who competed on nearby Lake Lanier. The athletes apparently had no complaints about the temporary housing—except for a late-night fire alarm that once deprived some of sleep. Dennis McCafferty, "City puts its oar in, ends up a winner; Trial run: A rowing championship goes smoothly in Gainesville, giving the community pre-Olympic practice." *The Atlanta Constitution* (Atlanta, GA), 01 July 1995, pp. E/2.
147. Joe Drape, "Update '94: Two Years and Counting Annual Olympics Report," *Atlanta Journal-Constitution*, 18 September 1994, sec. G, p. 15.
148. Brenau College, *Bubbles* (Gainesville, GA; Brenau College, 1995), 127. Hereafter, references to this source are indicated as "*Bubbles* (1995)."
149. *Aurum* (formerly *Bubbles*) (Gainesville, GA: Brenau College, 2000), 96.
150. St. Louis Rowing Club, "Results--2004 Head of the Hooch, November 6-7, 2004," http://stlouisrowingclub.com/regattas/2004_hooch.pdf (accessed 18 May 2013).

151. "Regatta Central," https://www.regattacentral.com/regatta/entries/?job_id=772&org_id=675 (accessed 18 May 2013).
152. "Brenau crew earns bronze," *Gainesville Times*, 30 March 2009, http://www.gainesvilletimes.com/archives/16819/ (http://www.gainesvilletimes.com/archives/16819/).
153. Kim Butler, "My Story," Kim Butler: Letting Go Blog, entry posted 27 September 2010, http://kimbutler.theworldrace.org/?filename=bio (accessed 18 May 2013).
154. Brenau College, *Bubbles* (Gainesville, GA; Brenau College, 1997), 84–85. Hereafter, references to this source are indicated as "*Bubbles* (1997)."
155. *Aurum* (formerly *Bubbles*) (Gainesville, GA: Brenau College, 2000), 96.
156. "Brenau," http://www.ssacsports.com/stats/2002-03/Volleyball/bre.htm (accessed 21 March 2014).
157. Dan Washburn, "Two ex-Trojans give Brenau a needed spark," *Gainesville Times* (Gainesville, GA), 28 October 2001, sec. E, p. 1.
158. "2009 Volleyball," http://www.brenautigers.com/sport/7/6.php (accessed 18 May 2013).
159. "Andre Ferreira will serve as interim coach of Golden Tigers Volleyball Team," Brenau University Update, 11 October 2011, http://update.brenau.edu/2011/10/11/andre-ferreira-will-serve-as-interim-coach-of-golden-tigers-volleyball-team/ (accessed 18 May 2013).
160. "Brenau (Ga.), NAIA Volleyball," NAIA Official Statistics, http://www.dakstats.com/WebSync/Pages/Team/TeamStats.aspx?association=10&sg=WVB&sea=NAIWVB_2013&team=1924&tab=2 (accessed 17 March 2014).
161. *Bubbles* (1997), 86.
162. Brenau University, "2012 Cross Country Coaches," http://www.brenautigers.com/coach/10/3.php (accessed 18 May 2013).
163. *Aurum* (formerly *Bubbles*) (Gainesville, GA: Brenau College, 1999), 122.
164. Brenau University, "Cheer on the Crouching Tigers," Brenau News, 6 September 2011, http://www.brenautigers.com/article/578.php (accessed 18 May 2013).
165. "Cheerleading Season Outlook," http://www.brenautigers.com/outlook/10/8.php (accessed 17 March 2014).
166. Ibid.
167. Brenau University, "Brenau University 2007 Golden Tigers Softball Camp" http://www.brenau.edu/athletics/softballbrochure.pdf (accessed 22 August 2007).

168. Brenau University, "2011 Softball," http://www.brenautigers.com/sport/8/2.php (accessed 18 May 2013).
169. "Brenau softball eliminated in national tournament," *Gainesville Times*, 22 May 2012, http://www.gainesvilletimes.com/section/176/article/67863/ (accessed 18 May 2013).
170. Gordon Leslie, "Bays to Spearhead Brenau's New Women's Basketball Program"; *S.S.A.C. Sports*, 24 August 2005, http://www.ssacsports.com/article/493.php (accessed 18 May 2013).
171. Hometownhall.com, "Golden Tigers Basketball opens with a Bang," 13 November 2006, http://www.hometownhall.com/sports/college/golden-tigers-basketball-.shtml (accessed 24 August 2007).
172. "Team Career Stats," http://www.dakstats.com/WebSync/Pages/Team/TeamStats.aspx?association=10&sg=WBB&sea=NAIWBB_2013&team=6877&tab=2 (accessed 21 March 2014).
173. "2011-12 Basketball Coaches," http://www.brenautigers.com/coach/9/1.php (accessed 21 March 2014).
174. Gordon Leslie, "Bays to Spearhead Brenau's New Women's Basketball Program," *S.S.A.C. Sports*, 24 August 2005, http://www.ssacsports.com/article/493.php (accessed 21 March 2014).
175. "Brenau to add track and field program," *Gainesville Times*, 23 November 2011, http://www.gainesvilletimes.com/archives/59634/ (accessed 18 May 2013).
176. Ibid.
177. "Brenau to introduce women's golf program in 2013," *Gainesville Times*, 12 December 2012, http://www.gainesvilletimes.com/section/176/article/76959/ (accessed 13 December 2012).
178. Lee Johnson, "Brenau looking to expand again; School may use fields near Pacolet Milliken plant for athletics," *Gainesville Times*, 19 December 2012, http://www.gainesvilletimes.com/section/6/article/77309/ (accessed 20 December 2012).

Chapter 9

Student Success at Shaping Space

Secret Societies at Brenau

History suggests that in the ongoing negotiation between students and College personnel to refine the character of Brenau College, the students enjoyed some successes, but often came up short. Brenau students seem to have had very little input in the development of the College's curriculum. Likewise, the faculty and administration generally made policy decisions on matters like admissions (at least concerning race and gender) absent student contributions. Students enjoyed some success in shaping rules of conduct at Brenau and in negotiating the development of athletics on campus, but even those changes saw, at times, significant faculty and staff member involvement. Ultimately, in the many contests between Brenau students and College personnel to create what each group perceived as an ideal college, students enjoyed the most success in shaping Brenau's secret societies, its sororities and secret student clubs. Because of their clandestine nature, these groups operated largely beyond the reach of Brenau's faculty and staff and afforded students great autonomy to create within these spheres their preferred version of collegiate space.

There is no universally accepted definition of what a collegiate "secret society" is. One might think of them simply as groups comprised of college students (both men and women) that each try to differing degrees to keep various aspects of their affairs hidden from the public. These aspects might include such things as "secret passwords, grips, costumes, and strange initiation ceremonies."[1] Secret clubs and societies have existed at American colleges for centuries. The first to be founded was likely the F.H.C. Society, which existed at the College of William & Mary as early as 1750 and claimed Thomas Jefferson as a member.[2] Perhaps the most well-known collegiate secret society is the mysterious Skull & Bones Society of Yale University, which was founded in 1832 and whose rumored alumni include many rich and powerful individuals.[3] There are and have been many collegiate secret societies in the United States.[4] At least one such group and, at older and/or larger schools, often more are associated with practically every major college and university in the country, including Brenau.

Since the College's inception, several secret societies have existed at the institution at one time or another. These were particularly popular during the early twentieth century. The 1901 *Bubbles* yearbook suggested that the first to come to campus was a group called ΚΚΦ.[5] Not much at all is known about it, but the group's four members claimed a Greek motto ("Κακŵγ Κλδσμεν Φρενιον"), which, sadly, defies translation. Other clandestine groups would follow. Such groups have been similar to sororities in that both secret clubs and societies and Brenau's sororities did much behind closed doors. They differ in that Brenau's secret clubs simply never styled themselves as sororities nor did they publicize activities such as formal dances or socials as did sororities. Put another way, sororities maintained a public face that secret groups and clubs largely eschewed.

John E. Sites, a former dean at Brenau, wrote about the College's secret clubs in a memorandum dated November 27, 1973. He described the Tri-Kappas, a group that was active on campus around 1912 and whose trappings bore something of a resemblance to those of the Ku Klux Klan.[6]

Sites also indicated that another group called only "G.S.G." operated at Brenau in 1912, but that it left behind only a single strange photograph in the *Bubbles* yearbook to mark its existence.[7] Sites wrote that in 1914, the "Sphinx" society formed at Brenau. It lasted over ten years and never had more than around a dozen members. Sites noted, "The dress of the organization was long embroidered white robes with every part of the body covered except for the eyes [which actually sounds more "Klan-like" than the garb of the Tri-Kappas...]. They included a long pair of black beads, and if that were not strange enough, it was noted that the song of the group was 'The Old Oaken Bucket.'"[8] In 1915, another group, the "Mercurites," came to Brenau and stayed briefly.

Then, in 1919, two societies established themselves at Brenau: the "Skulls" and the "Stabs." The *Bubbles* of 1919 related that the latter group's motto was a "dark secret" and that their symbol was a knife and skull. (See Figure 37.) A 1919 edition of the *Alchemist* described the Stabs' rivals, the Skulls. It read:

> A new feature has been added to the several other organizations of social clubs, the name of which is "Skulls." The organizers held their initial meeting Sunday evening...At this meeting, the members decided upon the secret proceedings and mystic operations as are customary to make its followers realize the honor and seriousness of the entrance into such a club. Each "Skull" was sworn in by a flowery oath of allegiance and made to realize more keenly that each Sunday evening at an appointed hour and place, she is required to hang out a smile and banish all thoughts of the outer world from regions supposed to be inhabited by the brain.[9]

The Skulls ended their meeting by discussing "matters of grave importance" until their hostess served refreshments that consisted of "a lovely ice course."[10]

The College yearbooks revealed that the Skulls, the Stabs, and Brenau's other secret societies generally shared several common traits. All groups typically adopted particular costumes, created secret passwords and rituals, and had their own songs, flowers, and/or slogans. These features would have served to foster cohesion within the group while, at the same time, distinguishing the club from outsiders. None of Brenau's various secret clubs had many members. Yearbook photographs consistently revealed just a handful of women (seldom more than ten) in any club. Smaller numbers would have made for more intimacy, which would also have brought the group closer together. Finally, examining many years' worth of the *Bubbles* revealed that secret clubs tended to be very short-lived. Few lasted more than a decade. Most came and went in only one or two years, probably because student interests turned to other pastimes.

Only one secret society at Brenau has enjoyed any longevity. According to a description published annually in the *Bubbles* yearbooks during the late 1930s and 1940s, "The H.G.H. Senior Society exists to promote the interests of Brenau College, and to serve the welfare of the college student body as a whole, without regard to personal, social, class or political affiliations."[11] Dean Sites wrote that the organization formed in 1935. The initials are believed by many to stand for "Highest Given Honor," though nothing available in the Brenau Archives can precisely substantiate this and, moreover, current members of the organization disavow that meaning. The *Bubbles* declared that, "In May of each year the Society will select seven new members from the Junior class of the college, who in turn will select, at the proper time, their own successors. Thus, it is proposed that the H.G.H. Society will continue to serve the college so long as the college shall endure."[12]

Only Brenau's best could earn membership in H.G.H. The *Bubbles* noted that:

> Election to membership in H.G.H. is based on merit and merit alone. Everything a student does from her entrance into the college, to serve the college, in the class room, in the debate forum, on the concert stage, in dramatic productions, in contributing to and administering college publications, in the Y. W. C. A., in athletics,

or any other constructive curricular or extra curricular activity, will bring her that much nearer the goal of H.G.H.[13]

Dean Sites specified that initiates were to be "the most outstanding seven members of the Junior Class" and that "membership in the Society has traditionally been the highest honor the school can offer, as it gives recognition to the achievements of the previous three years of the student's college life."[14] Merit alone determined selection. The *Bubbles* asserted that, "Merit is so emphasized that a girl may secure election if she deserves it, even if she has personal enemies in the Society" and that "neither politics nor fraternal considerations play any part in the election of H.G.H."[15] Election to the group was a stamp that "indicates character and achievement" and the society sought young women that were "leaders in large public affairs, who are marked by such qualities as courage, generosity, kindness and high moral character."[16] According to the *Bubbles*, the society would admit "only students whose loyalty to Brenau College is proved and beyond question."[17] Dean Sites reiterated this point and wrote, "It was said of this group, in the time of their founding, that no service, task, or calling would be too great nor too demanding for the members of this group to perform."[18]

Though the identity of the members within the group is known from year to year, specifically what the group has done for Brenau is unknown because H.G.H. operates in other respects mostly in secret. One former Brenau student described the slim extent to which the society operated in public. She wrote:

> There is one secret society at Brenau University, and it's highly regarded on campus and taken very serious [sic]. They're called "Horses" – it's seven women in the senior class who are without a doubt dedicated to Brenau. Nobody knows what they do (though we know that they somehow "contribute" to the campus and we know who they are because they wear circular pins...and if you yell out "HORSE!" they have to stop whatever they're doing and bow their heads for seven seconds, etc.), but it's a huge thing here....When they tap their seven "ponies" for the next year,

everybody waits in the cold to see it, they bless the houses at the beginning of each year, etc.[19]

The student concluded by saying that H.G.H. did "have a skull and bones on their pins" and that "in their picture in the yearbook (where they're dressed in their black robes, sitting on the steps of Bailey [Hall] facing left...), they have a skull and bones banner in front of them."[20] Examining several editions of the *Bubbles* revealed that the H.G.H. yearbook portrait is indeed consistently as the student described from year to year—the seven members of the group are always photographed at night sitting in a lambda shape facing to their right on the steps of Bailey Hall. (See Figure 38.) Another photograph from a private collection displayed online for a time until 2013 showed that at initiation, Society members apply what appears to be electrical tape to their faces to form a capital letter "H" on each cheek and a capital letter "G" on their forehead.

A newspaper article published in the February 6, 2008, edition of the *Alchemist* seems to verify some of what this student and the yearbooks related about the society and likewise offered additional details on H.G.H. The articled described the first component of the H.G.H. initiation ritual in some detail. It read:

> Students of Brenau know when "tapping" is close. Ribbons, bearing the society's colors are tied to the sundial located in Sorority Circle. It's believed by many that where the bows are faced suggest where the next horse lives.[21]

For that year, tapping occurred on January 20 as "residents of Brenau stood in Sorority Circle and waited in anticipation."[22] The all-night affair began when the current H.G.H. members assembled around a small sculpture of a sundial displayed in the Sorority Circle lawn before leaving to collect the new inductees to the society (the "ponies"). The current members led the ponies, their heads bowed, through campus to the sundial. There, graduated members of H.G.H. who had returned to campus for the ceremony were "asked to bow the ponies' heads farther down as they stand in Sorority Circle."²³ After this ceremony of "revealing," inductees were not allowed to leave campus for seven weeks. During this period, to continue earning membership in the society, the ponies would be found from time to time around campus "in horsey mode." This meant that they would wear the letters "H. G. H." in white on their faces while performing various chores and tasks for the College, generally at night. The article went on to say that after those seven weeks, the juniors and seniors would travel to Panama City, Florida, presumably for some initiation ceremony because, "After their return to Gainesville, the 'ponies' bear the symbol of the honor society."²⁴ The article intimated that some initiates have declined membership in the Senior Honor Society over the years. It stated, "Ponies that do not wish to remain members are allowed to remove themselves within the first seven weeks of membership."²⁵ These students would become known as "fallen horses."

In describing some of the lore surrounding H.G.H., the article noted that particular colors apparently held meaning to the society. H.G.H. members "wear circular black pins bearing certain symbols in gold" to identify themselves and will occasionally wear the letters "H. G. H." in black on their faces.²⁶ Also, each of the seven members of H.G.H. has one of the following colors associated with her: red, orange, yellow, green, blue, purple and white.²⁷ Nothing is known about the significance of the colors. In addition to colors and lettering, the newspaper related that, "the society uses the monuments on campus to symbolize qualities of H.G.H."²⁸ The monuments important to the society were:

> The sundial in Sorority Circle, the flagpole near the Student Owens Center, the Japanese sculpture near the Gazebo, the Brenau Ideal, and the sculpture near Wilkes Hall, the Astronomer's Stone in Sorority Circle, and the stone black plaque between the two benches in Sorority Circle.²⁹

The article suggested that each monument has its own name that is known to H.G.H. members. The paper stated nothing about the significance of each monument to the society.

Perhaps just as interesting as the *Alchemist* article reporting on the H.G.H. Senior Honor Society were several of the comments posted online from readers about the article. As might be expected, most of the comments consisted of a sentence or two either lauding or criticizing the society for one reason or another, but one set of comments is particularly interesting. A person claiming to be a jilted fiancé of an H.G.H. member posted four paragraphs of text commenting on the article. Besides being rather poorly written and riddled with grammatical errors, the postings purportedly exposed some of the secret workings of the society as told to the vengeful author by his ex-fiancé. For example, the author of these posts described what supposedly happens with initiates on the Panama City trip. Also, according to him, H.G.H. stands not for "highest given honor" but rather for a "higher giving hand."[30] Although other seemingly-informed commentators challenged his veracity, this author's posts do include quite a bit of detail that might be quite challenging to fabricate—assuming anyone would even take the time to do so.

One point that no source speaks to is why there is an equine association with the Senior Honor Society. Presumably, there is some reason why society members are called "horses" as opposed to something else. Perhaps the women in H.G.H. are regarded as the "workhorses" of the College. One can only speculate because, appropriately enough for a secret society, H.G.H. members seem to be very tight-lipped about their clandestine club.

One H.G.H. alumna member who graduated around 2008 (who wished to remain anonymous) revealed very little when interviewed about the society via email in 2011. The former member was able to confirm that H.G.H. does not stand for "highest given honor," but she could not disclose what the initials actually represent. Additionally, she was able to verify that both the horse and particular colors hold significance to H.G.H. but could not elaborate further on either. She did stress that, "At all times, in all actions, the Society is doing what it believes is in the best interest of Brenau" and noted that "members of the Society work behind the scenes to do anything they can to assist the University at any time."[31] Importantly for the institution, she said this assistance could take a tangible form: The interviewed H.G.H. alumna (who was pursuing a career as an attorney) indicated that, among alumnae, "members of the Society are the largest monetary donating group to Brenau."[32]

What is clear about H.G.H. and Brenau's other secret societies is that they were student-led and that they operated largely beyond the reach of the College faculty and staff in many respects. To borrow a reference from Sherlock Holmes, this is best evidenced by the dog that did not bark.[33] There is nothing in the Brenau Archives that suggests that Brenau's governors exercised much control at all over these secretive groups. Although various pieces of correspondence or entries in the faculty meeting minutes books indicated that Brenau's faculty and administration had power over other groups on campus, nothing exists to suggest that secret societies were similarly controlled.

Secret groups like H.G.H. have not been the only student organizations at Brenau to operate largely beyond the reach of College personnel. Social sororities have also long existed at Brenau and have, for the most part, operated independently in many respects from the College's faculty and administration. The establishment of sororities at Brenau College continued a centuries-old tradition of fraternity life in America. Student Greek-letter societies had existed in the country since the founding of Phi Beta Kappa at the College of William and Mary in 1776.[34] Prior to the mid-nineteenth century, such societies existed for and admitted only men. Then, in 1851 and 1852, women at Georgia's Wesleyan Female College in Macon founded Alpha Delta Pi and Phi Mu from two existing literary societies and, in so doing, gave birth to women's sororities.[35]

In her book *The Education of the Southern Belle*, Christie Anne Farnham described the origin of sororities at early southern women's colleges. Farnham analyzed student letters and journals and determined that many young women at antebellum women's colleges in the South were profoundly homesick. In the absence of relatives and loved ones from back home, students forged very close ties of friendship with schoolmates. Opportunities to do this abounded because students actually socialized a great deal at their colleges. Farnham posited that as groups of young women formed networked friendships, cliques emerged at their colleges as students were included and excluded by their peer groups. Farnham asserted that, "Through these practices of inclusion and exclusion, young women constructed their position in the social world of the school."[36]

Literary clubs modeled after those at men's colleges grew out of this process of construction. Typically, southern women's colleges had two such societies that would hold debates (or at least lively conversations) with each other. Over time, these clubs often developed into secret societies and adopted Greek letters. These early societies competed fiercely for new members, at times literally rushing down to the train station as trains pulled in to begin combing through the ranks of new students for suitable recruits. Farnham revealed that social background and personality mattered more in selection for membership to these nascent sororities than anything else, which suited the class-conscious antebellum South perfectly. She concluded, "It is not surprising that the first sorority would begin in the slave South, where hierarchy was an integral part of the social fabric and distancing oneself from social inferiors was an imperative of the lady of chivalry."[37]

Historian Diana Turk picked up about where Farnham left off in examining sororities in her book entitled *Bound by a Mighty Vow: Sisterhood and Women's Fraternities, 1870–1920*. She used the Kappa Alpha Theta sorority as a case study for her analysis, which was not confined solely to the South. Turk argued that the first women to attend college, who were also the founders of the first sororities in the 1800s, were out to prove themselves to be the equals of men. Taking men's fraternities as their model, sorority founders created secret rules and rituals for their groups. These women emphasized intellectual achievement, chose careers over marriage, and asserted a new role for their gender, one that stretched beyond "the old occupations of home-making and teaching."[38] In so doing, Turk claimed that early sororities, "effectively redefined for themselves the feminine ideal, broadening it to include intellectual capacity along with the more socially accepted traits of morality and social grace."[39]

The second generation of sorority women, Turk wrote, was, by contrast, already accepted on college campuses. Having nothing to prove academically, these women focused on the social aspects of Greek life and concentrated on such things as "banquets, spreads, and cozies."[40] Sorority membership grew rapidly and sororities became image conscious, national organizations. Also, because sorority women were mostly white, middle-class, and Protestant, they felt threatened by "others," and so discriminated against Jews, Catholics, and blacks seeking membership. Resenting Greek "practices of exclusivity and elitism," many colleges banned sororities.[41] Sororities responded by trying to improve their image and to come across as being responsible, scholarly groups. Turk asserted that the campaign often worked and gained wider acceptance for sororities. By the 1920s, sororities were "permanent features of American campus life."[42] They were likewise permanent features at Brenau, a rare thing for a women's college.

The first widespread pubic mention of sororities at Brenau came in 1904, when the "Brenau Notes" section of the *Atlanta Constitution* related, "It is rumored that one or two well-known Sororities are to organize chapters here during the present term."[43] The first mention of a Greek organization by name in the paper came a half a year later when the *Constitution* reported that, "The Misses Knight entertained the Phi Mu Gamma Sorority Friday evening."[44] The "Notes" would continue to mention Brenau "sorority" and "fraternity" (the terms were used interchangeably) happenings for years.

In fact, Greek societies had apparently existed at Brenau for some time prior to making the society pages. In 1932, Brenau's annual student yearbook, the *Bubbles*, related the history of the Greek system at the College. It began:

> The early beginning of the sorority movement on the campus of Brenau may be seen as far back as 1900. In this year appeared the first organization bearing the Greek letter[s, the] Phi Gamma Alpha Club—which was a "society for the advancement of the mathematical science."[45]

The essay continued, noting that Phi Mu Gamma organized on campus in 1902. The *Bubbles* declared that "This was the first sorority on the campus."[46] The following year, a group called Alpha Beta Tau formed at Brenau. On April 14, 1910, Alpha Delta Pi granted a charter to this chapter. According to the *Bubbles*, this made AΔΠ "the first A. national sorority to appear on the campus."[47] This practice of smaller, local Greek letter groups forming at Brenau and then later being chartered by national sororities continued for several years.[48] Delta Delta Delta formed his way at Brenau in 1914 when members of three local Greek clubs joined together.[49] Zeta Tau Alpha likewise chartered in this manner on January 1, 1911, when it formed from a group called Pi Gamma Theta, which had appeared on campus in 1907.[50]

The *Bubbles* essay continued, describing how Brenau gained three more nationally prominent sororities. It read:

> On October 8, 1910, Phi Mu was established through the colonization of several Phi Mus from their Alpha chapter of Wesleyan College. In 1910 was also the beginning of Alpha Chi Omega as the local Eta Upsilon Gamma. It was granted the charter of that national on November 24, 1911. In 1913 appeared Nu Sigma which became in the same year Alpha Gamma Delta.[51]

Several more sororities followed these to campus. In 1921, Theta Upsilon granted a charter to a local Brenau group called Lambda Beta Psi, which had organized in 1918. The local Beta Beta club became Delta Zeta on May 13, 1924. Delta Phi Epsilon joined Brenau's Greek system on November

28, 1926. Also in 1926, Brenau's local society named Pi Gamma Theta originated. It would develop into Alpha Xi Delta in May of 1927. Finally, the *Bubbles* essay related that, "The Athenians were further augmented by the Delta Phi Sigmas who were petitioning Alpha Delta Theta. Their petition was granted in May of 1929."[52]

All in all, by the 1930s, Brenau claimed eleven sororities. Eight of these were or would become widespread, national organizations and six of these would prosper at Brenau into the twenty-first century. These six were Alpha Chi Omega, Alpha Delta Pi, Alpha Gamma Delta, Delta Delta Delta, Phi Mu, and Zeta Tau Alpha. Brenau's sororities have always been active within their respective national organizations and Brenau has for many years occasionally hosted large meetings of the regional and national organizations of some of the sororities.[53] The other three national sorority organizations that established chapters at Brenau at one time or another were Delta Zeta, Chi Omega, and Alpha Xi Delta. Delta Zeta folded at Brenau during the 1950s but was revived in 1962. That same year, Chi Omega established a chapter at Brenau. Delta Zeta went on to fold again at Brenau in 1978. Likewise, Chi Omega shut down its Brenau chapter in 2003. Brenau's chapter of Alpha Xi Delta, today a large national organization, had folded by 1941. Brenau's other two sororities that existed around this decade (Theta Upsilon and Delta Phi Epsilon) were national organizations, but were much smaller in scope. These had ceased to operate at the College well prior to mid-century.

All in all, throughout its history, Brenau has possessed a remarkable number of sororities for an institution of its modest size and all-female character. Indeed, only three other all-women's colleges (Spelman College in Atlanta, Bennett College for Women in Greensboro, North Carolina, and Stephens College in Columbia, Missouri) have chapters of nationally recognized social sororities. With eight national organizations represented, the Greek system at Brenau is both the largest of any women's college and the only one with official sorority houses.[54]

Exactly why Brenau, as a small women's college, has had such a vibrant Greek life when most other similar institutions have none is a matter of conjecture. In *A Century of Higher Education for American Women*, author Mabel Newcomer concluded that schools like Brenau should not have needed sororities. She wrote that, "The women's colleges more often than the others [coeducational colleges] have managed without sororities or other societies with limited memberships."[55] She attributed this to two things. First was the "very adequate dormitory facilities" of women's colleges.[56] Sororities popped up at coeducational campuses, Newcomer claimed, to satisfy housing needs of female students when colleges failed to offer women room and board options. Secondly, Newcomer claimed that sororities often existed to confer social prestige on members and that this was simply not needed at women's colleges because merely attending these colleges conferred, by itself, all the social prestige a student could need.[57]

Regarding Brenau, Newcomer was likely wrong on both accounts. During the early twentieth century (the period when Brenau women founded most of their sororities), housing at Brenau was frequently somewhat tight. Multiple promotional materials, advertisements, and articles about Brenau in early editions of the *Atlanta Constitution* constantly reiterated the point that Brenau was experiencing explosive growth and operating at or very near capacity. These materials also intimated that dormitory space was precious. In addition, it is probably no coincidence that all of Brenau's sororities very quickly acquired a chapter house or bungalow after organizing. This sorority housing would have been welcomed by Brenau's administration as well as its students to ease pressure on the College facilities and so sororities themselves would have been welcomed at Brenau.[58]

Just as Brenau officials should have welcomed sororities because of housing considerations, students at Brenau and other women's colleges might well have welcomed the coming of sororities for social reasons. Newcomer contended that sororities did not flourish at women's colleges because students at such places were not concerned with getting more social prestige than that they got simply by attending their well-respected schools. Yet, historians researching and writing after Newcomer have debunked this explanation of why sororities did not emerge at women's colleges. These historians have learned that social cliques and concern over family background and social status *did* strongly exist at women's colleges. From reading women's college student literature of the time, Helen Horowitz concluded that students in the northeastern women's colleges "divided themselves into sets, or cliques, which formed a hierarchical scale."[59] Pretty, popular young women from wealthy families, who had the right clothes, friends, and contacts, were on top and referred to as "swells." The young women who were different, quiet, too studious, and from modest economic backgrounds were on the bottom of the hierarchy. In between were "all-around girls," often direct and forceful women, fiercely loyal to their classes and colleges, who "dominated campus organizations" by holding meetings, handling club money, and the like.[60] The swells and the all-around girls at these schools probably would not at all have minded if additional organizations (like sororities) had existed to help sort-out social position or to further college ends.

Administrative officials at these and other women's institutions apparently *did* mind. Barbara Miller Solomon wrote that, "Some educators and students opposed sororities because their presence promoted exclusivity."[61] Amy Thompson McCandless observed that, "Despite the idealism expressed in sorority mottos, constitutions, and oaths, these organizations were often viewed suspiciously by the uninitiated. In the early decades of the twentieth century, many public colleges in the South opposed the introduction of exclusive organizations of any sort."[62] Public colleges were not alone in their disdain for Greek societies. McCandless continued, writing that, "Antifraternity feeling also led to the banning of sororities at private institutions" in the South.[63] Sweet Briar College, Hollins College, Salem College, and even Wesleyan itself, the mother of the first collegiate Greek-letter organizations for women, banned sororities for life.[64]

In fact, at women's colleges across the country, officials eliminated existing sororities and prevented new sororities from colonizing in an effort to prevent Greek-fostered exclusivity from developing on campuses. The administration at Brenau also discouraged exclusivity. From early on, Brenau's promotional materials made such claims as "a perfectly democratic spirit prevails in the institution."[65] College rules that prohibited practices like extravagant dress existed at Brenau since its inception and were meant to foster this "democratic spirit."

But try as they might, Brenau officials could not eliminate social distinctiveness entirely from their institution. Instead, they had to acknowledge that the College was "fortunate in having a large patronage among the wealthier classes of the South, who demand for their daughters the conveniences of life to which they have been accustomed at home."[66] Such young women as these would have been akin to the "swells" of the New England women's colleges. It is probable that they would not have objected to the presence of sororities at Brenau because they would have been among the most coveted members of such groups. In the running negotiation with students over the character of the College, Brenau officials ultimately assented to the existence of sororities on campus in part out of deference to these student attitudes.[67]

But sororities did not merely exist at Brenau; they thrived and enjoyed great acceptance on campus from early on. An article that appeared in 1908 in the *Atlanta Constitution* declared, "At Brenau the sorority life has fine expression."[68] It went on to say that, "Besides the sororities, there are literary, dramatic and social organizations of the lighter vein, while in both colleges, the one in Gainesville and in Eufaula, Alabama [a short-lived branch campus of Brenau] there are well organized departments of the Young Women's Christian Association."[69] The article clearly sought to convey the message that Brenau valued sororities as much as any of its other campus organizations. Indeed, the College actively encouraged their establishment and growth as indicated by a line in the 1910 catalog that read, "Any group of students who desire to do so may organize themselves into a sorority."[70] Brenau's administration supported its sororities in advertising as well. One promotional piece in the *Atlanta Constitution* read:

> One of the most modern essentials to the happiness of the school girl these days is the sorority. There are several of the best known national sororities at Brenau. Chapter houses, beautifully furnished, are provided, in which these sororities can give entertainments, etc.[71]

Brenau proactively supported sororities at a time when other southern women's colleges were going so far as to outright outlaw them.

Why the disparity? McCandless wrote that, early on, students and administrators at larger schools valued sororities because they "promoted a sense of sisterhood and recalled the family life that students left behind" when they left home to attend college.[72] This might have been true at Brenau as well, despite its more modest size, because Brenau students were often very far from home. In 1907, for example, the "Brenau Notes" column mentioned that Brenau claimed students from as far away as Iowa and Massachusetts. The College boasted, "While there are some state institutions that have a larger attendance than Brenau, there is no institution in this section, at least, that draws its patronage from such a wide area."[73] According to a 1910 publication about Brenau, "The present student-body includes representatives from twenty-five states of the Union."[74] Presumably, some of these young women who were very far from home would have been unable to see their families with any frequency owing to distance and so could have become very homesick. Sorority ties might have substituted for family ties to salve this homesickness and, in so doing, have earned the respect of the administration. Of course, this function for sororities would have lessened over time as transportation and telecommunications improvements kept students in better touch with families. Yet, by the time automobiles and telephones were readily available to Brenau students, sororities had irremovably entrenched themselves into the life of the College.

Besides helping young women develop friendships, the administration believed that the sororities taught lessons of responsibility and domesticity. Certainly, College officials would have been impressed by the sorority women who, according to a newspaper advertisement, had "resolved to do our part of the housework" on the little cottage they acquired as a sorority house.[75] College officials also appreciated how the sororities could develop leadership capabilities in women, a view expressed in the 1910 College catalog.[76] In addition, some sororities went so far as to donate money to Brenau. For example, the "Phi Mu Gamma society (Gamma chapter at Brenau)" donated an annual scholarship to Brenau on behalf of the Atlanta Woman's Club.[77] Finally, sororities supported good scholarship among their members. Several years of the Brenau student handbooks indicated that students had to maintain good grades to live in a sorority house or to participate in sorority rush.

Brenau's faculty members and administrators may also have appreciated the opportunity to use the sororities for their own ends in their negotiations with students. Solomon wrote that, "Administrators, early wary of the political power of these societies as a competing authority, at first tried to halt their development. In time, though, they found it useful to enlist sorority leaders along with those of student government, to control social behavior on campus."[78] Early editions of Brenau's yearbook, the *Bubbles*, did very often depict the leaders in sororities occupying other influential positions in organizations on campus, such as in the Student Government Association or the Y.W.C.A. By enlisting the support of those leaders, College personnel would have gained powerful allies in implementing social control on campus. Brenau officials actually acknowledged this outright by asserting that, "These organizations...under wise control can be made helpful in the disciplinary management of the institution."[79]

Later in the twentieth century, Brenau's administrators expressed other reasons for appreciating the College's sororities. In an address given to the Brenau College Board of Trustees in 1964, President Josiah Crudup related that, "Through our plan of seeking cooperation and financial support from national sororities, we have received financial aid from Chi Omega, Tri Delta, Phi Mu and Delta Zeta during the past twelve months."[80] In other words, Brenau liked sororities because it received funds from the national sorority organizations.

In a similar address given two years before, Dr. Crudup explained the arrangement that Brenau enjoyed with its sororities. He began by telling the board of Brenau's long Greek history and of its unique relationship with sororities regarding housing. Crudup said:

> One characteristic which makes Brenau College rather distinctive among the small women's colleges of America is the presence of national sororities on our campus. This has been a fact existing since the past century and some of the oldest sorority chapters in America are located on this college campus. The fact that Brenau owns and controls all of the sorority houses at Brenau College makes our situation even more unusual. The sorority houses at Brenau College have the same status as dormitories and they are owned by the College, but we give the right of occupancy only to the sorority members of each particular sorority. [81]

Brenau benefited greatly from this arrangement. It essentially got to house many students for half price in very fine residences. (See Figure 39.) Crudup continued:

> The administrative attitude at Brenau College has been that we will match funds with national sororities in making such improvements and additions to their houses as they desire. Brenau College then gives to that particular sorority the right of occupancy of that building as long as the chapter exists in good standing. All pay the same rate of board and room whether living in dormitories or sorority houses. In recent years, much improvement has been made in sorority houses here on this campus by working out plans with sorority national headquarters to match money with the College in financing these improvements. [82]

Crudup provided an example of this arrangement in action. He told the Trustees:

Recently, Delta Zeta Sorority has returned to the campus under this kind of plan and occupies the new building at 214 Prior Street. This sorority house has come into existence through a gift from the Citizens Bank and a contribution from Delta Zeta National headquarters. This brings the total to seven national sororities on campus now. [83]

This arrangement attracted other comers as well and Dr. Crudup indicated that Brenau had "turned to these other sources of financial aid in making progress."[84] Dr. Crudup related that, "This spring Brenau College has been approached by two other sororities wishing to establish chapters on this campus. These sororities are Sigma Kappa and Chi Omega, who have promised to contribute $10,000 each to the establishment of sorority houses for their chapters here." [85] In 1965, Dr. Crudup indicated to the Trustees that Brenau had received an "Alpha Delta Pi gift (pledge) of 10,000.00" to apply toward the renovations of its sorority house on Brenau's campus.[86] Dr. Crudup reported that, "Through cooperation with our Alpha Delta Pi National, plans have been made to add a wing onto the west side of [the] Alpha Delta Pi House which will provide for four additional bedrooms, a communal bathroom, an additional club room, a terrace and a new front porch. These plans also provide for the renovation of all old bathrooms into modern design with tile floors and walls."[87] Dr. Crudup indicated that the projected cost of the expansion and renovation would be $42,560—a hefty figure for the day—and intimated that the sorority's support was much appreciated. [88]

Besides gaining support for campus housing, Brenau also received support from its sororities in student recruitment. The November 24, 1969, edition of the *Alchemist* related that Brenau was "in the red financially" after 1936 when a tornado destroyed much of the front campus.[89] When Dr. Crudup arrived at Brenau as its new president, he had "neither the time nor the money to send out a traveling field representative to encourage high school seniors to attend Brenau."[90] The *Alchemist* reported, "It occurred to him to let the National Sororities do the advertising for him."[91] Dr. Crudup stipulated that Brenau's sororities had to maintain "a sufficient number of girls" living in any sorority house as a condition of establishing houses on the campus. So, the sororities advertised for Brenau, "encouraging the high school seniors to attend and join the sororities."[92] Ultimately, Dr. Crudup concluded, "Brenau had to have sororities to be what it is today. We have neither church nor state support but we have sorority support."[93]

Despite the advantages the presence of the sororities at the College conferred upon Brenau, there were disadvantages as well. For example, Brenau's experience indicated that institutional fears about sororities being too exclusive may have been well-founded. In examining the experience of women students at college, Solomon observed that, "Some students discovered that whatever talents or skills they possessed, their religious, ethnic, or racial identities either kept them on the fringes or barred them from particular activities."[94] At Brenau, religion appears to have been, at times, one such bar to entry to a sorority.

No one less than Brenau's president substantiated this. In 1964, Dr. Crudup received a letter from a Mrs. Doris D. Smith, who was a member of the Brenau class of 1963. Mrs. Smith wrote to Dr. Crudup to inquire about whether or not a young Jewish friend of hers and a prospective Brenau student, Freda Rosner, might be able to join a sorority. Dr. Crudup replied:

> I have been pleased to receive your letter today letting me know ...about Freda Rosner who will enroll in Brenau College this fall and asking me to give you information concerning the eligibility of Jewish girls for sorority membership here on the campus.
>
> I wish it were possible for me to give you accurate information concerning this matter, but this is one phase of sorority life in which I do not have accurate information. Since the rules and rituals of the sororities are closely held secrets within the sorority and these secrets seem to vary from one sorority to another, this information is not available. However, it has been my observation that most of the sororities do not extend bids to Jewish girls,

though they seem to extend a very warm friendship, though not membership, as in the case of [one] Myrna Sheftal.

About 18 years ago, I recall a very fine Jewish girl from Texas, Lita Bernstein, who was very popular and elected Vice President of the Student Government Association, but she was not a member of one of the sororities on the campus.[95]

Dr. Crudup closed his letter by writing, "I believe it would be of doubtful value and even hurtful to Freda if she receives encouragement with the idea that she will receive a bid from a sorority. I believe it will be much more helpful to point out to her that about half of the students do not join sororities and find a very happy life among many friends here on the campus."[96]

It is perhaps a sad irony that a Jewish woman attending Brenau at nearly the height of the Civil Rights movement could not expect to get a bid from a sorority. This is especially true in light of the fact that she might have easily found a Greek home at Brenau four decades earlier. In 1926, the Delta Phi Epsilon sorority chartered its Xi chapter at Brenau College.[97] Though officially non-sectarian since the 1970s, ΔΦE had long been identified as a predominantly (and, on some campuses at times, exclusively) Jewish sorority.[98] There appears to have been a strong Jewish connection to the chapter at Brenau. Though archival materials say nothing about Brenau's ΔΦE women as being Jewish, other sources do.

Rabbi H. Cerf Straus began publishing *The Southern Israelite* as a temple bulletin in Augusta in 1925, but it became so popular that it quickly expanded into a monthly newspaper. New owners acquired the *Israelite* around 1930, moved the paper to Atlanta, and greatly expanded its circulation. *The Southern Israelite* would change hands a few more times in the century as the newspaper continued to grow its readership, eventually becoming a weekly. All the while, *The Southern Israelite* covered any and all news about southern Jewry, including, for a time, announcements it printed in its "Society and Personals" section.[99] Some of these referenced Brenau women and their membership in the College's

Delta Phi Epsilon chapter. One such announcement related in 1929 that, "Mrs. Marcus Klausman attended the Semi-Centennial Exercises at her Alma Mater, Brenau College Conservatory, Gainesville, Ga. While there she was honored by the Delta Phi Epsilon and made a member of the sorority."[100] Another spoke of Miss Matilda Shapiro who "received her Bachelor of Arts Degree from Brenau College in 1929," where she was a member of Delta Phi Epsilon.[101]

These young women would actually have been among the first and the last ΔΦE sisters at Brenau. Xi chapter shut down in 1930 after only four years of operation. Why is unknown. The *Bubbles* yearbooks of the times never depicted many women as being in Delta Phi Epsilon, so paltry membership may have been a factor. Still, that this group existed at all where and when it did is rather remarkable. How many people would predict that a small, private institution in the Bible Belt of rural Georgia in the 1920s would have attracted any Jewish women at all, let alone enough to contemplate forming a sisterhood? Brenau's Delta Phi Epsilon chapter was, in fact, only the second Jewish sorority founded in the state of Georgia and the first founded at a private institution. Sigma Delta Tau established its Eta chapter at the University of Georgia in 1924, barely a year before ΔΦE came to Brenau.[102] No other Jewish sorority would appear at a private college in Georgia until 1959 when Alpha Epsilon Phi established itself at Emory University.[103] While this history of religious tolerance in Brenau's Greek system seems to have waned over time (if Freda Rosner's case is any indication), it seems to say something positive about the institution that it existed once at all.

Excepting the window in which ΔΦE operated, up until the last decades of the twentieth century, Brenau's sororities were Christian (indeed, mostly Protestant) bastions. They were also all white. Brenau as an institution did not racially integrate its student body in any true sense until the early1970s.[104] Roughly two more decades would pass before even a single African-American woman is depicted by the *Bubbles* as being a member of any national Panhellenic sorority. In the 1994 edition of the yearbook, a photograph shows that an African American young woman was a member of the Alpha Gamma Delta sorority.[105] Even the passing of another decade would not substantially integrate Brenau's sororities. By 2006, only one other sorority (Alpha Chi Omega) had apparently extended membership to a black woman if photographs in the yearbook can be taken as evidence of this. The rest of Brenau's older sororities had always been all-white up through around 2008, despite the fact that African American students have comprised about 25% of Brenau's student body for over a decade.

Perhaps because of this, black students at Brenau have, over time, elected to form their own Greek organizations. The 1980 edition of the *Bubbles* revealed that the College's African American women sought to forge ties of sisterhood almost as soon as Brenau integrated. The yearbook indicated that four young black women were members of Alpha Psi Theta, "a colony struggling to become national" that "was started in November of 1977."[106] Despite this early effort, it would not be until 1994 that an historically black sorority finally came to campus. In May of that year, a chapter of the Alpha Kappa Alpha sorority came on-line at Brenau.[107] Six years later, students established the Tau Eta Chapter of Delta Sigma Theta Sorority, Inc., at Brenau.[108] These organizations remain small in terms of membership at Brenau as compared to other sororities, though they do provide a strong sense of sisterhood among minority students.

Brenau's sororities have also apparently made membership decisions at one time or another for more esoteric reasons. Evidently, marriage was a bar to sorority membership for some time to such an extent that married women at Brenau who desired to go Greek formed their own sorority.[109] The 1974–1975 student handbook read, "Mu Rho Sigma, a sorority for women who are married or have been married, was founded at Brenau in May of 1974."[110] Very little information exists about the group and it was not mentioned anywhere on the College website as of May, 2013. According to the Brenau College *Student Handbook* published in 1985, the organization was apparently still on campus, although it is not clear how many members it attracted. It ceased to be sometime thereafter.

Another unusual factor Brenau sororities apparently considered for a time when selecting members was smoking preference. A letter sent by an anonymous "Brenau Alumna" to President Crudup in 1964 called his attention to "the serious problem of the smoking of cigarettes at the college" and indicated that:

> At present, for a Brenau girl to be considered at all by any of the sororities for membership she must smoke, or be willing to start smoking in order to be "one of the girls."[111]

Nothing suggests that Dr. Crudup pursued the matter, but it is interesting that a young woman went to the trouble to raise the issue at all.

The women who were granted entry into a Brenau sorority comprised a membership that has varied in number over time. Sorority membership in the early 1900s was relatively small. College yearbook photographic spreads seldom depicted more than ten or twelve young women in any chapter. By the 1930s, sorority membership had grown but still never comprised a very large percentage of the student body. The 1932 *Bubbles* revealed that membership in the several social sororities varied, with the smallest being Theta Upsilon and Alpha Chi Omega with 18 and 17 members, respectively. At the same time, Alpha Delta Pi had upwards of 30 young ladies as sisters. According to the 1931 *Brenau Bulletin*, the College of Liberal Arts enrolled a total of 323 students from over 20 states and territories whereas the Conservatory enrolled 170 students for a grand total of 493 students.[112] This means that fewer than 20% of the student body of the early 1930s affiliated with a sorority. Whatever their size, all of the Brenau sororities around the 1930s had well-appointed residential chapter houses or club houses that were used for meetings. These were formerly private residences adjacent to or near campus.

Sorority membership would increase after the 1930s. Examining the Brenau yearbooks reveals that at any given time since about the 1940s to the mid-1960s, roughly one-third to as much as one-half of Brenau's student body affiliated with a Greek sorority. A survey of one-hundred years of the *Bubbles* indicated that Brenau's sororities enjoyed their most robust periods in terms of membership in the late 1950s and early 1960s, again in the 1980s, and once more in the 2000s. By the 1950s, thirty (or thereabouts) women per chapter was the norm for membership and the chapters occupied dormitory-like house residences on campus. Sorority membership dipped some in the late 1960s and the early 1970s, but would rebound. By 1988, each of Brenau's seven sororities (ΑΧΩ, ΑΔΠ, ΑΓΔ, ΧΩ, ΔΔΔ, ΦΜ, and ΖΤΑ) could once again boast of thirty or more members. Yet, only a decade later in 1998, membership in any given chapter had decreased by anywhere from one-third to one-half. Around 2008, about 30% of Brenau Women's College students were Greek.[113] Each of the Women's College's six predominately white sororities (ΧΩ had folded by the mid-1990s) had around two-dozen members. The College's two sororities for African American young women (ΑΚΑ and ΔΣΘ), which were both relatively new, were smaller as each had about ten members. Membership in sororities continued to decline a bit over the next half-decade. By 2013, 23% of Brenau women participated in sorority life.[114]

Membership in Brenau's sororities often tracked national trends. For example, in his well-received book entitled, *Beer and Circus: How Big-Time College Sports Has Crippled Undergraduate Education*, Indiana University professor Murray Sperber addressed Greek organization membership since the 1960s. Sperber wrote, "The 1960s marked a low point for the collegiate subculture on American campuses; numerous fraternities and sororities downsized or closed their doors as some of their members, and many incoming students, joined the rebel subculture."[115] The anti-establishment sentiment of the age may have diminished sorority membership at Brenau as well since fewer young women joined. Likewise, Sperber wrote that "many fraternity and sorority chapters that were on life support at the beginning of the 1970s were thriving by 1980," which was the case at Brenau by 1988.[116] According to the *Encyclopedia of American Education*, this occurred as "the passage of state laws banning the sale of alcoholic beverages to persons under 21 [forced] student parties off campus into private facilities" like Greek houses.[117] Though Brenau sorority houses remained the property of the institution, they would have offered residents more autonomy than traditional dormitories owing to the exclusive and, at times, clandestine nature of the sororities. Around the mid-1990s, nationwide Greek membership "once again began plunging, as the number of students on financial aid increased and left fewer undergraduates able or willing to afford the hundreds of dollars in annual membership costs" that came with fraternity and sorority dues.[118] Brenau likewise experienced this contraction as each of its sororities saw membership decline by 30–50%.

Regarding Greek membership, what is interesting to note is that events particular to Brenau that might have been expected to reduce sorority numbers actually seemed to have had relatively little impact on recruiting. For example, one might expect that the creation of satellite campuses and online and weekend programs beginning in the mid-1980s would siphon off prospective sorority members from the Gainesville campus as young women took classes in these other formats. Yet, Brenau's sororities actually grew in size during these years. This is likely a testament to the institution's success at preserving the particular character and autonomy of the Women's College even as the University underwent many changes. Given that Brenau's sororities continue to present attractive social and housing options to Women's College students, it is likely that Brenau's Greek system will remain vibrant for some time to come.

Despite this vibrancy, there have been and are alternatives to going Greek at Brenau. By 1965, Brenau women who were not Greek had the opportunity to join the "Independents Organization." Regarding this group, the 1974–1975 *Student Handbook* said simply that, "Any student who lives on campus, is not a sorority member, and who wishes to support the activities of the Independents Organization shall be considered a member of the organization."[119] Language in the 1984–1985 *Handbook* might seem to be actually reactive against the Greek system at the College. Part of the organization's purpose was, "to encourage members' individualism as well as their active participation in campus and community events."[120] Moreover, the *Handbook* indicated that "During the week of Rush, the Brenau Independents Organization representatives shall be available to confer with incoming students."[121] Photographs of this group in the *Bubbles* in the 1970s did, indeed, present a stark contrast to group pictures of Brenau's sororities. Several African American women and a blind young woman were pictured as being members of the B.I.O., which contrasted starkly against the College's all-white sorority group photographs.

Since the founding of sororities at the College, members of Brenau's Greek system have been very active in many respects. In the early 1900s, some people considered many of the activities of the sororities to be newsworthy and these were included in the "Brenau Notes" section of the *Atlanta Constitution*. One edition of the "Notes" indicated that, "The Phi Mu Gamma Sorority entertained the Alpha Beta Taus Saturday evening. The hall was beautifully decorated with palms and cut flowers. A delicious salad course...was served."[122] This same edition of the "Notes" also mentioned another here-to-fore unpublished local Greek group in the *Constitution*, the Sigma Phi Epsilons, who had just elected new officers.[123] By February, 1906, Brenau had another Greek sorority (Sigma Theta Phi) on campus, which was actively reported on.[124] Beginning in about 1910, virtually all of the "Brenau Notes" became dominated by information regarding the sororities. The "Notes" described parties given by the Greeks and acknowledged guests at the sororities visiting from out-of-town, among other things.

Besides entertaining others, Brenau's early sororities were apparently themselves entertained upon occasion. Curiously, like the "Misses Knight" mentioned earlier, genuine sisters or pairs of young women often seemed to be entertaining sorority sisters. The "Brenau Notes" reported in one instance that, "Misses Lucy and Bessie Parker entertained the Sigma Phi Epsilon sorority on Monday afternoon with a tallyho ride. Their souvenirs were unique, being substantial lunch baskets with tin cups tied to them with a bow of red and white ribbon. The Misses Parker filled them with picnic dainties."[125] A subsequent edition of the "Brenau Notes" revealed that "Miss Villa Rhodes and Miss Bessie Burnett entertained the Sigma Theta Phi's" with another tally-ho party only a few weeks later.[126] (A "tally-ho ride," incidentally, seems to have been essentially an opportunity for several young women to don their finest clothes and be ridden around town in an opulently decorated carriage.) It appears that entertaining a sorority at functions like these might have served as a segue to becoming a member of that sorority. The practice did not persist much into the 1900s. Only a few years into the twentieth century, the size of Brenau's sorority chapters had grown too large to make entertaining in this fashion feasible.

Faculty members as well as students were associated with the early sororities at Brenau, either as entertainers at events or, apparently, as outright members. The "Brenau Notes" reported in one instance that, "Monday night Mrs. H. J. Pearce entertained the Sigma Theta Phi Society at a Japanese tea. All the girls wore Japanese costumes and all the decorations and refreshments carried the same idea."[127] In another instance, the "Notes" reported that, "Mrs. Mary Craft Ward, of Hartwell, has composed a two-step and dedicated it to the Alpha Tau Beta Society, of Brenau College. Mrs. Ward is a popular piano instructor at Brenau and a member of the Sorority."[128]

Faculty and/or staff members would, in fact, be associated with the sororities in one way or another throughout their existences up through the 1980s. Beginning in about the 1930s, every house had a hostess or house director that played a role in maintaining the chapter residence. Also, sorority houses were left in the care of a matron or a married couple for summer months when students left school to return home.[129] It should be noted that the responsibilities of these staff members appear to have been limited. Dedications in several editions of the *Bubbles* indicated that sororities generally thought very highly of their matrons.

Yet, nothing indicated that these sentiments truly translated into ceding total authority to house mothers. These staff members mainly performed tasks like monitoring guest visits or supervising house maids. Although the faculty and administration might have enjoyed having one of their own in a position of great power over a sorority, this never materialized.

Unlike the faculty and staff, sorority alumnae did play large and important parts in the life of chapters. Many editions of the *Brenau Girl* and the *Student Handbooks* contemplated that alumnae would be connected to rush events and cautioned sororities to make sure that their alumnae knew the rules. Also, over time, it is evident that several rushees were "legacies," which meant that their mothers and, in some cases, even their grandmothers, were members of a sorority at Brenau. Additionally, several editions of the "Brenau Notes" related that various alumnae of the early sororities would often come back to visit their chapters from time to time. Invariably, the "Notes" mention that the visitor was pleasantly entertained.

The involvement of alumnae in sorority life actually buttresses the idea that Brenau's sororities operated at arm's length from the faculty and administration. The support given by alumnae to sororities came in many forms. Brenau sorority women would have been able to look to their alumnae for guidance or resources. In the absence of this source of support, Brenau sororities may have been forced to negotiate with other sources for support. The most logical other source would have been the College faculty and administration. Consequently, the presence of sorority alumnae meant that Brenau sororities might have used their alumnae as surrogates for the faculty and administration, which would have let the sororities keep College officials at a greater distance.

Sorority entertainment and activity continued well into the twentieth century. The "Brenau Notes" section of the *Atlanta Constitution* and, later, the *Alchemist*, Brenau's student newspaper, reported on this on a myriad of occasions. Sororities held teas and socials around mid-century and, later, dances and fund-raising drives for various causes. Some of the events of the early part of the century seemed to be the most colorful. For example, the Brenau *Alchemist* described one Phi Mu Rush Party in November of 1924 this way:

> The guests were seated at small tables of four and the informal was rendered cabaret fashion during the course of the turkey dinner.
>
> Repeated encores were elicited for Miss Clarke's interpretations of a balloon and Oriental dance, while Misses Jeraldine Ellis and Charlotte Simpson gave a very delightful costume-portrayal of the tango.
>
> An appropriate violin selection by Miss Dorothy Lawrence, followed by Mrs. Corinne Turnipseed's exquisite rendition of "Smilin' Through" contributed a marked feature to the evening's enjoyment.
>
> At intervals during the dinner, Miss Katherine Redwine, dressed as a cigarette girl, distributed many interesting little favors to the group of diners.
>
> Music for the dancing was furnished by the Brenau Busters.[130]

This same edition of the *Alchemist* also described a Delta Zeta rush party, which was likewise a very colorful and entertaining dinner-dance.[131] In 1930, the *Alchemist* reported that the Alpha Chi Omegas "entertained the lady members of the faculty at a bridge party" whereas the Alpha Xi Deltas celebrated their Founder's Day with a banquet at Gainesville's posh Dixie-Hunt hotel.[132]

Socials with visiting men were also popular with Brenau's sororities in the 1930s. Mary Helen Hosch was a member of Tri-Delta sorority then and recalled:

> We had a formal dance every month and the boys came from all the colleges around—UGA, Emory, Tech, Clemson, Mercer, Atlanta Dental School—just all around. We wore evening dresses and just had a wonderful time. ... The dances were held in the sorority

houses and, see, if the boys knew girls in more than one sorority house, they could go where they knew another girl for a while, and some of the local boys went to all of the sorority houses![133]

Elizabeth Wheeler Thurmond was a member of Zeta Tau Alpha in the early 1930s and had similar recollections. Of her experiences in a sorority, she said:

> We had little things going like volunteering to help children, kindergartens and stuff. We really didn't have enough time to do too much. On Saturdays they didn't all leave campus like they do now. Saturdays are just closed down practically, aren't they? Then they stayed around. We had a lot of fun; I don't know that we did so much. And we used to have dances in our houses, sorority houses. We'd be so excited. Boys from Georgia, Tech, [and] Emory would come. Everybody was looking out and seeing how this house was doing, how many were over at the other house—they just sort of hopped around. That was a big deal.[134]

Interestingly, this tradition that was so popular at Brenau in the 1930s was unknown to the College in just the previous decade. Mrs. Lil Robinson and Mrs. Mary Foote Paris, who both started Brenau in 1926 and who both graduated in 1930 and were members of Zeta Tau Alpha and Alpha Chi Omega, respectively, were interviewed for the Brenau Archives in 1995. When asked about the activities "back then," Mrs. Robinson recalled, "Well, they didn't have the bashes the sororities have now. We never sponsored a dance—did your sorority?" Mrs. Robinson directed the question at Mrs. Paris, who replied, "Just within their own group. But not with boys to the house, no. The girls could have dates on weekends [and] all the dates were in the parlor over at Yonah Hall with a chaperone. You didn't go out; you stayed there with your date."[135] Along with dancing and dating, even the work in a sorority was fun. Elizabeth Wheeler Thurmond also recalled that, "I was president of Zeta House a couple of years, so that is why I stayed over there so much and some nights I'd just sleep on the sofa and not go home when we'd been through late,

late meetings. Always during Rush, we stayed up until 2 and 3 o'clock in the morning. It was fun and I enjoyed every minute of it."[136]

Sororities at Brenau have historically competed against one another in academic achievement, athletics, and at events such as Field Day. This competition and relations generally between Brenau's sororities appear to have been largely amicable. This seems to have been the case right from the start. Several early editions of the "Brenau Notes" described functions similar to the social mentioned earlier between the Phi Mu Gammas and the Alpha Beta Taus. Friendly competition and congenial association appear to have been the norm for subsequent decades as well. This was due in large part to the existence of a "Pan-Hellenic Association," which had been established at Brenau around May of 1911.[137] The Association served to "foster a spirit of mutual helpfulness among the sororities."[138] The Pan-Hellenic Association actually required amity among Greeks. Portions of Brenau's early student handbooks dealt with Greek relations promulgated by the association and had rules against bad conduct. For example, a portion of the 1925–1926 edition of the handbook (which would be repeated in subsequent years) read:

> No member of any sorority shall make a disparaging remark about any other sorority having a chapter in Brenau. It shall be the duty of every delegate to report to Pan-Hellenic any rumor or disparaging remark about any chapter at the first meeting after hearing the same, insisting upon investigation, that the chapter involved may be cleared, or proved guilty.[139]

Although a rule such as this probably helped to promote good relationships between sororities, it did not guarantee friendship. At times, competition between sororities could apparently become heated.

Perhaps the best example of this heated competition involved sorority rush.[140] Every edition of the *Brenau Girl* published at least some pages of technical rules about how sororities could grow their membership by courting new students. Indeed, these rules generally became more complicated over time, at least until the 1970s. The apparent aim of the rules was to place each chapter on a level playing field when it came to recruiting new members while giving new students time to settle into college. The 1925–1926 rules required, for example, that no sorority member wear her pin or so much as discuss her sorority with new freshmen women for six weeks. Also, official Pan-Hellenic-approved invitations had to be used to invite a young woman to join a sorority. Additionally, no "non-fraternity girl" could spend the night in any sorority house.[141]

About a decade later, rules had been added to limit expenses of certain rush events and these rules required sororities to submit an itemized account of expenses to the Pan-Hellenic Association to demonstrate their compliance with the set limits.[142] Also, the 1937–1938 "Instructions Concerning Bids" included a provision that "Two lawyers chosen by Pan-Hellenic shall deliver the bids" to pledges at an appointed day and time.[143] By 1945–1946, rules were more complicated still. Rushing had been divided into first and second semesters. Sorority sisters could not enter campus dormitories during rush. Also, stiff monetary penalties were spelled out for breaking rushing rules. For example, a sorority would be fined $50 for "contacting a rushee in any way whatsoever" outside of those ways prescribed and $50 for "having more than two dates per day with one girl."[144]

By 1955, the eighty-one page student handbook devoted fully eighteen pages to sorority life and rushing. Described therein was a "Preferential Bidding System" where sorority and rushee preferences were collected and matched to one another. Ideally, a rushee's top pick would be for a sorority that had also selected her as a top pick. If this was not the case, then a rushee's second choices would be matched up with the selections of the sororities. A neutral party was entrusted with this task of conducting the matching procedure. According to the rules, and reflecting the importance of this process, said party would be either "a lawyer, or other outsider, or the dean of women."[145] The rules in the nineteen-fifties also included a quota system for Greek membership so that no one chapter could snatch up too many pledges. Also, according to the rules, "The number of members in each sorority of Panhellenic shall not exceed forty," but this quota was subject to change as the association saw fit.[146]

By 1965, rushing rules had changed significantly. The *Student Handbook*, which was no longer called the *Brenau Girl*, listed only twenty-three brief rules and did not, as earlier versions had done, reproduce the by-laws of the Panhellenic Association (note new spelling). Some strictures were also relaxed. For example, upperclassmen were permitted to speak to freshmen during rush, but "only in a casual way without carrying on lengthy conversations."[147] Also, although no sorority member could "rush any girl during the summer," they were permitted to associate with incoming freshmen because the rule pertaining to this banned only "detailed" talk about a sorority.[148]

Roughly a decade later, rushing regulations had relaxed even further and the handbook devoted only a mere one-and-a-half pages to these rules. Absent from the 1974–1975 handbook were any rules regarding how or when a sorority member could speak with rushees. There was also no mention of fines, quotas, a bidding system, or minimum academic requirements for going Greek. The rules did prohibit sorority members from buying anything (such as dinner) for new students. Also, the Civil Rights Movement of the 1960s had left its mark on Brenau's Greek system —at least on paper—as a rule in the handbook indicated that, "Panhellenic sanctions no discrimination."[149]

The *Brenau Women's College Student Handbook of 1984 – 1985* saw something of a resurgence of Greek presence. This version reprinted the constitution of the Panhellenic Association and also presented four pages of by-laws. Aspects of these by-laws served to replace the "Rushing Rules" outlined in earlier handbooks. The rules were substantially relaxed. Perhaps most telling of this change was the stipulation that, "Except during rushing period, continuous open bidding shall be in effect during the college year for eligible women students."[150] Also, the regulations indicated that "A pledge may be initiated whenever she has met the requirements of the fraternity to which she has pledged."[151] These rules operated together to essentially say that sorority membership could grow throughout the year, which meant that Greeks must have been permitted to associate with non-Greeks year-round. Gone were the days when rules restricted how sisters could speak to rushees and when rules barred rushees from entering into sorority houses.

What is interesting about all of these regulations regarding sorority rush is what they communicate about aspects of Brenau sorority life. In some respects, there is truly a near-complete absence of any faculty or administrative involvement in sorority life. In these instances, Brenau's sororities were practically self-governing entities where student desires mattered most. The historical evidence suggests that Brenau's sororities had a great deal of latitude to conduct their own affairs and that they held this for decades. For example, College officials apparently never contested with the sororities over whom the sororities could admit into their ranks. Brenau permitted the sororities to include (or exclude) whomever they chose from membership. Also, in most respects, Brenau's faculty and staff left it up to the sororities to determine how their houses would be occupied. The sororities could only have gained and maintained such boons thanks to years of periodic direct or indirect negotiation with College personnel. Seen this way, Greek life has the potential to be one aspect of the negotiated college experience where Brenau's faculty and staff have little say compared to that of students.

Still, having little say is not the same as having no say at all. Other aspects about Brenau's sororities reveal that the ongoing negotiation between students and College officials was more two-sided. In some cases, College officials did exert their influence. For example, Brenau's faculty and staff dictated such things as how frequently the sororities could have formal socials. Also, at some times in the College's history, house directors ensured proper conduct of sorority members in houses that were technically owned by the College. Yet, even in the face of faculty and staff authority, students still contested for "their Brenau." Brenau officials might have cracked down further against such student action just as students might have rebelled in other respects. That the College and the students did not do either suggests that the negotiated arrangement regarding sorority life that emerged between College officials and students was acceptable to both parties. Perhaps the best evidence for this is simply the very existence of the sororities at Brenau. At virtually all other women's colleges, officials did away with sororities, at times much to the dismay of students. Brenau students knew they had a good thing in the form of their Greek system and so they worked to ensure that sororities added value to the institution. Faculty and staff members, in turn, left students much autonomy in Greek matters because Brenau derived benefits from the sororities like monetary assistance in developing College housing and assistance with student social control as sororities kept their members in line. Ultimately, the negotiation over Greek life at Brenau resulted in something like a "win-win" situation for the institution that persists to the present day.

Examining sororities and secret societies at Brenau does more than just shed light on the negotiations between students and College personnel to mold the institutional character of the College. We learn of a great irony from considering the darker nature of these groups. With respect to the secret societies, with their morbid symbols of skulls and knives, this nature is perhaps self-evident. Sororities, too, had their dark sides, which were perhaps less overt. Some regulations in the 1984 *Student Handbook* suggested this. Article VII of the by-laws banned all forms of hazing "which would reflect unfavorably on the fraternity system."[152] For example, blindfolding is mentioned specifically as something not condoned outside of specific sorority rituals. Also, Article X of the by-laws dealt with "Theft, Destruction of Greek Property." This was strictly forbidden by the Association. Curiously, though, the text read that "Theft or destruction of Greek property from *another* campus" (emphasis added) is what was prohibited.[153] This might imply that intra-campus theft did not occur. In any case, the fact that the Greek regulations included provisions banning hazing and theft suggest that both may have occurred in Brenau's sororities in the past to such an extent that they needed curbing via policy.

Ultimately, the existence of these last two regulations is illustrative of what is perhaps the most interesting thing about Greek life and secret societies at Brenau. When one thinks of morbid symbols, "hazing," and "theft," what probably comes to mind are *fraternities* and men's organizations, not sororities or women's organizations. For example, it is perhaps easy to imagine brother John "Bluto" Blutarsky and his confederates from Animal House giving pledges the third degree or swiping some prized artifact from a rival house on fraternity row. It is perhaps more difficult to mentally ascribe such behaviors to women. After all, whether it is reality or not, American society has arguably always tended to view women as being better-behaved and more passive than men. Indeed, women's colleges like Brenau initially developed as much to safeguard this feminine ideal as they did to educate women. Sororities and secret societies, in turn, developed to sequester women in secure houses or in private club meetings, to further perpetuate the feminine ideal of sisterhood, and, in the case of sororities, to cultivate the qualities society prized in women of nurturing others and of being socially able. Viewed this way, Brenau's sororities and secret organizations probably did just as much to subvert femininity as to support it.

To be sure, sororities and secret organizations at Brenau perpetuated feminine ideals. The myriad of accounts in the "Brenau Notes" of sorority women hosting teas, throwing parties and galas and the like support this notion. Yet, in other ways, Brenau's sororities and secret societies did little to perpetuate femininity and instead made women more the equals of men. For example, speaking of sorority houses, Horowitz observed that, "Buildings designed to protect femininity were subverted to its suppression."[154] This was true as sororities turned their houses into their homes. The earlier excerpt indicated that exactly this happened at Brenau. The faculty member who observed the sorority sister doing "other work not generally pursued by a girl of college age" was observing a young woman assuming the masculine role of home-repairer. As she and her sisters saved their pennies and worried about finances, they were leaving further behind their traditional, passive, gender-determined, stereotyped roles. Also, the sorority women at Brenau did more than merely "worry their pretty little heads" (as the saying goes) about the complexities of rush at the College. They grappled with those difficulties, negotiated amongst themselves and with College personnel, and developed sophisticated, necessarily complicated regulations to fairly govern sorority life. Brenau women in groups like H.G.H. even took on the weighty responsibility of doing anything for Brenau that they might be called upon to do as students or as alumnae. And, if the anonymous alumnae's account about smoking can be believed, sorority women sought to demonstrate that they were on equal footing with men by insisting that their members even adopt the same bad habits as men. In sum, the life of sororities and secret societies at Brenau saw young women demonstrate that they were both the equals of men and, at the same time, quite different from them as well.

Notes

1. Adam Parfrey and Craig Heimbichner, *Ritual America: Secret Brotherhoods and Their Influence on American Society - A Visual Guide* (Port Townsend, WA: Feral House, 2012), xviii.
2. "Shhhhh....It's A Secret," *W & M Style*, http://www.wm.edu/style/secret.php (accessed 18 March 2014).
3. See M. J. Stephey, "A Brief History of The Skull & Bones Society," *Time Magazine*, 23 February 2009, http://content.time.com/time/nation/article/0,8599,1881172,00.html (accessed 18 March 2014) for more about this group.
4. See "Collegiate secret societies in North America" at http://en.wikipedia.org/wiki/Collegiate_secret_societies_in_North_America for a description of several such societies (last accessed 18 March 2014).
5. *Bubbles* (Gainesville, GA: Brenau College, 1901), 102.
6. Memorandum dated 27 November 1973, written by Brenau Dean John E. Sites, published in Rigney, *Brenau College 1878–1978*, 66.
7. Ibid.
8. Ibid.
9. "'Skulls' – We Scalp 'Em," *Alchemist* (Gainesville, GA: Brenau College), vol. 7, no. 3 (8 November 1919), p. 3.
10. Ibid. Regrettably, there is little secondary literature on colleges' secret societies that would help to contextualize these organizations and their appearance at this particular point in time.
11. *Bubbles* (1945), no page number.
12. Ibid.
13. Ibid.
14. Memorandum dated 27 November 1973, written by Brenau Dean John E. Sites, published in Rigney, *Brenau College 1878–1978*, 68.
15. *Bubbles* (1945), no page number.
16. Ibid.
17. Ibid.
18. Memorandum dated 27 November 1973, written by Brenau Dean John E. Sites, published in Rigney, *Brenau College 1878–1978*, 68.
19. GreekChat.com, "Secret Societies" forum, http://www.greekchat.com/gcforums/archive/index.php/t-13261.html (accessed 18 May 2013).
20. Ibid.

21. "With an H, with an H, with an H.G.H." *Alchemist*, 6 February 2008, http://intranet.brenau.edu/dnn/StudentServices/CareerServices/JobBoard/tabid/92/mid/505/newsid505/1269/Default.aspx (accessed 21 May 2013).
22. Ibid.
23. Ibid.
24. Ibid.
25. Ibid.
26. Ibid.
27. Ibid.
28. Ibid.
29. Ibid.
30. Ibid.
31. Anonymous, interview by author, email, 2 August 2011.
32. Ibid. Former Brenau President Dr. John Burd did not confirm this and, indeed, wondered if this information could actually be determined. Comments to author, n.d., but communicated in edits to manuscript draft in 2013..
33. See Sir Arthur Conan Doyle, "The Memoirs of Sherlock Holmes: Silver Blaze," Project Gutenberg, available at http://www.gutenberg.org/ebooks/834 (accessed 18 May 2013).
34. For more information about college fraternities and sororities, see Jack L. Anson and Robert F. Marchesani, eds., *Baird's Manual of American College Fraternities* (Menasha, WI: G. Banta Co., 1991).
35. Wesleyan College, "History of the College" http://www.wesleyancollege.edu/about/history.cfm (accessed 18 May 2013).
36. Farnham, *Education of the Southern Belle*, 148.
37. Ibid., 154.
38. Diana B. Turk, *Bound by a Mighty Vow: Sisterhood and Women's Fraternities, 1870–1920* (New York, NY: New York University Press, 2004), 23.
39. Ibid., 35.
40. Ibid., 48.
41. Ibid., 161.
42. Ibid., 122.
43. "Brenau Notes," *Atlanta Constitution*, 9 October 1904, sec. C, p. 6.
44. "Brenau Notes," *Atlanta Constitution*, 7 May 1905, sec. D, p. 8.
45. *Bubbles* (1932), 145.
46. Ibid.
47. Ibid. The essay does not indicate what factors make a particular sorority an "A national." Presumably, it would be one with a large member-

ship and widespread footprint, whereas a "B national" would have these things to a lesser extent. The groups the *Bubbles* identified as "A" level had several chapters spread throughout the nation by the early twentieth century; the "B" level groups had expanded not nearly so far. See Anson and Marchesani, eds., *Baird's Manual*, for information about the spread of sororities.
48. For another example of this, note the instance in 1910 when the "Brenau Notes" reported that, "The Kappa Alpha Phi Sorority has nationalized and now affiliates with the Sigma Iota Chi." "Many Visitors at Brenau," *Atlanta Constitution*, 20 May 1910, p. 6.
49. The *Bubbles* essay spelled out how "Beta Sigma Omicron appeared in 1907 and in 1909 came Alpha Sigma Alpha. In 1914 these two joined forces with members of Phi Mu Gamma and were granted the charter of Delta Delta Delta. The other members of Phi Mu Gamma preferred to retain their status as a B. national." Ibid.
50. Ibid.
51. Ibid. See also "Phi Mu at Brenau," *Atlanta Constitution*, 12 October 1910, sec. B, p. 6; "Zeta Tau Alpha Enters Brenau," *Atlanta Constitution*, 15 January 1911, sec. A, p. 5.
52. *Bubbles* (1932), 145. While the months and years of the founding dates of all of the sorority chapters at Brenau are not in dispute, some conflicting information exists regarding the precise days upon which some chapters were founded. For example, the national organization website for Zeta Tau Alpha lists January 14, 1911, as the founding date for the Brenau chapter and not January 1 as the *Bubbles* proclaimed. See "Chapter Profile: Omicron," Zeta Tau Alpha, http://www.zetataualpha.org/cms400 min/FIVE/ChapterProfile.aspx?contactID=100015 (accessed 27 December 2012).
53. The earliest of these dates as far back as 1910. "To Sorority Delegates," *Atlanta Constitution*, 4 June 1910, p. 8.
54. While young women founded and nurtured several prominent sororities at a few women's colleges as far back as the mid-nineteenth century, very few women's colleges sustained Greek systems over time. A thorough search of the Internet websites of the following women's colleges conducted in July of 2012 revealed that each possessed no institutionally sponsored Greek sororities at all: Agnes Scott College, Alverno College, Barnard College, Bay Path College, Brescia University College, Bryn Mawr College, Carlow University*, Cedar Crest College, Chatham University, College of New Rochelle, College of Saint Benedict,

College of Saint Elizabeth, College of Saint Mary, Columbia College, Converse College, Cottey College, Hollins University, Judson College, Mary Baldwin College, Meredith College, Midway College, Mills College, Moore College of Art and Design, Mount Holyoke College, Mount Mary College, Notre Dame of Maryland University, Pine Manor College, Russell Sage College of The Sage Colleges, Saint Mary-of-the-Woods College, Saint Mary's College (IN), Salem College, Scripps College, Simmons College, Smith College, St. Catherine University*, Sweet Briar College, Trinity Washington University, University of Saint Joseph, Ursuline College*, Wellesley College, Wesleyan College, Wheelock College*, William Smith College, and Wilson College.(* Indicates an institution that, strictly speaking, is no longer a women's college since men are admitted to study in limited numbers. However, the percentage of women students at these institutions is at least 90%, vastly outnumbering that of male students.) Only a handful of present-day women's college students are able to join sororities. For example, students in The Women's College of the University of Denver and at the Douglass Residential College of Rutgers University would have access to the sororities attached to their respective greater universities that do maintain Greek systems. The women's colleges themselves maintain no sororities. (See http://du.orgsync.com/org/dugreeklife/home and http://getinvolved.rutgers.edu/fraternities-and-sororities (accessed 25 January 2013).) St. Catherine University maintains a group called "Lambda Sigma Tau," which is described as "a social/service sorority dedicated to serving the University community" (http://minerva.stkate.edu/offices/administrative/stu_ctr_act.nsf/pages/clubs (accessed 25 January 2013)). Also, students at the College of Saint Benedict may join a group called the Alpha Kappa Sigma Service Sorority (http://www.csbsju.edu/SALD/Clubs/AKS-Sorority-Constitution.htm (accessed 25 January 2013)). Both of these organizations are local in scope and are not purely social sororities. As of 2013, Mount St. Mary's College of Los Angeles has two social sororities at its Chalon campus, but neither could be considered truly national in scope. According to its website (http://www.sigmathetapsi.com (accessed 25 January 2013)), Sigma Theta Psi has nine chapters in California and one in Nevada. Theta Alpha Sigma is described as "a Catholic based service and social sorority" which, as of 2012, maintained one chapter at MSMC and another at California State University – Monterey Bay (http://www.msmcthetas.com/index.html (accessed 25 January 2013)). Only a handful of women's college students are able to become full-fledged members of

prominent national social sororities. African American women attending Carlow University have access to a "city-wide chapter" of Alpha Kappa Alpha that "unites women from several Pittsburgh colleges" (http://www.carlow.edu/policies/pdf/02-100_ugrad_student_handbook.pdf (accessed 25 January 2013)). Bennett College for Women in Greensboro, North Carolina, maintains its own chapter of Alpha Kappa Alpha, as well as chapters of Delta Sigma Theta, Sigma Gamma Rho, and Zeta Phi Beta (http://www.bennett.edu/sacs/docdirectory/StudentOrganizations.pdf (accessed 25 January 2013)). Spelman College has these sororities on campus as well and also has two service-oriented sororities (http://www.spelman.edu/student-life/student-life-and-engagement/sorority-life (accessed 25 January 2013)). Only Stephens College in Columbia, Missouri, and Brenau support chapters of sororities that are members of the National Panhellenic Conference (https://www.npcwomen.org/about/member-organizations.aspx (accessed 25 January 2013)). As of 2013, Stephens has two: Sigma Sigma Sigma and Kappa Delta (http://www.stephens.edu/campuslife/activities/#SOR (accessed 25 January 2013)). Brenau maintains six, all of which have chapter houses: Alpha Gamma Delta, Alpha Delta Pi, Alpha Chi Omega, Delta Delta Delta, Phi Mu, and Zeta Tau Alpha (http://www.brenaugreeks.com/greek-council (accessed 25 January 2013)).
55. Newcomer, *A Century of Higher Education for American Women*, 123.
56. Ibid., 124.
57. Ibid.
58. Examining several early editions of the *Bubbles* revealed that sororities all had club houses and that they had obtained them very soon after coming into existence at Brenau.
59. Horowitz, *Alma Mater*, 152.
60. Ibid., 156.
61. Solomon, *In the Company of Educated Women*, 107.
62. McCandless, *Past in the Present*, 142.
63. Ibid.
64. Ibid.
65. *Catalog* (1910), 76.
66. Ibid.
67. Some evidence suggests that it was this wealthier class of young women that joined sororities at Brenau. In an interview about life at Brenau in the late 1920s, Mrs. Lil Robinson indicated that, "The day students were not included in a whole lot of activities. If they were included they were

never elected to an office that I remember. ... Of course, if you were in a sorority you did enjoy activities there and you were close enough to take part. But so many of the town girls were not in sororities." Typed transcript of an interview with Mrs. Lil Robinson and Mrs. Mary Foote Paris conducted by Andrea Davis on 15 February 1995, p. 2; Box 1 of 1 (labeled "Dean of Women Files"), Brenau University Archives, Gainesville, Georgia. Since "town girls" did not join, sororities must have been made up mostly of out-of-town girls. These students would probably have come from wealthier families since maintaining a daughter at an out-of-town college would have been expensive and beyond the reach of many families.
68. "A Word About the Social Organization," *Atlanta Constitution*, 2 August 1908, sec. A, p. 5.
69. Ibid.
70. *Catalog* (1910), 65.
71. Display Advertisement—No Title, *Atlanta Constitution*, 15 December 1912, sec. A, p. 13.
72. McCandless, *Past in the Present*, 143.
73. "Brenau Opens Soon," *Atlanta Constitution*, 7 September 1907, p. 12.
74. *President Thomas Jackson Simmons...An Appreciation* (Gainesville, GA: Brenau College, c. 1910), 39; http://archive.org/stream/presidentthmasj00ross#page/38/mode/2up (accessed 25 January 2013).
75. See *supra*.
76. *Catalog* (1910), 65.
77. "Members of Brenau Sorority to Give Annual Scholarship," *Atlanta Constitution*, 21 March 1909, p. 10.
78. Solomon, *In the Company of Educated Women*, 107.
79. *Catalog* (1910), 65.
80. Crudup, "Report to the Board (May 29, 1964)," p. 4.
81. Crudup, "Report to the Board (June 1, 1962)," p. 10.
82. Ibid.
83. Ibid.
84. Ibid.
85. Ibid.
86. Crudup, "Report to the Board (June 4, 1965)," p. 7.
87. Ibid., 8.
88. Ibid.
89. Claudia Wiggins, "Dr. Crudup Talks About Student Unrest, Sororities," *Alchemist*, 24 November 1969, vol. LXI, no. 5, p. 8.

90. Ibid.
91. Ibid.
92. Ibid.
93. Ibid.
94. Solomon, *In the Company of Educated Women*, 107.
95. Letter to Mrs. Doris D. Smith, August 29, 1964 from Josiah Crudup. Dr. Crudup Files, Box 29 of 40, Folder 4, Brenau University Archives, Gainesville, Georgia. Mrs. Smith was a member of the class of 1963 who wrote to Dr. Crudup on this matter. She referenced Myrna Sheftal: "I have told Freda that if she makes herself desirable that perhaps she can at least be socially affiliated like Myrna Sheftal was in ZTA."
96. Ibid. Sororities at other colleges also excluded Jewish women from membership. Indeed, it was not until 1951 that the National Panhellenic Congress removed its non-Jewish policy. See Diana B. Turk, *Bound by a Mighty Vow: Sisterhood and Women's Fraternities, 1870–1920* (New York, NY: New York University Press, 2004).
97. Marianne Rachel Sanua, *Going Greek: Jewish College Fraternities in the United States, 1895–1945* (Detroit, MI: Wayne State University Press, 2003), 316.
98. See Marianne Rachel Sanua, *Going Greek: Jewish College Fraternities in the United States, 1895–1945* (Detroit, MI: Wayne State University Press, 2003) for more information about Delta Phi Epsilon. Shira Kohn wrote, "To appeal to a wider variety of students in hopes of boosting their numbers, two Jewish sororities, Delta Phi Epsilon and Phi Sigma Sigma, decided to rebrand themselves by moving away from any acknowledgement or celebration of their Jewish roots and identity. Slowly, they opened up several new chapters on campuses with few Jewish students, and today both have a majority of non-Jewish women as members." Shira Kohn, "A (Re)Consideration of Jewish Sororities," *Lilith Magazine* (fall 2011), http://www.lilith.org/pdfs/LILFa11_final1004_sororities%20.pdf (accessed 25 January 2013).
99. Digital Library of Georgia, "Southern Israelite: Georgia Historic Newspapers Information," http://dlg.galileo.usg.edu/CollectionsA-Z/sois_information.html?Welcome&Welcome (accessed 18 May 2013).
100. *Southern Israelite* (monthly), 14 June 1929 -- page 6 "Society and Personals."
101. Ibid., 30 September 1932 -- page 12 "Southern Notes."
102. Sanua, *Going Greek*, 314.
103. Ibid., 311.

104. A very small number of Hispanic young women from Central and South America and an even smaller number of Asians (apparently, two) enrolled at Brenau during the entire span of the twentieth century, but it is not clear that all were regular college students. Such students attended Brenau so infrequently, however, and in such small numbers that it would be a stretch to say that Brenau had integrated racially by their coming to campus.
105. *Bubbles* (1994), 99.
106. *Bubbles* (1980), 100.
107. The chapter would go on to become inactive during the 2002–2003 school year, but was revived in the following year. Brenau University, "Rho Eta History," http://studentdevelopment.brenau.edu/greek/AKA/RhoEtaHistory.htm (accessed 19 May 2008); visit http://rhoetaold.homestead.com/history.html (accessed 25 January 2013) to access a more current version of the Rho Eta website.
108. "Delta Sigma Theta, Inc.," Brenau University Greek Council, http://www.brenaugreeks.com/delta-sigma-theta-inc (accessed 25 January 2013).
109. It is doubtful Brenau was unique in this regard. An Internet search conducted in March of 2014 on multiple online Greek fora found several posts made by users who believed that, at one time, many sororities maintained policies that barred married women from joining.
110. *Handbook* (1974), 70.
111. Letter written anonymously by a "Brenau Alumna" dated 18 June 1964 to Dr. Josiah Crudup, President. Dr. Crudup Files, Box 29 of 40, Folder 4, Brenau University Archives, Gainesville, Georgia.
112. *Brenau Bulletin, vol. XXII, no. 4* (Gainesville, GA: Brenau College, 1931), 124–125.
113. GA College 411.com, "Brenau University-Women's College profile," http://www.gacollege411.org/campustour/undergraduate/521/Brenau_University__Womens_College/Brenau_University__Womens_College5.html (accessed 19 May 2008).
114. "College Profile: Brenau University," CollegeData.com, http://www.collegedata.com/cs/data/college/college_pg05_tmpl.jhtml?schoolId=5 13 (accessed 21 May 2013).
115. Murray Sperber, *Beer and Circus: How Big-Time College Sports Has Crippled Undergraduate Education* (New York, NY: Holt Paperbacks, 2000), 15.
116. Ibid., 16.

117. "Fraternity," *Encyclopedia of American Education*, published 25 June 2011, http://american-education.org/875-fraternity.html (accessed 21 May 2013).
118. Ibid.
119. *Handbook* (1974), 66.
120. *Handbook* (1984), 73.
121. Ibid.
122. "Brenau Notes," *Atlanta Constitution*, 16 October 1905, p. 5.
123. Ibid.
124. "Brenau Notes," *Atlanta Constitution*, 11 February 1906, sec. D, p. 8.
125. "Brenau Notes," *Atlanta Constitution*, 18 March 1906, sec. B, p. 5.
126. "Brenau Notes," *Atlanta Constitution*, 8 April 1906, sec. D, p. 9.
127. "Brenau Notes," *Atlanta Constitution*, 24 March 1907, sec. A, p. 2.
128. "Brenau Notes," *Atlanta Constitution*, 14 July 1907, sec. C, p. 8.
129. "Brenau Notes," *Atlanta Constitution*, 18 August 1912, sec. D, p. 10.
130. *Alchemist* (Gainesville, GA: Brenau College), vol. XII, no. 6 (3 December 1924), p. 3.
131. Ibid., 5.
132. *Alchemist* (Gainesville, GA: Brenau College), vol. XVI, no. 26 (16 April 1930), p. 4.
133. Typed transcript of an interview with Mary Helen Hosch conducted by Andrea Davis on Friday, 27 February 1995, p. 1–2; Box 1 of 1 (labeled "Dean of Women Files"), Brenau University Archives, Gainesville, Georgia.
134. Elizabeth Wheeler (Lib) Thurmond, Brenau student (1929–1933), interviewer unknown, typed transcript, date unknown, p. 4; Box 1 of 1 (labeled "Dean of Women Files"), Brenau University Archives, Gainesville, Georgia
135. Typed transcript of an interview with Mrs. Lil Robinson and Mrs. Mary Foote Paris conducted by Andrea Davis on 15 February 1995, p. 1; Box 1 of 1 (labeled "Dean of Women Files"), Brenau University Archives, Gainesville, Georgia.
136. Elizabeth Wheeler (Lib) Thurmond, Brenau student (1929–1933), interviewer unknown, typed transcript, date unknown, p. 4; Box 1 of 1 (labeled "Dean of Women Files"), Brenau University Archives, Gainesville, Georgia.
137. "Brenau Notes," *Atlanta Constitution*, 14 May 1911, sec. E, p. 11.
138. *Handbook* (1937), 46.
139. *Handbook* (1925), 29.

140. While the origins of the term "sorority rush" are not settled, one scholar has asserted that its use is probably related "to the slang for courting a girl by heaping insistent and numerous favors upon her." C. S. Johnson, *Fraternities in Our Colleges* (New York, NY: National Interfraternity Foundation, 1972), 254.
141. *Handbook* (1925), 31.
142. *Handbook* (1937), 54.
143. Ibid.
144. *Handbook* (1945), 52.
145. *Handbook* (1955), 60. Note that while the dean of women might be involved with rush, her role was strictly to sort ballots. She would have exercised no authority over determining membership selection.
146. Ibid.
147. *Handbook* (1965), 89.
148. Ibid., 90.
149. *Handbook* (1974), 60.
150. *Handbook* (1984), 70.
151. Ibid.
152. Ibid.
153. Ibid., 71. Incidentally, the penalty for violating this provision of the regulations was a fine of "up to, but not exceeding, $100" (71). In the big scheme of things, this probably could not really be seen as a harsh punishment, which might suggest that some hijinks might have been expected and winked at.
154. Horowitz, *Alma Mater*, 178.

Conclusion

Brenau University Today

With enrollment topping 800 students annually and its endowment over $25 million, Brenau University's Women's College is rare among American institutions of higher education in the twenty-first century because it remains a viable (perhaps, in some respects, even thriving) women's college. Indeed, that it simply still exists at all is saying something. Around the mid-twentieth century, roughly 300 women's colleges operated in the United States. These institutions provided higher education to women at a time when not all state and private colleges admitted women. By 1970, that number had whittled down to 230. The decline was likely the result of a great drop in enrollment at women's colleges as young women opted to attend other public or private institutions that had become coeducational over the years. In a sense, then, women's colleges were falling victim to their own success. Over time, formerly male-only institutions saw how well women performed in women's colleges, which induced them to open their doors to women students who then came in large numbers. In the 1970s, 108 women's colleges converted to coeducation themselves while another 46 women's colleges closed their doors outright. This trend of attrition would continue for many years. By 2007, only 58 women's colleges remained in existence in the United

States.¹ Just five years later, only 47 institutions claimed membership in the Women's College Coalition of America.² Brenau is one of them.

Many educators lament the disappearance of women's colleges because these institutions can play such an important role in women's education. They remove the element of competition with men for academic honors, leadership positions on campus, etc., and thereby give women much more space for intellectual and character development. When many women's colleges were closing or going co-ed to make ends meet, Brenau's Women's College stayed its course—and actually grew. In the 2007–2008 academic year, the Women's College alone enrolled close to a record 930 students at Brenau, a 50 percent increase over what enrollment had been just four years earlier.³ Though annual enrollment numbers would subsequently dip below this peak, by 2013, the Women's College still enrolled over 800 students.⁴

Precisely what accounts for Brenau's longevity when so many similar institutions have changed or failed is not easy to discern. A myriad of factors have no doubt contributed to the University's success over the years. What is evident, though, is that the Brenau of today is a product of its past. Every event, large and small, in the history of the institution contributed to placing Brenau on its present trajectory. Moreover, these events—especially the most significant ones—would, at some level, typically be the product of subtle and not-so-subtle negotiation between Brenau's students and its faculty and administration.

Throughout its history, Brenau's students and Brenau's officials have, as remarkably cohesive groups, each sought to refine the College to create what could be termed "their Brenau." Each party to the ongoing negotiation at the institution sought to construct an ideal college experience based upon their desires and perceptions. Each side achieved varying degrees of success in the negotiations at different times and on different matters during the long life of the College.

Brenau's faculty and staff have historically held much sway over academic matters. They set degree requirements and scholastic standards and expected students to satisfy and adhere to them. At any time in Brenau's history, the students would have generally complied for the sake of simply being able to graduate. Fortunately for students, Brenau was frequently progressive in its academic policymaking. The College created "home ec.," business, and education programs sooner than many of its regional peers and likely inaugurated in higher education the practice of counting art and music courses as elective credit toward baccalaureate degrees. Little suggests that students ever participated much in negotiations with College officials over academic matters such as these. Yet, even pitted as they were against the mighty ivory tower, students have not been entirely unarmed. From time to time, Brenau students did petition the faculty and administration or otherwise negotiated successfully for changes at the College that related to academics. In addition, students shaped academic life at Brenau when they elected to study in some programs and declined to study in others. Brenau actually discontinued several academic programs as a result of low student enrollment and created other programs (even entire satellite and virtual campuses) in an effort to attract and retain students.

Besides controlling academic matters, Brenau's faculty and staff governed the composition of Brenau's student body. For much of the twentieth century, Brenau officials implemented policies to ensure that only whites would attend the College. Compared to some other similarly situated institutions, some of these policies were quite novel and well-calculated to long perpetuate segregation at the College. Although the federal government forced other private colleges and universities to integrate for having taken federal funding for this or that, Brenau avoided integrating for many years thanks to its policy of not accepting any funding at all from government sources. While this did prevent desegregation from occurring for many years at the Women's College even when it was going on elsewhere, Brenau's stance probably cost the institution thousands of dollars in government support. Had Brenau students wanted their college to integrate—and it is not entirely evident that they did or did not—history suggests that their views on the matter would have been given scant attention by College officials if Brenau's foray into admitting male students in the 1970s is any indication. Rather, Brenau's faculty and administrators set policies for the College on such things as student recruitment largely absent student input.

Finally, it was the institution's faculty and staff that have controlled Brenau's built and landscaped environment throughout its history. They determined when to build what and where and oversaw the development and maintenance of all campus structures and grounds. Nothing suggests that there was a great deal of student input in these processes for much of the institution's history. Still, even though students were not much involved in any direct negotiation over the institution's physical spaces, they did personalize their own club houses and sorority houses to great extents. Also, students co-opted many landmarks and monuments on campus for their own purposes. Although this would do nothing like confer ownership upon students, the interest they asserted may at times have been substantial enough to incline officials to treat with them regarding certain components of Brenau's built environment.

Although Brenau students were scarcely party to negotiations in these realms at all, other negotiations with the faculty and staff demonstrated a more notable degree of give-and-take. Student discipline at Brenau was one area in which students, though ultimately subject to faculty and administrative authority, had a great deal of say-so. Throughout the history of the College, officials entrusted Brenau students with an exceptional degree of self-government. Through their student government association, which is one of if not *the* oldest at a southern women's college, Brenau women negotiated often and with a great deal of solidarity with College officials over disciplinary regulations. Over time, the students enjoyed remarkable success in changing or eliminating rules that governed their behavior. For example, in the early twentieth century, Brenau students could not date, smoke, ride in cars with men, see movies, or wear shorts in public. Even though students still remained ultimately subject to College authority by virtue of having enrolled themselves at

Brenau, over the course of several decades, Brenau women successfully petitioned for permission to do all of these once-forbidden things. Indeed, Brenau students gained some of these freedoms far earlier than their counterparts at several other southern women's colleges.

Students arguably enjoyed even greater successes in negotiating with the faculty and staff over other matters. There is much more to college than professors, textbooks, and attending classes. John R. Thelin observed that as American colleges developed, "undergraduates… created an elaborate world of their own within and alongside the official world of the college."[5] In this world, student clubs, secret societies, athletic teams, campus traditions and the like emerged and became key components of the college experience. Indeed, some students have been more interested in this "extracurricular" aspect of college than in their studies. Since the founding of Brenau College and its predecessor, the Georgia Baptist Female Seminary, students negotiated doggedly (and, often, successfully) with College officials to create the extracurricular world they wanted.

The products of these negotiations are chiefly apparent in the few surviving editions of the *Alchemist*, Brenau's student newspaper, in newspaper columns referred to as "Brenau College Notes" or "Brenau Notes" in the *Atlanta Constitution* newspaper, and in a hundred years' worth of Brenau's annually-published student yearbook, the *Bubbles*. All of these sources began publication around the turn of the twentieth century. All would, for several decades, substantiate that students refined "their Brenau" through the traditions they created and passed down and through the sporting, cultural, and extracurricular organizations and practices they founded and maintained. Indeed, Brenau students probably enjoyed their greatest success in their negotiations with faculty members and administrators in creating and maintaining their sororities, secret societies, early sporting groups, and traditions. The products of some of these negotiations have made Brenau unique.

No other women's college has a Greek system as established, as large, as active, and as old as Brenau's. Brenau was the first women's college in the state of Georgia and possibly the first in the South to play intercollegiate athletics. Also, as of 2012, Brenau has arguably the most successful small-college athletic program in the state—if not the entire region—judging by the several conference and national titles it has held. Brenau's H.G.H. Senior Honor Society is one of the oldest and one of the very few secret societies in existence at a women's college today. Finally, Brenau has many captivating, long-lived traditions thriving at its Gainesville campus that create cohesion between its many students. Brenau students have kept these traditions alive over time and have formed organizations, populated them, elected officers, and held events and functions—all with relatively little (if any) meaningful interference or involvement on the part of the College faculty and/or the administration.

Brenau's faculty members and administrators were likely quite content with this arrangement. Paraphrasing Frederick Rudolph, Thelin contended that:

> student initiated activities had a discernible life cycle. In the initial stage, an activity would surface informally and even spontaneously among undergraduates. If a particular activity enjoyed sustained popularity, it attracted scrutiny from the administration and then attempts at either official abolition or control. Such administrative efforts usually failed and the activity would resurface in the form of a renegade organization. Ultimately the administration would try to control or co-opt the activity by assimilating it into the formal structure (and covenants) of the college.[6]

This life cycle is, in essence, an ongoing negotiation between college students and college personnel, one of several, in fact, that occur between these two sides. This life cycle was and is discernible at Brenau and confers benefits upon the institution.

On the surface, many of Brenau's several student organizations (especially groups like the secret societies or the sororities) might appear to be bastions of student agency, places where Brenau students held virtual sway. Indeed, to an extent, such organizations were quite autonomous.

Yet, beneath the surface, more was going on. To accomplish their aims, Brenau College officials at various times in the institution's history have been happy to enlist the help of some of these student groups. Brenau's faculty and staff and even Brenau's own student body relied upon the College's student organizations to police student conduct and to encourage conformity. This was clearly evident in several ways.

As an example, one way this dynamic functioned is apparent in the workings of the College's honor societies. Faculty members selected students for membership in these based upon their scholastic accomplishments and good behavior—things college personnel prize above all else in students. Desirous of membership in the societies, many students studied hard and behaved, much to the faculty's relief. The faculty and staff at Brenau utilized other student organizations in like fashion in an attempt to gain the upper hand in the negotiations over how Brenau would be. At the same time, Brenau students used these same organizations to encourage other students—particularly new students—to fill the roles they were expected to play at the College. When, for example, College officials left sororities, sports clubs, and secret organizations alone to thrive, they did so knowing that those organizations would actually do a good measure of policing and disciplining the student body on behalf of the faculty and staff. Professors did not have to tell students to study; students studied because the sports team they wanted to play on or the sorority they wanted to join set high academic standards for membership. College officials did not have to tell students to dress properly or to behave as ladies; things like sororities or Brenau's Student Government Association demanded that their members conform or face stern social consequences. Clearly, Brenau's students and Brenau's faculty and staff have not always been working at cross purposes in their negotiations to refine the Brenau college experience—but they have always been working.

Some of this work occurred formally. Formal negotiations between Brenau's students and College officials often took place at meetings of Brenau's faculty and staff when students either sent petitions for official consideration or appeared in person to make requests. The vast majority of these personnel meetings were regularly scheduled monthly events; the remainder were "called" meetings when the faculty and staff assembled to address some extraordinary circumstances. The Brenau Archives holds two books of minutes from these meetings that span roughly the first half of the twentieth century. I analyzed the *Faculty Meeting Minutes Book for Twenty-five Years (1922–1947)*, treating it as a sample of faculty-student interaction occurring at Brenau. By determining exactly how much formal negotiation went on between Brenau students and the Brenau faculty and staff in meetings for this long period, it is possible to reasonably infer how often formal negotiation has occurred between these groups throughout the entire life of the institution.

According to the minutes book, the Brenau faculty and staff met no fewer than 211 times between September of 1922 and the end of the academic year in 1947. The College was still relatively young during this era that saw the Roaring Twenties, the Great Depression, and World War II all pass by. This was a period long before that when one might expect many institutions of higher learning to routinely involve students in important decision making. Yet, this is exactly what occurred at Brenau.

The minutes book shows that Brenau officials received at their meetings right at 90 official student petitions or recommendations during this 25 year sample, an average of 3.6 a year or roughly two a semester. Virtually all issued from recognized student groups such as the Discipline Committee or the Student Government Association, which are both quite old. Their significant motions related to a wide range of subjects. Students advanced proposals touching on everything from recommended sentences for rule breakers handed down by the committee on discipline to attendance policies to requests to modify school rules to petitions to alter the College break schedule and academic calendar. That the faculty and staff received such petitions at all in their meetings suggests a solid willingness to negotiate with students regarding the character of the

Brenau collegiate experience. More remarkably, though, is the fate of the student requests.

Brenau officials very seldom denied student petitions. Over fully a quarter-century, more than 90% of the time, the faculty and staff essentially partnered with students to shape what Brenau would be by granting the student petitions, either in whole (usually) or in part. Less than ten percent of student efforts to negotiate with College officials to create or amend institutional policy failed in just over two-dozen years. Significantly, some of the student petitions that did fail did so by close margins. This suggests that even when the students came up short in formal negotiations with the faculty and staff, officials still gave student requests very serious consideration. At the same time, such a high success rate illustrates how students and faculty & staff members did not have to work at cross-purposes to create a college experience desired by both.

One suspects that, in addition to formal negotiations like those that occurred in faculty & staff meetings, students and College personnel have as well long engaged in informal parleys to craft Brenau college life. There has certainly been ample opportunity for this. Students and College personnel have had over a century to talk after class, to meet during office hours, to chat during performance intermissions, etc., about things great and small. Any of these instances and a thousand others would have provided students and Brenau's faculty and staff with a venue from which they could try to reach an agreement or compromise about something through discussion—the essence of negotiation. Had records of such discussions ever been kept, they might have informed even further how the collegiate experience at Brenau formed through conciliation.

The informal and formal college-shaping negotiations that have taken place at Brenau over the years between students and officials are not processes unique to the Gainesville women's college. Such negotiations have long occurred at all colleges and universities to varying degrees. Indeed, the practice should only have proliferated in recent decades as many colleges and universities have liberalized since the 1960s and have become more receptive to student input across the board. Yet, if what happened at Brenau was not unique, it might in some respects still be conspicuous. For instance, more formal negotiating may have generally gone on at Brenau than at neighboring institutions if a comparison of petitioning activity during a particular several-year period is any indication. The student newspaper of the University of Georgia, the *Red and Black*, which covered in exceptional detail everything related to UGA, could report on only a dozen student petition efforts between 1922 and 1930.[7] During the same eight year period, the North Georgia College faculty meeting minutes indicated that students petitioned officials only three times: twice to expand some aspect of senior privileges and once "for repeal of the regulation requiring compulsory attendance at church."[8] By comparison, Brenau women petitioned their College faculty and staff on a variety of topics around thirty times during the same several-year period. It might also be saying something that Brenau established its student government association earlier than any other women's college in the region. That might suggest that Brenau women wanted an organized entity of their own to better engage in formal discourse with College officials. Given all of this, it would seem that the people connected to Brenau have, for some time, been both more willing and more able than others elsewhere to collaborate in fashioning their college into what it would become.

In a letter written to Jean-Baptiste Leroy in 1789, the venerable Benjamin Franklin turned a now-famous phrase: "In this world nothing can be said to be certain, except death and taxes." To these, Franklin might have added another certainty: That as long as there are colleges and universities, there will be negotiations between college students and college faculty and staff members to bring into being at their institution what each constituency regards as an ideal collegiate experience. The result of the long-term give-and-take, the back-and-forth between the two sides, is frequently the emergence of a remarkable place of learning that endears itself to many. This is Brenau. It is wholly apropos that the very meaning of this name is "gold as refined by fire." Like smiths at a forge fixated on a masterpiece, Brenau's students and Brenau's faculty and staff hammer away in their perpetual negotiations to refine their college. The work of art they have created and will continue to create is, for them, akin to gold and something to be treasured just as dearly—a women's college that is exceptionally brilliant, extraordinarily valuable, and exceedingly rare.

Notes

1. Heather Geraci, "'Better Dead than Coed?' Survival and Decline of Single-Sex College in the United States." Paper presented at the annual meeting of the American Sociological Association, Marriott Hotel, Loews Philadelphia Hotel, Philadelphia, PA, 12 August 2005, http://citation.allacademic.com/meta/p_mla_apa_research_citation/0/2/1/2/9/pages21296/p21296-1.php (accessed 21 May 2013). See also Leslie Miller-Bernal and Susan L. Poulson, eds., *Challenged by Coeducation: Women's Colleges Since the 1960s* (Nashville, TN: Vanderbilt University Press, 2005) for more information on the decline of women's colleges.
2. "Colleges & Universities by Name," WomensColleges.org: The Women's College Coalition, http://www.womenscolleges.org/colleges/byname (accessed 21 May 2013).
3. Will Success Spoil Single-gender Education at Brenau?" *Brenau Window*, Fall 2007, http://artsweb.brenau.edu/brenauwindow/Fall2007/Single-gender_article.pdf (accessed 21 May 2013).
4. "College Profile: Brenau University," CollegeData.com, http://www.collegedata.com/cs/data/college/college_pg01_tmpl.jhtml?schoolId=513 (accessed 21 May 2013).
5. Thelin, *History of American Higher Education*, 64.
6. Ibid., 65.
7. These efforts were: A petition from seniors to abolish third term exams (*Red and Black*, 31 March 1922, p. 3, http://redandblack.libs.uga.edu/xtf/view?docId=news/1922/rab1922-0089.xml&query=petition&brand=rab-brand (accessed 25 January 2013)); a student petition to a Dean asking that the defunct UGA Glee Club be revived (*Red and Black*, 26 January 1923, p. 1, http://redandblack.libs.uga.edu/xtf/view?docId=news/1923/rab1923-0009.xml&query=petition&brand=rab-brand (accessed 25 January 2013)); a petition to eliminate term exams for juniors and seniors was circulated, intended for the faculty (*Red and Black*, 13 February 1924, p. 1, http://redandblack.libs.uga.edu/xtf/view?docId=news/1924/rab1924-0041.xml&query=petition&brand=rab-brand (accessed 25 January 2013)); sophomore women sent a petition to "university authorities" to request a name change for a building (*Red and Black*, 13 October 1926, p. 3, http://redandblack.libs.uga.edu/xtf/view?docId=news/1926/rab1926-0155.xml&query=petition&brand=rab-brand (accessed 25 January 2013)); the senior

class would often submit a petition to the faculty asking that they be excused from taking their last semester final examinations, a petition which the faculty would "quietly ignore" (*Red and Black*, 14 May 1926, p. 4, http://redandblack.libs.uga.edu/xtf/view?docId=news/1926/rab19 26-0108.xml&query=petition&brand=rab-brand (accessed 25 January 2013)); students petitioned to organize a "home study" department (*Red and Black*, 5 November 1926, p. 5, http://redandblack.libs.uga.edu/xtf/view?docId=news/1926/rab1926-0181.xml&query=petition&brand=rab-brand (accessed 25 January 2013)); around 18 November 1927, UGA students were circulating a petition to eventually put to the faculty to lengthen the Thanksgiving holiday (*Red and Black*, 18 November 1927, p. 4, http://redandblack.libs.uga.edu/xtf/view?docId=news/1927/rab1927-0 204.xml&query=petition&brand=rab-brand (accessed 25 January 2013)); students submitted a petition to alter chapel services (*Red and Black*, 18 March 1927, p. 6, http://redandblack.libs.uga.edu/xtf/view?docId=news/ 1927/rab1927-0078.xml&query=petition&brand=rab-brand (accessed 25 January 2013)); students presented a petition to the chancellor asking that a new history of art course be created (*Red and Black*, 27 May 1927, p. 3, http://redandblack.libs.uga.edu/xtf/view?docId=news/1927/rab19 27-0139.xml&query=petition&brand=rab-brand (accessed 25 January 2013)); students submitted to the faculty a petition to have an electrified fence removed from campus (*Red and Black*, 2 March 1928, p. 5, http:// redandblack.libs.uga.edu/xtf/view?docId=news/1928/rab1928-0053.xml& query=petition&brand=rab-brand (accessed 25 January 2013)); students submitted a petition to admit freshmen to some events traditionally open only to upperclassmen (*Red and Black*, 18 October 1929, p. 1, http:// redandblack.libs.uga.edu/xtf/view?docId=news/1929/rab1929-0169.xml& query=petition&brand=rab-brand (accessed 25 January 2013)); the faculty granted a student petition requesting a spring dance (*Red and Black*, 14 March 1930, p. 1, http://redandblack.libs.uga.edu/xtf/view?docId=news/ 1930/rab1930-0055.xml&query=petition&brand=rab-brand (accessed 25 January 2013)).

8. *North Georgia College & State University Faculty Minutes 1896–1930*, http://archive.org/details/facultyminute18961930nort (accessed 21 May 2013). According to the minutes: On December 9, 1922, the faculty issued a reply to a "request from Student Council of December 4, 1922" that expanded slightly senior privileges for seniors in good standing (p. 436); on November 6, 1923, the faculty considered a petition from the senior class to again expand senior privileges (p. 446); and the minutes of the faculty

meeting for December 15, 1922, described a request from North Georgia's president. He indicated, "The Student Council having appealed to the Faculty for repeal of the regulation requiring compulsory attendance at church...Therefore, I request that you [the faculty] signify by a 'yes' or 'no' whether or not you think it wise to grant [this] petition." Twelve professors replied "yes," one replied "no," and two abstained (p. 445).

Figures

All photographs are the property of Brenau University unless otherwise indicated and are used with permission. Originals are stored in the Brenau University Archives in the Brenau Trustee Library in Gainesville, Georgia. Unless otherwise indicated, neither a photographer's name, a photograph title, nor an exact date upon which an image was created is available.

Figure 1. Students of the Georgia Baptist Female Seminary circa 1890.

Figure 2. Brenau students circa 1920.

Figure 3. Brenau students in 1938 in a photograph taken by Ramsey (Gainesville, Georgia) entitled, "Tri-Delta Chapter 1938."

Figure 4. Brenau students entertaining dates from nearby Riverside Military Academy circa 1955.

Figure 5. Students participating in Brenau's annual spring Class Day event circa May, 1980.

Figure 6. Brenau students circa 1992.

Figure 7. Brenau students in 2013.

Source. Photograph by Nick Dentamaro for Brenau University taken on April 13, 2013, which appeared in David Morrison, "Alumnae Reunion Weekend & May Day 2013," *Brenau Window*, winter 2012–2013, http://window.brenau.edu/articles/may-day-2013/ (accessed 17 June 2013).

Note. A caption for the same photograph appearing on Brenau's Facebook page (https://www.facebook.com/brenauuniversity, accessed 17 June 2013) read, "Mycharia Spurling is revealed as H.J. the tiger to the Women's College students in Pearce Auditorium during the Class Day at Brenau University's Alumnae Reunion Weekend. During the program the student who was secretly portraying H.J. for the year is unmasked."

Figure 8. Dr. H. J. Pearce and Prof. Azor Van Hoose.

Figure 9. Dr. Josiah Crudup.

Figure 10. Dr. James T. Rogers.

Figure 11. Dr. John S. Burd.

Figure 12. Dr. Edward L. Schrader.

Figure 13. Image showing damage caused by the tornado of April 6, 1936 to Brenau's campus.

Figure 14. Domestic science laboratory circa 1950.

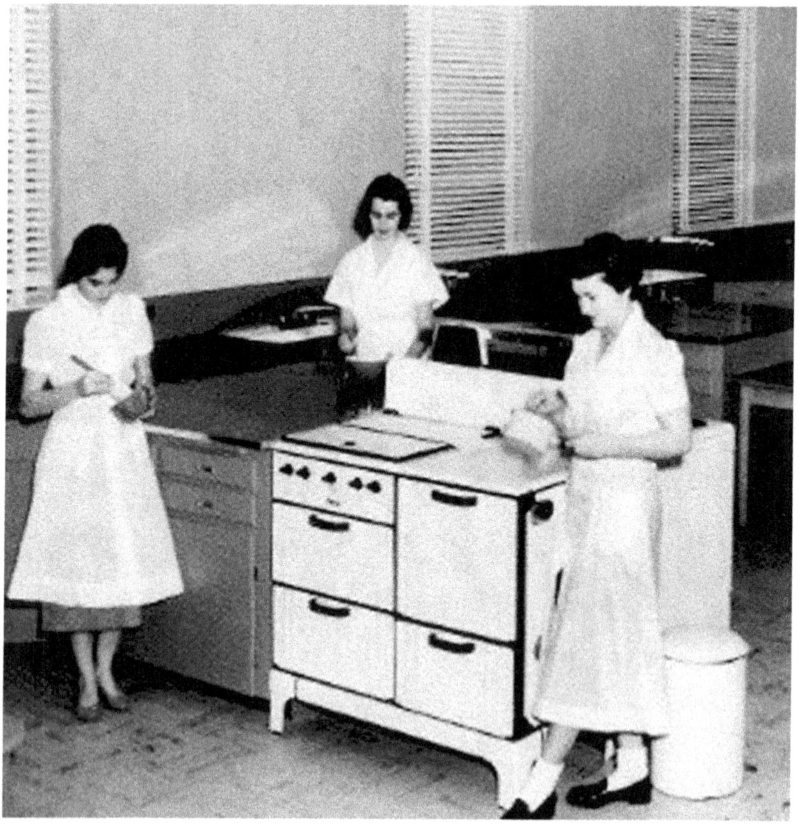

Figure 15. A sample of music performed at Brenau in the early 1900s.

Overture to "Elizabeth," Rossini—Lillian Reese, Ward Parker, Della DeLoach and Hattie Bowden.

"In May Time," Speaks; "Thou art like unto a flower." Cantor—Carrie Chambers.

"Sandalphon," Longfellow—Agnes Donalson.

Music to Shakespeare's "Midsummer Night's Dream," Mendelssohn—Emily Spence, Emma L. Rowe, Camille Callaway and Mattie Alford.

(a) "The Woodpecker," Nevin; (b) "Bercouse," Strelezki—Mary Wartmann.

"Hungarian Fantasie," Liszt-Bulow—Haidee McKenzie. (Orchestral part on second piano by Obie McKenzie.)

Waltz from "Romeo and Juliet," Gounod—Mattie R. Tilson.

"The Mustard Plaster." Reading—Mary Lucy Turner.

"When Roses Bloom Again," Cantor—Mary A. Boone.

Racoczy march, Liszt—Ida Kohn, Pearl Hutchinson, Hattie Clements and Allie Hayes.

Source. "Notes from Brenau," *Atlanta Constitution*, 20 December 1903, sec. B, p. 9.

Figure 16. Brenau Choral circa 2007.

Figure 17. Brenau students in a 2005 production by the Gainesville Theatre Alliance.

Figure 18. The Tri-Kappa Society of Brenau College.

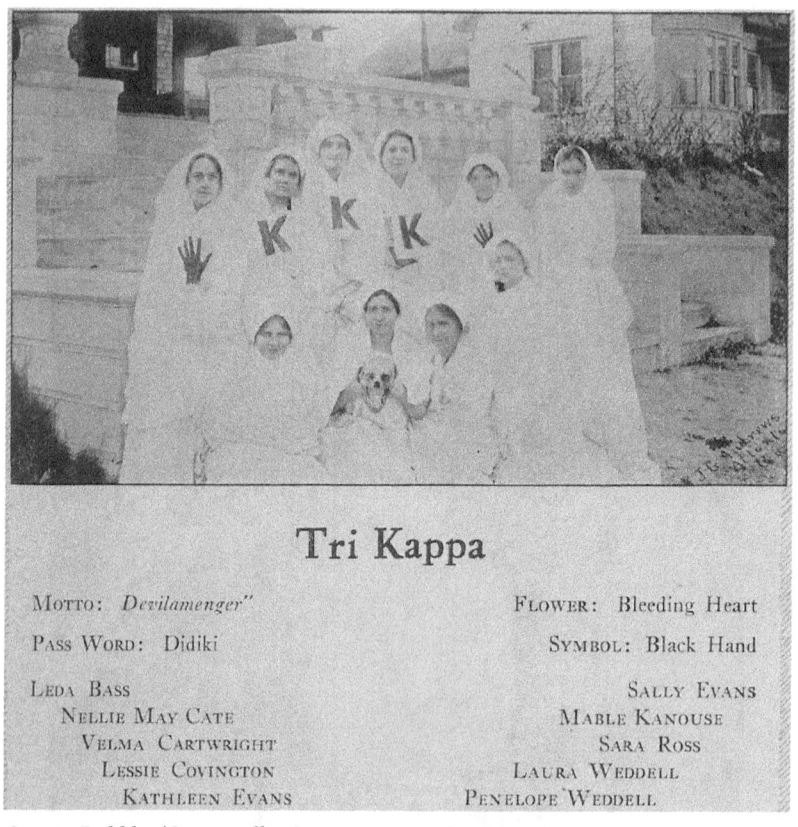

Source. *Bubbles* (Gainesville, GA; Brenau College, 1912), no page number.

Figure 19. The Georgia Baptist Female Seminary circa 1879.

Figure 20. Wilkes Hall circa 1920.

Figure 21. Photograph of the lobby of Yonah Hall circa 1900.

Figure 22. From left to right, Yonah Hall, East Hall, Bailey Hall, and Pearce Auditorium circa 1940.

Figure 23. Interior of Pearce Auditorium (circa 1920), featuring the ceiling painting entitled, "Aeneas at the Court of Dido."

Figures 525

Figure 24. Simmons Memorial Hall circa 1940.

Figure 25. Brenau Trustee Library circa 2002.

Figure 26. The Crow's Nest circa 1925 showing elevated seniors and underclassmen.

Figure 27. Elements of Brenau's Japanese gardens designed by Shogo Joseph Myaida.

Figure 28. The Brenau campus in the early 1900s, depicting several halls connected to form a single, large edifice.

528   THE HISTORY OF BRENAU UNIVERSITY, 1878–2013

Figure 29. The Alpha Delta Pi house circa 1920, which was typical of the several sorority cottages at Brenau during this era.

Figure 30. May Day at Brenau circa 1925.

Figure 31. R.A.T.T. week at Brenau circa 1995.

530   The History of Brenau University, 1878–2013

Figure 32. One of Brenau's mysterious Dare Stones.

Figure 33. Brenau's early aquatic facilities.

Figure 34. A field day sports team (of sophomore baseball players) also showing appropriate costume for gym activities (circa 1920).

Figure 35. Brenau students playing volleyball circa 1950. (Note as well the presence of archery targets and bars for stretching in the upper left-hand corner of the frame.)

Figure 36. Brenau soccer circa 2011.

Figure 37. The Stabs as depicted in the Bubbles circa 1920.

Figure 38. Brenau's H.G.H. Society.

Figure 39. One of Brenau's several stately sorority houses.

TABLES

Table 1. Number of Men and Women on the Brenau Faculty by Year.

Year	Men	Women	Percentage of Women Faculty
1900	7	11	61%
1910	15	22	59%
1920	18	27	40%
1930	10	18	64%
1940	18	26	59%
1950	14	23	62%
1960	19	18	49%
1970	29	28	49%
1980	34	48	59%

Table 2a. Undergraduate degrees offered by Brenau over time.

Degree	1900	1910	1920	1930
A.B. or B.A. (Bachelor of Arts, a.k.a. the "Classical Degree")[1] B.S. (Bachelor of Science, a.k.a. "the Scientific Degree")[2] B.L. (Bachelor of Letters, a.k.a. the "Literary Degree")[3]	Brenau had "schools," akin to modern departments. "At the completion of any one of the schools a certificate of proficiency in that school is awarded; a certain number of such certificates entitles the holder to a ... degree."[4] Brenau required four years of subjects like history, math, and English for all degrees. Students focused on one subject, but had to take outside courses. Hence, classic or literary students would take courses in, e.g., the sciences.[5] Students with parental permission could substitute courses in art, music, etc., for courses in their school and so earn a collegiate degree while getting conservatory training.[6]	A.B., B.S., or B.L. degrees required "fifteen hours per week for eight terms" studying core subjects like math and English and elective courses in a major area.[7]	Brenau had converted to the semester system and required 120 hours for an A.B., B.S., or B.L. degree. A major required a minimum of 24 semester hours of credit and a minor required half as much. Students could both major and minor in several departments, which generally embraced the typical subjects offered at liberal arts colleges. Brenau required students to earn 60 semester hours during their junior and senior years.[8]	Students took 48 hours of "required courses" and some "courses with options," which let students choose a course from a list.[9] Students also took elective courses and courses in their major and minor to earn 120 hours. Students could major in "English Language and Literature, Latin, French, Spanish, German, Mathematics, Philosophy and Education, History and Political Science, the Biological Sciences, the Physical Sciences, Chemistry and Home Science."[10] Conservatory work could apply to degrees.

[1] *Catalog* (1900), 21.
[2] Ibid.
[3] Ibid.
[4] Ibid., 23.
[5] Ibid., 30. The catalog presented a table with year-to-year course requirements for the several degrees.
[6] See *Catalog* (1900), 33, for a description of the elective course.
[7] *Catalog* (1910), 15.
[8] *Catalog* (1920).
[9] *Catalog* (1929), 43.
[10] Ibid., 44.

Table 2b. Undergraduate degrees offered by Brenau over time (cont.)

Degree	1900	1910	1920	1930
L.I. degree ("Licentiate of Instruction")[11]		"The L.I. degree is a new course intended to be something of a Normal Course…adapted to young women wishing to teach."[12] Students learned pedagogy, spelling, grammar, geography, and history. This degree required slightly fewer credits than a bachelor's degree and could be finished in two years.[13]		"By completing certain specified courses in the department of Education, and satisfying requirements of the Junior College diploma, it is possible for a student to secure, in two years, both the Junior College diploma and the Junior College Professional Teachers Certificate, qualifying the student to teach in [Georgia] elementary schools."[14]
B.O. (Bachelor of Oratory)[15]		One fourth of the BO requirements were "Literary Interpretation & Expression"; another quarter was split among English (mostly) and math. The remaining requirements were general education courses and recitations of passages that gradually increased in rigor over the course of several years.[16]		
B.D. (Bachelors of Domesticity)[17]		For "girls who desire to spend two or three years in college to fit themselves for the duties of society and home."[18]	The bachelor's degree was replaced by a "Certificate in Household Economics," which required the completion of 20 hours of "Household Economics" and "thirty semester hours, in addition" of college courses.[19]	

---

[11] *Catalog* (1910), 15.
[12] Ibid.
[13] Ibid. Most normal schools that trained teachers required three years of study.
[14] *Catalog* (1929), 48.
[15] *Catalog* (1910).
[16] Ibid., 16.
[17] Ibid.
[18] Ibid.
[19] *Catalog* (1921), 43.

Table 2c. Undergraduate degrees offered by Brenau over time (cont.)

Degree	1900	1910	1920	1930
Mus.B. (Bachelor of Music)				Awarded after mastering a course in piano, strings, voice, or organ by learning four years' worth of progressively challenging pieces, studying three years of music theory, and playing from memory a public recital of material akin to the hardest pieces learned during study.
Associate in Arts			Required 45 hours of "Freshman and Sophomore" courses, namely six hours of: (a) English; (b) a foreign language; (c) a 2nd language; (d) history; (e) math or logic & introductory philosophy; (f) a physical science; (g) a biological science or in household economics; (h) and 3 in general psychology, plus electives to total 60 hours.[20]	The 1930 catalog indicated that, "It is a matter of record that only a small proportion of students entering college…are able to complete a four year college course. Accordingly for such students a diploma from the Junior College division is awarded by Brenau College upon the satisfactory completion of the requirements of the Freshman and Sophomore years." Brenau required 60 hours for the certificate.[21]
Certificate in "Secretarial Studies and Public Accounting."				Brenau offered a two-year certificate in stenography and typewriting.[22]
B.S. in Education				

[20] Ibid., 43.
[21] *Catalog* (1929), 47.
[22] *Catalog* (1939), 85.

Table 2d. Undergraduate degrees offered by Brenau over time (cont.)

Degree	1940	1950	1960	1970
A.B.[23] B.S.[24] B.L.[25]	The B.S. and the B.L. were gradually eliminated, though the B.S. would later be offered again; the A.B. remained continuously offered.	The "Brenau Plan" only offered an A.B. with majors in such subjects as "English Language and Literature, Speech Arts, Foreign Languages, Psychology, Mathematics and Physics, Sociology and Economics, History and Political Science, Biology, Chemistry, and Music." "Core" courses made up one-third of the degree; the remainder consisted of courses in the major area and elective course work. Also, the catalog indicated that students required a "C" average to graduate.[26]		
L.I. degree				
B.O.				
B.D.				
Mus.B.				
Associate in Arts			The A.A. basically required meeting all "core" requirements and completing some elective courses.	
Certificate in "Secretarial Studies and Public Accounting."	Required a year each of college courses (English, history, etc.) and courses like typing, shorthand, stenography, etc.[27]	Brenau discontinued the certificate but continued teaching business-related courses as electives through a department of "Commerce."[28]		
B.S. in Education	Offered in "Physical Education and Biological and Natural Science" until all degrees but the A.B. were eliminated.[29]		Resumed.	

[23] *Catalog* (1900), 21.
[24] Ibid.
[25] Ibid.
[26] *Catalog* (1949), 43.
[27] *Catalog* (1939), 117.
[28] *Catalog* (1949), 55.
[29] *Catalog* (1939), 117.

Table 2e. Undergraduate degrees offered by Brenau over time (cont.)

Degree	1980	1990	2000
A.B. or B.A.[30] B.S.[31] B.F.A., B.B.A.[32]	Quarter system now used; required courses comprised about one-third to one-half of a Bachelor's degree. Majors in traditional liberal arts subjects and business administration, criminal justice, broadcasting and journalism, allied health, and several sub-disciplines of education. Also a general studies major and several "pre-professional" programs. Bachelors of Fine Arts and of Business Administration were also added to Brenau's degree offerings around this time. Each consisted of a similar distribution of core, elective, and major courses as the B.A.	Reversion to semester system; otherwise, requirements for bachelor's degrees largely unchanged from previous decade.	Largely unchanged from previous decade.
Mus.B.	Resumed. Roughly one-third to one-half of the degree components were required general education courses and a handful of electives; the remainder consisted of courses mostly in music theory and/or education and courses focused on voice or piano performance.	Largely unchanged from previous decade.	
Associate in Arts	Largely unchanged from previous decade, requiring roughly half of the credit requisite to earning a bachelor's degree in general education and a few elective courses.	Largely unchanged from previous decade.	
B.S. in Education	Resumed. Courses designed to develop content matter expertise coupled with pedagogy courses comprised roughly half the degree. General education courses and a few elective courses comprised the remainder.	Largely unchanged from previous decade.	

[30] *Catalog* (1900), 21.
[31] Ibid.
[32] *Catalog* (1980).

Bibliography

Where appropriate, the full citations for all Brenau catalogs/bulletins and student handbooks referenced throughout this work are abbreviated simply as "*Catalog ([XXXX])*" or "*Handbook ([XXXX])*," with "XXXX" representing the year of publication. Thus, for example, the abbreviation for the "*Brenau Bulletin, 1949–1950 v. XXXXI n. 3* (Gainesville, GA: Brenau College, 1949), 17" would be "*Catalog* (1949), 17." Copies of all catalogs and handbooks are available in the Brenau University Archives in Gainesville, Georgia.

The minutes of many years' worth of the Brenau College faculty meetings are recorded in two volumes housed in the Brenau University Archives: *Brenau College Faculty Journal for Twelve Years (1910–1922)* and *Faculty Journal for Twenty-five Years* (which contains minutes from 1923 to 1948). The volumes are not well-paginated, but entries are listed chronologically by date. Where appropriate, the full citations for these volumes throughout this work are abbreviated simply as "*Faculty Journal (12 years)*, [entry date]" and "*Faculty Journal (25 years)*, [entry date]."

As president of Brenau, Dr. Josiah Crudup delivered a report to the Brenau College Board of Trustees at their annual meeting held in late May or early June of each year. Typewritten transcriptions of these reports are filed in chronological order in folders located in several boxes of the "Dr. Crudup Files" collection of the Brenau University Archives in Gainesville, Georgia. Where appropriate, the full citations of each of these sources (e.g., Josiah Crudup, "A Report to the Board of Trustees of Brenau College (Friday, May 29, 1953)." Dr. Crudup Files, Box 34 of 40, Folder 10, Brenau University Archives, Gainesville, Georgia)) will be abbreviated as follows: Crudup, "Report to the Board ([date])."

Brenau published annually a student yearbook entitled *Bubbles* for most of its history. These hardbound books contained around one-hundred-fifty or so glossy pages of photographs of Brenau people, groups, events, and places and brief descriptions or captions accompanying the photographs. The vast majority of *Bubbles* editions contained only black-and-white photographs, though color photographs came into usage after the 1980s. Though most editions of *Bubbles* were paginated, not all were. Beginning in the 1990s, Brenau changed the yearbook name from *Bubbles* to *Aurum*. By this time, the publication was a much leaner version of what it had been. The Brenau Archives contain at least one copy of the annual yearbook for each year of the University's existence dating back to the nineteenth century. Where appropriate, the full citations for these volumes throughout this work are abbreviated simply as *Bubbles* or *Aurum (*[year of publication]*)*.

PRIMARY SOURCES

MANUSCRIPT COLLECTIONS

Brenau University Archives (Gainesville, Georgia)

College and University Catalogs (in chronological order)

Twenty-Second Annual Catalogue of Brenau College and Brenau Conservatory. Atlanta, GA: The Foote & Davis Company, 1900.

Thirty-second Annual Catalogue of Brenau College-Conservatory, 1910, v. 1, n. 2. Gainesville, GA: Brenau College, 1910.

President Thomas Jackson Simmons...An Appreciation. Gainesville, GA: Brenau College, c. 1910. Available from http://archive.org/stream/presidentthmasj00ross#page/38/mode/2up; Internet; accessed 25 January 2013.

Brenau College Catalogue, 1920–1921, v. XI, n. 2. Gainesville, GA: Brenau College, 1920.

Bibliography

Brenau College Catalogue, 1929–1930, v. XXII, n. 2. Gainesville, GA: Brenau College, 1929.

Brenau College Catalogue, 1931–1932, v. XXII, n. 4. Gainesville, GA: Brenau College, 1931.

Brenau College Catalogue, 1939–1940, v. XXXI, n.3. Gainesville, GA: Brenau College, 1939.

Brenau Bulletin, 1949–1950 v. XXXXI n. 3. Gainesville, GA: Brenau College, 1949.

Brenau College Bulletin 1960–1961, v. L, n. 1. Gainesville, GA: Brenau College, 1960.

Brenau College Bulletin 1970–1971, Annual Catalogue Edition, Vol. LX, No. 1. Gainesville, GA: Brenau College, 1970.

Brenau College Catalog, 1978–79. Gainesville, GA: Brenau College, 1978.

Brenau College 1980–1981 Undergraduate Bulletin. Gainesville, GA: Brenau College, 1980.

Brenau College 1980 Graduate Bulletin. Gainesville, GA: Brenau College, 1980.

Brenau College Catalog, 1988–1990. Gainesville, GA: Brenau College, 1988.

Brenau University Undergraduate and Graduate Catalog. Vol. 107, No. 1. Gainesville, GA: Brenau University, 1990.

Brenau University Undergraduate and Graduate Catalog. Vol. 110, No. 1. Gainesville, GA: Brenau University, 1992–1993.

Brenau University Undergraduate and Graduate Catalog. Vol. 115, No. 1. Gainesville, GA:

Brenau University, 1998.

Brenau University Undergraduate and Graduate Catalog. Vol. 117, No. 1. Gainesville, GA: Brenau University, 2000.

Annual Catalog, Vol. 122. Gainesville, GA: Brenau University, 2006.

Brenau University Undergraduate and Graduate Catalog 2007–2008. Vol. 123. Gainesville, GA: Brenau University, 2007.

Brenau University Undergraduate and Graduate Catalog 2008–2009. Vol. 124. Gainesville, GA: Brenau University, 2007.

College Student Newspapers
Seminary Signal (Gainesville, Georgia), April, 1895.

Alchemist (Gainesville, Georgia), 1900 – .

College Yearbooks
Bubbles. Gainesville, Georgia: Brenau College, 1900 – .

Aurum (formerly *Bubbles*). Gainesville, GA: Brenau College, 1998 – .

Interviews (transcribed)
Hosch, Mary Helen. Transcription of interview conducted by Andrea Davis on 27 February 1995. Dean of Women Files, Box 1 of 1, Brenau University Archives, Gainesville, Georgia.

Robinson, Lil and Mrs. Mary Foote Paris. Transcription of interview conducted by Andrea Davis on 15 February 1995. Dean of Women Files, Box 1 of 1, Brenau University Archives, Gainesville, Georgia.

Thurmond, Elizabeth Wheeler (Lib). Transcription of interview (interviewer unknown, date unknown). Dean of Women Files, Box 1 of 1, Brenau University Archives, Gainesville, Georgia.

Webster, J. Allen. Transcription of interview (interviewer unknown, date unknown). Dean of Women Files, Box 1 of 1, Brenau University Archives, Gainesville, Georgia.

Institutional Self-Studies
Brenau College, An Institutional Self Study, Under the Auspices of The Southern Association of Colleges and Schools, September 1969 – May 1971. Gainesville, GA. Brenau College. Brenau University Archives, Gainesville, Georgia.

Brenau College, An Institutional Self-Study Under the Auspices of The Southern Association of Colleges and Schools, September, 1979

Bibliography

– May, 1981. Gainesville, GA. Brenau College. Brenau University Archives, Gainesville, Georgia.

Brenau: The Professional College, An Institutional Self-study under the Auspices of The Southern Association of Colleges and Schools, 1984–1986. Gainesville, GA. Brenau College. Brenau University Archives, Gainesville, Georgia.

Burd, Dr. John S. "Brenau College: Self-Study Report Georgia Department of Education." 15 December 1990. Gainesville, GA. Brenau College. Brenau University Archives, Gainesville, Georgia.

Meeting Minutes

Brenau Trustees, "Minutes of Meeting of Trustees of Brenau College (Friday, June 4, 1965)," William Clark Files, Box 7 of 7, Folder 3, Brenau University Archives, Gainesville, Georgia.

Brenau College Faculty Journal for Twelve Years (1910–1922), Brenau University Archives, Gainesville, Georgia.

Faculty Journal for Twenty-five Years (1922–1947), Brenau University Archives, Gainesville, Georgia.

Memoranda

"Freshman Mortality 1929–1939." Registrar Files, Box 1 of 1, Folder 8, Brenau University Archives, Gainesville, Georgia.

Winfield, Ella D. "Enrollment of Brenau College." Undated, but likely prepared in 1950, the last year of data provided in the memo. Registrar Files, Box 1 of 1, Folder 6, Brenau University Archives, Gainesville, Georgia.

Letters and Correspondence

Anonymous "Brenau Alumna" on June 18, 1964 to Dr. Josiah Crudup, President. Dr. Crudup Files, Box 29 of 40, Folder 4, Brenau University Archives, Gainesville, Georgia.

Crudup, Josiah. "Letter of January 16, 1951, from Dr. Crudup to Mr. Thomas C. Law." Dr. Crudup files, Box 35 of 40, Folder 7, Brenau University Archives, Gainesville, Georgia.

----------. "April 6, 1964 letter to the Honorable Carl Elliot, Congressman, United States House of Representatives, Washington, D.C." Dr. Crudup Files, Box 34 of 40, Folder 9, Brenau University Archives, Gainesville, Georgia.

----------. "May 28, 1964, letter to the Honorable Carl Elliot, Congressman, United States House of Representatives, Washington, D.C." Dr. Crudup Files, Box 34 of 40, Folder 9, Brenau University Archives, Gainesville, Georgia.

----------. "Letter to Mrs. Doris D. Smith, August 29, 1964." Dr. Crudup Files, Box 29 of 40, Folder 4, Brenau University Archives, Gainesville, Georgia.

----------. "Sept 1, 1964, letter to Mr. Malcolm Reese, Chairman of School Committee, Committee of 1000, Perry, Georgia." Dr. Crudup Files, Box 34 of 40, Folder 9, Brenau University Archives, Gainesville, Georgia.

Yust, Walter. "Letter from the editor, Encyclopedia Britannica, to Dr. Josiah Crudup inquiring about the vital statistics of the college for publication in the Encyclopedia's 1950 Britannica's Book of the Year, dated October 21, 1949." Registrar Files, Box 1 of 1, Folder 6, Brenau University Archives, Gainesville, Georgia.

Reports to the Board of Trustees

Crudup, Josiah. "Report to the Board of Trustees of Brenau College (Monday, May 28, 1945)." Dr. Crudup Files, Box 34 of 40, Folder 10, Brenau University Archives, Gainesville, Georgia.

----------. "Report to the Board of Trustees of Brenau College (Friday, May 27, 1949)." Dr. Crudup Files, Box 34 of 40, Folder 10, Brenau University Archives, Gainesville, Georgia.

----------. "A Report to the Board of Trustees of Brenau College (Friday, May 29, 1953)." Dr. Crudup Files, Box 34 of 40, Folder 10, Brenau University Archives, Gainesville, Georgia.

----------. "A Report to the Board of Trustees of Brenau College (Friday, May 31, 1957)." Dr. Crudup Files, Box 35 of 40, Folder 5, Brenau University Archives, Gainesville, Georgia.

----------. "A Report to the Board of Trustees of Brenau College (Friday, May 30, 1958)." Dr. Crudup Files, Box 35 of 40, Folder 5, Brenau University Archives, Gainesville, Georgia.

----------. "A Report to the Board of Trustees of Brenau College (Friday, September 23, 1960." Dr. Crudup Files, Box 29 of 40, Folder 5, Brenau University Archives, Gainesville, Georgia.

----------. "A Report to the Board of Trustees of Brenau College (Friday, June 2, 1961)." Dr. Crudup Files, Box 29 of 40, Folder 5, Brenau University Archives, Gainesville, Georgia.

----------. "A Report to the Board of Trustees of Brenau College (Friday, June 1, 1962)." Dr. Crudup Files, Box 29 of 40, Folder 5, Brenau University Archives, Gainesville, Georgia.

----------. "A Report to the Board of Trustees of Brenau College (Friday, May 29, 1964)." Dr. Crudup Files, Box 29 of 40, Folder 5, Brenau University Archives, Gainesville, Georgia.

----------. "A Report to the Board of Trustees of Brenau College (Friday, June 4, 1965)." Dr. Crudup Files, Box 29 of 40, Folder 5, Brenau University Archives, Gainesville, Georgia.

Student Handbooks (in chronological order)

Official Hand-Book of Information, 1925–1926. Gainesville, GA: Brenau College, 1925.

Culler, Louise, ed. The *Brenau Girl: Official Handbook of Information, 1937–1938.* Gainesville, GA: Brenau College, 1937.

Duncan, Marguerite, ed. *Official Handbook of Information, 1945–1946.* Gainesville, GA: Brenau College, 1945.

Allen, Sarah, ed. *Students' Handbook, Brenau College 1955–1956.* Gainesville, GA: Brenau College, 1955.

Fargason, Patsy and Cheryl Gibbons, eds. *Students' Handbook, Brenau College 1965–1966.* Gainesville, GA: Brenau College, 1965.

Thrasher, Margie, ed. *Student Handbook, Brenau College, 1974–1975*. Gainesville, GA: Brenau College, 1974.

Duncan, Jody and Lynn Smith, eds. *Brenau Women's College Student Handbook 1984–1985*. Gainesville, GA: Brenau University, 1984.

Other Collegiate Primary Sources

Catalogue of the Baptist Female University, Raleigh, North Carolina, 1899–1900. Raleigh, NC: Edwards & Broughton, Printers and Binders, 1900.

Thirty-Sixth Annual Catalogue. Pittsburgh, PA: Pennsylvania College for Women, 1905.

Quarterly Bulletin 1909–1910. Raleigh, NC: Meredith College, 1909.

The Sixth Year Book of Sweet Briar College. Sweet Briar, VA: Sweet Briar College, 1911.

Bulletin of Sweet Briar College: State of the College. Sweet Briar, VA: Sweet Briar College, 1960.

Anderson College Student Handbook for Women. Anderson, SC: Anderson College, 1968.

The Lotus Yearbook. Raleigh, NC: Peace College, 1973.

GOVERNMENT and REFERENCE PUBLICATIONS

"Civil Rights Act of 1964." (Pub.L. 88–352), *United States Statutes at Large*, 78 Stat. 241 (July 2, 1964).

"Surplus Property Act of 1944." (49 USC 47151), *Code of Federal Regulations* (1944).

"Title IX of the Education Amendments of 1972 to the Civil Rights Act of 1964." (Pub. L. 92–318), United *States Statutes at Large*, 86 Stat. 235 (June 23, 1972).

INTERVIEWS

Burd, Dr. John S. Immediate past president, Brenau University. Interview by author, 23 September 2010, Gainesville, Georgia. Tape recording.

Bibliography

Member of H.G.H. Senior Honor Society. Email interview by author, 02 August 2011. (The interviewee requested that her name be withheld from publication.)

Southerland, Dr. James E. Former history professor, Provost, and Vice President for Academic Affairs. Telephone interview by author, 03 November 2006, Gainesville, Georgia. Written notes.

Staff member of the Brenau University Office of Admissions. Interview by author, 31 October 2006, Gainesville, Georgia. Written notes. (The interviewee requested that her name be withheld from publication.)

LEGAL RECORDS and COURT CASES

Brown v. Board of Education of Topeka, Kansas, 98 F. Supp. 797 (1951), 347 U.S. 483 (1954), 349 U.S. 294 (1955).

Frasier v. Board of Trustees of the University of North Carolina, 134 F. Supp. 589 (M.D.N.C. 1955).

Hall, Samuel. "The Laws of Harvard College (1790)." *18th-Century Reading Room.com.* Available from http://18thcenturyreadingroom.wordpress.com/2006/02/23/item-of-the-day-the-laws-of-harvard-college-1790/. Internet; accessed 18 June 2013.

Plessy v. Ferguson, 163 U.S. 537 (1896).

MEETING MINUTES

Minutes of the Georgia Baptist Convention, April 19, 20, 21, and 23, 1887, Gainesville, Georgia, as cited in Rigney, Eleanor. *Brenau College 1878–1978: Enriched by the Past, Challenged by the Future.* Gainesville, GA: Brenau College, 1978.

NEWSPAPERS and PERIODICALS

Atlanta Constitution, 1868–1929.

Atlanta Journal-Constitution, 1985– .

Chatsworth Times, 17 May 1951.

Chicago Tribune, 26 April 2006.

Gainesville Eagle, 1877–1878.

Gainesville Times, 1977–2004.

Macon Telegraph, 10 September 1887.

Montgomery Advertiser, 1 August 1901.

New York Times on the Web, 3 September 1981.

The Red and Black (Athens, Georgia), 1920– .

REPORTS

Reports on the Course of Instruction in Yale College: By a Committee of the Corporation and the Academical Faculty. New Haven, CT: H. Howe, 1828.

Ford Foundation. "Archives: Ford Foundation Annual Report 1957." Available from http://www.fordfound.org/Archives/item/1957/text/101. Internet; accessed 5 July 2008.

BOOKS

DuBois, W.E. Burghardt. *The College-bred Negro: Report of a Social Study Made Under the Direction of Atlanta University*, Together with the Proceedings of the Fifth Conference for the Study of the Negro Problems, held at Atlanta University, May 29–30, 1900. Atlanta, GA: Atlanta University Press, 1900. Available from The Digital Library of Georgia in DJVU format at http://fax.libs.uga.edu/E185x5xA881p/aup05/ . Internet; accessed 18 June 2013.

Fuller, Hubert Bruce. *History of the Baptist Denomination in Georgia*. Atlanta, GA: Jas. P. Harrison & Co. Printers and Publishers, 1881. Available from http://www.ebooksread.com/authors-eng/hubert-bruce-fuller/history-of-the-baptist-denomination-in-georgia-alt/page-129-history-of-the-baptist-denomination-in-georgia-alt.shtml. Internet; accessed 2 December 2012.

Mitchell, Wesley Clair (ed.). *Income in the United States, its Amount and Distribution, 1909–1919*, Issue II. New York, NY: National Bureau of Economic Research, 1922.

Pearce, Heyward J. *Philosophical Meditations*. Boston, MA: The Stratford Company, 1917.

Rosser, Mary. *President Thomas Jackson Simmons and Mrs. Simmons: An Appreciation*. Gainesville, GA: Brenau College and Conservatory, 1910. Available from http://catalog.hathitrust.org/Record/009587573 . Internet; accessed 17 December 2012.

Weld, Thomas and Peter Hugh. "New England's First Fruits: In Respect to the Progress of Learning in the College at Cambridge in Massachusetts-bay (1640)..." In *Collections of the Massachusetts Historical Society*, ser. I., Vol.1, 1792, 242–248.

ARTICLES

Adams, Michael F. "State of the University 2000." State of the University Address, 12 January 2000. Available from http://president.uga.edu/index.php/speeches/sotu/state_of_the_university_2000/. Internet; accessed 16 June 2013.

American Association of University Professors. "Censure List." Available from http://www.aaup.org/our-programs/academic-freedom/censure-list. Internet; accessed 18 June 2013.

Gainesville Parks and Recreation Division. "Allen Creek Soccer Complex." Available from http://www.gainesville.org/allen-creek-soccer-complex . Internet; accessed 18 June 2013.

Northeast Georgia History Center. "About the History Center: Brenau University." Available from http://www.negahc.org/about/. Internet; accessed 18 June 2013.

PHOTOGRAPHS

All images reprinted in this manuscript are the property of Brenau University or their affiliates and are used with permission. The University Archives contain a rich collection of images numbering into the several thousands. Mostly photographs, these images issue from all eras of the University's existence and depict a myriad of subjects. Not all of this vast image collection has been organized or filed. Most of the images in this manuscript may be located in a box labeled "Brenau Photos from the past," which is housed in the Brenau University Archives in Gainesville, Georgia. For virtually all images, neither the name of the illustrator/photographer nor the exact date upon which the image was created is available. Additionally, no titles exist for most of the images.

SECONDARY SOURCES

BOOKS

Akers, Samuel Luttrell. *The First Hundred Years of Wesleyan College, 1836–1936.* Savannah, GA: Beehive Press, 1976.

Alvey, Edward. *History of Mary Washington College, 1908–1972.* Charlottesville, VA: University Press of Virginia, 1974.

Anson, Jack L. and Robert F. Marchesani, eds. *Baird's Manual of American College Fraternities.* Menasha, WI: George Banta Publishing Company, 1991.

Ayers, Edward L. et. al, *American Passages: A History of the United States.* Boston, MA: Wadsworth Cengage Learning, 2009.

Bainbridge, Judith T. *Academy and College: The History of the Woman's College of Furman University.* Macon, GA: Mercer University Press, 2001.

Banet-Weiser, Sarah. *The Most Beautiful Girl in the World: Beauty Pageants and National Identity.* Berkeley, CA: University of California Press, 1999.

Blandin, Isabella Margaret Elizabeth. *History of Higher Education of Women in the South prior to 1860.* Washington, DC: The Neale Publishing Co., 1909.

Boas, Louise Schutz. *Woman's Education Begins; the Rise of the Women's Colleges.* Norton, MA: Wheaton College Press, 1935.

Boorstin, Daniel. *The Americans: The National Experience.* New York, NY: Vintage Books, 1965.

Boren, Mark Edel. *Student Resistance: A History of the Unruly Subject.* New York, NY: Routledge Press, 2001.

Bibliography

Brandt, Allan M. *The Cigarette Century: The Rise, Fall, and Deadly Persistence of the Product That Defined America.* New York, NY: Basic Books, 2009.

Brekus, Catherine A. *Strangers and Pilgrims: Female Preaching in America, 1740–1845.* Chapel Hill, NC: University of North Carolina Press, 1998.

Bronner, Simon J. *American Children's Folklore.* Atlanta, GA: August House Publishers, Inc., 2006.

Cardozier, V.R. *Colleges and Universities in World War II.* Westport, CT: Greenwood Publishing Group, Inc., 1993.

Chait, Richard. *The Questions of Tenure.* Boston, MA: Harvard University Press, 2005.

Cobban, Alan B. *The Medieval English Universities: Oxford and Cambridge to c. 1500.* Berkeley, CA: University of California Press, 1988.

-----------. *The Medieval Universities: Their Development and Organization.* London, UK: Methuen and Co., 1975.

Cogan, Frances B. *All-American Girl: The Ideal of Real Womanhood in Mid-Nineteenth-Century America.* Athens, GA: The University of Georgia Press, 1989.

Converse, Florence. *The Story of Wellesley.* Boston, MA: Little, Brown and Company, 1915.

Cornelius, Roberta D. *The History of Randolph-Macon Woman's College.* Chapel Hill, NC: The University of North Carolina Press, 1951.

Cowan, Ruth Schwartz. *More Work for Mother: The Ironies of Household Technology from the Open Hearth to the Microwave.* New York, NY: Basic Books, 1983.

Eisenmann, Linda. *Higher Education for Women in Postwar America, 1945–1965.* Baltimore, MD: Johns Hopkins University Press, 2006.

Faragher, John Mack and Florence Howe. *Women and Higher Education in American History.* New York, NY: W. W. Norton & Company, 1988.

Farnham, Christie Anne. *The Education of the Southern Belle: Higher Education and Student Socialization in the Antebellum South.* New York, NY: New York University Press, 1994.

Fletcher, Adam. *Meaningful Student Involvement: Guide to Students as Partners in School Change 2nd edition.* Olympia, WA: SoundOut.org, 2005.

Frost, S. E. *Education's Own Stations: The History of Broadcast Licenses Issued to Educational Institutions.* New York: Arno Press and The New York Times, 1971.

Gelernter, Mark. *A History of American Architecture.* Manchester, UK: Manchester University Press, 1999.

Gordon, Lynn D. *Gender and Higher Education in the Progressive Era.* New Haven, CT: Yale University Press, 1990.

Grob, Gerald N. *The Deadly Truth: A History of Disease in America.* Boston, MA: Harvard University Press, 2002.

Grumet, Madeleine R. *Bitter Milk: Women and Teaching.* Amherst, MA: University of Massachusetts Press, 1988.

Haller, John S. and Robin M. Haller. *The Physician and Sexuality in Victorian America.* Urbana, IL: University of Illinois Press, 1974.

Hamilton, Frances Dew and Elizabeth Crabtree Wells. *Daughters of the Dream: Judson College 1838–1988.* Marion, AL: Judson College, 1989.

Harris, Ellen T. *Henry Purcell's Dido and Aeneas.* New York, NY: Oxford University Press, 1990.

Harwarth, Irene, Mindi Maline, and Elizabeth DeBra. "Women's Colleges in the United States: History, Issues, and Challenges." Report prepared for the National Institute on Postsecondary Education, Libraries, and Lifelong Learning of the Office of Educational Research and Improvement in the Department of Education. Available from http://www.eric.ed.gov/PDFS/ED409815.pdf . Internet; accessed 18 June 2013.

----------. "A Closer Look at Women's Colleges." United States Department of Education (July 1999). Available from http://www2.ed.gov/pubs/WomensColleges/index.html . Internet; accessed 18 June 2013.

Bibliography

Haskins, Charles Homer. *The Rise of Universities*. Ithaca, NY: Cornell University Press, 1957.

Horowitz, Helen Lefkowitz. *Alma Mater: Design and Experience in the Women's Colleges from Their Nineteenth-Century Beginnings to the 1930s*. New York, NY: Alfred A. Knopf, 1984.

Inscoe, John C. *Writing the South Through the Self: Explorations in Southern Autobiography*. Athens, GA: University of Georgia Press, 2011.

Johnson, C. S. *Fraternities in Our Colleges*. New York, NY: National Interfraternity Foundation, 1972.

Johnson, Mary Lynch. *A History of Meredith College*. Raleigh, NC: Meredith College, 1956.

Kaestle, Carl F. *Pillars of the Republic: Common Schools and American Society, 1780–1860*. New York, NY: Hill and Wang, 1983.

Kelley, Mary. *Learning to Stand & Speak: Women, Education, and Public Life in America's Republic*. Chapel Hill, NC: Published by the Omohundro Institute of Early American History and Culture, Williamsburg, Virginia, by the University of North Carolina Press, 2006.

Kibler, Lillian Adele. *The History of Converse College, 1889–1971*. Spartanburg, SC: Converse College, 1973.

Knight, Lucian Lamar. *A Standard History of Georgia and Georgians: Volume Five*. Chicago, IL: The Lewis Publishing Company, 1917.

Knipp, Anna Heubeck and Thaddeus P. Thomas. *The History of Goucher College*. Baltimore, MD: Goucher College, 1938.

Leonard, John William. *Woman's Who's Who of America: A Biographical Dictionary of Contemporary Women of the United States and Canada*. New York, NY: The American Commonwealth Company, 1915.

Lucas, Christopher J. *American Higher Education: A History*. New York, NY: St. Martin's Press, 1994.

MacLean, Nancy. *Behind the Mask of Chivalry: The Making of the Second Ku Klux Klan*. New York, NY: Oxford University Press, 1994.

Marcus, Maeva, ed. *The Documentary History of the Supreme Court of the United States, 1789–1800: Volume 8.* New York, NY: Columbia University Press, 2007.

Marsden, George M. *The Soul of the American University: From Protestant Establishment to Established Nonbelief.* New York, N.Y.: Oxford University Press, 1996.

McCain, James Ross. *The Story of Agnes Scott College: 1889–1939.* Atlanta, GA: Agnes Scott College, 1939.

McCandless, Amy Thompson. *The Past in the Present: Women's Higher Education in the Twentieth-Century American South.* Tuscaloosa, AL: The University of Alabama Press, 1999.

McEwen, Mildred Morse. *Queens College: Yesterday and Today.* Charlotte, NC: Heritage Printers, Inc. for Queens College Alumni Association, 1980.

McGrath, James. *Should Students Share the Power? A Study of Their Role in College and University Governance.* Philadelphia, PA: Temple University Press, 1970.

McNair, Walter Edward. *Lest We Forget: An Account of Agnes Scott College.* Atlanta, GA: Tucker-Castleberry Printing, Inc., 1983.

Michener, James. *Sports in America.* New York, NY: Random House, 1976.

Miller-Bernal, Leslie and Susan L. Poulson, eds. *Challenged by Coeducation: Women's Colleges Since the 1960s.* Nashville, TN: Vanderbilt University Press, 2005.

Mjagkij, Nina and Margaret Spratt, eds. *Men and Women Adrift: The YMCA and the YWCA in the City.* New York, NY: New York University Press, 1997.

Nash, Margaret A. *Women's Education in the United States 1780–1840.* New York, NY: Palgrave MacMillian, 2005.

Newcomer, Mabel. *A Century of Higher Education for American Women.* New York, NY: Harper & Brothers Publishers, 1959.

Nidiffer, Jana and Carolyn Terry Bashaw. *Women Administrators in Higher Education: Historical and contemporary Perspectives.* Albany, NY: State University of New York Press, Albany, 2001.

Bibliography

Niederer, Frances J. *Hollins College: An Illustrated History.* Charlottesville, VA: University of Virginia Press, 1973.

Norton, Jr., William L. *Historic Gainesville & Hall County: An Illustrated History.* San Antonio, TX: HPN Books, 2001.

Noverr, Douglas A. and Lawrence Ziewacz. *The Games They Played: Sports in American History, 1865–1980.* Chicago, IL: Nelson-Hall, 1983.

Oates, Mary J., ed. *Higher Education for Catholic Women: An Historical Anthology.* New York, NY: Garland Publishing, Inc., 1987.

O'Reilly, Jean and Susan K. Cahn, Eds. *Women and Sports in the United States: A Documentary Reader.* Boston, MA: Northeastern University Press, 2007.

Parfrey, Adam and Craig Heimbichner. *Ritual America: Secret Brotherhoods and Their Influence on American Society - A Visual Guide.* Port Townsend, WA: Feral House, 2012.

Pearce, Haywood J. *Philosophical Meditations; Talks to College Girls.* Boston, MA: The Stratford Company, 1917.

Pierson, George W. *A Yale Book of Numbers: Historical Statistics of the College and University 1701–1976.* New Haven, CT: Yale University Press, 1983.

Pieschel, Bridget Smith. *Loyal daughters: One hundred years at Mississippi University for Women, 1884–1984.* Oxford, MS: University Press of Mississippi, 1984.

Powers, Jane Bernard. *The "Girl Question" in Education: Vocational Education for Young Women in the Progressive Era.* Washington, DC: Falmer Press, 1992.

Punter, David. *A Companion to the Gothic.* Malden, MA: Blackwell Publishing, Ltd., 2001.

Read, Florence. *The Story of Spelman College.* Princeton, NJ: Princeton University Press, 1961.

Rieser, Andrew. *The Chautauqua Moment: Protestants, Progressives, and the Culture of Modern Liberalism.* New York, NY: Columbia University Press, 2003.

Rigney, Eleanor. *Brenau College 1878–1978: Enriched by the Past, Challenged by the Future.* Gainesville, GA: Brenau College, 1978.

Rudolph, Frederick. *The American College and University: A History.* New York, NY: Alfred A. Knopf. 1962. Reprint, Athens, GA: The University of Georgia Press, 1991.

Sanua, Marianne Rachel. *Going Greek: Jewish College Fraternities in the United States, 1895–1945.* Detroit, MI: Wayne State University Press, 2003.

Savory, Jerold J. *Columbia College: The Ariail Era.* Columbia, SC: R. L. Bryan, 1979.

Sharma, Rajendra Kumar and Rachana Sharma. *Social Psychology.* New Delhi: Atlantic Publishers and Distributors, 1997.

Sizer, Theodore R. *The Age of the Academies.* New York, NY: Teachers College Press, 1964.

Smith, W. R. L. *Charles Lewis Cocke: Founder of Hollins College.* Boston, MA: The Gorham Press, 1921.

Solomon, Barbara Miller. *In the Company of Educated Women: A History of Women and Higher Education in America.* New Haven, CT: Yale University Press, 1985.

Spalding, Phinizy. *Higher Education for Women in the South: A History of Lucy Cobb Institute, 1858–1994.* Athens, GA: The University of Georgia Press, 1994.

Sparks, Linda. *Institutions of Higher Education: An International Bibliography.* Westport, CT: Greenwood Publishing Group, 1990.

Spears, Betty and Richard A. Swanson. *History of Sport and Physical Education in the United States.* 3rd ed. Dubuque, IA: Wm. C. Brown, 1988.

Sperber, Murray. *Beer and Circus: How Big-Time College Sports Has Crippled Undergraduate Education.* New York, NY: Holt Paperbacks, 2000.

Stohlman, Martha Lou Lemmon. *The Story of Sweet Briar College.* Sweet Briar, VA: Alumnae Association of Sweet Briar College, 1956.

Thelin, John R. *A History of American Higher Education.* Baltimore, MD: Johns Hopkins University Press, 2004, 2011.

Tucker, Susan and Beth Willinger (eds.). *Newcomb College, 1886–2006: Higher Education for Women in New Orleans.* Baton Rouge, LA: Louisiana State University Press, 2012.

Turk, Diana B. *Bound by a Mighty Vow: Sisterhood and Women's Fraternities, 1870–1920.* New York, NY: New York University Press, 2004.

Turner, Paul Venable. *Campus: An American Planning Tradition.* Cambridge, MA: M.I.T. Press, 1984.

Twombly, Wells. *200 Years of Sports in America: A Pageant of a Nation at Play.* New York, NY: McGraw Hill, 1976.

Verbrugge, Martha H. *Able-Bodied Womanhood: Personal Health and Social Change in Nineteenth-Century Boston.* New York, NY: Oxford University Press, 1988.

Veysey, Laurence R. *The Emergence of the American University.* Chicago, IL: University of Chicago Press, 1965.

White, Robert. *A Witness for Eleanor Dare: The Final Chapter in a 400 Year Old Mystery.* San Francisco, CA: Lexikos, 1992.

Willis, Jeffrey R. *Converse College.* Charleston, SC: Arcadia Publishing, 2001.

Woody, Thomas A. *A History of Women's Education in the United States.* 2 vols. New York, NY: Science Press, 1929. Reprint, New York, NY: Octagon Books, 1966.

Woodward, C. Vann. *Tom Watson: Agrarian Rebel.* New York: Macmillan, 1938. Reprint, New York, NY: Oxford University Press, 1963.

Young, Elizabeth Barber. *A Study of the Curricula of Seven Selected Women's Colleges of the Southern States.* New York, NY: Teachers Colleges, Columbia University, 1932.

ARTICLES or BOOK CHAPTERS

Banet-Weiser, Sarah and Laura Portwood-Stacer. "'I just want to be me again!': Beauty pageants, reality television and post-feminism." *Feminist Theory,* vol. 7 (2006), 255- 272.

Barnes, L. Diane. "Booster Ethos: Community, Image, and Profit in Early Clarksburg." *Journal of West Virginia History,* vol. 56 (1997): 27–

42. Available from http://www.wvculture.org/HiStory/journal_wvh/wvh56-2.html. Internet; accessed 18 June 2013.

Baumann, Roland M. "A History of Recording Black Students at Oberlin College and the Story of the Missing Record." Available from http://www.oberlin.edu/archive/holdings/finding/RG5/SG4/S3/2002intro.html. Internet; accessed 18 June 2013.

Boney, F. N. "'The Pioneer College for Women': Wesleyan over a Century and a Half." *Georgia Historical Quarterly*, vol. 72 (fall, 1988): 519–32.

Brenau Magazine (fall, 2007). "Will Success Spoil Single-gender Education at Brenau?" Available from http://artsweb.brenau.edu/brenauwindow/Fall2007/Single-gender_article.pdf . Internet; accessed 18 June 2013.

Brenau University. "2007 Volleyball Team Review." Available from http://www.brenautigers.com/sport/10/6.php . Internet; accessed 18 June 2013.

----------. "Adding Value to Our Community." Available from http://alum.brenau.edu/development/value.cfm. Internet; accessed 22 August 2007.

----------. "Brenau Crew." Available from http://news.brenau.edu/athletics/crew/team.cfm. Internet; accessed 16 October 2007.

----------. "Brenau Tapped to Host Prestigious Phi Kappa Phi Honor Society Chapter." Available from http://www.brenau.edu/PR/news/prarticle.cfm?ID=320. Internet; accessed 7 October 2007.

----------. "Brenau University 2007 Golden Tigers Softball Camp." Available from http://www.brenau.edu/athletics/softballbrochure.pdf. Internet; accessed 22 August 2007.

----------. "Coach's Page." Available from http://www.brenau.edu/athletics/soccer/coach.cfm. Internet; accessed 26 August 2007.

----------. "Delta Sigma Theta Sorority (Brenau Chapter)." Available from http://studentdevelopment.brenau.edu/greek/DST/AboutDST.htm. Internet; accessed 19 May 2008.

----------. "Discover Brenau: Facts and Figures." Available from http://www.brenau.edu/about/facts.htm. Internet; accessed 21 January 2008.

Bibliography

----------. "Georgia Senator Steen Miles, Brenau University Celebrate Martin Luther King Day 2007." Available from http://www.brenau.edu/PR/news/prarticle.cfm?ID=284. Internet; accessed 8 September 2007.

----------. "James D. (Jim) Young." Available from http://www.brenau.edu/athletics/swimming/coach.cfm. Internet; accessed 23 August 2007.

----------. "Orientation Information." Available from http://www.brenau.edu/EWC/OrientationOnline/GainesvilleCampus.htm. Internet; accessed 13 September 2007.

----------. "Rho Eta History." Available from http://studentdevelopment.brenau.edu/greek/AKA/RhoEtaHistory.htm. Internet; accessed 19 May 2008.

----------. "Soccer Schedule and Scores." Available from http://www.brenau.edu/athletics/soccer/schedule.cfm. Internet; accessed 27 August 2007.

----------. "Uniquely Brenau: Pearce Auditorium." Available from http://www.brenau.edu/about/Uniquely/pearce.htm. Internet; accessed 29 December 2007.

"Brenau Undergraduate Viewbook." Jensen Design Studio. Available from http://jensendesignstudio.com/wp-content/uploads/2011/11/brenau_viewbook_spreads.pdf . Internet; accessed 19 October 2012.

Bryant, J.C. "Mercer University." *The New Georgia Encyclopedia*, 15 September 2008. Available http://www.georgiaencyclopedia.org/nge/Article.jsp?id=h-1448. Internet; accessed 17 December 2012.

Buttimer, Brendan J. "Catholic Church." *New Georgia Encyclopedia*, 10 December 2005. Available from http://www.georgiaencyclopedia.org/nge/Article.jsp?id=h-2922. Internet; accessed 27 October 2012.

Chait, Richard and Cathy A. Trower. "Where Tenure Does Not Reign: Colleges with Contract Systems." *New Pathways: Faculty Career and Employment for the 21st Century Working Paper Series Inquiry #3*, American Association for Higher Education, Washington, DC, 1997. Available from http://www.eric.ed.gov/ERICWebPortal/detail?accno=ED424814. Internet; accessed 19 January 2013.

CollegeData.com. "College Profile: Brenau University." Available from http://www.collegedata.com/cs/data/college/college_pg01_tmpl.jhtml?schoolId=513 ; Internet; accessed 28 January 2011.

College Tennis Online. "Brenau University (Ga.) Women Past Rankings." Available from http://www.collegetennisonline.com/BrenauUniversity(Ga.)-W-Tennis/Home.aspx . Internet; accessed 18 June 2013.

Colton, Elizabeth Avery. "Standards of Southern Colleges for Women." *The School Review*, vol. 20, no. 7 (Sep., 1912): 458–475.

Converse College. "History of Converse College." Available from http://www.converse.edu/about/our-mission-history?nav=1 . Internet; accessed 18 June 2013.

"Deaths: Dr. J. W. Bailey." *Charlotte Medical Journal*, vol. 61 (January – June, 1910). Available from http://archive.org/stream/charlottemedical611910char#page/n5/mode/2up. Internet; accessed 14 February 2013.

DeBell, Camille. "Ninety Years in the World of Work in America." *Career Development Quarterly*, vol. 50, no. 1 (Sept., 2001): 77–88.

Dismukes, Camillus J. "North Georgia College Under the Trustees." *The Georgia Historical Quarterly*, vol. 56, no. 1 (Spring, 1972): 92–100.

Dyer, Candice. "She Speaks for Herself." *Brenau Window*, Summer, 2011, pp. 8–11.

----------, "Miss Hacksaw: Trody Trow!" *Brenau Window*, Spring, 2010, pp. 6 – 9.

Emory University. "Stability and Growth: Harvey Warren Cox's Presidency." Available from http://emoryhistory.emory.edu/people/presidents/Cox.htm. Internet; accessed 18 June 2013.

English, Thomas H. *Emory University 1915–1965 - A Semicentennial History*. Atlanta, GA: Higgins-McArthur Co., 1966.

Farmer, Jared. "Review of *Massacre at Mountain Meadows: An American Tragedy* by Ronald W. Walker, Richard E. Turley Jr. and Glen M. Leonard." *BYU Studies*, vol. 47, no. 3 (2008): 175–179.

Bibliography 565

Fiene, Karen. "A Tale of Three Campuses: Planning and Design in Response to Cultural Heritage at Mills College, the University of California, Berkeley, and Stanford University." *Planning for Higher Education*, 1 April 2011. Available from http://www.readperiodicals.com//201104/2325179311.html#ixzz1SkmwngW7. Internet; accessed 14 February 2013.

Fletcher, Adam. *Meaningful Student Involvement: Guide to Students as Partners in School Change 2nd edition.* Olympia, WA: SoundOut.org, 2005. Available from http://www.soundout.org/MSIGuide.pdf . Internet; accessed 3 January 2013.

GA College 411.com. "Brenau University-Women's College Profile." Available from http://www.gacollege411.org/campustour/undergraduate/521/Brenau_University_Womens_College/Brenau_University_Womens_College5.html. Internet; accessed 19 May 2008.

Gardner, Sarah E. "Helen Dortch Longstreet (1863–1962)." *The New Georgia Encyclopedia*, 25 May 2007. Available from http://www.georgiaencyclopedia.org/nge/Article.jsp?id=h-881. Internet; accessed 30 November 2012.

Georgia Institute of Technology. "Tech Timeline – 1885." Available from http://livinghistory.gatech.edu/new/timeline/timelineFrame.html . Internet; accessed 18 June 2013.

Geraci, Heather. "'Better Dead than Coed?' Survival and Decline of Single-Sex College in the United States." Paper presented at the annual meeting of the American Sociological Association, Marriott Hotel, Loews Philadelphia Hotel, Philadelphia, PA, 12 August 2005. Available from http://citation.allacademic.com/meta/p_mla_apa_research_citation/0/2/1/2/9/pages21296/p21296-1.php . Internet; accessed 18 June 2013.

GreekChat.com. "Secret Societies" Forum. Available from http://www.greekchat.com/gcforums/archive/index.php/t-13261.html. Internet; accessed 18 June 2013.

Griffin, Richard W. "Wesleyan College: Its Genesis, 1835–1840." *Georgia Historical Quarterly* vol. 50 (March, 1966): 54–73.

Grillo, Jerry. "A Work in Progress." *Georgia Trend*, vol. 16, no. 2 (Oct 01, 2000): 88.

Guess, Andy. "Board Rights vs. Alumni Rights." *Inside Higher Ed.* Available from http://www.insidehighered.com/news/2007/10/05/trustees. Internet; accessed 20 January 2013.

Gurr, Steve. "Gainesville." *New Georgia Encyclopedia.* Available from http://www.georgiaencyclopedia.org/nge/Article.jsp?id=h-766 . Internet; accessed 18 June 2013.

Hall, Jacquelyn Dowd. "'To Widen the Reach of Our Love:' Autobiography, History, and Desire." *Feminist Studies*, vol. 26, no. 1 (spring 2000): 231–248.

Harris, Robin O. "'To Illustrate the Genius of Southern Womanhood:' Julia Flisch and Her Campaign for the Higher Education of Georgia Women." *Georgia Historical Quarterly*, vol. LXXIX, no. 3 (fall, 1996): 506–531.

Herbst, Jurgen. "The First Three American Colleges: Schools of the Reformation." *Perspectives in American History*, vol. 8 (1974): 7–52.

Hometownhall.com. "Brenau Tigers Soccer season wrap up..." 23 December 2006. Available from http://www.hometownhall.com/sports/college/brenau-tigers-soccer-seas.shtml. Internet; last accessed 30 August 2007.

----------. "Golden Tigers Basketball opens with a Bang." 13 November 2006. Available from http://www.hometownhall.com/sports/college/golden-tigers-basketball-.shtml. Internet; accessed 24 August 2007.

Hout, Michael and Claude S. Fischer. "Religious Diversity in America, 1940–2000." Paper prepared for submission to the Sociology of Religion Session, Annual Meeting of the ASA, Chicago, IL, August 2001.

Inter-University Consortium for Political and Social Research. "Study 00003: Historical Demographic, Economic, and Social Data: U.S., 1790–1970." Ann Arbor, MI: ICPSR. Available online at http://www.icpsr.umich.edu/icpsrweb/ICPSR/studies/3 .Internet; accessed 18 June 2013.

Jaschik, Scott. "Male Impact." *Inside Higher Ed*, 19 July 2005. Available from http://www.insidehighered.com/news/2005/07/19/men. Internet; accessed 19 January 2013.

Kennard, June A. "Review Essay: The History of Physical Education." *Signs: Journal of Women*, vol. 2, no. 4 (summer, 1977): 835–842.

Kirby, David. "The Maconian Renaissance? Candice Dyer's Street Singers Plumbs the Mystery of Macon Music." *Georgia Music Magazine*. Available from http://georgiamusicmag.com/the-maconian-renaissance/. Internet; accessed 1 December 2012.

Kohn, Shira. "A (Re)Consideration of Jewish Sororities." *Lilith Magazine*, Fall 2011.

Lang, Susan. "How competition for the best students, faculty and facilities -- and rankings -- sends tuition soaring." *Cornell Chronicle*, 8 November 2006. Available from http://www.news.cornell.edu/stories/Nov06/tuition.so.much.sl.html. Internet; accessed 17 October 2012.

Lavender, Catherine. "The New Woman." Available from http://www.library.csi.cuny.edu/dept/history/lavender/386/newwoman.html. Internet; accessed 10 May 2013.

Leslie, Gordon. "Bays to Spearhead Brenau's New Women's Basketball Program." S.S.A.C. Sports, 24 August 2005. Available from http://www.ssacsports.com/article/493.php. Internet; accessed 18 June 2013.

Lizzio, Alf and Keithia Wilson. "Student Participation in University Governance: The Role Conceptions and Sense of Efficacy of Student Representatives on Departmental Committees." *Studies in Higher Education*, vol. 34, no. 1 (February 2009): 69–84.

Lorence, James J. "Gainesville State College." *New Georgia Encyclopedia*, 21 October 2005. Available from http://www.georgiaencyclopedia.org/nge/Article.jsp?id=h-1440. Internet; accessed 19 January 2013.

Lynn, Susan. "Gender and Progressive Politics: A Bridge to Social Activism of the 1960s." In Joanne Meyerowitz, ed., *Not June Cleaver: Women and Gender in Postwar America, 1945–1960*. Philadelphia, PA: Temple Univ. Press, 1994.

Mahefkey, Ann. "Brenau University." *New Georgia Encyclopedia*, 6 June 2006. Available from Available from http://www.georgiaencyclopedia.org/nge/Article.jsp?id=h-1449. Internet; accessed 18 January 2013.

Mallon, William T.. "Standard Deviations: Faculty Appointment Policies at Institutions Without Tenure." In Cathy A. Trower, ed., *Policies on Faculty Appointment: Standard Practices and Unusual Arrangements*. Bolton, MA: Anker Publishing, Inc., 2000.

Martin, Caryl L. "The Evolution of Intercollegiate Athletics at Wesleyan College: A Historical Perspective." *Journal of the Georgia Association of Historians*, vol. 19 (1998): 54–106.

[no author]. "Birte and Paula Host Rotarians." *The Rotarian: An International Magazine*, May 1954.

McCandless, Amy Thompson. "Maintaining the Spirit and Tone of Robust Manliness: The Battle against Coeducation at Southern Colleges and Universities, 1890–1940." *NWSA Journal*, vol. 2, no. 2 (spring, 1990): 199–216.

Miller, Starr. "Was This Voice First to Question the Value of Homework?" *The Clearing House*, vol. 29, no. 6 (February, 1955): 359.

Mitchell, S. A. "Academic Freedom and Tenure: Report of Committee A." *Bulletin of the American Association of University Professors*, vol. 20, no. 2 (February 1934): 97–104.

Mjagkij, Nina and Margaret Spratt, eds. *Men and Women Adrift: The YMCA and the YWCA in the City*. New York, NY: New York University Press, 1997.

Noble, Jeanne. "The Higher Education of Black Women in the Twentieth Century." In John Mack Faragher and Florence Howe, eds., *Women and Higher Education in American History*. New York, NY: W.W. Norton & Co., 1988.

Northeast Georgia History Center. "About Us." Available from http://www.negahc.org/about/ . Internet; accessed 18 June 2013.

Perkins, Linda M. "The Education of Black Women in the Nineteenth Century." In John Mack Faragher and Florence Howe, eds., *Women and Higher Education in American History.* New York, NY: W.W. Norton & Co., 1988.

Petersons.com. "Brenau University." Available from http://www.petersons.com/college-search/brenau-university-000_10004140.aspx . Internet; accessed 18 June 2013.

Princeton Review. *Complete Book of Colleges.* New York, NY: Princeton Review Publishing, 2004.

Ravitch, Diane. "American Traditions of Education." In Terry M. Moe, ed., *A Primer on America's Schools.* Stanford, CA: Hoover Institution Press, 2001.

Riess, Steven A. "The Historiography of American Sport." *OAH Magazine of History*, vol. 7 (Summer 1992). Available from http://faculty.umf.maine.edu/walter.sargent/public.www/FYS%20Sports_12/Riess%20sports%20history%20overview.pdf . Internet; accessed 18 June 2013.

Romine, Scott. "Katharine Du Pre Lumpkin (1897–1988)." *The New Georgia Encyclopedia*, 15 April 2009. Available from http://www.georgiaencyclopedia.org/nge/Article.jsp?id=h-491&sug=y. Internet; accessed 30 November 2012.

Rosenberg, Rosalind. "The Limits of Access: The History of Coeducation in America." In John Mack Faragher and Florence Howe, eds., *Women and Higher Education in American History.* New York, NY: W.W. Norton & Co., 1988.

Rury, J. L. "Who Became Teachers? The Social Characteristics of Teachers in American History." In D. Warren, ed., *American Teachers: Histories of a Profession at Work.* New York, NY: Macmillan, 1989.

Samford University. "History of Samford University." Available from http://www.samford.edu/universityhistory/ . Internet; accessed 18 June 2013.

Schwager, Sally. "Educating Women in America." *Signs*, vol. 12, no. 2 (winter, 1987): 336.

Simpson, Michael W. Review of *A History of American Higher Education* by John R. Thelin. *Education Review*, 12 September 2004. Available from http://www.edrev.info/reviews/rev303.htm. Internet; accessed 12 October 2012.

Sparkes, Boyden. "Writ on Rocke." *Saturday Evening Post*, 26 April 1941.

Spencer, Taronda. "Spelman College." *New Georgia Encyclopedia*, 6 June 2006. Available from http://www.georgiaencyclopedia.org/nge/Article.jsp?id=h-1460. Internet; accessed 27 October 2012.

St. Louis Rowing Club. "Results--2004 Head of the Hooch, November 6–7, 2004." Available from http://stlouisrowingclub.com/regattas/2004_hooch.pdf . Internet; accessed 18 June 2013.

Swail, Watson S. "Legislation to Improve Graduation Rates Could Have the Opposite Effect." The *Chronicle of Higher Education*, vol. 50, no. 20 (January 23, 2004): B16.

Taylor-Colbert, Alice. "Brief History and Traditions of Shorter College: The Shorter Heritage." Available from http://www.shorter.edu/about/history.htm . Internet; accessed 18 June 2013.

Theriot, Nancy. "Towards a New Sporting Ideal: The Women's Division of the National Amateur Athletic Federation." *Frontiers: A Journal of Women Studies*, vol. 3, no. 1 (spring, 1978): 1–7.

Tolley, Kim. "The Rise of the Academies: Continuity or Change?" *History of Education Quarterly*, vol. 41 (summer, 2001): 225–38.

U.S. Department of Education Office for Civil Rights. "Historically Black Colleges and Universities and Higher Education Desegregation." Available from http://www2.ed.gov/about/offices/list/ocr/docs/hq9511.html . Internet; accessed 18 June 2013.

Vassar College. "Chronology, [various years]." Available from http://chronology.vassar.edu/ . Internet; accessed 13 June 2013.

Veltri, S., Banning, J.H., & Davis, T.G. (2006). "The community college classroom environment: Student perceptions." *College Student Journal*, vol. 40, no. 3 (Sept. 2006): 517–527.

Vincent, Leonard S. "B. J. Kaston, American Araneologist 1906–1985: A Biography and Bibliography." *Journal of Arachnology*, vol. 14 (1987): 283–291.

Virginia Historical Society. "The Civil Rights Movement in Virginia." Available from http://www.vahistorical.org/civilrights/massiveresistance.htm. Internet; accessed 18 June 2018.

"Virginia Supreme Court Rules for Randolph College Over Its Move to Coeducation." Chronicle of Higher Education, 6 June 2008. Available from http://chronicle.com/article/Virginia-Supreme-Court-Rules/41 106. Internet; accessed 18 June 2013.

Waskiewicz, Lyn. *Brenau College District. National Register of Historic Places designation report.* Washington, DC: U.S. Department of the Interior/National Park Service, 1978.

Welch, Mary. "Roslyn Wallace Was Here." *Brenau Window* (Spring, 2010): 10–11.

Wells, Elizabeth Crabtree. "Judson College." *Encyclopedia of Alabama.* Available from http://www.encyclopediaofalabama.org/face/Article.jsp?id=h-2492. Internet; accessed 13 February 2013.

Welter, Barbara. "The Cult of True Womanhood: 1820–1860." *American Quarterly,* vol. 18 (1966): 151–74.

Wesleyan College. "History of the College." Available from http://www.wesleyancollege.edu/about/history.cfm . Internet; accessed 18 June 2013.

Wikipedia. "Coeducation." Available from http://en.wikipedia.org/wiki/Coeducation#Years_U.S._educational_institutions_became_coeducational. Internet; accessed 18 June 2013.

----------. "Timeline of women's colleges in the United States." Available from http://en.wikipedia.org/wiki/Timeline_of_women%27s_colleges_in_the_United_States ; Internet; accessed 18 June 2013.

THESES and DISSERTATIONS

Corley, Florence. "Higher Education for Southern Women: Four Church-Related Women's Colleges in Georgia, Agnes Scott, Shorter, Spelman, and Wesleyan, 1900–1920." Ph.D. diss., Georgia State University, 1985.

Harris, Darin S. "Polishing Cornerstones: Tift College, Georgia Baptists' Separate College for Women." Ph.D. diss., Georgia State University, 2008.

Rice, Kathleen George. "A History of Whitworth College for Women." Ph.D. diss., University of Mississippi, 1985.

Sanseviro, Michael Lenard. "Student Government Presidents' Perceptions of their Role in Institutional Decision-Making at a Two-year Public College." Ph.D. diss., Georgia State University, 2007.

Winn, Evelyn Barksdale. "A History of Columbia College." Master's thesis, University of South Carolina, 1928.

Index

academy, xvii, 4–9, 14–15, 26, 29, 46, 52, 76, 83, 100, 193, 201–202, 209, 223, 283, 301, 347, 396, 422, 506

accreditation, xx, 1, 51–53, 56, 73, 98, 108, 110, 117, 124–125, 127–130, 145, 157, 166, 171–173, 182, 200, 212, 218, 248, 258

administration, xvi–xvii, xix–xxi, xxiv–xxv, 2, 15, 22, 31–32, 37–39, 43, 55, 61–62, 68, 72–73, 75–76, 80, 82–91, 111, 117, 124, 129, 131–133, 137, 141, 145, 157, 160, 162–163, 165, 167, 177, 194–195, 200, 204, 212–213, 215–216, 218, 220–222, 225–226, 233–234, 242, 244, 249, 269–272, 274, 283, 286, 297, 313, 319, 321–325, 338, 340, 379–380, 395, 403–405, 427, 430, 435, 439, 447, 452–457, 468, 474, 481, 490–494

admission requirements, xxi, xxv, 25, 41, 44, 48, 51–52, 55, 80, 85, 97, 199, 215, 217, 220, 223, 230–231, 234, 247, 408, 439

adult education. *See under* Brenau University Learning and Leisure Institute (B.U.L.L.I.)

advertisements, xviii, 21, 34, 38, 46, 140, 145, 147, 153, 176, 279, 283, 377, 382, 452, 455, 458

affordability, xviii, 39

African-Americans, 227, 231, 237, 461

age (of students), 61

Agnes Scott College, 19, 29, 44, 93–94, 96, 98, 105, 107–108, 123, 125, 136, 172, 177–178, 193, 205, 343, 364, 369, 378, 391, 406, 416, 480

Agnes the Ghost, 297

Alabama Brenau, 105–106, 162, 454

Alchemist, The, 20, 49, 61, 65, 77, 80, 104, 107–108, 110, 149–151, 154–155, 157, 179, 181, 197–199, 214, 217–220, 231, 234–235, 237, 271, 273, 276, 279–289, 298, 301, 303–310, 316, 321, 325, 339, 342, 352, 357, 360, 365, 370–371, 385–386, 392, 398, 405, 408–409, 412–416, 429, 431–432, 441, 444, 446, 458, 468–469, 478–479, 483, 486, 493, 498

alcohol, 356–357

Alpha Chi Omega, 450–451, 462–464, 470, 482

Alpha Delta Pi, 245–246, 260, 413, 447, 450–451, 458, 463–464, 482, 528

Alpha Gamma Delta, 214, 413, 450–451, 462, 464, 482

Alpha Xi Delta, 451, 469

alumnae, xv, xviii, 2, 18, 21, 29, 42, 56–61, 69–70, 74, 80, 102–103, 108–109, 111, 127–128, 143, 152, 158, 166, 182, 213, 224, 236, 238, 245, 247, 252, 259, 285, 291–293, 307, 335, 342, 368, 440, 446–447, 463, 468, 477, 485, 509

alumnae giving, 60

American Association of
  University Professors (A.A.U.P.),
  82–84, 87, 111–112
Andrews, Jay, 281, 305
annual. *See under* Bubbles
applicants, 44, 51–53, 55, 125–126,
  133, 167, 194–195, 198–199, 202,
  205, 211, 288
aquatics, 420
archery, 388, 408, 410–412, 414, 532
architecture. *See under* campus
  architecture
art, xv, xix–xx, 2–5, 8, 33, 35, 49, 54,
  57, 75, 116, 119, 123–124, 130,
  132, 136, 141, 143–145, 154–156,
  159–162, 168–169, 171, 180, 182,
  189, 207, 217, 219, 223, 243–244,
  249, 254, 264, 275, 279, 361, 426,
  461, 463, 481, 491, 499, 501, 524
  collection, 152–153, 277
  fine arts, xxii, 1, 53, 74, 131, 146,
    150, 152–153, 157–158, 246,
    271, 324–325
associate degrees, 1, 58, 72, 77, 148,
  218, 473–474
Athens, Georgia, 19, 25, 29, 65, 79,
  102, 136, 149, 166, 276, 280, 347,
  352, 390, 396
athletics, xv, xxiii–xxiv, xxvi, 13,
  20, 23, 30–31, 40, 53, 88, 116,
  227, 250, 265, 270–271, 334,
  336–338, 373–377, 379, 381–386,
  388–392, 395–398, 400, 402–418,
  420–421, 424–428, 431–432,
  434–437, 439, 442, 464, 471, 485,
  494–495, 531
Atlanta, Georgia, 1–2, 19, 21, 25,
  29, 34, 36, 39, 42, 44–47, 59,
  65–66, 71, 76–77, 91, 93–97,
  99, 103–105, 107–108, 110, 117,
  119–121, 123, 134, 138–139,

Atlanta, Georgia (*continued*),
  141–142, 146–151, 155–157,
  162–163, 170–172, 175–181,
  183–184, 189, 197, 202–205,
  208, 229, 231, 233–234, 236–237,
  253, 256–257, 263, 266, 271, 273,
  276, 281, 293, 299, 301, 303–304,
  308–310, 313, 315, 326, 341,
  346–347, 352, 354, 359, 362,
  364–367, 369–371, 377–378,
  380–381, 385, 391–392, 396, 398,
  403, 406, 415, 417–418, 420–421,
  423–424, 429–430, 433–435,
  449, 451–452, 454–456, 460, 466,
  468–469, 479–480, 483, 486, 493,
  517
Atlanta Journal-Constitution, The,
  21, 39, 59, 77–78, 108, 110, 146,
  149, 163, 177, 181, 183–184, 203,
  234, 253, 257, 271, 273–274, 281,
  293, 303, 308, 383, 392, 398, 415,
  417–418, 421, 429–430, 433–435,
  449, 455, 466–468, 471, 476,
  479–480, 486, 493
attendance policies, xxiii, 37, 45–47,
  313, 322–328, 346, 359, 365, 496,
  498, 502
auditorium, 77, 148–149, 153, 178,
  201, 243–246, 249, 251, 290, 292,
  295, 308, 322, 332, 346, 380, 509,
  523–524
Audubon, 248, 264
Aurum, The, 1, 67, 281, 364,
  434–436
automobiles, 77, 283, 300–301, 337,
  340–341, 348–350, 352, 358, 377,
  455, 492
Aya Takeda Uyehara, 253–254, 266

bachelor degrees, xix–xx, 2, 8–9,
  25, 49, 51, 53, 64–65, 79–81,

bachelor degrees (*continued*), 102, 105, 110, 116, 121, 123–124, 130–131, 133, 135, 141, 143–146, 148–150, 154, 156–159, 161–162, 165–167, 171, 177, 189, 217, 229, 249, 263, 280–281, 283, 327, 336, 375, 388, 400–401, 407–408, 410, 461, 466, 479–480, 484, 491, 517, 538–542
Bachman, Blaire, 420
badminton, 388, 408, 411
Bailey Hall, 242–243, 245, 248, 262, 299, 338, 377–378, 444, 523
ballet, 156–157, 181, 412
Banet-Weiser, Sarah, 286–287, 306
Baptists, xxii, 2, 10, 30, 34, 39, 44–46, 51, 62–67, 69, 72, 75, 103, 105, 117, 119, 127, 134, 136, 138, 140, 158–160, 193, 242–243, 255, 271, 274–275, 279, 304, 322–323, 326, 334, 339, 343, 365, 368, 377, 379–380, 493, 503, 521
baseball, 374, 376, 388, 391, 396, 398–400, 407–408, 531
basketball, xxiii–xxiv, 374, 376, 382–383, 388, 392, 396–399, 402, 404–407, 409–411, 413–414, 416, 426, 430, 437
beauty pageant. *See under* Miss Brenau
black students, 48, 187, 190, 195, 197, 212–213, 227, 462
Blake, Amanda, 58, 102
Board of Trustees, xvi, xxi, 3, 5, 20, 23, 53, 58, 65, 68–70, 72, 74–75, 82, 85, 105–106, 109, 123, 125, 127–128, 130, 143, 150, 153, 166, 168, 172–175, 184, 194, 201, 203–208, 210–211, 220–221, 225, 230, 232–233, 235–236, 245–249, 252–253, 262–264, 301, 456–458,

Board of Trustees (*continued*), 503, 525
bookkeeping, 118, 139–140, 158
bowling, 337, 380–381, 412, 414
Brenau Academy, 52, 100, 201–202
Brenau Ideal, The, 170, 445
"Brenau Notes," 21, 39, 77–78, 110, 149, 177, 181, 253, 257, 271, 273, 303, 383, 392, 398, 429–430, 449, 455, 466–468, 471, 476, 479–480, 486, 493
Brenau Plan, 130
Brenau University Learning and Leisure Institute (B.U.L.L.I.), 167, 184
Brenau Window, 56, 97, 101–102, 111, 183, 434, 500, 509
Bridwell, Dr. Jim, 280
broadcasting, 59, 131, 145, 249, 280–281, 305
Bubbles, The, 47, 98, 102, 108, 195–196, 212, 214, 224, 231, 238, 271–272, 274, 280–281, 285–286, 291–292, 298, 303, 305, 360, 367, 371, 383, 388, 392–393, 396, 400, 405–408, 410, 416–417, 421–423, 429–436, 440–444, 449–451, 456, 461–464, 466–467, 478–480, 482, 485, 493, 520
budget, 128, 144, 221–222
buildings. *See under* campus architecture
bulletins, 15, 20, 23, 25, 30, 34–36, 38, 43–45, 49–51, 53, 56, 59, 72, 76–77, 80–81, 84, 92–100, 104–112, 120, 130–131, 135, 139–140, 145, 147–148, 150, 154, 158–159, 161, 164, 170, 173–184, 222, 226, 232, 236–237, 261, 264, 275, 319, 322, 325, 328, 358,

bulletins (*continued*), 364–365, 369, 378–379, 384–386, 388, 391–392, 407, 413–416, 429–432, 454, 456, 460, 463, 482–483, 485
Burd, Dr. John S., 74–75, 109, 128–129, 151–153, 161–162, 164, 173–174, 179–180, 182–184, 220, 224–225, 234–237, 247–251, 264, 390, 417, 420, 432, 434–435, 479, 513
Burd, Dr. Patricia, 74, 109
business, 1–2, 7, 42, 52, 70, 72, 74, 116, 120, 126, 131, 133, 138–141, 158, 160–163, 165, 167, 174, 202, 249, 272, 281, 311, 325, 409, 491
Butchart, Dr. Ronald E., 28, 175, 229, 231

Cabell, Ed, 155
Camp Takeda, 254, 407
campus architecture, xxii, 1, 61, 74, 126, 153, 171, 178, 200, 203–204, 206, 239–245, 247, 251–252, 254–262, 270, 290, 294–295, 328, 342, 344, 353, 377, 381, 396, 403, 476, 492, 494
campus master plan, 242
campuses, satellite, xx, 2, 136, 166, 465
cardplaying, 312, 322
careers, 3, 13, 15, 133, 137, 161, 449
Castelli, Leo, 153, 180
catalog. *See under* bulletins
Catholicism, 10, 27, 46–48, 97, 274, 303, 348, 449, 481
ceremonies, 36, 56, 96, 109, 118, 145, 171, 197–198, 200, 210, 217, 225–226, 231, 237, 277, 284–287, 291, 298, 306–309, 356, 440, 444–445, 509, 529
Cezanne, Paul, 153

championships, 40, 399–400, 417–420, 424–425, 435
chapel, xxiii, 26, 29, 110, 178, 246, 274, 313, 324–326, 359, 501
chaperones, 300, 331, 346–348, 356, 358, 383, 470
charter, 119
Chase, William Merritt, 153
Chautauquas, 121, 299–300, 309–310, 382
cheating, 313, 318, 358
cheerleaders, xxiv, 405, 425, 436
Chi Omega, 450–451, 457–458, 462–464, 470, 482
choir, 151, 179
choral, 151, 518
Christian, 6, 45, 61, 110, 192, 200, 253, 273, 275, 324, 326, 358, 454, 461
church, xxiii, 18, 29, 44–46, 63–64, 72, 97, 105–106, 131, 133–134, 205–207, 214, 238, 315, 322–325, 336, 347, 351, 365, 459, 498, 502
Clark, Dr. William K., 73, 213, 234
classes, xxiv, 2, 34, 44, 46, 51–53, 56, 102, 122, 140, 142–143, 156, 158, 161–162, 167, 184, 187, 207, 216, 218, 225, 287, 289–291, 300, 308, 314, 324, 327–328, 336, 338, 366, 374, 398, 409, 411, 414, 453–454, 465, 493
  See also freshmen, sophomores, juniors, *and* seniors
classical curriculum, 8, 12, 18, 118, 134
clothing, 38, 152, 250, 337
clubs, xviii, xxii–xxv, 16, 39–41, 47, 49, 53, 58–59, 61–62, 70, 72, 90, 103, 134, 149, 154–155, 167, 179, 196–197, 227, 246, 256–257, 266, 269–275, 287, 298–299, 303,

clubs (*continued*), 316–317,
320–321, 325–326, 340, 363–364,
383–385, 388, 398, 404–407,
410–411, 416–417, 421–424, 435,
439–443, 446–448, 450, 453, 456,
458, 460, 463, 476–477, 481–482,
492–496, 498, 500
coaches, 77, 81, 417–427, 434–437
coeducation, xxii–xxiii, 10, 13–14,
16, 27, 66, 109, 136, 175–176,
183, 191–193, 195, 202, 216–222,
228–231, 235, 343, 354, 397,
403–404, 406, 430, 452, 479,
489–490, 500
collegiate way, 12, 32–33, 374
colors, 402
commencement, 109, 200, 237, 277,
356
commercial education, xix, 124,
133, 138–141, 158
committees, 55, 71–72, 75, 80,
82–85, 111, 175, 220–223, 233,
236, 245, 283, 345, 348, 353, 371,
403, 496
community, 2, 12, 15, 25, 72, 87,
128, 151, 161, 165, 167, 216,
218–219, 222, 227, 249–250,
256, 261, 264, 270, 279–281, 284,
287, 295, 323–324, 375, 415, 424,
427–428, 435, 466, 481
concerts, 77, 151, 202, 213, 220, 299,
301, 336, 341, 442
conduct, 220, 313, 358, 495
conformity, xxii, 270–271, 284,
286–287, 289, 495
conservatory, xix, 11, 35, 76–78, 81,
91–92, 104–106, 116, 119–120,
146–152, 154, 156–158, 175–176,
178–179, 255, 257, 384, 392, 461,
463
Converse College, 19, 29, 45, 95–96,

Converse College (*continued*), 98,
106, 111, 123, 125, 143, 157,
171–172, 182, 206–207, 226, 232,
307, 316, 362, 368, 481
cost, xviii, 35–37, 53, 71, 92–93,
127, 137, 139, 188, 208–210, 249,
259–260, 278, 391, 458, 465, 491
cotillion, 298, 350, 410
cottages, xxii, 34, 143, 240, 246,
255–258, 328, 456, 528
courses, xix–xx, xxiii–xxiv, 3–4,
8, 36, 40, 49, 78, 116, 119–120,
122–124, 131–132, 134, 139–141,
143–145, 148, 150, 152, 154, 156,
160, 162–164, 167, 171, 184, 218,
318, 399, 407–408, 413–415, 491
coursework, 8, 116, 134, 157, 163,
412
crew. *See under* rowing
cross country program, xxiv, 424,
426, 436
Crow's Nest, 251–252, 259,
290–292, 356–357, 526
Crudup, Dr. Josiah, xix, xxi, 72–73,
84, 101, 108, 125–130, 172–174,
199–213, 215, 221, 231–234, 236,
247, 253–254, 266, 338, 342, 368,
456–460, 463, 483–485, 511
curfews, xxiii, 333, 352–353
curriculum, xvii, xix–xx, xxv, 3–4,
6–9, 12–14, 18, 23, 29, 32, 44,
88, 116–122, 124, 130–132, 134,
138, 140, 143, 150–152, 154, 160,
164, 168–169, 177, 189, 223, 234,
269–270, 376, 385, 389, 395, 399,
408, 427, 439
Cushman Club, 154

Dahlonega, 48, 65, 136, 219, 301,
310, 385, 396, 403–404, 406
dance, 54, 146, 148, 153, 156–157,

dance (*continued*), 182, 225, 247, 249, 254, 285–286, 293, 298, 353, 385, 410, 412, 414, 425, 469–470, 501
dances, 298, 346, 350, 396, 409–410, 440, 468–470
Dare Stones, 296–298, 309, 530
dating, xxiii, 20, 45, 52, 90, 102, 152, 195, 197, 243, 261, 276, 279, 283, 294, 313, 320–321, 341, 350–355, 357, 359, 370, 407, 470, 472, 480, 506
debating, 272, 275–276, 278, 297, 304, 442, 448
debt, 66, 126, 128–129, 200, 204–205, 248
degree requirements, xx, 132, 144–145, 150, 154, 161, 165, 223, 413, 415, 490
degrees, xx, xxvi, 1, 9–10, 14, 23, 32, 42, 46, 56–58, 60, 65–66, 73, 76, 81, 86, 110, 116–117, 119, 121, 123–124, 129–132, 135, 138, 141, 143–146, 148, 150–151, 154, 156–159, 161–163, 165, 167–169, 189–190, 194, 219, 223, 225, 229, 234, 258, 306, 314, 366, 388, 395, 403, 407–409, 411, 425, 461, 476, 490, 492
Delacroix, Eugène, 153
Delta Delta Delta, 416, 432, 450–451, 457, 464, 469, 480, 482, 505
Delta Phi Epsilon, 47, 97, 366, 450–451, 460–461, 484
Delta Sigma Theta, 462, 464, 482, 485
departments, xix, 76, 120–121, 138, 140–141, 148, 155, 402, 454
desegregation, xxi, 191, 201–203, 205, 207, 210–211, 215, 226,

desegregation (*continued*), 229–230, 238, 491
diaries, 21
Dido, 243–244, 263, 524
dining, 32, 36, 89, 221, 242–243, 254, 324, 331, 338, 351, 382
discipline, xxii–xxiii, xxvi, 11, 17, 23–24, 88, 123, 134, 169, 206, 234, 274–275, 311–313, 315–317, 319–321, 334, 340, 345, 348, 358–359, 364, 403, 456, 492, 495–496
discrimination, xxv, 12, 98, 188, 191, 193, 205, 226, 449, 473
disease. *See under* illness
dissent, 70–71, 85
diversity, xviii, 2, 39, 41, 46, 48, 96, 187–188, 199, 227
Dixie-Hunt Hotel, 69, 127, 173, 469
doctoral programs, 80, 168, 184–185
Dodd, Ed, 250
domestic science. *See under* home economics
domesticity, 17–18, 124, 143–144, 178, 456
donorship, 167, 209
drama, 145, 148, 153–155, 181, 225, 236, 273, 325, 399, 442, 454
dress code, xxiii, 311, 334–336, 338–339, 360, 386, 388, 409
drinking, 312, 339, 357, 381
drugs, 357
DuBois, W. E. B., 189, 194–195, 229, 231
Dyer, Candice, 59, 97, 102, 292, 294–295, 308–309

education, xv–xvii, xix, xxi–xxiv, 1–18, 20, 24–30, 33–35, 37, 41–42, 49, 54–55, 57, 60, 65, 67, 73–75, 82–83, 86–87, 89, 91–93,

Index

education (*continued*), 95–96, 103, 109, 111–112, 116, 118–119, 121–122, 124, 131–139, 141, 145, 151, 153–154, 156–165, 167–168, 170–172, 176, 183, 188–195, 201–203, 206, 208–209, 217–218, 220, 229–231, 235–236, 240–241, 247, 261, 269, 278, 284–285, 299–300, 303–304, 306, 312, 317, 326, 336, 344, 363, 373–376, 378–379, 384–385, 387–388, 390, 395, 397–399, 402, 404, 406–408, 410, 412–415, 421, 430, 447, 452, 464, 479, 482, 485–486, 489–491, 500

Eisenmann, Linda, 16, 28

electives, xix, 116, 122–124, 132, 144–145, 162, 171, 408, 491

Elixir, The, 59, 277–279, 304
See also literary journals

elocution, 35, 118, 146, 153

Emory University, 36, 66, 71, 93, 104, 107, 172, 205, 296, 423, 461, 469–470

endowment, 2, 10, 38, 69–70, 72, 74, 108, 125–129, 155, 173–174, 489

engagement, 12, 14, 49, 62, 149, 214, 252, 275–276, 322, 326, 376, 404, 407, 410, 416, 423, 427, 482, 497

enrollment, xvii, xx, 2, 10, 37, 39, 41, 48, 50–51, 72, 74–75, 98, 108, 127–128, 146, 158, 166, 169, 173, 189–191, 201–202, 205, 210–211, 214–217, 224–225, 241, 254, 318, 430, 489–491

entertainment, 155, 179, 223, 273, 299–302, 325, 357, 468

entrance examinations, 51

epidemics, 378

equipment, 66, 149, 233, 250, 382, 391, 410

Europe, 2, 40, 66, 68, 76, 121, 148, 156, 197, 244, 276

Evening and Weekend College, 1, 50, 59, 74, 117, 162–165, 183, 224–226, 228, 277, 318

exclusivity, 402, 449, 453–454

excursions, 379

Executive Council, 85, 90, 319, 325, 330, 337, 340, 356

exercise, xxi, xxiii, 87–88, 282, 352, 374–376, 379–386, 397, 414–415

exhibitions, 153, 250

expansion, 162–163

expenses, 35–36, 41, 209, 472

expulsion, 88, 316, 319, 321, 328, 339, 346, 348–349, 353–354, 357–359

extracurricular activities, 12, 269–271, 278, 398, 493

extravagance, 38–39

facilities, xxii–xxiv, 35, 93, 126, 148, 151, 162, 190, 202, 252, 258–259, 265, 267, 380–382, 396, 415, 427, 452, 465, 531

faculty, xv–xxv, 12–13, 16–17, 20, 22–23, 31–32, 39, 52, 55, 58, 60–62, 66, 69–73, 76–82, 84–91, 93, 100, 106–107, 111–113, 115–117, 122–126, 129, 132–133, 135, 139, 144–148, 150–151, 153, 155, 157, 164, 166–167, 169, 172, 174–175, 179, 183–184, 187–188, 198, 205, 207, 212–213, 215, 217, 219–224, 226, 228, 233–234, 242, 245–247, 249, 256–258, 270–275, 278, 280, 282–284, 286, 288, 291–292, 295, 297–298, 300–302, 306, 312–314, 317–330, 334, 340, 344–345, 347–350, 353–359, 361, 365–366, 368–371, 373, faculty (*continued*), 379–380, 382–385, 388, 395, 397, 399, 403–405, 407–409, 413, 427, 429–431, 439, 447, 456, 467–469, 474–476, 490–502, 537

Farnham, Christie Anne, 3–4, 8, 18, 25, 27–28, 91, 118–119, 170, 285, 306, 378, 447–448, 479

fashion, 2, 38, 117, 146, 152, 180, 242, 336, 339, 383, 385, 387, 410, 467, 469, 495

fees, 15, 35–38, 127, 209, 259, 399

femininity, xxii, xxiv–xxv, 239–240, 285–286, 412, 476

feminist, 13–14, 16, 110, 137, 141, 286–287, 306

fencing, 383, 388, 391, 399, 408–409, 414, 417

Ferrata, Chevalier, 76

field hockey, 388, 399–400, 402, 406, 408, 416

finances, 7, 127–128, 477

fishing, 385, 420–421

fitness, 51, 74, 167, 376, 381, 387, 389, 427

founder, 193

founding, xv, 2, 10, 31, 45, 48, 57, 62–63, 65, 100, 103, 115–116, 168, 181, 197, 216, 239, 250, 271, 284, 313, 326, 328, 354, 363, 395, 421, 425, 443, 447, 466, 480, 493

fountain, 252, 259, 397

French, xvii, 3–4, 6, 8–9, 51, 80, 117–118, 243, 245, 358

freshmen, 34, 52, 197–198, 227, 284, 286–292, 298, 301, 310, 332, 353, 356, 374, 409, 411, 425, 431, 472–473, 501

funding, xxi, 44, 53, 75, 169, 199, 204–205, 207, 211, 249, 491

Gainesville, xv, xxi, 1–2, 20–21, 25, 27, 30, 35, 40, 42, 46–47, 50, 57, 62–70, 72, 74, 76–77, 83, 92–93, 95–106, 108–110, 112, 127, 146, 148, 151, 153–156, 161–164, 168–169, 172–175, 178–185, 193, 200, 217–219, 227, 231–237, 242–243, 245–246, 249–250, 252–254, 257, 259, 261–267, 279–281, 283, 292–294, 296, 299–301, 303–310, 329, 346–348, 351, 356, 363–371, 377–380, 392–393, 396, 404, 406–407, 415–416, 418–420, 422–424, 426–427, 429–437, 445, 454, 461, 465, 469, 478, 483–486, 494, 497, 503, 505, 519–520

Gainesville Theatre Alliance, 49, 53, 155, 181, 287, 519

galleries, 152–153, 180, 244, 246, 249

gambling, 322, 339

games, 300, 352–353, 374, 382, 386, 388, 390, 396–400, 402–406, 409, 412–416, 421–424, 426, 429, 432, 435

gardens, 59, 250, 252–254, 265–266, 290, 527

gender, xviii–xix, xxi–xxii, 11, 14–16, 28, 32–33, 49, 74, 81–82, 177, 187–188, 191, 195, 216–217, 278, 304, 413, 439, 449, 477, 500

gentlemen callers, 346, 350, 370

Georgia Baptist Female Seminary, xxii, 2, 5, 8, 10, 15, 34, 39, 44–45, 51, 62–69, 75, 103–105, 117, 119, 127, 134–136, 138–140, 146–147, 158–160, 175–176, 178, 193, 195, 240, 242–243, 255–256, 271, 275, 279, 304, 326, 334, 339, 343, 368, 377, 379–380, 391, 493, 503, 521

Index 581

ghosts. *See under* Agnes
Gibbs, Florence Reville, 58, 102
Golden Tigers, 417–419, 421–422, 425–426, 434, 436–437
golf, 337, 388, 408, 410, 412, 414, 417, 426–427, 437
government. *See under* student government
grades, 51–52, 136, 167, 204, 401, 456
graduate and professional school attendance, 56
graduate degrees, xx, 18, 25–30, 49, 58–59, 66, 72–73, 76, 78, 80–82, 92–93, 95, 97, 99, 103–104, 106, 113, 121, 127, 135–136, 141, 148, 155, 161–162, 165–168, 171–172, 176–179, 184–185, 189, 213, 217, 219, 227, 229–230, 234, 238, 241–243, 245, 250, 252, 259–261, 265, 267, 276, 280, 289, 309, 316, 325–326, 330–334, 336, 346–347, 352–353, 355, 358, 365, 368–369, 377, 382, 390–391, 423, 432, 478, 490
graduates, xix, xxii, 3, 18, 43, 51–53, 56, 60–61, 91, 103, 136, 143, 190, 200, 216, 227, 232, 285, 354, 398
See also alumnae
graduation, 56, 96, 118, 145, 171, 210, 225–226, 291, 298, 306
Greek system, 309, 450–451, 461, 465–466, 471, 473–475, 493
See also sororities
groups. *See under* organizations
gymnasium, 241, 258, 288, 298, 335, 338, 376, 380–382, 384–387, 391, 396–397, 409, 414–415, 425–427, 531
gymnastics, xxiv, 373, 376, 385, 395,

gymnastics (*continued*), 398–399, 409

Hall County, 63, 103, 135, 146, 163, 178, 183, 210–211, 217, 427
Hammond, Jim, 155
handbook, 20, 98, 170, 273, 291, 306, 317–320, 322–325, 327–328, 330–338, 341–343, 345–360, 363–371, 381, 386, 388, 392, 399–401, 409–412, 414–415, 420–421, 429, 431–432, 434, 456, 462–463, 465–466, 468, 471–473, 475, 482, 485–487
Harrison, Belinda, 103, 227
hazing, 289, 293, 475–476
health, xxiii, 1, 167, 169, 191, 208, 239, 258, 277, 339, 342–343, 376–379, 381, 383, 390–391, 399, 407, 413–414
Helping Outstanding Pupils Educationally (H.O.P.E.) Scholarship, 23, 41, 86, 95, 228
Herbst, Jurgen, 2, 25
H.G.H. Senior Honor Society, xxv, 261, 442–447, 477, 479, 494, 535
homecoming, 223, 298
home economics, 17–18, 116, 124, 133, 141–145, 159–160, 177–178, 456, 491, 516
homemaking, 133, 145
homosexuality, 17, 49, 98, 413
Honor Code, 317–319, 358
honor societies, 53–55, 104, 270–271, 495
Honors Program, 163
Horowitz, Helen, 17–18, 28, 33, 43, 91, 239–241, 255–258, 261, 266, 316, 336, 339, 363, 368, 397, 453, 476, 482, 487

horses. See *under* H.G.H. Senior
   Honor Society
Hosch, Helen, 367, 369, 469, 486
house mothers, 340, 468
housing, xxiii, 2, 32, 34, 41, 91, 126,
   143, 164, 206–207, 212, 227, 234,
   241–243, 246–247, 255–257,
   260, 292, 328–329, 331–334, 338,
   340–342, 344–345, 352–353,
   367, 381–382, 435, 452, 456–459,
   464–465, 470, 472, 475
Hunt, Aurora Strong, 69, 127

illness, 63, 293, 296, 322, 324, 326,
   375, 377–378, 391, 407
Independents Organization,
   465–466
innovation, xx, 7, 74, 111, 116–117,
   119, 122–124, 136, 157–158, 160,
   163, 168–169, 403, 421
integration, xv, xxi, 12, 15, 20, 23,
   73, 123, 188, 191, 193, 195, 199,
   202–204, 207, 209–214, 226–228,
   233–234, 238, 462, 485
interclass competition, 374, 388,
   400, 405, 413
intercollegiate athletics, xxiv,
   13, 30, 88, 374, 386, 397, 400,
   402–406, 416–418, 420, 494
international students, 30, 40, 48,
   54, 57, 95, 97, 151, 187, 227, 276,
   303, 418–419, 433
intramurals, 389, 402, 406, 409,
   412–413, 415–416, 427, 475

Jadot-Rops, Princess Lucie Shirazi,
   152
Japanese influences, 66, 79,
   252–254, 265–266, 418, 445, 467,
   527
jazz, 156, 280–281, 293, 330

Jewell family, 247, 427
Jewish students, 46–48, 326, 449,
   459–461, 484
Johns, Jasper, 153, 180
journalism, 21, 54, 75, 111, 245, 280,
   297
Judson College, 19, 29, 45, 96, 140,
   227, 237, 481
juniors, 34, 118, 251, 288, 290–292,
   298, 327, 347, 351–352, 356, 374,
   406–409, 425–426, 442–443, 445,
   500

Kaston, Dr. Benjamin Julian, 78,
   110
Kelley, Mary, 15, 26, 28
Krannert, Ellnora Decker, 57, 101
Ku Klux Klan, 196–197, 231,
   440–441, 520

lakes, 253–255, 289, 300, 351, 357,
   384–385, 421, 423, 435
landmarks, 259, 261, 492
landscaping. *See under* gardens
League of Women Voters, 272, 303
legends, 292, 296
lesbians. *See under* homosexuality
liberalism, 83, 343, 360, 497
librarians, 57, 81, 164, 275, 293
library, 20, 32, 35–36, 57, 74, 104,
   107, 124, 126–127, 152, 173, 178,
   220, 229–230, 237–238, 242,
   246–248, 262–264, 266, 274–275,
   329–330, 336, 342, 484, 503, 525
Lichtenstein, Roy, 153
literary department, 34, 399
literary magazine, 15, 20–21, 59,
   257, 267, 276–279, 304
literary societies, 36, 53, 272,
   275–276, 447–448, 454

Index

locations. *See under* satellite campuses
Lochstampfor, Coach Mike, 422, 435
Longstreet, Helen Dortch, 57, 78, 101
love, 53, 110, 115, 183, 244, 272, 277–278, 294–295, 413
Lumpkin, Katharine Du Pre, 58, 102

magazine, 56, 97, 101–102, 111, 183, 434, 500, 509
maids, 212, 332–333, 367, 468
majors, 2, 49, 54, 108, 120, 130–131, 145, 156–157, 165, 409, 412
male students, 216–219, 224–226, 481, 492
marriage, xxiii, 3, 15, 17, 50, 57, 60, 119, 152, 253, 277–278, 354–355, 412, 449, 462, 467, 485
mascot, 402, 425
master's degrees. *See under* graduate degrees
Matthews, Annabel, 57
May Day, 198, 231, 284–287, 291, 306–309, 509, 529
McCandless, Amy Thompson, 16, 18, 28, 91, 123, 134, 136, 143, 160, 171, 175, 177, 182, 312, 343–344, 360, 362, 369, 386, 392, 402, 430, 453, 455, 482–483
medical technology, 146
men, xix–xxiii, 3, 6–10, 14–15, 17–18, 23, 59, 62, 66, 72, 111, 118, 121, 129, 137–138, 140, 160–161, 176, 181, 188–190, 193, 199, 215–220, 222, 224–226, 228–229, 234–237, 240–241, 255, 258, 264, 285–286, 298, 304, 312, 334, 339, 344–350, 360, 373–375, 395, 400, 402, 413, 421, 428, 440,

men (*continued*), 447–448, 469, 476–477, 481, 490, 492, 537
Mercer University, 29, 62, 65, 72, 93, 108, 172, 199, 208, 469
Mills, Dr. Hugh M., 73
minorities, 188, 248
Miss Brenau, 227, 286–287, 409, 411, 415
mission, 170, 281
monuments, 78, 289, 306, 316, 363, 444–446, 492
morality, 87, 118, 120, 170, 257, 275, 295, 311, 443, 449
movies, 283, 346–347, 349–350, 355–357, 370, 492
Mu Rho Sigma, 316, 355, 462
museum. *See under* Northeast Georgia History Center *or* galleries
music, xix, 5, 8, 11, 33, 35, 54, 57, 59, 74, 76–78, 102, 104, 116, 119, 123, 131, 133, 145–152, 155, 157–158, 160, 171, 175–176, 178, 246, 249, 280–281, 293, 330, 380, 469, 491, 517
music school. *See under* conservatory
musical, 76–77, 133, 141, 148–151, 273, 300, 325–326, 331
musicians, 77

Nash, Margaret A., 14, 26
natatorium, 73, 247, 338, 380–381, 415
National Association of Intercollegiate Athletics (N.A.I.A.), 417–420, 422, 425–426, 433–434, 436
negotiation, xvi, xviii–xxvi, 22–24, 31, 37, 60–62, 69, 76, 82, 84,

negotiation (*continued*), 88–91, 116, 132–133, 146, 169, 188, 215, 222, 226, 228, 241, 258–260, 270–272, 275, 283–284, 286, 290, 292, 295, 302, 311–313, 319–320, 334, 340, 343–344, 347, 359, 361, 373–374, 384, 395, 397, 427, 439, 454, 456, 468, 474–475, 490–499
Newcomer, Mabel, 7, 27, 452
Newman Club, 47, 97, 274, 348
newspaper. *See under "Alchemist"*
night riding, xxiii, 311, 348–350, 358–360
Northeast Georgia History Center, 74, 250, 264–265
Nott, Prof. Beth, 80
nursing, 2, 54, 131, 146, 161, 163, 165, 167–168, 178, 184, 210–211, 217, 225–226, 233, 272, 338, 408

Oglesby Hall, 246, 387
Olympics, 247, 415, 418, 423, 435
online offerings, xx, 1, 25, 49–50, 74, 100, 103, 167–168, 184, 188, 238, 262–263, 266, 281–282, 306–308, 433, 444, 446, 465, 485
opera, 76, 148, 151, 244
oratory, 78, 119, 153–154, 245, 300, 382, 398–399
orchestra, 147, 151, 179, 273
organ, 35, 77, 110, 148–149, 243
organizations. *See under* sororities, clubs
Overton, Florence M. and Overton Hall, 78, 245, 382
Owens Student Center, 245

pageants. *See under* "Miss Brenau"
paintings. *See under* art
Panhellenic Council, 214, 273, 461,

Panhellenic Council (*continued*), 473, 482, 484
Pan-Hellenic Council, 257, 471–472
parents, 41, 126, 172, 174, 209, 223, 234, 291, 296, 313, 315, 322, 343–344, 355, 377–378, 382–383
Parker, Dr. Elizabeth, 57, 101, 466–467
parties, 298, 300–301, 310, 350, 410, 465–466, 476
paternalism, 32
P.E. requirements, 407
Pearce Auditorium, 148–149, 153, 178, 243–246, 249, 251, 290, 292, 295, 308, 509, 523–524
Pearce, Jr., Dr. Heyward Jefferson, 296
Pearce, Mrs. Heyward Jefferson, 68, 72, 467
Pearce, Sr., Dr. Heyward Jefferson, xix, 66–71, 82, 84, 88–89, 106, 115, 120, 127, 170, 244, 285, 296, 355, 358, 396, 404–405, 467, 510
performances, 39, 76–78, 133, 147–151, 154–157, 179, 202, 225, 249, 273, 286, 295, 298, 300, 325–326, 330, 332, 335, 497
petitions, 90, 162, 319, 321–323, 325, 330, 340, 344, 347, 451, 491, 495–498, 500–502
Pfefferkorn, Prof. Otto, 77
Philomathesian, 276
Phi Mu, 257, 387, 447, 449–451, 456–457, 464, 466, 469, 471, 480, 482
physical culture, xv, xxiii, 20, 116, 154, 373, 377–381, 383–386, 388–389, 395
physician, 242, 375, 377–378, 384, 390, 407, 413–414
piano, 35, 106, 148–151, 179,

piano (*continued*), 292–293, 330, 467
plays. *See under* Gainesville Theatre Alliance
pledging. *See under* sororities
policymaking, xxi, 187, 224, 491
pool, 211, 243, 247, 292, 338, 380, 387, 400–401, 409, 414–415
Pottorf, Darryl, 153
prayer, 323, 361, 397
prejudice, 46, 191, 194, 197, 212
presidents, xvi, xix, xxi, 20, 55, 57, 62–63, 66, 68, 71–75, 80, 82–85, 88, 92, 101, 104–112, 115, 122, 127–128, 130, 134, 143–144, 152–153, 162, 199–201, 206–207, 210, 212–213, 217, 220–221, 225, 227, 233–234, 236–238, 244–249, 253, 259, 266–267, 275, 285, 296, 313, 316, 319, 321, 325, 342, 354, 358, 365, 368, 377, 382, 390, 404, 427, 456, 458–460, 463, 470, 479, 483, 485, 502
privileges, 315, 319, 321, 345–347, 350, 356, 360, 498, 501
professors, xv–xxv, 12–13, 16–17, 20, 22–23, 31–32, 36, 39, 41, 52, 55, 58, 60–62, 65–73, 76–91, 93, 100, 106–107, 111–113, 115–117, 120–126, 129, 132–135, 138–139, 144–151, 153, 155, 157, 164, 166–167, 169, 172, 174–175, 179, 183–184, 187–188, 198, 205, 207, 212–213, 215, 217, 219–224, 226, 228, 233–234, 238, 242, 245–247, 249, 256–258, 270–275, 278, 280, 282–284, 286, 288, 291–293, 295–298, 300–302, 306, 312–330, 334, 340, 344–345, 347–350, 353–359, 361, 365–366, 368–371, 373, 379–380, 382–385, 388, 395, 397–399, 403–405, 407–409, 413,

professors (*continued*), 424, 427, 429–431, 439, 447, 456, 464, 467–469, 474–476, 490–502, 537
promotion, xxiii, 34, 63, 204, 275, 292, 373, 377, 379, 381, 384, 453, 455
See also tenure
Protestant, xviii, 33, 45–46, 366, 449, 461
publications, student. *See under* "*Alchemist*," "*Elixir*," "*Bubbles*," "*Aurum*"
punishments, 321, 328, 349

quadrangle, 1, 178, 241, 251–252
quarantine, 378

R.A.T.T. Week, 197, 287–290, 306–307, 529
race, xviii, xxi, xxv, 14, 32, 48–49, 58, 95, 98, 188, 190–191, 194–199, 201, 204–205, 212–213, 215, 217, 226–227, 230, 439, 459
racism, 189, 191, 196
radio station, 59, 108, 145, 203, 249, 280–283, 300, 305, 352
Rankin, Jeannette, 78–79
rankings, 2, 81, 89, 93, 103, 418–419, 425, 433
Rauschenberg, Robert, 153
Ray, Dr. Helen, 75
recitals, 39, 77, 110, 149–151, 154, 156–157, 179, 181, 201, 249, 293, 300, 335
recreation, 243, 254, 258, 286, 341, 351, 377, 381–382, 385, 410–415, 431, 435
recruits, 212, 227, 420, 448, 458, 492
regulations, xxii, 31, 45, 90, 194, 198, 256, 258, 312–313, 315,

regulations (*continued*), 317–318, 321–322, 331–334, 336, 338–339, 341, 344, 346, 353, 358–359, 361, 411, 473–477, 487, 492

relationships, 48, 89, 217, 220, 290, 354–355, 457, 471

religion, xviii, xxi, xxiii, xxv, 10, 18, 27, 29, 32–33, 44–48, 63–64, 66, 72, 96–98, 103, 105–106, 116, 131, 133–134, 167, 205–207, 214, 238, 274, 303, 311, 315, 322–326, 336, 347, 351, 365–366, 449, 459, 461, 481, 498, 502

Renoir, Pierre-Auguste, 153

retention, 51, 80, 84, 87–88

Rigney, Eleanor, 11, 27, 39, 41–43, 53–54, 68, 94–95, 100, 104, 106–107, 117–118, 170, 231, 274, 304, 478

rituals, 442, 444, 448, 459, 475, 478

Riverside Military Academy, 46, 273, 283, 301, 310, 347, 396, 429, 506

Rogers, Dr. James T., 73–74, 109, 217, 417–419, 423, 512

Rosenquist, James, 153

Roueché, Dr. Michelle, 151, 179

rowing, xxiv, 374, 376, 384–385, 395, 402, 407, 423–424, 426, 435–436

Rudolph, Frederick, 6, 12–13, 25–27, 32, 91, 269, 312, 362, 494

rules, xxi–xxiii, xxv–xxvi, 23–24, 31, 44–45, 85, 87–88, 194, 223, 235–237, 274, 287–288, 311–317, 319–324, 326–334, 337, 343–363, 365, 369, 374, 409, 415, 439, 448, 454, 459, 468, 471–474, 492, 496

runners, 418, 424–425

rush, 301, 456, 466, 468–469, 471–474, 477, 487

salaries, 69–71, 107, 126, 129

satellite campuses, xx, 2, 136, 152, 162, 166, 465, 491

scholarships, xvii–xviii, 11, 16, 18, 28, 38, 41, 53–54, 75, 86, 95, 100, 167, 169, 286, 297, 329, 416, 456, 483

Schrader, Dr. Edward L., 75, 109–110, 259–260, 267, 427, 514

science, 1, 8, 13, 26, 35, 51, 116, 118, 120–121, 124, 126, 131, 133, 135, 141–145, 147, 159–160, 162, 170–171, 177, 247, 252, 272, 388, 408, 450, 516

sculpture, 153, 444–445

secret societies, xv, xxiv, 20, 97, 196, 231, 269–271, 366, 439–441, 447–448, 475–478, 493–494

secretarial program, xix, 131, 140, 145

segregation, xxi, 58, 73, 187–188, 190–192, 195, 197, 199, 201–205, 207–210, 212–215, 226–227, 491

Sellars Gallery, 153, 246

seminary, xxii, 2, 5–6, 8–10, 15, 34, 39, 44–45, 51, 62–69, 75, 103–105, 117–119, 127, 134–136, 138–140, 146–147, 158–160, 175–176, 178, 189, 193, 195, 240, 242–243, 255–256, 271, 275, 279, 304, 326, 334, 339, 343, 368, 377, 379–380, 391, 493, 503, 521

Seminary Signal, 279, 339, 368

seniors, 34, 118, 154, 251, 288–292, 298, 308, 320, 327, 333, 346–347, 351–353, 355–356, 374, 398, 407–408, 419, 425, 429, 431, 443, 445, 458–459, 500–501, 526

Seven Sisters, 10, 17

Shorter College, 18, 29, 44, 68, 75,

Shorter College (*continued*), 86, 96, 98, 104–106, 108, 110, 140, 208, 230, 417
Simmons, Dr. Thomas J, 68
Simmons, Lessie Southgate, 68, 105–106, 274
single-gender education, 11, 14, 74, 108, 216–217, 500
Skulls, The, xxv, 441, 475, 478
Smithgall, Lessie, 249, 419
smoking, xxiii, xxv, 311–313, 339–343, 347, 351, 358–361, 368–369, 463, 477
soccer, xxiv, 388, 400, 406, 408–412, 421–422, 426–427, 434–435, 533
socials, 440, 468–469, 474
softball, xxiv, 409, 411–412, 414–415, 425–427, 431, 436–437
Solomon, Barbara Miller, 14, 28, 141, 177, 376, 391, 453, 456, 459, 482–484
solos, 156, 295
sophomores, 34, 53, 118, 198, 287–292, 298, 307, 332, 351–352, 356, 374, 411, 426
sororities, xxiv, 41, 47–48, 53–55, 97, 196, 199, 205, 212, 234, 251–252, 259, 271–272, 286, 293, 296, 298, 302, 304, 309, 326, 333, 335, 338, 342, 347, 353, 355, 412, 416, 439–440, 444–445, 447, 450, 452–455, 460–461, 475, 479–486, 493–495
   fluctuations in membership, xxv, 449, 459, 462–464, 474
   houses, xxii, 2, 240, 246, 255–258, 260, 328–329, 331–332, 337, 340–341, 346, 351, 451, 457–458, 465, 467, 470, 474, 476, 492, 528, 536
   integration of, 214

sororities (*continued*)
   membership, 464
   rushing, xxv, 301, 448, 456, 466, 468–469, 471–474, 477, 487
Southerland, Dr. James E., 80, 111, 169, 212, 216, 233–234, 262
Southern Association of Colleges and Schools (S.A.C.S.), xxii, 1, 45, 52, 55–58, 62, 71, 73, 79, 84, 93, 99–101, 108, 124–132, 135, 138, 144, 146, 163, 165, 168, 171–172, 182, 191, 193, 200, 207, 212, 218, 230–231, 246–247, 252, 255, 258, 261, 271, 273–274, 280–281, 283–284, 319–320, 326, 332, 378, 404, 412, 416, 421, 423, 437, 456, 487
Spade Hunt, 290, 307–309
Spelman College, 18–19, 29, 44, 96, 105, 107, 190, 193, 451, 482
Sphinx, 441
sports, xxiii–xxiv, 250, 265, 334, 336–338, 373–377, 382–383, 386, 388, 390–391, 395, 400, 402, 405–416, 421, 424–428, 432, 434–435, 437, 464, 485, 495, 531
   See also athletics
Stabs, xxv, 441, 534
staff, xv–xviii, xx–xxiii, xxv, 22–23, 31–32, 60–62, 76, 78, 80–81, 88–91, 107, 115–117, 129, 132–133, 146, 150–151, 155, 164, 187–188, 215, 218, 220–222, 224, 226, 228, 230–231, 243, 258, 264, 270–275, 278, 280–284, 286, 292, 295, 297–298, 301–302, 308, 312–313, 317, 319–323, 334, 347, 354, 384, 397–398, 404, 416, 427, 433–434, 439, 447, 467–468, 474–475, 490–493, 495–499
standardized tests, 51

state clubs, 39, 41, 406
stenography, xix, 124, 133, 138–141, 158
Stewart, Kris, 426
student government, xviii, 61–62, 90, 103, 165–166, 203–204, 209, 214, 222–223, 227, 236, 270–271, 273, 289, 314–318, 320, 322–323, 325, 327, 340, 361–367, 369–370, 456, 460, 474, 491–492, 495–496, 498
students, xv–xvii, xix, xxi–xxiii, xxvi, 1, 3, 6, 9, 15–17, 22–23, 31, 34–37, 42, 44, 46–47, 50–56, 58, 60, 62, 69, 72, 76–78, 80–82, 88–91, 93–95, 97, 108, 111, 115–117, 121–123, 126, 128, 130, 132–133, 135, 139–144, 146, 148–151, 153–160, 162–163, 165–169, 172, 180–181, 183–185, 188, 191–193, 198, 204–205, 208–210, 215, 220–223, 228, 235–236, 239–241, 249–253, 255–260, 264, 269–284, 286, 289–292, 294–303, 308, 311–364, 366–369, 373–376, 378–389, 391, 395–400, 402–403, 405–416, 421, 423–424, 427–428, 439–440, 443–445, 448, 452–457, 459–460, 463–467, 471–475, 477, 482–485, 489–491, 493–499, 501, 503–509, 519, 532
   age, 2, 61
   demographics, xxiv–xxv, 14, 25, 45, 152, 487
   first-generation, 43
   geographic diversity of, 39, 41
   male, 216–219, 224–226, 481, 492
   nontraditional, xx, 161, 164
   race, 40, 48–49, 187, 189–190, 194–197, 207, 212–214, 227,

students
   race (*continued*), 229, 462
   socioeconomic status, xviii, 11, 32–33, 38–39, 43, 449
Students In Free Enterprise (S.I.F.E.), 81–82, 272
studios, 246–247, 249
Swedish gymnastics, 376
swells, 453–454
swimming, xxiv, 243, 247, 254, 292, 338, 368, 381, 387–388, 399–401, 405, 408, 410–411, 413–417, 419–420, 426, 433–434
symbols, 445, 475–476
symphony, 147, 151, 179, 273

teachers. *See under* faculty
teams (sports), 389, 407, 427
television, 58, 249, 280, 282, 294, 300, 306, 332
tennis, xxiii–xxiv, 40, 74, 249, 253–254, 264, 288, 300, 335–336, 374, 376, 381–383, 387, 391, 396–397, 399–400, 402, 405, 408–409, 411–412, 416–419, 424, 426, 433, 435
tenure policy, 74, 82–87, 111–113, 212, 223, 314
   See also promotion
termites, 411–412, 415, 431
theatre, 74, 82, 131, 146, 154–155, 157, 181, 225, 245, 249, 254, 295, 346, 356–357, 519
   See also Gainesville Theatre Alliance
Thelin, John R., 8–9, 12–13, 27–28, 91, 118, 170, 269, 303, 373, 390, 493–494, 500
theology, 118, 133
Thomas, Lera Millard, 59, 102

Index

Thurman, Rachel, 49, 98
Times, The Gainesville, 102, 109–110, 173, 178, 180, 184–185, 233, 252, 261, 264–266, 292, 299, 305, 307–309, 415, 418–420, 424, 426–427, 433–434, 436–437
tornado, 70, 127, 173, 250, 458, 515
tournaments, 400, 408–409, 412–413, 415–416, 418, 422, 426, 437
town girls, 329, 483
track, xxiv, 8, 301, 374, 387, 391, 398–400, 424, 426, 437
traditions, xv, xix, xxii, 11–12, 20, 26, 81, 91, 96, 104–105, 119, 132, 135, 144–145, 149, 160, 192, 197, 204, 210, 219, 241, 251–252, 256, 261–262, 265, 269–271, 277, 279, 284, 286–287, 289–292, 296, 298–302, 306–309, 317–318, 332, 336, 375, 386, 402, 447, 465, 470, 477, 493–494
Trustees. *See under* Board of Trustees
tuition, 5, 34–37, 41, 69, 92–94, 127, 159, 209, 217
typhoid, 378
typing, 139, 141

underclassmen, 198, 252, 291, 407, 526
undergraduate degrees, xx, 2, 8–9, 25, 51, 53, 64–65, 80, 123–124, 130–131, 135, 141, 143–145, 150, 154, 158–159, 161–162, 165, 189, 217, 388, 400, 407–408, 461, 480, 538–542
undergraduates, xx, xxiv, 1–2, 25, 34, 43, 52–53, 61, 91, 93, 95, 100, 108, 122, 124, 131–132, 151, 154, 161, 164–165, 168–169, 174–175,

undergraduates (*continued*), 182, 184–185, 188, 197–198, 222, 224, 227, 229–230, 237, 251, 264–265, 269–270, 284, 286–292, 298, 301, 307–308, 310–311, 327, 332–333, 346–347, 351–353, 355–356, 364, 374, 406–409, 411, 415–416, 419, 422, 425–426, 429, 431–432, 445, 458–459, 464–465, 472–473, 485, 493–494, 500–501, 526, 538–542
uniforms, 36, 122, 338, 386, 412, 415, 425
University of Georgia, 25, 29, 36, 56, 65, 80, 92, 102, 149, 157, 168, 172, 179, 203, 214, 229, 276, 280, 303–305, 317, 390, 396, 416–417, 420, 433, 461, 469, 498, 500–501
utopia, 240

Vardeman, Johnny, 110, 173, 252, 254, 264–266
vice, 68, 74–75, 80, 111, 212, 233–234, 238, 290, 296, 325, 460
Victorian, 148, 242, 375, 385, 390
violin, 148–149, 469
virtues, 324, 386, 397
vocationally-oriented programs, 133, 145–146, 162
voice department, 76, 148
volleyball, xxiv, 388, 398–400, 405, 409, 411, 414, 424, 426, 436, 532

W.B.C.X., 59, 108, 145, 203, 249, 280–282, 300, 305, 352
Wages, Bete Todd, 152
Wallace, Dr. Roslyn E., 59, 102
Wallis Field, 249, 251
Walters, Jim, 245–246
Ward, Del, 59
Warhol, Andy, 153
Watson, Thomas E. "Tom," 96, 189,

Watson, Thomas E. "Tom," (*continued*), 248, 264
Weekend College. *See under* Evening and Weekend College
Wesleyan College, 9, 18–19, 29–30, 44, 96, 105, 107, 136, 140, 171, 173, 193, 227, 237, 378, 421, 426, 447, 450, 453, 479, 481
Wheeler Alumni House, 74, 247
Wilkes, Rev. William C., 62–66, 193, 242–243, 255, 445, 522
womanhood, cult of, 115, 117, 285, 335, 375–376, 390
womanly virtue, 256, 343
Woody, Thomas, 5–7, 9, 13–14, 26–28

yearbook, xxiv, 20, 38–39, 45, 47, yearbook (*continued*), 98, 102, 108, 195–196, 212, 214, 224, 227, 231, 238, 271–272, 274, 280, 285–286, 291–292, 298, 303, 305, 360–361, 367, 371, 383, 388, 392–393, 396, 398, 400, 405–408, 410, 416–417, 421–425, 429–436, 440–444, 450–451, 456, 461–464, 466–467, 478–480, 482, 485, 493, 520, 534
Yonah Hall, 243–244, 251, 255, 345, 350–351, 370, 470, 522–523
Young Women's Christian Association (Y.W.C.A.), xxii, 246, 271, 273–275, 284, 303–304, 319, 326, 341, 442, 456

Zeta Tau Alpha, 450–451, 464, 470, 480, 482, 484

www.ingramcontent.com/pod-product-compliance
Lightning Source LLC
Chambersburg PA
CBHW071429300426
44114CB00013B/1365